IFIP Advances in Information and Communication Technology

359

IFIP – The International Federation for Information Processing

IFIP was founded in 1960 under the auspices of UNESCO, following the First World Computer Congress held in Paris the previous year. An umbrella organization for societies working in information processing, IFIP's aim is two-fold: to support information processing within its member countries and to encourage technology transfer to developing nations. As its mission statement clearly states,

> *IFIP's mission is to be the leading, truly international, apolitical organization which encourages and assists in the development, exploitation and application of information technology for the bene t of all people.*

IFIP is a non-profitmaking organization, run almost solely by 2500 volunteers. It operates through a number of technical committees, which organize events and publications. IFIP's events range from an international congress to local seminars, but the most important are:

- The IFIP World Computer Congress, held every second year;
- Open conferences;
- Working conferences.

The flagship event is the IFIP World Computer Congress, at which both invited and contributed papers are presented. Contributed papers are rigorously refereed and the rejection rate is high.

As with the Congress, participation in the open conferences is open to all and papers may be invited or submitted. Again, submitted papers are stringently refereed.

The working conferences are structured differently. They are usually run by a working group and attendance is small and by invitation only. Their purpose is to create an atmosphere conducive to innovation and development. Refereeing is less rigorous and papers are subjected to extensive group discussion.

Publications arising from IFIP events vary. The papers presented at the IFIP World Computer Congress and at open conferences are published as conference proceedings, while the results of the working conferences are often published as collections of selected and edited papers.

Any national society whose primary activity is in information may apply to become a full member of IFIP, although full membership is restricted to one society per country. Full members are entitled to vote at the annual General Assembly, National societies preferring a less committed involvement may apply for associate or corresponding membership. Associate members enjoy the same benefits as full members, but without voting rights. Corresponding members are not represented in IFIP bodies. Affiliated membership is open to non-national societies, and individual and honorary membership schemes are also offered.

Jiří Hřebíček
Gerald Schimak   Ralf Denzer (Eds.)

Environmental Software Systems

Frameworks of eEnvironment

9th IFIP WG 5.11 International Symposium, ISESS 2011
Brno, Czech Republic, June 27-29, 2011
Proceedings

 Springer

Volume Editors

Jiří Hřebíček
Masaryk University, Institute of Biostatistics and Analyses
Kamenice 126/3, 625 00 Brno, Czech Republic
E-mail: hrebicek@iba.muni.cz

Gerald Schimak
Austrian Institute of Technology GmbH (AIT)
2444 Seibersdorf, Austria
E-mail: gerald.schimak@ait.ac.at

Ralf Denzer
Environmental Informatics Group (EIG)
Goebenstr. 40, 66117 Saarbrücken, Germany
E-mail: ralf.denzer@enviromatics.org

ISSN 1868-4238   e-ISSN 1868-422X
ISBN 978-3-642-26878-6   ISBN 978-3-642-22285-6 (eBook)
DOI 10.1007/978-3-642-22285-6
Springer Heidelberg Dordrecht London New York

CR Subject Classification (1998): I.2, H.4, H.3, C.2, H.5, D.2

Preface

1 ISESS ++ (Ralf Denzer)

1.1 IFIP WG 5.11 and ISESS

The International Symposium on Environmental Software Systems (ISESS) is one of several overlapping forums discussing issues of Environmental Information Systems, Environmental Decision Support Systems, Environmental Software Systems, Environmental Informatics, Eco-Informatics or Enviromatics – whichever of the terms you prefer at a certain time of day.

ISESS was founded by Gerald Schimak and myself in 1995, with great support from the German Informatics Society Working Group 4.6 "Computer Science for Environmental Protection" and the International Federation for Information Processing (IFIP) Working Group 5.11 "Computers and Environment."

Like many things, ISESS started over a couple of drinks (how else, for a German), when a visiting friend, David Russell from Pennsylvania State University, issued an invitation to organize some sort of workshop or conference on his campus. When we prepared for the first ISESS at Penn State, it was at best "a shot in the dark," although I am prepared to swear every oath that neither the Pink Panther nor Inspector Clouseau had any part in the plot.

The symposium has been held in a number of countries since: the United States, Canada, Austria, New Zealand, Switzerland, Portugal, the Czech Republic, Spain, Italy; in some years, joint sessions were held in conjunction with the biannual meeting of IEMSS (International Environmental Modelling and Software Society). ISESS is an official IFIP event which is directly supported by WG 5.11.

The WG itself was led by Giorgio Guariso (1991–1999), myself (1999–2005) and Dave Swayne (2005–2011). Several individuals have served as vice-chairs or as secretaries of the WG and many members of the WG have been active supporters for a long time without holding an official position.

1.2 Jiri's Question

Jiri Hrebicek, the General Chairman of this ISESS 2011 in Brno, has asked me to say a few words in the introduction of these proceedings about where we are now and where we might go in the coming years – our field of work, our WG 5.11 and our conference ISESS. Jiri is particularly interested in opinions regarding what R&D should be fostered, and how the WG and ISESS may support the process to discuss them. I also understand that he is interested in discussing where the contribution of our community can have maximum impact. My dear Jiri: How can any one individual hope to make some sense of such a question? On top of that, have you considered that as a professor I *already* gossip too much?

The first simple answer to your question would point you to other people and be: *go and ask the end users about their needs*. The problem with this simple answer is that it will only deliver a partial answer, for the following reasons:

a) The real end users are often not the deciders of investments, even less deciders of corporate information and communication (ICT) strategies.
b) If at all, they can only indirectly influence priorities of research (for instance through policies which reflect societal needs).
c) If you ask individual users from different domains, you will always get an entirely fragmented picture of individual needs.
d) These needs change all the time with new environmental issues popping up.

This approach will not tell you which type of R&D is needed broadly. It leaves you with multiple *micro-level views*.

A second simple answer to your question would also point you to other people and be: *go ask the people who have the big picture*, for instance, those who define large-scale ICT policies or those who prepare mind-boggling visionary large-scale projects. I am not sure if this will give you a lot of *concrete* answers to your question, because naturally such efforts stay at a *macro-level view* for at least some of their time.

What you would like to know, Jiri, may be at a level in between these two views, and I think that our scientific community already has some answers, although you may have to collect them from many sources and make some systematic sense of them. The ISESS forum is hopefully contributing to this process.

1.3   Vision of an IT Infrastructure for Decision Making

If there is a dominant topic recently, then it is the notion of a networked information infrastructure which allows users of different domains, expertise and capabilities to share information and services, and which provides them with the necessary information for their decisions at anytime, anywhere, on-demand and in an ad-hoc fashion if needed. In Europe, the terms "single information space for the environment" (SISE) and "shared environmental information system" (SEIS) have been introduced, and although other parts of the world may use other words, they are often after the same thing. The various efforts, for instance, in Australia to build a continent-wide information resource for the water domain is very similar. Along with this vision, activities to provide fundamental services as a baseline are underway, as pointed out in the paper "eEnvironment: Reality and Challenges for eEnvironment Implementation in Europe" of Hrebicek and Pillmann in these proceedings. One might ask the questions: Why has this notion been so dominant recently? Is it more like a high-level political wish, or a nice-to-have wish, is this vision really reflecting the needs of a majority of end users? In order to discuss this question, we can consider several types of applications.

For those applications that require integration across (geographic, political, organizational, domain) boundaries, it is obvious that they are supported by a SISE. Such applications may be at continental scale or cross-boundary applications.

Then there is a type of application that requires a high degree of flexibility in the combination of existing information and services, maybe because the decisions taken are too complex and cannot be completely predefined, or due to the fact that it is simply too expensive to build a dedicated software system supporting them. Such applications include those that have to react to unforeseen factors. A SISE which supports on-demand information processing of "whatever is available out there" in an efficient way clearly supports these applications.

Finally there are applications that do not necessarily need to rely on the SISE, but which may just become more efficient because end users are relieved of stupid, time-consuming tasks, or which could greatly improve their performance if respective services were available in the infrastructure.

Where we are with the vision of an ICT infrastructure for environmental decision making is anybody's guess, and it is also somewhat subjective. It is essential that more and more applications using the SISE come on-line in real life (and not in R&D projects *alone*). For this, *all* barriers preventing integrated distributed work flows need to be coped with. Only if end users and organizations get value and quality for money from the SISE will there be a growing awareness that it is worth investing in it oneself.

1.4 Some of the Gossip

As part of the preparation of this preface, and after writing chaps. 1.1 to 1.3, I contacted 25 individuals (not including Gerald and Jiri) who have been important contributors in this line of work for quite a while, in academia, government and industry. I received 12 replies and will try to summarize the majority of the opinions in terms of achievements, deficits and opportunities. It is interesting to note that most replies received included not only technological but also many "soft factors."

1.5 Achievements

Environmental data and information management are generally considered very mature and the underlying technology is solid. Sensor networks and earth observation give access to an ever-increasing amount of observation data, and it can be expected that in the future there will be more (cheap, mobile) sensors producing types of data not available today.

The achievements in data and service standards and their practical importance are recognized and have greatly improved inter-operability at least at the syntactical level. There has been considerable progress at the conceptual level of distributed services; for instance, the use of the service-oriented architecture (SOA) paradigm and application of reference models have demonstrated that multiple autonomous organizations can connect via this paradigm.

Spatial data infrastructures are being consolidated at a national level, and coordinated international activities are progressing toward the integration of heterogeneous information sources. There is also some drive toward providing geospatial applications and data over reduced barriers.

The simulation of environmental phenomena has reached an unprecedented level of detail, and it is quite possible to embed complex models in decision support systems, maybe for the first time really "from a local to a global scale." Concepts are underway toward flexible modeling as well as decision support frameworks that make the implementation of concrete systems more affordable.

Interactive, graphics-based systems, particularly those which make information on the Internet available for local use, have contributed to the transfer of information to stakeholders and have improved the confidence in applying decision theory as part of finding a solution to a given problem.

In terms of "soft factors" it is noted that – at least for those working regularly in our application area – some common understanding of terminology has been reached between modelers, IT specialists and application specialists. Common problems have been identified and examples of good practices are known.

The scientific communities have become broader rather than narrowed down. Several individuals note that 15 years ago one would have thought of classic environmental media, whereas today fields like industrial ecology, sustainable development and risk management are part of many systems being built.

1.6   Deficits

The majority of individuals have expressed the opinion – in one way or other – that there are several large gaps between what has been made available *at the conceptual level*, and what is done *in practice*, an opinion which I share in most cases.

At the data level, there is a gap between the ever-increasing availability of data and the lack of easy discovery and access – the issue of ownership being part of the problem. There is also a large gap between data and data semantics, including the quantification of uncertainties which would be needed for larger-scale data sharing among specialists of different fields. As data sharing involves individuals from neighboring disciplines (and sometimes remote disciplines), and because decision making today often requires the involvement of experts from many disciplines, the issue of semantics is of on-going importance, and there is hope that mainstream IT will deliver improved concepts and tools.

At the level of supporting end users with decision support systems, several individuals express the opinion that there have been too many prototypes and too few "real-world" decision support systems (DSS) that are used on a daily basis by decision makers. This is probably the case and may be due to the fact that these systems are often quite complex and may need considerable improvement in usability. One colleague thinks that there may have been too much focus on the technological side and that "we may have lost the customers in the process." I share this opinion partially, but I do not know what the alternative would have been; I think that for complex DSS we are still in the phase of experimentation, and more driven by the technology side. In any case it will be necessary to get more DSS on the end user desk.

There is a particularly large gap between sophisticated design concepts and how systems are being built today. For instance, many applications are still completely hard wired and there is a lot of re-inventing of the wheel (why should it be different in our line of work...). Although high-level concepts and software engineering paradigms (like reference models, systematic use of SOAs and so forth) exist, they do not even make it into the requirements of public tenders in many cases. There seems to be a general lack of knowledge, even in some self-announced software companies, that these concepts even exist, and what they mean in the context of an application project or an IT strategy of a customer. Perhaps these concepts have not been sufficiently communicated and practical training is a necessity.

The current level of service standardization is also not considered sufficiently mature, which is particularly important because the availability of more generic services would both promote inter-operability and re-use, i.e., this could have a considerable impact. This is particularly the case for services going beyond the classic "discovery and access" services, supporting higher-level analysis, for instance, for data fusion, simulation or semantic inter-operability. There is also a need of concepts for tailoring generic services to application domains.

The "softer" deficits mentioned belong to several categories. First of all there is the issue of digital rights and making more existing data available for general use. Secondly there is the above-mentioned lack of competence of a considerable number of the players in "the ICT team." There is a lack of training in the application of sophisticated and proven concepts developed since the mid-2000s. It also seems to be the case that there are still project developers out there who have not understood what proper user involvement is, which leads to a poor record of performance for at least some decision support systems. At the same time, customers seem to have a need to better identify how they can avoid hiring a bad software company.

1.7 Opportunities

Several individuals identify opportunities through a more "systematic approach." On one hand this can be a clearer foundation based on a "solid understanding of the nature of data, information and knowledge," but this would also apply to improved use of semantics for annotation, which would in turn improve discovery, access and use of information resources. Proper tools to cope with uncertainty and complex systems with multiple feedback loops are under this category and semantics could also be used to describe models in order to improve their use. A better way to communicate uncertainty and risk could be of great benefit for stakeholders.

In more practical terms, the use of reference models for corporate and multi-organization ICT strategies is considered a key factor in organizing the SISE. Improved use of standards, in particular to foster the creation of thematic profiles of generic services, is considered necessary toward this goal. It is also expected that the increasing number of sensors will support new types of applications not available today. It will also be beneficial to improve high-level frameworks and reference models toward better support of distributed service orchestration, trust-worthiness and robustness. Improved computational analysis, for instance, in the area of data fusion, should become part of the generic service framework.

A number of recent ICT developments are considered good opportunities as well. One can, for instance, imagine synergies between social networks and decision making, including volunteered information and presentation of information in virtual worlds. The area of mobile applications is considered a key opportunity, because mobile location-based Apps for everyday use could reach a much larger number of users more easily. This could also include computer vision for monitoring purposes.

Cloud computing and virtualization are a new type of platform that could help to turn systems into trusted services, and they allow for new types of business models through alternative service delivery.

It was interesting to see that the largest number of comments regarding "soft factors" came under the question regarding opportunities for the coming years. First of all there is a need to show more concrete examples of identifying and adopting good practices, and communication in the scientific community regarding good practices is worth fostering. For decision support systems it would be important to identify "cohorts of environmental decision makers" who exist in significant numbers, which may be just another way of saying that we need to go toward more standardized (although maybe domain-specific) products. It would be valuable if one could quantify the benefits of ICT-supported decision making and if the scientific community could give some better "proof" that systems really help decision makers to make better decisions.

Several individuals see considerable opportunities in reaching out to larger scientific communities, for instance, in the area of sustainability, industrial ecology or the interface between environment and health. Collaboration across societies and scientific communities in particular at the interface to modelers is considered particularly important. Improved funding for real interdisciplinary projects between ICT and application teams would help to bridge gaps as well. A SISE will also need organizational and legal frameworks beyond the ICT.

1.8   Conclusions

Despite the long list of deficits in the previous chapter, which reflect practical deficiencies, we have seen many successful applications of ICTs in different areas of environmental management, sustainability, risk management and so forth. But we have also seen far too many "prototypes-only" and far too many badly designed systems that are quietly buried by their end users after a short period of time. I think that the WG, in collaboration with other scientific communities, can make a contribution by spreading information about good practices and by involving even broader communities, both in terms of discipline and of geography. My personal opinion as a computer scientist is that it is our responsibility to seek the communication with the end user, and not the end user's responsibility to find us.

2   Framework of ISESS 2011 (Jiri Hrebicek)

2.1   Predecessors of ISESS 2011

The first and second proceedings of the International Symposium on Environmental Software Systems (ISESS 1995 and ISESS 1997) were published and printed by official IFIP publisher Chapman&Hall:

- R. Denzer, D. Russell, G. Schimak (eds.), Environmental Software Systems, Chapman & Hall, 1996, ISBN 0 412 73730 2.
- R. Denzer, D. A. Swayne, G. Schimak (eds.), Environmental Software Systems Vol. 2, Chapman & Hall, 1998, ISBN 0 412 81740 3.

Then IFIP changed publisher and the third proceedings of ISESS 1999 were published and printed by official IFIP publisher Kluwer:

- R. Denzer, D. A. Swayne, M. Purvis, G. Schimak (eds.), Environmental Software Systems Vol. 3 - Environmental Information and Environmental Decision Support, Kluwer Academic Publishers, 2000, ISBN 0 7923 7832 6.

The fourth and fifth proceeding of ISESS 2001 and ISESS 2003 were published and printed by the organizers of the symposium themselves under IFIP ISBN:

- D. A. Swayne, R. Denzer, G. Schimak (eds.), Environmental Software Systems Vol. 4 - Environmental Information and Indicators, International Federation for Information Processing, 2001, ISBN 3 901882 14 6.
- G. Schimak, D. A. Swayne, N.T. Quinn, R. Denzer (eds.), Environmental Software Systems Vol. 5 - Environmental Knowledge and Information Systems, International Federation for Information Processing, 2003, ISBN 3 901882 16 2.

In a similar way the sixth and seventh proceedings of ISESS 2005 and ISESS 2007 were published by the organizers but this time on CD and USB under IFIP ISBN:

- D. A. Swayne, T. Jakeman (eds.), Environmental Software Systems, Vol. 6 - Environmental Risk Assessment Systems, International Federation for Information Processing, 2005, IFIP ISBN 3-901882-21-9
- D. A. Swayne, J. Hrebicek (eds.), Environmental Software Systems, Vol. 7 - Dimensions of Environmental Informatics, International Federation for Information Processing, 2007, IFIP ISBN: 978-3-901882-22-7.

The eight proceedings of ISESS 2009 were published again on a USB, but not under IFIP ISBN:

- D. A. Swayne, R. Soncini-Sessa (eds.), Environmental Software Systems, Vol. 8, 2009, C.R.L.E University of Guelph ISBN: 978-3-901882-364.

2.2   Collaboration with IFIP and Springer

The editors of these proceedings decided to use the new IFIP publishing channel, which is Springer, and to publish the ISESS 2011 proceedings electronically (as a CD) in the IFIP *Advances in Information and Communication Technology* (AICT) series.

The IFIP AICT series publishes state-of-the-art results in the science of information and communication technologies. The scope of the series includes: foundations of computer science; software theory and practice; education; computer applications in technology; communication systems; systems modeling and optimization; information systems; computers and society; computer systems technology; security; artificial intelligence; and human – computer interaction.

The principal aim of the IFIP AICT series is to encourage education and the dissemination and exchange of information about all aspects of computing.

One of the goals of this event is to merge the knowledge and interests of members of WG 5.11 "Computers and Environment" and the ISESS 2011 conference dedicated to information exchange among scientists and businesses involved in the development and use of environmental informatics for the delivery of state-of-the-art eEnvironment services in Europe and worldwide.

Therefore the conference focuses specifically on the following topics:

- eEnvironment and Cross-Border Services in Digital Agenda for Europe
- Environmental Information Systems and Services—Infrastructures and Platforms
- Semantics and Environment
- Information Tools for Global Environmental Assessment
- Services and Environmental Tools for Urban Planning and Climate Change Applications and Services

ISESS 2011 is a meeting place for experts on leading-edge technologies, and it aims to foster the standardization and integration of environmental data and information flows, which are essential pre-requirements for managing our natural resources in a framework of sustainable development.

ISESS has become open to governmental institutions, international and intergovernmental organizations, environmental agencies and networks, scientists, academicians, politicians, businesses, public administration and decision makers in the field of environmental information, experts from ICT industry, specialists of theoretical and applied informatics, consultants, students and the concerned public.

The editors hope that you find new knowledge and ideas in the IFIP AICT proceedings of ISESS 2011 and from its website, where you can read reviewed contributions of authors and experts on leading-edge ICT technologies for environments of the above-mentioned topics.

3 Vision of IFIP WG 5.11 (Gerald Schimak)

Since many years now, IFIP WG 5.11 "Computers and Environment" is running, under the umbrella of IFIP, this ISESS conference series. We hope that this conference will turn out to be as fruitful as all its predecessors and proves once again as the R&D reference event in Enviromatics.

The vision and mission of the WG 5.11 was always to foster the improved application of information technology in environmental research, monitoring, assessment, management and policy. This is still valid but over the last few years the picture has changed slightly and new challenges have popped up.

Challenges, stemming from requirements realizing a SISE and SEIS or when setting up the Strategies for the Digital Agenda for Europe, demand for new services, new collaboration strategies in decision making and cross-border information exchange. This is not only valid for Europe but also applicable worldwide, if we consider the ICT needs in GMES or GEOSS in ICT and eEnvironment.

In order to achieve our mission mentioned above my personal vision and hopefully also the one of IFIP WG 5.11 for the future is:

- To establish a platform / forum among and between ICT and environmental professionals.
- Hold knowledge-centric conferences worldwide to exchange information about state-of-the-art technology and prepare the ground for the future.
- Provide expert advice to government, multinational organisations and industry.
- Provide strategy and policy makers with intuitive ICT concepts and solutions.

One of the first upcoming tasks of WG 5.11 will be the adoption of our WG member list of well-known experts in the fields of ICT and the environment domain as well as from related sectors like energy or mobility.

Acknowledgments

The editors are grateful to all authors for their valuable contributions to the conference and the members of the Programme Committee for reviewing more than 100 submitted abstracts. Special thanks go to the representatives of the International Federation for Information Processing, DG Information Society and Media of the European Commission as well as the Joint Research Centre for their kind support and useful advice with respect to the collaboration and organization of ISESS 2011.

We would like also to thank Masaryk University, its Institute of Biostatistics and Analyses, the Ministry of Environment of the Czech Republic, and the Technology Centre AS CR for the scientific and organizational support of this conference, the company SYMMA and Aleš Martínek for their administrative support, and Miroslav Kubásek and Jakub Gregor—the conference Web administration and editorial team—for their enormous work on the ISESS website.

Last but not the least we thank all partners involved in the preparation of this conference as well as all sponsors for their valuable cooperation and patience.

June 2011

Jiří Hřebíček
Gerald Schimak
Ralf Denzer

Organization

Program Committee Chairs

Jiří Hřebíček (Chair)	Masaryk University, Czech Republic
Gerald Schimak (Vice-chair)	Austrian Institute of Technology, Austria
Arne J. Berre	SINTEF, Norway
Ralf Denzer	Saarland University of Applied Sciences, Germany
Ladislav Dušek	Masaryk University, Czech Republic
Lars Gidhagen	Swedish Meteorological and Hydrological Institute, Sweden
Ivan Holoubek	Masaryk University, Czech Republic
Martin Kaltenböck	Semantic Web Company & OGD Austria, Austria
David Swayne	University of Guelph, Canada

Publication Chair

Jiří Hřebíček	Masaryk University, Czech Republic

Program Committee Members

Alessandro Annoni	European Commission, Joint Research Centre, Italy
Robert Argent	Centre for Environmental Applied Hydrology, University of Melbourne, Australia
Ioannis N. Athanasiadis	Democritus University of Thrace, Xanthi, Greece
Guiseppe Avelino	Telepatio, Italy
Vladimir Benko	Slovak Environmental Agency, Slovak Republic
Raul Carlsson	Chalmers University, Sweden
Giorgio Guariso	University of Milan, Italy
Werner Geiger	Research Center Karlsruhe, Germany
Albrecht Gnauck	Brandenburg University of Technology Cottbus, Germany
Reiner Güttler	Saarland State University for Applied Sciences, Germany

Gavin Fleming	CSIR Water Environment and Forestry Technology, Republic of South Africa
Steven Frysinger	James Madison University, USA
Jiří Hradec	Czech Environmental Information Agency, Czech Republic
Karel Charvát	Czech Centre for Science and Society, Czech Republic
Anthony Jakeman	Australian National University, Australia
Stefan Jensen	European Environment Agency, Denmark
Martin Kaltenböck	Semantic Web Company & OGD Austria, Austria
Kostas Karatzas	Aristotle University, Greece
Jana Klánová	Masaryk University, Czech Republic
Milan Konečný	Masaryk University, Czech Republic
Horst Kremers	CODATA - Germany, Germany
Daniel Vidal-Madjar	Centre National d'Etudes Spatiales, France
Colette Maloney	European Commission, DG INFSO, Belgium
Patrick Maué	University of Münster, Germany
Thomas Maurer	Federal Institute of Hydrology, Germany
Jaroslav Myšiak	FEEM, Venice, Italy
Tomas Pariente	Atos Origin, Spain
Thomas Pick	Ministry of Environment of Lower Saxony, Germany
Werner Pillmann	International Society for Environmental Protection, Austria
Tomáš Pitner	Masaryk University, Czech Republic
Jaroslav Pokorný	Charles University, Czech Republic
Nigel Quinn	Berkeley Research Lab and University of Berkeley, USA
Iva Ritschelová	Czech Statistical Office, Czech Republic
Andrea E. Rizzoli	IDSIA, Schwitzerland
Bernt Röndell	European Environment Agency, Denmark
Ivica Ruzic	Rudjer Boskovic Institute, Croatia
Miquel Sànchez-Marrè	Technical University of Catalonia, Spain
Alberto Susini	Geneva Labour Inspectorate (OCIRT), Switzerland
Olga Štěpánková	Czech Technical University, Czech Republic
Thomas Usländer	Fraunhofer IOSB, Germany
Irina Zálišová	EPMA, Czech Republic

Additional Reviewers

Jose Mario Caridad	University Cordoba, Spain
Denis Havlík	Austrian Institute of Technology, Austria
Miroslav Kubásek	Masaryk University, Czech Republic

Table of Contents

Invited Talks

eEnvironment and Cross-Border Services in Digital Agenda for Europe

Environmental Information Systems and Services – Infrastructures and Platforms

Semantics and Environment

Information Tools for Global Environmental Assessment

Climate Services and Environmental Tools for Urban Planning and Climate Change Applications and Services

Erratum

eEnvironment: Reality and Challenges for eEnvironment Implementation in Europe

Jiří Hřebíček[1] and Werner Pillmann[2]

[1] Masaryk University, Institute Biostatistics and Analyses,
Kotlářská 2, 611 37 Brno, Czech Republic
[2] International Society for Environmental Protection,
Bechardgasse 24/12, A-1030 Vienna, Austria
hrebicek@iba.muni.cz, pillmann@isep.at

Abstract. The White Paper on eEnvironment introduced the content of eEnvironment at the Ad hoc Committee on eDemocracy of the Council of Europe in 2007. The Recommendation CM/Rec(2009)1 of the Committee of Ministers of the Council of Europe to member states on electronic democracy (e-Democracy) specified eEnvironment in more detail. The objective is that any citizen can be informed about environmental matters and can use this information for active participation in decision making and environmental protection.

Now, eEnvironment is one of the pillars of eDemocracy and a member in the "eFamily" like eParticipation and eGovernment. The paper describes the reality and challenges for eEnvironment implementation with respect to the Digital Agenda for Europe and the European eGovernment Action Plan 2011-2015. Furthermore it formulates some ideas for embedding eEnvironment in a Shared Environmental Information System and linked it to the vision of a Single Information Space in Europe for the Environment.

Keywords: eEnvironment, eGovernment, eDemocracy, SISE, SEIS, GMES, GEOSS, Europe 2020, Digital Agenda for Europe, European eGovernment Action Plan.

1 Introduction

The White Paper on eEnvironment[1] introduced the content of eEnvironment at the Ad hoc Committee on eDemocracy of the Council of Europe in 2007. This paper outlines eEnvironment as the part of eDemocracy[2] [1], a framework of Shared Environmental Information System (SEIS)[3] [2], Global Monitoring for Environment and Security (GMES)[4] and Global Earth Observation System of Systems (GEOSS)[5] [3], [4] and the

---

[1] http://www.bmeia.gv.at/fileadmin/user_upload/bmeia/media/AOes/
e-Democracy/4575_18___eacces_to_environm___info.pdf
[2] http://en.wikipedia.org/wiki/E-democracy
[3] http://ec.europa.eu/environment/seis/index.htm
[4] http://www.gmes.info/
[5] http://www.earthobservations.org/gci_gci.shtml

J. Hřebíček, G. Schimak, and R. Denzer (Eds.): ISESS 2011, IFIP AICT 359, pp. 1–14, 2011.

important part of the Single Information Space in Europe for the Environment (SISE)[6] [2], [5] and introduces current trends in the European Union (EU). Both the visions and challenges of eEnvironment and its potential for further sustainable development of the Environment are discussed. It takes into account tasks and roles of a Digital Agenda for Europe (DAE), cross-border eEnvironment services, the SEIS as a part of the Europe 2020 strategy and the European eGovernment Action Plan 2011-2015 (COM(2010) 743). To accomplish the goals of the EU 2020 Strategy and its flagship initiatives, Innovation Union[7] and DAE, we need advanced communication infrastructures, information technologies, smart applications and services that should be based on a new generation of networks, on the Internet of the Future[8].

Therefore, shared environmental data, information and services will be combined in eEnvironment with environmental knowledge for public in order to participate and support government decisions to foster environmental protection and sustainable development in the EU.

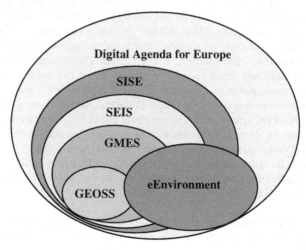

Fig. 1. eEnvironment as the subset of a Digital Agenda for Europe, SISE, SEIS, GMES and GEOSS

2 Introduction to eEnvironment Vision

2.1 eEnvironment and eDemocracy

The Recommendation CM/Rec(2009)1 of the Committee of Ministers of the Council of Europe to member states on electronic democracy (*eDemocracy*) of 18 February 2009 settled out recommendations, principles and guidelines concerning eDemocracy which are designed to apply to eDemocracy the democracy and human rights principles established, inter alia, by existing Council of Europe instruments and other international instruments.

---

[6] http://ict-ensure.tugraz.at/en/index.php/ensure/Content2/SISE
[7] http://ec.europa.eu/research/innovation-union/index_en.cfm
[8] http://www.future-internet.eu/

It determined 72 principles, rules and regulatory frameworks of eDemocracy in the Appendix to Recommendation CM/Rec(2009)1. It also includes Principle 40 of eDemocracy, where is officially specified eEnvironment as: *"eEnvironment is the use and promotion of Information and Communication Technology (ICT) for the purposes of environmental assessment and protection, spatial planning, and the sustainable use of natural resources, and includes public participation. Using ICT to introduce or enhance public participation can improve democratic governance in respect of environmental issues."*

This principle was specified in the Explanatory memorandum to Recommendation CM/Rec(2009)1 of the Committee of Ministers to Member States on eDemocracy, where it is described in the Sectors on eDemocracy as items 87-89:

87. *eEnvironment includes the use of ICT-based systems for access to and the dissemination of environmental data and information as well as the establishment of ICT-supported monitoring systems and repositories for environmental knowledge.* eEnvironment thus makes it possible to forecast and monitor the impact of natural and man-made factors and other pressures on the environment, and to determine the current state of the environment, which in turn makes it easier to formulate potential responses because it is possible to draw on a broader, more widely disseminated knowledge base.

88. *Spatial planning and spatial cohesion are both basic components of the eEnvironment field, and as such constitute major challenges for nation states and regional and local authorities.* In May 2008, the Congress of Local and Regional Authorities of the Council of Europe adopted a report and recommendation on *"Electronic democracy and deliberative consultation on urban projects."*[9].

89. The *Aarhus Convention*[10] includes provisions calling on contracting parties to use electronic information tools to provide public access to environmental information. To this end, the Parties to the Aarhus Convention set up a task force to facilitate its implementation through the effective use of ICT tools (Aarhus Clearing house[11]) designed to provide public access to environmental information.

The above eDemocracy principles for eEnvironment were reflected in European legislation and influence the idea of the SISE and particularly for the SEIS [4], [5], where very important role had recent development which has been the entering in force of the INSPIRE Directive 2007/2/EC in May 2007[12] supporting the 88. principle. This established an infrastructure for spatial information in Europe to support environmental policies in EU, and policies or activities which may have an impact on the environment[13]. It is supported by the prototype INSPIRE geoportal[14] for discovery

---

[9] http://wcd.coe.int/ViewDoc.jsp?id=1278871&Site=Congress&BackColorInternet=e0cee1& BackColorIntranet=e0cee1&BackColorLogged=FFC679
[10] http://www.unece.org/env/pp/
[11] http://aarhusclearinghouse.unece.org/
[12] http://eur-lex.europa.eu/LexUriServ/LexUriServ.do?uri=CELEX:32007L0002:EN:NOT
[13] http://inspire.jrc.ec.europa.eu/index.cfm

and viewing of spatial data sets and services. The prototype INSPIRE geoportal currently accesses a limited number of discovery and view services and therefore only a few metadata for spatial data sets and services can be found and viewed. These will increase as more services become available from the EU Member States.

2.2 Development of eEnvironment Infrastructure

The development of an ICT infrastructure for the SISE and the SEIS (generally for eEnvironment) started during the Sixth Framework Programme (FP6)[15] 2002 – 2006. The majority of funding under the respective actions in ICT went into technical preparation of the SISE (architectures, concepts, services, reference models etc). It has continued in the Seven Framework Programme (FP7)[16] 2007 - 2013, particularly in the last two years to permit an easy discovery of European environmental service nodes on the web and their adaptive chaining (or composition) on demand.

The EU actively supports the concept of SEIS and SISE through its research programmes. In previous (e.g. FP6) and the currently active (FP7) framework programme, there is a multitude of research projects (DIADEM, DIVINE, EarthLookCZ, GEM-CON-BIO, GENESIS, GIGAS, HUMBOLDT, ICT-ENSURE, INTAMAP, LENVIS, ORCHESTRA, SANY, TESS,)[17] that address key aspects of a common environmental information system supporting the 87. and 89 principles of eDemocracy. The same is also true for the CIP[18] umbrella programme and especially its ICT-PSP programme[19].

It took full advantage of international open standards including the program *Interoperability Solutions for European Public Administrations* (ISA)[20]. It capitalizes on the experience gained since 1999 with the two previous programmes IDA II (Interchange of Data between Administrations) and IDABC (Interoperable Delivery of pan-European eGovernment services to public Administrations, Businesses and Citizens). ISA will run from 2010 to 2015 with a financial funding of 164 million Euros.

The development of the SISE in FP7 included generic semantics frameworks and dynamic ontology services for the discovery of and access to distributed environmental resources in a multilingual multi-domain context.

Challenges and new tasks of eEnvironment were summarised by authors of [5] in 2010:

- Establish *eEnvironment national/regional environmental information web centres in the Member States of EU* or equivalent sources of information as the part of the SEIS that will stimulate and promote public access to information and public participation in environmental decision-making; promote access to electronically stored environmental information by establishing and maintaining community web access points;

---

[14] http://www.inspire-geoportal.eu/index.cfm
[15] http://ec.europa.eu/research/fp6/index_en.cfm
[16] http://ec.europa.eu/research/fp7/index_en.cfm
[17] http://ec.europa.eu/environment/seis/related_projects.htm
[18] http://ec.europa.eu/cip/
[19] http://ec.europa.eu/cip/ict-psp/index_en.htm
[20] http://ec.europa.eu/isa/

- Establish *one-stop access point(s) for citizen and related eGovernment services*[21], with coordinated input from the relevant public authorities and/or linkages to other similar sites;
- Develop *human capacity for the use of ICT tools* of SISE, SEIS, GMES and GEOSS to promote the implementation of eEnvironment through comprehensive and forward-looking training and education strategies for public officials;
- Promote the European Commission's efforts to develop the *institutional capacities of public authorities* to monitor, collect, organize, store and disseminate environmental data, information, services and knowledge in an easily accessible and user-friendly manner *in GMES*;
- Ensure the availability *of commonly readable, user-friendly and easily transferable formats* (as standards) of SISE, SEIS, GMES and GEOSS for environment-related data, information, services and knowledge. Develop and apply comprehensive ICT tools of eEnvironment, including specific training programmes linking the use of ICT tools to the promotion of good environmental governance in EU member states;
- Promote the *involvement of different stakeholders* representing both SEIS, GMES and GEOSS providers and its users, including civil society and private sector institutions, in the development and use of ICT tools with a view to improving the accessibility, as well as the availability, of environmental information and knowledge to the public;
- Maintain a *national SEIS web site* with data and information related to the nationwide implementation of eEnvironment, which will serve also as the national node of the SEIS clearing-house mechanism;
- Designate *national/regional contact points in SEIS and GMES* responsible for collecting, managing and updating the information contained in the national node and for providing the necessary information for the central node of the SEIS clearing-house mechanism at EEA, and undertake to disseminate information to the public on the clearing-house mechanism; and
- Develop *capacity for public officials* managing and updating information for the national node of SEIS in the *Shared European National State of the Environment*[22] (SENSE) project, and for providing the necessary information for the central node of the clearing-house mechanism at European Environment Agency (EEA).
- Develop methods and protocols for service chaining in SISE and for the management of the effects of uncertainty propagation through service chaining, which will be included into the ICT infrastructure for eEnvironment.

The *eEnvironment* implementation through SEIS and the "State of Environment Report" (SOER) 2010[23] has contributed to high quality information and services

---

[21] http://ec.europa.eu/information_society/activities/egovernment/index_en.htm

[22] http://svn.eionet.europa.eu/projects/Zope/wiki/SENSE

[23] SOER 2010, http://www.eea.europa.eu/soer, was the fourth State and Outlook Report on the European environment produced by the European Environment Agency (EEA). This "report" produced by the EEA for 2010, covered 38 countries, on the current state of the environment, how we got to that state, what that state might be by 2020, what is being done and what could be done to improve that state.

provision and it will thus provide Europe's backbone infrastructure for *eGovernment /
eParticipation*[24] */ eDemocracy* services in the Environment Matters; it will also provide a powerful ICT tools to support rapid knowledge-based decision making for
sustainable development at all levels (national, regional, local), as integrated information from various environmental impacts (related with economic and social items)
will be available on real-time.

It will boost competiveness and innovation of European ICT industry. Finally,
SOER 2010 is a substantial contribution of EU to global ICT tools under development
(in Digital Agenda for Europe goals implementation) in order to support global governance for sustainable development, such as is done in the GEOSS.

2.3   eEnvironment and Digital Agenda for Europe

The *Digital Agenda for Europe* (COM (2010) 245)[25] is one of the seven flagship
initiatives of the Europe 2020 Strategy (COM(2010) 2020 final)[26], that set out to
define the key enabling role that the use of ICTs will have to play if Europe wants to
succeed in its ambitions for 2020. It outlines seven priority areas for action, namely:

1.   Creating a Digital Single Market to deliver the benefits of the digital era.
2.   Improving the framework conditions for interoperability between ICT
     products.
3.   Enhancing Internet trust and security.
4.   Increasing access to fast and ultra fast Internet.
5.   Boosting cutting-edge research and innovation in ICTs.
6.   Enhancing digital literacy, skills and social inclusion.
7.   Applying ICTs to address social challenges such as climate change, rising
     healthcare costs and the ageing population.

In its *Key Action 16* and *other actions the Digital Agenda for Europe* proposes a
Council and Parliament Decision by 2012 to ensure mutual recognition of
e-identification and e-authentication across the EU, based on online *"authentication
services"* to be offered in all Member States (which may use the most appropriate
official citizen documents – issued by the public or the private sector).

The Digital Agenda for Europe sets eGovernment within a comprehensive set of
measures aimed at exploiting the benefits of ICT across Europe. At a time of highly
constrained public resources, ICT can help the public sector develop innovative ways
of delivering its services to citizens while unleashing efficiencies and driving down
costs.

The availability of innovative technologies such as social networks has increased
the expectations of citizens in terms of responsiveness when accessing all kinds of
services on line. However, cross-border eGovernment services are few and, even
where eGovernment services are offered, the majority of EU citizens are reluctant to
use them. There is clearly a need to move towards a more open model of design, production and delivery of online services, taking advantage of the possibility offered by

---

[24] http://ec.europa.eu/information_society/activities/egovernment/policy/eparticipation/
index_en.htm
[25] http://eur-lex.europa.eu/LexUriServ/LexUriServ.do?uri=COM:2010:0245:FIN:EN:PDF
[26] http://eur-lex.europa.eu/LexUriServ/LexUriServ.do?uri=COM:2010:2020:FIN:EN:PDF

collaboration between citizens, entrepreneurs and civil society. The combination of new technologies, open specifications, innovative architectures and the availability of public sector information can deliver greater value to citizens with fewer resources.

Furthermore the Digital Agenda for Europe (DAE) proposes:

- Support by 2012 seamless cross-border eGovernment services in the single market through the *Competitiveness and Innovation Programme* and *Interoperability Solutions for European Public Administrations (ISA) Programme*[27] issued from the ISA;
- Review by 2011 of Directive 2003/4/EC *"Public Access to Environmental Information"*;
- Work with Member States and stakeholders to *implement cross-border e-Environment services*, notably advanced sensor networks;
- Define by 2011 concrete steps in a *White Paper* on how to inter-connect e-procurement capacity across the single market; and
- Set an example of open and transparent eGovernment by creating and implementing an ambitious *eCommission 2011-2015 action plan*[28] including full electronic procurement.

Member States of the EU should follow these tasks formulated by the DAE i.e.:

- Make *eGovernment services* fully *interoperable*, overcoming organizational, technical or semantic barriers and supporting communication protocol IPv6[29];
- Ensure that the *Points of Single Contact function* as fully fledged eGovernment centres beyond the requirements and areas covered by the *Services Directive* [7];
- Agree by 2011 on a common list of key cross-border public services that correspond to well-defined needs - enabling entrepreneurs to set up and run a business anywhere in Europe independent of their original location, and allowing citizens to study, work, reside and retire anywhere in the EU. These key services should be available online by 2015.

2.4 eEnvironment Services in the Digital Agenda for Europe

The term *"eEnvironment services"* in the Digital Agenda for Europe (DAE) includes all computer-based tools that support the environment conservation process and encompasses services ranging from the simple provision of environmental information to sophisticated reporting and information processing.

According to the DAE eEnvironment services that focus on ICT development in the environment domain are somewhat underdeveloped or "fragmented along national borders".

The current approach to these challenges is embedded in the SEIS Communication (COM/2008/0046 final)[30] and some recent projects (Reportnet[31], PortalU[32] and

---

[27] http://ec.europa.eu/isa/
[28] http://ec.europa.eu/information_society/activities/egovernment/action_plan_2011_2015/docs/action_plan_en_act_part1_v2.pdf
[29] http://ipv6.com/
[30] http://eur-lex.europa.eu/LexUriServ/LexUriServ.do?uri=CELEX:52008DC0046:EN:NOT

WISE[33]). The SEIS recognises the need to address several key steps in the ways data are created and shared, where the notion of centralised systems for reporting "are progressively replaced by systems based on access, sharing and interoperability".

The eEnvironment services can be a valuable tool for interested persons, researchers, and decision makers. They can address general policy-related subjects, or specific environmental study areas [6]. These areas can be grouped as follows:

- Air quality.
- Ozone depletion.
- Climate change.
- Biodiversity.
- Terrestrial.
- Water.
- Waste.
- Agriculture.
- Energy.
- Fishery.
- Transport.

eEnvironment services, as a category of *eGovernment services*, are either still under-developed, or fragmented along national borders[34]. This is a challenge that the digitalization of public services is facing as a whole. In extension to overcome these barriers, firstly the EU law in this area among others should be reviewed and modernized. Secondly, innovative solutions such as advanced sensor networks can help fill gaps in the required environmental data.

The project NESIS[35] has identified requirements and ICT solutions for environmental information sharing, refers to the European ICT policy context (top-down approach), as well as to the specific needs and related solutions of environmental data-sharing, as dealt by (bottom-up approach) in recent projects and initiatives.

The top-down approach grounds on the political context/evolution and refers to the priorities of the current EC initiatives. Overall, concerns about information-sharing in public agencies and government in the EU are grounded in the activities of eGovernment. At the EU level, the *European Interoperability Strategy* (EIS)[36] was devised to ensure appropriate governance, organisation and processes in line with the EU policies and objectives, together with trusted information exchange. The ISA carry

---

[31] http://www.eionet.europa.eu/reportnet

[32] http://www.portalu.de/ingrid-portal/portal/_ns:YUxhbmd1YWdlU3dpdGNNofGMwfGQw/

[33] http://www.water.europa.eu/

[34] Austria: http://www.nesis.eu/index.php?option=com_wrapper&view=wrapper&Itemid=157,
Czech: http://www.nesis.eu/index.php?option=com_wrapper&view=wrapper&Itemid=147,
France: http://www.nesis.eu/index.php?option=com_wrapper&view=wrapper&Itemid=163,
Germany: http://www.nesis.eu/index.php?option=com_wrapper&view=wrapper&Itemid=146,
Sweden: http://www.nesis.eu/index.php?option=com_wrapper&view=wrapper&Itemid=154
UK: http://www.nesis.eu/index.php?option=com_wrapper&view=wrapper&Itemid=190

[35] http://www.nesis.eu/

[36] http://ec.europa.eu/idabc/en/document/7772.html

forward the *European eGovernment Action Plan from 2010 to 2015*[37], with a particular focus on "back-office" solutions that support EU policies and activities and avoid barriers to interoperability across borders.

The EIS suggested that a top-down view and definition of criteria and contents should be accompanied by actions supporting concrete projects at a grassroots level (bottom-up approach), with similar considerations present in the ISA. By addressing real examples, that test existing guidelines against concrete needs, it is hoped that new and possibly reusable services/tools can be produced to meet these demands in a range of contexts.

This brings an impulse for new progress in the area of eEnvironment. The plan to provide eEnvironment communication to all citizens of the EU in the DAE will enable citizens to be informed about environmental matters and to use monitored, collected, processed, evaluated and visualized data, information and knowledge, and thus allow an active participation of citizens in decision making in environmental protection and sustainable growth.

SEIS proposed the set of principles on the basis of which the collection, exchange and use of environmental data and information should be organised in the future:

- Manage information close to source.
- Share information.
- Support fulfilment of reporting obligations.
- Assess state of the environment.
- Assess effectiveness of policies.
- Support design of new policies.
- Support (public) participation.
- Allow comparison on appropriate geographic scale.
- Make information on the environment publicly available.
- Support multilingualism.
- Base IT on open source.

A key step in the implementation of the SEIS (eEnvironment services) approach will be to modernise the way in which information required in various pieces of environmental legislation is made available, through a legislative instrument that should follow the SEIS Communication and probably revise the current "Standardised reporting directive" No. 91/692/EC[38]. Such a revision should also provide an immediate opportunity to repeal a limited number of obsolete reporting requirements, and lead to further simplification and modernization along the following lines [9]:

- to help to stimulate further streamlining of information requirements in thematic environmental legislation, with a coherent and up-to-date overall framework;
- to stimulate similar developments in international conventions, which according to estimates are responsible for around 70% of environmental reporting requirements to which EU Member States are subject;

---

[37] http://ec.europa.eu/information_society/activities/egovernment/
action_plan_2011_2015/index_en.htm
[38] http://eur-lex.europa.eu/LexUriServ/site/en/consleg/1991/L/01991L0692-20031120-en.pdf

- to encourage improvements in the way that data collection and exchange within EU Member States is organized.

2.5 eEnvironment Services and European Neighbourhood

The EEA was assigned by EC Directorate-General EuropeAid Co-operation Office (EC/DG AIDCO)[39] to carry out a project for gradually extending the SEIS principles (eEnvironment services) to the European Neighbourhood Policy[40] to South and East neighbours and the Russian Federation (ENP). The ENPI-SEIS project[41] aims to improve environmental monitoring and data and information sharing by gradually extending the SEIS principles to the European neighbourhood. The project will run over the period 2010-2014.

The overall goal of the ENPI-SEIS project is to promote the protection of the environment in the countries of the ENP area. In order to achieve this, the project aims towards a set of measurable and specific objectives:

- to identify or further develop environmental indicators and scorecards suitable for the design and review of environmental policies, supporting the monitoring and compliance with various national, regional and international obligations and targets;
- to improve capacities in the field of monitoring, collection, storage, assessment, and reporting of environmental data in the relevant environmental authorities including the national statistical systems, in compliance with reporting obligations to international agreements and in coordination with relevant regional initiatives;
- to set up national and regional environmental information systems in the countries of the ENP area that are in line with the SEIS, and
- to track progress of the regional environmental initiatives (ENP, Eastern Partnership, Horizon 2020)[42].

The main outcomes of the ENPI-SEIS project will address the three SEIS components - cooperation, content and infrastructure - through enhanced networking with the national capacities on environmental information. Furthermore, it will promote open, public access to information through compatible and freely available exchange tools.

2.6 eEnvironment and Open Government Data Initiative

Many projects supporting the ambitious efforts of SISE and SEIS (including eEnvironment services), which are now in progress, were presented during the European conference of the Czech Presidency of the Council of the EU: *Towards eEnvironment - Opportunities of SEIS and SISE: Integrating Environmental Knowledge in Europe*[43] in Prague on March 25-27, 2009 [8].

---

[39] http://ec.europa.eu/europeaid/index_en.htm
[40] http://ec.europa.eu/europeaid/where/neighbourhood/index_en.htm
[41] http://enpi-seis.ew.eea.europa.eu/
[42] http://www.h2020.net/en/review-monitoring-and-research/the-project-enpi-seis.html
[43] http://www.e-envi2009.org

The Conference *Sharing Environmental Information*[44] was held in Brussels on November 29,2010 – December 1,2010 and brought in its Conclusion a new initiative connected to Open Government data: "*8. Initiatives towards enhancing the availability of data and information produced or commissioned by government or government controlled entities such as the Open Government data initiative*[45] *is welcomed.*"

This conference brought together representatives from the EEA member and cooperating countries, EEA and the European Commission (EC). The participants reflected mainly on the implementation of the SEIS. In the conference conclusions, the participants encouraged the EC to publish the SEIS Implementation Plan as soon as possible.

They also emphasised the benefits of mutually supportive interaction between SEIS, INSPIRE and GMES processes. The participants also recommended that SEIS, through the use of relevant ICT, should be closely connected to the Digital Agenda for Europe as part of the EU strategy 2020.

The public sector holds a gold mine of environmental information. Much of environmental data that public authorities gather are not used or serve only a limited purpose. The release of non personal public data (environmental, geographical, demographic, statistical data etc…) in particular when provided in a machine readable format allows citizens, and businesses to find new ways to use it and to create new innovative products and services.

The European eGovernment Action Plan 2011 - 2015 has given the central role of national governments in the implementation of this action plan the EC's main responsibility is to improve the conditions for development of cross-border eGovernment services provided to citizens and businesses regardless of their country of origin. This includes establishing pre-conditions, such as interoperability, eSignatures[46] and eIdentification[47]. These services strengthen the internal market and complement EU legislative acts and their effectiveness[48] in a number of domains where ICT can improve delivery of services; such as in procurement, justice, health, environment, mobility and social security, and support the implementation of citizens' initiatives with ICT tools.

The vision Open Government data is fulfilled by the European Open Government data initiative (OGDI)[49] that is a free, open-source, cloud-based collection of software assets that government organizations can take advantage of. They can load and store public data using the Microsoft Cloud[50], using the Windows Azure Platform[51].

---

[44] http://ew.eea.europa.eu/meetings-and-events/sharing-environmental-information

[45] http://opengovernmentdata.org/

[46] http://ec.europa.eu/information_society/policy/esignature/index_en.htm

[47] http://ec.europa.eu/information_society/policy/esignature/action_plan/index_en.htm

[48] Such EU legislative acts include: the Services Directive (2006/123/EC), the eSignatures Directive (1999/93/EC), the Procurement Directives (2004/17/EC and 2004/18/EC), the Data Protection Directive (95/46/EC), the Directive on the re-use of public sector information (2003/98/EC), the Infrastructure for Spatial Information in the European Community (IN SPIRE Directive 2007/2/EC), the public access to environmental information Directive (2003/4/EC).

[49] http://www.govdata.eu/en/europeanopen.aspx

[50] http://www.microsoft.com/en-us/cloud/1/home.aspx?fbid=vL9l-4EikW6

[51] http://www.microsoft.com/windowsazure/

eEnvironment legislative background - Directive 2003/98/EC of the European Parliament and of the Council of 17 November 2003 on the re-use of public sector information (PSI Directive) - sets the legislative framework for the re-use of public information. It has introduced a common legislative framework regulating how public sector bodies should make their information available for re-use in order to remove barriers such as discriminatory practices, monopoly markets and a lack of transparency. All 27 EU Member States have implemented the PSI Directive into their national legal orders[52].

But Open Government is so much more than a legal requirement. Better access to Public Sector Information (PSI) can improve people's quality of life and make how they interface with government much easier. Plus, it can create new businesses and jobs while giving consumers more choice and greater value for money.

PSI is the single largest source of environmental information in Europe. It is produced and collected by public bodies and includes digital maps, meteorological, environmental, legal, traffic, financial, economic and other data. Most of this raw data could be re-used or integrated into new products and services, which we use on a daily basis, such as car navigation systems, weather forecasts, financial and insurance services.

Re-use of PSI means using it in new ways by adding value to it, combining information from different sources, making mash-ups and new applications, both for commercial and non-commercial purposes. Examples include real time traffic information and bus timetables together with maps downloaded to smart phones.

The Directive PSI has introduced a common legislative framework regulating how public sector bodies should make their information available for re-use in order to remove barriers such as discriminatory practices, monopoly markets and a lack of transparency. All 27 EU Member States have implemented the PSI Directive into their national legal orders.

OGDI uses the Windows Azure Platform for Windows Azure Platform to make it easier to publish and use a wide variety of public data from government agencies. OGDI is also a free, open source "starter kit" with code[53] that can be used to publish data on the Internet in a Web-friendly format with easy-to-use, open Application Program Interfaces (API's)[54]. OGDI-based web API's can be accessed from a variety of client technologies such as Silverlight, Flash, JavaScript, PHP, Python, Ruby, mapping web sites, etc.

Whether citizen wishing to use government data (e.g. environmental data), a government developer, or a "citizen developer", these open API's will enable citizen to build innovative applications, visualizations and mash-ups that empower people through access to government information. This site is built using the OGDI starter kit software assets and provides interactive access to some publicly-available data sets along with sample code and resources for writing applications using the OGDI API's.

---

[52] http://ec.europa.eu/information_society/policy/psi/rules/ms/index_en.htm
[53] http://ogdi.codeplex.com/
[54] Application program interface is a set of routines, protocols, and tools for building software applications.

3 Vision for Extending eEnvironment to a Single Information Space in Europe for the Environment

The idea to integrate the immense pan-European diversity of environmental information is a vision. A first step to foster the free flow of environmental information is done by eEnvironment, making distributed information sources available in the Web which meets the needs of administration, politics, research, business and the public.

The objective of the implementation of a *Single Information Space in Europe for the Environment* (SISE) is only conceivable in the medium term for selected areas of environmental relevance. Requirements and demands for such areas can be found in multiple sources, e.g. in the EU's 6th Environmental Action Plan, the Environmental Policy Reviews and in the Digital Agenda for Europe. Currently the idea of SISE is promoted by list of European projects as ICT-ENSURE[55], EnviroGrid BlackSee[56], GENESIS[57], NaturNet plus[58],TaToo[59] and ENVIROFI[60].

We see SISE as complementary activity to INSPIRE, GMES and SEIS, supporting mainly bottom up building ICT infrastructure for environment. First steps in the design and conceptual detailing of such an information space are done in the FP7 project ICT-ENSURE. The emphasis was put on some focus areas, where ICT are applied in control of Energy Consumption, increasing Energy Efficiency, analyses Climate Change, improve Sustainable Use of Natural Resources, monitor Biodiversity and use ICT for Industrial Ecology and for Sustainable Urban Development.

The FP7 ENVIROFI Future Internet project will address such important issues by specifying the requirements, and building conceptual prototypes, of the specific enablers of the environmental usage area in the Future Internet. It will bring these diverse stakeholder communities together to understand environmentally observed processes with higher spatial resolutions and contextual situation awareness at an unprecedented scale.

The SISE is seen as further step after eEnvironment services are fully implemented for "Public access to Environmental Information" in Europe". A structural design of the SISE including eEnvironment as an essential element can be found in [10].

4 Conclusion

This paper outlined some reality and challenges for eEnvironment implementation in Europe, which are required by the DAE and its implementation plan.

Acknowledgments. The above results have been developed during the ICT-ENSURE project "European ICT Environmental Sustainability Research". ICT-ENSURE was financed under the grant agreement number 224017 of the European Commission's 7th framework programme, by DG-INFSO Unit "ICT for Sustainable Growth".

---

[55] http://www.ict-ensure.eu
[56] http://www.envirogrids.net/
[57] http://www.genesis-fp7.eu/
[58] http://www.naturnet.org/simplecms/?menuID=66&action=article&presenter=Article
[59] http://www.tatoo-fp7.eu/tatooweb/
[60] http://www.envirofi.eu/

References

1. Karamagioli, E., Hřebíček, J., Legat, R., Schleidt, K.: Environmental Democracy via ICT; Public Participation via ICT Towards Sustainable Development. In: Leitner, C., Makolm, M.H.J., Traunmüller, R. (eds.) Eastern European eIGov Days 2010. Unleashing the Potential of e-Government: Beyond Simple Patterns of Electronic Service Delivery, pp. 177–194. Austrian Computer Society, Wien (2010)
2. Hrebicek, J., Pillmann, W.: Shared Environmental Information System and Single Information Space in Europe for the Environment: Antipodes or Associates? In: European conference of the Czech Presidency of the Council of the EU: Towards eEnvironment - Opportunities of SEIS and SISE: Integrating Environmental Knowledge in Europe, pp. 447–458. Masaryk university, Brno (2009)
3. Pillmann, W., Hrebicek, J.: Information Sources for a European Integrated Environmental Information Space. In: 23. International Conference on Informatics for Environmental Protection. EnviroInfo 2009. Environmental Informatics and Industrial Environmental Protection: Concepts, Methods and Tools, pp. 341–352. Shaker Verlag, Aachen (2009)
4. Pillmann, W., Hrebicek, J.: ICT for Public Access to Environmental Information. In: 8. Eastern European eIGov Days 2010. Unleashing the Potential of eGovernment: Beyond Simple Patterns of Electronic Service Delivery, pp. 195–202. Austrian Computer Society, Wien (2010)
5. Hrebicek, J., Legat, R., Schleidt, K.: eDemocracy & eEnvironment: Reality and challenges for eEnvironment implementation in Europe. In: 8. Eastern European eIGov Days 2010. Unleashing the Potential of e-Government: Beyond Simple Patterns of Electronic Service Delivery, pp. 167–176. Austrian Computer Society, Wien (2010)
6. Indicators and fact sheets about Europe's environment, http://www.eea.europa.eu/data-and-maps/indicators/#c7=all&c5=&c0=10
7. Handbook on Implementation of the Service Directive, http://ec.europa.eu/internal_market/services/docs/services-dir/guides/handbook_en.pdf
8. Hrebicek, J., et al. (eds.): Proceedings of European conference of the Czech Presidency of the Council of the EU: Towards eEnvironment - Opportunities of SEIS and SISE: Integrating Environmental Knowledge in Europe. Masaryk University, Brno (2009)
9. NESIS: Deliverable 6.2 – Towards the ICT implementation of SEIS, http://www.nesis.eu/index.php?option=com_content&view=article&id=142&Itemid=125
10. Pillmann, W., Pick, T., Hrebicek, J., et al.: Conceptual Detailing of a Single Information Space in Europe for the Environment. ICT-ENSURE Deliverable D7.2 (2010), http://ict-ensure.tugraz.at/en/index.php/ensure/Organisational-Content/Downloads-Resources/Deliverables/WP-7-SISE-Concept-Outline

Making Progress in Integrated Modelling and Environmental Decision Support

Anthony J. Jakeman[1], Sondoss El Sawah[1],
Joseph H.A. Guillaume[1], and Suzanne A. Pierce[2]

[1] Fenner School of Environment and Society and National Centre for Groundwater Research
and Training, The Australian National University, Canberra
[2] Jackson School of Geosciences, University of Texas, Austin
{tony.jakeman,sondoss.elsawah}@anu.edu.au

Abstract. Integrated modelling and environmental decision support are increasingly important as society tackles some of the most complex challenges of our generation, with impacts on future generations. When integrated modelling is successful, the results can be transformational yet the core elements for generating that success are not always clear. There is an elusive element to finding the best mix of methods, models and approaches for any given problem. This raises issues for repeatability and questions regarding how the emerging metadiscipline will converge in order to consistently achieve quality results or increased understanding of the processes that lead to success. Key challenges include the need to diagnose elements that lead to successful process, training for professional and technical competencies, and increased access to stable platforms and interchangeable models and modelling tools. This paper aims to summarize some of the key process and product related challenges of integrated modelling and environmental decision support.

Keywords: Integrated modelling, environmental decision support, modelling tools.

1 Introduction

Most environmental and sustainability issues we face today are known to be wicked or messy problems. Wicked problems arise in contexts where uncertainty and conflicts are rife (Rittel and Webber [1]). To manage these complex issues, we need to take a precautionary, adaptive and evidence-based approach that seeks to balance the needs of current and future generations. To help inform decision making and adaptive planning, there are several requirements:

- Engaging relevant interest groups in participatory processes to collectively frame the issues to be addressed, share knowledge and engender trust
- Modelling activities (both qualitative and quantitative) that acquire, systematize and integrate the knowledge about: the problem under scrutiny, data, information and perspectives in order to improve system understanding and clarify trade-off options

J. Hřebíček, G. Schimak, and R. Denzer (Eds.): ISESS 2011, IFIP AICT 359, pp. 15–25, 2011.
© IFIP International Federation for Information Processing 2011

- Managing the major sources of uncertainty in the decision making process by identifying, ranking, communicating and purposefully reducing the crucial components
- Creating stable and accessible information and knowledge-based systems that support efficient storage, processing and (re)-use of available data, knowledge and models
- Committing sufficient resources to the overall decision making process or, at least, using available resources efficiently be they financial, technical or facilitative.

This paper focuses on the role that integrated modelling can play in effectively and efficiently meeting decision support requirements. A worthwhile question then is: how far are we as an environmental modelling and software community along this path? To help address this question, the paper has three aims:

(1) Give a brief snapshot of the integrated modelling field and some of its key achievements and weaknesses that we can improve and build upon (Sections 2 and 3)
(2) Proffer some suggestions as to where we, as a community of modellers and software developers, would like to be in a decade or so in terms of providing major progress to support the environmental decision making process (Section 4)
(3) Discuss some of the opportunities that the modelling community can embrace to achieve such progress (Section 5).

2 Integrated Modelling

Undoubtedly there has been a lot of activity in the environmental modelling area since the use of computers has become routine. Indeed that activity has been growing and models are increasingly used to support environmental decisions. There is really no alternative to the use of modelling, a term and activity used here in the broadest sense. Indeed modelling is unavoidable and more necessary the messier the problem.

Integrated environmental modelling can be viewed as a "metadiscipline" which integrates knowledge and practices across multiple scientific fields (e.g. hydrology, ecology, economics, various social sciences) to improve understanding of the ecological, social and economic outcomes of management decisions. The challenge is to treat integrated modelling as a process that strives for credibility and accessibility. Ravetz [2] goes so far as arguing for evaluation of the process of integrated model development rather than the product, stating that in such circumstances *"the inherently more difficult path of testing of the process may actually be more practical."* We would argue the need for evaluation of both process and product and recognize the mutual support lent by each objective.

3 Where Are We Now?

The development and application of integrated modelling stand on a number of pillars or building blocks which constitute both the modelling process and content development (see Figure 1). These include: (1) models, (2) modelling guidelines, (3) participatory modelling, (4) modelling paradigms, (5) methods and tools, and (6) software/hardware technologies. The following sub-sections address these pillars.

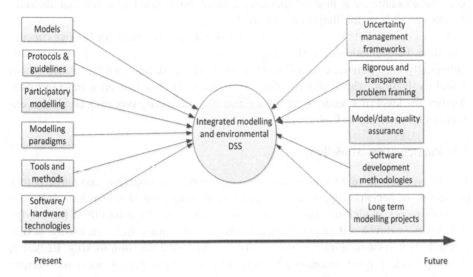

Fig. 1. Pillars in the field of integrated modelling and environmental decision support

3.1 The Legacy of Models

First of all we now have a legacy of disciplinary models for a wide range of bio-physical and socio-economic processes that is relevant for incorporating in integrated models and/or modelling. In each of hydrology, ecology, economics, and other enabling fields there is a very rich literature proposing, applying and (to a lesser extent) evaluating models of different types for different purposes utilizing a varying quantity and quality of data. In that literature there is much that can be learnt about the values of these models as component candidates for an integrated model. In the integrated modelling literature, Oxley et al. [3] discuss the difference between domain-specific research models and integrated policy-oriented models. They identify several criteria when considering a model for including as a component in an integrated model or integrated modelling exercise, such as: purpose/use of the integrated model, adequacy of represented processes, accuracy and resolution of data. Integrating, adapting and rebuilding are three strategies for incorporating existing models into an integrated platform. Each strategy has its own advantages and disadvantages in terms of development costs, flexibility of the end-product, and the degree to which user requirements are met. Advances in software development have provided technologies and tools that can effectively support the technical integration of models. This will be further discussed in Sub-section 3.6.

3.2 Protocols and Guidelines

Secondly, in line with the dual but mutually supportive premises of accentuating the process and evaluating the products of modelling, some accepted protocols and guidelines exist about how one develops models and software. Adopting good modelling practices improves the chances for the reusability and extendibility of models. The Position Paper [4] on the development and evaluation of environmental models is just one example of a host of literature and recommended practice that includes Refsgaard [5], Van der Sluijs et al. [6] and Lee [7].

A weakness to date that could easily be obliterated is the need for heavier concentration on the evaluation of models as products, most of which being reported remains pathetically thin. Bennett et al. [8] summarize quantitative and qualitative methods of model evaluation, which will hopefully help place the practice on a trajectory that clarifies the level of a model's credibility and, as a necessary reporting condition, explicitly characterizes its limitations.

3.3 Participatory Modelling

Thirdly, we now have a maturing literature on the role of modelling and participatory processes for decision support and a rapidly increasing pool of researchers dedicated to participatory modelling. This research line is informed by a wealth of knowledge and practices developed in psychological and social inquiry fields including: action research, soft systems thinking and cognitive/behavioural decision making. Becker et al. [9] provide a good summary of where and how participation enters the various stages of integrated modelling. Bousquet and Voinov [10] is a good introduction to "Modelling with stakeholders" and is evidence of the strong trend towards participatory modelling. A deficiency at present, however, seems to be that there is an imbalance in the research between there being too much science push and not enough stakeholder pull in general. There are two interrelated causes for this perceived gap. First, there has been little attention paid to systematically evaluating and demonstrating the practical impacts of the process and its products on decision making. Second, participatory modelling remains more of an art than a science. Whereas it is recognized that the research design highly depends on the project's context and purpose, there is still a lack of understanding of how/why a process works in practice to achieve a desired outcome. Recent work has started to recognise these drawbacks, such as Mathews et al. [11]. Perhaps it is just a matter of time until the value of the science is more recognised and this perceived imbalance reverses.

3.4 Paradigms for Integrated Modelling

Fourthly, we have some powerful paradigms or families for integrated modelling, each with their own suitability to different situations. These include

- Bayesian Networks
- Agent Based Models
- System Dynamics Models
- Coupled Complex Models , and
- Hybrids of these families.

The strengths and weaknesses of these paradigms in different contexts are characterized in [12], according to modelling purpose, nature of the data at one's disposal, the breadth of issues being addressed, capability of the paradigm for handling uncertainty, and disciplinary model components to be incorporated. As applications of these paradigms mount, the literature here is becoming increasingly helpful in illustrating what sort of utility they possess.

3.5 Methods and Tools

Fifthly, we have a myriad of methods and tools to assist with integrated modelling and the development of decision support systems [13]. These include:

- Data acquisition and analysis tools (e.g. GIS, data mining)
- Qualitative modelling methods (e.g. conceptual models)
- Scenario development methods (e.g. narratives and fuzzy cognitive maps)
- Participatory methods to elicit and synthesize multiple sources of knowledge
- Expert elicitation methods to obtain and incorporate expert opinion into models in cases where other information sources are limited or unreliable (e.g. Delphi techniques and fuzzy methods)
- Cost-benefit analysis methods
- Multi-criteria analysis tools
- Optimisation algorithms
- Sensitivity analysis
- Uncertainty analysis
- Modelling and statistical tools more generally.

3.6 The Software and Hardware Technology

Sixthly, the available software technology is advancing rapidly, perhaps much faster than the science of integrated participatory modelling. Many technologies have been, and can be further, leveraged to support integrated modelling. These include:

- Code coupling technologies such as APIs (e.g. interface wrappers), Open MI interfaces, and component modelling technologies (e.g. Active X)
- Digital communication and learning technologies, such as 3-D visualization and interactive gaming technologies [14]
- Distributed and parallel computing technologies, such as cloud computing.

4 Where Would We Like to Be?

4.1 Uncertainty Management

In keeping with the emphasis on process *and* product, a primary aim should be to identify and communicate the sources of uncertainty at all stages of the decision making process. And, as far as is necessary to meet end user needs, one should for example be clarifying trade-offs, and reducing and characterizing uncertainty, such that its effect on objectives can be described by propagating each uncertainty through all stages of that process. Importantly, the existence of residual uncertainty must be recognised and measures planned to address that uncertainty as it arises.

The stages of the decision making process include project scoping, problem framing, searching for options, analysis of candidates, deliberation, implementation and monitoring and evaluation. Reducing uncertainty in problem framing and in the model used for analysis is a key outcome for the more rigorous methods recommended in the next sections. However, it is also necessary to describe and communicate the underlying, often implicitly considered, uncertainties. Scenarios and multi-model techniques [15] can be used to capture multiple frames of a system and its drivers. There are numerous techniques for addressing uncertainty in the model structure and parameters [16], the merits of which are discussed in more detail in Section 3.3. In deliberation, implementation, and monitoring and evaluation, we must be clear about uncertainties accumulated from the rest of the process and their effect on the confidence that we can have in predicted outcomes. There is some belief that discussing the uncertainty in predictions weakens the credibility and authority of recommendations. It must however be acknowledged that uncertainty exists, whether it is explicitly discussed or not, and the risk of failure of decision support will be best minimised by consciously planning how that uncertainty is communicated. By explicitly considering the sources of uncertainty throughout the process, it becomes clear that much can be done to improve the way it is addressed; and indeed many methods already exist, for example to account for and quantify uncertainties in search through optimisation and planning data acquisition for monitoring.

Note that we do have frameworks and methods to better manage uncertainty more holisically [e.g. 17,18] but we require studies that apply these frameworks with appropriate tools so as to show the way the process can be enhanced and the confidence between outcomes predicted.

4.2 Problem Framing

Our observation is that in general much less time is given to framing the problem under scrutiny than is desirable. Although problem framing and structuring can be more critical than the computational techniques we use to generate solutions, there is a perceived temptation to rush to "writing equations and computer code" before developing a sufficient understanding of the problem at hand. A profound investigation of the situation context is the foundation for a rigorous modelling effort to achieve higher impact results. Otherwise we take the high risk of wasting resources on developing super-elegant but less relevant and less useful models. While the upfront cost of exploring the ambiguous elements of a modelling context may seem expensive, it is often worth the extra effort because it can yield results that a community or interest groups will value.

There is a wide range of problem structuring methodologies and techniques for exploring and framing issues in ambiguous and ill-defined decision making contexts including: soft systems methodologies [19], narrative analysis and value-focused thinking. Outputs from these inquiries (mainly qualitative insights) help modellers "get a sense" of how the system works, stakeholder values and issues of concern. This knowledge provides the basis for defining modelling purpose, use, design and functional requirements.

A key challenge facing modellers is how to translate qualitative stakeholder views and values into formal model inputs (i.e. scenarios) and outputs (i.e. indicators). It is observed that in many cases the link between stakeholder frames and models are weak, and the logic information flow is obscure, and sometimes, disconnected. This weakness may defeat the modelling purpose and undermine a model's credibility and relevance. Whereas this problem is inevitable given the different philosophical stances and natures underlying interpretive/soft framing and formal/hard modelling, there is still potential for bridging this gap, or at least transparently reporting inconsistencies. Promising steps in this direction include [20,21].

These concerns must be balanced with a determination to keep the model as simple as possible to meet the objectives. In some cases this will mean simplifying the objectives to obtain usefully accurate answers.

4.3 Model and Data Assurance, Uncertainty and Sensitivity

Much improved modelling practice is warranted and has several requirements. Placing more emphasis on specifying and assessing basic model limitations should be within easy reach. This is mostly a matter of the peer review community insisting more vigorously on researchers being more comprehensive in this regard. Some items in a list of limitations are easily specified and relate to the model assumptions, while others can be revealed by sensibility and sensitivity testing. Do the parameter values make sense? Are some parameters redundant? Is the fit of predictions to observations unacceptably poor under important conditions? Model performance evaluation, beyond perfunctory sensitivity analysis and basic calibration checks, are needed to advance the usability for real world problems.

Sensitivity analysis (SA) needs to be a common step in any complex model evaluation, and indeed could be applied much more in the model construction stage where alternative hypotheses are being entertained. But SA is typically applied in a perfunctory manner, for example merely changing parameters one at a time by some proportional amount after acceptance of the model. Saltelli and Annoni [22] illustrate the dangers of this simplistic practice. While methods of SA need to be better developed for complex models, including those with a strong spatial and multidisciplinary component, use of first cut methods like that of Morris and frequency domain analysis can be more widely applied as very useful screening tools.

Uncertainty analysis (UA) of a model, as opposed to the modelling process, is starting to receive increased attention. But it also needs to be more pervasive, and indeed eclectic. Much of the current focus on UA is either on sampling techniques like pseudo Monte Carlo or on sophisticated and computationally demanding Bayesian techniques where obtaining convergence seems to be an art. At best these methods seem most suited to single discipline models that are not overly complex. In many cases, simpler methods may suffice. Norton [23] for example argues and demonstrates the ease of algebraic SA, where operations in an equation can be combined to find the sensitivities of its output to variations in contributing factors. The challenge for UA is to find ways of propagating uncertainties between model components of an integrated model that have been analyzed individually in an manner that is appropriate for that model component. Another focus in UA should be augmented consideration of errors in input data that drives a model, on output data that is used to calibrate and/or assess performance, and on alternative model structure hypotheses. In the end what would be very advantageous is a catalogue of uncertainties and a ranking of them, preferably informed by their effect on the decision options to understand which uncertainties have crucial consequences.

4.4 Long Term Modelling Projects

Most integrated modelling and DSS development efforts are short term projects which are deemed completed upon the delivery of an end product in the form of a tool and/or final results report. Therefore, there is little attention paid to the post-implementation phases in the model's lifecycle, including: tools/results use, maintenance and summative evaluation. This impairs our understanding of how models are actually used in the policy domain and reduces chances for improvement. In addition, most projects are single shot event whereas increasing returns can be achieved through cycles of implementation. Whereas this observation has been made frequently in the integrated modelling literature [e.g. 24,25] we cannot perceive much improvement in this direction. Mysiak et al. [26] argue that the existing research funding mechanisms impede long term projects and widen the perceived gap between science and policy making.

4.5 Software Development Methodologies

A software development methodology is a prescriptive one that structures and coordinates the technical process of designing, implementing, and testing a software product. Existing software development methodologies provide a complementary framework of concepts, practices, methods and tools that can improve the effectiveness and efficiency of the modelling process and products. Using one of these methodologies enables modellers to apply mechanisms that explicitly incorporate usability aspects into the modelling process, such as: user-centred design and prototyping. To increase the awareness of the integrated modelling and software community about software development concepts, Verweij et al [27] present an IT perspective on the integrated modelling process.

5   How Do We Get There and What Are the Opportunities?

There is an enormous opportunity for members of the integrated modelling and environmental decision support community not only to contribute to the decision making process technically, but also to play a role as neutral broker. Teams are starting to emerge which express the combined overall scientific and participatory strengths - through engaging the interest groups, framing the problem with them and applying scientifically reputable tools.

In order to advance our metadiscipline, several strategies suggest themselves. One is to share the accumulated learnings obtained by those teams from studying messy problems. This will require mechanisms that encourage exchanges across research community boundaries to share problems and solutions.

Another strategy is to develop awareness in teams to select an integrated modelling and software approach that fits the problem well and to comprehensively apply tools that satisfactorily enhance the quality of the process and characterise the credibility of the product. Such an open mindset and capacity necessitates changes to the way that most modellers are educated. Researchers in the main tend to become modellers either from being motivated by the need to solve a problem that is in their sphere of interest or by coming through specific disciplines. In the former case many do not have modelling training. In the latter they may have more training but tend to have preferred ways of treating problems. What is required is a move towards an education and training focus on the discipline of modelling itself that emphasizes the problem context, while also providing exposure to a broad range of problem contexts, disciplines and methods. A modeller's satisfaction would then derive from the greater insights generated from looking for, finding and applying the most relevant tools to the problem – in stark contrast, say, to the rewards of applying approaches that fit within one's comfort zone. Better modelling training is essential. To some extent we have been going backwards with so few modellers able to write serious code. This is epitomized by the advent of the interface which has prevented many from seeing what's inside the models they use.

This education of modellers can take many shapes. One is to develop the relevant majors in undergraduate degrees or create professional training programs that advance modelling capacity for mid-career levels. Another is to insist on accreditation of modellers. A community of integrated modellers exists with too few points of contact. Developing a community of practice for integrated modelling with recognized access points, such as cyberinfrastructure hubs and workshops, makes sense to us.

Participatory modelling and greater consideration and documentation of the modelling process can also support ongoing improvement of modelling practice. In some cases, modelling in a participatory setting could be considered a service rather than a product (though it is very much a research service requiring much acumen). The focus is then on the model enabling social learning and building capacity, with both the model's development and use being facilitated by its creators. This improves the modeller's capacity to evaluate the model, and helps ensure it has made an impact regardless of the fate of the product. Documentation of the modelling process to the extent that it is recoverable [28], and consideration of future re-use of the model, can also facilitate adaptive modelling, such that new work is aware of and builds on past experiences. A database of documented recoverable experiences and their evaluation can provide inspiration for better methods to tackle overlooked but often essential tasks, as well as provide evidence for revision and evolution of best practice guidelines.

What such an agenda implies about research infrastructure has been discussed in [29] and bears repeating. "Plainly a new research and education effort as broad and as discipline-spanning as the one outlined above poses some questions about the adequacy of present research, education and training arrangements. It implies time scales of the order of a decade, funding on a scale allowing continuity for a community large enough to make significant progress on broad and demanding issues, and a means of getting researchers and research users from very different backgrounds to talk to each other and learn each others' perspectives and priorities. It also poses hard practical problems in sourcing, testing, describing, providing access to and archiving data."

References

1. Rittel, H., Webber, M.: Dilemmas in a General Theory of Planning. Policy Sciences 4, 155–169 (1973)
2. Ravetz, J.R.: Integrated Environmental Assessment Forum: Developing Guidelines for "Good Practice." Darmstadt University of Technology. ULYSSES WP-97-1, ULYSSES Project (1997)
3. Oxley, T., McIntosh, B.S., Winder, N., Mulligan, M., Engelen, G.: Integrated Modelling and Decision-Support Tools: a Mediterranean Example. Environmental Modelling and Software 19, 999–1010 (2004)
4. Jakeman, A.J., Letcher, R.A., Norton, J.P.: Ten Iterative Steps in Development and Evaluation of Environmental Models. Environmental Modelling and Software 21, 602–614 (2006)
5. Refsgaard, J.C., Henriksen, H.J., Harrar, W.G., Scholten, H., Kassahan, A.: Quality Assurance in Model Based Water Management – Review of Existing Practice and Outline of New Approaches. Environmental Modelling and Software 20, 1201–1215 (2005)
6. Van der Sluijs, J.P., Craye, M., Funtowicz, S., Kloprogge, P., Ravetz, J., Risbey, J.: Combining Quantitative and Qualitative Measures of Uncertainty in Model Based Environmental Assessment: the NUSAP System. Risk Analysis 25, 481–492 (2005)
7. Lee, N.: Bridging the Gap Between Theory and Practice. Environmental Impact Assessment Review 26, 57–78 (2006)
8. Bennett, N.D., Croke, B.F.W., Jakeman, A.J., Newham, L.T.H., Norton, J.P.: Performance Evaluation of Environmental Models. In: Swayne, D., et al. (eds.) Proceedings International Environmental Modelling and Software Society, Ottawa, Canada (2010), http://www.iemss.org/iemss2010/proceedings.html
9. Becker, A., Soncini-Sessa, R., Castelletti, A., Hattermann, F.F., Willems, P., Stalnacke, P., Laurans, Y., de Lange, W.J.: How can Models Help Implementing the Water Framework Directive? In: Hattermann, F.F., Kundzewicz, Z.W. (eds.) Water Framework Directive: Model Supported Implementation. A Water Manager's Guide. IWA Publishing, London (2010)
10. Bousquet, F., Voinov, A.: Modelling with Stakeholders. Environmental Modelling and Software 25, 1268–1281 (2010)
11. Matthews, K.B., Rivington, M., Blackstock, K.L., McCrum, G., Buchan, K., Miller, D.G.: Raising the Bar? The Challenges of Evaluating the Outcomes of Environmental Modelling and Software. Environmental Modelling and Software 26, 247–257 (2011)
12. Jakeman, A.J., Letcher, R.A., Chen, S.: Integrated Assessment of Impacts of Policy and Water Allocation Change Across Social, Economic and Environmental Dimensions. In: Hussey, K., Dovers, S. (eds.) Managing Water for Australia: the Social and Institutional Challenges, pp. 97–112. CSIRO Publishing (2007)
13. De Ridder, W., Turnpenny, J., Nilsson, M., von Ragmmby, A.: A Framework for Tool Selection and Use in Integrated Assessment for Sustainable Development. Journal of Environmental Assessment Policy and Management 29, 423–441 (2007)
14. Hartig, F., Horn, M., Drechsler, M.: EcoTRADE – A Multi-Player Network Game of a Tradable Permit Market for Biodiversity Credits. Environmental Modelling and Software 25, 1479–1480 (2010)
15. Rojas, R., Kahunde, S., Peeters, L., Batelaan, O., Feyen, L., Dassargues, A.: Application of a Multimodel Approach to Account for Conceptual Model and Scenario Uncertainties in Groundwater Modelling. Journal of Hydrology (in press)

16. Guillaume, J.H.A., Croke, B.F.W., El Sawah, S., Jakeman, A.J.: Implementing a Framework for Managing Uncertainty Holistically. In: Watermatex 2011, San Sebastian, Spain (2011)

17. Walker, W.E., Harremoës, P., Rotmans, J., van der Sluijs, J.P., van Asselt, M.B.A., Janssen, P., von Krauss, M.P.K.: Defining Uncertainty: A Conceptual Basis for Uncertainty Management in Model-Based Decision Support. Integrated Assessment 4(1), 5–17 (2003)

18. Guillaume, J., Pierce, S.A., Jakeman, A.J.: Managing Uncertainty in Determining Sustainable Aquifer Yield. In: Groundwater 2010 Conference, October31-November 4 (2010)

19. Rosenhead, J.: What's the Problem: An Introduction to Problem Structuring Methods. Interface 26(6), 117–131 (1996)

20. Kok, K.: The potential of Fuzzy Cognitive Maps for Semi-Quantitative Scenario Development, with an Example from Brazil. Global Environmental Change 19, 122–133 (2009)

21. Kok, K., van Delden, V.: Combining Two Approaches of Integrated Scenario Development to Combat Desertification in the Guadalentin Watershed, Spain. Environment and Planning B 36, 49–66 (2009)

22. Saltelli, A., Annoni, P.: How to Avoid a Perfunctory Sensitivity Analysis. Environmental Modelling and Software 25, 1508–1517 (2010)

23. Norton, J.P.: Algebraic Sensitivity Analysis of Environmental Models. Environmental Modelling and Software 23, 963–972 (2008)

24. Toth, F.: State of the Art and Future Challenges for Integrated Environmental Assessment. Integrated Assessment 4, 250–264 (2003)

25. Letcher, R.A., Jakeman, A.J.: Application of an Adaptive Method for Integrated Assessment of Water Allocation Issues in the Namoi River Catchment, Australia. Integrated Assessment 4, 73–89 (2003)

26. Mysiak, J., Bazzani, G., Tamaro, M., et al.: Review of Model Based Tools with Regard to the Interaction of Water Management and Agriculture. Chapter 3. In: Vanrolleghem, P. (ed.) Decision Support for Water Framework Directive Implementation. IWA Publishing, London (2011)

27. Verweija, P.J.F.M., Knapena, M.J.R., de Wintera, W.P., Wiena, J.J.F., te Rollera, J.A., Sieberb, S., Jansen, J.M.L.: An IT Perspective on Integrated Environmental Modelling: The SIAT Case. Ecological Modelling 221, 2167–2176 (2010)

28. Checkland, P.: Model Validation in Soft Systems Practice. Systems Research 12(1), 47–54 (1995), doi:10.1002/sres.3850120108

29. Jakeman, A.J., Letcher, R.A., Norton, J.P., et al.: Outstanding Research Issues in Integration and Participation for Water Resources Planning and Management. Chapter 15. In: Castelletti, A., Soncini-Sessa, R. (eds.) Topics on System Analysis and Integrated Water Resource Management, Elsevier, Amsterdam, ch. 15, pp. 273–289. Elsevier, Amsterdam (2007)

Microsoft Open Government Data Initiative (OGDI), Eye on Earth Case Study

Zdeněk Jiříček and Francesa Di Massimo

Microsoft s.r.o., BB Centrum, Building Alpha, Vyskočilova 1461/2a
140 00 Praha 4, Czech Republic
zdenekj@microsoft.com
Microsoft Italy, Centro Direzionale San Felice, Palazzo A
Via Rivoltana 13, 20090 Segrate (MI), Italy
frandim@microsoft.com

Abstract. European Open Government Data Initiative is introduced as a free, open-source, cloud-based collection of software assets that government organizations can take advantage of. They can upload and store public data into the Microsoft Cloud, while leveraging the Windows Azure Platform and environment. Important case study of Windows Azure Platform are presented.

Keywords: Open Government Data, Cloud Computing, Public Sector Information, Eye on Earth, Windows Azure Platform.

1 Open Data Driving Open Government

Open Government is transforming the way organizations across the world handle data and make it available to citizens and communities, and is based on common principles of transparency, participation, and collaboration. Publishing digital data produced and collected by public bodies is a way to realize a piece of Open Government. Overall, this initiative aims at making it easier to publish and reuse a wide variety of public data. This includes mapping, meteorological, legal, traffic, financial, economic, and demographic data. Typically, it doesn't include personal or identifiable information.

1.1 The Open Government Challenge

As much of public data sits on different - and commonly incompatible - systems, the main challenge is delivering interoperability to enable its wider distribution and reuse. Interoperability enables governments to unlock data from disparate locations and make it available in an array of e-government services, while taking into consideration security and privacy aspects. By using emerging protocols, smart tagging, semantics, and document format standards, it is now possible to extract data from incompatible systems. New, simple and accessible ways of using the data are already enabling services that benefit both local and global communities, while there's still a lot of potential in front of us.

J. Hřebíček, G. Schimak, and R. Denzer (Eds.): ISESS 2011, IFIP AICT 359, pp. 26–32, 2011.
© IFIP International Federation for Information Processing 2011

1.2 Why is Public Data So Important?

In the European Union (EU), the Public sector information (PSI) Directive[1] sets the legislative framework for the reuse of public information. But Open Government is so much more than a legal provision. Better access to Public Sector Information (PSI) can improve people's quality of life and make their interaction with government much easier. Unlocking the potential of Government data, some analysts are already talking about "Government as a platform". Besides that, using government data can create new businesses and jobs while giving consumers more choice and greater value for money.

2 The European Open Government Data Initiative (European OGDI) Solution

European OGDI[2] is a free, open-source, cloud-based collection of software assets that government organizations can take advantage of. They can upload and store public data into the Microsoft Cloud[3], while leveraging the Windows Azure Platform[4] and environment.

As an open platform, Windows Azure also lets developers use variety of programming languages, such as .NET, PHP, Ruby, Python and more. The European OGDI data repository is continuously being added to and is fully compliant with the PSI Directive principles:

- *Availability:* Enables governments to publish open data in a reusable format and already includes over 60 different government datasets.
- *Transparency:* Empowers citizens with more visibility of governments' services.
- *Added Value*: Enables independent software vendors (ISV) to develop new applications that create more economic value locally.
- *Non-discriminatory:* Developers working on new applications and services can use the free and customizable source code. It can be used to publish data on the internet in a web-friendly format with easy-to-use, open Application Programming Interfaces (API), which can be accessed from Silverlight, Flash, JavaScript, PHP, Python and Ruby among others.
- *Non-exclusivity*: Available as open source starter kit on Codeplex portal[5].

2.1 Overcoming Barriers towards Open Government

In Europe, there is untapped economic potential from reusing public data. That's why the European Commission (EC) has issued a PSI directive public consultation to

---

[1] Directive 2003/98/EC of the European Parliament and of the Council of 17 November 2003 on the re-use of public sector information,
http://eur-lex.europa.eu/LexUriServ/LexUriServ.do?uri=CELEX:32003L0098:EN:NOT
[2] http://www.govdata.eu/en/index.aspx
[3] http://www.microsoft.com/en-us/cloud/1/home.aspx?fbid=vL9l-4EikW6
[4] http://www.microsoft.com/windowsazure/
[5] http://ogdi.codeplex.com

understand more about the barriers. The findings will inform future amendments to the Directive. In summary, Microsoft's view of the current barriers are:

1. Prevalence of open data that is published to application-specific, non-reusable formats that also lack terminology and data consistency.
2. Cost of provisioning and delivery. Data is most often stored on servers within public bodies, not readily available for external, scalable access.
3. Open data frameworks should be publicly available for developers independently on programming languages, together with tools, sample code and documentation to make it easier to re-use the data.
4. More focus is required on publishing open data to the Cloud to improve cost efficiency, to enable reuse features and give non-discriminatory availability for developers and software developers.

2.2   Why Use the Cloud for Open Data?

The Cloud[6] is a highly effective way to publish large amounts of open data quickly and inexpensively without having to invest in a dedicated server infrastructure.

More and more Open Government projects are being hosted in the Cloud. Cloud platforms, such as Windows Azure, provide inherent benefits for Open Government projects, including:

- It supports a variety of standards, languages and protocols, thus realizing specific interoperability[7] (Interoperability elements[8] of a cloud platform).
- As a service provider, Microsoft must comply with regulatory requirements of the governmental entities within whose jurisdictions Azure operates, in order to ensure compliance and management of security risks. Windows Azure operates in the Microsoft Global Foundation Services (GFS) infrastructure, portions of which are ISO27001 certified. ISO27001 is recognized worldwide as one of the premiere international information security management standards. Windows Azure is in the process of evaluating further industry certifications. In addition to the internationally recognized ISO27001 standard, Microsoft Corporation is a signatory to Safe Harbor and is committed to fulfill all of its obligations under the Safe Harbor Framework.
- Unlimited amounts of government data can be hosted in the Cloud without additional server hardware and management. Government data becomes even more valuable with greater local relevance. For example, city and local authorities generate rich data about local transportation, construction projects, budgeting and civic facilities.
- The Cloud is highly scalable and you only pay for what is used, so it's ideal for hosting government data which may show varying transaction volumes.

---

[6] http://en.wikipedia.org/wiki/Cloud_computing
[7] http://blogs.msdn.com/b/interoperability/archive/2010/12/27/
quicksteps-to-get-started-with-php-on-windows-azure.aspx
[8] http://blogs.msdn.com/b/interoperability/archive/2010/07/22/
interoperability-elements-of-a-cloud-platform-outlined-at-oscon.aspx

- As government open data is non-PII (Personally Identifiable Information), it is often not constrained by the same data protection issues as, for example, online email or document sharing. As a result, Cloud open data solutions can be hosted internationally.
- Azure Data Market enables government agencies to charge ISV's for the data reuse and consumption and enables ISV's to charge their application users for the services they offer on top of the data. (example: data.gov[9]).

2.3 Open Data Projects Using Microsoft Technologies

Examples of Open Government initiatives that are already reusing public data, and leveraging Windows Azure and other Microsoft technologies:

- Live map of the London Underground train network in close to real time[10];
- France health establishments and their locations[11];
- France Personal services establishments and their locations[12];
- Parking for Disabled in the City of Rennes[13];
- Waste collection points in the City of Rennes[14];
- Trees species in Paris for people allergic to pollen[15];
- Glass recycling collection points in the City of Paris[16];
- Easy access to data compiled and Produced by Government Authorities for Swedish Parliament composition[17];
- Eye on Earth[18] utilizes Windows Azure, Silverlight, Bing Maps.
- City of Edmonton[19];
- VanGuide[20] utilizes Windows Azure, OGDI, Bing Maps, Silverlight, Windows Phone 7.
- Miami 311[21] utilizes Windows Azure, Silverlight, Bing Maps, CRM.

2.4 Open Data Terms of Use

The Reuse of the Data published[22] on OGDI web is regulated by the Terms of Use[23] that the Government Agency publishing the Data will attach to the Datasets.

---

[9] https://datamarket.azure.com/browse/filter/publisher~55daae4c-da44-438c-aec3-690a0d3ba623/
[10] http://traintimes.org.uk/map/tube/
[11] http://www.govdata.eu/samples/INSEE/INSEESante.html
[12] http://www.govdata.eu/samples/INSEE/INSEEServices.html
[13] http://www.govdata.eu/samples/rennes/rennessh.html
[14] http://www.govdata.eu/samples/rennes/rennespaven.html
[15] http://www.govdata.eu/samples/paris/parisarbreseu.html
[16] http://www.govdata.eu/samples/paris/pariscolonnesverre.html
[17] http://www.offentligadata.se/Apps.aspx
[18] http://www.eyeonearth.eu
[19] http://data.edmonton.ca
[20] http://vanguide.cloudapp.net/
[21] http://miami311.cloudapp.net
[22] http://dev.govdata.eu/

3 Case Studies

3.1 Environmental Data Sharing: Eye on Earth a Cloud-Based, Web 2.0 Solution

An agency of the European Union, the European Environment Agency (EEA) provides independent and reliable information on the environment for policy makers and the general public. The EEA is working toward raising environmental awareness across Europe by delivering easy-to-understand information about a number of environmental topics—among them, water and air quality. It also encourages citizens to contribute their own observations about the environment around them. Working with Microsoft, it developed the Eye On Earth platform, based on the Windows Azure cloud services operating system. Users can view water or air quality from the 32 member countries of the EEA, using high-definition Bing® Maps.

The EEA has also launched the Environmental Atlas of Europe, which features stories told by eyewitnesses about their first-hand experiences of climate change. Both solutions can help broaden awareness of the impacts of environmental change and help people in Europe make better-informed choices about their environment.

Eye On Earth is supported by cloud services operating system Windows Azure, which works seamlessly with the existing infrastructure, and helps developers quickly deploy new features. The service-based architecture and cloud operating system provide the same level of reliability as an enterprise datacenter, but they offer greater agility, ensuring Eye On Earth can very quickly scale to meet rapid growth in data and traffic.

For WaterWatch, the EEA experiences peak demand during the summer months as people plan their holidays and seek information about the water quality at their destinations. Hundreds of thousands of citizens access the application during its busiest periods, and demand is growing rapidly. AirWatch users are also likely to be increasingly interested in ozone levels in summer when air circulation is more stagnant due to the warmer weather, trapping toxins and pollutants. Cloud technology allows the EEA to easily respond to large-scale peaks in demand.

Bing Maps for Enterprise provides high-resolution satellite images and aerial photography across Europe and beyond. And it's easily customized, so the agency can incorporate its environmental data into the mapping technology with ease.

Data is fed into Microsoft® SQL Azure™ (a cloud-based database service built on Microsoft SQL Server data management software) every hour. The powerful database supports rapid retrieval of information, making it possible for Eye On Earth to process and deliver data in real time. In addition, the Microsoft Silverlight 3 browser plug-in delivers a seamless media experience, providing users with highly interactive features and Deep Zoom functionality.

Determined to make the application as interoperable as possible, the EEA offers a Microsoft® ASP.NET version of the application allowing everyone to participate, independent of their device. This makes the tools accessible to people with Windows computers using Internet Explorer® and the Firefox browser, Macintosh users with the Safari browser, and people with Linux machines.

With Eye On Earth, the EEA brings the most advanced environmental modeling to citizens across Europe, and encourages them to participate. The data is made available to other interested parties such as urban traffic control, tourism, or healthcare

---

[23] http://dev.govdata.eu/Terms

Fig. 1. Eye On Earth platform. Example of Eye On Earth reading, filtered by location for Copenhagen, Denmark.

systems—helping organisations and citizens work together to address climate change, using data that has never before been available on such a scale.

3.2   Open Data Applications: Rennes – Waste Collection Points

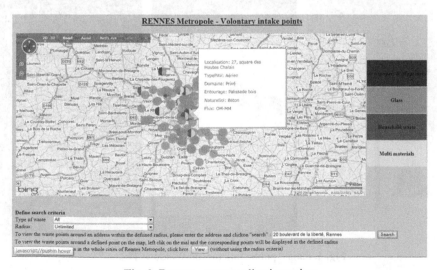

Fig. 2. Rennes – waste collection points

3.3   Open Data Applications: Paris – Sorting on Streetside Trees

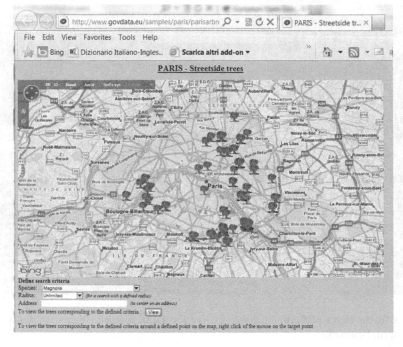

Fig. 3. Paris – sorting on streetside trees

3.4   Open Data Applications: Paris – Public Toilettes on Windows Phone 7

Fig. 4. Paris – public toilettes on Windows Phone 7

Environmental Statistics at the CZSO:
Past Development and Future Trends

Iva Ritschelová[1,2], Egor Sidorov[1,2], and Jiří Hřebíček[3]

[1] Czech Statistical Office, Na padesátém 81,
100 82 Praha 10, Czech Republic
[2] Jan Evangelista Purkyně University, Faculty of Environment
Králova výšina 3132/7, 400 96 Ústí nad Labem, Czech Republic
[3] Masaryk University, Institute of Biostatistics and Analyses
Kotlářská 2, 611 37 Brno, Czech Republic
iva.ritschelova@czso.cz, egor.sidorov@ujep.cz,
hrebicek@iba.muni.cz

Abstract. One of the very important aims of the Czech Statistical Office (CZSO) is to produce national statistical data on environmental development among others. During the last two decades one could trace the constantly increasing interest and attention to environmental statistics both at the international, national and regional level. Being a sustainability management tool, its content has been consequently improving and extending along with the changing political priorities and stakeholder interests. The paper describes the development path of the environmental statistics at the CZSO, makes an assessment of its historical development, current state, and presents the expected future development trends in the field.

Keywords: environment, statistics, history, development, Czech Republic.

1 Introduction

The Czech Statistical Office (CZSO) is an official national statistical institution of the Czech Republic. Being a coordinator of the State Statistical Service its main goal consists in acquisition of data and consequent production of statistical information on social, economic, demographic, and environmental development of the state. Based on acquired data CZSO yields a reliable and consistent image about the state of the arts and development of the society according to various user needs.

The recent stress laid on environmental protection stimulated by discussions and policies both at international and national levels leads to the stable demand for high quality environmentally related statistics from the variety of stakeholders. This interest is primarily motivated by the need to assess the environmental state as well as to define and describe environmental-economic interrelations that are highly influencing economic activity, employment, foreign trade, price level, etc. This is undoubtedly the reason for growing interest among politicians, as well as businessmen in the range of quality environmentally related statistics suitable for complex environmental-economic analyses.

J. Hřebíček, G. Schimak, and R. Denzer (Eds.): ISESS 2011, IFIP AICT 359, pp. 33–46, 2011.
© IFIP International Federation for Information Processing 2011

In reaction to this demand the CZSO has been actively developing production of environmentally related statistics. The following paper maps the main factors that have influenced its recent development and present a bottom line of its current state. The special attention is devoted to key factors and trends that are expected to significantly influence future development in the field.

2 Development of the Environmental Statistics at the CZSO

Legislation development may be considered to be one of the most significant factors influencing the content of the official environmental statistics produced by the CZSO. Concerning the development of the Czech state environmental policy before 1989 one can mention several legislative acts focused on water, forests and general nature protection that appeared in 1950's. In 1960's the land and air legislation came into being. In 1970's the water law was accepted. As a result of foreign pressure the pact on distance trans-border pollution was signed up in 1980's. Furthermore act on protection and exploitation of mineral resources came into being. However, with a view to planned economy peculiarities, proprietorship model and prevailing political priorities environmental problems have been underestimated and mistreated for the long time (see e.g. Ritschelová et al., 2006). Since there was no political demand for relevant data, one can state that environmental statistics at that time was limited to data closely related to agriculture with no particular environmental purpose.

The development of the environmental policy in Europe followed the general trend of moving from end-of-pipe technologies and pollution abatement practices that were prevailing in the 60's-70's of the 20th century up to the so-called integrated technologies and cleaner production of the last decades. Concerning the Czech Republic mainly administrative methods of environmental policy were used in the beginning of the 90's. The primary transformation of the Czech economy during that period was connected with significant activities aimed at improving the environmental state that belonged among the most problematic in the Central Europe of that time. In the first half of the 90's the important changes of environmental protection, especially in the legislative sphere, took place.

During that period legislation has consequently covered the variety of environmental domains, state institutions and environmental funding processes. In addition to acts establishing the Ministry for the Environment (1989), Czech Environmental Inspectorate and State Environmental Fund (1991) number of environmental regulations either newly appeared, or were updated. The most important legislative regulations included acts concerning waste (1990, 1991, and 1992), air protection (1991), general environment, protection of nature and the landscape, and environmental impact assessment (1992). These were often stimulated by the European legislative framework. In reaction to these processes the CZSO has started regular waste generation survey in 1992.

In the second half of the 90's the First State Environmental policy of the Czech Republic (1995-2001) was developed. It has clearly pointed out the priorities based on the generally accepted environmental protection principles and set up time frames for single aims. Environmental legislative process of that time was predominately concentrated on the enforcement of post 1989 acts. One should point out the act stipulating right for environmentally related information was adopted in 1998.

Number of the newly introduced measures enabled to achieve the required level of environmental quality through economic restructuring, decreasing the extent of the chosen economic activities, and implementing the new predominately end-of-pipe technologies. These measures placed very high requirements on number and volume of investment projects financed both form the public and private sources. Under these circumstances the demand for data on environmental expenditures naturally occurred within the variety of stakeholder groups. The CZSO had been collecting relevant statistics since 1986 and therefore could offer respective data.

The development of the legislation in the beginning of the new century was connected to entering the EU. The Second State Environmental Policy was accepted in 2001. It mainly reflected the requirements to the EU members and was predominately focused on the fastest implementation of the European environmental legislation. The policy promoted the sustainable development principles and put stress on incorporation of environmental aspects within the sectoral policies. During that time the Czech legal regulations transposed several tens of European environmental directives. The European accent on sustainability promotion demands complex interdisciplinary data from the so-called environmental accounts among others. At present environmental accounting is one of the most actively developing sphere of environmentally related statistics in the CZSO. According to the Recommendation of the Statistical Program Committee (EC) the regular, timely, production of the key environmental accounts modules is expected from national statistical offices. The CZSO is actively taking part in these activities.

Environmental accounts provide a link between economy and environment. The main guideline for implementation of environmental accounts is called System of Integrated Environmental and Economic Accounts [11]. It is based on the same framework as national accounts [2], [8]. Environmental accounting seems to be the best platform for confronting environmental and economic information and serving as a basis for sustainable development assessment. Only such complex statistical overview of the problem area is capable of supporting sustainability-related decision making at regional and national levels.

The Third State Environmental Policy was accepted in 2004 along with the entering the EU and defined agenda until the year 2010. The contemporary legal system of the Czech Republic responds to all new legal environmental regulations adopted by the European Community. Apart from the so-called administrative tools, one can also see the increasing role of the economic tools represented by fees, environmental taxes, emission permits, etc along with the Czech environmental policy development. Several projects performed by the CZSO were related to these issues as well.

As one can see all the above mentioned institutional conditions during two last decades were actively supporting the interest in high quality environmental statistics. These requirements have also been consequently finding respective reflections in the activities of the Czech Statistical Office. The CZSO environmental department was established in 1993. Its personnel capacity have been fluctuating around 8-9 employees during the whole period of its existence. Today 6 persons are involved into preparation of environmental statistics: 1.5 persons (full time equivalent) are engaged into environmental protection expenditure surveying, 2 persons deal with waste survey, 1 person prepares water statistics, and 1.5 persons perform activities in the sphere of environmental accounting.

It is clear that not all environmental domains are covered by statistical surveys. However one should also mention that a significant part of data is being collected from other administrative sources (i.e. ministries and other bodies of the State Statistical Service). In this case CZSO additionally plays an active integrative role that consists in collecting, aggregating and confronting of available environmentally related statistical data. This enables providing a more complete picture of environmental-economic situation in the country.

3 Own Statistical Surveys and Overtaken Data

3.1 Statistical Survey on Environmental Expenditure

Environmental protection expenditure may be divided into investment and non-investment (i.e. current) expenditure. For a long period of time environmental protection investment was measured as a part of statistical surveys that weren't primarily focused at environmental issues. For example, during 1986-2001 respective questions were incorporated within the investment survey of the CZSO. One should mention that only investment into fixed environmentally related assets was covered at that time. [7,8]

During 1986-1990 environmental investment activities were surveyed both at the macroeconomic level (as total environmental fixed assets investment), as well as at the level of particular investment projects, defined as single constructions and other investment activities leading to improvement of the current environmental state. The latter included all environmentally related constructions with granted construction permission and with the budget over CZK 5 million. Those eventually included constructions individually subsidized from the state budget. Data were currently monitored starting from construction permission grant till final building approval.

All investment activities were broken down into four categories: 1. water quality control, 2. protection of ambient air, 3. waste management, and 4. soil reclamation related to mining and waste dumping activities. During 1992-1995 those were additionally extended by protection activities against physical factors influencing environment, i.e. activities reducing noise level, electromagnetic field intensity, or radioactivity.

The structure of financial sources has been surveyed since 1992. For instance in 1993 the following five categories of financial sources were used within environmental investment activities survey:

1. own sources,
2. loans,
3. support from public budgets,
4. sources from abroad, and
5. other sources.

However, one of the shortcomings of this survey was that its results covered only a limited number of constructions. Furthermore single types of financial sources were not unambiguously defined. For example, in case of financial sources obtained from the State Environmental Fund one could classify them as state subsidies, as well as other sources.

Within the framework of harmonizing the survey with the European standards in 1996 the CZSO has changed the environmental investment definition and classification. The new classification became to a large extent similar to the so-called *Classification of Environmental Protection Activities* (CEPA) adopted by the Conference of European Statisticians in 1994. In this respect environmental investment activities were grouped into 6 categories:

1. water pollution control (excl. groundwater),
2. air pollution control and climate protection,
3. waste management,
4. landscape and nature conservation,
5. reduction of the impact of physical factors, and
6. soil and groundwater protection.

Another important change was connected with the extension of the financial limit of the covered environmental investment types. Since then investment activities with budgets less CZK 5 million were also included. State environmental fund was introduced as an additional financial source, i.e. since 1996 the total of 6 financial source types had been surveyed. National Property Fund was included among other sources.

After the new budget structure was adopted by the Ministry of Finance of the Czech Republic in 1997, its specification of environmental expenditures became very close to the one specified by the CZSO. Particular investment projects survey was cancelled. Through the noticeable progress in the sphere of environmental investment survey methodology, its information capacity was still very limited. In particular due to the fact that it still didn't cover non-investment expenditure.

In 2002 environmental investment survey was performed on the one hand as a part of the annual business survey covering selected production industries and, on the other hand, as a part of the annual survey for government institutions. That year CZSO introduced a new environmental activity classification compatible with the 2000 version of CEPA that has been used up to now. It contains the total of 9 categories, including the following:

1. protection of ambient air and climate,
2. wastewater management,
3. waste management,
4. protection and remediation of soil, groundwater and surface water,
5. noise and vibration abatement (excluding workplace protection),
6. protection of biodiversity and landscapes,
7. protection against radiation (excluding external safety),
8. research and development, and
9. other environmental protection activities.

Classification of financial resources was also updated in 2002 reflecting the changes in model of economic relations in the country. Such finance sources as loans and financial assistance, and issue of securities, free transfers, nonmonetary deposits, etc. were newly introduced.

One of the most significant changes took place in 2003 when the first non-investment expenditure data were introduced for the first time. Non-investment data introduction led to adoption of the targeted Annual survey on environmental protection expenditure. These updates enabled more complex presentation of national environmental protection expenditure. One should mention that in the beginning it covered only business sector. Separate Annual survey covering only investment into long-term fixed assets for government institutions was used until 2005. Since 2006 both business and public sector data have been collected by a *Single environmental protection expenditure survey* (ZP 1-01 survey). [3]

A year later ZP 1-01 survey was additionally extended by environmental fees and charges data. At that time it covered non-financial enterprises in the following fields: agriculture, forestry, mining of mineral resources, manufacturing industry, production and distribution of electricity, gas, water, surface and underground transport, aircraft transport with the number of staff higher than 20 and more (NACE rev.1 codes 01, 02, 10-40, 41, 60, 62). Furthermore the survey covered all non-financial enterprises in the field recycling of secondary raw material and waste disposal (NACE rev.1 codes 37, 90) regardless their size. Finally it included all governmental institutions and municipalities with more than 500 citizens (NACE rev. 1 code 75).

Table 1. Survey of Environmental Expenditure in 2003-2009. [Source: CZSO]

year	2003	2004	2005	2006	2007	2008	2009
Number of respondents	8 039	11 648	11 463	15 288	15 143	11 467	11 705
Response, %	74	57	62	66	82	82	84

Upon introduction of CZ-NACE rev. 2 in 2008 the current ZP 1-01 survey covers chosen units from CZ-NACE 01, 02, 03, 05-33, 35, 36, 49, 51, 52, 58 with 50+ employees and CZ-NACE 37, 38, and 39 regardless number of employees, municipalities with 500+ inhabitants, budgetary organizations and state funds.

As one can see environmental protection expenditure survey has underwent many phases and experienced multiple methodological changes. Today the CZSO has a relatively extensive time series on environmental investment expenditure (1986-2009), accompanied by a shorter time series of non-investment expenditure (2003-2009 for business and 2006-2009 for public sector), as well as revenues from by-products and services (2003-2009 for business and 2006-2009 for public sector). The survey data is used before all to fulfill the reporting duty within the Structural Business Statistics regulation. It is widely used for preparation of printed publications and variety of electronic outputs produced either by the CZSO itself or in cooperation with the Ministry for the Environment (MfE) of the Czech Republic. One should mention among others such publications as Environmental Protection Expenditure in the Czech Republic[1], Report on the Environment in the Czech Republic[2], Statistical Yearbook of the Czech Republic[3], or e.g. Regional Statistical Yearbooks[4].

The main domestic data users are MfE and Czech Environmental Information Agency (CENIA). Information is also widely used within co-operation with international organizations. For instance based on gentlemen agreement the CZSO regularly fills out *OECD/Eurostat Environmental Protection Expenditure*[5] and *Revenue Joint Questionnaire*[6]. One should mention however, that only about 5 percent of required data is being filled out at present. One of the strengths of the survey is that information on environmental revenues and taxes is being collected by its means. Both of them belong to highly discussed topics with a view to political situation in the EU. The first is closely related to Europe 2020 strategy supporting environmental technologies and eco-innovations. The second one corresponds to the so-called environmental tax reform (activities in this field in the Czech Republic have been slowed down lately before all with a view to economic recession and restrictive fiscal policy of the current government).

Concerning the future development in the area of environmental expenditure statistics one should state that under the current circumstances the policy of the CZSO is neither to introduce new surveys, nor to support the extension of existing ones. The aim is not to increase administrative burden as well as not to increase budget requirements. In this respect one should rather expect reduction of survey activities in future. However on the other hand legislative activity at the EU level has a potential to motivate extension and development of the survey under review. This would be the case if *Environmental Protection Expenditure Account* (EPEA) module would be introduced among others within the environmental economic accounts regulation. National activities aimed at reducing public budgets and international policy supporting environmental activities are the two contradictive factors that would influence the future development in the area of environmental expenditure statistics. One can expect that along with the overcoming of the economic recession impacts interest in relevant statistical data would consequently increase.

3.2 Waste Production Survey

CZSO has been making statistical surveys in the field of waste generation and waste treatment since the 80's. After two single-standing one-time surveys of waste dumps and waste production performed by the former Federal Statistical Office in 1980 and 1987 waste generation surveys have been performed on the regular annual basis since 1992. [9]

Through the number of existing critiques (e.g. coverage only of special and hazardous waste, or publishing only aggregated statistics due to individual data issues,

---

[1] http://www.czso.cz/csu/2010edicniplan.nsf/engp/2005-10

[2] http://rocenka.cenia.cz/stat_rocenka_2009/index.htm

[3] http://www.czso.cz/eng/redakce.nsf/i/statistical_yearbooks_of_the_czech_republic

[4] http://www.czso.cz/eng/edicniplan.nsf/aktual/ep-1#10

[5] http://epp.eurostat.ec.europa.eu/statistics_explained/index.php/
Environmental_protection_expenditure

[6] http://epp.eurostat.ec.europa.eu/portal/page/portal/product_details/
publication?p_product_code=KS-EC-05-001

etc.) statistical questionnaire on wastes in 1993-1996 period established a relatively good basis for further time series creation. This enabled tracing development in the field of production and management of the certain types of waste in the Czech Republic.

Before 1994 surveys were solely focused at disposal and utilization of waste by establishments in order to eliminate double counting possibility connected with transfer of waste between several economic agents. However, strong demand for flow data related to waste transfers between units resulted in extension of survey in 1995 by introducing the name and identification number of the waste acceptor. Based on confronting acceptor organizations with the registers of dump operators and waste incineration facilities one could identify the way of disposal of up to 60 % of the transferred waste.

The survey covered companies classified according to their principle economic activity by such CZ NACE rev. 1 codes and 01, 10-41, 45, 55, 601, 602, 62, 747, 7481, 851, 852, 90, 9211, and 93 with 25+ employees.

The 1998 statistical survey of waste production and disposal was maximally adapted to the requirements of the new act on waste and its regulations for implementation. The main changes included switching to a new waste catalogue, new coding system of waste disposal and utilization ways. These changes were regarded to be the most complex, e.g. due to the fact that the new coding system was regarded to be relatively complicated especially for smaller economic agents. Additional changes consisted in inclusion of other waste category into survey and extension of number of respondents.

In 2002 a new act on waste entered into force. The newly adopted act fully complies with waste management laws and regulations of the EU. The surveyed data is classified according to groups of the official waste catalogue among others. The survey enables production data on waste generated by enterprises (broken down by hazardous and other waste), waste generated by municipalities (including separately collected categories), waste management (recovery, disposal, etc.). This information is supplemented by data on consumption of waste as secondary raw material for producing selected products.

The 2002 survey population included enterprises and sampled municipalities (CZ-NACE code 751). The enterprises group covered units with 20+ employees with the principal economic activity in CZ-NACE codes 01, 02, 10-36, 38-41, 45, 502, 55, 601-602, 62, 642, 747, 7481, 851, 852, 9211, and 93. Furthermore, units classified to CZ-NACE 37 (Recycling) and 5157 (Wholesale of waste and scrap) and units classified to CZ-NACE 90 (Sewage and refuse disposal, sanitation and similar activities) with no limit on the number of employees, were also included in the survey.

In order to reduce reporting burden the so-called "rotating model" approach to respondent selection is used since 2009. It consists in regular surveying of the most significant business entities (according to generated waste, business branch, or pursuant to the number of employees). The remaining "rotational" part of respondents is inquired once every three years with the rest of the data being mathematically imputed. This approach enabled reducing of respondent number by almost a half.

Table 2. Waste Production Survey in 1998-2009 [Source: CZSO]

year	1998	2002	2004	2006	2008	2009
Number of respondents	14 461	17 741	19 085	17 875	17 363	9 787
Response, %	64	69	76	81	79	84

Among the main data users directly using data on waste are e.g. such national institutions as Ministry for the Environment and its affiliate Czech Environment Information Agency, Ministry of Industry and Trade, variety of research and development institutions and, of course, media. The collected data is a part of the following regular publications: Statistical Yearbook of the Czech Republic, Generation, Recovery and Disposal of Waste in the Czech Republic, Regional Statistical Yearbooks, Statistical Environmental Yearbook of the Czech Republic, and Report on the Environment of the Czech Republic among others. The last two publications are joint outcomes of CZSO and the MfE.

Among international users one can name e.g. Eurostat and its data users, as well as national statistical institutions of the EU member states. For more than a decade the CZSO has been transferring waste related data to Eurostat. During 1995-2004 the national data reporting was performed according to the so-called Eurostat/OECD Joint Questionnaire on Waste. In 2006 the environmental statistics department changed the report structure in accordance with EC waste directive for which the CZSO is a national responsible institution. One should expect that the range of possible data users is far more extensive. Since the CZSO publishes the majority of data on its web pages, significant amount of regular data users remain anonymous, since they obtain them indirectly via internet.

Concerning the future development of waste production survey one should mention, that act on waste has been updated recently. The most important changes concern the definition and specification of secondary raw materials. Under the current political and economic conditions producers are getting more and more motivated to transform waste into secondary raw materials and to actively use them as production inputs. In reaction to these changes the CZSO has prepared an update of waste production survey. As a result the new survey would support control and development of national Raw Materials policy due to more precise and complete tracing of material flows of waste as well as secondary raw materials e.g. by covering export and import flows. Under institutional conditions of the Czech Republic the waste statistics is also being currently surveyed by the MfE. However, since its actions are limited by the waste-related legislation, and novelization processes involving number of stakeholders are difficult and time consuming, the MfE has no power to follow the new material flow trends so operatively. This also highlights flexibility of national statistical office in reflecting current socio-economic reality.

Issues of raw materials safety are paid an exceptional attention at the European level at present. Secondary raw materials are looked at as a strategically important input into production process. Under these circumstances one can expect that extended waste (and secondary raw materials) production survey would be consequently improved and developed in future according to various stakeholder needs.

3.3 Environmental Accounting

Key modules of environmental accounting in the CZSO include Air Emissions Accounts, Economy-Wide Material Flow Accounts (EW-MFA), and Module for Environmental Protection Expenditure and Revenue. Pilot projects focused at Environmental Taxes by Economic Activity and Environmental Goods and Service Sector were completed as well. One should state that all these modules are still more or less a work in progress. As it was already mentioned, even environmental expenditure survey that has been developing since 1986 is not complete enough to prepare Environmental Protection Expenditure Account (EPEA) according to the requirements described in [11].

However, wide range of methodological work and pilot applications of respective results is currently performed in all key environmental accounts modules. These activities are actively supported by the Recommendation of the Statistical Program Committee (EC) suggesting to provide regular and timely production of the key environmental accounts modules. Eurostat in its turn provides active financial and methodological support to member countries in order to intensify research and development activities in this area. Since no legal base exists in this problem field, at present the majority of data is based upon gentlemen agreements between Eurostat and national statistical institutions. At present some of them transfer data on chosen modules on the basis of other already existing data sources. For instance those include e.g. data on Economy-Wide Material Flows Accounts (based on data from agricultural, industrial and trade statistics), on air emissions accounts (based on the data of air emission inventories), or data on environmental taxes (based on of tax and government finance statistics).

In the meantime proposal for a Regulation on European environmental economic accounts is discussed. The current proposal concerns only the collection of data on emissions, environmental taxes, and material flow accounting. One can expect however, that other modules would be added in future upon the progress in the field of methodology and pilot application (e.g. Environmental Goods and Services Sector (EGSS), EPEA, energy accounts, Resource Use and Management Expenditure Accounts (RUMEA), water, waste, forest accounts, Environmentally Related Transfers (Subsidies) accounts or probably the most problematic ecosystem services accounts).

The first attempt to compile Air Emissions Accounts in the Czech Republic was performed with the support of project of the Ministry for the Environment in 1998. National Accounting Matrix including Environmental Accounts (NAMEA) integrated framework was used for these purposes. The pilot project covered such pollutants as SO_2, NH_3, NO_x, and HCl. As a result of the project time series for time period 1992 and 1995 occurred.

The next project took place in 2004-2005 and was focused on data of 1998, 1999, and 2003. Its aim was to make a step forward and to find a way for regular annual compilation of NAMEA for air emissions in the Czech Republic. In this respect a close cooperation with the Czech Hydro-meteorological Institute (CHMI) was established. This project significantly extended the amount of pollutants covered by the NAMEA framework. In addition to previous results such pollutants as CO_2, N_2O, CH_4, NMVOC, CO, PM10, Hg, Pb, Cd, As, Zn, Cr, Se, Cu, Ni were covered completely, and CO2 bio, HFCs, PFCs, SF6 were covered partly. No data were identified for CFCs and HCFCs. Consequently in 2008 another project was completed. At that time NAMEA Air reporting tables containing 1995–2006 time series were reported to Eurostat. All project results were also used at national level e.g. in reports on the environment of the Czech Republic, or for State environmental policy development and assessment. In 2010 NAMEA Air data collection project continued based on a new compilation guide.

The first attempts of Material Flow Accounts (MFA) preparation in the Czech Republic for years 1990–2003 were performed by the Charles University Environment Centre as a part of its research and development activities. In the following years the CZSO in cooperation with Environment Center carried out a common project aimed at routine MFA preparation process development. As a result of this project the Czech MFA time series for the years 1993–2004 were compiled. Data were collected in close cooperation with Ministry of Industry and Trade and Czech Geological Survey among others. At present CZSO disposes of quite extensive economy-wide material flow time series: domestic extraction is covered for the period 1990-2009, import is covered for 1999-2009, and export is covered for 1999-2009 period. In the close future it is also planned to map outputs of the economy.

As it was mentioned, Environmental Taxes by Economic Activity and Environmental Goods and Service Sector statistics are currently in the phase of development. [5] In 2009-2010 the CZSO has got two respective Eurostat grants in order to develop methodology for routine data collection. The aim of the pilot Environmental Taxes by Economic Activity compilation project was to determine data sources for sectoral breakdown of environmental taxes and fees in the Czech Republic additionally broken down into four categories: energy taxes, pollution taxes, resources taxes, and transport taxes. Totally 12 taxes and fees matching the environmental tax definition were specified for these purposes in cooperation with Charles University Environment Center and chosen tax recipients. As a result of the project time series of energy, resources and transport taxes from 1995 to 2008 and pollution taxes from 2001 to 2008 were created in a demanded structure.

Methodology for Environmental Goods and Services Sector data collection was developed in cooperation with Jan Evangelista Purkyne University. The project was focused at possibilities of environmental goods and services related data from yearly industry and production and environmental protection expenditure surveys, core industries conventional statistics as well as government expenditure statistics. As a result of the project time series of environmental goods and services related data for 2005-2009(2008) were developed. Research related to these and other environmental accounting modules in the CZSO would continue in future.

4 Discussion

Even through the fact that the extent of voluntary business environmental reporting activities is constantly increasing, the role of the state statistical service in the field of producing environmental statistics still holds its exceptional position. The main reason for that is that only centralized state authority is capable of providing objective, standardized, quality and complete environmental statistics. These parameters make it a suitable tool for supporting of decision making at different levels. Furthermore only official statistics can be sufficiently specific and take into account the local conditions as well as particular interests of different policy makers. Being a producer of wide range of other economic and social statistics national statistical office is capable of ensuring the compatibility of different data for the purposes of multidimensional analyses. In this respect official statistics is the most appropriate or even the only data source for promoting sustainable development principles.

One of the critical issues in promoting sustainability consists in analysis of interaction between the economy and the environment. It is widely accepted that the best available approach to the economy description and analysis is based on using national accounting framework. The contemporary System of National Accounts (SNA) is an internationally acknowledged accounting standard at the macro-economic level. The SNA has historically acquired a good reputation of a tool supporting policy-making at different levels. The majority of countries today widely use such SNA-generated indicators for defining objectives and evaluating results of different policies.

The development of the national accounting system has gone a long way from narrow focus at purely economic activities to the wide range of social, economic, and environmental issues. With a view to the constantly changing needs of decision and policy makers as well as other stakeholders, the conventional national accounting system is being constantly transformed and updated in order to meet them.

Significant part of changes is motivated by growing environmental concerns. They have stimulated numerous critiques of the conventional System of National Accounts and brought an idea of linking economic and environmental data. Speaking about the national accounting, the most up-to-date approaches to this linking are discussed in the System of Integrated Environmental and Economic Accounting (SEEA). [2] It comprises several categories of accounts, among which one can find environmentally adjusted accounts. These accounts consider how the existing SNA might be adjusted to reflect defensive expenditure, depletion, and degradation and consequently calculate the environmentally adjusted NDP among others.

Through the common agreement about linking the conventional economic and newly developed environmental accounting systems there is a wide debate about the form of their integration. Some experts argue for the complete greening of national accounts, i.e. integrating environmental concerns into conventional SNA that would consequently adjust main economic indicators. The main argument is that conventional SNA does not provide comprehensive welfare measures and therefore policy- and decision-makers do not get indicators they are actually interested in. Greening of accounts is expected to eliminate this problem.

The other group of experts argues for maintaining explicit distinction between the two accounting systems. The rationale for that is connected with the following two reasons. First, it is the need to maintain consistency with already available historical time series of indicators produced by the SNA. Second, is the conservative principle of accounting preventing from direct incorporation of data retrieved by various non-market evaluation techniques into the conventional national accounting.

According to our opinion, the most sensible way is to choose the second conservative approach to linking economic and environmental accounting systems and continue using satellite accounts that were firstly introduced in the SNA 1993. The SEEA is still a work in progress containing number of unsolved methodological issues. In number of cases it provides only discussion and/or overview of possible approaches rather than an action plan. Currently the third version of the SEEA is being prepared. However, one can expect that complete consensus on all arguable points would not be reached in this version either. This conservative approach would enable the development of environmental accounting, provide comparable environmental-economic data, and preserve the consistency of conventional national accounts. One should admit that the SNA can not be (and probably should not be) flexible enough to follow all the newly borne concepts and theories.[6]

Additional argument is that environmental accounts are closely related to environmental statistics. In case environmental accounts become part of national accounts the link between accounts in physical and money units may be damaged or become less straightforward. It is a matter of vital importance to preserve direct relation between monetary statistics and physical environmental data. Not only it enables the control of data quality, but it also helps to explain economic processes and provides logical interpretations of different environmental-economic phenomena. In this respect the satellite accounts approach is the right solution for making the whole system more suitable for satisfying the growing information needs of both decision-makers and other stakeholders involved into variety of issues.

5 Conclusion

As one can see political interest in environmentally related statistics has been rapidly increasing during the last two decades. The main reasons for that are twofold. First, the alarming environmental problems required legislative actions. These processes created demand for environmental statistics enabling prioritization of respective problems. On the other hand, environmental actions significantly influence economic activities, motivate structural changes and involve number of other related socio-economic consequences. These factors created demand for quality environmental accounting information. As one can see, all these institutional conditions were and are still actively supporting the interest in complex environmentally related statistics.

As key integrative part of the national statistics service the Czech Statistical Office has been making active steps to meet these rapidly changing institutional requirements. One should also note that significant number of environmentally related statistics is also collected due to various command and control purposes. Even through the fact that not all environmental domains are covered by statistical surveys, CZSO data accompanied by these data cover the most important spheres of environmental issues.

Regarding the political demand for environmental data and increasing pressure from variety of other stakeholders, the future of environmentally related statistics is determined by setting up a legal background on the compilation of environmental accounts. One can expect that these activities would support development of environmental satellite accounts and provide complex and comparable data for environmental-economic analyses at the European level. These processes, however, would be obviously slowed-down in reaction to the overall economic situation and consequent reduction of budgets of national statistical institutions. Furthermore, in conditions of overall administrative burden optimization, actions increasing the reporting burden become less and less politically acceptable. In addition to the current stage of methodological development and preparedness of single member countries, this is one of the main reasons why the currently proposed regulation reduces field of action to the three core modules only, with the rest to be consequently added in future. These contradictory factors would determine development in the field in the upcoming years.

References

1. Barroso, J.M.: Europe 2020 - Presentation of J.M. Barroso, President of the European Commission, to the Informal European Council of February 11, 2010, http://ec.europa.eu/eu2020/index_en.htm
2. Congressional Budget Office. Greening the National Accounts. Congressional Budget Office, Washington, D.C (1994), http://www.cbo.gov/ftpdocs/48xx/doc4886/doc11.pdf
3. CZSO. Indicators on Environmental Protection Expenditure. Agriculture, Forestry and Environment Statistics Department, CZSO, Prague (2008)
4. EUROSTAT. Environmental Statistics and Accounts in Europe. Eurostat, Luxembourg (2010)
5. EUROSTAT. The Environmental Goods and Services Sector. Office for Official Publications of the European Communities, Luxembourg (2009)
6. Leinen, J.: Report on the proposal for a regulation of the European Parliament and of the Council on European environmental economic accounts. Committee on the Environment, Public Health and Food Safety 17 (November 2010), http://www.europarl.europa.eu/sides/getDoc.do? pubRef=-//EP//NONSGML+REPORT+A7-2010-0330+0+DOC+PDF+V0//EN
7. Ritschelova, I., et al.: Environmental Policy. Selected Chapters. Jan Evangelista Purkyně University in Ústí nad Labem, Ústí nad Labem (2007)
8. Ritschelová, I., Hájek, M.: K metodice zjišťování výdajů na ochranu životního prostředí. Finance a úvěr 2, 110–117 (1998)
9. Ritschelová, I.: Determinantion of Waste Production in CR. Eurostat - Work session on environmental statistics, Lysebu – Norway, Working Paper No. 13 (1996)
10. Šimonová, L.: Statistika odpadů v ČR a Evropě. In: Žák, M (Ed.) Účetnictví a reporting udržitelného rozvoje (na mikroekonomické a makroekonomické úrovni). pp. 31—34, Linde nakladatelství s.r.o., Praha (2009)
11. United Nations et al. Handbook of National Accounting — Integrated Environmental and Economic Accounting (2003), http://unstats.un.org/unsd/envAccounting/seea2003.pdf

The National Secretariat GEOSS/GMES – Implementation of GEOSS and GMES in the Czech Republic

Jaromír Adamuška[1] and Simona Losmanová[2]

[1] Ministry of the Environment of the Czech Republic, Vršovická 65, Prague 10,
100 10, Czech Republic
jaromir.adamuska@mzp.cz
[2] CENIA, Czech Environmental Information Agency, Litevská 8, Prague 10,
100 05, Czech Republic
simona.losmanova@cenia.cz

Abstract. The aim of the article is to present the role and activities of the National Secretariat GEOSS/GMES (NS). Existence of the NS was declared by the Czech Governmental Resolution No. 229/2009. This resolution requires activities of two ministries – the Ministry of the Environment and the Ministry of Education, Youth and Sports to coordinate Czech activities related to international programmes GEOSS and GMES. The goal of GEOSS and GMES is building up an integrated and sustainable system by sharing and providing information services on the environment, especially those based on Earth observation and remote sensing technologies. The article explains the Czech approach to the coordination of GEOSS/GMES. The coordination is necessary for efficient exploitation of the first-emerged services and also for expanding information to the user´s community. The NS Work Plan 2011 was introduced at the beginning of this year and some goals have already been achieved.

Keywords: GMES, GEOSS, GEO, European Commission, National Secretariat, environment, data, users, services, coordination, remote sensing.

1 Introduction

The Czech Republic is actively participating in the European programme Global Monitoring for Environment and Security (GMES) by expanding awareness about GMES at the national level through the implementation of developing knowledge and best practices into a governmental management system in the Czech Republic. GMES is often presented as the second pillar of the EU space policy after the Galileo programme. However, GMES is not only related to space. The GMES programme consists of three elements: the space component, the in-situ component and services driven by the user´s needs.

There are many definitions of GMES. All of them reflect the original idea from the Baveno Manifesto in 1998. Some parts of GMES can be emphasized by different interest groups. Maybe the most accurate description of GMES is the one which says that GMES is a framework for sustainable, standardized and operational services used for efficient management of environmental, ecological and social threats. Moreover, different approaches to GMES increase the importance of this programme as the EU

J. Hřebíček, G. Schimak, and R. Denzer (Eds.): ISESS 2011, IFIP AICT 359, pp. 47–50, 2011.
© IFIP International Federation for Information Processing 2011

contribution to the worldwide GEOSS (Global Observation System of Systems) initiative developed by The Group on Earth Observation (GEO).

After more than 12 years of continuous effort, GMES finally advanced to the pre-operational phase. The most important milestone was the issuing of Regulation No. 911/2010 [1], which entered into force on 9 November 2010. This regulation shifted GMES from an initiative to a programme or, in other words, to the stage when GMES gained its own budget, and also enforced its relevance and importance. Not surprisingly, an increase of claims and a growth of the agenda concerning the coordination between the EU and Member States is anticipated. The key aspect is a usage of the maximum potential that this programme brings. Each Member state has a different approach how to tackle this issue. This article describes the Czech approach to the coordination of GMES activities within the Czech Republic.

2 Czech Approach to GMES

The Czech Republic has been increasing its involvement in the European programme Global Monitoring for Environment and Security (GMES) by different actions since November 2010 in order to be very well-prepared for the year 2014 when GMES should be fully operational. The first step of the Czech Republic's involvement within the GMES initiative emerged at the end of 2006. At that time, the Czech government approved the engagement of the Czech Republic with GEO and agreed to the building up of the integrated and sustained GEOSS, as well as agreed with its participation in GMES. The competence for the coordination and carrying out of these issues has been given to two ministries: the Ministry of the Environment (MoE) and the Ministry of Education, Youth and Sports (MoEYS). The MoE includes those connected with the environment – major users or potential data producers (or service providers). The MoEYS represents the research sector – institutions which are able to participate in the developing and the designing of services and associated technologies. In 2006, GMES was in its early stage and had the status of an initiative. Particular projects were exclusively funded from the EU Framework programme (FP6 and later from FP7). The first aim of those projects was to develop pilot services based on existing data sources to prove potential and possibilities, need and usage of GMES. After finishing these projects, it was necessary to maintain the vital built-up services (Framework Programmes for R&D do not intend to operate project outputs). To cope with this issue was crucial and it was due to one of these mentioned cases which led to the preparation of the new legislation to underpin GMES.

This context was also reflected at the national level. The priority was to set up an organizational framework for the coordination of GMES activities within the Czech Republic and to ensure the consultation of prepared EU legislation between 2007 and 2010. It proceeded through both ministries which were involved at the national level as well as through Czech delegates from the GMES Advisory Council of the EU. In relation to the increasing need for better GMES coordination, the Czech government authorized the MoE and the MoEYS in spring 2009 to establish the National Secretariat of GEOSS/GMES (NS) as an operational body to deal with GMES and GEOSS issues. This particularly gave power to the NS to regulate and advise public institutions for the purchasing of remote sensing data. The NS was established in July 2010 and has been in full operation since November 2010. The NS consists of four members from the most relevant institutions coming under both ministries: a secretary from the MoE who is responsible for official communication within national authorities and two GMES specialists – the first one represents CENIA, Czech Environmental Information Agency; focusing on user´s needs, community and overlaps to INSPIRE and SEIS. The second specialist comes from the Czech Space Office and he specialises in the research aspects of GMES and the funding of projects through the EU Framework Programme. The fourth member of the NS is a representative of the Czech Hydrometeorological Institute covering GEOSS, atmosphere, hydrology, climate and meteorology.

The first completed goal of the NS was to launch the Czech portal (www.gmes.cz) at the end of 2010. This portal provides comprehensive information about GMES and GEO activities in a bilingual version – Czech and English. Visitors may find here useful information about the evolution of GMES and GEOSS along with the structure scheme of the NS. Services like downloading documents, signing for newsletters or asking questions are offered via the e-mail address: info@gmes.cz. A calendar with interesting events such as project calls, conferences, seminars and workshops is

Fig. 1. The Czech portal www.gmes.cz

updated regularly together with news section [2]. Another step was the completion of the document called "Strategy of the Implementation of GEOSS and GMES in the Czech Republic 2011-2013". This internal document represents a road map type plan and summarises the aims and priorities of the activities for the NS members. At the same time, the strategy presents the main principles and spheres of the NS work and specifies its particular activities.

Members of the NS represent the Czech Republic within the EU and sit within different bodies. One of them is the recently established User Forum managed by the GMES Bureau which is driven by the EU General Directorate for Enterprise and Industry (DG ENTR). The second one is the GMES Committee (GC). In fact, the Czech Republic is represented at the GC´s meetings by two delegates independently nominated by the MoE instead of the NS´s members. In spite of this, they closely and independently cooperate with the NS (consultation of voting instructions, etc.). The NS can also cover delegate's participation if the need arises. Currently the NS is helping to find the best suitable candidate for the Security Board.

There is also an active cooperation with the Ministry of Transport and the Ministry of Interior as an example of interaction on the highest institutional level. The communication with other relevant public authorities is secured by the Coordination Board of GEOSS/GMES (CB). The CB, consisting of various public representatives, shall collect GEOSS/GMES positions and needs of other resorts. The CB recommendations help the Ministry of the Environment to specify main NS´s forehead activities.

3 Conclusion

Considering the tight time frame, the National Secretariat of GEOSS/GMES (NS) has achieved a lot. The necessity for the coordination procedures connected with remote sensing data is undisputable. The NS was established not only as the advisory body and as the coordinator, but was also created for saving national expenditures. Therefore, the NS will be the main contact point for relevant public institutions to discuss their needs. The NS will provide them with correct information about available remote sensing data and opportunities to engage themselves with GMES projects. It is very important to highlight the fact that remote sensing data coming from the EU to Member States should be free for public authorities. The NS will provide information about GMES and GEOSS through different types of media (internet website, oral presentations, leaflets). The NS will motivate experts from research or academic institutions and also support SMEs to benefit from GMES. The NS will also ensure consultation of the EUs strategic and legislative materials. Overall, the NS will help the Czech Republic to eliminate or to reduce information gaps by close cooperation among institutions.

Future advantages will depend on the quality of cooperation among all parties involved.

References

1. Regulation of the European Parliament and of the Council of 22 September 2010 on the European Earth monitoring programme (GMES) and its initial operations (2011-13), http://ec.europa.eu/enterprise/policies/space/files/gmes/regulation_%28eu%29_no_911_2010_en.pdf
2. GEOSS/GMES in the Czech Republic, http://www.gmes.cz/en

Vision and Requirements of Scenario-Driven Environmental Decision Support Systems Supporting Automation for End Users

Sascha Schlobinski[1], Ralf Denzer[2], Steven Frysinger[2,3],
Reiner Güttler[2], and Thorsten Hell[1]

[1] cismet GmbH, Altenkesseler Strasse 17, 66115 Saarbrücken
[2] Environmental Informatics Group (EIG), Goebenstrasse 40, 66117 Saarbrücken, Germany
[3] James Madison University, Harrisonburg, Virginia, USA 22807
sascha.schlobinski@cismet.de

Abstract. This paper discusses the vision and requirements of a highly interactive workbench which supports decision makers using distributed resources including models as automated components of an integrated environmental decision support system. The concepts discussed are results of the SUDPLAN project, an EU FP7 project which aims at developing advanced tools for climate change adaptation for city planners and city managers. To this end, SUDPLAN incorporates access to climate change models and model results as an important common service. This paper provides an overview of SUDPLAN, with special emphasis on the highly interactive Scenario Management System. It also includes an overview of the user requirements derived through a user-centred design process engaging highly diverse user representatives of four pilot application cities.

Keywords: workflow automation; data infrastructures; visualization; climate change; environmental decision support system.

1 Introduction

The Sustainable Urban Development Planner for Climate Change Adaptation (SUDPLAN) is intended to help municipal decision makers and their scientific consultants consider the possible impacts of climate change as they make medium to long-term plans for development or modification of their cities [1]. In order to do this, they will need access to sophisticated climate modeling results pertaining to their region, which in turn requires downscaling of modeling results from global climate models [2].

A major contribution of SUDPLAN is to make such models and related data sets and services available to decision makers who would normally not have access to them, along with data and information describing their impact in the local context.

This is achieved through a flexible workbench framework that may be readily adapted to different regions and different decision problems. By taking a systematic approach, which has been inherited from the FP6 projects ORCHESTRA [3]) and SANY [4], SUDPLAN is compliant with existing infrastructures supporting the

J. Hřebíček, G. Schimak, and R. Denzer (Eds.): ISESS 2011, IFIP AICT 359, pp. 51–63, 2011.

emerging Single Information Space in Europe for the Environment [5]. In addition, developing the requirements for SUDPLAN in close cooperation with four distinct pilot cities has made it possible to achieve a remarkable level of flexibility and adaptability.

2   The SUDPLAN Vision

The principal idea of the SUDPLAN project is to develop an easy-to-use web-based planning, prediction, and decision support tool. This is to be used in an urban context, based on a 'what-if' scenario execution environment, and is designed to help assure a population's health, safety, and quality of life as well as the sustainability of investments in utilities and infrastructures within the context of a changing climate.

SUDPLAN provides a new and visionary capacity to link existing environmental models, information and sensor infrastructures, spatial data infrastructures, and climatic scenario databases, providing visualisation of long-term forecasts of environmental factors for urban subsystems such as buildings, transportation, landscapes, and water management systems. Decision makers will be able to evaluate the risks of such phenomena as river flooding, storm water runoff, and elevated air pollution levels for existing or planned urban areas subject to a changing climate.

The planning of urban infrastructure is typically based on a statistical evaluation of historical data. Traditionally, for example, such data are used to quantify the maximum river runoff during a 100-year period, the most intense rainfall occurring within a similar period, or the risks associated with a concurrent air pollution event and heat wave. But the temperature increase, changes in precipitation and air pollution levels, and variation in storm patterns expected to occur during the coming decades may invalidate those historical analyses and necessitate new assessments based on forecasted climate scenarios. SUDPLAN will make it possible for city planners to include such analyses in a simple and cost-effective manner.

Sustainable cities will require an integrated planning approach. Using SUDPLAN, planners will be able to assess some of the most important environmental factors. Sustainability is approached during both present and predicted climate scenarios which are simulated by regional climate models derived through down scaling from global climate models. This means there will be modeling at the European scale, from which SUDPLAN services may be used to further downscale future climate variables to the urban scale, where they can be used as input to local models implemented over planned or existing urban areas and visualised using a variety of techniques [6].

SUDPLAN provides urban planners and decision makers with a web-based scenario management environment. This tool will allow them to manage scenarios, and to execute, visualise and compare them with each other and with real developments over 3-space and time, in order to carry out scenario-based prediction, damage assessment, planning, and training. SUDPLAN uses 3D/4D modeling, as well as simulation and visualisation coupled with existing resources, such as sensor networks, and provides ready access to integrated and high quality information regarding urban environmental factors for both current and future scenarios. SUDPLAN allows on-the-fly combination and production of forecasts from different types of models, sensors, and geospatial information in 2D and 3D (such as land use and topography).

3 The Scenario Management System Requirements

Early in the development of the SUDPLAN vision it was recognized that different cities would be concerned with different decision problems requiring different analytical tools and data sets. In order to arrive at the specification of a platform flexible enough to suit many such application contexts, a variant of user-centered design [7] was employed.

In conventional user-centered design, representative users of a software application are engaged to help with the design process through a variety of needs assessment techniques in a process which is usually iterative. Carefully done, the ultimate design is then much more likely to suit the needs of the application's targeted users.

To apply this process to SUDPLAN – which is not a single application but a framework for applications – it was necessary to identify representative application contexts and then carry out the user-centred design process for each of them. Once this was accomplished the resulting application requirements could be compared in order to discern common elements and structural features.

Four pilot urban application contexts were chosen: Linz (Austria), Prague (Czech Republic), Stockholm (Sweden), and Wuppertal (Germany). Each of these pilots was interested in different decision problems, and each had somewhat different decision makers (and other users) who would be of interest.

3.1 Needs Assessment

The first step towards the requirements specification [8] included interviews with the people involved in the pilot applications, and assessment and documentation of other relevant aspects. The interviews were carried out with a strong focus on the following important goals:

- identifying the users involved in each pilot's decision process and their role (e.g. direct or indirect users of the system)
- discerning the decisions the pilot application must support
- learning what information and data (amount, representation, flow) will be required
- identifying visualisation and interaction needs
- discovering available subsystems.

The second step consisted of the identification of the tasks the user(s) of the SUD-PLAN applications must be able to perform. The identified tasks were decomposed into a hierarchy of sub-tasks simple enough to enable identification of the resources (data and services) needed to perform the lowest level tasks. This step resulted in definitions of the pilots which served as the basis for plans that document the identified tasks and associated use-cases necessary for the analysis and extraction of functional requirements. The SUDPLAN platform requirements reflect these use-cases and tasks. In addition, SUDPLAN platform requirements are also derived from experience in other projects [9],[10], the literature, and general software engineering and interaction design practice.

3.2 User Requirements Derivation

A key step in the specification of user requirements is the definition of the users. It was possible to develop a generalized definition of primary, secondary and tertiary users in a way which was generic across the application contexts of the four pilots.

SUDPLAN users are described in three basic categories:

- Analysts are those who will be using the SUDPLAN applications on a regular basis to carry out analyses in order to arrive at an environmental management decision. In some cases they may be the decision makers, and in some cases they may be supporting the decision makers. The precise nature of their tasks depends on the particular decision problem they are addressing (e.g. flood management, air quality control, etc.)
- Modellers are those people who develop, integrate, and/or configure mathematical models to be used within SUDPLAN applications.
- System Managers are those people who install and maintain SUDPLAN applications and carry out general system administration tasks.

Characterizing SUDPLAN pilot users in a generic way simplified the data gathering and generalization process, and facilitated derivation of requirements for a platform that could support these users in their various geographic and management contexts.

3.3 User Requirements Overview

User requirements were divided into four categories:

- Common user requirements
- Requirements of analysts
- Requirements of modellers
- Requirements of system managers

While the user requirements described here are important, individually they are not necessarily unique. But their integration into a *single platform supporting families of environmental decision support systems* is. *Looking at the entire information processing chain for all involved stakeholders in a holistic way* is the essential character of the SUDPLAN Scenario Management System.

3.3.1 Common User Requirements

Not surprisingly, the common user requirements (i.e. those shared by all three categories of user) included state-of-the-practice attention to usability and user-centered design. After all, SUDPLAN implementations will no doubt be complex, and therefore the user interfaces need to be as easy to use as possible. This is especially critical when it comes to users from specific disciplines interacting with interdisciplinary aspects of the modelled system. To the extent possible, users should not have to educate themselves outside of their disciplines in order to effectively use the system. Table 1 summarizes in more detail the common user requirements.

Table 1. Common User Requirements Summary

Category	Requirement	Rationale
Usability	User-centered design	Systematic user-centered design helps ensure that the intended users are successful and improves overall productivity.
	User Errors	Preventing or successfully mitigating user errors is necessary to ensure a productive outcome of the users' use of the system.
	Short-term Memory	Avoiding a reliance on the users' short-term memory significantly increases productivity, reduces error rates, and increases user satisfaction.
	Contextual Help	When users are expected to provide input to an application they may need clarification or explanation of the input that is expected of them.
	Ease of Learning	Users should be able to learn how to use the user interface easily and to readily understand its functionality.
	Memorability	Users should be able to readily remember how to use the user interface.
	Transparency	Users should not need to have technical knowledge outside of their domain.
Automation	Recurring Task Automation	There are tasks which must be performed repeatedly. Allowing the users to automate such tasks will greatly enhance ultimate productivity.
	Recurring Task Configuration	Recurring tasks will generally require configuration of input data, parameters, and other variables.
Profiling	Profiling of the User Interface	User interfaces generally allow configuration by users to suit their needs or preferences. Keeping these configurations in a profile prevents any given user from having to reconfigure the application each time they use it.
	Establishment of User Groups	Some aspects of the user interface configuration may be associated with categories of users rather than individual users.
	Profiling of Automation Tasks	Automatically recurring task configurations should be stored in a profile to allow users to re-establish similar task executions without having to completely re-enter configuration information.
	Profiling of Business Processes	Applications will often require combinations of information and services requested from diverse sources, and these request transactions will need to be configured. Saving of request transaction profiles will help users to streamline their analyses by avoiding extensive reconfiguration.

3.3.2 Requirements of Analysts

Over and above these common requirements, which apply to all user categories, one particular category of user – analysts – has very specific requirements. One area of significance to analysts is the management of the tremendous amount of information which must be brought to bear in their analyses. Finding, validating, and managing input data, along with appropriate management and display of results are key to this user's function.

Besides this, the nature of the human decision making process, often a 'what if' process, requires that the system be highly interactive, allowing them to manipulate parameters and see corresponding changes in the results as soon as possible thereafter. This necessitates technical approaches such as caching and preloading to facilitate manipulation of large data sets and/or model results.

In addition, analysts need to be able to control the modelling and analysis process itself. This implies the ability to manage the models involved in a simulation scenario, and to have relatively convenient access to models and modelling results regardless of whether the models execute quickly or take a great deal of time to complete. Various techniques (such as asynchronous and pre-calculated model execution) are required to support this flexibility. The ability to save and share model execution scenarios is a natural extension of this.

Finally, and of at least as much importance, is the need to display, report, and publish the results of analyses. Decision-making requires cognitive access to the information that is relevant to the decision. This includes visualization of data to the analyst, as well as reporting of data to other stakeholders and, ultimately, publishing of results to a larger community, possibly to include the general public. Table 2 summarizes in more detail the requirements of analysts.

Table 2. Analyst Requirements Summary

Category	Requirement	Rationale
Information Management	Information Source Management	An information-intensive application must facilitate the finding, storing, and utilization of information within the application in order to support user success and satisfaction.
	Management of Related Knowledge	Besides actual input data, there may be other information valuable to the analyst, and this information needs to be readily accessible to the users.
	Distributed Information Sources	Applications will often rely on data from multiple external sources.
	Output Data Management	Applications will produce results in a wide variety of forms. These data need to be easily accessible to and manipulated by the analysts.

Table 2. (*continued*)

	Result Processing Management	Given the complexity of applications, output data resulting from primary analytical techniques may need to be post-processed by the user, and system support for these activities is necessary.
	Information Product Management	Information products produced by analysts must be stored and managed in an organized and accessible fashion.
	Coordinate Conversion	Information products produced throughout the platform must be easily convertible to other spatial reference systems.
	Tracing	The system should support the tracing of user and system component interactions.
Interactivity	General Interactivity Requirements	The system shall support analysts by including design features which facilitate manipulation of elements of the modelled system (e.g. parameters, variables, input data).
	Responsiveness	When the analyst has manipulated an input to the modelling system, the system needs to provide an immediate response to this change in situations where that makes sense and is possible.
	Local Data Copy	Pre-fetching and caching data locally can greatly improve the users' experience of interactive exploration of the data.
	Differential Data Download	Many data sources contain data that only infrequently change. Fetching of "changes only" in combination with pre-fetching and caching can therefore greatly improve the system responsiveness.
Model Management	Initial and Boundary Conditions	Mathematical models require parameters describing initial and boundary conditions of the model. It is essential that users be assisted where possible in choosing and establishing those conditions.
	Condition Sets	Particular combinations of initial and boundary condition parameters can be stored as a set, and then reused in subsequent model runs.
	Synchronous Model Execution	Models which generally run to completion quickly can be run by users who choose to wait for completion.
	Asynchronous Model Execution	Since some models will take considerable time to complete, users may choose to run these models asynchronously.

Table 2. (*continued*)

	Model Set Execution	Extending the concept of asynchronous model execution, users can run multiple instances of the same model combination with varying sets of parameters, producing a "family" of results.
	Pre-calculated Model Execution	For computationally intensive models limiting the number of times the model has to be executed, and using stored results from previous runs, can help model combinations which use these results to execute in a timely fashion, and can also reduce redundant use of computational resources.
	Model Status	Computationally intensive models can take considerable time to execute, and during their execution analysts will need to be able to check their status.
Scenarios	Establishing Scenarios	Users need to be able to specify the values for parameters within a scenario (including initial and boundary conditions), as well as the particular models to be included for each scenario.
	Scenario Management	As users define scenarios, they will need to be able to manage them.
Visualisation	3D/4D Visualisation	Analysts need to carry out exploratory data analysis on 3- and 4-dimensional data sets, and therefore need visualization support for these data.
	Spatial Visualisation	Environmental data are very often spatial in nature, and therefore require geo-spatial visualization techniques.
	Temporal Visualisation	Environmental phenomena are dynamic in nature, and therefore often require the use of visualization techniques representation variation of one or more variables as a function of time.
	Spatio-temporal Visualisation	More complex environmental data sets vary in both time and space.
	Visualisation of a Model Run Result	Many model runs will generate spatial and/or temporal data which need to be visualized to be interpreted by the analyst.
	Comparison of Model Run Results	Analysis of the results from multiple comparable model runs (such as under different scenarios) requires the ability to simultaneously represent model results visually.

Table 2. (*continued*)

Result Documentation and Annotation	Documentation of a Model Run	The results of each model run needs to be annotated before being stored in order to facilitate search and recovery.
	Documentation of Scenario Set Execution	In addition to storing annotations about individual model runs, analysts will need to annotate scenario sets as well.
Information Products	Creation of Information Products	The value of an analysis can be greatly enhanced by producing information products which are also accessible to other stakeholders. Analysts will require system support to help them generate such information products.
	Report Generation	Basic reports making the results of scenario execution accessible to non-analysts are necessary in order to communicate the results to the other stakeholders.
	Export	In order to support the generation of information products beyond basic reports, the analyst will need to be able to export artefacts (such as model execution results or visualized data) to other formats for use of external tools.
Sharing	Information Sharing	Information regarding an application, including but not limited to input data, should be readily shared between consenting analysts to facilitate collaboration and efficiency.
	Result Sharing	The results of model and scenario set execution can be useful for analysts working on the same or related applications, and should be readily shared along with their documentation annotations.
	Information Product Sharing	Multiple analysts might be producing similar information products to communicate their results. Sharing of these products encourages efficiency and consistency.
	Automation Sharing	The configuration of automation tasks can become complex for some complicated modelling systems. Sharing these configurations for re-use brings increased efficiency and quality control.
	Annotation Sharing	Sharing of annotations among analysts working on the same data sets can increase their efficiency and support additional quality control.

Table 2. (*continued*)

Publishing	Information Publishing	Analysts may wish to make their data and other information available to other web-based services, and therefore need a mechanism for publishing this information to the Internet.
	Web Publishing	Results such as visualizations and information products, may be shared as web content in order to enhance the value added by the analyses.
	Web Publishing Standards	Adherence to standards will increase the availability of information to the wider community.

3.3.3 Requirements of Modellers

Modellers have somewhat narrower requirements, focused as they are on the fine-tuning and integration of models into the decision support system framework. Since they are generally somewhat more specialized than the analysts, their needs are also more specific. But because they are involved with the integration of models (not all of

Table 3. Modeller Requirements Summary

Category	Requirement	Rationale
Model Management	Model Integration	Integrating models into an application, possibly with other models, means that the modeller needs to be able to specify the role of the model(s) within the application and to make the necessary connections between the model(s) and other components of the application.
	Model Configuration	Modellers need to be able to configure models by specifying those data which are necessary for the model but which will not be under the control of the analyst.
Model Calibration and Validation	Model Calibration	If an application provides access to sufficient measurement data, it may be desirable to calibrate the model(s) used within the application to those data.
	Model Validation	If an application has access to sufficient measurement data, using these data to validate the model(s) can increase confidence in the results of the model(s) within the context of the application.
	Model Versions	If different versions of a model are available it is necessary for these versions to be managed in such a way that analysts can distinguish their features and employ the correct version for their needs.

which are necessarily within their specialty) they require particular help in the areas of assumption harmonization and calibration/validation of integrated models [11]. They must also be supported in coping with a range of versions of particular models, and require assistance in distinguishing the nature of their differences. Table 3 summarizes in more detail the requirements of modellers.

3.3.4 Requirements of System Managers

Finally, system managers have particular requirements. These include provision for user identification and authorization, and extend to the representation of authorized users to external systems with their own authentication requirements. The system manager may be responsible for integration of data, sensor data, services, and models into a platform configuration supporting the analysts, and will therefore require support for all of these tasks. Table 4 summarizes in more detail the requirements of system managers.

Table 4. System Manager Requirements Summary

Category	Requirement	Rationale
Platform Management	User Management	In order to manage access to an application the system manager needs to be able to specify users and groups of users to the system.
	Security and Rights Management	System managers need to be able to specify which users are authorized to have what level of access to which parts of the application.
Integration	Data Source Integration	An application may use data from a variety of sources. The system manager needs to be able to integrate these data sources into the application for the system analyst.
	Sensor Service Integration	Applications may use sensor services that are either local to the application or that are distributed and accessible via the web.
	Service Integration	Applications may use other non-modelling services that are either local to the application or that are distributed and accessible via the web.

4   Architecture and Status of Implementation

An overview of the overall architecture of SUDPLAN has been described elsewhere [12]. The first version of the system has been finalised during the first project year, and will be extended and upgraded during the next 2 years.

The Scenario Management System itself is based on the *cids* geospatial application framework of cismet GmbH [13]. This framework has been developed over more than 10 years [14] and has applications in a number of environmental management and planning applications.

SUDPLAN provides a contemporary example of a family of decision support systems which, though each sibling has uniquely individual needs, offers an economy of resemblance that allows expeditious development. The SUDPLAN pilot applications' disparate contexts and needs might challenge decision support system developers not approaching the problem as systematically as SUDPLAN has done. Yet in this case, these pilot applications yielded to a framework which played on the structural similarities of these applications, while acknowledging their differences.

These interim observations and results must finally, of course, be evaluated as the pilot systems are released to their intended decision makers. Such evaluation is still ahead. It will also be interesting to ascertain, if the opportunity arises, how much of the success of SUDPLAN depends on certain similarities between the pilots, i.e. that they were all urban contexts, and that the predominant issue was climate change. Experimental application of the SUDPLAN framework to other application contexts will go a long way toward answering this question.

Acknowledgements

SUDPLAN is a Collaborative Project (contract number 247708) co-funded by the Information Society and Media DG of the European Commission within the RTD activities of the Thematic Priority Information Society Technologies.

References

Denzer, R., Schlobinski, S., Gidhagen, L.: A Decision Support System for Urban Climate Change Adaptation. In: Proceedings of the 44th Hawaii International Conference on System Sciences (HICSS-44), CDROM. IEEE Computer Society, Los Alamitos (2011)

Gidhagen, L., Denzer, R., Schlobinski, S., Michel, F., Kutschera, P., Havlik, D.: Sustainable Urban Development Planner for Climate Change Adaptation (SUDPLAN). In: Proceedings of ENVIP 2010 workshop at EnviroInfo2010, "Environmental Information Systems and Services - Infrastructures and Platforms, Bonn, October 6-8. CEUR-WS, vol. 679 (2010) ISSN 1613-0073, urn:nbn:de:0074-679-9

Usländer, T. (ed.): Reference Model for the ORCHESTRA Architecture (RM-OA Version 2.1), OGC Best Practices Document, Open Geospatial Consortium (2007),
http://portal.opengeospatial.org/files/?artifact_id=23286

Douglas, J., Usländer, T., Schimak, G., Esteban, J.F., Denzer, R.: An Open Distributed Architecture for Sensor Networks for Risk Management. Journal Sensors 8, 1755–1773 (2008)

SEIS EC: Towards a Shared Environmental Information System (SEIS) (2008),
http://www.eurlex.europa.eu/LexUriServ/LexUriServ.do?uri=COM:
2008:0046:FIN:EN:PDF

Gidhagen, L., Denzer, R., Schlobinski, S., Michel, F., Kutschera, P., Havlik, D.: Sustainable Urban Development Planner for Climate Change Adaptation (SUDPLAN). In: Proceedings of ENVIP 2010 Workshop at EnviroInfo2010, "Environmental Information Systems and Ser-vices - Infrastructures and Platforms, Bonn, October 6-8. CEUR-WS, vol. 679 (2010) ISSN 1613-0073, urn:nbn:de:0074-679-9

Preece, Rogers, Sharp: Interaction Design: Beyond Human-Computer Interaction, 2nd edn. Wiley, Chichester (2007)

SUDPLAN: Sustainable Urban Development Planner for Climate Change Adaptation - Requirements Specification (June 30, 2010), A public version will be available in 2011 at http://www.smhi.se/sudplan/Results

Usländer, T., Denzer, R.: Requirements and Open Architecture of Environmental Risk Management Information Systems. In: van der Walle, B. (ed.) Information Systems for Emergency Management, pp. 344–368. M. E. Sharpe Publishers (2010) ISBN 978-0-7656-2134-4

Havlik, D.: SANY Final Activity Report (D1.1.5.1 Publishable Final Activity Report) (2010), http://sany-ip.eu/filemanager/active?fid=320

Frysinger, S.P.: Integrative Environmental Modeling. In: Clarke, K.C., Parks, B.E., Crane, M.P. (eds.) Geographic Information Systems and Environmental Modeling. Prentice Hall, Englewood Cliffs (2002)

Denzer, R., Schlobinski, S., Gidhagen, L.: A Decision Support System for Urban Climate Change Adaptation. In: Proceedings of the 44th Hawaii International Conference on System Sciences (HICSS-44), CDROM. IEEE Computer Society, Los Alamitos (2011)

Schlobinski, S., Hell, T., Denzer, R., Güttler, R.: Ein Werkzeug für die Entwicklung integrierter Fachanwendungen im Umfeld verteilter Daten- und Service-Infrastrukturen. In: Proceedings AGIT Conference, Salzburg (in press, 2011)

Güttler, R., Denzer, R., Houy, P.: An EIS Called WuNDa, Environmental Software Systems. Environmental Information and Decision Support, vol. 3, pp. 114–121. Kluwer Academic Publishers, Dordrecht (2000)

OGD2011 – Requirements Analysis for an Open Data Strategy (in Austria)

Martin Kaltenböck

Semantic Web Company, OGD Austria, Lerchenfelder Gürtel 43, 1160 Vienna, Austria
m.kaltenboeck@semantic-web.at

Abstract. The OGD2011 project launches the 1st Open Government Data Conference Austria and brings together international and national experts in the area of Open Government Data as well as representatives of the main four open data stakeholder groups: politicians, citizens, industry and the public administration in Austria for the first time in 2011 in Vienna. But OGD2011 is more than a conference: in the course of four workshops with representatives of the 4 mentioned stakeholder groups in Spring 2011 the expectations & requirements of these groups as well as challenges & threats and open questions & important issues of the open data process in Austria have been evaluated and analysed. As an output of this analysis as well as of the conference the OGD2011 project team publishes the OGD White Book Austria. This paper gives an overview over the outcomes of the OGD2011 project.

Keywords: open government data, open data, requirements, analysis.

1 Introduction

To analyse the requirements of an open government data strategy for Austria as well as to evaluate expectations, challenges and threats of open data itself, relevant representatives of the four main stakeholder groups were identified and invited to stakeholder workshops: politicians, citizens, industry and public administration (as well as the additional stakeholder groups: media and academia). The participants for these workshops were chosen to ensure a homogeneous workshop group per stakeholder workshop (e.g. for the politicians workshop members of all Austrian main parties were invited as well as representatives from local, regional and national governments). Every workshop was moderated by two persons of the area of public administration research and was documented by 2 members of the OGD2011 team. In the forefront of the workshops the participants have been invited to prioritize the relevant topics of open data for their respective workshop (12 topics were given for this preparation). On the basis of this prioritization the workshop agendas have been created and the workshops have been accomplished along the highest weighted open data topics of the prioritization of the respective stakeholder group. The minutes of the 4 workshops have been compacted and reports have been created out of the minutes. As a final step these reports have been compared with each other as well as populated by additional research results, additional publications and the outcome of about ~ 40 meetings with representatives of the 4 stakeholder groups that took place along the

J. Hřebíček, G. Schimak, and R. Denzer (Eds.): ISESS 2011, IFIP AICT 359, pp. 64–69, 2011.

OGD2011 process. The outcome of this is published in the OGD2011 White Book Austria. As follows you can find the main identified topics to keep in mind for an open data process/strategy.

2 Need for Definitions

As one of the first steps for an open data strategy / process it was identified that there is a strong need to create definitions to ensure further discussion on open data on the basis of a common understanding. As there are different legal issues and frameworks as well as cultures and languages in the EU 27 countries these definitions need to be created for every nation. The following terms needed a deeper look in the OGD2011 project: open government, open government data, linked open government data, public sector information. After the clarification of such definitions together with the relevant stakeholders it is on the one hand possible to trigger a political process on open data as well as on the other hand to ensure that all stakeholders as well as the community and the interested public are talking about the same things.

3 Open Government: Transparency and Democracy, Participation and Collaboration

When starting to discuss open data as a measure for the digital infrastructure of a country the stakeholders that have to become active first are politicians as well as the public administration. One of the strongest arguments of open data is to enable open government: more transparency of processes and decisions made by the politics and the administration, what then becomes a key factor for better democracy on the basis of a better understanding between citizens – politicians – public administration. This new open government paradigm could also lower disenchantment with politics and can be achieved by a stronger involvement (participation) of the citizens in public processes and decision making processes as well as in enabling collaboration between all open data stakeholders. To ensure this open government there is a strong need for a commitment on open data by the highest levels of politics as well as public administration.

4 Legal Issues

A further criteria that is very important in the course of an open data process for a country is to identify and discuss legal issues for this open data strategy. As laws and regulations differ very strong between EU27 countries these legal issues can hardly be transferred from one country to the other. Existing laws and regulations have to be evaluated and maybe adapted for this. In many EU27 countries the ground principles of the EPSI directive (European Public Sector Information Directive, came into force on 17 November 2003 approved by the Council of Ministers – see: http://ec.europa.eu/information_society/policy/psi/index_en.htm) have already been implemented into national laws. That means that these laws could be a very good starting point for additional needed legal changes in information re-use. For example in Austria the 'IWG: Informationsweiterverwendungsgesetz' (the IWG came into force on 18 November 2005, see: http://www.ris.bka.gv.at/) is the existing law for this. Furthermore the issue of pro-active information provision by public administration as well as public liability and disclaimers of liability for open data need to be discussed and regulated in the course of a nationwide open data strategy.

5 Impact on Society

As open data is a relatively novel field of data and information provision there is also a tremendous impact on society. New cultural techniques are needed in several fields: in the field of data interpretation, analysis and visualization – along the whole data handling mechanisms and techniques. Because open data is not useful if the data is not used! Furthermore the handling of crowd sourcing mechanisms, of stronger ways of e-participation and collaboration between citizens, politics and public administration needs to be taken into account and last but not least there is also a need for a change inside the public administration – as open data changes the used ways of data management and publishing as well as it the lowers the borders between citizens and the public administration. That means on the one hand that we do need to discuss and implement new methods in media and data literacy (from ground school up to adult education) as well as on the other hands we need to discuss and manage change processes inside of the public administration. Furthermore issues of privacy and data protection need to be discussed and solved here.

6 Innovation and Knowledge Society

One main issue why we are talking about Open Government Data is to strengthen the information society in Europe by enabling innovation and the knowledge society. This means that it is of very high importance to ensure that there is free available data to look at, take it and play with it to ensure these innovation mechanisms. As Prof. Nigel Shadbolt of the University of Southampton, one of the leading experts in UK in the open data process, pointed out: 'open the data and the Apps will flow'.

Important to mention here is to think also about technical issues of Open Government Data: putting the term 'Linked' in front of it supports strongly the creation of knowledge out of interlinked data. Linked Open (Government) Data principles ensure that information (and things) is interlinked and thereby context is provided and can be used to create new knowledge.

7 Impact on Economy/Industry

When basic structures of an Open Government Data strategy are discussed for a country it is very important not to forget the stakeholder group of industry to be involved in the Open Data strategy and the OGD process as well as in the concrete implementation/realization. Industry will benefit of Open Government Data – as information is one of the most important goods/resources of our service-oriented economy in Europe (as it is also for industry for e.g. enabling better decision making in the area of market intelligence et al.). The impact of Open Government Data on economy is split into direct impact (as commercial revenues and thereby taxes, foundation of new companies, etc.) and indirect economic impacts (as lower unemployment and several areas of the national economy as e.g. health and many others). This area of economic impact needs to be studied more in detail as it lacks a little bit of figures and measurements at the moment – but this can be done in the course of the 1st year of an open data strategy. As a first point it is very important to involve the economy/industry of a country as an important stakeholder.

8 Licenses, Models for Exploitation, Terms of Use

Coming from economic impact initiated by Open Government Data there is a strong need to discuss all issues of licensing as well as exploitation models and terms of use for this Open Government Data. Providing licenses ensures several issues: 1) giving the users of the data legal compliance as it is clear what the users are allowed to do with the data, 2) giving the data provider a disclaimer of liability and 3) learn about the usage of the data (e.g. when a license includes the obligation to refer to the data source when using a data set). Based on this, exploitation models need to be discussed and developed: this is important on the one hand for the public administration as there are lots of data sets require a fee at the moment and on the other hand for the industry that wants to set up new business models on top of the data. Issues as 'freemium models' (some data for free to enable innovation and 'better data' cost a fee), service level agreements (permanence, performance, stability, timeliness, etc.) et al need to be discussed here.

9 Data relevant Aspects

Coming to the data itself then, there are lots of things to take into account. Type and scale of data that can be provided as Open Data – as a first step there is a strong need to manage an internal inventory of data in the public sector – said this does not mean that existing data sets cannot be provided as soon as possible at a single point of access (as for instance a data catalogue) to ensure to use the 'low hanging fruits' – but in the long run every data set needs a look at to decide whether to open it or not and when to open it and how to open it. The OGD2011 project shows, as well as a deeper look on existing open data activities, that to open up the 'basic data' is a very good approach (geo data, statistical data etc.) at the beginning to ensure the provision of a basic data infrastructure that users can work with.

Furthermore the following aspects need to be taken into account: formats, permanence & timeliness, raw data, meta data, data granularity, completeness, data quality et al.

10 Data Governance

Beside the concrete aspects of the data itself there is also a lot to think about the data surroundings, the data governance. Origin and source of data, information on the process of data harvesting/collection, information about how to interpret (maybe provision of a reference interpretation) need to be given together with the data (best as a part of the provided meta data). For this topic the expertise of the respective domain experts is needed and highly recommended. Data governance is one of the most important topics to ensure an efficient usage of the data. For example an Open Government Data Stakeholder Survey of 2010/2011 managed by the EU project LOD2 (http://www.lod2.eu) has shown that the main issue of trusting a data set is the data sets origin / source.

11 Applications and Use Cases

Clearly the usage of the data is an important issue for every Open Data activity, too – because the data is absolutely useless if the data is not used. Taking a look at best practices in EU27, the US, Australia and New Zealand can help a lot here. Beside the above mentioned issues of data literacy there is a strong need to pro-actively involve users in the Open Data process. Competitions can help a lot to generate visibility and to ensure a first output in the area of use cases & ideas, data analysis and visualizations and new and innovative applications on the open(ed) data. The best applications to name here are apps that generate a benefit for both: the citizens as well as the public administration.

12 Technological Aspects

Last but not least we do need a deeper look into the area of infrastructure and technology to really enable the power of Open Government Data. As mentioned before it needs to be mentioned again: Open (Government) Data is a measure for the digital infrastructure of a country - as the building of roads or as electricity – as we are talking about our information and knowledge society in Europe! On top of this infrastructure data integration, services and application et al. can be developed and realized. To ensure to bring the potential of Open Data to its full blown power it is important to keep in mind a few things to A) ensure the widest range of usage as well as B) to ensure the most useful & powerful way of usage. Said this means to A) provide data in several formats and B) also provide an API is important to ensure that as many users as possible are able to use the data, C) the use of open formats and standards for Open Data is important to lower barriers (& costs) for the usage, D) the provision of a single point of access to the data (a data portal / catalogue) where users can find all of the data very quick and easy, E) provision of all data in human AND machine readable formats, F) in the mid- and long-term provision of the data following the W3C linked open data principles (see: http://en.wikipedia.org/wiki/Linked_Data) to enable the most powerful way for the usage of data (including the provision of context) as well as to ensure interoperability. Linked Data is also the direction the European Commission goes: so that interoperability between EU27 can be enabled in the future using linked open data standards and principles. This approach can also be seen by Sir Tim Berners Lee the director of W3C in his 5 star model of Open Government Data (http://www.w3.org/DesignIssues/LinkedData.html).

13 Conclusion

Summarising the output of the OGD2011 project there are several issues and areas that need to be taken into account when starting an Open Government Data strategy for a nation (or city or region etc). This starts at the need of definitions over open government and legal issues to issues around the impact on society and economy/industry. Beside this data relevant issues need to be analysed, discussed and clarified as licenses, data governance and technological aspects. From a planning perspective a 2 phase approach seems to be the right one:

a) starting with low hanging fruits by providing existing open data at a single point of access (some basic data sets as postal codes, geospatial data, statistical data etc.) as early as possible and

b) for mid-term and long-term approach to start a comprehensive project by taking all above mentioned issues into account and see Open Government Data asa measure for the digital infrastructure of a country.

SISE Semantics Interpretation Concept

Karel Kisza[1] and Jiří Hřebíček[2]

[1] Masaryk University, Faculty of Infromatics, Botanická 68a Brno, Czech Republic
kkisza@mail.muni.cz
[2] Masaryk University, Faculty of Science, Research Centre for Toxic Compounds
in the Environment, Kotlářská 267/2 Brno, Czech Republic
hrebicek@iba.muni.cz

Abstract. The development of the complete and complex Single Information Space for the Environment in the Europe (SISE) covering all interactions among environmental information and knowledge using current ICT tools is practically impossible. A common methodology of building the conceptual model of the SISE, based on ontologies and associated technologies was developed at Masaryk University. The big challenge is to find the best way how to make ontology semantics available to the user using appropriate problem solving (search) interface. The paper shows the concept of a SISE semantic interpretation, related summary of used technologies. The concept combines main advantages of ontologies and expert systems - the ontology semantics and the rule based on application are used for searching information and issuing predictions.

Keywords: Semantics, SISE, ontology, expert system.

1 Introduction

The paper presents a semantic idea of interpretation of theoretical model of the Single Information Space for the Environment in Europe (SISE). The Hrebicek and Pilman theoretical conceptual model [4] was compared with an upper ontology concept of the SISE [2].

The developed conceptual model of the SISE enables an implementation of the vision of development for an integrated, modern, common, shared and sustained Single European Information Space infrastructure for environmental information exchange and environmental management in Europe. The upper ontology concept of SISE was not suitable for more specific tasks (e.g. for the implementation of effects of environmental information), where the detailed level of the solution is needed. In this case it was necessary to use a more detailed model, which is much more specific than the upper ontology model (European ICT Environmental Sustainability Research, 2010) [3], [4].

Currently the research and development of shared environmental information system [3] focuses on the improvement of search results by using semantic web technologies [7]. Internet users without special knowledge in environmental topics should

J. Hřebíček, G. Schimak, and R. Denzer (Eds.): ISESS 2011, IFIP AICT 359, pp. 70–76, 2011.
© IFIP International Federation for Information Processing 2011

be enabled to find all available information for their special requirements by placing a request as simple as possible.

There is a big amount of various kind of ontological model in the environmental research area. These models are built both for systems in various fields (domain ontology) and for systems in business companies (application ontology). Domain ontology defines a domain based set of terms and relations, which should be independent of any problem solving method. Application ontology contains terms and relations unique to particular problem solving method. This customization allows to separates out control and procedural knowledge. The use of pre-defined domain ontologies enable users to reduce the available search space. Ontological concepts relevant to a problem domain are supplied to the user allowing them to focus their query. A more advanced interface would allow the user's query to use their terms and map that to an underlying domain.

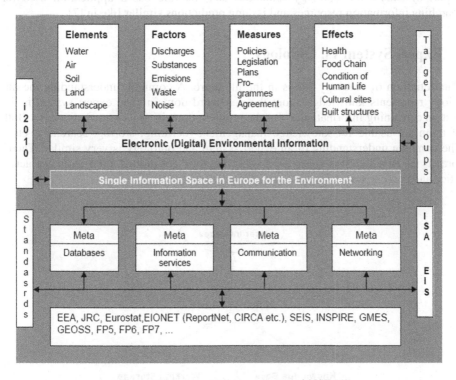

Fig. 1. Hrebicek and Pilman concept of SISE [4]

The big challenge is to find the best way how to make ontology semantics available to the user using appropriate problem solving (search) interface. Problem solving methods are defined as reasoning strategies for solving certain problem types. Here expert systems come to be used.

Since their appearance in the 1970's, rule based expert systems have found applications in a variety of domains ranging from control systems for power plants to help systems. They are mainly used for tasks like diagnostics or predictions. The typical scenario consists of interviewing the user in order to acquire facts that are used afterwards to generate the predictions or diagnostics. Many common expert systems have a reduced number of observable facts and the intelligence of the system is used only for the process of generating the prediction [6]. Most of them do not take into consideration the importance of this set of observable facts. The limited number of observable facts induces a generality problem that affects the quality of the observable facts.

Experts systems are capable of performing complex tasks in their specific field of expertise. They use a vast amount of explicit and tacit domain knowledge - domain ontology which should support problem solving method. A problem solving method is called an interface engine (in expert systems terminology).

The paper tries to show the idea of ontology semantic interpretation and related summary of used technologies, based on modern expert systems combined with ontological models platform. This concept combines main advantages of ontologies and expert systems - the ontology semantics and the rule based application used for searching information resources and issuing predictions similar like in [7].

2 Expert System vs. Ontology

The definition of ontology varies in the literature. A common understanding the ontology represents knowledge about the real word domain. The expert system is the system containing information about the problem domain in its knowledge base. Both of them are usable for knowledge management (defining, storing, searching, etc.). The common understanding of an expert system and ontology is very similar. Therefore, as the first step it is necessary to describe their definitions, their main characteristics and comparison.

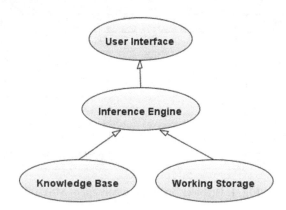

Fig. 2. Expert system schema

2.1 Expert System

Expert systems are mainly computer application which enables both algorithmic and non-algorithmic expertise for solving particular types of problems. Basically they are composed from four basic parts as is seen in Figure 2:

- Knowledge Base – declarative representation of the expertise represented in IF … THEN … rules;
- Working Storage – the data that is specific to problem being solved;
- Inference Engine – the heart of the system which derives recommendation from the knowledge base and working storage;
- User Interface – component for input queries from users.

Expert systems recognize three basic types of knowledge:

- Descriptive (conceptual) knowledge (stored in knowledge base) – describes the concepts in the given domain and the relations among them. Each defined concept should be described by relation to already existing concepts.
- Procedural knowledge (stored in knowledge base) – clearly describes the procedures (actions) which should be processed in particular situation
- Factual knowledge (stored in working storage) – means the facts formalization. Especially facts describing particular situation or problem which should be solved

2.2 Ontology

Very precise definition of ontology in the context of computer and information science has been written by Tom Gruber [1]: "An ontology defines a set of representational primitives with which to model a domain of knowledge or discourse. The representational primitives are typically classes (or sets), attributes (or properties), and relationships (or relations among class members). The definitions of the representational primitives include information about their meaning and constraints on their logically consistent application." In the context of database systems, ontology can be viewed as a level of abstraction of data models, analogous to hierarchical and relational models, but intended for modeling knowledge about individuals, their attributes, and their relationships to other individuals.

2.3 Expert System and Ontology Combination Advantages/Disadvantages

It is necessary to accept the limitations of the technology upon which current knowledge-based systems are built. An inference engine alone doesn't provide an expert system. The main parts of each knowledge based systems are knowledge. As was mentioned in above text the limited number of observable facts induces a generality problem that affects the quality of the observable facts. Existence of many huge ontology models in various areas, their complexity and tolls supporting their development help to solve the lack of observable facts in expert systems based on ontology.

Moreover, it is usual in practice that two systems are using the same terms which mean different, sometimes completely contradictory, things. Ontology can help to pin down precisely what these differences are. More than serve as meta-data model, ontology can help to aggregation of more existing expert systems without loose of interoperability.

One of the tasks which have to be solved concerning SISE is to find the best way how to make ontology semantics available to the user using appropriate problem solving (search) interface. Experts systems are capable of performing complex tasks in their specific field of expertise, which should help to solve this task.

3 Ontology Based Expert System

As was stated in above text, the knowledge base should be the (SISE) ontology (mainly implemented in OWL). The main architecture concept of expert system based on ontology can be seen in the Figure 3.

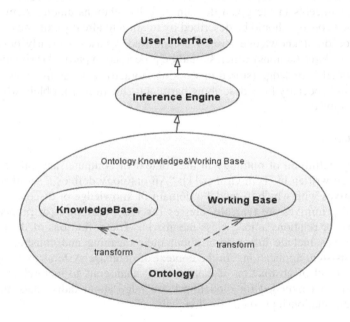

Fig. 3. Expert system based on ontology concept

The Ontology Knowledge&Working Base is in fact the ontology model transformed to expert system knowledge and working base. The idea of transformation is described in the next part. The Inference Engine is the mechanism which applies the axiomatic knowledge present in the knowledge base to the problem-specific data leading to the conclusion. The User interface component is responsible for communication between user and expert system.

4 Idea of Implementation

For implementation idea will be used JESS the Rule Engine for the JavaTM Platform as main implementation language [8]; ROWL - Rule Language in OWL and Translation Engine for JESS [5] to transform ontology to expert system rules; and ontology written in OWL.

As the first step is it is necessary to transform ontology (written in OWL in this case) to the knowledge and working base for expert system written in JESS. It can be done by using ROWL. It enables users to frame rules in RDF/XML syntax using an ontology in OWL. Using XSLT stylesheets, the rules in RDF/XML are transformed into forward-chaining *defrules* in JESS. The main principle of using ROWL can be seen on the Figure 4.

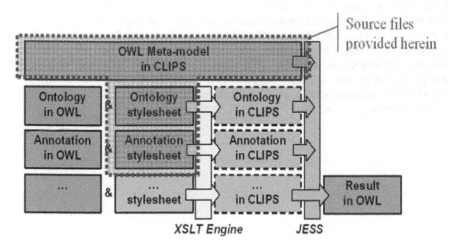

Fig. 4. OWL inference engine using XSLT and JESS – overall architecture [8]

Whole ontology model is transformed using style sheets (XSTL Engine) to ontology usable in JESS and can be used in expert system.

5 Conclusion

There was discussed the concept of combination of expert system and ontology in the paper. This concept is based on classical expert system architecture, where knowledge and working base is based on ontology. It has been discussed advantages and disadvantages of such combination and possibilities of this approach contribution to solve SISE task concerning finding the best way how to make ontology semantics available to the user. Finally, there were described the idea of implementation of this concept using new technologies (JESS, OWL, ROWL).

References

1. Gruber, T.: Encyclopedia of Database Systems, Liu, L., Tamer Özsu, M. (eds.). Springer, Heidelberg (2009)
2. Hřebíček, J., Kisza, K.: Conceptual Model of Single Information Space for Environment in Europe. In: Proceedings of the iEMSs Fourth Biennial Meeting: International Congress on Environmental Modelling and Software (iEMSs 2008), pp. 735–742. iEMSS, Barcelona (2008)

3. Pillmann, W., Hřebíček, J.: Information Sources for a European Integrated Environmental Information Space. In: EnviroInfo 2009. Environmental Informatics and Industrial Environmental Protection: Concepts, Methods and Tools. 23. International Conference on Informatics for Environmental Protection, pp. 341–352. Shaker Verlag, Aachen (2009)
4. Hřebíček, J., Pillmann, W.: eEnvironment and the Single Information Space in Europe for the Environment. In: EnviroInfo 2010. 24th International Conference on Informatics in Environmental Protection, pp. 45–55. Shaker Verlag, Aachen (2010)
5. JESS - the Rule Engine for the JavaTM Platform, http://www.jessrules.com/
6. Merritt, D.: Building Expert Systems in prolog. Amzi! inc., Lebanon (2000)
7. Pariente, T., Fuentes, J.M., Angeles, M., González, S., Yurtsever, S., Avelino, G., Rizzoli, A., Nesic, S.: A Model for Semantic Annotation of Environmental Resources: The TaToo Semantic Framework. In: Hřebíček, J., Schimak, G., Denzer, R. (eds.) ISESS 2011. IFIP AICT, vol. 359, pp. 429–437. Springer, Heidelberg (2011)
8. ROWL: Rule Language in OWL and Translation Engine for JESS, http://mcom.cs.cmu.edu/OWL/ROWL/ROWL.html

Flood Management and Geoinformation Support within the Emergency Cycle (EU Example)

Petr Kubíček[1], Eva Muličková[1], Milan Konečný[1], and Jitka Kučerová[2]

[1] Department of Geography, Masaryk University of Brno,
Kotlarska 2, 611 37 Brno, Czech Republic
{kubicek,mulickova,konecny}@geogr.muni.cz
[2] Czech Hydrometeorological Institute, Kroftova 43, 616 67 Brno, Czech Republic
jitka.kucerova@chmi.cz

Abstract. Paper describes the state-of-the-art of flood management both in the Czech Republic and in the broader framework of EU. Special focus is given to geoinformation and cartographic issues within consecutive parts of emergency management cycle used in European Union countries (prevention, preparation, response, and recovery phases). For each phase an adaptive mapping solution is outlined. The principles of adaptive cartography and its applications are described.

Keywords: Floods, geoinformation, adaptive mapping, context.

1 Introduction

The goal of crisis management activities is to reduce the degree to which a community condition is worsened by a disaster relative to its pre-disaster condition [2]. The field of crisis management usually divides any situation into four components (phases) that roughly correspond to the before – called *preparedness*, during – called *response*, and after phase (*recovery*) of any particular event. The last but not least *mitigation (*and *prevention)* phase is concerned with minimizing the effects of possible disasters by mandating policies and regulations that will lessen the effects of hypothetical disaster. Each of these phases put particular demands on emergency managers and responders, and each can be informed and improved by the application of geospatial data and tools. These phases follow one another in a continuous cycle, with a disaster event occurring between preparedness and response phase (Fig.1). Geospatial demands vary across the phases of disaster as well as across hazard types. Geospatial resources and processes thus must be able to adapt and respond to follow the changing demands.

In the case of crises management geospatial services can provide a unified environment allowing visualizing, analyzing, and/or editing data from various data sources within a single client. The main theoretical approach proposed for the crises management cartographic support is so called adaptive cartography. This method is based on the idea of geodata visualization automation and adjustment according to situation, purpose and user's background [9,10,8]. Adaptive maps are still supposed to be maps, i.e. correct, well legible, visual medium for spatial information transmission.

J. Hřebíček, G. Schimak, and R. Denzer (Eds.): ISESS 2011, IFIP AICT 359, pp. 77–86, 2011.

While all map modification processes are incorporated in electronic map logic, users can affect adaptive map just indirectly by a context.

Geospatial demands vary across the phases of disaster as well as across hazard types. Geospatial resources and processes thus must be able to adapt and respond to follow the changing demands. In order to document the adaptation process we are presenting the example of flood management and proposing the cartographic contexts and possible data sources for particular phases of disaster management cycle. Remainder of the text is structured as follows: Chapter 2 brings overview of flood management in the Czech Republic – it describes its legal framework and points out some activities and responsibilities. Chapter 3 analyses the current flood (geo)information resources according to the phase of the flood situation it relates to. Chapter 4 describes the adaptive mapping approach applied to the flood and defines selected contexts.

2   Flood Management in the Czech Republic

The causes and consequences of flood events vary across the countries and regions of Europe. Flood risk management should therefore take into account the particular characteristics of the areas and ensure relevant coordination within river basin districts and promote the achievement of environmental objectives. This fact led to the establishment of Directive 2007/60/EC of the European parliament and of the council of 23 October 2007 on the Assessment and Management of Flood Risks [4]. Based on this directive member states shall make available to the public flood relevant documents and information - namely the preliminary flood risk assessment, the flood hazard maps, the flood risk maps and the flood risk management plans.

For each type of documents the following is then recommended:

- The preliminary flood risk assessment – states, for which part of river basin district, the flood risk assessment will be accomplished. Only selected river basin areas will be further processed.
- The flood hazard maps, the flood risk maps - show the potential adverse consequences associated with different flood scenarios, including information on potential sources of environmental pollution as a consequence of floods.
- The flood risk management plans - It should focus on prevention, protection and preparedness. The elements of flood risk management plans should be periodically reviewed and if necessary updated, taking into account the likely impacts of climate change on the occurrence of floods.

2.1 Legal Framework

In the Czech Republic flood protection is in focus of many legislative documents. The pivotal one is the Act of 28 June 2001 on Water and Amendments to Some Acts (The Water Act), which defines flood prevention, floodplain zones, flood activity degrees, flood plans, flood inspections, flood prediction services, rescue activities etc. Beside this Act, there is a huge number of other important legislative regulations settled in another Acts. They are concerned with, e.g.:

- definition of crises situations, crises management bodies and financial issues (Act No. 240/2000),
- determination of cooperation among Integrated Rescue System units, definition of their tasks and roles (Act No. 239/2000)
- definition of military assistance in the case of extraordinary event (Act No. 219/1999)
- definition of public administration competencies (Act No. 128/2000)
- specification of life, health and property protection in the case of disaster events (Act No. 133/1985)
- specification of the state subsidy in the case of disaster event (Act No. 363/1999).

Protection itself is secured according to Flood Management Plans and, in the case that crisis situation is declared, according to Crises and Emergency Plans. Protection against the natural floods is controlled by Flood Authorities that are (on territorial basis) responsible for organization of flood prevention and response; further they administer and coordinate the activities of other responsible actors within flood prevention and response. Character and activity of Flood Authorities are specified for two periods – beyond flood and during flood; their specification in hierarchical order is shown in Table 1.

Table 1. Flood Authorities beyond and during flood on different hierarchical levels

	Beyond flood	During flood
Municipality level	Municipality authorities	Flood Staff of the Municipality
District level	Authorities of the Municipalities with Extended Powers	Flood Staff of the Municipalities with Extended Powers
Regional level	Regional authorities	Flood Staff of the Region
State level	Ministry of the Environment, Ministry of the Interior	Central Flood Staff

2.2 Activities in the Flood Management

Flood management is very complex set of tasks. Flood Authorities are responsible of coordination of activities of different user groups. It includes e.g. units of the Integrated Rescue System (Fire Rescue Service of the Czech Rep., Police of the Czech Rep., Ambulance Service etc.), River Basin Districts Authorities, Watercourse managers, etc. These users are responsible for different tasks in flood management; some of them can (or must) be supported by geoinformation.

Watercourse managers and managers of touched object (or other subjects ordered by Flood Authorities) are responsible for Flood Security Activities (e.g. measures against water pollution, removing blockades of ice) that must be coordinated with the River Basin Authorities. Fire Rescue Service (FRS) as one of the component of Integrated Rescue System (IRS) has many tasks within Flood Rescue Activities (e.g. evacuation, rescue of citizens), Flood Security Activities (e.g. flood survey, indication of dangerous areas) and Organizational Activities (e.g. coordination of rescue works).

Flood Authorities are responsible for planning (e.g. compilation of Flood Plan), organizing (e.g. local early warning), and securing (e.g. health care and emergency supply).

3 Flood Related Spatial Data and Services to Support Activities within the Disaster Management Cycle

In the following chapters we will review existing geospatial support for prevention activities (Risk Assessment), preparation activities (Pre-impact activities) and response activities (Emergency management).

3.1 Geoinformation for Prevention – Flood Zone Mapping, Insurance Maps, Flood Risk Mapping

The main role of geospatial support within this particular part of cycle is to identify the potential areas of risk and minimise future losses of both lives and assets.

According The Water Act (No. 254/2001) Flood zone is an area that can be flooded during the natural flood event. Its extent is proposed by the particular watercourse manager for discharges occurring once per 5/20/100 years. Its delimitation is given by Legal notice No. 236/2002 and is based e.g. on hydrological data, on regulations of water structures influencing flood discharges, on longitudinal and cross sections of the river etc. Project of flood zone is elaborated on the ground map of the Czech Republic 1:10 000. Besides the flood zone also *Active zone of flood area* is determined. It is an urban area that influences drainage during floods.

Almost all property insurances in the Czech Republic use Flood Risk Assessment Tool (FRAT) developed by Swiss Re to identify high exposed risks. Users can be located by the address (street, house number, and city) or interactively on the map. The system generates information on the flood risk exposure of the selected location and displays it on-screen. The tool distinguishes four different flood risk zones: Zone 1: very low flood risk, Zone 2: low flood risk, Zone 3: medium flood risk, Zone 4: high flood risk. The insurance flood zones database is available not only for the main watercourses but also for local streams with drainage basin larger than 20 sq km.

The Czech Republic adopted the Flood Directive 2007 and proposed the national methodology for flood mapping. The methodology is based on matrix of risk [1] and is closely connected to the standard database established, operated and administrated within the Czech water management. It comprises following main procedures: identification of the flood hazard, determination of vulnerability and semi-quantitative implication of flood risk by four-degree scale. The final methodology result is flood risk map combining information about danger and vulnerability of objects and activities in the floodplain. Landscape vulnerability is represented by objects and activities occurring in landscape. Resulting flood risk zones show areas where maximal acceptable risk is exceeded. The reached values of the flood danger in the corresponding colour scale are indicated inside each such highlighted area. For detail description of the corresponding methodology see [7].

3.2 Geoinformation for Preparation – Integrated Warning Service System, Flood Modelling

Preparation or pre-disaster phase is characterised by a combination of warning services and spatially depending flood forecasts initiating the whole set of activities.

Integrated Warning Service System (IWSS), a component of Integrated Rescue System of the Czech Republic, is meteorology and hydrology warning service for the Czech Republic. IWSS is provided jointly by Central Forecasting Office (CPP) of the Czech Hydrometeorological Institute (CHMI) [2] (within Ministry of the Environment) and the Department of Hydrometeorological Services of the Military Geographical and Hydrometeorological Office (within Ministry of Defence). IWSS provides evaluation of up-to-date meteorological and hydrological data, information and forecasts and delivering integrated warning information. The part of Central Forecasting Office (CPP) is Warning and Information Office; its main activity is to alert in the case of dangerous meteorological phenomena (e.g. heavy rain, snow cover, snowdrift, strong wind, frost in vegetation time) and other weather phenomena (smog, dangerous air substance transmission etc.).

Czech Hydrometeorological Institute (CHMI) employs two hydrological models for discharge prediction – HYDROG and AQUALOG.

HYDROG is rainfall-runoff model for flood simulations and discharge prediction. Inputs are discharges, controlled water reservoirs run-offs and precipitation; in winter also data about temperature and snow cover.

AQUALOG is programming tool for simulation, prediction and run-off management and water quality in real time and in the past. It allows numeric simulations of creation and melting of snow cover, rainfall-runoff transformation, simulation and management on reservoirs, and modelling of diffuse processes on surface waters.

3.3 Geoinformation for Response – Flood Management Plan

When flood becomes a reality than it is necessary to follow certain strategy in order to minimise the potential flooding impact. Flood Management Plans are sources of information for this part of disaster cycle. The Flood Management Plan is divided to factual, organisational, and graphic parts.

Factual part includes information necessary for securing specific object, municipality, complex basin or other territory, directive limits for declaration of degrees of flood activity, informs about the possibilities to influence discharge, etc. Organisational part includes list of names and addresses, describes communication links between involved persons, specify tasks for people and organization concerned with flood protection, assists with securing local early warning system etc. Graphic part includes following maps: Flood Committees & Evacuation Places, Gauging stations & Precipitation Station, Flood areas, Watercourse and water structures, Transportation.

There are four types of Flood Management Plans (FMP) corresponding with hierarchical order of flood authorities – FMP of the Czech Republic, FMP of the Region, FMP of the Municipalities with Extended Powers, FMP of the Municipality and the fifth one (Other Flood Management Plan) that is done for the buildings and parcels that either lay in the floodplain or can influence the progress of the flood.

4 Adaptive Mapping in Crisis Management

Chapter 3 documented exiting sources of geoinformation and services related to floods. Flood management plans offers set of analytical maps; they are sources of essential information but in time limited situations in preparation and response phase may be not effective. They are thematically oriented (e.g. transportation, gauging stations) but not task oriented. Existing maps have predominantly information function, i.e. it inform about "what is where". But modern cartography can offer more; it can shift map to decision-making tool. So called *adaptive mapping* [9] brings to crisis management opportunity to be more effective by adaptation of cartography outputs to needs of users. User is supplied only by the information that is necessary for decision making and is given in the most comprehensive form for the user. Context in which the geographic data are presented plays the key role; thus the term *context cartography* is also used. Cartography visualization (e.g. map) is adapted to user's context. Context is the set of characteristics dealing with the user, environment and the purpose [9,8,14,5].

The aim of adaptive mapping is to facilitate different users to work over the same data. Even though the context maps portray the same objects and phenomena, the knowledge the users get from it depends on the task they are responsible for. The visualization reflects the role the object plays in decision making process, e.g. object school play different roles in task of flood prediction and in task of navigation. In the former case, the maps supply the knowledge about the *"object of social character with people that need special protection"*. In the later, the school plays the role of *"object that eases orientation"*. Cartography model for each context map must reflect this fact; different roles of the same object in reality are expressed by different map symbols and in different implications.

4.1 Conceptual Framework – Study "FLOOD"

Our approach followed the idea of [5] and modified it with the respect to cartography visualization in crisis management.

Context is the set of factors that influence legibility and usability of the map [9]. There is an indefinite number of such factors and thus it is necessary to chose those with the highest influence.

We distinguish three main context types:

1. Identity context. This type of context refers to questions like *"Who will use the map? Who is responsible for what?"*. This context influences the visualization since users having diverse professional background are using different visualization methods and map symbols. Further, this information is used for authorization rights purposes, i.e. which data (data layers, properties) can be managed and administered by the user. For example POLICE can edit information about roads, watercourse managers about objects on the river, etc.
2. Functional context. It deals with questions *"How the map will be used? What is the function of the map in the decision making process?* We can distinguish three groups of users: users that only needs to know "what is where" - function INFO), user that needs to update status of spatial objects (e.g. bridge is destroyed, road is

closed) – function CONTROL, and users who need to create new object (e.g. place where intervention is necessary, place of ice blockage) – function ORGANIZE.

3. Emergency core context. It is the most complex one. It refers to the issue of data content. Within it two particular questions are dealt: *What?* and *When?*

Question *WHAT?* implies the *ACTIVITY*, e.g. *What activity should be supported with the map?* Activity embodies the range of tasks that the user is responsible for. It is the most crucial factor that determinates the specific view of the reality; by familiarity with the knowledge that user must get to be able to perform decision making it is possible to guess about relevance of spatial object and thus to define map content. Following five main activities were defined for the event FLOOD:

- *PREDICTION AND PROGRESS* - development and expected progress of the flood
- *TECHNICAL SUPPORT* – technical support in inundation area – support of Flood Security Activities
- *RESCUE* – evacuation of the citizens
- *ORGANIZATION* – organization of power and means
- *PUBLIC INFORMATION* – information for public about flood development, evacuation etc.

Question WHEN? specifies the *STAGE*, e.g. *In what phase of the emergency event the activity is realised?* The crisis management is not limited to the response phase of the event but pass the entire disaster management circle. We can specify four phases of crisis management circle [11] that correspond to the four *STAGES*:

- *prevention* (out of the flood)
- *preparation* (shortly before the flood)
- *response* (during the flood)
- *recovery* (after the flood)

Figure 1 illustrates which emergency core contexts are defined based on the activity and the stage. For example, to realize the activity *rescue* in *preparation phase* user chose the context *evacuation preparation* for which data content is defined.

Activity and stage are parameters that primarily define map content, e.g. what should be on the map. The other parameter is *OPERATIONAL RANGE* that relates to *WHERE?* and deals with questions like *Where the event takes place? What is the event extent? What is the activity extent?* This parameter does not influence the map content "thematically" but tackle the problem how many information can be portrayed on the map so that it is still legible. It influences character of generalization; it must be not only quantitative but also semantically based.

Five basic operational ranges were defined:

- one for detailed information – e.g. part of floodplain: *LOCAL*
- three due to hierarchical system of flood management: *REGION, DISTRICT, MU-NICIPALITY*
- one due to the necessity to flood monitoring in natural borderlines: *CATCHMENT*

Map scale of the corresponding operational range spans from large (i.e. 1:5 000 – 1:2 000) for LOCAL to small (i.e. 1:500 000 – 1: 1 mil.) for REGION and CATCHMENT to capture appropriate (administrative or natural) unit. Operational range is

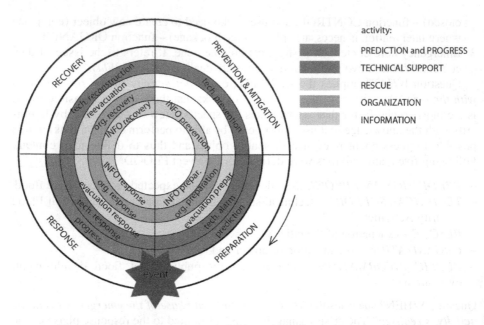

Fig. 1. Emergency core context definition within disaster management circle

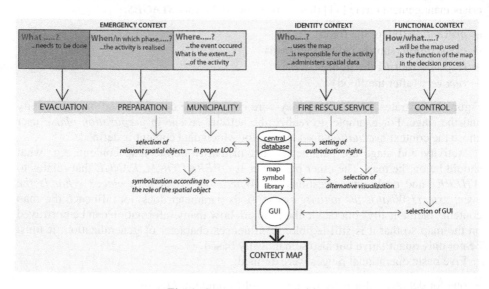

Fig. 2. Context map composition

assigned to each emergency core context and defines in which level of detail information will be (most probably) used. Users are not limited to work in the dedicated operational range but out of it they may get less information.

4.2 Context Composition

Appearance and functionality of final context map will be set by the combination of all particular contexts: identity, functional and core emergency. The user can define, for example, the context map by the following profile:

> Identity context: Fire Rescue Service
> Functional context: control
> Emergency core context: evacuation + preparation

Content of the invoked map will be to ensure the evacuation (emergency accommodation, access roads etc.), symbology and access rights for fire rescue service will be called out and GUI will allow editing of attributes (e.g. user can change the status of evacuated building to *evacuation terminated*). Process of context map composition is illustrated on figure 2.

5 Conclusion

Paper described state of the art within flood case of emergency management cycle and has shown a wide variety of both users' requirements and available geoinformation sources. In accordance with [6] and [10] we can conclude that intuitive interfaces and dynamic visualization are highly demanded. Thus the adaptive cartographic visualization with simple associative icons and symbols can significantly improve the communication. [15] documented that an adaptive cartographic (context based) approach applied for integrated rescue system operators led to lighter maps which were more efficient than existing overloaded multipurpose maps. In the next phase we plan to fully implement the adaptive approach for a selected flood management area and consequently test the cognitive issues for selected tasks within the emergency cycle.

References

1. Beffa, C.: A Statistical Approach for Spatial Analysis of Flood Prone Areas. In: International Symposium on Flood Defence, D-Kassel, p. 8 (2000)
2. Czech Hydrometeorogical Service, http://www.chmi.cz
3. Committee on Planning for Catastrophe: Successful Response Starts with a Map: Improving Geospatial Support for Disaster Management, p. 197 (2007)
4. COUNCIL OF THE EUROPEAN UNION: DIRECTIVE 2007/60/EC OF THE EUROPEAN PARLIAMENT AND OF THE COUNCIL of 23 October 2007 on the assessment and management of flood risks (2007)
5. Dey, A.K., Abowd, G.D.: Towards a better understanding of context and context-awareness. In: Proceedings of the CHI 2000 Workshop on The What, Who, Where, When, and How of Context-Awareness, The Hague, Netherlands (2000)
6. Diehl, S., Neuvel, J., Zlatanova, S., Scholten, H.: Investigation of user requirements in the emergency response sector: the Dutch case. In: Proceedings of the Second Gi4DM, Goa, India, CD ROM, September 25-26, p. 6 (2006)

7. Drbal, K., Dráb, A., Friedmannová, L., Horský, M., Levitus, V., Říha, J., Satrapa, L., Štěpánková, P., Valenta, P.: The Methodology for the Flood risks and Flood hazards map making. Bulletin of the Ministry of the Environment XX(4), 4–70 (2010) (in Czech)
8. Erharuyi, N., Fairbairn, D.: Task-Centred Adaptation of Geographic Information to Support Disaster Management. In: van Oosterom, P., Zlatanova, S., Fendel, E.M. (eds.) Geoinformation for Disaster Management, pp. 997–1008. Springer, Heidelberg (2005)
9. Friedmannová, L., Konečný, M., Staněk, K.: Adaptive maps for crises management. Kartografické Listy 15, 41–50, 127 (2007)
10. Kubíček, P., Ludík, T., Mulíčková, E., Ráček, J., Šafr, G.: Process Support and Adaptive Geovisualisation in Emergency Management. In: Geographic Information and Cartography for Risk and Crisis Management - Towards Better Solutions, 1st edn. Lecture Notes in Geoinformation and Cartography, pp. 335–348, 14. Springer, Heidelberg (2010)
11. Lumbroso, D., et al.: Review report of operational flood management methods and models, FLOODsite Project Report No. T17-07-01 (2007)
12. Mulíčková, E., Šafr, G., Staněk, K.: Context map – a tool for cartography support in crisis management. In: 3rd International Conference on Cartography and GIS, Nessebar (2010)
13. Pequet, J.: A Conceptual Framework and Comparison of Spatial Data Models. Cartographic Journal 2(4), 66–113 (1984)
14. Reichenbacher, T.: Adaptive Methods for Mobile Cartography. In: The 21st International Car-tographic Conference Durban 2003, Proceedings on CD-ROM (2003)
15. Staněk, K., Friedmannová, L., Kubíček, P., Konečný, M.: Selected issues of cartographic communication optimization for emergency centers. International Journal of Digital Earth 3(4), 316–339 (2010)

Capturing of Uncertainty by Geographical IS in Decision Support for Selected Aspects of Quality of Life

Jitka Machalová

Faculty of Business and Economics, Mendel University in Brno, Zemedelska 1,
613 00 Brno, Czech Republic
jitka.machalova@mendelu.cz

Abstract. Quality of life has currently been intensively studied and assessed by using a variety of indicators. Information and communication technologies, or more precisely geographical information technologies, prove invaluable in this process. It is clearly difficult to quantify and spatially localize the quality of life. Fuzzy sets allow the capturing of uncertainty. This article deals with the integration of fuzzy sets into a geographical IS to capture, analyse and evaluate selected aspects of the quality of life.

Keywords: Fuzzy Sets, Geographical IS, Quality of Life.

1 Introduction

Information systems are used for decision support at all levels of management. Information systems can be viewed as models of specific parts of reality (storage, human resources etc.). They save information about the modelled reality in the form of data; the data are then restructured, analysed and presented to decision-makers by the systems at appropriate times, in requested quality, form, volume and content. Information systems capable of modelling landscapes and the processes running in landscapes are known as geographic information systems, or geo-information systems (GIS).

There are certain setbacks in using models generated by such systems. A typical disadvantage of every model is its simplification of the modelled reality. One of the major simplifications in models based on GIS, is the use of binary logic, for example, if we need to mark an area as waterlogged or dry. Any decision maker, however, who implements these models uses natural language working with uncertainty, for example: the area is "slightly" or "substantially" waterlogged. The tool to work with such uncertainty is the theory of fuzzy sets. Implementation of fuzzy sets in geographic information systems allows us to model, analyse and evaluate the modelled processes better.

A good example of the application of fuzzy sets could be a request to evaluate the quality of life in a specified area. In scientific literature, the term quality of life (QOL) has been discussed by classic psychologists, such as C. G. Jung. First attempts to measure the quality of life were made in treatment of patients. The findings were published in the field of medicine, especially in psychiatry, oncology and geriatrics.

J. Hřebíček, G. Schimak, and R. Denzer (Eds.): ISESS 2011, IFIP AICT 359, pp. 87–100, 2011.
© IFIP International Federation for Information Processing 2011

Later, the term quality of life and attempts to measure it can be seen in social sciences. One approach seeks to specify objective conditions for quality of life. The other approach monitors subjective human perception as satisfaction with one´s own life. In the last ten years we can see attempts to measure the quality of life from the perspective of marketing and management. The need for sustainable development forces us to compromise between the need for protecting the environment and its maximal use. The number of tools for measuring the quality of life is growing, as they become more specialized in several domains of this kind of assessment.

This work deals with the integration of fuzzy sets into geographic information systems in order to capture, analyse and evaluate selected aspects of the quality of life. The main ideas on the aspects of the quality of life, collectively known as the "well-being factor" will be presented and applied to a representative area in South Moravia in the Czech Republic.

2 Modelling of Landscape Phenomena

Information about landscape phenomena (elements with a relation to a location on Earth) is saved in the form of geographical data in geographic information systems. Spatial data or geographical data are data which are related to specific places in space with known location at the required level of detail [8].

2.1 Geodata and Map Algebra

Storage of high volume data sets is now managed by geodatabases [11]. The data is usually saved in a vector or raster format as thematic layers. Data in vector format has two parts: a spatial and descriptive i.e. attribute part. The spatial part typically uses the rules of vector graphics; the descriptive part uses rules of relational database systems. In the case of geodata storage in the raster format, the layer is represented by a square network of cells or pixels, where a specific value, a number from a specific domain, is assigned to each cell.

The choice of geodata storage depends on many factors. One of the important factors is the need of spatial analysis, performed on the data. Spatial analysis is a process we use to obtain information from geodata. We can use a map algebra apparatus for data saved in the raster format. The map algebra makes it possible to combine raster layers using different mathematical operations and a map algebra language. The map algebra is a tool which allows us to process the raster representation of reality by using the map algebra language. We can carry out map algebra operations with one or more layers. The operations or functions are divided into local, zonal, focal and global ones [14]. The result of a local function is a change of value of one layer cell. A focal function changes cell values based on values of the neighbouring cells. These functions are mostly used in flow analyses. Zonal functions change values of cells based on values in another layer. A global function concerns the whole layer and is used for example, in distance analyses such as costs or timing.

Functions are built from operators and operands. Operands can be: arithmetic (plus, minus, times etc.), Boolean (true, false), relational (greater than etc.) as well as specialized, such as bit shifts, accumulative, combinatorial assignment operators. The operands are values stored in a cell or cells of layers used in the spatial analysis (Fig. 1).

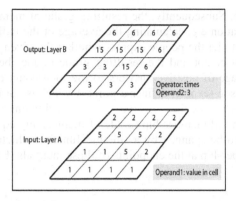

Fig. 1. Example of map algebra used with an arithmetic operator on one layer

2.2 Fuzzy Logic

The basic advantage of fuzzy logic is its ability to mathematically describe information expressed in words. In other words, it enables us to work with ambiguous terms often used in human language. Fuzzy logic permits us to use ICT resources to discern the meanings of "less" or "significantly" based on mutual comparison. The possibility to search for information based on ambiguous or incomplete values with an option to find incorrectly saved information [5] is also an advantage.

Suppose there is an element a. We have to decide, whether it belongs to a given set or not. Each element a in a domain D will be assigned an integer z, $z \in <0;1>$, which expresses the grade of membership in the set. Value 0 means: completely not included in the set; value 1 means: fully included in the set. If we have a set of elements, where each element is characterized by a grade of membership, we call this a fuzzy set [16]. The traditional set can be understood as a special case of the fuzzy set, $z \in Z, Z \equiv \{0;1\}$.

Numbers z define a membership function. The traditional sets with exact borders h_1, h_2 can be defined as follows:

$$MF(a) = 1, \text{ if } a \in <h_1;h_2> \tag{1}$$
$$MF(a) = 0, \text{ if } a \notin <h_1;h_2> \tag{2}$$

Fuzzy sets can be expressed as follows:

$$A = (a, MF(a)), \text{ if } \forall a \in D, \tag{3}$$

where $MF(a)$ is a membership function of element a in domain A with values in closed interval $<0;1>$. Range of the values of the function MF can be either the whole interval $<0;1>$ or only few selected values.

The MF function and its range can be defined by an expert in the given field or by using operations research methods. The former is used when we model the semantics of words of a natural language. The meaning of words is a subjective matter. When possible, we can ask a number of people to make a statement. There are two ways of doing this. The first option is to let the subjects to express themselves using a number or a graphic scale in order to determine whether a given element satisfies the researched expression. Subsequently, the resulting grade of membership is found using a statistical evaluation e.g. calculating the average of the individual observations. The second option is to let the people express whether the given element satisfies the researched expression or not and the resulting grade of membership will be determined as the percentage of positive answers to the total count of answers. In a real situation, a single person (expert) defines a point A which is not included in the studied set, a point D which is another extreme value not belonging to the set, an interval of values $<B;C>$ with full membership (grade of membership equals 1), and intervals $<A;B>$ and $<C;D>$ to be spanned by a suitable function which approaches the extreme grades of membership at the endpoints of these intervals (Fig. 2).

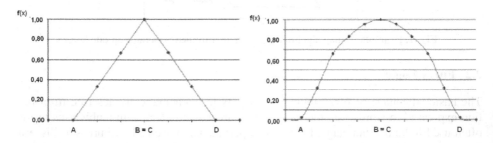

Fig. 2. Linear and parabolic membership function of a fuzzy set

To a great extent, a fuzzy set is determined by the membership function it is associated with. The selection of a membership function influences the borders of the fuzzy set.

3   Principles of Fuzzy Sets Integration into Geographic IS

As mentioned above, GIS are able to model the landscape around us. Some elements of landscapes for example plots, have exact borders. However, it is difficult to delimit the borders of some phenomena, such as waterlogging. It is often unclear, how to correctly define for example the possible limits of land slopes. Fuzzy sets are particularly suitable and useful because of their ability to capture the uncertainty when modeling the aspects of the quality of life. In these cases it appears necessary to introduce uncertainty into the GIS in the form of fuzzy geoelements.

Fuzzy geoelement is a geoelement which in addition to a geometry, topology, attributes and time also has its own membership function. The basic fuzzy geoelements are a fuzzy point, fuzzy line and fuzzy polygon [10].

Each type of the fuzzy geoelement depends on a membership function. Its modeling is based on the concrete membership function. In raster information storage, values of each cell are calculated on the basis of the membership function and a distance of the cell from cells with the value of a membership function equal to one.

Fuzzy point is a fuzzy geoelement given by the ordered triad F, A, M, where F is a membership function, A (with coordinates x, y) is a cell with a value of the membership function equal to one, and M is a set of description (attribute) values of the fuzzy point [10] (Fig. 3).

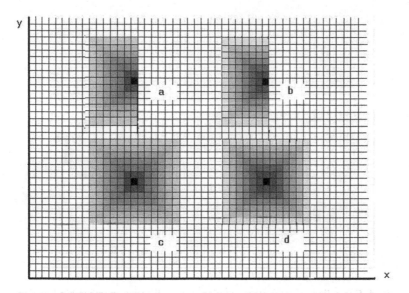

Fig. 3. Fuzzy point in raster representation with different membership function

Fuzzy line is a fuzzy geoelement given by the ordered n+2-tuple F, A_1, A_2, ..., A_n, M, where F is a membership function and A_1 to A_n are neighbouring cells with the membership function equal to one. A_i only has neighbours A_{i-1} and A_{i+1}, A_1 only has a neighbour A_2, and A_n has only A_{n-1}. M is a set of description values of the fuzzy line [10] (Fig. 4).

Fuzzy polygon is a fuzzy geoelement given by the ordered n+2-tuple F, A_1, A_2, ..., A_n, M, where F is a membership function and A_1 to A_n are neighbouring cells with the membership function equal to one, which fill contiguous space. M is a set of describing values of the fuzzy polygon. Fuzzy polygon, which meets requirements of the previous definition, is a fuzzy line [10] (Fig. 5).

The cell A is a cell of fuzzy geoelement P just if it has the membership function of the fuzzy geoelement P greater than 0.

To make fuzzy geoelements applicable in spatial analyses, it is necessary to define geometrical and topological relations. When Euclidean metrics is used, a position of each cell is defined as the position of its centre, and the distance between two cells is defined as the distance between their centres.

There are three types of distances between fuzzy points:

1. minimal – minimum of distances of the fuzzy geoelement cells with the grade of membership greater than 0,
2. mean – minimum of distances of the fuzzy geoelement cells with the grade of membership equal to 0.5,
3. simple – minimum of distances of the fuzzy geoelement cells with the grade of membership equal to 1.

Two fuzzy lines are continuous only if there is a cell with the membership function value equal to 1 with both lines.

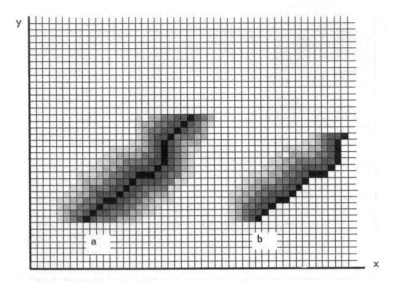

Fig. 4. Fuzzy line in raster representation with a different membership function

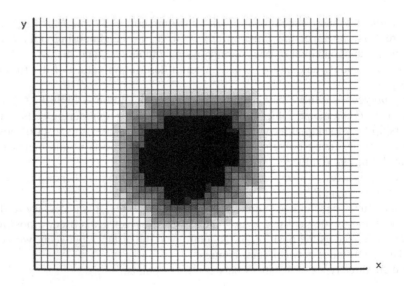

Fig. 5. Fuzzy polygon in raster representation

Two fuzzy polygons are neighbouring only if there is at least one cell which has the membership function value greater than 0 with the first fuzzy polygon, and at the same time, there is a neighbouring cell (with a common border) having the membership function value greater than 0 with the second fuzzy polygon.

Two fuzzy polygons are simple neighbours if there is at least one cell having the membership function value equal to 1 with the first fuzzy polygon, and at the same time, there is a neighbouring cell (with a common border) having the membership function value equal to 1 with the second fuzzy polygon.

Fuzzy polygon P contains a second fuzzy polygon Q if each cell of the fuzzy polygon Q with non-zero membership function value has also non-zero membership function value with the second polygon P [10].

As described above, fuzzy sets provide an option to capture the uncertainty, or vagueness typical for human language. However, the necessity to describe the reality using binary logic causes inaccuracies, which can consequently lead to poor decisions. For example, how can we exactly specify low level of traffic? Fuzzy sets make it possible to capture, analyse and present such "fuzzy" information. The use of fuzzy sets in similar situations is contingent on the following three steps:

1. Correct definition of types of membership functions and the values A, B, C and D (Fig. 2)
2. Assurance of good-quality input data, where the quality is given by precision, authenticity and recency [7].
3. Modelling fuzzy sets defined by experts and execution of spatial analyses over these sets.

Solution of the first two steps is not the main contribution of this article. As noted above, the correct definition of fuzzy sets is up to experts in the given research area. The second step can be critical for the success of the project, because especially with raster data, it requires a compromise between the resolution (number of cells per inch, called DPI) and the size of the file storing the information (in MB, or TB). We usually encounter performance limits of computers at this stage of the analysis, or cluster computers where the analyses are processed.

The article is innovative especially by the approach used in solving the third step. Because the full use of the mentioned methods to provide a comprehensive methodology for assessing the quality of life would be beyond the scope of this article, the article will be focused only on the specific aspects of the well-being factor.

4 Application to the Well-Being Factor

The methodology described above will be applied to one of the quality of life indicators – the well-being factor. The study has been carried out on a sample region in South Moravia in the Czech Republic. The area is 150 km^2. It is relatively densely and evenly populated. There are several small municipalities present, including a regional centre – a town. The landscape is flat with undulating parts and hills. It is used for agriculture; forests are present as well. We can find factories here and also an area unaffected by industry.

The well-being factor is a summary criterion which means a low density of buildings, traffic, noise, light and smell pollution [13]. In the Czech Republic, the well-being factor is understood as a landscape characteristic comprised of the following factors: visual (the visual contamination of scenery), acoustic (the noise level not reaching or exceeding threshold limits), odor (not reaching hygienic limits, but dominant in a negative sense) and emotional disturbance of well-being factors [12].

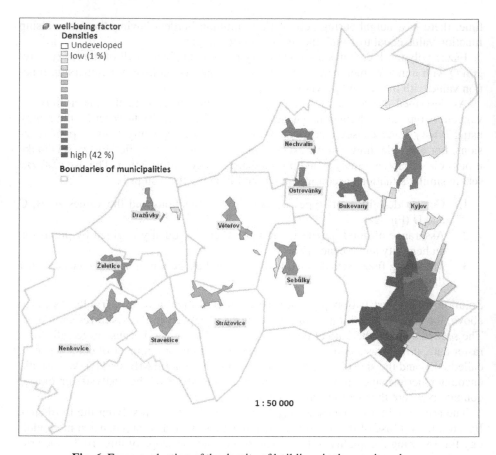

Fig. 6. Fuzzy evaluation of the density of buildings in the monitored area

The density of buildings differs from population density[1]. The density of buildings is reported as the percentage of the built-up area to the total area. It is possible to use vector layers of buildings and utility buildings as input data. These layers have to be rasterized, reclassified and merged to a binary raster layer of buildings using map algebra (1 – built-up, 0 – un-built). Using cadastral maps and land plans we will define the built-up area of a municipality and the built-up areas such as country house areas outside the built-up area of the municipality. In these areas, the percentage of the built-up area will be calculated in reference to the total area and expressed using fuzzy sets (Fig. 6) with a linear membership function. Point A = 1 %, B = C = 42 % – the maximal density (Fig. 2). The following geographic representation is not expressed as fuzzy sets, because the monitored areas have fixed boundaries also defined in the land plans.

---

[1] Population density is measured as the number of inhabitants per square kilometer. In the Czech Republic, it represents 130 inhabitants/km^2, in the monitored area 150–200 inhabitants/km^2.

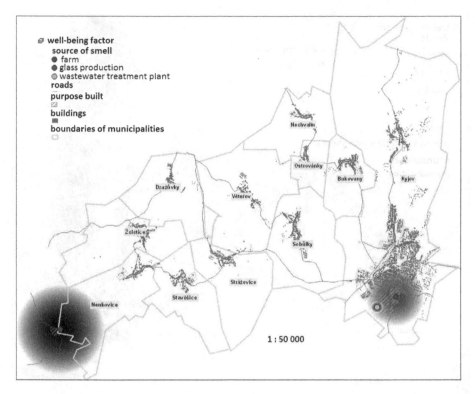

Fig. 7. Fuzzy evaluation of the sources of odor in the monitored area

Odor is a very subjective matter. For the purpose of standardization, relevant legislation regarding odor and its acceptable limits was enacted (Act No. 86/2002 Coll., Decree No. 362/2006). It sets limits for each substance in appropriate units which represent acceptable odor pollution. The well-being factor however, is often affected by values below the legal threshold. There are three sources of odor in the monitored area: a glass factory (arsenic, chromium, cadmium and airborne dust), a sewage water treatment facility (phosphorus) and a cattle and poultry farm (ammonia). The given scenario represents a fuzzy set with a parabolic membership function. Two points, A and D were set, both 1.500 m far from the farm, 500 m far from the sewage water treatment facility and 1.000 m far from the glass factory. The point $B = C$ was set in each source of odor. The figure 7 visualizes the influence on the well-being factor in reference to the character of each source of odor.

There is a personal and public transportation in the monitored area. The transportation takes place on public roads. The quality of life in the area is affected by noise caused by the traffic on the roads and by the quality of roads during their usage. In addition the distance from stops and the time distance from the regional centers while using the public transportation also affects the quality of life.

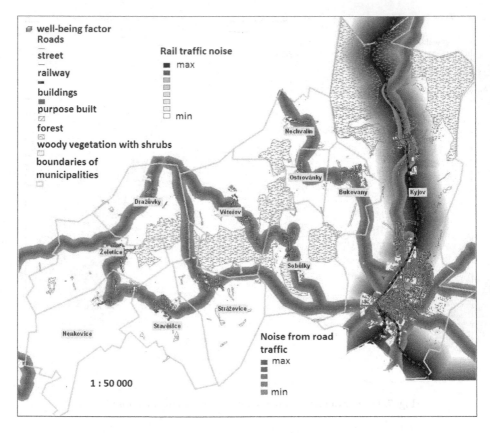

Fig. 8. Fuzzy evaluation of the source of noise in the monitored area

According to the data published by the World Health Organization, a long-term noise burden above 55 dB is harmful and can cause a variety of illnesses. Noise above 65 dB is reported by physicians as in the long-term unbearable and demonstrably harmful to health [1]. Strategic noise maps have been published on the basis of the obligation to create and disclose noise maps. This obligation was stipulated by the European Directive No. 2002/49/EC relating to the assessment and management of environmental noise,. However this is done only for those urban areas and road systems, where more than 6 million cars pass annually. Road traffic has a 95 percent share in the proven annoyance by noise [1].

The noise map of the Czech Republic classifies areas into 7 zones according to the noise level. This classification however, was not made with fuzzy sets. Our monitored area is not included in the noise map. In 2005, the Road and Motorway Directorate of the Czech Republic prepared a summary map of the number of cars passing measure points in 24 hours. According to the results, the intensity of traffic is relatively low and stable on the public roads, with values from 1 500 to 3 000 cars in 24 hours [3].There were also local measurements carried out in the streets under the auspices of the municipal authorities. The result is that most streets are used for private transportation of the locals. Another source of noise is a non- electrified state-owned railway.

There are no other important sources of noise caused by industry present in the monitored area.

Buildings, vegetation and terrain relief are important in the elimination of the spread of noise. The landscape is relatively open and flat with one major hill. The input data for analyses are the layers of buildings, utility buildings, forests, greenery with scrubs and slopes. In order to get a qualified analysis, the layers must be rasterized first and then reclassified in accordance with the influence on the noise elimination.

Furthermore, a summary layer of the elements eliminating noise must be created using map algebra. The layer then inputs together with the membership function of the spread of noise into the function of spreading. The result is a pair of fuzzy layers presenting the noise caused by the railway and road (public roads + streets) traffic (Fig. 8).

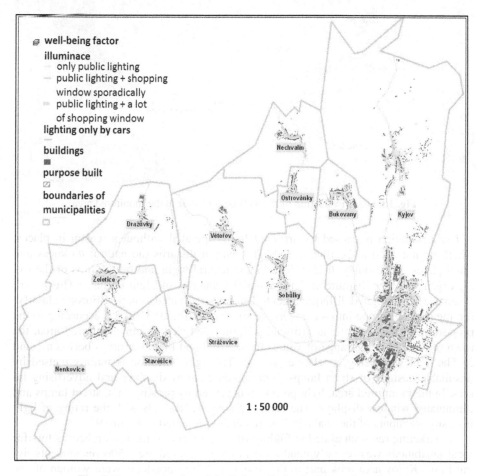

Fig. 9. Fuzzy evaluation of the light pollution in the monitored area

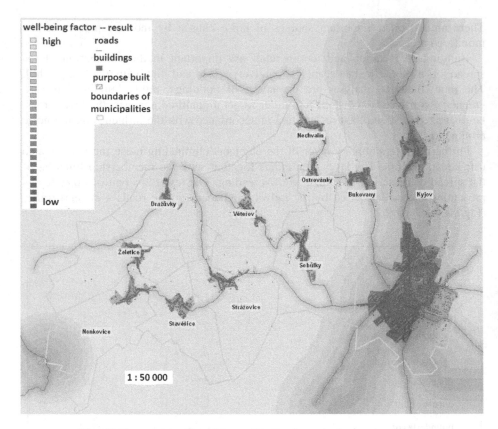

Fig. 10. Fuzzy evaluation of the well-being factor in the monitored area

Light pollution is caused by artificial light, operated without a reason in places, which do not need to be illuminated. This way it disturbs the natural darkness and often glares dangerously. It also disturbs the natural night and biorhythms of the living organisms. The Institute of Science and Technology of Light Pollution (Insituto di Scienza e Tecnologia dell'Inquinamento Luminoso) created a map of Europe classifying the area in Europe into 4 categories,in the range from 0.33 to 27, according to the proportion of the natural and artificially illuminated sky. In our monitored area, the town of Kyjov has the range of values from 3 to 9 and the other areas between 1 and 3. The light well-being is relative present. The light pollution is mainly caused by unsuitable designs of street lamps, illuminated window displays and advertising lasers. In the monitored area, light pollution is caused by passing cars, street lamps and illuminated window displays. The layers of streets and roads with the rating of light intensity are inputs of the analysis. The result are presented in Figure 9.

A marketing research aimed at finding the importance of the researched factors for local inhabitants was recently conducted in the monitored area. 506 respondents living in the Kyjov area took part in the research. 300 respondents were women of age between 22-66 years with the prevailing secondary education. In addition, controlled interviews were conducted with all mayors of surrounding villages. The survey showed clearly that respondents attached the lowest importance which influences the subjective well-being to light pollution and the highest importance to traffic noise. The respondents found the density of buildings as fair; an excessive density of buildings would negatively affect their well-being factor. Odor pollution was found as important as the noise pollution by the respondents of areas affected by odor.

The resulting well-being factor was created using map algebra where the input operands were the layers of the density of buildings, smell, noise and light pollution; the operator is addition. The operands are multiplied by a coefficient which emerged from the marketing research (Fig. 10).

Well-being factor = 2 × the density of buildings + 4 × the smell pollution + 5 × the noise pollution + the light pollution

5 Conclusions

The result of the analyses is the spatial presentation of the well-being factor. The presentation assigns a well-being factor value of the resulting fuzzy layer to each place of the monitored area. According to the known facts that the well-being factor is mostly influenced by the built-up area, noise, odor and light pollution, the lowest value of the well-being factor can be found in the built-up area and the areas in the neighbourhood of roads or the railway. The highest values of the well-being factor in built-up areas are in the village of Věteřov which is off the main roads. The lowest value of the well-being factor can be found in the regional centre – the town of Kyjov. This can be credited to railway transport, several main streets, two sources of odor and the highest values of the light pollution. The well-being factor is only one of the factors influencing the quality of life. It is completely in accordance with current trends of people moving from the urban areas to rural calm, but within the grasp of the city. Comprehensive modelling of the spatial aspects of the quality of life is a subject of further research.

The use of fuzzy layers and map algebra can better capture the uncertainty natural to human thinking expressed in language. Unlike the traditional geoelements, the fuzzy geoelements are able to model selected spatial phenomena more accurately. Therefore the results reflect the modelled reality better.

References

1. Bernard, M.: Analysis of results of the strategic noise maps,
   http://aa.ecn.cz/img_upload/analyza.doc
2. Czech Astronomical Society: Light Pollution,
   http://www.astro.cz/znecisteni/
3. Directorate of Roads and Highways: Trafic intensity in 2005 in the Czech Republic (2005),
   http://www.rsd.cz/Silnicni-a-dalnicni-sit/Intenzita-dopravy
4. Hrebicek, J., Soukopova, J., Kutova, E.: Standardization of Key Performance Indicators for Environmental Management and Reporting in the Czech Republic. International Journal of Energy and Environment 4, 169–176 (2010)

5. Klir, G.J., Yuan, B.: Fuzzy Sets and Fuzzy Logic. Prentice Hall, New Jersey (1995)
6. Konecny, M., Zlatanova, S., Bandrova, T.L. (eds.): Geographic Information and Cartography for Risk and Crisis Management. Springer, Heidelberg (2010)
7. Lake, R.: Virtual Globes as Essential Services?, http://www.galdosinc.com/archives/533
8. Longley, P., Goodchild, M.F., Maguire, D.J., Rhind, D.W.: Geographic Information Systems and Science. John Wiley & Sons Ltd., Vancouver (1981)
9. Machalova, J.: Modeling of chosen selectable factors of the develop of tourism with geographic IT and Fuzzy sets using. In: Acta univ.agric.et silvic Mendel., Brun., vol. LVIX(1), pp. 189–198 (2011)
10. Machalova, J.: Definition of fuzzygeoelements in raster representation for decision-making. In: International Symposium Digital Earth, pp. 242–244. Masaryk University, Brno (2004)
11. Prochazka, D.: On Development of Search Engine for Geodata. In: Acta univ.agric.et silvic Mendel., Brun., vol. LVIII(6), pp. 389–398 (2010)
12. Sklenička, P.: Protection of Landscape Character in Process EIA. In. Zpravodaj EIA, Ministery of the Environment of the Czech Republic, Praha (2002)
13. Swanwick, C.: Land use consultants. Landscape Character Assessment – Guidance for England and Scotland. The Countryside Agency – Scottish Natural Heritage, Edinburgh (2002)
14. Tomlin, C.D.: Geographic Information Systems and Cartographic Modeling. Prentice Hall, New Jersey (1990)
15. Wilson, J.P., Gallant, J.C.: Terrain Analysis: principles and applications. John Wiley & Sons Ltd., Vancouver (2000)
16. Zadeh, L.A.: Fuzzy sets. Inf & Control (1965)

Knowledge-Based Service Architecture for Multi-risk Environmental Decision Support Applications

Stuart E. Middleton and Zoheir A. Sabeur

IT Innovation Centre, University of Southampton, Gamma House,
Enterprise Road, Southampton SO16 7NS, United Kingdom
{sem,zas}@it-innovation.soton.ac.uk

Abstract. This paper describes our work to date on knowledge-based service architecture implementations for multi-risk environmental decision-support. The work described spans two research projects, SANY and TRIDEC, and covers application domains where very large, high report frequency real-time information sources must be processed in challenging timescales to support multi-risk decision support in evolving crises. We describe how OGC and W3C standards can be used to support semantic interoperability, and how context-ware information filtering can reduce the amount of processed data to manageable levels. We separate our data mining and data fusion processing into distinct pipelines, each supporting JDL inspired semantic levels of data processing. We conclude by outlining the challenges ahead and our vision for how knowledge-based service architectures can address these challenges.

Keywords: OGC, SWE, SOA, semantics, data fusion, environmental risk management, crisis management.

1 Introduction

Multiple environmental risks, including those leading to crisis events, require fast and intelligent access to relevant spatial-temporal environmental information with meaningful thematic context by decision makers. The potentially very large and heterogeneous information generated from such data sources should be critically integrated and coherently presented alongside uncertainty information such as sensor accuracy or modelling error estimations. The handling of such information complexity requires agile and information channelling, supported by intelligent data filtering, mining and fusion.

This paper describes our work to date on environmental service oriented architecture implementations for multi-risk environmental management and decision-support. The work described spans two projects, SANY [8] and TRIDEC [10], and covers application domains where very large, high report frequency information sources are processed in challenging timescales in order to support multi-risk decision making in evolving crises.

Our approach to implementing knowledge-based service architectures is to use standards from the Open Geospatial Consortium (OGC) and World Wide Web Consortium (W3C). These support semantic interoperability, allowing metadata driven

J. Hřebíček, G. Schimak, and R. Denzer (Eds.): ISESS 2011, IFIP AICT 359, pp. 101–109, 2011.

automation when integrating new data sources. We also propose the use of the Business Processing Execution Language (BPEL) to achieve agility for our data processing services, and the identification of clear semantic levels for each data fusion & mining processes under a structured Joint Directors of Laboratories (JDL) type data fusion framework.

Finally, we propose context-ware information filtering methods to intelligently filter and index raw information events and tailor processing.

2   Problem Statement

We now live in an information age with increasing volumes of information from affordable means of communication, monitoring and observation systems. This information is more accessible to much larger communities of multi-disciplinary users than ever before. Such large volumes of data, and associated high reporting event frequencies, require data to be stored, intelligently retrieved, analysed and efficiently distributed to groups of collaborating users.

The domain of air quality monitoring, marine risk management and geo-hazard risk management in urban areas has been examined in the SANY project [8]. These applications areas are characterised by their use of in-situ sensors & sensor networks, remote sensing data and contextual information. Decision timescales range from minutes to days, with tens of sensor stations reporting measurements and dataset sizes in the gigabyte range. For example, in the area of bathing water quality risk management, beach attendants need to receive alerts about microbial contamination risks levels of exceedance under the EC bathing water directives. Exceedence levels are predicted from a fusion of meteorological and hydrological sensor measurements fed into simulation data models.

The domains of natural crisis management and industrial drilling operations are being examined within the on-going TRIDEC project [10]. These domains are characterised by having survey data sizes in the terabyte range, which are likely to increase to petabytes of data in the next decade. These application domain areas use a variety of information and data sources, such as sensor networks with hundreds of sensors, camera streams, textual data and social networking web 2.0 sites.

While oil drilling operation decision-making timescales range from hours, for planning decisions, to few seconds for detecting drilling operation system anomalies, the intergovernmental agencies decision timescales, for tsunami warning, range from an hour down to few minutes, depending on the distance a tsunami will travel before impacting on the coastline.

3   Developing a Knowledge-Based Service Architecture

Semantic interoperability within communities, and also between traditionally disparate communities is a major challenge to overcome. The W3C community has developed standards for the semantic web such as XML, RDF and OWL. The OGC [5] SWE standard set [9] has also been developed to handle different sensor types (in-situ, remote sensors, video, models, etc.) from a variety of different disciplines such as those in environmental sciences, defence, crisis management, and spatial application domains covering marine, atmospheric, terrestrial biodiversity and so forth.

SWE is a suite of OGC standards consisting of three standard XML encodings (SensorML, O&M, SWE Common) and four standard web service interfaces (SOS, SAS, SPS, WNS). The SWE standards are predicated on a service oriented architecture (SOA) approach. UncertML is an emerging standard [11] for representing statistics and different mathematical distribution types that the SWE working group are currently discussing with a view to integration into their next generation of standards. It can be seen in Figure 1 that standards now exist to support knowledge-based services working in a variety of different domain layers.

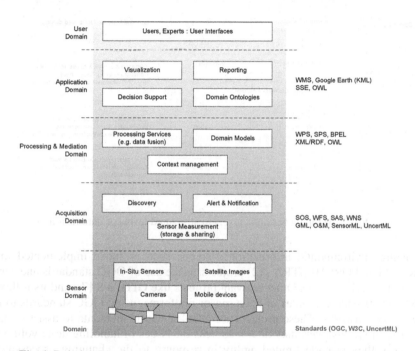

Fig. 1. Relationships between different domain layers and available standards

As sensor systems become ever larger and more inter-connected we are seeing the volumes of data being shared moving from gigabytes to petabytes (especially in satellite systems [2]). In these circumstances, the need for context-aware data filtering and processing becomes important for achieving critical information management and decision-support. By using different types of context (e.g. a decision support task context or trust model in a data source) intelligent information filtering algorithms can reduce the volume of relevant data which needs to be processed. Context-aware algorithms can also improve the effectiveness of data mining and data fusion approaches by helping to steer algorithms according to the temporally evolving needs of decision makers in a crisis.

The underlying work on knowledge-based service architecture, through projects such as SANY and TRIDEC, consists of identifying semantically well-defined levels of data fusion, motivated by JDL data fusion information model [3]. The separation of the semantic layers involved in data processing allows us to implement structured and specialized processing units that can be orchestrated into agile processing pipelines, which could be well suited to respond to the constantly changing requirements of multi-risk environmental decision support applications. These semantic layers can be seen in Figure 2.

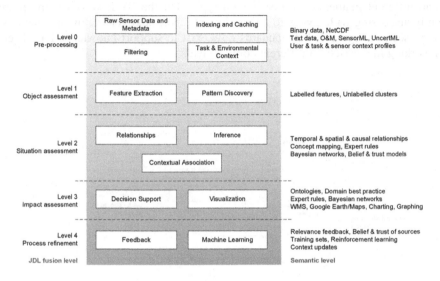

Fig. 2. Mapping semantic layers to structured levels of data fusion

Existing environmental information systems, such as those implemented in the OSIRIS [6] and ORCHESTRA [12] projects, make use of OGC standards and service orchestrated architectures. Other relevant projects like GITEWS [7], and its follow-on DEWS [1], provide examples of open sensor platforms, using OGC standards to integrate sensor networks. These projects use OGC semantic metadata to assist semantic interoperability, however, they do not address the issues of handling large volumes of data. Also, they provide limited agility in response to the changing processing requirements of dynamic decision support situations that occur in risk management. The novel approach which we aim to adopt is the coupling of de-facto data fusion methodologies, state of the art scalable processing architectures and semantic technology in order to overcome the above mentioned shortcomings.

4 Knowledge-Based Services for In-Situ Sensors and Sensor Networks

The SANY project [8] focused on interoperability of in-situ sensors and sensor networks, assuring sensor data could be easily processed and used as a basis for decision support. The sensor service architecture (SensorSA) is the fundamental architectural framework of the SANY project for the design of sensor-based environmental applications and their supporting service infrastructure.

The SensorSA is a service-oriented architecture (SOA) with support for event processing and a particular focus on the access, management and processing of information provided by sensors and sensor networks. The foundation for the SensorSA is the ORCHESTRA project architecture (RM-OA) [12] and the OGC SWE architecture. The knowledge-based service architecture in SANY is a concrete example implementation [4] of the SensorSA architecture principles. This is shown in Figure 3.

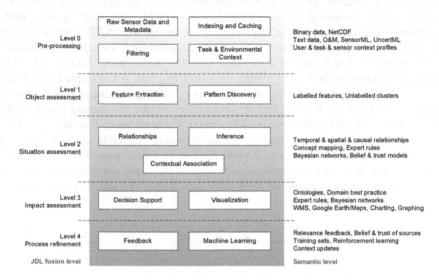

Fig. 3. Knowledge-based service architecture [SANY]

All sensor data in SANY was obtained directly from a sensor observation service (SOS). In SANY SOS's provided access to both sensor measurement datasets and fusion processing result sets. Sensor datasets contained measurements for air pollution, meteorology, ground displacement and more. Whenever a web processing service (WPS) or sensor planning service (SPS) needed data it used a SOS client.

Because sensor data was represented using both the SWE observation and measurement (O&M) model and UncertML, sensor metadata (units, measurement types, sensor accuracy etc.) was directly available to be used by the SANY processing services. Much of SANY's data fusion pre-processing was thus automated, using metadata to aggregate data from separate distributed SOS's. Examples of this are the use of metadata to identify identical phenomenon for dataset merging and the use of unit metadata to validate data value ranges. In SANY new sensor datasets from SOS's could just be 'plugged in'.

An example of the type of data processing work performed in SANY is spatial interpolation of meteorological data, for subsequent input into a bathing water quality data-driven model. The semantic level of fusion in SANY was mostly a combination of pre-processing (level 0) and impact assessment (level 3).

For complex multi-service workflows in SANY a BPEL orchestrator service was used to execute workflows involving SOS's, WPS's and SPS's. The results of these workflows would be sent to the decision support services, making use of geospatial mapping services and advanced visualizations (e.g. Google Earth 3D visualizations). In this way, raw sensor data, data fusion results and the uncertainty context associated with this data could be made available to decision makers.

5 Knowledge-Based Services for Real-Time and Multi-modal Data

In the on-going TRIDEC project [10] we are building on the approaches developed within in SANY, focussing on the challenges associated with handling very large scale multi-modal data sources in real-time. In common with SANY we are using OGC and W3C standards to achieve semantic interoperability. To achieve scalability and performance we will employ a message oriented middleware (MOM), allowing sensor measurements to be sent as events on a message bus. An example of an event is a set of measurements taken over a sample period. Using a message bus allows us to employ complex event routing, and dynamically configure this routing based on the current decision support requirements and context. Context-aware filtering of events, as described in figure 4, is essential as we are planning to handle up to a thousand multi-modal data sources, each source measuring in real-time tens of properties with sampling at periods down to the millisecond range. It is simply not possible to naively receive and process this amount of unfiltered data within the decision making time window of our applications.

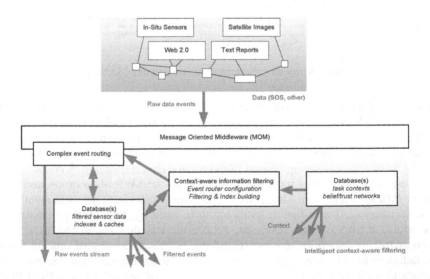

Fig. 4. Illustration of intelligent context-aware information filtering [TRIDEC]

Because crisis situations are dynamically changing, the decision making task context is modelled in real-time. Up-to-date task context allows the knowledge-based services' processing framework to re-configure itself in an agile fashion, through re-focussing of processing services to answer the questions required by decision makers at any given evolutionary stage of a crisis. OGC SWE services, such as sensor planning services (SPS's) and web processing services (WPS's), can be used to control the specific processing steps in a number of processing pipelines. A BPEL orchestrator can enact specific pipeline workflows. However, it will need to be controlled by a choreography component dynamically linking the questions decision makers need to answer to known pipelines capable of generating the answers.

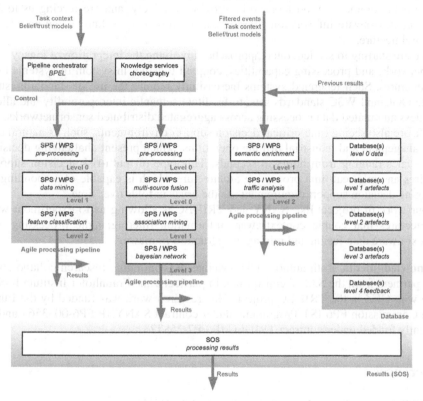

Fig. 5. Illustration of an agile processing framework for knowledge-based services [TRIDEC]

Each processing step provides result data at a different semantic level. An example of a processing step would be feature extraction, annotating a fused multi-sensor data feed with metadata to describe temporally correlated patterns. Each processing pipeline provides the processing steps needed to build up evidence that is able to answer a specific 'question' of interest to a decision maker. An example of a pipeline would be a set of several processing steps generating reports, in real-time, on sensor correlations matching conditions where a drilling 'kick' looks likely to occur.

The use of multi-modal data sources is a challenge in itself. Sensor data, text, video and image data all present their own processing requirements. Our agile processing framework allows us to include semantic enrichment processing steps into our pipelines, facilitating annotation of real-time information feeds with metadata suitable for multi-level semantic processing.

6 Conclusions

Environmental information systems are becoming more and more complex as they increase in scale and scope. As sensor systems become more advanced, the data volumes also increase, both in terms of data sizes (petabyte datasets) and message throughput (hundreds of sensors reporting measurements multiple times per second). These data volumes are too large to be processed naively, and are forcing us to develop context-aware information filtering capabilities into our knowledge-based service architecture.

We are starting to see federated approaches involving the integration of legacy sensor networks and processing capabilities, coupled together in system of systems type architectures. Such federated systems increasingly require the use of standards, such as the OGC and W3C standards sets, to facilitate semantic interoperability and allow seamless automated data processing across aggregated distributed sensor networks.

We are also seeing time-critical decision support environments, such as natural crisis management and industrial drilling operations, which present challenging decision time scales ranging from hours to seconds. This type of multi-risk decision support requires an agile real-time processing architecture which is capable of responding to changing decision support requirements as the crisis unfolds over time.

Our work in projects like SANY and TRIDEC is allowing us to experiment with architectures that couple context-aware information filtering, agile processing and context-aware data fusion and mining in a structure framework.

Acknowledgments. Both authors acknowledge the continuing research collaboration with partners from the SANY consortium, in particular the Fraunhofer Institute IOSB. Also with GFZ in the TRIDEC project. This research work was funded by the European Commission FP6 IST Programme under contract SANY IP FP6-0033564 and is currently funded under contract TRIDEC IP FP7-258723.

References

1. DEWS project, Distant Early Warning System, FP6-045453,
   http://www.dews-online.org
2. Gehrz, R.D.: The NASA Spitzer Space Telescope. Review of scientific instruments 78, 011302 (2007)
3. Lambert, D.A.: A blueprint for higher-level fusion systems. Information Fusion 10(1), 6–24 (2009)
4. Middleton, S.E. (ed.): SANY fusion and modelling architecture, OGC discussion paper, OGC ref 10-001 (2010)
5. Open Geospatial Consortium (OGC), http://www.opengeospatial.org/ogc
6. OSIRIS project, Open architecture for Smart and Interoperable networks in Risk management based on In-situ Sensors, FP6-0033475, http://www.osiris-fp6.eu/
7. Rudloff, A., Flueh, E.R., Hanka, W., Lauterjung, J., Schöne, T.: The GITEWS Project (The German-Indonesian Tsunami Early Warning System), 3rd General Assembly European Geosciences Union (2006)
8. SANY project, Sensors Anywhere, FP6-IST 0033564, http://www.sany-ip.eu

9. Sensor Web Enablement (SWE),
   http://www.opengeospatial.org/projects/groups/sensorweb
10. TRIDEC project, Collaborative Complex and Critical Decision Support in Evolving Crises, FP7-258723, http://www.tridec-online.eu
11. Uncertainty Markup Language: UncertML, v1.0.0, http://www.uncertml.org
12. Uslander, T. (ed.): RM-OA: reference model for the orchestra architecture, OGC best-practice document, OGC ref 07-097 (2007)

GMES – The EU Earth Observation Programme

Ondřej Mirovský

Czech Space Office, Prvního Pluku 17, Prague 8, 186 00, Czech Republic
mirovsky@czechspace.cz

Abstract. The paper describes evolution, recent development and structure of the Global Monitoring for Environment and Security (GMES) programme, which is a European tool how to bring data produced within Earth Observation capacities closer to daily use for numerous international, national and even regional users. GMES will help to ensure sustainable flow of accurate and timely data to monitor changes of our environment and will be a helpful tool to manage and coordinate fast emergency response.

Keywords: GMES, European Union, European Commission, European Space Agency, European Environmental Agency, services, data, environment, security.

1 Introduction

The planet Earth is recently going through ages of rapid change of its surface, biosphere, atmosphere and climate, which has impact on both nature and people inhabiting this planet. In order to be able to monitor these changes, Earth Observation (EO) gives us powerful tool how to get detailed information on global scale in a short of time.

European Union (EU) is in terms of environmental issues global leader and needs accurate and timely information to fulfil all monitoring and reporting demands as well as data for quick emergency response. Therefore, Global Monitoring for Environment and Security (GMES) as the European Initiative for the establishment of a European capacity for Earth Observation was launched.

2 GMES – From the GMES Programme

A key driving element, having contributed to the establishment of GMES, was the paradox of having so much data produced within current Earth Observation systems on one hand and lack of good quality and timely data delivered to decisions makers on the other hand. Thus, in 1998 in Baveno (Italy) representatives of numerous institutions in this field concluded together with European Commission (EC) and European Space Agency (ESA) to establish European capacity for Earth Observation named GMES.

However, it was not only need to ensure data for Europe, but GMES bears also greater geostrategic importance of having autonomous system not dependent on

J. Hřebíček, G. Schimak, and R. Denzer (Eds.): ISESS 2011, IFIP AICT 359, pp. 110–114, 2011.

non-European systems, where still recently EU depends almost from 60% on foreign EO systems. EU commitment in this field is also a good tool to support European spaces industry, research and development while are all targeting to help to meet goals of the EU Lisbon strategy [1] and also EU 2020 strategy [2].

During last few years GMES has received wider importance within EU and in 2004 GMES was recognized in the Communication from the Commission to the European parliament and the Council (COM 2004 65) [3] followed by the resolution of the Parliament giving "green" light to further develop GMES.

Further on GMES found substantial basis to its development via finances from Seventh Framework Programme (FP7) in the domain of SPACE research. In the period 2007- 2013, 1.2 billion EUR were made available to develop GMES. In 2010 key step forward to make GMES a real programme was taken by the adoption of the regulation No. 911/2010 (Regulation of the European Parliament and of the Council on the European Earth monitoring programme (GMES) and its initial operations 2011–13), which entered into force on 9th November 2010 [4]. In accordance with the Regulation, the EU provides €107 million, of which €43 million are foreseen for the initial operation of GMES services and €64 million for the GMES Space Component [5].

3 Architecture of GMES

The GMES federates a wide range of observational networks and data providers, exploiting the most recent observation techniques and technologies, for developing edge-cutting information products to end-users. In principle, the GMES observational infrastructure composes of two main components – space and in situ.

3.1 Space Infrastructure

The space component shall ensure sustainable provision of satellite derived Earth observation data to all GMES services. The architecture of the component is derived from service requirements provided by the user communities. ESA and EUMETSAT are two main European actors in this area who should play the major role in co-ordination, implementation and operational running of the infrastructure [6].

Key elements of this component will be sets of 6 satellites systems named Sentinels, which shall cover all space born data needs for all services. These satellites will acquire radar and optical data, information on atmospheric chemistry and many other needs. First satellites on the orbit are expected in 2013. It is also a key aspect of benefits of GMES programme that Sentinel satellite systems are synergic logical follow up of some already existing satellite systems widely used in Europe (e.g. SPOT and ENVISAT).

3.2 In-Situ Infrastructure

The in situ component is based on an observation infrastructure owned and operated by the large number of stakeholders coordinated, in some cases, in the frame of European or international networks. In situ observation activities and associated infrastructure derive from a range of national, EU and international regulatory requirements and agreements or form part of research processes. None was created to meet the needs of

GMES, and they cover a much wider field than the GMES services. By this reason European Environmental Agency was appointed to co-ordinate the consolidation of in-situ networks for GMES purposes [7].

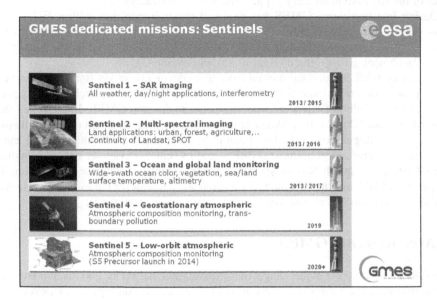

Fig. 1. GMES Sentinel satellites [source ESA]

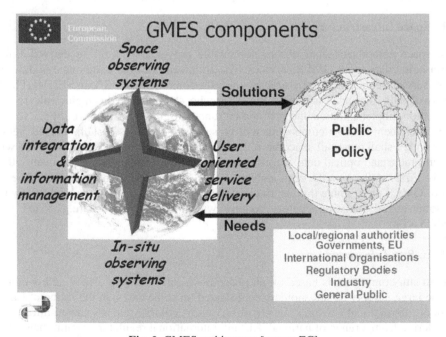

Fig. 2. GMES architecture [source EC]

3.3 Users

Another key element of the GMES will be final users. Users are here to define their needs to both space and in-situ elements in order to get from the system such data they can instantly use for their daily needs. User-driven principle shall be applied in both elements – for the design of satellite systems as well as on in-situ data processing to final users. What European users need most are ready-made tailored data.

4 GMES Services

Bringing GMES into reality of daily life involves sets of services, which are now in pilot phase with the future transition into operational services. Today we have six basic GMES services under development tackling most needed information for European users.

Land monitoring service is now being developed under GEOLAND 2 [7] project and it is dedicated to cover land monitoring needs for Europe including topics as land cover changes, agro-environmental issues, spatial planning, forest monitoring etc. For the domain of **marine** applications project MyOcean is now processed to cover monitoring of the ocean and seas in order to get better data on maritime security, natural recourses, oil spill prevention etc [8].

Emergency response service of GMES is covered by project SAFER [9], which gathers activities towards to a rapid mapping and provision of online information during emergency situations. The scope of this service goes even on global level, when this service has the potential to work worldwide. **Atmosphere services** of GMES are recently under MACC [10] project, when core of this task is to deliver data on air quality, climate, monitor sand and dust storms, UV radiation risks etc. Lastly, G-MOSAIC project is now running to cover **security** GMES services. Core of activities is in the provision of geo-spatial information in support of EU external relation policies for Security related activities [11].

Recently, another service covering GMES **climate change monitoring** is prepared to be initiated in 2012.

5 GMES – Operational EO Service

After twelve years GMES has now entered its operational phase through many research projects financed by the EU, ESA and Member States aimed to develop future operational services and infrastructure. The services are being developed to meet the needs of a wide range of users who rely on accurate environmental and security data and information. Operational, continuous and sustainable delivery of information has not yet been achieved. Further investment is therefore necessary, in Space infrastructure in particular, in order to fill the remaining gaps in GMES services and to guarantee their long-term sustainability and reliability. In addition, a common approach between the various partners involved in the development of GMES needs to be further enhanced, to avoid the possibility of a duplication of efforts. GMES is also creating opportunities for increased private sector usage of new information sources. It will trigger partnerships between research and service providers, many of them small and medium enterprises. Thus, while not likely in the short to medium term, the development of market opportunities could eventually determine the proportion of public investment [12].

6 Conclusion

Earth Observation encompasses a powerful set of advanced technologies which in combination with in situ (ground-based, airborne etc.) measurements provides products and services supporting solutions to international challenges such as security threats, environmental degradation and climate change. The GMES initiative reflects the European decision to develop its own, independent observation capabilities. At this time GMES starts the transition into real operational services delivering data where needed and has a unique potential to be a very successful approach how to maintain our planet safe and healthy. For its success, future strong commitment of its main key players – European Commission and European Space Agency is needed together with the voice of member states of the EU and other international bodies.

References

1. EU Lisbon strategy,
   http://ec.europa.eu/archives/growthandjobs_2009/
2. EU 2020 strategy, http://ec.europa.eu/europe2020/index_en.htm
3. COM (2004) 65, COMMUNICATION FROM THE COMMISSION TO THE EUROPEAN PARLIAMENT AND THE COUNCIL, Global Monitoring for Environment and Security (GMES): Establishing a GMES capacity by 2008 - (Action Plan (2004-2008))
4. Regulation of the European Parliament and of the Council on the European Earth monitoring programme (GMES) and its initial operations 2011-13,
   http://download.esa.int/docs/GMES/
   GMES_Regulation_911-2010_FINAL.pdf
5. ESA GMES, http://www.esa.int/esaLP/SEMEAN1PLFG_LPgmes_0.html
6. GMES Observational Infrastructure,
   http://ec.europa.eu/gmes/obser_infra.htm
7. Geoland 2, http://www.gmes-geoland.info/
8. MyOcean,
   http://www.myocean.eu.org/index.php/project/objectives
9. SAFER, http://safer.emergencyresponse.eu/site/FO/
   scripts/myFO_accueil.php?lang=EN
10. MACC, http://www.gmes-atmosphere.eu/
11. G-MOSAIC, http://www.gmes-gmosaic.eu/
12. Kolar, J., Mirovsky, O.: The Czech EU presidency: a gateway to GMES for users from Central and Eastern Europe, Window on GMES (March 2009) ISSN 2030-5410,
    http://www.boss4gmes.eu/index.php?id=103&no_cache=1

Can Volunteered Geographic Information Be a Participant in eEnvironment and SDI?

Peter Mooney and Padraig Corcoran

Department of Computer Science,
National University of Ireland Maynooth (NUIM),
Maynooth, Co. Kildare. Ireland
{peter.mooney,padraig.corcoran}@nuim.ie

Abstract. We investigate the potential role Volunteered Geographic Information (VGI) can play in eEvironment and various Spatial Data Infrastructures (SDI) on a local, regional, and national level. eEnvironment is the use and promotion of ICT for the purposes of environmental assessment and protection, spatial planning, and the sustainable use of natural resources. An SDI provides an institutionally sanctioned, automated means for posting, discovering, evaluating, and exchanging geospatial information by participating information producers and users. A key common theme shared by both definitions is public participation and user-centric services. We pose the research question: is VGI (an example of public participation and collaboration) is ready to participate in eEnvironment and SDI?

Keywords: VGI, OpenStreetMap, SDI, Spatial data.

1 Introduction

On first glance VGI appears to have all of the required ICT ingredients to provide a dynamic picture of the environment. VGI's ability to leverage large numbers of dedicated "citizen sensors" [5] is unprecedented. As a consequence the amount of VGI available on the Internet today has grown enormously in the past few years. Initiatives such as Wikimapia, Google Mapmaker, OpenStreetMap (OSM), geotagging in Flickr, geolocation in Twitter, Geonames, etc have seen VGI become a "hot topic in GIS research" [15] and is now one of the rapid growth areas of GIS. Recently VGI (such as OpenStreetMap) has begun to provide an interesting and feasible alternative to traditional authoritative spatial information from National Mapping Agencies and corporations. However the fact that VGI is a spatial form of the user-generated content in Web 2.0 has raised serious concerns and reservations within the GIS, Geomatics and Environmental Science communities [15,14] about its quality, accuracy, sustainability, and fitness for use/purpose. Kessler et al [11] points out that compared to other projects building on user contributed content, such as Wikipedia, VGI remains on the GIS periphery and consequently has been restricted to web-based mapping applications [8] and not considered for involvement in "serious geomatics applications" [17]. De Longueville et al

J. Hřebíček, G. Schimak, and R. Denzer (Eds.): ISESS 2011, IFIP AICT 359, pp. 115–122, 2011.

[13] (also in [12]) comments that work-flows have been implemented to create, validate, and distribute VGI datasets for various thematic domains but its exploitation in real-time and its integration into existing concepts of Digital Earth, such as SDI, still needs to be further addressed". SDI are created for specialists and experts with the goal of making diverse and heterogeneous data available and accessible. Gouveia et al [6] stress that the development of SDI, throughout the world, has facilitated improved public access to environmental information because of its inherently spatial characteristics. As GPS and web-enabled mobile devices have become ubiquitous we feel that it is important to leverage these new information sources and work towards stronger integration capabilities. Our paper attempts to make a case for VGI as a participant in eEnvironment and SDI.

2   Overview of Related Literature

Citizens, experts and non-experts alike, are increasingly participating in the process of generating continuous spatial information and collaborating with others in problem-solving tasks. This highlights the transition of the role of users from just mere data consumers to active participants and providers [2]. Traditionally, SDI building follows a top-down approach. This scenario leads to the provider-consumer paradigm, where only official providers like National Mapping Agencies (NMAs) and other environmental agencies, centrally, manage and deploy resources according to institutional policies. In this approach end-users can only be consumers [2]. However, VGI has changed this. There has been a transition in the role of users from just mere "data consumers to active participants and providers" [2]. Budhathoki et al [1] argue that SDI and VGI are not separate entities but are complementary phenomena. Budhathoki et al believe that these phenomena can be brought within a "single framework where the role of the user of SDI is re conceptualized to *produser* (producer and consumer of spatial data [2]) and VGI is included in the SDI-related processes. To enhance consumption of spatial data from SDI Omran and van Etten [16] suggest using a social network approach to spatial data sharing as a means of improving spatial data exchange in SDI. However, in a social network model (just as in VGI) there needs to be "a redefining of the rules about spatial data sharing and transferring more responsibility to more individuals in organizations [16]. Most SDI typically comprise of participants such as National Mapping Agencies (NMA), government agencies, private organizations, etc who have traditional or commercial roles in producing spatial information. Ho and Rajabifard [9] believe that this view "leaves a large part of society (community groups, concerned citizens) with none or nominal roles in SDI and are excluded or disengaged" where VGI is potentially left on the fringes. Research on SDIs and other spatial data sharing structures has not specifically considered the challenges facing grassroots data users. This is addressed by Elwood [3] who emphasizes the need for local data integration and accessibility to local users. SDIs are predicated on an assumption of openness to data sharing and exchange, conceptualizing data as a public good and assuming institutional and individual openness to sharing. In all likelihood, no single approach is wholly sufficient, given the social, political and technological complexity of spatial data sharing. Ho and Rajabifand [9] argue that as a visible representation of citizens' thoughts, observations, collected spatial and environmental data, VGI can be a "potential barometer for people's environmental concerns and attitudes and potentially lead to better citizen 'buy-in' to SDIs". This could also help inform the SDI managers what grassroots users and citizens currently require from an SDI.

In Section 1 we mentioned that VGI was not used in "serious applications" but there are some examples. Pultar et al [18] show applications to wildfire evacuation modeling and travel scenarios of urban environments. Over et al [17] develop prototype 3-D models using German OSM data. The "extensive produser (producer and consumer of spatial data [2]) base" in VGI referred to by Budhathoki et al [1] is a now large enough to be considered by SDI-related initiatives and eEnvironment. Some authors outline the problems in SDI development which are actually positives in VGI. Thellufsen et al [19] argue that the effective development of SDI is often a "fragmented" activity requiring inter-organization collaboration. Unfortunately many of the stakeholders in this collaboration resist "data sharing across organizational boundaries due to loss of control, power and independence. This is an area where VGI is very strong through the collaborative nature and ethos of the community based upon an inherent understanding and willingness to *share* data. Budhathoki et al [1] argue that VGI has harnessed a "large number of participants, without being coordinated by any formal organization, and without the lure of monetary or personal gain". Thellufsen et al [19] conclude that currently too many organizations, with spatial data useful for SDIs, are data "silo-minded" precisely at a time when they ought to be outreaching and co-operative. The authors suggest that these organizations should focus on building motivation awareness before actual solutions. In the next section we provide some results of analysis of OSM which provides some open questions for the inclusion of VGI in SDIs.

3   Using VGI in SDI: The OpenStreetMap Case Study

In this section we outline some results from some experimental analysis of OSM in Europe. To give an overview of some of the problems that VGI must tackle before becoming an active player in VGI we use the methodology of Grus et al [7] as well as some examples of the characteristics of OSM. Grus et al [7] developed a goal-oriented assessment view approach for assessing the realization of SDI goals and is demonstrated by its implementation in the Dutch SDI. As concluded by Giff and Crompvoets [4] SDIs must "not only to justify expenditure on their implementation but also to determine whether or not they are achieving their objectives". For this case-study we have analyzed the OSM databases for UK and Ireland, France, Germany, Austria, and Estonia. We show sample results under a number of headings: metadata, the nature of collaborative contributions, and data scale issues.

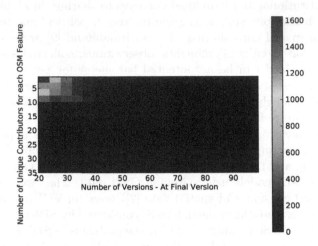

Fig. 1. A 2-D heat map histogram showing the distribution of the number of versions (*x* axis) against the number of unique contributors (*y*)

3.1   Metadata

Grus et al [7] suggest two metadata related indicators for SDI: *Metadata-standard applied in the national SDI geoportal* and *Metadata are produced for a significant fraction of spatial datasets*. Metadata can be inserted into the OSM database through the use of the accepted tagging structures. Tag keys such as "source","source:ref", "source:url" can be used as metadata to document the source of imported bulk data, tracing from aerial imagery, etc. Tags such as "note" and "attribution" can make specific statements about mapping techniques, errors, or other information useful to other mappers or users of the data. Tags offer OSM contributors with an opportunity to document their contributions. In the global OSM database the "source" tag is widely used of the 73 million objects using the source tag 51% are points, 47% are polygon, and 40% are relations. However our analysis shows this is dominated by bulk imports such as the French import of the EEA Corine Land Cover dataset. The "note" tag is used on five million objects: 5.8% of these are points, 1.74% of these are polygons, and 5.77% are relations. The tagging of OSM can rapidly degenerate into a folksonomy by leaving tagging up to individual contributors. But this can be seen as a flexibility which can grow to accommodate other metadata needs for example. Best practices, at the very minimum for bulk import or tracing of aerial imagery using OSM editors, can and should be implemented. All edits are tracked in OpenStreetMap so there is a clear trail of "who did what". While there are well known advantages in spatial data interoperability in using Dublin Core and ISO 19115 metadata schemes Kalantari et al [10]) argue that the folksonomy approach of VGI could have unpredicted advantages by leading to "more user-generated metadata potentially initiating richer metadata and better possibillty of user/creator updating".

3.2   Collaborative Contributions

In Figure 1 we show a 2-D heat map histogram of the distribution of the number of versions (x axis) of OSM polygons and polylines against the number of unique contributors (y) to each feature. 10, 000 "high edit" (more than 20 edits from OSM contributors) polygons and polylines from the UK and Ireland OSM databases were analyzed. Most of these features have a small number of contributors (≤ 5) while the number of versions (subsequent edits) of these features have a mean of 35 versions. We analyzed the complete historical record for these 10, 000 objects. Table 1 shows a summary of the time between edits of consecutive versions of the same object. Almost 42% of consecutive edits are separated by an editing time of 1 week to 1 month. Almost 38% of consecutive edits have 1 hour and 24 hours between them. The results in Table 1 gives an indication of the rate of change of the OSM database for these 10, 000 objects. To integrate the most up-to-date versions of these features into an SDI one must consider the time between edits. While almost half of edits (updates) happened with a period of 24 hours or more one must consider if the OSM database is changing too quickly for integration into an SDI.

Table 1. Distribution of time between consecutive edits for 10, 000

No. Edits	% of Edits	Time Between Edits
3, 866	3.30%	$\leq$ 5 minutes
11, 478	9.80%	5mins $\leq$ 30mins
2, 400	2.05%	30mins $\leq$ 1hour
12, 183	10.40%	1hr $\leq$ 2hr
21, 318	18.20%	2hr $\leq$ 12hr
11, 608	9.91%	12hr $\leq$ 24hr
3, 391	2.90%	24hr $\leq$ 1week
49, 084	41.91%	1week $\leq$ 1month
1, 784	1.52%	> 1month

3.3   Spatial Scale Issues

As Mooney and Corcoran [14] outline differences between countries in Europe to how spatial data is represented in the corresponding OSM database particularly in the number of nodes used to represent features. Differences in representation is an artefact of the different surveying and sampling methodologies employed by contributors to OSM. Figure 2 shows a plot of the mean spacing between nodes in landuse polygons in OSM for Estonia and Austria. Both Estonia and Austria have benefited from the donation of spatial data from Corine and Government sources respectively. It is evident from figure 2 that the scales of the two datasets are different. Grus et al [7] cite the inclusion of harmonized datasets within an SDI as an important indicator of a successful SDI.

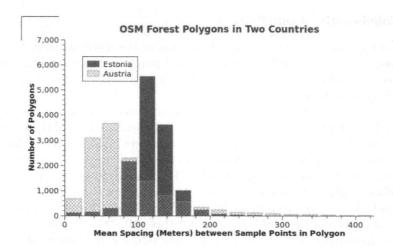

Fig. 2. Spacing between points in polygons in countries with government generated data

4   Conclusions

VGI is a rapidly evolving user-generated content movement. It's sustainability going forward into the long-term is uncertain. VGI will need to introduce improved management of contributions and contributors to prevent the spatial data moving indefinitely between a status of good and bad quality. Leveraging those dynamic updates (indicated in Table 1) is a key step to making the most of VGI. It is necessary that the VGI community can demonstrate that issues such as data quality (see Mooney and Corcoran [15]), scale and harmonization problems (Figure 2), etc can be detected effectively and efficiently. We agree with Budhathoki et al [1] that is "unlikely that VGI will completely replace SDIs". However, we believe that there is adequate scope and motivation for VGI to become a key stakeholder (both as spatial data producer and consumer) in SDIs. Diaz et al [2] remark that VGI is forcing the expert producers to rethink their traditional approaches of spatial production. Many open research questions remain. One of the key questions in relation to GIS is how VGI will interact with this community? As Budhathoki et al [1] (and Mooney and Corcoran [15]) remark "VGI is unlikely to satisfy the vast majority of institutional and professional GI producers whose requirements in terms of data quality, timeliness, and completeness are very strict". Can a suitable middleground between professional GI producers and VGI can be found? Wiemann and Bernard [20] indicates that "the full integration of VGI (such as OSM) within SDI is not yet possible". However we believe that the generation of knowledge from a variety of sources of spatial information can play a decisive role in building knowledge-based structures made accessible through the vehicle of SDI. Giff and Crompvoets [4] conclude that SDIs must "engage its users to clearly think through the processes involved in the provision of spatial information products and services". Engagement of users/communities is one of the most impressive characteristics of the VGI phenonema.

Acknowledgements

Dr. Peter Mooney is a research fellow at the Department of Computer Science NUIM and is funded by the Irish Environmental Protection Agency STRIVE programme (grant 2008-FS-DM-14- S4). Dr. Padraig Corcoran is a lecturer and post-doctoral researcher also at the Department of Computer Science NUIM. Dr. Corcoran is part of STRAT-AG which is a Strategic Research Cluster grant (07/SRC/I1168) funded by Science Foundation Ireland under the National Development Plan. The authors gratefully acknowledge this support.

References

1. Budhathoki, N., Bruce, B., Nedovic-Budic, Z.: Reconceptualizing the role of the user of spatial data infrastructure. GeoJournal 72, 149–160 (2008)
2. Daz, L., Granell, C., Gould, M., Huerta, J.: Managing user-generated information in geospatial cyberinfrastructures. Future Generation Computer Systems 27(3), 304–314 (2011)
3. Elwood, S.: Grassroots groups as stakeholders in spatial data infrastructures: challenges and opportunities for local data development and sharing. International Journal of Geographical Information Science 22(1), 71–90 (2008)
4. Giff, G.A., Crompvoets, J.: Performance indicators a tool to support spatial data infrastructure assessment. Computers, Environment and Urban Systems 32(5), 365–376 (2008)
5. Goodchild, M.F.: Neogeography and the nature of geographic expertise. Journal of Location Based Services 3(2), 82–96 (2009)
6. Gouveia, C., Fonseca, A., Cmara, A., Ferreira, F.: Promoting the use of environmental data collected by concerned citizens through information and communication technologies. Journal of Environmental Management 71(2), 135–154 (2004)
7. Grus, L., Castelein, W., Crompvoets, J., Overduin, T., van Loenen, B., van Groenestijn, A., Rajabifard, A., Bregt, A.K.: An assessment view to evaluate whether spatial data infrastructures meet their goals. In: Computers, Environment and Urban Systems, Corrected Proof (in press, 2010)
8. Haklay, M.: A comparative study of openstreetmap and ordnance survey datasets for london and the rest of england. Environment and Planning B: Planning and Design 37(4), 628–703 (2010)
9. Ho, S., Rajabifard, A.: Learning from the crowd: The role of volunteered geographic information in realising a spatially enabled society. In: Proceedings of GSDI 12 World Conference - Realising Spatially Enabled Societies, Singapore (October 2010)
10. Kalantari, M., Olfat, H., Rajabifard, A.: Automatic spatial metadata enrichment: Reducing metadata creation burden through spatial folksonomies. In: GSDI 12 Proceedings of the 12th Global Spatial Data Infrastructures Conference, pp. 773–779. GSDI (October 2010)

11. KeBler, C., Janowicz, K., Bishr, M.: An agenda for the next generation gazetteer: geographic information contribution and retrieval. In: Proceedings of the 17th ACM SIGSPATIAL International Conference on Advances in Geographic Information Systems, GIS 2009, pp. 91–100. ACM, New York (2009)
12. Longueville, B.D.: Community-based geoportals: The next generation? concepts and methods for the geospatial web 2.0. Computers, Environment and Urban Systems 34(4), 299–308 (2010)
13. Longueville, B.D., Ostländer, N., Keskitalo, C.: Addressing vagueness in volunteered geographic information (VGI) – A case study. International Journal of Spatial Data Infrastructures Research 5 (2009)
14. Mooney, P., Corcoran, P.: A study of data representation of natural features in openstreetmap. In: Weibel, R., Fabrikant, S. (eds.) Proceedings GIScience 2010: The Sixth International Conference on Geographic Information Science. LNCS. Springer, Heidelberg (2010)
15. Mooney, P., Corcoran, P., Winstanley, A.C.: Towards quality metrics for openstreetmap. In: Proceedings of the 18th SIGSPATIAL International Conference on Advances in Geographic Information Systems, GIS 2010, pp. 514–517. ACM, New York (2010)
16. Omran, E.E., van Etten, J.: Spatial-data sharing: Applying social-network analysis to study individual and collective behaviour. International Journal of Geographical Information Science 21(6), 699–714 (2007)
17. Over, M., Schilling, A., Neubauer, S., Zipf, A.: Generating web-based 3d city models from openstreetmap: The current situation in germany. Computers, Environment and Urban Systems 34(6), 496–507 (2010); GeoVisualization and the Digital City - Special issue of the International Cartographic Association Commission on GeoVisualization
18. Pultar, E., Raubal, M., Cova, T.J., Goodchild, M.F.: Dynamic gis case studies: Wildfire evacuation and volunteered geographic information. Transactions in GIS 13, 85–104 (2009)
19. Thellufsen, C., Rajabifard, A., Enemark, S., Williamson, I.: Awareness as a foundation for developing effective spatial data infrastructures. Land Use Policy 26(2), 254 (2009)
20. Wiemann, S., Bernard, L.: A comparative study of proprietary geodata and volunteered geographic information for germany. In: Painho, M., Santos, M.Y., Pundt, H. (eds.) Proceedings AGILE 2010: The 13th AGILE International Conference on Geographic Information Science, Springer Verlag, Guimarães (2010)

3D Modelling as a Tool for Landscape Restoration and Analysis

Jan Pacina, Kamil Novák, and Lukáš Weiss

Department of Informatics and Geoinformatics, Faculty of the Environment,
J. E. Purkyně University, Králova výšina 7, 400 96, Ústí nad Labem, Czech Republic
{Jan.Pacina,Kamil.Novak}@ujep.cz, Weiss.Lukas@email.cz

Abstract. The region of North-west Bohemia has been influenced by the open cast mining for more than the last hundred years. During this period has the coal mining activity become very intense leaving huge change on the landscape. We may require the original landscape for many purposes (historical, landscape renewal). One of the ways how to reconstruct the original shape of the landscape is the usage of historical maps and old aerial photographs made in the period before the dramatic georelief changes. As the data sources, we use the maps of the 3rd Military survey 1:25 000 after reambulation, aerial photographs taken in years 1938, 1952, 1995 and maps of stabile cadaster. The reambulated maps contain clearly readable elevation data (contour lines), which were used for reconstructing the original landscape. From processed aerial photographs we get the Digital Surface Model of the coal mines in different time periods.

Keywords: georelief reconstruction, 3rd Military survey, stabile cadaster maps, aerial photographs, digital surface model, volumetric analysis.

1 Introduction

The area between the towns Kadaň and Duchcov (North-west Bohemia, the Czech Republic) is a part of so called Black Triangle [3] with active coal mining activity. The Brown coal has been mined in this area for ages, but the mining has become very intense in the last 80 years. Brown coal is not located too deep in the coal basin, so the technology of open-cast mines is widely used in this area. The open-cast mining is a rather cheap technology of coal mining giving access to huge loads of brown coal, but with a destructive effect on the surrounding environment.

This region used to be focused on agriculture, with towns and little villages spread all over the basin. The coal mining followed by the heavy industry has changed the view and shape of this region a lot.

In this area there were 3 Hot Spots delineated– areas with landscape degraded by coal mining. Each of these Hot Spots has its significant structure, usage, problems and vision. Within Hot Spots there are the following areas (see Fig. 2):

- Jezeří castle – a historical castle built at the edge of Krušné hory (Ore Mountains). Currently endangered by geological instability and landslides.

J. Hřebíček, G. Schimak, and R. Denzer (Eds.): ISESS 2011, IFIP AICT 359, pp. 123–138, 2011.
© IFIP International Federation for Information Processing 2011

- Lake Most – an open-cast mine currently turned into a hydric recultivation (land-renewal). The town Most, destroyed in 1970', was originally settled in this area.
- Open-cast mine Bílina and dump Radovesice – one of the biggest active coal mines in the region.

The purpose of this paper is to show the possibilities of landscape restoration on these different Hot Spots using the technologies of GIS and 3D modeling. For this purposes we use the old maps of the region and historical aerial photographs, as these data sources are very relevant historical materials that could be used for this kind of task.

The landscape reconstruction requires elevation data from the period before the intensive coal mining activity and in some cases also data from different time periods.

This area has been closely mapped in 1930' thanks to its geographic location (which is close to the border with Germany) and the huge brown coal reserves. The maps of the 3rd Military survey 1:25 000 of this region were reambulated in the period 1934 – 1938 and in 1938 was the region covered with aerial photographs. The current state of the georelief within the coal mines cannot be easily obtained and the coal mining companies are not a well accessible data source at all. Here we have to use the aerial photographs for Digital Surface Model (DSM) and further on Digital Elevation Model (DTM) creation.

Fig. 1. Georelief change in the Basin of Most - 1960' and 2000 [11]

2   Data and Methods

In this paper we work with old maps and historical/current aerial photographs. Old maps used for this project are the maps of the 3rd Military survey 1:25 000 after reambulation and Stabile cadaster maps. Historical aerial photographs originate from the years 1938, 1953, 1987 and the recent aerial photographs from the year 2008.

2.1   Old Maps

The maps of the 3rd Military survey of this region were reambulated in 1930' apparently for the strategic purposes with upcoming of the 2nd World War. Elevation data are clearly readable in these maps in the form of contour lines and elevation points. The contour line interval is varying from 20m in flat areas to 2.5m in hilly areas. These maps are in scale 1:25 000 and are the primary source of historical data.

Other sources of historical maps are the Stabile cadaster maps 1:2880. These maps were created in the period 1826 – 1843 and they are one of the most reliable sources for land-use development analysis.

All maps covering the Hot Spots have to be georeferenced. Spline transformation implemented in ArcGIS was used to georeference the data. The spline transformation is a true rubber sheeting method and is optimized for local accuracy but not global accuracy. It is based on a spline function - a piecewise polynomial that maintains continuity and smoothness between adjacent polynomials. [2]

The spline transformation was chosen as it fulfills the position accuracy of the transformed requested for the DTM creation in this project.

Approximately 150 to 250 identical points were chosen in each map sheet of the 3rd Military survey (dependently on the input data) to secure the local accuracy. With respect to the map scale to a local accuracy were the Stabile cadaster maps georeferenced using approximately 30 identical points in each map sheet.

The transformation accuracy has been visually tested with the MapAnalyst application [5] by applying a regular square network on the transformed data.

Digitized contour lines are further on used for Digital Terrain Model (DTM) creation.

2.2 Aerial Photographs

All of the three Hot Spot areas are fully covered with aerial photographs from the years 1938, 1953, 1987 and 2008.

Aerial photographs have been processed in the standard way of photogrammetry using the Leica Photogrammetric Suite (for detail description of aerial image processing in this region, see [9] and [13]).

The historical images from the years 1938 and 1953 are not in a very good visual quality. The images are noisy, scratched, and affected by the contemporary technology of creation – this affects especially the selection of Ground Control Points (GCP's) and the automatic Digital Surface Model (DSM) creation from aerial images.

On the aerial images from the year 1938 and 1953 are within the Hot Spot areas large parts of the landcape that has changed a lot. The recent data are practically useless for processing the GCP's in these areas. Here were used partially the old maps (3rd Military survey) to locate the object on the historical aerial photographs, recent orthophoto for the surrounding areas without a significant change and the orthophoto from 1953 accessible at http://kontaminace.cenia.cz for the other areas.

The following aerial images were used for the different Hot Spots:

- Jezeří Castle – years 1953 and 2008,
- Lake Most – years 1953 and 2008,
- Open-cast mine Bílina – years 1938, 1987 and 1995.

2.3 DTM and DSM Creation

Several DTM's and DSM's were created under processing of the Hot Spots. We require DTM as an input for aerial image processing for defining the GCP's elevation information. Here we use the ZABAGED® [1] contour lines and digitized contour lines from the maps of 3rd Military survey.

Fig. 2. Hot Spots overview

Fig. 3. Jezeří castle at the edge of a coal mine (author's photo)

The DSM's are results of automatic image correlation. This method is used for automatic DSM extraction from aerial images with known orientation parameters with image overlap (in our case 60%). The extracted DSM's are the desired results for historical landscape restoration.

The precise methodology for DTM and DTM creation is described in [9].

2.4 Hot Spot Characterization

All of the processed Hot Spots are presented on Fig. 2. In each of the Hot Spot is the research focused on different topic, requiring slightly different methodology.

Fig. 4. The landscape change within the royal town Most [4] [10]

Jezeří Castle
The castle Jezeří is one of the biggest castles in the Czech Republic, founded in the 14th century. The castle is a part of the national cultural heritage, but it is highly endangered by the surrounding coal mines. The research in this Hot Spot is focused on the landscape and land-use development. The forest garden surrounding the castle and the castle itself are highly endangered by the surrounding coal mine and by landslides connected with the mining activity (see Fig. 3).

Lake Most
This Hot Spot is a significant example, how is the open-cast mining activity changing the landscape. Within this Hot Spot used to be the royal town Most, destructed in the 1970'. When the coal mine was depleted, it has been changed into a hydrical reculti-vation (over flooded mine) with future leisure time usage (see Fig. 4). Within this Hot Spot we focus on the georelief changes.

The open-cast mine Bílina
The open-cast mine Bílina is one of the largest active mines in the region. Several villages have been destroyed as the mine was spreading. In this Hot Spot, we focus on volumetric analysis – based on DTM'S and DSM's and we would like to summarize the whole amount of material that has been mined in the mine, or moved into the outer deposits.

Fig. 5. Landscape change in the surroundings of town Bílina

The Hot Spot Bílina is the largest area processed in this paper, thus in this paper we focus only on the selected area representing the main coal mine and its surroundings, excluding the dump Radovesice. See Fig. 6.

Fig. 6. The area for volumetric analysis within the open-cast mine Bílina

3 Analysis

The meaning of this project is to show the possible reconstruction works concerning the landscape restoration and the land-use analysis. Thus we focus on slightly different analysis in our investigation Hot Spots.

3.1 Castle Jezeří Analysis

The position of Jezeří castle is on the very edge of the open-cast coal mine Československá armáda (Czechoslovak army). The coal mining activity, that has stopped at the very edge of the Ore Mountains is causing geological instability resulting in very huge landslides in the surrounding localities.

The castle should be protected from sliding into the coal mine by a pillar, situated under the castle. The pillar is also located in the forest garden. In the past years huge landslides appeared also in the pillar (see Fig. 7). One task of this land modeling issue would be to evaluate the landslides, the amount of material that has slide and the landslides position.

This analysis requires very precise elevation data of this area, which are currently unreachable for public or scientific purposes, as they are the property of the coal-mining company. In the year 2012 would be this whole area a part of the national photogrammetry survey. Results of this survey will be very precise photogrammetric digital imagery that will be used to finish the analysis.

Fig. 7. Landslides at the pillar protecting the castle [11]

So far we have processed the aerial images from the year 1953 and 2008 that gave us precise DSM's of the whole area[1]:

- DSM_1953 – derived from the aerial photographs – year 1953,
- DSM_2008 – derived from the aerial photographs – year 2008.

We are able to compute the landscape change in this area, and to localize the potential landslides from the DTM analysis. On Fig. 9 the boundary between the original (un-changed) georelief and the georelief that has been affected by the coal mining activity is delineated. The boundary was derived based on the differences analysis of DSM_1953 and DSM_2008 (Fig. 8) and it represents the upper pillar boundary.

The area of Jezeří castle Hot Spot is fully covered by a series of historical map-ping. These maps will be used to analyze the land-use change during the period of

---

[1] Similar naming of DTM's and DSM's is used in the rest of this paper.

almost 200 years. The analysis will include maps of the 1st, 2nd and 3rd Military Survey, Stabile Cadaster maps and historical aerial.

3.2 Lake Most Analysis

The analysis of Lake Most is focused on the dramatic georelief change, when a town was under-mined and then changed into a lake. The whole analysis is based on DSM's produced from aerial images and DTM's derived from elevation data contained in current and historical maps.

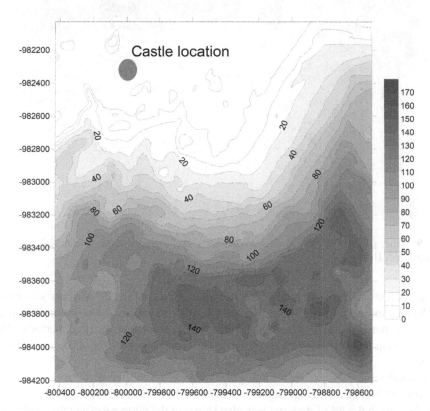

Fig. 8. Differences of Digital Surface Models created from the aerial photographs (Castle Jezeří Hot Spot) – years 1953 and 2008

Processing of the historical aerial images of this area was problematic, because the shape of the landscape has changed a lot during the past 60 years. As the source of elevation were in this case used the contour lines derived from the maps of the 3rd Military survey.

Fig. 9. Line delineating the boundary between the changed and unchanged georelief (Castle Jezeøí Hot Spot)

The analysis results have shown that the contour lines of the 3rd Military survey are not detailed enough. In our future work they will be replaced by contour lines digitized from derived digital state-map 1:5000 from corresponding time periods. This will even help us to reconstruct the relief in different time periods of the coal mining activity.

The analysis results are representing the total georelief change between the years 1953 and 2008 (Fig. 10). Huge amount of material has been removed (positive values) from the area, but a lot of material was also stored in the deoposits (negative values).

On Fig. 11 is presented visualization of DSM's from years 1953 and 2008 derived from aerial photographs, including two elevation profiles (visualized on Fig. 12 and Fig. 13). The *hillshade* analysis is used to make the visualization more readable.

The future scope of this Hot Spot analysis should be the georelief reconstruction in different time periods focused on the final state of over-flooded coal mine.

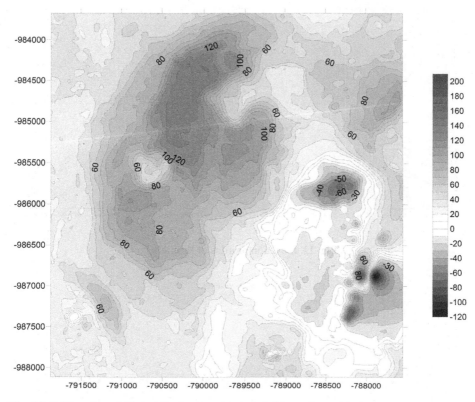

Fig. 10. Differences of Digital Surface Models created from the aerial photographs (Lake Most Hot Spot) – years 1953 and 2008

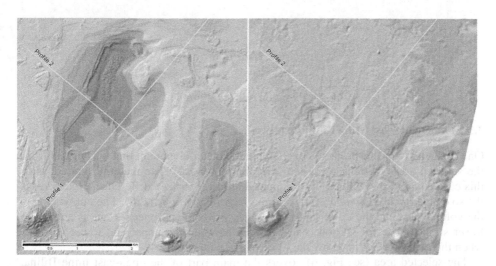

Fig. 11. Landscape change changes within the Lake Most Hot Spot. Left – year 2008. Right – year 1953. Lines are delineating Profile 1 and Profile 2.

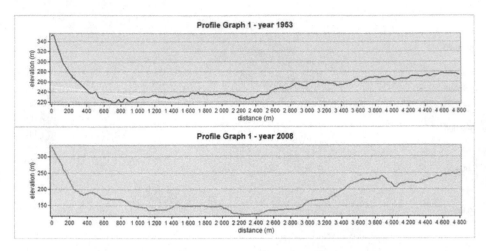

Fig. 12. Elevation profiles of Profile 1

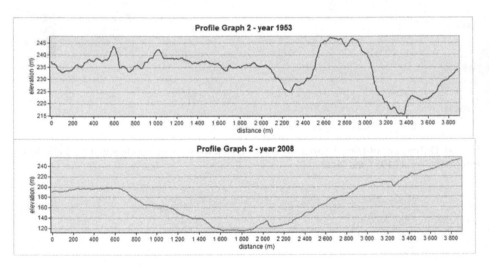

Fig. 13. Elevation profiles of Profile 2

3.3   The Open-Cast Mine Bílina Analysis

One of the tasks of this project is to evaluate the material amount that was mined from the selected areas or transported into the dump (deposit). The material amount is in this case equal to the volume of the upper and lower surface difference. Here we get the so called *Positive Volume (Cut)* and the *Negative Volume (Fill)*. The cut portion is the volume between the upper and lower surface when the upper surface is above the lower surface. The fill portion is the volume between the upper and lower surfaces when the upper surface is below the lower surface (see Fig. 14).

The selected area (see Fig. 6) covers the main part of the open-cast mine Bílina. The historical aerial photographs from the year 1938 do not cover the whole area of the coal mine, therefore the DTM derived from the 3rd Military survey map contours

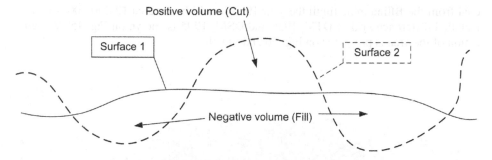

Fig. 14. Principle of volumetric analysis

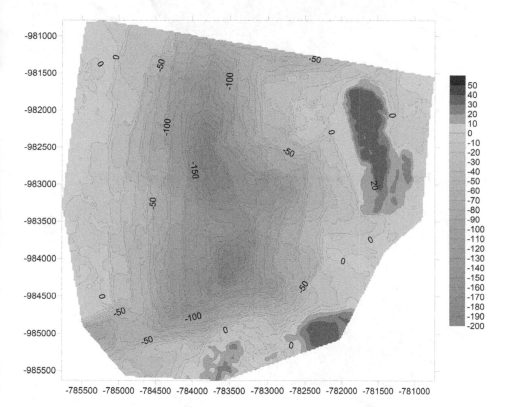

Fig. 15. Detailed difference grid of Digital Terrain Model – year 1936 and Digital Surface Model – year 1995

will be used for the volumetric analysis. The volume calculation from DTM_1936 would be proximate, as the DTM was interpolated from hand-vectorized contour lines.

The total Positive Volume (Cut) of the area is 44 363 951m3 and the Negative Volume (Fill) is 930 015 080m^3. One railway transport wagon can store up to 75m^3 of material - this means (based on this computation) that to transport the material and coal from the Bílina mine (until the year 1995) could be used ca 12 400 200 wagons. Detailed difference grid of DTM_1936 and DSM_1995 is shown on Fig. 15. Visualization of the area is presented on Fig. 16 and Fig. 17.

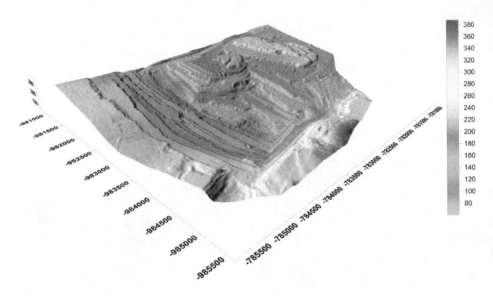

Fig. 16. Digital Surface Model of the open-cast mine Bílina – year 1995

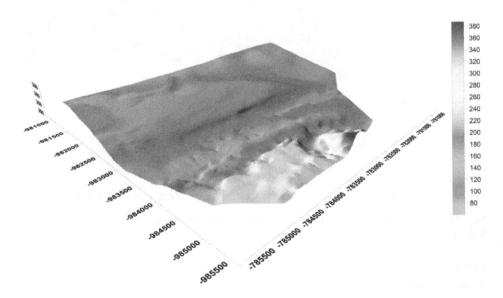

Fig. 17. Digital Terrain Model of former landscape of open-cast mine Bílina – year 1936

4 Conclusion

In this paper are presented the possibilities for reconstruction and analysis of irreversibly changed georelief, using aerial images and old maps.

The maps of the 3rd Military Survey are used as a source of elevation data in areas with a large change of the landscape and the maps of Stabile Cadaster (1:2880) are used for the landscape development analysis. The 3rd Military Survey maps are georeferenced using a spline transformation (rubber sheeting) with a huge number of identical points – 150 to 250 per map sheet. The Stabile Cadastre maps are due to it's scale transformed using approx 30 identical points per maps sheet. This transformation method provides for both map sources sufficient accuracy for the purpose of this project. A Digital Terrain Model (DTM) was interpolated from the hand-vectorized contour lines of the 3rd Military maps.

Within the area of the Basin of Most were chosen three Hot Spots - areas with landscape degraded by coal mining. Each of these Hot Spots has its significant structure, usage, problems and vision.

The Hot Spot Castle Jezeří is one of the biggest castles in the Czech Republic. Due to the surrounding active coal mining activity is this part of national cultural heritage endangered by geological instability and huge landslides in the castle surroundings. Within this paper the boundary between the changed and unchanged part of georelief, creating a security pillar preventing the castle from sliding down to the coal-mine was delimitated. The Digital Surface Models (DSM's) were derived from aerial photographs from the year 1953 and 2008. With these data we may perform a difference analysis which shows the total georelief change in this Hot Spots area. For the precise landslide analysis (and other possible relief movements) are required aerial photographs from the current time period, which will be available during the year 2012.

The Hot Spot Lake Most is an example of hydric recultivation – a former coal mine is turned into a lake. The interesting fact about this Hot Spot is that in 1970' there used to be the royal town Most (25 000 inhabitants), but the huge brown-coal layers located not very deep under the Earth surface led to the destruction of the town. The landscape in this area has changed many times during the active mining. The aim of this analysis is to show the georelief evolution during this period, focused on the area of the new lake and its surroundings. From the results presented in this paper we may see that a lot of material has been stored in outer deposits around the former coal mine. The analysis results have also shown that the usage of elevation data obtained from the 3rd Military Survey Maps do not give the results of required preciseness. For our future work we will use digital state-map 1:5000 covering the whole Hot Spot area with precise elevation data.

The Hot Spot Open-cast mine Bílina is one of the biggest active open-cast mines in this region. The analysis within this Hot Spot is focused on volumetric analysis of material that has been mined from the coal-mine area and stored in the outer deposits. Within this paper for computation of the volumetric I have used the elevation data from the 3rd Military Survey maps and DSM which is derived from the 1995 aerial photographs. The total amount of material mined in this area in the period 1936 – 1995 is 930 015 080m^3. Precise computations for the whole Hot Spot area may be found in [9] and [13].

References

1. Základní, Č.U.Z.K.: báze geografických dat ZABAGED ® [online]. [cit 2010-20-10], http://www.cuzk.cz/Dokument.aspx?PRARESKOD=998&MENUID=0& AKCE=DOC:30-ZU_ZABAGED
2. ESRI ArcGIS Desktop 9.3 Help [online]. [cit 2010-20-10], http://webhelp.esri.com/arcgisdesktop/9.3/
3. Ecological Center Most: Black Triangle [online]. [cit. 2011-13-4], http://www.ecmost.cz/ver_cz/aktualni_sdeleni/cerny_trojuhelnik.htm
4. Foto Mapy, Pohled na město Most [online]. [cit. 2011-13-4], http://foto.mapy.cz/original?id=14170
5. Jenny, B., Weber, A.: Map Analyst [online]. [cit 2011-15-4], http://mapanalyst.cartography.ch/
6. Mitas, L., Mitasova, H.: General variational approach to the interpolation problem. Computers and Mathematics with Applications 16, 983–992 (1988)
7. Mitas, L., Mitasova, H.: Interpolation by regularized spline with tension: I. Theory and implementation. Mathematical Geology 25, 641–655 (1993)
8. Neteler, M.: Open Source GIS: a GRASS GIS approach. Kluwer Academic Publishers, USA (2004) ISBN: 1-4020-8064-6
9. Pacina, J., Weiss, L.: Georelief reconstruction and analysis based on historical maps and aerial photographs. In: Proceedings of Symposium GIS Ostrava 2011, VSB - Technical University of Ostrava (2011) ISBN: 978-80-248-2366-9
10. Palivový kombinát Ústí, Napouštění Jezera Most [online]. [cit 2011-15-14], http://www.pku.cz/pku/site.php?location=5&type=napousteni_most
11. Sesuv půdy pod zámkem Jezeří [online]. [cit 2011-15-14], http://www.koukej.com
12. Štýs, S.: The Region of Most – A New Born Landscape, Ecoconsult Pons Most. CZ (2000)
13. Weiss, L.: Spatio-temporally analysis of georelief changes in Bílina region caused by the coal-mining activity. Faculty of Environment, J. E. Purkyně University. Diploma thesis (2011)

GINA (Geographical Information Assistant) Fresh Wind in Environmental Mapping

Zbyněk Poulíček, Boris Procházka, and Petra Bačíková

GINA Software s.r.o, U Vodárny 2a,
61600 Brno, Czech Republic
info@ginasystem.com

Abstract. GINA is a comprehensive software system for field workers allowing effective mapping of environment and situation. The GINA makes easier by its design the mapping works in the terrain and protects the collected data. It runs on hardware of Motorola Company which has sturdy design for work in the field and is perfectly adjusted to needs of field workers. By means of GINA System can be realized mapping projects in extravilans that wouldn't be even possible to do by traditional methods.

Keywords: GINA System, environmental mapping, online mapping, crowdsourcing.

1 Introduction

The aim of this document is introduction of innovative mobile system offering new methods for effective environmental mapping. The system is called GINA and it is a main product of GINA Software Company.

Fig. 1. GINA logo

1.1 GINA System

The core of the system is software for mobile equipment. It serves for collecting of geographical information and allows their exchange in real-time. Thanks to this the system is aimed not only for passive mapping but also allows remote management of people working in the field.

The mobile client offers a possibility to display and record huge amount of different information in the map. The user is not limit in any way and can have all the need information with him in the field. The GINA System offers many types of maps which are available directly in the field so the users can choose the most suitable

J. Hřebíček, G. Schimak, and R. Denzer (Eds.): ISESS 2011, IFIP AICT 359, pp. 139–143, 2011.

maps to fulfill current tasks. These maps are downloaded from the Internet so the users are not limited by the memory of the device and can use the whole map portfolio. Currently GINA System offers broadly available Internet maps such are OpenStreetMap and Bing Maps and also specialized types of map layers such as cadastral maps. The advantage of the system is its extensibility. The map portfolio can be very briskly extended of almost any digital map data according to customers' needs. For work in the low areas with low Internet Connectivity can be the maps also pre-cached in the device.

The system aims to increasing the productivity of field workers. It provides very comfortable user interface which is customizable according to customers' needs. The access to main functions for collecting of geographical information is very intuitive and makes the work with the software as simple as is man works with the paper map. The user can draw by curves and polygons by pen, can add pictograms into the map and to all the recorded information he can add an attachment which can be pictures taken by built-in camera, drawings, textual documents or other files. This way can be all the recorded information well documented. [1]

2   Usage Scenarios

Besides environmental mapping the GINA System is in use also by crisis management or corporate government. Thanks to its unique feature of real-time geographical information exchange it is a power tool for search & rescue missions and security operations. In such scenarios is very important for people in the field to have always the up-to-date information because it can mean the difference between life and death. The system allows interconnection of big number of field workers end even their groups. Besides the exchange of information by means of the map they can also use the benefits of integrated instant messaging and conference calls. This way makes GINA the crises management more effective and lowers the costs of it.

GINA System already approved to be a powerful tool for crises management in several scenarios. The system is in use in Haiti since April 2010 where it helps by several rescue and security missions. It is involved in the rescue mission of Hand for Help organization where it helps by coordination of rescuers and served for finding the most suitable location for the hospital. Since January 2011 it is in use also by mission Water for Haiti organized by Praga Haiti organization. The goal of the mission is sinking of tents of new wells in the area as there is a lack of drinking water. The current progress of the mission is available to public on website www.haitiwells.com [2]. Most widely is GINA in use by project ECHO Haiti which is a project of European Union. GINA helps by monitoring of political situation and cholera spreading. The up-to-date information is available on the website www.cholerahaiti.com [3]. Besides Haiti has been GINA system deployed also to Brazil when it helps by renovation of devastated areas after flood and also to Japan only few days after the earthquake in March 2011. In Japan was GINA used as a documentation tool for rescuers and the results are again available online on www.japansituation.com [4].

Fig. 2. Usage of GINA in Haiti by Hand for Help organization

3   Integration Possibilities

GINA System is very open platform to integration with other systems. Currently it is possible thanks to cooperation with National Instruments Company to integrate autonomous sensors into the system. Thanks to this can be the important values automatically measured and results are available to people in the field in real-time. This data are stored with chronological context for allowing the display of trends of measured values. Besides the measuring and tracking hardware GINA allows also integration with software systems such as ERP or CRMs.

4   Hardware Equipment

The GINA System contains of mobile client and PC Software. The software for the PC can run on almost any computer with Microsoft Windows installed. The mobile client requires Windows Mobile device and it is strongly recommended to use Motorola devices for which is the system aimed. Those devices are sturdy and are designed for work in the field. They have a big well readable screen; the battery can last up to 8 hours and all the data are preserved in persistent memory protects data in case of damage of the device. There are also available sturdy tablets supported by GINA System offering even bigger displays for comfortable work.

Fig. 3. Sturdy Motorola device

For recording of geographical point is used built-in GPS sensor. In Motorola devices are integrated the highest class GPS sensors. Despite the fact they don't support the TCM correction data is possible to reach a precision around 1 meter in open space which is sufficient for environmental mapping.

5   Services for Customers

GINA Software offers the following services in context of environmental mapping. It provides licenses of GINA System for the end-users and offers also assisted mapping services when the mapping in the field is done by dedicated workers of GINA Software Company. There is also available a simplified mobile client supporting almost every commonly available smartphone allowing to involve crowd in the mapping. This way can be very effectively mapped very large areas.

6   References of Usage

GINA System is used with high advantage in two main areas. The first one is surveys in extravilans (outside the city), where the rapid access to cadastral and satellite maps together with its precise location is desirable during the whole day. The system was, for example, used to localize very large fence (about 10 Kilometers) around habitat corridor whereas the whole localization was done during 1 day. The second area is environmental mapping of large areas and places. As the system is designed to input of single information (object in the country) very easily, it was able to map more than 13 hectares of areas counting more than 2000 different trees and 200 surfaces of bushes in 4 days. The next day has been generated the documentation according to submitter needs. Mapping large area was never so easy before.

7 Company Profile

GINA Software is a company established at the end of the year 2010 in the Czech Republic. The main product is GINA System which allows an effective management of field workers. The company also aims to ensuring the security of people by tracking of movement. GINA Software is Motorola ISV Partner and Microsoft Partner. [5]

References

1. GINA System, http://www.ginasystem.com
2. Haiti Wells (Project Water for Haiti), http://www.haitiwells.com
3. Cholera in Haiti, http://www.cholerahaiti.com
4. Japan Situation, http://www.japansituation.com
5. GINA Software Company, http://ginasoftware.com

Environmental Information Systems on the Internet: A Need for Change

Sven Schade[1], Barbara Fogarty[2], Michael Kobernus[3], Katharina Schleidt[4], Paul Gaughan[5], Paolo Mazzetti[6], and Arne-Jørgen Berre[7]

[1] Institute for Environment and Sustainability,
Joint Research Centre of the European Commission, Ispra, Italy
sven.schade@jrc.ec.europa.eu
[2] Dublin City University
barbara.fogarty@dcu.ie
[3] Norsk Institutt for Luftforskning, Norway
mike.kobernus@nilu.no
[4] Umweltbundesamt Östereich, Austria
katharina.schleidt@umweltbundesamt.at
[5] Marine Institute, Ireland
paul.gaughan@marine.ie
[6] Consiglio Nazionale delle Ricerche, Italy
mazzetti@imaa.cnr.it
[7] Stiftelsen SINTEF, Norway
arne.j.berre@sintef.no

Abstract. The cost effective delivery of scientific and policy requirements is a key driver for the realization of global sustainability research, integrated assessment and supporting innovative systems. The next generation of geospatial information infrastructures is proposed as a possible solution. Still, questions such as 'what does all this mean to environmental information systems' and 'what is expected to change', have only partially been answered. In this paper, we describe the recent challenges for eEnvironment services in Europe, specify desired capabilities and derive according requirements. We identify affected stakeholder communities and depict their involvement in the overall value chain of environmental knowledge generation. Specific examples illustrate individual needs, while a derived description of the value chain indicates more general outcomes. Developmental requirements of future information systems are discussed. The presented work answers the questions above by bridging the gab between stakeholder needs, Information and Communication Technology (ICT) development and higher level concepts, such as Digital Earth and Future Internet.

1 Introduction

The International Council for Science (ICSU) identified five scientific priorities, or Grand Challenges, in global sustainability research, including (i) development of observation systems needed to manage global and regional environmental change; (ii) improvement of the usefulness of forecasts of future environmental conditions and

J. Hřebíček, G. Schimak, and R. Denzer (Eds.): ISESS 2011, IFIP AICT 359, pp. 144–153, 2011.

their consequences for people; and (iii) investigation of institutional, economic and behavioral responses that can enable effective steps toward global sustainability [1]. A next generation of geospatial information infrastructures (Digital Earth) has been proposed as a possible solution, which provides more dynamic systems, new sources of information, and stronger capacities for their integration [2].

With the Europe 2020 strategy [3], especially under the umbrella of the Digital Agenda [4] and Innovation Union [5] flagship initiatives, the EU provided the required policy context for addressing the above mentioned Grand Challenges and for implementing a Digital Earth. The advent of Digital Science 2030 [6] indicates a growing importance. Here, among others, ICT-intense domains are challenged to develop innovative applications based on technological enablers, such as manifold sensors, simulation tools and scientific data infrastructures. The evolution of the Internet (Future Internet) [7] shall play a major role.

Yet, many questions remain unanswered. How do these high level concepts reflect reality? What does all this mean to environmental information systems? What is expected to change? Before these topics can be properly addressed, we have to carefully describe the recent challenges for eEnvironment services in Europe [8], specify desired capabilities and derive according requirements. Only if these are met, can we identify affected stakeholder communities, discuss suitable implementation frameworks and suggest sustainable development strategies.

This paper provides such groundwork. We review cases from three environmental spheres (terrain, atmosphere and marine) to illustrate the richness of applications across the borders of EU Member States, and the variety of stakeholders involved; examples range from classical monitoring and reporting, via downscaling of global environmental models to individual needs, to the inclusion of user contributed content into the value chain of environmental knowledge generation. We furthermore introduce some 'science fiction' services, in which we think outside the box of expected environmental applications.

The remainder of this paper is structured as follows. The next section presents viewpoints from three environmental spheres. It also includes a set of (science fiction) applications, which might become reality in the advent of new technologies and user communities. Thereafter, section 3 discusses possible generalization of the requested eEnvironment services and derives a common description of the underlying value chain. A suitable framework for developing required information systems is depicted in section 4. Given future developments in Information and Communication Technology (ICT), we put emphasis on the future of the Internet (or Future Internet). The paper concludes with a summary of our findings and an outlook to required future activities.

2 eEnvironment Services for Three Spheres

This section presents three concrete cases in which environmental information systems have to change in order to meet arising needs. Each section follows a similar structure. The overall context is defined first; followed by a discussion on the intended goals, steps to achieve them, derived case-specific requirements, and the resulting stakeholders. We specifically include issues of scalability, either in terms of spatial extent (from local to global) or in terms of amount of information to be processed when individualizing information (from global to local).

2.1 Terrain: Mapping Terrestrial Biodiversity

Terrestrial biodiversity provides an interesting case considering phenomena on land. The *UN Convention on Biodiversity* (CBD) and the EU have set a new target of halting the loss to biodiversity by the year 2020. Achieving this goal in the first place requires a solid basis and a new approach to current judging progress. Observational data on biodiversity has to be merged from all available sources while assuring high quality. Outreach groups for data survey can greatly widen the base from which observational data may be gleaned. This data can then be merged with existing data from research organizations as well as historic data available from museums. Scenarios on reporting biodiversity illustrate how humans that are supported by mobile devices, such as smart phones, can act as the main 'sensor' for data provision.

In order to maintain data quality when integrating data from multiple sources, future eEnvironment services will have to include mechanisms for context aware quality assurance of reported data. The initial quality assurance processing should at least account for:

1. *Spatial probability*, i.e. does this species fit into this bio-geographical region?
2. *Temporal probability*, i.e. can it be observed at this time of the year?
3. *Comparison with common mis-identifications*, i.e. providing the user with image of other types often confused with type identified - does the leaf of this species look like this?

Such a quality assurance process requires a semantic backbone for:

- *Structuring and storage of taxonomic information*, including both scientific and common species names.
- *Storing additional species information* as required for context aware quality assurance, i.e. bio-geographical regions of occurrence, types often wrongly identified as.
- *Semantic mapping between species lists*, against common opinion, scientific species names are not completely standardized across Europe.
- *Semantic annotation of external expert knowledge*, where a wide pool of external expert, for correct identification of species sighted, can be leveraged through crowd-sourcing mechanisms.

2.2 Atmosphere: Monitoring Individualized Pollen Exposure

On the atmospheric sphere, we concentrate on individual exposure assessment and air quality/meteorological alerts. Today, we have easy access to a great deal of information via television, radio and the World Wide Web. This includes pollution, pollen and meteorological data which are all relatively easily accessed in one or more dissemination channels. All this data contributes to a common sense, but it is not tailored to an individual user's needs. Relevancy of data and interpreting it are key issues for users today, especially with regards to pollen and pollution which directly affect as many as 25% of the population.

Future eEnvironment services should therefore aid individuals in tailoring information relevant to their specific requirements by providing personalized threshold alerts for air quality, meteorological conditions and pollen, as well as enabling the users to feed data back into the system which will then be used to further enhance the relevancy of the data to the user (Figure 1).

Fig. 1. Desired eEnvironment Services in the air quality domain

This personalization of the information becomes more achievable due to the increasing prevalence of GPS enabled 'smart' phones which will enable the system to assess the individual's exposure to pollution by recording the individual's coordinates and matching them with actual observation data with a higher degree of accuracy than is generally available to the public. In addition, by taking advantage of easier to use interface design we will enable the individual users to become part of the web of sensors by providing mechanisms for Voluntary Geographic Information (VGI) [9]. This data will feed back into the system and provide another layer of information to further enhance the existing infrastructure. An example of VGI could be a user reporting the prevalence of rag weed (to which he might be allergic) in an area where for which no data currently exists, thereby potentially alerting other sufferers of the existence of the allergenic plant.

2.3 Marine: Managing Marine Resources

The EU's marine waters support a wide range of economic and social activities. The *Integrated Maritime Policy for Europe* seeks to realize the significant potential of Europe's vast marine resources through the alignment of research and innovation capacity with relevant policy and market requirements. The *Marine Strategy Framework Directive (MFSD)* establishes a legally binding framework within which Member States shall take the necessary measures to achieve or maintain good environmental status in the marine environment by the 2020. The Directive constitutes the vital environmental component of the Union's future maritime policy, and is designed to achieve the full economic potential of oceans and seas in harmony with the marine sphere. The scale of the challenge is reflected in range of current monitoring requirements for the European marine environment which includes 70,000 km of coastline and an associated investment required of over €1 billion a year [10].

As new standards and approaches to the collection and management of marine data emerge [11, 12, 13] the next generation of decision based management tools must scale to transcend national borders and facilitate an ecosystem approach to the development of Europe's marine resources and related sectors including offshore energy, environmental monitoring, aquaculture and marine tourism.

Current observations of the marine environment are achieved using a variety of commercially available sensors deployed on static and mobile platforms both above and below water. Measurements can be taken from in-situ, air-borne, water-borne, space-borne or even human-borne sensing methods to measure various meteorological, oceanographic, geophysical and biological processes. The measurement spectroscopy used in these observations can also vary (UV, IR, visible, digital, analog etc.). Mission critical data includes information on meteorological and oceanographic data (e.g. wind, sea level pressure), sea states (namely wave conditions and water movements) and information on changes in the chemical status of the water. As a consequence, a generic approach is required for the description and integration of heterogeneous sensors and sensor data regarding marine observations. Challenges for the integration and interpretation of harvested data also include the ability to deliver large volumes of real time streaming data from advanced sensing platforms such as acoustic (e.g. hydrophones, sonar, ADCP, etc.) and video feeds. The ability to dynamically scale the response of distributed sensor networks in response to unpredictable environmental events is also likely to act as a key enabler in the realization of real time dynamic marine monitoring networks and the development of a range of associated products and services for marine sector activities.

New eEnvironment services will have to consider the need for secure, smart and fast mobile communications, agent-based middleware used to empower the marine stakeholder community to observe and operate in the marine environment. Diverse and heterogeneous data and information sources should be fused and prototyped for delivery on demand using multiple distributed services and might be presented via social networking internet technologies together with sensor web enablement and fusion services technologies (Figure 2).

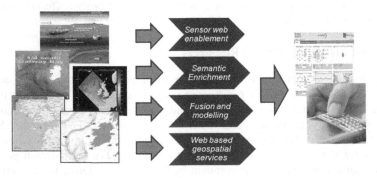

Fig. 2. Requirements for eEnvironment services for the marine sector

2.4 Beyond Foreseen eEnvironment Services

Beyond the cases outlined above (section 2), which are likely to become reality in the near future, we may expect even more sophisticated applications, such as:

- *A fully scalable, real-time environmental and social footprint*, which provides near real-time information about individuals or groups of individuals in terms of their waste production, CO_2 emission, water consumption, income, connections to other people and organizations etc.
- *Event tracing trough observation networks, tweets and newspaper articles*, in which for example natural disasters (but also political crises) are monitored from the causes, over the happening and direct responses, all the way to long term impacts, using the manifold information channels that are available.
- *Social networking with sensors and environmental models*, which basically enables the discovery of sensor networks, which may potentially be used as inputs to environmental models, but also serve as a communication platform for improving scientific models, and for informing about events, such as a predicted flood. This network might be even augmented with the social networking platforms of today.

Given the rapid development of ICT for environment during the last years and the growing citizen interests and technological capabilities, it is likely that also such or similar applications will become reality within this decade. We live in an era of growing user expectations on the one side and arising technological potential on the other side. Our information systems have to account for these frequent changes.

3 Generalization and Requirements Analysis

Given the information above and considering similar cases from other domains, we become able to extract generic components for environmental ICT applications and eEnvironment services. In this section, we introduce the roles, which are involved in generating knowledge about our environment and define the overall added-value chain. In a second step, we present common requirements for future eEnvironment services. In doing so, we provide a bridge between practical environmental applications and the wider political framework. The presented findings could equally be applied to other geospatial domains, not only to environment.

3.1 The Value Chain of Environmental Knowledge Generation

Analyzing the descriptions of section 2, we can extract a total of six roles, which contribute to the generation of environmental knowledge:

1. *Observer*, being the initial source of information about the environment. This may reach from sensor to citizen.
2. *Publisher*, making a resource, such as an observation, discoverable to a wider audience, e.g. by providing required resource descriptions (metadata).
3. *Discoverer*, being the entity that finds a resource based on all available descriptions.

4. *Service Provider*, making information or an environmental model accessible
    to (and usable by) the wider audience.
5. *Service Orchestrator*, being responsible for combining existing services in a
    way that they create information for a distinct purpose, i.e. environmental
    application focusing on a particular sphere on topic.
6. *Decision Maker*, consuming an environmental application in order to retrieve
    decision supporting material and making a final decision based on the infor-
    mation available.

Consequently, the process workflow can be summarized as in the figure below
(Figure 3). We call this workflow the *added-value chain of environmental knowledge
generation*. Notably, following this workflow services may themselves get published
in order to serve as building blocks for more complex eEnvironment solutions.

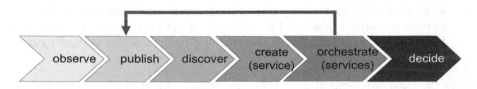

Fig. 3. The added-value chain of environmental knowledge generation

3.2 Overview of Stakeholders

The roles identified above (section 3.1) are played by a variety of individuals and
organizations. Most of these have been mentioned in the descriptions of desired services in section 2. In a nutshell, those can be defined as:

- *Citizens* of a particular social, political, or national community;
- *Environmental agencies* on sub-national, national and European level;
- *Public authorities* of national and regional and other level;
- *Industries* from the primary, secondary and service sector;
- *Platform providers* offering frameworks on which applications may be run;
- *Infrastructure providers* offering physical components and essential services;
- *Sensor network owners* holding the sensor and basic communication hardware.

Table 1 provides an overview of the manifold mappings between these stakeholders
and the different roles in the value chain of environmental knowledge generation. To
highlight only a few aspects: citizens can play all roles, they may even discover available information and provide new services ('mash-ups'). The decisions they may take
are on individual level, such as should "I travel through an area with bad air quality?"
All decisions that can be taken are strongly dependent on the stakeholder; industries
may use the environmental information for logistic or location planning, while the
owners of sensor networks may decide about the maintenance of their facilities.

Table 1. The added-value chain of environmental knowledge generation

	observe	provide	discover	create	orchestrate	decide
Citizens	x	X	x	x	x	x
Environmental agencies	x	X		x		x
Public authorities		X		x		x
Industries			x	x	x	x
Platform providers				x		
Infrastructure providers				x		
Sensor network owners	x	(x)	(x)			x

3.3 Requirements for a Next Generation of eEnvironment Services

Given all this, (i) what would be the needs for a next generation of eEnvironment services in Europe and (ii) what might be a suitable framework for establishing requested platforms and infrastructures? We address the first question in the remainder of this section. We outline the cases sketched above and derive functional and non-functional requirements. Available frameworks for future developments are addressed in the next section (section 4).

Re-visiting the sections above, we identify at least the following needs:

- discovery, access, visualization and publication of data sets;
- discovery, access, visualization, and planning of sensor observations;
- access to environmental models and simulations as services;
- transformation of data sets and harmonization of observations;
- composition and invocation of workflows;
- support and enforcement of data and service policies based on identity, licenses, trust chains, etc.;
- provision of objective, semi-objective and subjective observations by end users;
- access and use of controlled vocabularies, taxonomies, ontologies and annotations;
- integration with the Semantic Web and Web 2.0; and
- interoperability with existing and planned infrastructures in the context of:
  - o the most relevant initiatives at international level, such as INSPIRE, GMES, GEOSS; and
  - o relevant well-established communities, including research and e-government infrastructures.

Specific components (environmental enablers) should support these requirements. They should be designed and developed leveraging existing architectural approaches and technical specifications, and re-using/extending existing tools. Particular attention should be paid to open international standards and communities-of-practice specifications, and to open source components in order to make the resulting system more flexible and scalable (see also [14]).

4 Future Internet: A Framework for Implementing Change

In response to the world economic crisis in 2008, the European Commission formulated its long term vision in *Europe 2020* strategy [3], which emphasizes actions around three main priorities: (i) developing an economy based on knowledge and innovation (smart growth): (ii) promoting a more resource efficient, greener and more competitive economy (sustainable growth); and (iii) fostering a high-employment economy delivering social and territorial cohesion (inclusive growth). Seven flagship initiatives give substance to the strategy. They address innovation, youth and the labor market, digital agenda, resource efficiency, industrial policy in the global context, skills and jobs, and social and territorial cohesion respectively. In particular, the *Innovation Union* [5] initiative aims to improve conditions and access to funding for research and innovation in Europe, to ensure that innovative ideas can be turned into commercial products and services that create jobs and economic growth, whereas the *Digital Agenda for Europe* [4] outlines policies and actions to maximize the benefit of the Digital Revolution for all. The Digital Agenda foresees the action to "work with the Member States and stakeholders to implement cross-border eEnvironment services, notably advanced sensor networks". Then again, the concept of the *Future Internet* [7] is part of the Digital Agenda for Europe's efforts to deliver economic benefits from fast to ultrafast Internet and interoperable applications.

Considering the latter, the European Commission (EC) provided €90 million for funding Future Internet-related research in 2011, and a further €210 million in 2012-2013 through the *Future Internet Public Private Partnership* (FI-PPP) FP7 Programme. The FI-PPP aims to (i) to support an Internet-enabled service economy, (ii) to improve key ICT infrastructures of Europe's economy and society by making them better able to process massive amounts of data originating from multiple sources; (iii) to render the Internet more reliable and secure; and (iv) to allow real time information to be processed into real time services.

There is a clear opportunity to further develop the sustainability-innovation-growth triangle by dedicating a usage area of the FI-PPP to the environment. This provides an excellent frame for addressing the required environmental enablers, which have been identified in section 3. For optimizing the outcomes, the early and strong involvement of application areas from all environmental spheres is essential. Only in this manner, the current push of technological approaches can be balanced with applications' need, which eventually will lead to powerful and useful eEnvironment solutions.

5 Summary and Outlook

This paper outlined some changes, which are required for improving eEnvironment services. Three concrete cases were presented covering the terrestrial, marine and atmosphere domain; those were complemented by a set of more futuristic applications. Analyzing the various descriptions, we extracted a total of six involved roles and depicted a general workflow for environmental knowledge generation. Stakeholders have been identified for each of these roles and a set of requirement environmental enablers has been presented. The FI-PPP has been identified as a suitable frame for implementing the requested changes in Europe. The 'application pull' of requirements will be key to success. If we fail to clearly formulate and communicate these requirements we will miss a unique opportunity. We are just starting to investigate these issues and will work to analyze the underlying principles and consequences for the stakeholder communities. We hope to successfully contribute to the future of eEnvironment in this manner.

Acknowledgements. We thank the ENVIROFI (FP7 – 284898) project consortium for the lively discussions we had. This paper is based on our common findings.

References

1. Scientific Grand Challenges identified to address global sustainability – ISCU pre-publication, http://www.icsu-visioning.org/wp-content/uploads/GrandChallenges_Pre-publication.pdf (last accessed February 12, 2011)
2. Craglia, M., Goodchild, M., Annoni, A., Camara, G., Gould, M., Kuhn, W., Mark, D., Masser, I., Maguire, D., Liang, S., Parsons, E.: Next-generation digital earth: A position paper from the vespucci initiative for the advancement of geographic information science. International Journal of Spatial Data Infrastructures Research 3, 146–167 (2008)
3. Official Homepage of the European Commission Europe 2020 Strategy, http://ec.europa.eu/europe2020/index_en.htm (last accessed March 25, 2011)
4. Official Homepage of the European Commission Digital Agenda for Europe (DG Information Society and Media), http://ec.europa.eu/information_society/digital-agenda/index_en.htm (last accessed March 25, 2011)
5. Official Homepage of the European Commission Innovation Union, http://ec.europa.eu/research/innovation-union/index_en.cfm (last accessed March 25, 2011)
6. Accordino, F.: Digital Science and its impact on Scientific Societies. Presentation given at European Computer Science Summit Prague (CZ) (October 13)
7. European Future Internet Portal, http://www.future-internet.eu/ (last accessed March 25, 2011)
8. Hřebíček, J.(Chief ed.), Hradec, J., Pelikán, E., Mírovský, O., Pillmann, W., Holoubek, I., Bandholtz, T. (eds.) Proceedings of the European conference of the Czech Presidency of the Council of the EU TOWARDS eENVIRONMENT. Opportunities of SEIS and SISE: Integrating Environmental Knowledge in Europe. Masaryk University, Brno, Czech Republic (March 2009)
9. Goodchild, M.: Citizens as sensors: the world of volunteered geography. GeoJournal 69(4), 211–221 (2007)
10. Marine Knowledge 2020, MEMO/10/404, http://europa.eu/rapid/pressReleasesAction.do?reference=MEMO/10/404&format=HTML&aged=0&language=EN&guiLanguage=en (last accessed March 25, 2011)
11. Official Homepage of the Pan-European infrastructure for Ocean & Marine Data Management (SeaDataNet) project, http://www.seadatanet.org/ (last accessed March 25, 2011)
12. Official Homepage of the Water Information System for Europe (WISE) project, http://water.europa.eu/ (last accessed March 25, 2011)
13. Official Homepage of the European Marine Observation and Data Network (EMODNET), http://ec.europa.eu/maritimeaffairs/emodnet_en.html (last accessed March 25, 2011)
14. Interoperable Solutions for European Public Administrations (isa): European Interoperability Strategy (EIS) for European public services (December 16, 2010)

Geospatial Virtual Appliances Using Open Source Software

Christian Schwartze, Sven Kralisch, and Wolfgang-Albert Flügel

Department of Geoinformatics, Hydrology and Modelling, School of Chemical and
Earth Sciences, Friedrich-Schiller-University of Jena, Germany
christian.schwartze@uni-jena.de
http://www.geoinf.uni-jena.de

Abstract. The hype on the Cloud is based on promising cost savings
if, considering the new service platform concepts (IaaS, PaaS, SaaS) the
term comes with, IT resources will be used effectively. Therefore, the
trend is moving away from physical systems to more instant and short-
term environments and virtualization is increasingly taking on a key role
in various system architectures. This is already well accepted by a few
business units such as customer relationship management or marketing,
operated from *Salesforce.com* for instance [1]. However, earth scientific
offers featuring specialized functions and services on demand are still rare
but of great benefit in order to overcome the global changes in environmental conditions. Only one task from the field of model preprocessing
at the DGHM[1] was picked out for virtualization purposes and the results
will be introduced in the following.

Keywords: Virtualization, SaaS, Integrated Landscape Management,
ILMS, GRASS-GIS, Hydrological Modelling, HRU.

1 Brief Introduction to Virtualization

Virtualization in all its forms creates simulated computer environments to meet
the requirements of streamlined and economical IT infrastructures, not least
due to the increasing awareness of *Green-IT*. In general, software virtualization
techniques are aimed at running multiple and various operating systems on one
single machine, whether on client or server[2]. In the sections below, the option
of system virtualization using a *Virtual Machine Monitor* (VMM) is considered.
The fact that the terms VMM and VM (*Virtual Machine*) were already outlined
in the remarks by Popek and Goldberg [2] in the mid 1970s does not let it seem
very new, contrary to the trend news currently announced. The two definitions
stated in [2] are as follows:

---

[1] Department of Geoinformatics, Hydrology and Modelling, University of Jena.
[2] Alternative approaches to realize virtualization use the hardware directly, which is
not taken into account in this paper (see e.g. *Xen* or *Microsoft Hyper-V* for such
"bare metal" solutions).

J. Hřebíček, G. Schimak, and R. Denzer (Eds.): ISESS 2011, IFIP AICT 359, pp. 154–160, 2011.
© IFIP International Federation for Information Processing 2011

[...], the *Virtual Machine Monitor* provides an environment for programs which is essentially identical with the original machine [...] in complete control of system resources.

A *Virtual Machine* is taken to be an efficient, isolated duplicate of the real machine.

Hence, the VMM, also referred to as *hypervisor*, can be understood as an abstraction layer operating either at hardware or operating system level of a physical system. In the case presented, a so-called *type-2-hypervisor* has to be used which means that the VMM is hosted by the operating system and takes care of hardware emulation (e.g. network) for each VM or rather virtual guest system. Typical representatives of that hypervisor strategy are *Microsoft Virtual PC*, *VMware Workstation* or *Oracle VirtualBox*. The latter one and its features will be described in the next section as this free software is applied in the presented example.

Compared to the container-based virtualization mechanism shown on the right of figure 1, the VMM approach provides the advantage of running guest machines on their own and native kernels with the result that the range of coexistent VM's is wider and less limited. But the freedom of choice of almost any x86 operating system is paid with small performance losses. Using modified and tuned guest kernels as it will be referred to in the next section is only one way to address these lacks if VMM based software virtualization is requested.

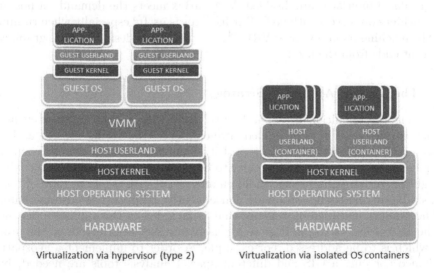

Virtualization via hypervisor (type 2)   Virtualization via isolated OS containers

Fig. 1. Left: System virtualization using a type-2-hypervisor. **Right:** Isolated runtime environments as provided by *OpenVZ* and *FreeBSD Jails* for instance are using one common kernel which manages all resources (network, memory etc.) needed by the OS containers (host userlands). Other kernels within each container are not allowed.

2   VirtualBox

In 2007 *VirtualBox* [3] entered the highly competitive market segment of virtualization solutions and started to become available for end users. Originally developed by the German software company *Innotek* under the influence of previous business relationships (e.g. *Microsoft*), VirtualBox was bought by *Sun Microsystems* one year later. With its acquisition by *Oracle* in 2010, the software's official name is now *Oracle VM VirtualBox*.

Significant motivation for choosing VirtualBox (in its binary edition[3]) was less the large number of supported platforms, but rather the following features from a developers point of view:

- The supplied programming interfaces (in C and Python) open up opportunities to access VMM functionality such as managing or launching virtual machines from 3rd party tools. Thus, the operation of a virtual system using VirtualBox is easy and comfortable to script, which in turn is important for use on servers.
- Virtual machines packaged and distributed as *Virtual Appliances* (see section 2.1) guarantee rapid deployment and due to the industry-standard *Open Virtualization Format* (OVF) they are deployable on various virtualization platforms as long as the hypervisor comes with support for that format. This feature was added in version 2.2 of VirtualBox.
- By providing methods to start virtual machines in a special mode where graphical interfaces are disabled, VirtualBox meets the demands of hosting machines on servers with no GUI frills. This is useful especially when running the machine remotely (over VRDP[4]) or even if it is desired to hide graphical front ends from the user.

2.1   The Virtual Appliance Strategy

Extending the definition in [4], a *Virtual Appliance* can be interpreted as a service consisting of a pre-installed, pre-configured operating system and an use-oriented application stack on top of it. The resulting software environment is typically delivered as an OVF archive to be run in virtual machines and enables straightforward distribution and maintenance of software as unique units. Efforts in installation and configuration are consequently minimized at customer site.

The number and kind of software that is included in the appliance depends on the field of use, or to put it more precisely and service-oriented, on the problem which is to be addressed. For example, in order to implement a geospatial appliance not only a GIS and different spatial analysis tools are needed, but also standardized protocols for serving georeferenced data over the network are of high importance. *Web Map Service* (WMS), *Web Feature Service* (WFS) or

---

[3] An open source edition (VirtualBox OSE) is provided for commercial purposes, but does not include all features.

[4] VirtualBox extends the *Remote Desktop Protocol*, but any standard RDP client can be used.

other OGC[5] compliant standards may come into consideration according to the requirements and specific application context. In the present case, a *Web Processing Service* (WPS) [5] will be applied as attention is paid to providing an almost automated workflow for preprocessing purposes of distributed hydrological simulation models (section 3).

Since a customized appliance should already bring along the underlying operating system it can be advantageous to choose one with a small footprint tailored to the package of software and drivers actually required (e.g. no window system, no USB, etc.), and even at best with a kernel that is optimized for hypervisors. These characteristics fully apply to *Ubuntu JeOS*[6] - a minimized derivative of Ubuntu Linux which runs smoothly as a guest on virtualization technologies including VirtualBox [6].

3   Integrated Landscape Management System

The Integrated Landscape Management System (ILMS) developed at DGHM provides an integrated, modular software platform and covers different steps of environmental system analysis and planning in a flexible and user-friendly workflow [7]. As shown on the left of figure 2, this includes ILMS*info* (management, analysis, visualization and presentation of different types of data using the web-based RBIS [8]), ILMS*image* (remote sensing module for object-oriented image analysis [9]), ILMS*gis* (derivation of modelling entities) and ILMS*model* (component-based environmental modelling using the JAMS framework [10]).

By applying the virtualization approach mentioned above to ILMS, a GRASS-GIS based solution has been implemented that aims at subdividing river catchments into *Hydrological Response Units* (HRU) [11]. These designated areas may be considered as spatially distributed entities aggregating common land use, topography or soil type, for instance, and are used in the JAMS/J2000 model suite of ILMS*model*. In general, the developed tools integrated in the process chain use open source software wherever possible.

3.1   HRU Virtual Appliance Solution

HRUs are generally delineated by means of GIS overlay analysis and specific methods individually adapted to different extensions on the HRU concept, such as topological flow routing. In order to address this challenge, GRASS-GIS had to be extended by Python scripts and additional software components to cover the following HRU processing steps:

1. Physiographic data input and preparation, i.e. DEM, soils, land use
2. Remove depressions (sinks) in the DEM, derive slope and aspect (D8 flow algorithms)

---

[5] The *Open Geospatial Consortium* is an international and non-profit organization focusing on geospatial standards.

[6] Abbreviation for *Just enough Operating System*.

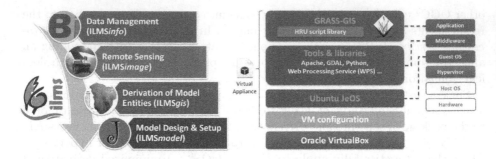

Fig. 2. Left: ILMS components for storage and analysis of watershed related data and timeseries, object-based and automated image classification, generation of model entities and environmental model development/application. **Right:** Main application stack of HRU service appliance

3. Reclassification of slope and aspect data
4. Calculate flow accumulation and flow direction
5. Delineate stream network, subbasins and basins based on outlets (D8, recursive upslope)
6. Generate data overlay of all input and calculated maps
7. Dissolve small areas in the overlay outcome (subbasin-by-subbasin)
8. Route water flow, support for N:1 and N:M routing (including flow rates) between HRUs (and HRU/reach)
9. Collect statistics for each HRU, e.g. average slope, soil type, centroid, elevation

As *PyWPS* [12], an implementation of the WPS standard in Python language, comes with native GRASS-GIS support, consequently almost all tasks previously listed are implemented as WPS compliant Python modules (HRU script library, see on the right of figure 2). Thus, the process development profits especially from the temporary GRASS-GIS session management and progress reports available through PyWPS. While each of the above-mentioned processes is performed by HTTP/GET request, the corresponding XML response document either contains literal outputs or more complex results (e.g. GeoTiff maps) respectively given as an URL. The latter is true, for example, at the time when step 9 is completed and will return a final HRU shapefile.

3.2   QGIS Integration

The free available *QGIS* [13] provides great mapping and data visualization capabilities and the option of writing extensions in C++/Python. For this reason, the platform was chosen to integrate a wizard that not only guides the user through the several delineation steps, but also manages communication between the QGIS plugin (WPS client) and the virtual appliance (see figure 3).

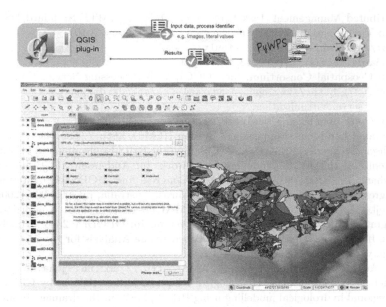

Fig. 3. The delineation wizard in QGIS acts as a client and sends requests to the geospatial appliance that includes all components for data processing

4   Summary

Using the delineation of spatially distributed model entities as an example, this paper illustrated the technical background and implementation of a geospatial appliance with focus on the deployment under VirtualBox. Due to the standardization of software environments designed for hypervisors, applications can be easily packaged and distributed to users. It is not just that the encapsulated solution stacks are installable without large installation costs and knowledge of included software, but also the additional security they provide since application errors have no impact on other hosted virtual machines.

Beyond the technical details, it was demonstrated how the VMM approach can be used in order to set up a GRASS-GIS based service which is applicable for sustainable land and water management in accordance with the ILMS workflow. During the implementation of required HRU processes, particular attention was paid to usability and the opportunity to easily extend the process chain and this is why a modular structured QGIS plugin was developed.

References

1. Salesforce.com, http://www.salesforce.com/
2. Popek, G.J., Goldberg, R.P.: Formal requirements for virtualizable third generation architectures. Communications of the ACM 17, 412–414 (1974)
3. Oracle VM VirtualBox, http://www.virtualbox.org

4. Distributed Management Task Force, Inc. (DMTF), DMTF Standard DSP0243, Open Virtualization Format Specification 1.1.0 (January 2010), http://www.dmtf.org/sites/default/files/standards/documents/DSP0243_1.1.0.pdf
5. Open Geospatial Consortium, Inc. (OGC), Web Processing Service (WPS) 1.0.0 (June 2007), http://www.opengeospatial.org/standards/wps
6. Ubuntu server virtualization, http://www.ubuntu.com/business/server/virtualisation
7. Integrated Landscape Management System (ILMS), http://ilms.uni-jena.de
8. Kralisch, S., Zander, F., Krause, P.: Coupling the RBIS Environmental Information System and the JAMS Modelling Framework. In: Anderssen, R., Braddock, R., Newham, L. (eds.) 18th World IMACS Congress and MODSIM09 International Congress on Modelling and Simulation, Cairns, Australia, pp. 902–908 (2009)
9. Matejka, E., Reinhold, M., Selsam, P.: IMALYS - an automated and database-integrated object-oriented classification system. In: GEOBIA 2008 - Pixels, Objects, Intelligence: Geographic Object Based Image Analysis for the 21st Century, Calgary, Canada (2008)
10. Jena Adaptable Modelling System (JAMS), http://jams.uni-jena.de
11. Flügel, W.-A.: Delineating Hydrological Response Units (HRU's) by GIS analysis for regional hydrological modelling using PRMS/MMS in the drainage basin of the River Bröl, Germany. Hydrological Processes 9, 423–436 (1995)
12. PyWPS Development Team: Python Web Processing Service (PyWPS), http://pywps.wald.intevation.org
13. Quantum GIS project (QGIS), http://www.qgis.org

How to Analyse User Requirements for Service-Oriented Environmental Information Systems

Thomas Usländer and Thomas Batz

Fraunhofer IOSB, Fraunhoferstr. 1,
76131 Karlsruhe, Germany
{thomas.uslaender,thomas.batz}@iosb.fraunhofer.de

Abstract. Environmental Information Systems (EIS) allow the user to store, query and process environmental information and visualize it in thematic maps, diagrams and reports. Although service-orientation is the predominant architectural style of EIS there is no design methodology that brings together the requirements and the expert knowledge of EIS users with the services and information offerings of existing EIS, and, in addition, explicitly obeys the guidelines and constraints of geospatial standards of the Open Geospatial Consortium (OGC) as side-conditions. This paper focuses on the analysis phase as a prelude to service-oriented design. It proposes a way of gathering, describing and documenting user requirements in terms of extended use cases which may then be used to perform the abstract design step following SERVUS which denotes a Design Methodology for Information Systems based upon Geospatial Service-oriented Architectures and the Modelling of Use Cases and Capabilities as Resources.

Keywords: Service-oriented architecture, service-oriented analysis and design, requirements analysis, environmental information system, SERVUS.

1 Introduction

Environmental Information Systems (EIS) allow the user to store, query and process environmental information and visualize it in thematic maps, diagrams and reports [3]. More advanced functions cover advanced mapping functions of environmental data such as geospatial predictions and simulations (e.g. geo-statistical interpolation algorithms) or geospatial visual analytics techniques by combining data mining and information visualization techniques. In order to cope with this variety of functions, EIS are inherently componentized and distributed. This trend is also due to the need for collaboration between the various public and private stakeholders involved and various environmental science disciplines [1].

From the technological point of view EIS are information systems that deal with geospatial information and services with a reference to a location on the Earth. EIS are associated with heterogeneous sensors and/or environmental models that deliver measured or calculated observations about environmental phenomena. Basically, EIS provide a restricted view upon the environment which is limited by temporal, spatial and thematic boundaries. Information fusion is then enabled by a loose coupling of

J. Hřebíček, G. Schimak, and R. Denzer (Eds.): ISESS 2011, IFIP AICT 359, pp. 161–168, 2011.
© IFIP International Federation for Information Processing 2011

EIS whereby the actual configuration of the resulting system-of-systems is dependent upon the environmental question to be answered.

These system requirements are best met by the principles of Service-oriented Architectures (SOA) [3] as a "framework for integrating business processes and supporting IT infrastructure as secure, standardized components – services – that can be reused and combined to address changing business priorities" [7]:

- SOA principles enable the sharing of geospatial information and services and their composition across organizational and administrative boundaries in a loosely-coupled but controlled manner. This is essential for EIS as environmental phenomena are not limited to boundaries drawn by humans.
- Effective and flexible interactions between EIS require an agreement within the developer community about the syntax and semantics of service interfaces and information models. Thus, as a crucial side-condition in the design of infrastructures for EIS, geospatial interoperability standards of ISO and the Open Geospatial Consortium (OGC) have to be considered.

There are several initiatives on national, European and world-wide scale that define geospatial SOAs as an underlying foundation for EIS, e.g. the Sensor Service Architecture (SensorSA) as a result of the European research project SANY [4]. However, one of the challenges is the design of applications that exploit the potential and the capabilities of such geospatial service networks. Software service engineering emerges as an own research discipline, strongly inheriting from the principles of software engineering, but enhancing them towards the open-world assumption of the SOA approach, i.e. a world of "unforeseen clients, execution contexts and usage" of services operating in "highly complex, distributed, unpredictable, and heterogeneous execution environments" [8]. Numerous methodologies for service-oriented analysis and design have been described in the literature and partly embedded in software development tools [2].

The deficiency today is that there is no design methodology that brings together the requirements and the expert knowledge of EIS users with the capabilities (i.e. services and information offerings) of existing EIS, and, in addition, explicitly obeys the guidelines and constraints of geospatial standards as side-conditions, which are, for the design of EIS, the reference model [10] and derived geospatial architectures of the OGC such as the SensorSA.

This paper describes a method for the co-development of requirements and capabilities of EIS (section 2) as a necessary prelude for a service-oriented design of EIS (section 3) and the analysis of user requirements (section 4). Section 5 concludes the paper with a project reference where this approach is being used.

2   Co-development of Requirements and Capabilities

Taking requirements and capabilities as a conceptual foundation, the kernel challenge for a service-oriented design of EIS boils down to the question of how the requirements of the user can be assessed against the already existing capabilities of service platforms. Basically, functional, informational and qualitative requirements at one

abstraction layer (A) have to be semantically matched to capabilities of another abstraction layer (B) taking side conditions into account (figure 1).

A pre-requisite to the matching is the discovery of possible capabilities which may
fulfill the requirements. These are called *candidate capabilities*. The matching activity selects among the candidate capabilities those who fit best to the requirements,
taking side conditions, such as the need to deliver standards-compliant services, explicitly into account. Discovery and matching need some associated semantic description of both requirements and capabilities in order to be effective. Such *semantic
descriptions* give meanings to the terms used in the specifications, e.g. by means of
semantic annotation to ontologies. Their representation forms range from text in combination with a glossary in which all important terms are defined for a given project
up to specifications in description logics.

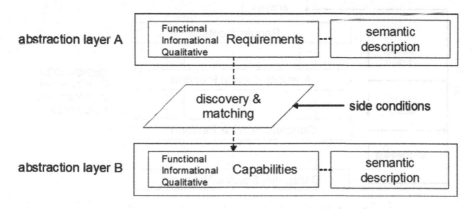

Fig. 1. Mapping of Requirements to Capabilities [3]

The discovery and matching problem repeatedly occurs when user requirements
are broken down into multiple steps across several abstraction layers. In fact, capabilities turn into requirements for the next design step. Furthermore, there is a widely
recognized need to package the development of requirement artifacts on a higher
abstraction level and the development of architectural artifacts on a lower level into
one single design step, leading to a so-called co-development of requirements (e.g.
use cases, section 4) and architectural artifacts, e.g. service specifications or information models [9]. This requires a step-wise refinement of the design artifacts:

1. The **Analysis** step in which the user analyses the problem and expresses the outcome in the form of user requirements. Example: A use case that requests to "get
   a diagram containing the average nitrate concentration of the groundwater bodies in the Upper Rhine Valley of the last 10 years".
2. The **Abstract Design** step in which the user requirements are transformed by the
   system designer into system requirements which then have to be matched with
   the capabilities of an abstract service platform, i.e. a service platform that abstracts from the peculiarities of service platform technologies. Example: Provide
   a service that enables to "get observation values with a sampling time in the

interval [2000-01-01, 2009-12-31] for the environmental parameter "nitrate" for all groundwater monitoring stations that are located in the Upper Rhine Valley".

3. The **Concrete Design** step in which the capabilities of the abstract service platform turn into requirements for the design of the concrete service platform and finally result in a specification of its capabilities. Example: The *getObservation* operation request of the OGC Sensor Observation Service.

4. The **Engineering** step in which the specified capabilities of the concrete service platform have to be implemented as service components and deployed in the context of a service network.

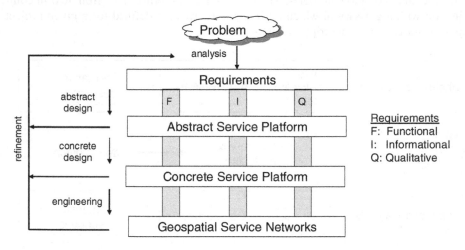

Fig. 2. Analysis, Design and Engineering Steps [3]

In the following a method for the *analysis* step is presented as a prelude of the SERVUS Design Methodology [3]. SERVUS focuses on the *abstract design* step as presented in the following section.

3   The SERVUS Design Methodology

SERVUS denotes a Design Methodology for Information Systems based upon Geospatial Service-oriented Architectures and the Modelling of Use Cases and Capabilities as Resources (SERVUS). SERVUS describes individual design activities that are interconnected by a common modelling environment interconnecting the Enterprise, Information and Service Viewpoint of geospatial architectures [10].

SERVUS relies upon a semantic resource model (see its UML specification in figure 3) as a common modelling language to which both use cases and capabilities may be mapped. Hereby, a resource is an information object that is uniquely identified, may be represented in one or more representational forms (e.g. as a diagram, XML document or a map layer) and support resource methods that are taken from a limited set of operations whose semantics are well-known (uniform interface). A resource has own characteristics (attributes) and is linked to other resources forming a resource network. Furthermore, resource descriptions may refer to concepts of the domain model (design ontology) using the principle of semantic annotation, yielding so-called *semantic resources*. The basic idea of the SERVUS resource model is derived from the Representational State Transfer (REST) architectural style for distributed hypermedia systems as conceived by Fielding [5].

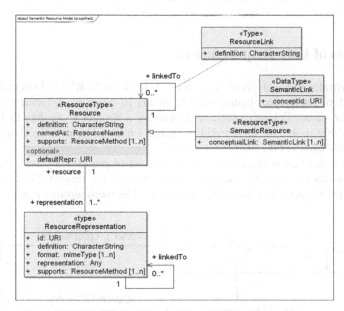

Fig. 3. SERVUS Semantic Resource Model [3]

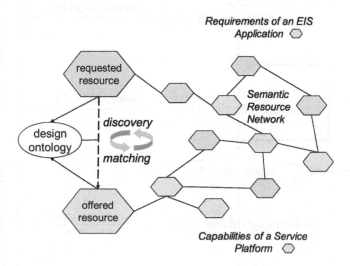

Fig. 4. Discovery and matching of requested and offered resources [3]

The abstract design step is then understood to be an iterative discovery and matching activity: *requested resources* derived from user requirements have to be mapped to fitting *offered resources* that represent the information objects being accessed and manipulated by geospatial services.

Hence, in the analysis step the set of *requested resources* has to be identified. This paper illustrates how user requirements may be captured through the identification and description of extended application uses cases.

4   Analysis of User Requirements

Figure 5 illustrates the analysis phase as a prelude of the SERVUS Design Methodology. As part of the project planning there needs to be some agreement of how to document use cases. For this continuous activity a project space has to be created which preferably should be supported by a project management server that is accessible by all participants of the analysis process.

As a first step of an analysis iteration loop a set of preliminary use cases (UC) is identified, mostly be those thematic experts who drive the project. For each of them an entry in the project space has to be generated. The methodology proposes that use

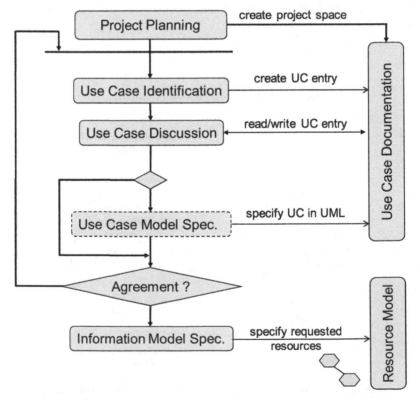

Fig. 5. Analysis phase of the SERVUS Methodology

cases are initially described in structured natural language but already contain the list of requested resources. This small extension with respect to the approach of Cockburn [11] heavily facilitates the transition to the abstract design step (here: the specification of the information model in UML) but is still very easy to understand by thematic experts. Hence, this description is the language which is used in the UC discussion that takes place in workshops that are facilitated by the system analyst. Depending on the level of agreement that can be reached the iteration loop is entered again in order to refine or add new use cases.

In order to identify inconsistencies and check the completeness of the UC model, the system analyst may transform the semi-structural UC description into formal specifications in the Unified Modelling Language (UML). However, these UML diagrams should still be on a high abstraction level such that a discussion with the end-user is possible. However, in addition to the usual UML use cases they already comprise the links to the set of requested (information) resources, their representation forms and the requirements to create, read, write or delete them. An example of such a use case diagram is contained in these proceedings [12].

Once an agreement is reached about the set of use case descriptions and related UML specifications it is then up to the system analyst to specify the resulting information model taking the (semantic) resource model (see above) as a modeling framework.

5 Conclusion and Outlook

The usability of the analysis method presented in this paper as a prelude to the SERVUS Design Methodology [3] has been validated in various facilitated workshops with users and software architects when analyzing user requirements for extensions of the EIS of the German federal state of Baden-Württemberg [6]. It is now applied to a related project that aims at analyzing the requirements for an information system that shall support the implementation and documentation of the Integrated Rhine Programme along the Upper Rhine valley in Germany [12]. These interdisciplinary projects comprise a multitude of stakeholders of different organizations. It can be stated that the application of this methodology heavily facilitates the discussion with the thematic experts and accelerates the consensus finding process. As a positive side effect, especially when being supported by a dedicated Web-based information management server, it decreases the burden of editing requirements analysis documents and helps in ensuring their consistency.

Service-orientation will be the major design paradigm for newly developed and future environmental information systems. However, in order to exploit its potential, it must be accompanied by powerful service-oriented design methodologies as a tool for system designer but also by adequate service-oriented analysis methodologies for system analysts that are tailored to the expertise and language of the thematic experts. It is the goal of the resource-oriented paradigm of the SERVUS Design Methodology to provide a modelling bridge between these two worlds of thinking.

References

1. Schimak, G. (ed.): Environmental Knowledge and Information Systems. Elsevier Special Issue 20(12) (2005)
2. Kohlborn, T., Korthaus, A., Chan, T., Rosemann, M.: Service Analysis - A Critical Assessment of the State of the Art. In: European Conference of Information Systems (ECIS 2009), Italy (2009)
3. Usländer, T.: Service-oriented Design of Environmental Information Systems. PhD thesis of the Karlsruhe Institute of Technology (KIT), Faculty of Computer Science. KIT Scientific Publishing (2010) ISBN 978-3-86644-499-7,
   http://digbib.ubka.uni-karlsruhe.de/volltexte/1000016721
4. Usländer, T. (ed.): Specification of the Sensor Service Architecture, Version 3.0 (Rev. 3.1). OGC Discussion Paper 09-132r1. Deliverable D2.3.4 of the European Integrated Project SANY, FP6-IST-033564 (2009)
5. Fielding, R.T.: Architectural Styles and the Design of Network-Based Software Architectures. Doctoral dissertation, University of California, Irvine (2000)
6. Keitel, A., Mayer-Föll, R., Schultze, A.: Framework Conception for the Environmental Information System of Baden-Württemberg (Germany). In: Hřebíček, J., et al. (eds.) Proceedings of Towards eEnvironment, pp. 461–468 (2009) ISBN 978-80-210-4824-9
7. Bieberstein, N., Bose, S., Fiammante, M., Jones, K., Shah, R.: Service-Oriented Architecture (SOA) Compass – Business Value, Planning and Enterprise Roadmap. IBM Press developerWorks Series (2006) ISBN 0-13-187002-5
8. van den Heuvel, W.J., Zimmermann, O., Leymann, F., Lago, P., Schieferdecker, I., Zdun, U., Avgeriou, P.: Software Service Engineering: Tenets and Challenges. In: Proceedings of ICSE 2009 Workshop - Principles of Engineering Service Oriented Systems (PESOS), IEEE Computer Society, Los Alamitos (2009)
9. Pohl, K., Sikora, E.: The Co-Development of System Requirements and Functional Architecture. In: Krogstie, et al. (eds.) Conceptual Modelling in Information Systems Engineering, pp. 229–246 (2007)
10. Percivall, G. (ed.). OGC Reference Model Version 2.0, Open Geospatial Consortium Document 08-062r4 (2008), http://orm.opengeospatial.org/
11. Cockburn, A.: Writing Effective Use Cases. Addison-Wesley, Reading (2001) ISBN-13: 9780201702255
12. Usländer, T., Junker, R., Pfarr, U.: Towards User Requirements for an Information System of the Integrated Rhine Programme. In: Hřebíček, J., Schimak, G., Denzer, R. (eds.) ISESS 2011. IFIP AICT, vol. 359, pp. 651–656. Springer, Heidelberg (2011)

Building an Environmental Information System for Personalized Content Delivery

Leo Wanner[1], Stefanos Vrochidis[2], Sara Tonelli[3], Jürgen Moßgraber[4], Harald Bosch[5], Ari Karppinen[6], Maria Myllynen[7], Marco Rospocher[3], Nadjet Bouayad-Agha[1], Ulrich Bügel[4], Gerard Casamayor[1], Thomas Ertl[5], Ioannis Kompatsiaris[2], Tarja Koskentalo[7], Simon Mille[1], Anastasia Moumtzidou[2], Emanuele Pianta[3], Horacio Saggion[1], Luciano Serafini[3], and Virpi Tarvainen[6]

[1] Dept. of Information and Communication Technologies, Pompeu Fabra University
[2] Centre for Research and Technology Hellas, Informatics and Telematics Institute
[3] Fondazione Bruno Kessler
[4] Fraunhofer Institute of Optronics, System Technologies and Image Exploitation
[5] Institute for Visualization and Interactive Systems, University of Stuttgart
[6] Finish Meteorological Institute
[7] Helsinki Region Environmental Services Authority
leo.wanner@upf.edu, stefanos@iti.gr, satonelli@fbk.eu,
juergen.mossgraber@iosb.fraunhofer.de,
harald.bosch@vis.uni-stuttgart.de, ari.karppinen@fmi.fi,
Maria.Myllynen@hsy.fi, rospocher@fbk.eu, nadjet.bouayad@upf.edu,
ulrich.buegel@iosb.fraunhofer.de, gerard.casamayor@upf.edu,
Thomas.Ertl@vis.uni-stuttgart.de, ikom@iti.gr,
Tarja.Koskentalo@hsy.fi, simon.mille@upf.edu, moumtzid@iti.gr,
pianta@fbk.eu, horacio.saggion@upf.edu, serafini@fbk.eu,
Virpi.Tarvainen@fmi.fi

Abstract. Citizens are increasingly aware of the influence of environmental and meteorological conditions on the quality of their life. This results in an increasing demand for personalized environmental information, i.e., information that is tailored to citizens' specific context and background. In this work we describe the development of an environmental information system that addresses this demand in its full complexity. Specifically, we aim at developing a system that supports submission of user generated queries related to environmental conditions. From the technical point of view, the system is tuned to discover reliable data in the web and to process these data in order to convert them into knowledge, which is stored in a dedicated repository. At run time, this information is transferred into an ontology-structured knowledge base, from which then information relevant to the specific user is deduced and communicated in the language of their preference.

Keywords: environmental information service, environmental node discovery, knowledge, personalization, infrastructure, services.

J. Hřebíček, G. Schimak, and R. Denzer (Eds.): ISESS 2011, IFIP AICT 359, pp. 169–176, 2011.
© IFIP International Federation for Information Processing 2011

1 Introduction

Citizens are increasingly aware of the influence of environmental and meteorological conditions on the quality of their life. One of the consequences of this awareness is the demand for high quality environmental information that is tailored to one's specific context and background (e.g. health conditions, travel preferences, etc.), i.e., which is personalized. Personalized environmental information may need to cover a variety of aspects (such as meteorology, air quality, pollen, and traffic) and take into account a number of specific personal attributes (health, age, etc.) of the user, as well as the intended use of the information. So far, only a few approaches have been proposed with a view of how this information can be facilitated in technical terms. All of these approaches focus on one environmental aspect and only very few of them address the problem of information personalization [1], [2], [3]. We aim to address the above task in its full complexity.

In this work, we take advantage of the fact that nowadays, the World Wide Web already hosts a great range of services (i.e. websites, which provide environmental information) that offer data on each of the above aspects, such that, in principle, the required basic data are available. The challenge is threefold: first, to discover and orchestrate these services, second, to process the obtained data in accordance with the needs of the user, and, third, to communicate the gained information in the user's preferred mode. To address this problem, we need to involve a considerable number of rather heterogeneous applications and thus an infrastructure that is flexible and stable enough to support a potentially distributed architecture. In what follows, we first outline the process of the discovery of the environmental services (also referred to as *nodes*) in the Web. This is considered as the prerequisite step for enable the retrieval capabilities of the system. Then, we describe briefly the tasks involved in the processing of the data obtained from the environmental nodes until their delivery to the user, and finally present the infrastructure designed to accommodate for both the discovery itself and the posterior tasks.

2 Discovery of Environmental Nodes

As already pointed out above, the web hosts a large amount of environmental (meteorological, air quality, traffic, pollen, etc.) services, which include both (static or dynamic) public webpages that offer environmental information worldwide, as well as dedicated environmental web services with free access. Especially the number of meteorological services that cover each major location is impressive. However, the fact that environmental information is highly distributed and available in heterogeneous forms and formats makes the problem of the discovery and extraction of information from webpages that provide environmental information a serious challenge. Still, it can be considered to be a problem of domain-specific web search, such that methodologies from this area can be applied to implement a node discovery framework.

We apply two types of methodologies of domain search: (a) the use of existing search engines for the submission of domain-specific automatically generated queries, and (b) focused crawling of predetermined websites [4]. To perform the queries generated by combining domain information from ontologies and geographical input obtained by geographical web services, we use a web search API (e.g., as offered by Yahoo). The queries are expanded by keyword spices [5], which are domain specific keywords extracted with the aid of machine learning techniques from environmental websites. In parallel, a set of predefined environmental websites is further enriched using a focused crawler, which is capable of exploring the web in a directed fashion in order to collect other nodes that satisfy specific criteria related to the content of the source pages and the link structure of the web.

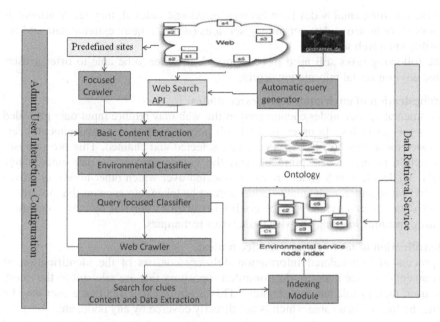

Fig. 1. Architecture for the discovery of environmental service nodes

The output of the search is post-processed in order to:

(i)   separate relevant from irrelevant nodes;

(ii)   categorize and further filter the relevant nodes with respect to the types of environmental data they provide (air quality, pollen, weather, etc.);

(iii)   parse the body and the metadata of the relevant webpages in order to extract the structure and the clues that reveal the information presented;

(iv)   identify internal and external links of the retrieved webpages, which can be further explored by crawlers. The determination of the relevance of the nodes and their categorization is done using a classifier that operates on a weight-based vector of key phrases and concepts from the metadata and content of the webpages. The proce- dure of the exploration of the external links is recursive and terminated by a manu- ally-set threshold. The information obtained with respect to each relevant node is indexed in a repository as its finger print, which can be accessed and retrieved by the system through the data retrieval service.

The whole discovery procedure is automatic, however an administrative user could intervene through an interactive user interface, in order to select geographic regions of interest to perform the discovery, optimize the selection of keyword spices and parameterize the training of the classifiers. Figure 1 shows the architecture of the discovery of environmental service nodes.

3 Processing, Orchestration and Retrieval of Environmental Nodes

Once the environmental nodes have been detected and indexed, they are available as data sources or as active data consuming services (if they require external data and are accessible via a web service).

The following tasks still need to be resolved, in order to be able to offer a user-tailored environmental information service.

1. Orchestration of environmental service nodes:
Environmental service nodes encountered in the web may require input data provided by other service nodes. In order to obtain all necessary data, the environmental service nodes must thus be "orchestrated", i.e., selected and chained. This presupposes the selection of appropriate protocols and the use of appropriate data interchange formats. To decide which nodes are to be selected over which other nodes, or which nodes fit best together, node quality criteria must be taken into account that are measured by data uncertainty and service confidence metrics derived by using statistical measures, machine learning and visual analytics techniques.

2. Identification of user relevant service nodes:
The process of user-tailored information delivery consists of the identification of environmental service nodes in the compiled repository that are relevant to the query of the user, their profile and their context. This is not trivial, given that a user may be moving, be located in an area which is not directly covered by any node, etc.

3. Extraction and distillation of the data from the webpages of the nodes:
To distill the data from webpages, advanced natural language processing techniques are needed for webpage parsing, information extraction and text mining. Although these techniques can be tuned to deal with the presentation mode of environmental (i.e., air quality, meteorological, traffic, etc.) data and information, the task of webpage scraping remains a very challenging task. In particular, given a service node, all and only the relevant data (e.g. all the temperature measurements for a city reported in a weather forecast website, but not advertisements) must be extracted.

Given the fact that much information in environmental websites is encoded as images and maps, we also plan to employ image analysis, with the goal to extract information from them.

4. Converting the data into content:
In order to guarantee a motivated orchestration of heterogeneous environmental service nodes and offer user-tailored decision support services and environmental information production, we need to convert the data into structured unified content, which will allow for application of intelligent reasoning algorithms. To this end, the extracted environmental information is integrated into an environmental knowledge base (KB).

Our KB, which is codified in the standard semantic web ontology language OWL [8], covers environmental content such as meteorological conditions and phenomena, air quality, and pollen, as well as other relevant environment-related content essential for the targeted user-tailored service: travel and traffic information, human diseases, geographical data, monitoring station details, user profile details, etc. In addition, the KB is also capable of formally representing the description of the user's inquiry.

The current version of the KB contains around 202 classes, 143 attributes and properties, 463 individuals[1]. Its Description Logic (DL) expressivity is $ALCHOIQ(D)$. The KB has been obtained by (i) including customized version of currently available ontologies (e.g., parts of the SWEET ontology), (ii) automatically extracting key concepts from domain relevant text sources, and (iii) manually adding additional properties and attributes.

5. Fusion of environmental content:

Environmental service nodes may provide competing or complementary data on the same or related aspect for the same or the neighboring location. To ensure the availability of a most reliable and comprehensive content as basis for further processing stages, the content proceeding from these nodes must be fused. As already in the case of node orchestration, this implies an assessment of the quality of the contributing services and data.

6. Assessment of the content with respect to the needs of the user:

Once the data from the nodes have been incorporated into the KB, they need to be evaluated and reasoned about in order to infer how they affect the addressee, given his/her personal health and life circumstances and the purpose of the request of the information. For instance, a citizen may request information because he/she wants to decide upon a planned action, be aware of extreme episodes or monitor the environmental conditions in a location.

7. Selection of user-relevant content and its delivery:

Not all content in the KB is apt to be communicated to the addressee: some of it would sound trivial or irrelevant. Intelligent content selection strategies that take into account the background of the user and the intended use of the information are thus needed to decide which elements of the content are worth and meaningful to be communicated. To deliver the selected content, techniques are required that present the content in a suitable mode (text, graphic and/or table) in the language of the preference of the addressee.

8. Interaction with the user:

The interaction between the system and the user is also an important aspect of this work. The user must be able to formulate the problem in a simple and intuitive format – be it based on natural language or on graphical building blocks. The user should also receive the generated information in a suitable form and, as already mentioned above, in the language of his/her preference.

---

[1] These data refer to the "empty" KB, i.e. without considering any environmental data coming from the nodes.

4 Service-Oriented Infrastructure

In order to accommodate for all tasks described above, we opt for a service-based architecture. This architecture is based on a methodology which has been developed in ORCHESTRA [6] for risk management, and which has been extended in SANY [7] to cover the domain of sensor networks and standard-based sensor web enablement. The focus of this methodology is on a platform neutral specification. In other words, it aims to provide the basic concepts and their interrelationships (conceptual models) as abstract specifications. The design is guided by the methodology developed in the ISO/IEC Reference Model for Open Distributed Processing (RM-ODP), which explicitly foresees an engineering step that maps solution types, such as information models, services and interfaces specified in information and service viewpoints, respectively, to distributed system technologies.

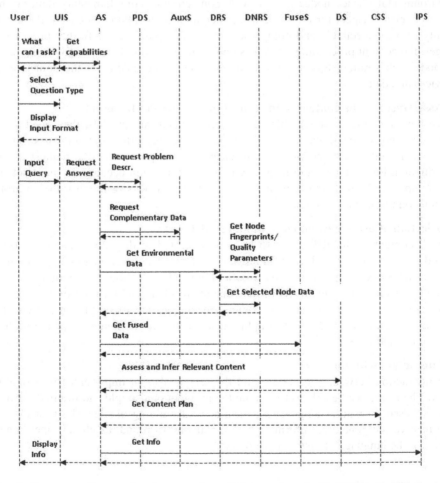

Fig. 2. Sequence diagram for the execution of the services for delivery of environmental information

We defined application-specific major tasks and actions as abstract service specifications, which can be implemented as service instances on a specific platform. Web service instances for these services are currently being developed, which can be redefined and substituted as needed.

Figure 2 displays a simplified sample workflow with the major application services in action. Two services are not cited in Figure 2 since they are consulted by nearly all other services: the Knowledge Base Access Service and the User Profile Management Service. The figure also does not include the services related to data discovery (Figure 1) and information distillation from webpages.

A main dispatcher service (called Answer Service, AS) controls the workflow and the execution of the services. First, the user interacts with the system via the User Interaction Service (UIS). In the case that the user is unsure with respect to the types of information they can ask for, he/she can inquire this information by requesting it from the Problem Description Service (PDS).

To ensure a full comprehension of the problem or user generated question, we decided to operate with controlled graphical and natural language input formats. Once the user has chosen what kind of question he wants to submit to the system, the UIS provides the user the corresponding formats. Thereupon, the user can formulate his/her query, which is subsequently translated by the PDS into a formal ontology-based representation understood by the system. After the problem description is generated, this is passed by the UIS to the AS as a "Request Answer" inquiry. Then, the AS assesses what kinds of data beyond environmental data are required to answer the query of the user and solicits these data from the Auxiliary Services (AuxS). For instance, such services can provide travel route information in the case that the user's query concerns the environmental conditions for a bicycle tour from A to B.

After having acquired the complementary data, the AS can request from the Data Retrieval Service (DRS) the environmental data needed to answer the user query. The DRS solicits these data from the environmental nodes that were identified by the Data Node Retrieval Service (DNRS) as relevant to the user's query and the complementary data. The DNRS retrieves this information from the data node repository after the node discovery phase has taken place.

As already mentioned, the retrieved nodes may deliver complementary or competing data of varying quality (to keep the presentation simple, we dispense with the illustration of the orchestration of service nodes). The Fusion Service (FS) applies uncertainty metrics to obtain the optimal and maximally complete data set, which is passed by the AS to the Decision Service (DS). The DS converts the data set into knowledge, or content, in that it relates it to the knowledge in our KB, reasons about it, and assesses it from the perspective of its relevance to the user. From this content, the Content Selection Service (CSS) compiles a content plan, which contains the knowledge to be communicated to the user as the answer. The Information Production Service (IPS) takes the content plan as input and generates information in the language and mode (text, table, or graphic) of the preference of the user, which then is passed to the user.

5 Outlook

We are currently implementing the described service infrastructure – including the environmental node discovery. The first operational prototype of the service will be available for demonstration by early summer 2011.

Acknowledgments. This work is partially funded by the European Commission under the contract number FP7-248594 "Personalized Environmental Service Configuration and Delivery Orchestration" (PESCaDO).

References

1. Karatzas, K.: State-of-the-art in the dissemination of AQ information to the general public. In: Proceedings of EnviroInfo, Warsaw, vol. 2, pp. 41–47 (2007)
2. Peinel, G., Rose, T., San José, R.: Customized Information Services for Environmental Awareness in Urban Areas. In: Proceedings of the 7th World Congress on Intelligent Transport Systems, Turin (2000)
3. Wanner, L., Bohnet, B., Bouayad-Agha, N., Lareau, F., Nicklass, D.: MARQUIS: Generation of User-Tailored Multilingual Air Quality Bulletins. Applied Artificial Intelligence 24(10), 914–952 (2010)
4. Wöber, K.: Domain Specific Search Engines. In: Fesenmaier, D.R., Werthner, H., Wöber, K. (eds.) Travel Destination Recommendation Systems: Behavioral Foundations and Applications, pp. 205–226. CAB International, Cambridge (2006)
5. Oyama, S., Kokubo, T., Ishida, T.: Domain-Specific Web Search with Keyword Spices Awareness in Urban Areas. IEEE Transactions on Knowledge and Data Engineering 16(1), 17–24 (2004)
6. Usländer, T. (ed.): Reference Model for the ORCHESTRA Architecture Version 2.1. OGC Best Practices Document 07-097 (2007) ,
   http://portal.opengeospatial.org/files/?artifact_id=23286
7. Usländer, T.: Specification of the Sensor Service Architecture, Version 3.0 (Rev. 3.1). OGC Discussion Paper 09-132r1. Deliverable D2.3.4 of the European Integrated Project SANY, FP6-IST-033564 (2009), http://portal.opengeospatial.org/files/?artifact_id=35888&version=1
8. World Wide Web Consortium: OWL Web Ontology Language Reference,
   http://www.w3.org/TR/owl-overview/

Using Negotiation for Dynamic Composition of Services in Multi-organizational Environmental Management

Costin Bădică[1], Sorin Ilie[1], Michiel Kamermans[2],
Gregor Pavlin[2], and Mihnea Scafeş[1]

[1] University of Craiova, Software Engineering Department, Romania
{costin.badica,sorin.ilie,mihnea.scafes}@software.ucv.ro
[2] Thales Nederland B.V., D-CIS Lab Delft, The Netherlands
{gregor.pavlin,michiel.kamermans}@d-cis.nl

Abstract. This paper discusses an efficient solution to contemporary situation assessment problems found in environmental management applications. The targeted problems are inherently complex and require processing of large quantities of heterogeneous information by using rich domain knowledge dispersed through multiple organizations. We assume a collaborative solution based on the Dynamic Process Integration Framework, which supports systematic encapsulation of heterogeneous processing services, including human experts. The encapsulation allows dynamic composition of heterogeneous processing services using advanced self-configuration mechanisms for optimal selection of service providers. Self-configuration is based on a framework for development of cooperative multi-issue one-to-many service negotiations. The framework allows the definition of: negotiation protocols, negotiation subjects composed of multiple negotiation issues, properties of negotiation issues, deal spaces, and utility functions of participant stakeholders. We show how this framework can be used for dynamic composition of workflows spanning multiple organizations in a disaster management information system.

Keywords: workflow, software agent, service negotiation.

1 Introduction

The increased complexity of socio-economic systems in combination with natural hazards might create conditions that, if not properly assessed, can evolve into dangerous incidents, for example chemical disasters. These are extremely complex and heterogeneous phenomena that can threaten the population as well as the natural environment. For example, places such as harbors as well as highly industrialized areas (e.g. the port of Rotterdam, the Netherlands) are constantly exposed to such risks because many companies are using, transporting and/or processing dangerous chemical substances in their neighborhood. Agencies specialized in environmental protection and emergency management are continuously monitoring the situation with the goal of taking corrective actions when things tend to go wrong. For example, DCMR[1] in the Netherlands and

---

[1] DCMR Milieudienst Rijnmond, http://www.dcmr.nl/

J. Hřebíček, G. Schimak, and R. Denzer (Eds.): ISESS 2011, IFIP AICT 359, pp. 177–188, 2011.

DEMA[2] in Denmark are two environment management organizations that protect the people and the environment against chemical hazards. They are specialized in solving complex environmental management problems by applying systematic procedures that are aimed, for example, at monitoring the situation and, when needed, act in order to discover the source of an incident, handle the chemical substance(s), secure the area and eventually decide on whether to evacuate (part of) the population or take other protective or corrective measures.

Actually, many contemporary applications require reasoning about complex processes and phenomena in real world domains including crisis management, environmental management, and project management. For example, in crisis management advanced information processing is required for various tasks, including (i) identification of critical situations, (ii) impact assessment which takes into account possible evolution of physical processes, (iii) planning and evaluation of countermeasures and (iv) decision making. These tasks are characterized as very complex situations that require a fast and efficient response through flexible and dynamic collaboration between various actors including emergency units, local and/or regional authorities, human experts, a.o., as well as systematic processing of large quantities of very heterogenous information, based on rich expertise about different aspects of the physical world. Usually underlying business processes involve interactions that cross organizational and geographical boundaries and that are highly dynamic and unpredictable in nature, thus demanding flexible composition of problem solving and reasoning patterns that cannot be captured using traditional workflow technologies.

Unfortunately, the processing requirements usually exceed the cognitive capabilities of a single human expert; an expert typically does not have knowledge of all the relevant domain methods and can only process limited amounts of available information. On the other hand, full automation of decision making processes in such settings is not feasible, since the creation of the required domain models as well as the inference are intractable problems. Therefore, complex assessment is often carried out in systems which can be characterized as *professional bureaucracies* [1], a class of organizations in which the skills are standardized, the control is decentralized to a great extent and the experts do not have to share domain knowledge.

We introduce a service oriented architecture called Dynamic Process Integration Framework (DPIF) that supports inter-organizational collaborative information processing in dynamic and distributed workflows. DPIF allows seamless integration of heterogeneous domain knowledge and processing capabilities into coherent collaborative processes. Processes are encapsulated by software agents, each using identical interaction protocols and collaboration interfaces for service provision and consumption. The DPIF combines Multi Agent Systems (MAS) [9] and a service oriented paradigm in new ways which facilitate implementation of hybrid collaborative reasoning systems with emergent problem solving capabilities. In contrast to traditional MAS approaches [9], the DPIF facilitates integration of human cognitive capabilities right into problem solving processes in workflows; humans are not mere users of an automated system, but contribute as processing resources. From the problem solving perspective, the humans experts can be viewed as a specific type of processing modules, integrated into the

---

[2] Danish Emergency Management Agency, http://www.brs.dk/

overall processing system via assistant agents. Each expert is associated with a DPIF assistant agent, which collects all the relevant information and disseminates the conclusions/estimates to the DPIF assistants of other interested service providers. In other words, DPIF assistant agents dynamically connect service providers into information processing workflows and facilitate automated information dissemination. In addition, some of the reasoning processes might be automated, which would speed up the assessment and increase quality. However, full automation of complex assessment processes is likely to be unacceptable or even impossible.

The DPIF is a service-oriented approach which supports dynamic and decentralized creation of workflows that facilitate collaborative problem solving. The DPIF supports efficient composition of heterogenous processing services provided by different human experts and computational processes. Each process provides a well-defined reasoning service in the form of an estimate, prediction, cost, etc. The inputs of a process are provided by other processes or by direct observations, like sensor measurements or human reports. Processes are wrapped as DPIF agents that support standardized interaction protocols. Each agent registers in the DPIF system (i) the services that the expert/automated process can provide and (ii) the types of services supplying the inputs that are required to provide the services of the expert.

By using the registered services, agents distributed throughout different networked devices can autonomously form workflows enabling collaborative processing of human experts and automated processing tools. The DPIF supports service composition which explicitly takes into account the characteristics of *professional bureaucracies*. Service composition in such settings can be achieved through service matching and discovery based on local domain knowledge supplemented with a finer level of control based on one-to-many service negotiation. Each expert or automated process "knows" which types of information (i.e. other service types) are required for providing his or her specific services. Service negotiation allows us to filter potential links found through service discovery, using additional dynamically-adjustable service parameters, rather than relying on a perfect matching at the service discovery level.

The paper is structured as follows. We start in Section 2 with the introduction of a utilization scenario in the domain of environment management. The scenario is formalized using the DPIF model of agents and services. We follow in Section 3 with a discussion of the dynamic formation of multi-organizational workflows using the DPIF model of service composition. Then in Section 4 we show using an example extracted from the utilization scenario how service negotiation can help tuning the DPIF service compositions. In the last section of the paper we briefly summarize our conclusions.

2   Environment Management Scenario

We illustrate our approach by using an example derived from a real world use case investigated in the FP7 DIADEM project[3]. For the sake of clarity but without the loss of generality we assume a significantly simplified scenario. In a chemical incident at a refinery a leaking chemical starts burning which results in harmful fumes. The impact

---

[3] http://www.ist-diadem.eu

of the resulting fumes is assessed through a service composition involving collaboration of human experts, as depicted in Figure 1 and explained below:

- *The* Control Room *operator is triggered by the* Gas Detection *system about the possible presence of a chemical incident caused by the leak of a dangerous gas.*

- *The* Control Room *uses the information provided by the* Gas Detection *system and applies local knowledge about the industrial environment to determine the source of the incident. Consequently, it requests a report of the situation from the factory via the* Factory Representative. *The* Factory Representative *replies with report that confirms the incident and provides information about the type of escaping gas.*

- *The* Control Room *directs a field inspector denoted by* Chemical Adviser 1 *to the location of the incident.* Chemical Adviser 1 *has appropriate expertise to estimate the quantity of the escaping gas and to propose mitigation measures at the refinery.*

- *Health complaints are reported. We assume that they also arrive to the* Control Room *via the* Gas Detection *system. Consequently, the* Control Room *dispatches a chemical expert that holds expertise in estimating the gas concentration in the affected area. This expert is denoted as* Chemical Adviser 2.

- *The* Chemical Adviser 2 *requires information about the meteorological conditions, the source of the pollution, and the quantity and type of escaping fumes in order to estimate the zones in which the concentration of toxic gases has exceeded critical levels and to identify areas which are likely to be critical after a certain period of time. We assume that* Chemical Adviser 2 *gets the weather information from the* Control Room *and the information about the source, quantity, and type of the escaping gas from* Chemical Adviser 1. *The* Chemical Adviser 2 *makes use of domain knowledge about the physical properties of gases and their propagation mechanisms.*

- *In addition, the* Chemical Adviser 2 *guides fire fighter* Measurement Teams *which can measure gas concentrations at specific locations in order to provide feedback for a more accurate estimation of the critical area. This interaction between* Chemical Adviser 2 *and* Measurement Teams *involves negotiation to determine the optimal providers of appropriate measurements.*

- *A map showing the critical area is supplied by the* Chemical Adviser 2 *to a* Health Expert. *He uses additional information information on populated areas obtained from the municipality to estimate the impact of the toxic fumes on the human population in case of exposure.*

Analyzing the utilization scenario, we were able to identify an initial list of stakeholders that are involved in the collaborative incident resolving process. Each stakeholder is mapped onto a DPIF software agent that keeps track of services provided by the stakeholder, as well as services that are required by each provided service – see Table 1. For example, *Chemical Adviser 2* provides output service *Map of High Concentration Zones* producing a map of the critical area. In order to provide service *Map of High Concentration Zones* she consumes three input services called *Information about Source, Weather Report* and *Concentration Measurements* providing her with i) information about the source, ii) weather and iii) concentration measurements in the interest area, respectively.

The workflow shown in Figure 1 is not hard-coded in a centralized place. Rather, this workflow is dynamically composed using the DPIF service composition model. Composition of services is achieved through service matching and discovery based on local domain knowledge. Each expert or process has complete knowledge of which types of

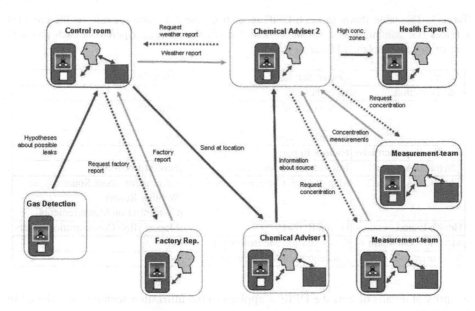

Fig. 1. Workflow for sample scenario

services he/she can provide to the community – the set of *output services*, as well as the types of services that are needed from the community to provide the output services,i.e. a set of *input services*. Consequently, the DPIF does not require centralized service ontologies describing relations between services and centralized service composition methods. However, a global lightweight ontology of services is necessary to align the syntax and semantics of services at the configuration of an assistant agent, prior to joining the overall system. Such configuration based on aligned services descriptions is key to runtime service composition resulting in dynamic workflows [6].

3   Dynamic Workflows

A basic workflow element in the DPIF is abstracted as a local process representing either the reasoning process of a human expert or an automated system implemented by a computational procedure. Each local process corresponds to a function that takes values of n input variables $x_1, x_2, \ldots, x_n$ and produces the value of an output variable $y = f_y(x_1, x_2, \ldots, x_n)$. For example, the local process of the *Chemical Adviser 2* described in Table 1 implements the following function:

$$x_{Map\ of\ High\ Concentration\ Zones} =$$
$$f_{Map}(x_{Information\ about\ Source}, x_{Weather\ Report}, x_{Concentration\ Measurements})$$

In the DPIF, a local process is wrapped as a DPIF software agent. The values of the input variables are provided by the input services of the DPIF agent, while the value of the process output is produced by an output service of the DPIF agent. More details about the architecture and design of the DPIF framework can be found in [5]. In what follows

Table 1. This table shows for each DPIF agent from the utilization scenario (i) the provided services (see column labeled *output service*) and (ii) the services required for each provided service (see column labeled *input service*)

Agent	Output Service	Input Service
Gas Detection	Hypothesis	n/a
Control Room	Send at Location	Hypothesis Factory Report
	Weather Report	n/a
Factory Representative	Factory Report	n/a
Chemical Adviser 1	Information about Source	Send at Location
Chemical Adviser 2	Map of High Concentration Zones	Information about Source Weather Report Concentration Measurements
Health Expert	Health Report	Map of High Concentration Zones
Measurement Team 1	Concentration Measurements	n/a
Measurement Team 2	Concentration Measurements	n/a

we present details of how the DPIF is applied to the utilization scenario introduced in Section 2.

It is interesting to note that the expertise of a human expert that is represented by a DPIF agent of type *Chemical Adviser 2* is local in the sense that the processing associated to its function $f_{Map\ of\ High\ Concentration\ Zones}$ encapsulates it, while only the external interfaces of this function are visible in the DPIF framework to allow dynamic formation of workflows through service composition based on service matching and discovery. For example, the output *Map of High Concentration Zones* of the agent *Chemical Adviser 2* can be matched using the service name with the input *Map of High Concentration Zones* of the agent *Health Adviser*.

Similarly, the local process of the *Health Adviser* described in Table 1 realizes the following function:

$$x_{Health\ Report} = f_{Health\ Report}(x_{Map\ of\ High\ Concentration\ Zones})$$

A function that is reduced to direct observation of its output variable can be noticed for the DPIF agents of type *Measurement Team* as follows:

$$x_{Concentration\ Measurements} = f_{Concentration\ Measurements}()$$

Inputs to a certain function ($f_{Health\ Report}$ for example) can be supplied by other DPIF agents (*Chemical Adviser 2* for example), thus dynamically forming a collaborative workflow. From a global perspective this workflow formation can be seen as a function composition that is realized in the DPIF using service composition. The dynamic composition process continues until a function is obtained in which all variables have been assigned a value. The resulting function obtained through service composition represents a mapping between directly observable variables (i.e. $x_{Concentration\ Measurements}$ for example, which is provided by *Measurement Team* agents) and hidden variables of interest ($x_{Health\ Report}$ for example). An example of composite function that yields the value of interest $x_{Health\ Report}$ is:

$$x_{Health\ Report} = f_{Health\ Report}($$
$$f_{Map\ of\ High\ Concentration\ Zones}($$
$$x_{Information\ about\ Source},$$
$$x_{Weather\ Report},$$
$$x_{Concentration\ Measurements}$$
$$)$$
$$)$$

4 Self-configuration Using Service Negotiation

In the DPIF, communication links between local processes in agents are facilitated firstly using service discovery: whenever an agent supplying some service (we will call this service the parent service, and the agent implementing it the manager) in a workflow requires data relating to some other service (we will call this required service the child service, and the agent implementing it the contractor), a communication link needs to be established between the manager agent and the contractor agent. However, there are two important aspects that affect whether and why links are established: i) we might have several agents in the system that provide the same service, i.e. that are able to realize the same task, and ii) we cannot always assume that an agent providing a service will automatically agree to supply the service asked for by a requesting agent. For example, the provider might be overloaded, or it might even consider that establishing a link is inappropriate, given the current context.

In addition, service discovery alone can only offer links between agents based on a broad level of service matching, while for solving a particular problem, a finer level of control is required to match services on additional parameters. Establishing links is based on one-to-many service negotiation. Rather than performing perfect matching with service discovery, negotiation allows us to filter potential links found through service discovery based on additional service parameters.

Negotiation is a process that describes the interaction between one or more participants that must agree on a subject by exchanging deals or proposals about this subject [3]. Negotiation about a service that one or more participants agree to provide to other participants is called *service negotiation*. We have developed a conceptual framework for service negotiation that is used in the DPIF. The framework is generic and it addresses negotiation protocols, negotiation subjects and decision components. Due to space restrictions we only briefly review the framework here. Details of the conceptual framework can be found in [2], while a brief description of the design and implementation is given in [7].

Our protocol supports one-to-many negotiations and it defines two roles: manager and contractor [8,4]. The manager is the agent that requests a service and thus initiates the negotiation. The contractor is the agent that is able to provide the service requested by the manager. A set of generic negotiation steps are defined: (i) negotiation subject identification and negotiation announcement (initiation of negotiation), (ii) bidding, i.e. making proposals and counter-proposals, (iii) deciding whether an agreement or a conflict was reached, and (iv) termination.

Negotiation subject comprises the service description and a subset of the service parameters that are important decision factors during negotiation (i.e. their current values are taken into consideration when selecting the appropriate service providers). During negotiation, these parameters are considered *negotiation issues*. Thus, when the negotiation designer configures the service, he also defines the negotiable parameters of the service (i.e. negotiation issues).

Negotiation issues are described by properties including their name, data type, and monotonicity. The name of the issue uniquely identifies the issue in a negotiation subject. The data type of the issue describes the type of the value the issue is allowed to take. It can be as simple as a number or string or more complex, as required for example to describe a geographical location or a date/time value. The monotonicity specifies whether the manager prefers higher values to lower values of this issue. Possible values are: (i) INCREASING if the agent prefers high utility values of the issue and (ii) DECREASING if the agent prefers low utility values of this issue.

An important characteristic of service negotiations in DIADEM is that they are *cooperative*. Cooperativity stems from the fact that the overall goal of negotiation participants is the optimization of the response for situation assessment in a chemical incident. Negotiations for a certain service provision are carried out only with agents that are able to provide the required service (i.e. that possess the domain knowledge or physical capabilities that are needed to provide the service). Provider agents will usually accept to offer their services if they are currently able to do so (for example if they posses all the necessary resources). During a negotiation: (i) the manager is the leading decision factor that looks to optimize the assignment of the negotiation task to the best available contractor(s); (ii) the contractor(s) make their best proposals for serving the manager, taking into account their current duties and availability, thus preserving their autonomy according to the principles of professional bureaucracy.

Service parameters can be classified into 4 classes: (i) DYNAMIC that specifies that the issue value is not fixed by the manager, i.e. the contractor can propose different values for the issue; (ii) FIXED that specifies that the issue value is fixed by the manager, i.e. if the contractor proposes a different value for the issue than the corresponding local utility of the issue is zero; (iii) CONDITION that specifies that the issue value is fixed by the manager, but if the contractor proposes a different value for the issue than the total utility of the proposal is zero; normally a contractor that cannot meet the issue value requested by the manager must decide to not bid because the utility of her bid will be zero; (iv) TRIVIAL that means that the issue is not taken into account in the computation of the bid utility, although it can be set in the request of the manager and consequently, it can be taken into account in the negotiation by the contractor and help her to make a more informed decision if and what to bid.

Negotiation participants in either manager or contractor role use utility functions to measure their preferences over deals. In our framework the manager uses a weighted additive utility function to evaluate proposals and to select the service provider. Each negotiation issue i has a weight $w_i \in [0, 1]$ and a partial utility function f_i. Note that weights are normalized i.e. $\sum_i w_i = 1$. Intuitively, the weight of an issue represents the relative importance for the manager of that issue in the set of all issues associated to a negotiation subject. The partial utility of an issue i maps the issue domain D_i to a value in the interval $[0, 1]$, i.e. $f_i : D_i \rightarrow [0, 1]$. The definition of function f_i depends on the domain of the issue. For example, a possibility to define the partial utility function of a real valued issue with $D_i = [x_{min}, x_{max}]$ is as follows:

$$f_i(x) = \frac{|x - x^*|}{|x_{max} - x_{min}|}$$

where x^* is the reference value assigned by the manager to the issue i and $|x - y|$ is the distance between x and y (note that the distance actually depends on the data type of the negotiation issue). Note that a negotiation issue for which the partial utility is defined as a distance from the reference value (that represents the optimal value from the manager point of view) has always a DECREASING monotonicity.

Let I be the set of negotiation issues partitioned into sets $I^\uparrow$ and $I^\downarrow$ of issues with INCREASING and DECREASING monotonicity. The utility function of a proposal $x = (x_i)_{i \in I}$ has the following form:

$$u_m(x) = \sum_{i \in I^\uparrow} w_i * f_i(x_i) + \sum_{i \in I^\downarrow} w_i * (1 - f_i(x_i))$$

The utility function of the contractor agent can be defined as $u_c(x) = 1 - effort(x)$. Here $effort(x)$ represents the total effort that must be deployed by contractor agent c to be able to provide the terms and conditions required by call for proposals proposal x. The contractor will obviously choose to propose a deal that maximizes her utility, i.e. that minimizes the required effort for achieving the task required by the manager. In practice, function $effort(x)$ can take into account several factors, including for example the cost of providing service x, the existing commitments of agent c that were previously contracted and are not yet finalized, and/or the amount of resources that are required to provide the service. Obviously, a higher number of commitments not finalized yet of agent c or a higher cost of providing x will result in a higher value of $effort(x)$ and consequently to a lower value of the utility $u_c(x)$.

Let us suppose that *Chemical Adviser 2* agent plays the role of manager looking for a provider for the service *Measure Gas Concentration*. The optimal selection of the service provider takes into account: the location where the measurement must be performed, the quality of the measurement, and the duration for performing the measurement. Additionally we assume that the measurement quality is given as a percentage and that the maximum time frame for performing the measurement is 100 minutes. The description of the negotiation issue, together with the manager proposal are given in Table 2.

Weights of negotiation issues must be normalized as follows:

$$w_{Location} = \tfrac{1}{6}$$
$$w_{Quality} = \tfrac{2}{6}$$
$$w_{Deadline} = \tfrac{3}{6}$$

Table 2. Negotiable issues and manager request

Issue	Location	Quality	Deadline
Reference value	*loc*	100	11:47 AM
Weight	1	2	3
Data type	REGION	NUMBER	DATE
Boundary	n/a	100	100
Negotiable	FIXED	DYNAMIC	DYNAMIC

Table 3. Contractors' bids

Issue	Location	Quality	Deadline
Bid Value (1)	*loc*	70	11:58 AM
Bid Value (2)	*loc*	100	00:12 PM

Let us assume that there are two *Measurement Teams* in the system and each of them decides to bid with an offer for providing the service *Measure Gas Concentration*. Their bids are shown in Table 3.

The utility of the bid of the first *Measurement Team* is computed as follows:

$$u_{Location_1} = \tfrac{1}{6} \times (1 - \tfrac{0}{1}) = 0.166$$
$$u_{Quality_1} = \tfrac{2}{6} \times (1 - \tfrac{30}{100}) = 0.233$$
$$u_{Deadline_1} = \tfrac{3}{6} \times (1 - \tfrac{11}{100}) = 0.445$$

$$u_{MT_1} = u_{Location_1} + u_{Quality_1} + u_{Deadline_1} = 0.844$$

The utility of the bid of the second *Measurement Team* is computed as follows:

$$u_{Location_2} = \tfrac{1}{6} \times (1 - \tfrac{0}{1}) = 0.166$$
$$u_{Quality_2} = \tfrac{2}{6} \times (1 - \tfrac{0}{100}) = 0.333$$
$$u_{Deadline_2} = \tfrac{3}{6} \times (1 - \tfrac{25}{100}) = 0.375$$

$$u_{MT_2} = u_{Location_2} + u_{Quality_2} + u_{Deadline_2} = 0.874$$

Chemical Adviser 2 agent uses these equations to compute the utilities of each bid received from *Measurement Team* agents. Then *Chemical Adviser 2* applies a strategy that allows it to either immediately select the winning bid or to decide if to continue the negotiation using a new iteration. Let us assume that *Chemical Adviser 2* applies a strategy that considers acceptable only those bids valuating above a given threshold value. If none is above the threshold then *Chemical Adviser 2* can perform a second iteration either by relaxing the conditions of the call for proposals (for example by decreasing the required quality of the measurements or by extending the deadline for performing the measurements) or by decrementing the threshold, thus giving a new chance to the

Measurement Team agents to update their bids. If at least one bid is considered acceptable then *Chemical Adviser 2* can decide to accept one or more *Measurement Team*
agents to contract the *Measure Gas Concentration* service. Assuming for example a
threshold of 0.85, according to this algorithm *Chemical Adviser 2* will select the second
Measurement Team after the first iteration.

5   Conclusions

This paper presents a solution which supports automated organization of experts which
collaboratively solve complex problems found in contemporary environmental and crisis management applications. In particular, the approach combines the Dynamic Process
Integration Framework (DPIF) and automated negotiation. DPIF is a wrapper technology which supports encapsulation and combination of heterogeneous processing
capabilities in collaborative problem solving processes found in complex real world
domains, such as environmental management. DPIF provides a technically sound infrastructure in which advanced negotiation processes can be systematically embedded.
Experts and automated processes are wrapped such that their services become composable and negotiable.

Negotiation is achieved through an additional software layer that enhances DPIF
agent communication with flexible service negotiation protocols. This negotiation layer
allows definition and configuration of service negotiation protocols in agent-based collaborative processes. In particular our framework supports flexible configuration of
multi-issue negotiation subjects, properties of negotiation issues, deal spaces, and utility
functions of participant agents. An example covering use of utility functions in a sample
negotiation scenario was discussed in detail, emphasizing how service negotiation can
improve the selection of optimal service providers in environment management.

Acknowledgement

The work reported in this paper was carried out as part of the Diadem project:
http://www.ist-diadem.eu. The Diadem project is funded by the E.U. under
the Information and Communication Technologies (ICT) theme of the 7th Framework
Programme for R&D, ref. no: 224318.

References

1. Argente, E., Julian, V., Botti, V.: Multi-Agent System Development Based on Organizations.
   Electronic Notes in Theoretical Computer Science, vol. 150, pp. 55–71. Elsevier, Amsterdam
   (2006)
2. Bădică, C., Scafeş, M.: Conceptual Framework for Design of Service Negotiation in Disaster
   Management Applications. In: Bai, Q., Fukuta, N. (eds.) Advances in Practical Multi-Agent
   Systems. Studies in Computational Intelligence, vol. 325, pp. 359–375. Springer, Heidelberg
   (2010)
3. Jennings, N.R., Faratin, P., Lomuscio, A.R., Parsons, S., Sierra, C., Wooldridge, M.: Automated Negotiation: Prospects, Methods and Challenges. Group Decision and Negotiation 10(2), 199–215 (2001)

4. Paurobally, S., Tamma, V., Wooldridge, M.: A Framework for Web service negotiation. ACM Transactions on Autonomous and Adaptive Systems 2(4) (2007)
5. Pavlin, G., Kamermans, M., Scafeş, M.: Dynamic Process Integration Framework: Toward Efficient Information Processing in Complex Distributed Systems. Informatica 34, 477–490 (2010)
6. Penders, A., Pavlin, G., Kamermans, M.: A Collaborative Approach to Construction of Complex Service Oriented Systems. In: Essaaidi, M.M., Michele, Bădică, C. (eds.) Intelligent Distributed Computing IV. Studies in Computational Intelligence, vol. 315, pp. 55–66. Springer, Heidelberg (2010)
7. Scafeş, M., Bădică, C., Pavlin, G., Kamermans, M.: Design and Implementation of a Service Negotiation Framework for Collaborative Disaster Management Applications. In: Proc.International Conference on Intelligent Networking and Collaborative Systems INCOS 2010, pp. 519–524 (2010)
8. Smith, R.G.: The Contract Net Protocol: High-Level Communication and Control in a Distributed Problem Solver. IEEE Transactions on Computers 29(12), 1104–1113 (1980)
9. Wooldridge, M.: An Introduction to MultiAgent Systems, 2nd edn. John Wiley & Sons, Chichester (2009)

data.reegle.info – A New Key Portal for Open Energy Data

Florian Bauer[1], Denise Recheis[1], and Martin Kaltenböck[2]

[1] REEEP – The Renewable Energy and Energy Efficiency Partnership, Wagramerstrasse 5, 1400 Vienna, Austria

[2] Semantic Web Company, OGD Austria, Lerchenfelder Gürtel 43, 1160 Vienna, Austria

{Florian.Bauer,Denise.Recheis}@reeep.org,
m.kaltenboeck@semantic-web.at

Abstract. The paper discuss the information gateway *data.reegle.info*, which is at the forefront of this development, is consuming and publishing energy related data in a machine-readable format so as to allow the flexible sharing and re-use of information in new and innovative ways. It filters and enriches content by sorting and adding pertinent information from various reliable sources. It enables data providers to easily link and publish datasets in a standardised, machine-readable format. In this way it can be easily accessible, and shared with 3rd parties. This is a real benefit for the users of reegle which targets policy- and decision makers, developers and the general public with an interest in renewable energy and energy efficiency, with a focus on developing countries.

Keywords: semantic web, open government data, energy data, linked data.

1 Introduction

Over the last few centuries knowledge and information has become much more widely available. It is no longer limited to a select few; more often it is available to anyone, anywhere with an internet connection and access to a computer. A major step forward was the invention of the printing press, resulting in greater access to information, higher literacy rates and improved levels of education. This sharing of knowledge has been radically transformed again recently with the onset of the internet combined with rapid technology advances. Linked Open Data is the next step along those lines, offering us opportunities to use the latest technologies and techniques available to share pertinent, up-to-date information, from a wider variety of sources free for use and re-use. One of the main challenges now is to sort through this ever increasing volume of information, of varying quality; to select the most relevant, up-to-date and reliable information from the different sources and formats in use; and to make this information available in a useful, reliable and standardised way.

Several governments and official agencies have pledged to make all their collected data publicly available, a move that makes sense considering it is public money that is being spent on gaining this data. These days, such data is published on the internet, meaning there is more and more of it available online. Sharing data is expected to

J. Hřebíček, G. Schimak, and R. Denzer (Eds.): ISESS 2011, IFIP AICT 359, pp. 189–194, 2011.

deliver more transparency, efficient public service and better use and re-use of data in the public and commercial domains.

Especially in the field of (clean) energy, it is crucial to have access to latest and accurate datasets and to be able to link, compare and mash-up this information to provide decision makers, financiers and project developers with the necessary set of information to accelerate the marketplace of clean energy. The Renewable Energy and Energy Efficiency Partnership (REEEP) has taken up the challenge of developing and running a web portal (http://www.reegle.info), which acts as a single point of access to these datasets, offering its datasets according to the Linked Open Data W3C Standards and enriching its own information with relevant data from other open data providers to offer the full benefit of information on clean energy to the user.

Linked Data best practise will allow the extension of the worldwide web to a global data space that can connect data from various domains like scientific data, businesses but also film and radio programmes. New applications using Linked Open Data can incorporate new data appearing on the web automatically by recognizing its relevance, and thus the user will receive more holistic results. reegle is joining this movement by providing and using Open Data from renewable energy related themes, and by offering its own applications as well as making its data available for applications of external sites. By using only high-quality sources, concerns about the trustworthiness of data are appeased for users as well as developers working with data retrieved through reegle.

1.1   Linked Open Data W3C Standards

When great amounts of data are published, it is important to structure, catalogue and document it in a way that makes it retrievable – not only by humans but also by machines. In order to make data actually re-useable, the distribution of raw data is crucial. This raw data has to be in a well defined machine-readable, structured format.

The Linked Data standards, techniques and technologies allow information to be published in an open and standard format with common web based access methods. This standard web-based data format allows data of various kinds, vocabularies, sources, semantics and authors to be federated, queried and analyzed. It is based on the "Resource Description Framework" (RDF) – a very open and general way to publish and consume data[1].

1.2   SKOS and RDF Format

SKOS (Standard Knowledge Organisation System)[2] is a formal and controlled vocabulary used in the context of the semantic web for creating taxonomies, thesauri and ontologies. Knowledge organized in such a way uses, for example, the Resource Description Framework (RDF) which encodes the information in a way that it can be used in decentralized metadata applications. RDF triples consist of a subject, a predicate and an object. The subject and object are labelled as a `skos:Concept`. The predicate describes the "properties" between subject and object, which could be

---

[1] W3C eGov Wiki (http://www.w3.org/RDF/)
[2] SKOS (http://www.w3.org/2004/02/skos/)

`skos:broader` if the subject is a child of the object, like for example if "jeans" were the subject then the predicate to its object "trousers" would be `skos:broader`. So RDF is built from classes/concepts and the properties between them, and each class and property has its own unique identifier URI.

This "third dimension" added when converting data to RDF triples allows mashups to be created with data from various sources to give it new meaning. This adds lots of value and results in highly interesting and informative applications, especially in the context of resource and energy data.

1.3 Thesauri

Thesauri[3] use controlled vocabulary in the sense of a closed list of named subjects as a means to index subjects/concepts. SKOS thesauri use a concept/subject-based classification. Controlled vocabulary has the advantage over uncontrolled vocabulary in that it avoids the use of different terms for identical subjects/concepts, like misspellings, old-fashioned names or simply singular forms. Information, data can be retrieved by its metadata which describes objects which are connected to the subjects/concepts they are about and which are used to classify the objects. An improvement over old-fashioned term-based thesauri is the fact that a concept/subject-based thesaurus allows poly-hierarchies, meaning that a subject/concept can have more than one broader relation. Each concept will always have the same narrow relations, whatever its broader concept may be.

Thesauri are a powerful way to classify objects and term subjects/concepts and to provide a way of searching for and browsing data. Furthermore thesauri enable very powerful search based applications as for instance similarity mechanisms et al. To handle this amount of data becoming available now as open data, filter mechanisms and categorization are more crucial than ever.

1.4 The reegle Thesauri

In fact, the reegle thesaurus consists of several thesauri covering the subjects of renewable energy technologies as well as climate compatible development. Having been built with the software PoolParty[4], it boasts full Linked Data capabilities and it is based on W3C principles which allow linking with other LOD[5] sources. Having developed a controlled vocabulary for the fields it covers, the reegle thesaurus is capable of structuring and categorizing the many concepts of clean energy. As a hand-crafted piece of work, it can be adjusted when required but operates and powers some of reegle's most important features without the need for constant man power.

The fact that several domain experts from engineering as well as international development have contributed to the reegle thesaurus ensures a high quality and relevance for reegle users. They have the benefit of vast knowledge combined with the comfort and ease of a modern web-tool.

---

[3] Thesaurus (http://en.wikipedia.org/wiki/Thesaurus)
[4] http://poolparty.punkt.at
[5] Linked Open Data

2   reegle.info as a Linked Open Data Publisher/Consumer

"reegle.info", the gateway for high quality information on renewable energy and energy efficiency acts as a main information source for more than 90,000 users per month in the clean energy sector. It is an offshoot from The Renewable Energy & Energy Efficiency Partnership (REEEP, http://www.reeep.org), a non-profit, specialist change agent aiming to catalyze the market for renewable energy and energy efficiency, with a primary focus on emerging markets and developing countries.

Originally launched in 2006, reegle was designed as a specialist search engine for renewable energy and efficiency issues. It didn't publish any content of its own, but eventually it developed further and an actors catalogue was produced for reegle. Two years later reegle underwent its first total make-over when a regular energy blog and a small glossary were introduced, and outreach could be expanded. Still, reegle was promoted foremost as a search engine and the website's design strongly focused on this feature.

Through experience and feedback, it became more apparent that user's tended to benefit more from reegle's secondary features, and more features were added. A reegle map visualizing energy statistics and potentials was introduced and again well-perceived by the public. As an ever evolving dissemination tool, it was decided in 2010 to add reegle to the LOD cloud as a user and producer of Open Data.

The new data portal (data.reegle.info), launched in 2011, has established reegle as a publisher and consumer of Linked Open Data in the energy sector in an innovative design. This means that data provided on reegle can be located and re-used by 3rd parties for free, and content is enriched by all relevant data from the LOD (Linked Open Data) cloud. It now provides key datasets free for re-use using Linked Open Data W3C standards. These datasets include extensive energy facts, a set of more than 1700 key stakeholders (actors catalogue) and a comprehensive thesaurus/glossary describing the clean energy sector. On www.reegle.info all available information is enriched by data from other data providers, resulting in comprehensive information dossiers, like the country energy profiles which summarize the most important energy related information (e.g. Regulations, Statistics, Organizations …) for all countries worldwide. reegle data is already being used by external developers to enrich their own information systems as openei.org or the Solar-Med-Atlas (http://dev.geomodel.eu/solar-med-atlas/) and thus proves its relevance.

This new development once again reinforces reegle's position as a one-stop-shop in the field of renewable energy, energy efficiency and climate compatible development. The energy sector is a vivid example of how Open (Government) Data can be utilized and benefits development and implementation of energy policies, targets and helps decision makers and project developers alike not only by offering the latest relevant data but also by offering new ways of using it.

2.1   The data.reegle.info SPARQL Endpoint

The SPARQL[6] endpoint[7] at reegle.info offers developers to retrieve data on energy statistics, key stakeholders and individual country energy profiles as well as the whole reegle.info thesaurus on clean energy for free and unlimited re-use.

---

[6] SPARQL as the query language of the semantic web offers a powerful API to retrieve data and manage complex queries over several data sources.

[7] http://semanticweb.org/wiki/SPARQL_endpoint

As an example, a user could send a query regarding reegle stakeholders in energy and efficiency NGOs active in the Czech Republic. The query would look like this:

```
PREFIX foaf: <http://xmlns.com/foaf/0.1/>
PREFIX dcterms: <http://purl.org/dc/terms/>
PREFIX reegle: <http://reegle.info/schema#>

SELECT ?actor ?name
WHERE {
  ?actor a foaf:Organization.
  ?actor dcterms:subject <http://reegle.info/categories/11>.
  ?actor foaf:name ?name. FILTER (lang(?name) = "en" )
  ?actor reegle:activeIn <http://reegle.info/countries/CZ>.
}
```

(Example from data.reegle.info/developers/sparql-intro)

The user will receive a list of all relevant stakeholders, each with its own unique identifier, for example LaGuardia Foundation with its URI (Unified Resource Identifier) http://reegle.info/actors/2423. This information can be used by developers for any application they can think of, free and without strings attached.

3   Benefits for reegle Users

3.1   Glossary, Web Search

Both glossary and intelligent web search are powered by the thesaurus. The glossary makes use of linked data principles and displays Wikipedia definitions beside reegle' own definition and informs the reader of synonyms, abbreviations or other terms that describe an identical "unit of thought"; they are included in the thesaurus as skos:prefLabel and skos:altLabel which allows for one preferred label and several alternative labels. Other sources like suitable glossaries or thesauri can easily be integrated to contribute more information when need arises. The web search can be refined through choosing related terms from the thesaurus in a box which can be ticked and which then will be added to the original terms. Related searches are also offered on basis of narrower terms at the bottom of the page. Auto-complete is another convenient measure that is offered, and common spelling errors are accounted for be including them as skos:hiddenLabel in the thesaurus. reegle users can thus find what they are looking for by refining their search and because the reegle web search operates on carefully pre-selected websites, reliability of the retrieved information is guaranteed.

3.2   Visualizing Knowledge

The reegle thesauri don't only power the intelligent web search and clean energy glossary in the ways just described, but PoolParty also allows a visual display of all the hierarchical and associative relations of a concept. This can really benefit understanding complex and abstract concepts, and by clicking onto the relations the user can dig deeper into a subject and get the full graphic display for each unit of thought.

3.3   Country Energy Profiles - A reegle Mash-Up

Following reegle's re-launch in 2011, it now boasts comprehensive and well-arranged energy-related information on all of the world's countries and regions. These profiles are not researched and written by a person, but they are an example of making use of open data that is freely available for re-use. Valuable documents from REEEP's own database such as the regulatory overview and the reegle stakeholders (actors) are presented in the brand-new reegle design and this information is now for the first time enriched with easy-to-understand reegle graphs showing energy demand, production and emissions amongst other key facts retrieved from trusted sources, such as UN data and the World Bank. A short general description and the flag of each country is contributed by DBpedia[8] and traditional "links" to relevant web pages documents or other relevant information round up these comprehensive dossiers.

This new asset is attracting a lot of project developers, decision makers and other interested parties because they can now gain a complete overview in a user-friendly format, getting the relevant facts from the major sources in one place as well as re-use them for free.

Another advantage is that new sources that suit the high quality requirements are regularly reviewed and can be added very easy to improve reegle's country energy profiles by such information.

4   Outlook

The ever increasing information flow can bring about many chances and opportunities, but now is the time to make some considerations and choose the right formats and create the right applications to show the public what can be done with Linked Open Data. One of the recent projects are the reegle.info country energy profiles which link and mash up data from different sources into one comprehensive package and offer machine-readable links to country information in other relevant data sources world-wide. reegle is determined to partake in this exiting development and be at the forefront of open energy data and to underline this progression it has just been re-launched in a new, modern and user-friendly design highlighting its most important features.

References

1. The World Wide Web Consortium (W3C), http://www.w3.org/
2. W3C eGov Wiki, http://www.w3.org/egov/wiki/Linked_Data
3. The Renewable Energy & Energy Efficiency Partnership (REEEP), http://www.reeep.org/
4. Garsho, L.: Metadata? Thesauri? Taxonomies? Topic Maps! Making sense of it all (2004), http://www.ontopia.net/topicmaps/materials/tm-vs-thesauri.html#N412
5. Campell, L., MacNeill, S.: The Semantic Web, Linked and Open Data; A Briefing Paper (2009)
6. Linked Data – Connect Distributed Data across the Web, http://linkeddata.org/
7. Bizer, C., Heath, T., Berners-Lee, T.: Linked Data, The Story So Far. International Journal on Semantic Web and Information Systems 3, 1–22 (2009)

---

[8] Wikipedia datasets (http://dbpedia.org/About)

GENESIS, a Flexible Solution for Building Networks of Collaborative Environmental Services

Stephane Bonnot[1], Simone Gianfranceschi[2], Steven Smolders[3], Marc Gilles[4],
Thomas Holzer-Popp[5], and Marc Erlich[6]

[1] Thales Alenia Space France, 100 Boulevard du Midi 100,
F-06156 Cannes la Bocca Cedex France
Phone: +33 4 92 92 69 31; Fax: +33 4 92 92 69 31
stephane.bonnot@thalesaleniaspace.com
[2] INTECS, 5 Via E. Giannessi, Ospedaletto, I–56121 Pisa, Italy
Phone: +39 050 96 57 411; Fax: +39 050 96 57 400
simone.gianfranceschi@intecs.it
[3] GIM, 5 Interleuvenlaan, B-3001 Heverlee, Belgium
Phone: .+32 16 40 30 39; Fax: +32 16 40 69 39
steven.smolders@gim.be
[4] Spacebel, 5-7 I. Vandammestraart, B-1560 Hoeilaart, Belgium
Phone: +32 2 658 20 11; Fax: +32 2 658 20 90
marc.gilles@spacebel.be
[5] DLR, 20 Münchener Str. Wessling 82234, Germany
Phone: +49-8153-28-1382
thomas.holzer-popp@dlr.de
[6] Artelia, 6 Rue de Lorraine, 38432 Echirolles, France
Phone: +33 4 76334281
marc.erlich@arteliagroup.com

Abstract. The GENESIS project, partially funded by the European Commission
(DG INFSO in the FP7 framework) provides an efficient Web-based software
solution that can be used by all kind of actors involved in environment management and health services in Europe. The solution takes aboard various leading-edge technologies like multi-linguality and ontologies, sensor networks,
near-real-time data fusion, dynamic work flows, portlet-based customizable
portal and many more. A set of multi-thematic pilots is developed based on the
GENESIS solution as a proof of concept.

Keywords: FP7 GENESIS, OGC, ISO, SOA, INSPIRE, Thematic Applications, Air Quality, Water Quality.

1 Introduction

The current situation of Environment management and Health actors is characterized by
numerous barriers to efficient cooperation and sharing of resources, mainly caused by:

- Scattered services, data and catalogues,
- The lack of standardization of legacy system.

J. Hřebíček, G. Schimak, and R. Denzer (Eds.): ISESS 2011, IFIP AICT 359, pp. 195–207, 2011.
© IFIP International Federation for Information Processing 2011

The GENESIS project has the objective of defining and developing an efficient solution based on advanced ICT to constitute collaborative information networks, integrating existing systems.

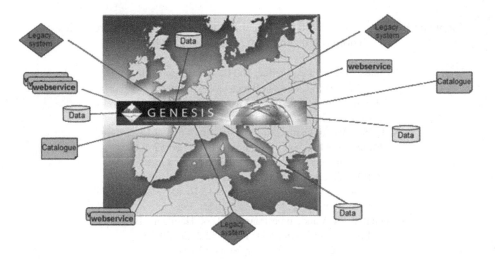

Fig. 1. GENESIS thematic-neutral collaborative framework

The GENESIS system is willing to offer an efficient solution to:

- Build integrated Environment & Health information systems easily accessible through Web interfaces, with collaboration of remote information systems or actors (at regional, national and European levels).
- Support environmental monitoring processes, and assessment of environment impact on health.
- Help all actors to get enhanced access to the geo-spatial information or services available all over Europe, independently from their location.
- Help data / services providers to upgrade their existing information systems, to promote standards and interoperability, in relation with INSPIRE and environment policy directives.
- Help thematic communities to build for their own purposes new applications or services related to Environment & Health by chaining various services (data access, viewing, processing, …)

2   Genesis Solution

The GENESIS software solution is based on an "INSPIRE Compliant" Service Oriented Architecture (SOA) composed of a set of secured, standardised Web Services and customisable Web Service Clients that can be easily deployed in a Web Portal.

The Web Services that are made available cover the full chain from discovery of data and services to the exploitation of processing results. Interested parties can select single Open Source services or make use of the GENESIS integrated solution. Within the GENESIS SOA, these services are deployed using the SOAP protocol bindings to enable service orchestration by a central workflow controller and a common authentication and authorisation mechanism. Most Web Service interfaces that are employed in this project are compliant with the most recent OGC Specifications that are either recently adopted or are under definition with technical work related to the standard definition and maturation performed within the GENESIS project (e.g. Sensor Catalogue Service).

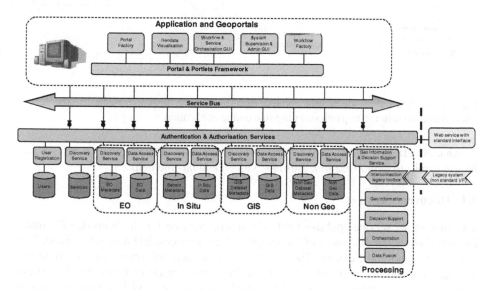

Fig. 2. GENESIS architecture based on the INSPIRE guidelines

The GENESIS architecture illustrated in the previous picture will be described in more details in the following sub sections. The GENESIS system also includes the tools as for example an interconnection legacy toolbox to easily integrate Thematic data and processing so that "Thematic" Information System can be built as an instantiation of (a subset of) the services and client building blocks that GENESIS delivers combining generic services with specific "thematic" processing components as shown on the following figure.

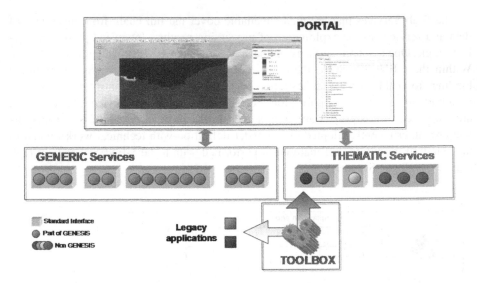

Fig. 3. GENESIS thematic-neutral collaborative framework with its "toolbox", the legacy interconnection solution to painlessly plug-in existing application

An extra effort is added to on information dissemination to promote GENESIS and its use thanks to demonstration, tutorials, videos and on-line help

2.1 Discovery Services

The first set of services publish OGC Catalogue Service for the Web (CSW) Interfaces and allow the discovery of Geographic Web Services, EO data set (series), GIS data set (series) and Sensors. These catalogues of meta-information allow both the management and discovery of metadata of the various resource types. Most of these metadata sets are managed using the ebRIM information model in which different extension packages can be expressed for different types of metadata, but the discovery mechanism is common for all metadata types.

Additionally, because all of the metadata for the different resource types are expressed in ebRIM, new associations between different resource types (e.g. EO Product collections and Sensors) can be added to link previously unassociated metadata. Additional important associations or classifications can also be added to enhance the semantics of the metadata to improve the discovery significantly e.g. retrieving of EO collection information based on sensor characteristics and navigate from EO collection information to the associated sensor description. The catalogue service components come with a graphical user interface to manage the catalogue configuration, allow metadata discovery and editing and bulk metadata harvesting.

Two different implementations are being validated and integrated with the GENESIS Portal: one is based on the ERDAS COTS and the second one is based on the Buddata ebXML Registry open source catalogue services. Both catalogue products provide an implementation of the latest CIM, EOP and Sensor Discovery OGC specifications. The Buddata ebXML Registry core components ahev also been integrated

Fig. 4. Buddata catalogue administration tool easing the management of meta-data harvesting, manual update etc...

in the legacy Interconnection Toolbox. This tools provides an advanced catalogue management creation interface and implements an INSPIRE compliant Façade allowing the access to the metadata stored in EbRim format via an ISO Application Profile client.

2.2 Data Access Services

A second set of services allows accessing vector, raster or sensor measurement data in accordance with the latest versions of the OGC Web Service interfaces (OGC WFS, WCS, SOS). Not only data access services but also the portrayal services that render these data sets into map images (and exposed using the OGC Web Map Service Interface Specification) are covered within this task.

These data access services are all implemented using SOAP bindings to allow orchestration and the use of the Web Service Security Specifications. The INSPIRE SOAP Primer and proposition for WSDL are used as the basis for the SOAP implementation which will be released as Open Source Software.

To handle Non Geodata access, a web-based tool is developed to allow the design of complex data models by non-expert users. The tool allows designing the data model and to instantiate a Web Feature Service and a corresponding datastore to publish this type of data. Such a web service instance implements the WFS-T specification with SOAP bindings. The modern web-based GUI allows drag and drop of model components and sharing of data models with peers.

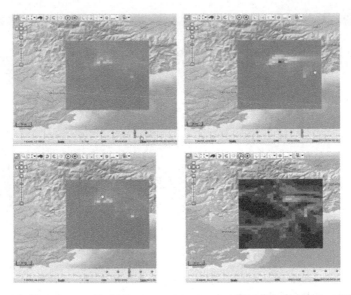

Fig. 5. Time Series of coverage maps animated by GeoData Visualisation Portlet

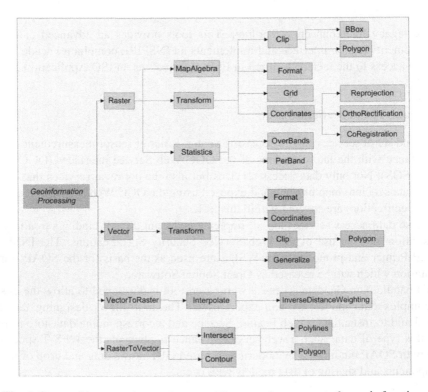

Fig. 6. Geographic processing services providing a ready-to-use set of generic functions

2.3 Data Processing Services

A third set of services deals with data processing including data fusion, geo data processing and decision support services. The data fusion services covers several aspects such as merging of several data formats, execution of thematic algorithms expressed with OpenMath language using a computation engine, processing of alerts. In addition a set of robust geographic processing web services have been developed that cover typical GIS and EO processing requirements. All these services are using the OGC WPS interface with SOAP binding and some improvements to support long running processes and asynchronous messaging using WS-Addressing. Tools have been developed to support the deployment of such services and to automatically generate the configuration files for instantiating the GENESIS WPS client interfaces inside the GENESIS Portal.

These processing services produce results that may need to be archived for later discovery and access. This is the purpose of the Archiving and Resources Management Services (ARMS) also published as specific OGC WPS profile which can store data on different servers such as FTP, WFS, WCS in a consistent way with extracted result meta-information inserted in a connected catalogue. Reporting services have been added to present data according to customizable report template and to some selected file format (PDF, HTML, ...). Reporting services are available as web services that can be invoked either from a dedicated reporting portlet user interface or from any other web service client.

2.4 Orchestration Services

On top of these web services, a workflow engine allows to chain and or automate web services execution e.g. processing chains, execution of simultaneous search requests in several remote catalogues. The orchestration is facilitated by the ARMS that provide a durable persistence of several types of resources and also a uniform way to address them using a URN. This should solve the classical input/output parameters mapping issues in the processes chaining. To remove the complexity of designing service orchestrations (based on WS-BPEL standard), an Orchestration Design GUI allows non-technical users to construct orchestration workflows in a very simple manner by drag-and-drop of preconfigured "services" onto a workflow area. This GUI produces output according to the BPEL4WS1.1 and OASIS WS-BPEL2.0 standards and deploys this output via to a WPS-T interface to the either the PEtALS EasyBPEL engine either to the Oracle BPEL engine following the GENESIS philosophy to propose several alternatives for the different components among COTS and Open Source Software solutions.

2.5 Genesis Service Portal

A generic portal proposes user interfaces to interact with the previously defined web services (orchestration services, discovery services, processing services ...). The portal is components (portlets) based allowing easy integration of additional web user interface components compliant with JSR-286. It includes a number of templates that allows to easily instantiate portal user interface to interact with remote web services based on standards interfaces such as OGC CSW, WPS...

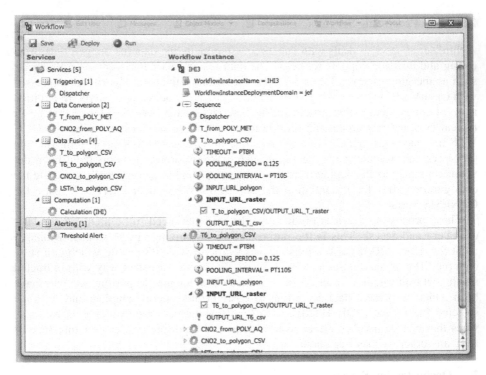

Fig. 7. Orchestration design tool allowing to simply chain services with any BPEL knowledge

A portal factory toolkit simplifies the portal customization in terms of look and feel (themes), portlets available on the different portal pages. The portal proposes standard portlet such as news, user management and also new portlets such as decision support, system supervision. Thanks to its connection to a SKOS repository with multilingual terms, the catalogue user interface on the portal shall allow users to define queries on catalogues based on terms of their own language. One of these dedicated portlets, the Geodata Visualisation provides a graphical user interface to interact via a map with the different data access services (WMS, WCS, SOS...) offering the user not only to select features on the map such as an area of interest but also to display processing results such as animated map, all kinds of data charts...

A security layer based on relevant international standards (WS-Security, XACML SAML,...) including the authentication and authorization services protects the access to the services based on rules configured in front of each service provider site. These rules authorize the access to the service based on the identity of the service invoker (generally user on the portal) and also based on the service input message information.

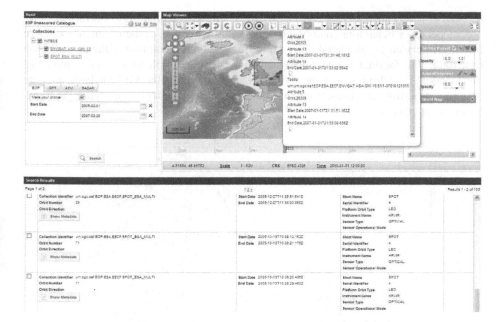

Fig. 8. Portal Earth Observation Products Catalogue Client

3 Genesis Pilots

To validate the pertinence of the GENESIS solution, our pilots deploy thematic applications based on our components with the aim of fulfilling the requirement of their
own users. As can be seen in the following descriptions, this covers a quite large
range of topics.

The pilot AQ-1 in Bavaria (Germany) aims at supporting the derivation and application of an Integrated Health Index (IHI) for the combined impact of meteorological
(temperature variations, humidity) and air quality (ozone, nitrogen dioxide, particulate
matter) parameters for elderly people affected by COPD (Chronic Obstructive
Pulmonary Disease). In the diagnosis mode medical information from regional ambulance databases is used to train the IHI algorithm. GENESIS provides specific visualization tools for data screening and standard pre-processing tools for the integration of
the environment and health data with a spatial background data set, i.e. postal code
areas. As the statistical analysis needs to deal with large data amounts to assure statistical significance from potentially different databases, the GENESIS solution offers a
high benefit for this analysis work. With the IHI algorithm designed, daily forecast
maps of the IHI for all Bavaria and adjacent regions are calculated as baseline for
information services for citizens affected by COPD or medical staff. The IHI calculation and visualization use web processing and web-GIS functionalities provided by
the GENESIS solution.

The pilot AQ-2 uses GIS technology to trace statistical trajectories of individual
persons and population groups throughout the day in the Greater London area. Here
the underlying GMES information used are daily forecast maps of high resolution

(i.e. street level) air pollutant concentrations. Using GIS technology and further datasets of person's behaviour (indoor, outdoor, way to work, ….) the pollutant exposure for single persons is calculated, fully exploiting the high resolution of the air pollution base data. This facilitates epidemiological studies, for example to assess the impact of the London Low Emission Zone. GENESIS tools enable the GIS analysis and the integration of different datasets into a standardized environment simplifying the transfer of the approach tested to other regions.

Fig. 9. The six GENESIS pilots covering 6 countries and 3 thematic topics (Air Quality, Water Quality and Health)

In the area around Nice, pilot AQ-3 investigates the derivation and application of a health risk index for air pollution and pollen information regarding elderly people affected with asthma. This region has significant episodes of pollen and high pollutant concentrations and is inhabited by large population and many tourists during summer. The collaboration with hospitals and pharmaceutical networks provides medical information for the development and validation of the approach. GENESIS supports the integration of the different data sets and their joint processing. In addition, an interactive interface to collect patient feedback on their individual health conditions related to the forecasted risk index is beeing designed and demonstrated using GENESIS tools.

The pilot WQ-1 – Oder/Odra estuary deals with the question of trans-boundary river basin management.. The pilot aims to forecast, inform and alert the population in case of a biological or accidental pollution risk. It addresses issues like accidental contamination, transport of pollutants and risks of virus infections in the estuary as well as the water transparency during summer. The principal aim of the Oder/Odra estuary pilot is the provision of an online information system for users interested in the hygienic water quality of the Oder/Odra lagoon. The system also supports sanitary inspectors in deciding about a bathing ban on the beaches. The interface between scientific insights and their implications for the water quality on the one hand and the users and their concerns on the other hand will be provided by an interactive website to be developed in the last year of the GENESIS project.

In second Water Quality Pilot (WQ-2), the site of Villerest artificial lake on the Loire river is used as a model to study and test the relevance of the application of remote sensing techniques combined with in-situ monitoring of cyanobacteria concentration in a large-sized aquatic ecosystem. This site was chosen because it shelters every year a proliferation of the toxic cyanobacteria Microcystis Aeruginosa. These proliferations are difficult to be monitored because of the strong heterogeneity of the spatial distribution of the cyanobacteria. This heterogeneity requires multiple samplings to obtain a good estimation of the intensity of the proliferation on the scale of the reservoir, especially to anticipate the problems arising in particular locations of the lake such as the bathing, recreational and fishing zones.

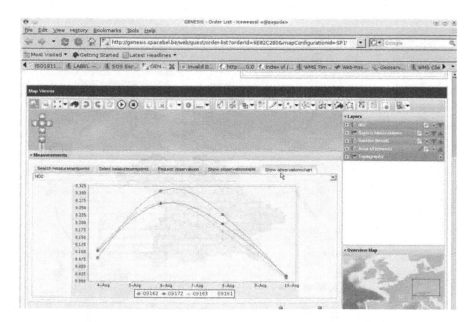

Fig. 10. AQ1 Pilot example – Average NO2 density time series for selected Bavarian sites

206   S. Bonnot et al.

The last pilot focuses on Lake Constance is a transboundary lake shared between Germany, Switzerland and Austria and the important drinking water reservoir. More than 4 Mio inhabitants are supplied by the clean lake water without considerable treatment. In recent years a comprehensive information system called Boden-seeOnline was developed in a cooperative research project. To enhance the ability of BodenseeOnline to serve as a decision support system, the GENESIS Project framework is used. The pilot has a special part of the project as it only started during the last year of the project to check that it was possible to address a new application with GENESIS generic components. They are using the same software package and receive support as if they were real external users, allowing to validate the soundness of the GENESIS approach.

4 Genesis Actors

In order to efficiently set up such system, different roles have been identified. *Technology developers* implement the various generic components based on the most appropriate and up to date technology. These generic components are then instantiated by *service providers* to implement the needed services with the support of thematic experts. These different services are then progressively connected together by the *system integrators*.

Once the system has been integrated, it can be validated by the *experts* and then finally offer to the *end users* which can be the man in the street as well decision makers.

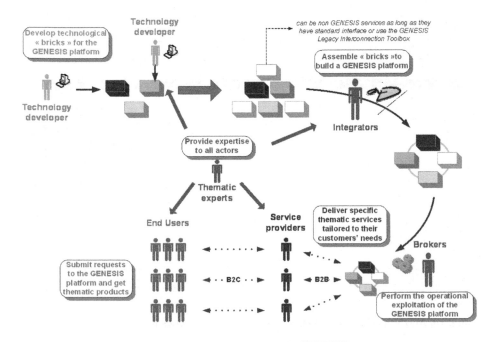

Fig. 11. All actors involved in GENESIS

Note that this full lifecycle is implemented inside the FP7 GENESIS project. A dedicated team is in charge of the system integration and maintenance of a reference platform where all most GENESIS components are installed. This system on this reference platform is validated with end-to-end scenarios representative of thematic usage. Within the GENESIS project itself, the system performance and robustness is further experimented through six different thematic pilots, covering various aspects of Air Quality and Water Quality monitoring, such as integrated health index computation in Bavaria (Germany), daily pollutant exposure for individual persons in London, trans-boundary river basin management Oder Odra estuary (Poland)...

5 Conclusion

GENESIS solution proposes a number of components including a Portal and Web Services based on up to date standards, technologies and European directives such as INSPIRE. Users have the choice of selecting isolated components or to rely on the integrated system to build their environmental application. The project is in its final stage working in parallel on the exploitation plan and the last validation phase by different pilot applications in the Air Quality and Water Quality domain.

Reference

1. FP7 GENESIS Public Web Site, http://www.genesis-fp7.eu/ (including a download page for the GENESIS Open Source components and a forum dedicated to user support)

An Environmental Decision Support System for Water Issues in the Oil Industry

Ralf Denzer[1], Fernando Torres-Bejarano[2], Thorsten Hell[3], Steven Frysinger[1,4], Sascha Schlobinski[3], Reiner Güttler[1], and Hermilo Ramírez[2]

[1] Environmental Informatics Group (EIG), Goebenstrasse 40, 66117 Saarbrücken, Germany
[2] Mexican Petroleum Institute (IMP), Eje Central Lázaro Cárdenas
152 Mexico D.F., Mexico
[3] cismet GmbH, Altenkesseler Strasse 17, 66115 Saarbrücken
[4] James Madison University, Harrisonburg, Virginia, USA 22807
ralf.denzer@enviromatics.org

Abstract. Many decision makers are hindered in their daily work by "un-integrated" systems which can force them to move data around between tools which are only more or less compatible. Because environmental models play an important role in environmental decision support systems, the integration of models into user-friendly integrated decision support systems is essential to the support of such users. This paper presents a decision support system supporting users involved in the protection of the Coatzacoalcos River in Mexico near the largest agglomeration of petrochemical installations in Mexico, which are operated by the Mexican oil company Petroleos Mexicanos. At the same time, the area is densely populated and important for agriculture.

The system was built in a collaboration of the Mexican Petroleum Institute, the Environmental Informatics Group, and cismet GmbH and is based on cismet's geospatial application suite called *cids*. It integrates several tools and models into a holistic, user-centered application.

Keywords: Environmental decision support; environmental information systems; oil pollution; environmental model integration.

1 Introduction

Management of environmental challenges is inevitably complex. Many technical disciplines are involved, and a tremendous amount of information must be interpreted in order to arrive at rational and effective management decisions. Even highly trained environmental managers are challenged by the breadth of the decision problems they face.

Therefore, environmental information systems that can help environmental managers to arrive at high-quality decisions are indispensable. The present paper describes an environmental decision support system (EDSS) that integrates mathematical process models of environmental phenomena with geographic information systems (GIS) technology in order to support petroleum facility managers as they attempt to determine which resource management actions will be most effective in the reduction of

J. Hřebíček, G. Schimak, and R. Denzer (Eds.): ISESS 2011, IFIP AICT 359, pp. 208–216, 2011.

surface water degradation related to petroleum processing within an important watershed in Mexico.

The Coatzacoalcos River in Mexico is challenged by several petroleum processing facilities. An environmental decision support system, called ANAITE, has been developed to help environmental managers minimize the impact of oil processing on the surface water quality of the river. The ANAITE EDSS is described in this paper.

2 Requirements of End Users

In any interactive computing system, understanding the needs and capabilities of the users is essential to a successful design of the systems to support them. This is certainly true of environmental decision support systems, whose users are often technically trained but not completely comfortable with information technology, or even all of the technical aspects of the decision problems they face.

That is the case with the ANAITE decision support system. The first version of the system targets a primary user who is a technical manager of an oil processing facility. This type of user is trained in process, chemical, or environmental engineering, and is trying to determine which interventions at this facility will achieve the greatest gains in water quality for the invested resources.

ANAITE is heavily based on sophisticated mathematical models of hydrodynamics and the advective-dispersive transport of pollutants. However, it is important to know that the primary end users of the system are *not* modelers. They will very likely be aware of the existence and use of mathematical models describing water quality, and it is assumed that they value, and to some extent trust the results of such models, at least under circumstances appropriate to their use. But their interest is for the EDSS to insulate them from technical details of the model so that they can, instead, focus on their domain, namely making operational decisions that will impact water quality.

2.1 Focus on What Is Needed

The principal upon which ANAITE, like other effective environmental decision support systems, is based is that decision makers facing multidisciplinary problems *cannot* be experts in all aspects of these problems. Scientists, mathematicians, engineers, and other specialized experts may have produced, in their respective domains, important insights that would be extremely relevant to a particular decision problem. However, if these insights are not delivered to decision makers in an accessible form, they will not help. Indeed, they may hinder high quality decision making by so thoroughly obfuscating the decision making process that even "good guesses" are hard to make. Stated more succinctly, decision makers need "computer support which provides everything that they need, but *only* what they need" [1].

2.2 Needs Analysis

In an interactive process between the project partners, a systematic analysis of the users' needs was carried out. While a few different categories of users were identified, the first among these – the primary user – is the environmental manager already mentioned. The first version of the ANAITE EDSS focuses on this primary user. This analysis shows that the environmental manager making the decisions about how best to invest in pollution mitigation needs to use models but, though technically trained, is not a modeler. Therefore, a key requirement of the ANAITE EDSS is the ability to integrate sophisticated mathematical models of water quality and pollutant behavior without requiring the user to interact directly with these models.

It also became clear that access to available data about the catchment in question would be critical – again without expecting the decision maker to know how to find or manipulate these data. And representations of these data would need to be easy to interpret, with representations specifically designed for the particular decisions the user needs to make. This means that the EDSS would have to make it particularly easy to access and represent environmental data, and, following an important precept of good human/computer interface design, allow movement of data between various domains, to include conventional data plots, spatial representations, analytical tools and so forth in an integrated fashion.

The first level analysis reveals use cases in the following major areas

- Administrative-level activities (maintenance of users, data, information sources, external services etc.)
- Management, display and visualization of facility-related information (chemical plants, their location, extent, risks and so forth)
- Management, display and visualization of data related to the geography of the area (population, installations, etc.)
- Notification, reporting, potentially alerting
- Configuration of models and model runs, including choice of initial conditions
- Execution of models, documentation of model runs
- Visualization of simulation results, in context with geographic and facility-related information, various cross-sections through data both in time and space
- Storing and management of simulation results
- Management and execution of complete simulation ensembles (i.e. simulations with variations over parameters and initial conditions)

All use cases have in common that users be relieved from notorious time consuming tasks like managing model input and output data sets, moving data between tools and overcoming intricacies of tool incompatibility. Therefore a holistic solution is needed both for data/model/system management and for scientific analysis including interactive visualization.

3 Details of the Application

Using the *cids* platform (which will be described in chapter 4), it was straightforward to design an EDSS that gives users direct access to data from various sources, to see this information in a spatial context, and to drill down into more in-depth information to help them understand what they're looking at. Figure 1 shows the main screen of the ANAITE EDSS.

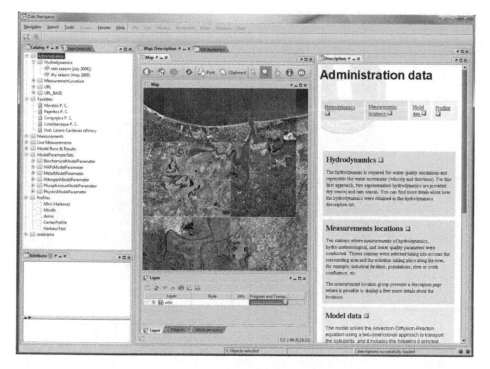

Fig. 1. Main screen of ANAITE

The user can interact with the information using three main paradigms: 1) the catalog (left part of main screen), 2) a spatial view (center part), and 3) data, model results and so forth including background information (rightmost part of main screen, as well as various other tabs). It is worth noting the obvious importance given to the spatial display of information. Environmental management problems are fundamentally spatial, and environmental managers are keenly aware of "place" when it comes to making management decisions. Therefore, spatial representations of the sort provided by geographic information systems (GIS) are a natural component of an EDSS. But a GIS itself is not an EDSS, primarily because standard GIS products provide far more options than are needed by a decision maker, and therefore are not well customized for users. Rather, elements of GIS are drawn into successful EDSS implementations only as needed. The ability to use spatial data already available from GIS datasets further promotes the use of compatible GIS components in EDSS implementations. Figure 2 shows an ANAITE screen in which GIS maps of the Coatzacoalcos River region are made available to the decision maker in a way which does not require them to be GIS experts.

A particularly useful characteristic of the ANAITE EDSS is that the users need not take special action to move data from the non-spatial to the spatial domain. When they discover a data set of interest, perhaps a set of water quality measurements made during a particular study, they need only drag this data set onto the spatial display window for the system to use embedded spatial information in the data to represent

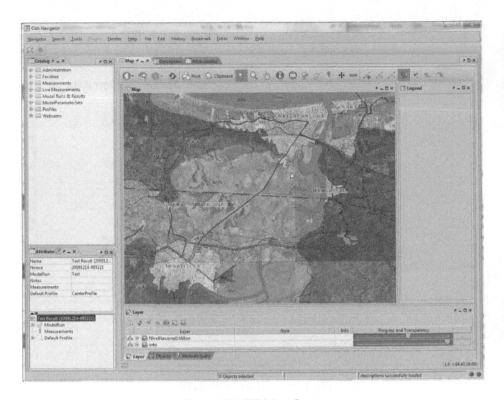

Fig. 2. ANAITE Maps Screen

them on the map. This sort of capability removes the burden of data formatting and management expertise from the primary user and allows them to focus instead on their environmental decision domain. Systems lacking such support generally preclude use by decision makers not possessing significant information systems expertise, which is one reason that many EDSS implementations in the past have gone unused by real decision makers.

ANAITE is designed to support "what if" scenario analyses in which the environmental manager postulates different values for chemical discharges into the river, at different locations, in order to see what impact these changes might have at various points along the river. A significant level of human analysis is required to compare the results of various scenarios, because water quality requirements or expectations generally differ at different locations. For example, one location might be where a town has an intake for a drinking water supply, another might include a swimming beach, and a third might be an important fishery. Acceptable variations in water quality for these three examples must be judged in their social, as well as technical, contexts, a task only effectively done by a human being.

To do this requires representation of the modeling and simulation results to the environmental manager in a way which is readily interpreted by them, and generally using a variety of techniques. For example, in Figure 3 one can see an overview of water quality variations computed by the various models for a scenario in their spatial context, along with information about co-located social structures.

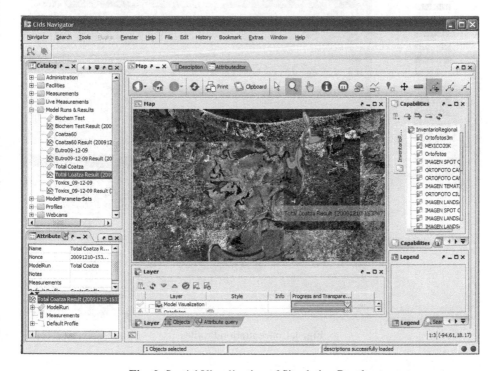

Fig. 3. Spatial Visualization of Simulation Results

In Figure 4 one can see these same results with a more precise representation of their quantitative values, albeit without most of the spatial context present. This flexibility of representation, again without the requirement of special information systems expertise, is a great facilitator of high quality decision-making.

4 System Platform

ANAITE has been implemented using the geo-spatial application suite *cids* of cismet Gmbh. *Cids* is both a distributed integration platform for distributed geo-spatial environments, and a highly integrated software development environment for interactive geo-spatial systems.

Cids has been developed and improved over more than 10 years and has been heavily driven by the WuNDa city information system [2]. At the core is a distributed integration platform (Figure 5) which is capable of integrating information and processes from a variety of different systems such as GIS systems, standard databases,

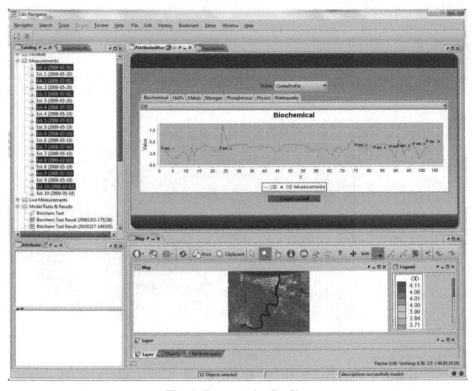

Fig. 4. Concentration Profiles

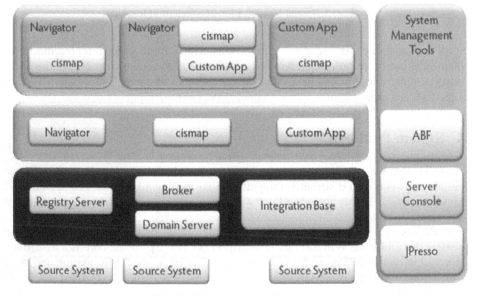

Fig. 5. *cids* platform architecture

document management systems, computational systems like models and so forth. The platform is particular useful for workflows which need a combination of information and processes from different source systems.

The core contains a domain-based service layer and a distributed meta database (registry server, broker, domain server, integration base), which jointly manage the network of attached data sources and services. Spatial services are integrated according to OGC standards, and the platform is compliant with OGC standards as well. The management of the service network is carried out with a variety of systems management tools, with a Netbeans-based *cids*-IDE (named ABF) in the centre. The platform includes distributed user management, authorisation and domain management for customisation according to the structure of the organisation and workflows. The platform includes a sophisticated access management component and can be personalised for user groups and individual users. Computational processes like the ANAITE models are generally integrated through OGC WPS compliant services.

The end user usually interacts with the system through two types of applications. The Navigator is a standard application deployed with all installations. It can be used to manage the information in the network and is particularly useful for cross-system search and retrieval, in space, time and topic. The Navigator is often used for *ad hoc* activities, which have not been pre-defined as work flows. The Navigator views are usually customised to the information classes which the particular organisation manages (both for space and themes).

The second type of applications are Custom Applications, specialised spatial/non-spatial workflows which support specific end user tasks. These CustomApps can also be shown inside the Navigator using a Plugin mechanism.

The ANAITE implementation is based on the Navigator.

5 Integration of Models

The integration of models into an EDSS raises both technical and scientific issues. From a technical perspective, it causes some overhead for application developers. In the case of ANAITE, the wrapping of the models was not really done in a systematic way, due to constraints of time and resources in the project. Model integration usually goes along with integration of sensor information and integration of model results. In ANAITE all computational processes have been integrated in an *ad hoc* fashion by wrapping them into *arbitrary* web services. Results are stored back into the sensor data bases and as OGC compliant layers for visualization.

In order to integrate models and associated input and output data sets, including sensors, in a systematic way, one should usually use standards of the OGC SWE suite and similar standards including the WPS specifications (Web Processing Service) [3]. A systematic approach to linking such models, including related sensor information, should include approaches like the ones forwarded in SANY [4]. Projects like SUD-PLAN [5] [6] are currently advancing such systematic concepts.

But from a scientific perspective, model integration includes important *conceptual* issues such as harmonization of modeling assumptions, and the application of model calibration and validation techniques [7]. While beyond the scope of the present paper, it is important to recognize that one cannot simply "plug" two models together and expect the results to be meaningful. In the case of ANAITE, the hydrodynamic and advective-dispersive models were co-developed in a way which ensured their compatibility. The cids platform then allowed them to be integrated, as a partnership, into the resulting environmental decision support system.

References

1. Frysinger, S.P.: Environmental Decision Support Systems: A Tool for Environmentally Conscious Management. In: Madu, C.N. (ed.) Handbook for Environmentally Conscious Manufacturing, Kluwer Academic Publishers, Dordrecht (2001)
2. Güttler, R., Denzer, R., Houy, P.: An EIS Called WuNDa, Environmental Software Systems. Environmental Information and Decision Support, vol. 3, pp. 114–121. Kluwer Academic Publishers, Dordrecht (2000)
3. Douglas, J., Usländer, T., Schimak, G., Esteban, J.F., Denzer, R.: An Open Distributed Architecture for Sensor Networks for Risk Management. Journal Sensors 8, 1755–1773 (2008)
4. Havlik, D.: SANY Final Activity Report (D1.1.5.1 Publishable Final Activity Report) (2010), http://sany-ip.eu/filemanager/active?fid=320
5. Gidhagen, L., Denzer, R., Schlobinski, S., Michel, F., Kutschera, P., Havlik, D.: Sustainable Urban Development Planner for Climate Change Adaptation (SUDPLAN). In: Proceedings of ENVIP 2010 Workshop at EnviroInfo2010, "Environmental Information Systems and Services - Infrastructures and Platforms", Bonn, October 6-8. CEUR-WS, vol. 679 (2010) ISSN 1613-0073, urn:nbn:de:0074-679-9
6. Denzer, R., Schlobinski, S., Gidhagen, L.: A Decision Support System for Urban Climate Change Adaptation. In: Proceedings of the 44th Hawaii International Conference on System Sciences (HICSS-44), CDROM. IEEE Computer Society, Los Alamitos (2011)
7. Frysinger, S.P.: Integrative Environmental Modeling. In: Clarke, K.C., Parks, B.E., Crane, M.P. (eds.) Geographic Information Systems and Environmental Modeling. Prentice Hall, Englewood Cliffs (2002)

Open Environmental Platforms:
Top-Level Components and Relevant Standards

Dumitru Roman[1], Sven Schade[2], and Arne J. Berre[1]

[1] SINTEF, Oslo, Norway
{dumitru.roman,arne.j.berre}@sintef.no
[2] Institute for Environment and Sustainability,
Joint Research Centre of the European Commission, Ispra, Italy
sven.schade@jrc.ec.europa.eu

Abstract. We present our ideas of an open Information and Communication Technology (ICT) platform for monitoring, mapping and managing our environment. The envisioned solution bridges the gap between the Internet of Things, Content and Services, and highly specific applications, such as oil spill detection or marine monitoring. On the one hand, this environmental platform should be open to new technologies; on the other hand, it has to provide open standard interfaces to various application domains. We identify core components, standards, and needs for new standard development in ICT for environment. We briefly outline how our past and present activities contribute to the development of the desired open environmental platform. Future implementations shall contribute to sustainable developments in the environmental domain.

Keywords: open environmental platform, infrastructure, architecture, standards.

1 Introduction

The Shared Environmental Information System (SEIS)[1] is one of three recent major initiatives along with the INSPIRE Directive (European Parliament and Council 2007) and the Global Monitoring for Environment and Security (GMES)[2] undertaken by Europe to collect and share environmental information for the benefit of the global society. ICT have an essential role to play in the context of environmental information systems as they provide the necessary support in terms of tools, systems and protocols to establish a dynamic environmental space of collaboration in a more and more sophisticated digital world. Core challenges are not only related to providing seamless environmental data access to public authorities, businesses and the public at large, but also to allowing for interoperable environmental services based on Web technologies, and stimulating new market opportunities[3]. ICT for environmental collaboration is widely recognised as a major step for addressing complex management issues including adaptation to climate change and sustainable management of urban environment.

---

[1] http://ec.europa.eu/environment/seis/, last accessed 11th January 2011
[2] http://www.gmes.info/, last accessed 11th January 2011
[3] http://ec.europa.eu/information_society/digital-agenda/, last accessed 11th January 2011

J. Hřebíček, G. Schimak, and R. Denzer (Eds.): ISESS 2011, IFIP AICT 359, pp. 217–225, 2011.

The European Commission recently funded several projects[4] in the area of ICT for Sustainable Growth, with a core focus on ICT for Environmental Services and Climate Change aiming at providing the foundations for an infrastructure for monitoring, predicting and managing the environment and its natural resources.

Current research problems addressed by such projects are centred on frameworks, methods, concepts, models, languages and technologies that enable enhanced environmental service infrastructures and platforms (e.g. the ENVISION project [7]). Environmental Information Systems are migrating towards being provided as Software as a Service (SaaS) and will benefit from the utilization and specialization of emerging Infrastructures as a Service (IaaS) and Platforms as a Service (PaaS) as this is emerging under the umbrella of Cloud computing as well as the evolution of the Future Internet[5] with its three core pillars: an Internet of Services, where applications live in the network, and data becomes an active entity, an Internet of Content, where most of the contents are generated by end-users, and an Internet of Things (IoT), where every electronic device will be an active participant in the network [11]. Cost effective design, development and deployment of environmental models and applications in this context requires novel platforms to emerge, and inter-connect, inter-operate and inter-work with each other and with platforms for other verticals. Of particular interest are the architectural foundations of infrastructures and platforms supporting flexible discovery and chaining of distributed environmental services and content, and showing how they combine synergistically to enable better collaborations on the scale required by Future Internet connected environments. This will foster a greater understanding of how open environmental service infrastructures and platforms can enable enhanced collaboration between public authorities, businesses and the general public for a better management of the environment and its natural resources. In this paper, we look at the architectural foundations of open environmental infrastructures and platforms, and propose top-level components of an open architecture (Section 2). We also identify standards relevant to architectures of environmental infrastructures and platforms (Section 3). Standards of ICT for environment are addressed in most detail. We conclude this paper with some challenges (Section 4).

2   Top-Level Components of the Environmental Monitoring Platform

The basic architecture of the suggested open environmental platform is depicted in Figure 1. The core platform (three layers in the middle) bridges the gap between the Internet of Things and end-user applications, such as marine monitoring or air quality monitoring and reporting. A relation of the suggested components with the Internet of Services and Internet of Content is depicted in addition. In the remainder of this section, we detail each of these layers (from bottom to the top). Notably, the complete environmental platform may be offered as a service in itself and by this mean implement the Platform as a Service (PaaS) concept.

---

[4] http://cordis.europa.eu/fp7/ict/sustainable-growth/environment_en.html,
   last accessed 11th January 2011.
[5] http://www.future-internet.eu/

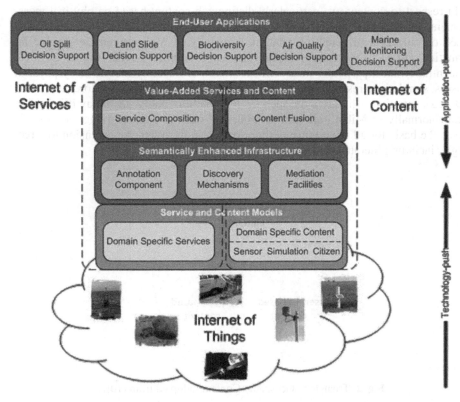

Fig. 1. Top-level Components of the Open Environmental Platform

2.1 Service and Content Models

On the bottom level of the platform (Service and Content Models), the diverse re-sources that are available from the IoT are aggregated into domain specific compo-nents, which encapsulate content, as well as access and processing services that are adopted to domain specific needs. We put particular emphasis on the use of open standards and flexibility of the proposed platform. We have to account for new tech-nologies that need to be integrated (technology-push).

Functionalities, non-functional aspects, as well as behaviours of the objects pro-vided by the IoT need to be encapsulated and properly described in order to create a certain level of abstraction on top of which other added-value services can be created. At this level, depending on the types of objects that need to be abstracted, various types of services are created that hide the technicalities and access details of the IoT objects. Examples of such services include sensor services (accessing real-time sensor data well defined interfaces), data services (providing access to relatively static data such as geographical features), or processing services (providing access to geospatial processing, simulations, and other resource-intensive processes). An important chal-lenge here is the development of proper conceptual models for services, that can be customized and extended for different domains.

In respect to content, we particularly distinguish content based on physical measurements by sensors, content based on environmental simulation/models, and content based on citizen contributed information, especially on Volunteered Geographic information (VGI) [3]. Taking air quality as an example, current values for CO_2 concentration on a particular measurement station are usually measured by physical sensors, simulations result in an areal coverage of CO_2 or in temporal forecasts of the CO_2 concentration, while reports, such as 'it's smelling badly' or 'today it is hard to breath normally in Milan', are part of VGI. For us, this content triangle (Figure 2) serves the basis for all environmental information in the Web. An extension to a rectangle, including literature based content, could be discussed.

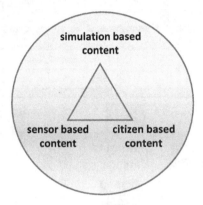

Fig. 2. Triangle of Geospatial Content (adopted from [10])

Specific content models rely on vocabulary generation, conceptual data modelling, and encodings that have to be developed in each specific domain. Inputs from the IoT are wrapped according to each (domain) specific model including required adapters on data types and values. In order to ease interoperability within and across domains, it is desirable to establish a common generic model for integrating content coming from each of the identified kinds of sources (sensor, citizen and simulation) more easily. Nevertheless, the actual integration task is part of the next layer.

2.2 Semantically Enhanced Infrastructure

At its intermediate layer in Figure 1 (Semantically Enhanced Infrastructure), the Open Environmental Platform provides harmonized access to the IoT. It facilitates semantic discovery based on annotations. Harmonized access to the IoT is provided in form of mediators that provide encapsulating services.

Semantic annotation should be used to describe the intended interpretation of services and content. Resource descriptions shall make use of existing domain vocabularies and ontologies. This requires (i) tools for creating vocabularies, ontologies and resource descriptions, and (ii) according storage facilities. Discovery mechanisms shall facilitate these descriptions and provide human users and machines with the capabilities to search for desired services or content using their own expressions or a predefined set of domain terms/concepts. For example, users may be provided with terms in English, French and German, whereas the initial resources are only described in English. Once a resource or a set of resources has been discovered, users have to be able to retrieve it. This process may include mediation, i.e. the translation of the initial domain model of a provided resource into that of the consumer. Apart from natural language translations, this may include unit conversions or more sophisticated schema mapping rules [12].

2.3 Value-Added Services and Content

The third layer of the architecture (Value-Added Services and Content) supports the creation of added value products by offering methodologies and facilities for content fusion and service composition. This layer makes use of the semantic discovery and mediation mechanisms provided by the semantically enhanced infrastructure and to access services or content coming from physical sensors, (environmental) simulations and citizen, as well as contextual information on the targeted added value chain.

The design of service compositions for creation of added-value services on top of atomic services encapsulating the different object provided by the IoT, requires the use a graphical language to allow for user-friendly specification of service chains by domain experts as well as users with little technical skills. The composition language needs to provide a sufficient level of abstraction, while still enabling sufficient level of detail so that the graphical service compositions can be used to generate complete executable service descriptions. The composition language must be able to compose different kinds of services including sensor, data, and processing services, as well as to express control and data flow dependencies between such services. A language based on (a subset of) the emerging Business Process Modelling Notation (BPMN) standard [6], extended with declarative features for flexible modelling of compositions and explicit treatment of data mediation and uncertainty would be a proper candidate for addressing the representational needs of environmental service compositions.

Given the harmonised access to data and the specified context, for example using air quality data for calculating individual exposure indexes, Content Fusion components provide the means for streamlining the available data to a particular use. Sabeur et al. proposed four fusion levels [8]:

o   Fusion level 0 provides prepossessing of data, such as smoothing, interpolation, and re-formatting;
o   Fusion level 1 offers algorithms for auto-correlation and Fourier analysis and the like, in order to identify objects or trends in the incoming data;
o   Fusion level 2 includes phenomenology models for estimating and refining previous fusion results; and
o   Fusion level 3 provides prediction and correction information, for example based on Kalman filtering.

The value added content can be exposed after each of the fusion steps and may serve input to multiple further processing steps. In this way, it provides manifold contributions to the Internet of Content. Notably, the modelling and propagation of uncertainties should be considered in the complete fusion process. This will require a quantification of initial errors and vagueness in the raw data coming from the lower levels of the proposed platform.

2.4 End-User Applications

Complementary to the technology-push, novel developments have to account for arising user requirements (application-pull). Otherwise, implementing sophisticated technology solutions, which are not used in the mid- and long-term, might be exciting, but remain a unprofitable exercise. In the following we outline a subset of the manifold applications, which should be supported by open environmental platforms. Their specific technical and non-technical requirements will help to sharpen the specifications of the components on the lower layers of the proposed solution and thereby to develop a flexible solution for information systems that account for all environmental spheres, including the atmospheric, terrestrial and marine domains.

Ground instabilities caused by *mud flows, landslides* or *ground failure* may cause significant physical and socio-economic damage in many regions of the world. Being able to correctly forecast such phenomena for proper prevention and mitigation implies the availability of and access to relevant environmental models, data, and services, and the ability of combining them in meaningful ways. Issues such as finding a landslide risk model with specific characteristics, which produces the required output data that fits given input data, chaining models for creating value added services such as landslide risk assessment models and making them accessible for the wider community pose great challenges for discovery and composition of both services and content.

Biodiversity related applications add user-contributed content as an important aspect to data acquisition. While many environmental monitoring applications reply on classical sensors, and environmental simulation and modelling, the biodiversity community retrieves large amounts of information from volunteers, which post their observations on species occurrences on diverse networking platforms. Birdwatch[6] provides one of the many impressive examples, in this case related to the occurrence of birds. The handling, quality assurance, and integration of such information is public authority data, such as protected sites, particularly challenges content fusion and semantic content descriptions.

Among others, *air quality monitoring* bear the challenge of assessing individualized exposure. Today, we have easy access to a great deal of information via television, radio and the World Wide Web. This includes pollution, pollen and meteorological data which are all relatively easily accessed in one or more dissemination channels. All this data contributes to a common sense, but it is not tailored to individual user needs. Relevancy of data and interpreting it are key issues for users today, especially with regards to pollen and pollution. The envisioned platform shall therefore aid the users in tailoring information relevant to their individual requirements, which again poses requirements on the functionalities for implementing the added value chain from general purpose to individualised information.

For the *marine domain*, the challenge is to create synergies with the market and with policy needs that are necessary to deliver significant value added to Europe from its vast marine resources. Enabling technology platforms are currently deployed across a range of existing marine related sectors including shipping, security and logistics, environmental monitoring and offshore energy. Next generation platforms

---

[6] http://www.birdwatch.co.uk/

have to dissolve national borders. They shall address these developments in respect to distributed sensing, and wireless and cable communications. In the marine domain, *oil spills* are an extremely sensitive topic. Accidental oil releases to the sea may have severe environmental, social and economic consequences, with vital natural resources and human enterprises being at risk. For oil spill decision making, it is essential to be able to predict the fate and effects of the spilled oil. Fate prediction requires data on the spill (location, time, amount, oil type), the environmental conditions (wind, current), and geography (sea depths, coast line). Effects prediction is based on data about natural resources (e.g. fish populations). Being able to combine such data (possibly made available through service) in real-time for prediction of the fate of the oil spill implies sophisticated discovery, composition, and integration mechanisms.

3 Relevant Standards

Open standards play a key role for interoperability between emerging environmental platforms. By only briefly pointing to standards etc. which have to be considered at the surrounding levels, we particularly focus on required standards on ICT for environment.

Depending on the exact field, end-user applications have to account for a large series of legal documents and standards. The UN Convention on Biodiversity, Clean Air for Europe, and the Marine Strategy Framework Directive are only some examples of these European and global Directives, Regulations and Strategies effecting particular environmental thematic areas. In total several hundred of similar texts apply to environmental monitoring on European and national level.

Value added services and content partially involve mainstream ICT standards, such as Business Process Modelling Notation (BPMN) [6] or Business Process Execution Language (BPEL) [5] for service composition. However, special standards and best practises exist for the environmental (and wider geospatial) community. Most notably, these include:

o   ISO 19119 (Geographic information — Services) [4] is a standard defined by the Technical Committee 211 (TC211) of the International Standardisation Organization (ISO). It defines the architecture patterns for service interfaces used for geographic information and presents a geographic services taxonomy which includes human interaction services, model/information management services, geographic processing services (spatial, thematic, temporal) and communication services. The standard includes guidelines for the selection and specification of geographic services from both platform-neutral and platform-specific perspectives. In fact, the various types of services proposed by this standard are relevant for all layers in Figure 1 where spatiotemporal aspects are relevant.

o   The Sensor Web Enablement (SWE) of the Open Geospatial Consortium (OGC) [1] provides standardized interfaces and metadata encodings that aim to enable real time integration of heterogeneous sensor webs into the information infrastructure. Sensor Model Language (SensorML), Observations & Measurements (O&M), Sensor Observations Service (SOS) are the most important specifications provided by SWE. These standards become highly relevant in relation to value added content and services. SWE standards currently undergo a phase of broad acceptance.

o   The Worl Wide Web Consortium (W3C) Semantic Sensor Network Incubator Group[7] developed ontologies that define the capabilities of sensors and sensor networks, and provides semantic annotations of a key language used by services based sensor networks. On top of its Semantic Web standards (RDF, OWL), W3C is setting the standards foundations for semantic interoperability (see also below).

The Semantically Enhanced Infrastructure layer serves the building blocks to the higher-level value-added components. Here, standards of the W3C Semantic Web community, such as the Resource Description Framework (RDF)[8] and the Web Ontology Language (OWL)[9] should be applied.

4   Challenges and Outlook

The realization of the desired open platform faces several challenges. For us, these include (ordered from the bottom layer of the platform to the top):

o   Interoperability in a heterogeneous environment: Dealing with resource discovery, processing support, service interfacing, and intermodal operation between heterogeneous types of resources. All of the above required semantically rich and extendible data models.

o   Advanced data mining: Including the handling of large volumes of data, pattern recognition depending on context, and data flow processing.

o   Data fusion with uncertainty analysis: Involving uncertainty and the combination of data and processing, but also the economic value of information from source to consumer. Security mechanisms and error-propagation are some of the required tools.

o   Dynamic service composition: Considering run-time identification of suitable service components, their bindings and execution.

o   User support: Covering generation of templates for end-user applications, best practices for application development and training.

As many prototype solutions already exist, issues of scalability, robustness, and quality of service are central to all of the listed issues [9]. An integrated approach, which is easy to instantiate, remains to be developed. The required balance between application-pull and technology-push can only be reached if the gap between platform developers and intended users can be bridged. This aspect is the most crucial for successful implementation.

We are currently addressing these issues within numerous de- (or loosely) coupled research projects. The Europe 2020 strategy[10] and two of its seven flagship initiatives (the Digital Agenda and Innovation Union) provide possibilities for long term funding.

---

[7] http://www.w3.org/2005/Incubator/ssn/wiki/Main_Page, last accessed 11th January 2011.
[8] http://www.w3.org/RDF/ http://www.w3.org/RDF/
[9] http://www.w3.org/TR/owl2-overview/
[10] http://www.europe2020.org/?lang=en, last accessed 11th January 2011.

Acknowledgements. The presented research has been partially funded by the ENVIROFI FP7 project (FP7-2011-ICT-FI-284898) and ENVISION project (249120).

References

1. Botts, M., Percivall, G., Reed, C., Davidson, J.: OGC® Sensor Web Enablement: Overview and High Level Architecture. In: Nittel, S., Labrinidis, A., Stefanidis, A. (eds.) GSN 2006. LNCS, vol. 4540, pp. 175–190. Springer, Heidelberg (2008)
2. European Parliament and Council. Directive 2007/2/EC of the European Parliament and of the Council of 14 March 2007 establishing an Infrastructure for Spatial Information in the European Community (INSPIRE). Official Journal on the European Parliament and of the Council (2007)
3. Goodchild, M.: Citizens as sensors: the world of volunteered geography. GeoJournal 69(4), 211–221 (2007)
4. ISO/TC211. 19119 Geographic Information - Services. ISO/TC211 Standards (2005)
5. OASIS, Web Services Business Process Execution Language Version 2.0. Committee Specification. OASIS WS-BPEL TC (2007)
6. OMG. Business Process Modeling Notation (BPMN) Version Beta 1 for version 2.0 - OMG Document Number: dtc/2009-08-14 (August 2009)
7. Roman, D., Schade, S., Berre, A.J., Bodsberg, N.R., Langlois, J.: Environmental Services Infrastructure with Ontologies – A Decision Support Framework. In: 23rd International Conference on Informatics for Environmental Protection (EnviroInfo 2009), Berlin, September 9-11, pp. 287–295. Shaker Verlag, Aachen (2009)
8. Sabeur, Z., Middleton, S., Veres, G., Zlatev, Z., Salvo, N.: Generic Sensor Data Fusion Services for Web-enabled Environmental Risk Management and Decision-Support Systems. In: European Geophysics Union, General Union Assembly, Vienna (May 2010)
9. Schade, S.: A Sensor Web for the Environment in Europe. In: Lemke, M. (ed.) 2nd Usage Area Workshop: Future Internet Initiative, Brussels, Belgium, June 21-22 (2010)
10. Schade, S., Craglia, M.: A Future Sensor Web for the Environment in Europe. In: EnviroInfo 2010, Cologne/Bonn, Germany (2010)
11. Vermesan, O., et al.: Internet of Things Strategic Research Roadmap. CERP-IoT 2009, Report Available at http://ec.europa.eu/information_society/policy/rfid/documents/in_cerp.pdf
12. Wache, H., Vögele, T., Visser, U., Stuckenschmidt, H., Schuster, G., Neumann, H., Hübner, S.: Ontology-Based Integration of Information - A Survey of Existing Approaches. In: IJCAI 2001 Workshop: Ontologies and Information Sharing, Seattle, WA (2001)

Best Practice Network GS SOIL
Promoting Access to European, Interoperable and INSPIRE Compliant Soil Information

Katharina Feiden[1], Fred Kruse[1], Tomáš Řezník[2], Petr Kubíček[2], Herbert Schentz[3], Einar Eberhardt[4], and Rainer Baritz[4]

[1] Coordination Center PortalU at the Lower Saxony Ministry of Environment and Climate Protection, Archivstr. 2, 30169 Hannover, Germany
[2] Masaryk University, Department of Geography, Laboratory on Geoinformatics and Cartography, Kotlářská 2, 61137 Brno, Czech Republic
[3] Umweltbundesamt GmbH, Spittelauer Lände 5, 1090 Vienna, Austria
[4] Federal Institute for Geosciences and Natural Resources, Information Systems Soil and Hydrogeology, Stilleweg 2, 30655 Hannover, Germany
gssoil@portalu.de

Abstract. INSPIRE provides the framework for the establishment of a European Spatial Data Infrastructure. The cross-border use and applicability of data requires that specific standards and rules are fulfilled by data providers. Such rules are currently being developed as data specifications. Soil as a theme in the INSPIRE annex III is included in this process, and was selected as the target theme for the EU best practice network GS SOIL „Assessment and strategic development of INSPIRE compliant Geodata-Services for European soil data". The project contributes to the harmonization and provision of interoperable soil geodata in Europe. The main deliverable of the project is the web portal http://gssoil-portal.eu/, which provides information, data management tools and links to data sources. Examples are the soil specific multilingual thesaurus, a metadata editor and catalogue service, provision of WMS and prototype WFS.

Keywords: INSPIRE, spatial data infrastructure, geoportal, soil data, metadata, data quality, thesaurus, controlled vocabulary, application schema, data specification.

Introduction

The best practice network is co-funded by the European Community programme eContentplus, by the European Commission DG Information Society and Media in the duration from June 2009 – May 2012.

The network consortium comprises 34 partners from 18 EU member states. Project Coordinator is the Coordination Center PortalU at the Lower Saxony Ministry of Environment and Climate Protection (Germany). Overall 24 partners out of the consortium are soil data providers and will make the data available for the project. Hence,

J. Hřebíček, G. Schimak, and R. Denzer (Eds.): ISESS 2011, IFIP AICT 359, pp. 226–234, 2011.
© IFIP International Federation for Information Processing 2011

a complex and high quality data basis in a European context is assured. Beyond that, European institutions are also involved via the advisory board, as the European Environment Agency and the Joint Research Center of the EC.

The partners will establish and operate a network of services for spatial datasets and metadata. This network includes distributed services for data transformation, discovery, view and download. The final result of the project will be a central GS SOIL Portal, where European soil data from heterogeneous sources will be bundled. In order to ensure cross-border usability of the portal and related services, aspects of multilingualism and data interpretation will be considered thoroughly.

The project will extensively support the implementation of the INSPIRE requirements on basis of available experience in selected European countries and regions on different organizational levels. The planned results of the project are [3]:

- A consolidated soil-related theme catalogue and consolidated soil-related theme content-framework standards,
- An INSPIRE compatible metadata profile for spatial soil datasets, dataset series and services,
- Generic application schemes for soil information [12],
- A web portal (GS SOIL Portal) which provides access to all project soil data, including [8], [9], [10]
    - a view service which provides access to spatial soil data,
    - discovery and view of the INSPIRE conform metadata for the provided soil maps [5], [6],
    - interoperable spatial soil datasets (for exemplary soil products),
    - case studies on cross-boarder delivery of harmonised soil data access [7],
    - Best practise guidelines for
        - creating and maintaining metadata for soil database [12],
        - and for data harmonization.

The GS SOIL Portal

The GS SOIL community provides a centralized web access point for standardized, interoperable and INSPIRE compliant European soil information. In the GS SOIL Portal http://gssoil-portal.eu all soil related information from web pages, over databases to data catalogues will be made available and accessible [4]. Search results will be ranked and listed in shared result lists. Spatial soil data from OGC compatible Web Mapping Services (WMS) and Web Feature Services (WFS) will be visualized in a map viewer. For all tasks within the project the GS SOIL Portal will be used as a platform for an improved access to soil data. GS SOIL Portal has been built in an iterative cycle, adopting the relevant INSPIRE Implementing Rules (Network Services and related) and on the basis of the InGrid software designed for the German Environment Information Portal (PortalU) [17]. Also general open tools and services will be provided for re-use by the project partners (data / service providers) and later technical integration of services and underlying geospatial data sets. Particular focus will be placed on mutual harvesting (CSW) with external systems. The current version of the GS SOIL Portal is already available in 13 project languages.

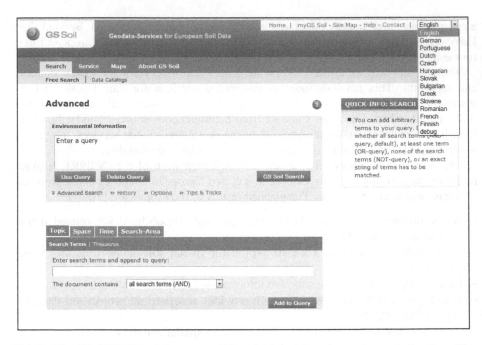

Fig. 1. The GS SOIL Portal (www.gssoil-portal.eu) and its advanced search function. The interface is available in 13 languages.

The product harvesting, as well as the development of so-called content-framework standards (terminology, reference material and definitions to compare soil data), are based on a substantial search for existing soil data in European countries. The result has been implemented into a catalogue of soil data existing in Europe with a specific focus on products provided through web-services.

Data Quality, Data Management and Metadata

In GS SOIL two soil data relevant metadata profiles (the first one for datasets and dataset series while the second is intended for describing a service) compliant to IN-SPIRE metadata and ISO standards were developed in 2010. Subsequently, metadata proposed by the GS SOIL community was delivered as reference material to the Thematic Working Group for the sections dealing with metadata and data quality in the first version of INSPIRE Annex III Data Specification on soil. INSPIRE Data Specifications contain requirements (that are legally mandated) and recommendations [13], [14]. On the other hand, INSPIRE Data Specifications may be hardly readable by data providers that are not aware of all underlying standards. Thus, it complicated to get an overall picture. GS SOIL Best Practice Guidelines for creating and maintaining metadata for soil databases are intended to overcome this insufficiency.

Proposed Best Practice Guidelines are covering both – metadata and data quality aspects. This approach consists of several steps, including

- a review of the GS SOIL metadata profile with respect to newly published INSPIRE documents (e.g. Commission Regulation 1089/2010 on interoperability of spatial data sets and services or new version 1.2 of Technical Guidelines on INSPIRE metadata),
- connections between dataset metadata and feature-level metadata through a feature catalogue,
- user-friendly guidelines for data providers who would like to describe their soil-related databases,
- the GS SOIL metadata profile applied on two real soil datasets as examples,
- guidelines on how to manage soil metadata in two or more languages,

Metadata element name	Data Quality – Positional accuracy – Absolute or external accuracy
Definition	Closeness of reported coordinate values to values accepted as being true.
ISO 19115 number and name	18. dataQualityInfo
ISO/TS 19139 path	dataQualityInfo
INSPIRE obligation / condition	Optional
INSPIRE multiplicity	0..*
Data type (and ISO 19115 no.)	117. DQ_AbsoluteExternalPositionalAccuracy
Domain	Lines 100-107 from ISO 19115
Implementing guidelines	This measure is for expressing of positional accuracy of point data (boreholes) only. Reported should be only one number expressing the positional accuracy according to the number of measured dimensions of soil dataset. Explicit formulas are defined in section 6.2. This result value is usually designated as Root Mean Square Error (RMSE) within GIS software. This is the only result to be reported within this metadata element. Following steps are recommended: 1. Recalculate resulting RMSE into metres, in case when resulting RMSE is in different units (for example GIS has calculated RMSE as 6 cm, i.e. recalculated RMSE is 0.06 m). 2. Write recalculated RMSE into the value metadata sub-element as a real number with a precision of 2 decimals (e.g. 1.85).Usage of decimal point is recommended. 3. Write "m" into the valueType metadata subelement
Example	value: **2.00** valueType: **m**

Example XML encoding	`<gmd:MD_Metadata ..`
	`    ..`
	`    <gmd:dataQualityInfo>`
	`    ..`
	`        <gmd:report>`
	`        <gmd:DQ_AbsoluteExternalPositionalAccuracy>`
	`            <gmd:result>`
	`[...]`

Fig. 2. Example of (data quality) metadata element structure as a part of GS SOIL Best Practice Guidelines for creating and maintaining metadata for soil databases

- brief information about the development of the soil specific multilingual thesaurus (which is in detail written in the following section)
- and examples on usage of soil metadata within INSPIRE, i.e. spatial data infrastructure framework (e.g. how to get from dataset metadata to view/download service or dataset itself as well as description of related aspects).

Best Practice Guidelines are established as a recommended set of steps to obtain the right value that should be reported within INSPIRE compliant metadata. All steps are written in user-friendly way while an end user does not have to be aware of underlying standardization documents to successfully create INSPIRE valid metadata with GS SOIL profile. The consortium partners decide for a selected and open tool to integrate the metadata into the GS SOIL portal (e.g. GeoNetwork, InGrid Editor etc.). These open tools were adopted to the defined metadata structure and are INSPIRE compliant.

Another specific part of Best Practice Guidelines is related to data quality issues that are currently divided into two main streams. The first is focused on analyzing the existing quality specifications and measures of compliancy specified within the data themes of Annex I as well as data quality evaluation according to the ISO standards (like ISO 19157, 15158, 19113, 19114). The second activity is focused on the discussion paper "Data quality in INSPIRE: from requirements to metadata" (from October 2010). This document [15], although only on the level of discussion paper, could seriously change the demands and also the viewpoints for defining the data quality for all INSPIRE spatial data themes, including soils.

Soil Specific Multilingual Thesaurus

Sharing metadata and/or data generally leads to the need of common semantics, a common set of concepts and a common controlled vocabulary. This is a fact well-known long before the existence of IT and IT networks, and has lead to controlled lists of physical units, chemical elements, species lists or even to complete vocabularies like the medical or pharmaceutics vocabularies. Today thesauri and/or ontologies have become state of the art within communities and international projects even when the participants do not want to share data but "just" want to exchange their knowledge. Public institutions who collect data/information/knowledge from various parties meet this well-known need establishing controlled vocabulary and making it accessible for their data providers. The European Environmental Agency e.g. uses and publishes GEMET, the GEneral Multilingual Environmental Thesaurus, Which is provided in 26 languages, as multilingualism is a need for any European collaboration, not only in the environmental sector. Referencing concepts of GEMET [12] is requested by the EU INSPIRE directive.

As GS SOIL aims to be INSPIRE compliant, GEMET has to be at least a part of the controlled vocabulary of that project. But GEMET represents a very general environmental vocabulary and needs more specific extensions for special domains, such as water, protected areas, air and – soil.

The GS SOIL Portal has a reference to a service for GEMET but for the reasons explained above, in addition to the preliminarily planned tasks, the GS SOIL community decided to establish a soil specific multilingual thesaurus in addition to the preliminarily planned tasks. This thesaurus shall be created as an extension of GEMET and shall contain the soil vocabulary of ISO11074 [16], the concepts of WRB [1] and concepts created and/or defined during the GS SOIL project.

Concerning the architectural aspects the thesaurus has to be linkable to the GS SOIL Portal and must be free and easily accessible. In order to make referencing GEMET as easy to handle as possible, it was decided to make the soil specific thesaurus not only semantically but also syntactically interoperable with this controlled vocabulary demanded by INSPIRE.

The architectural decisions and the willingness to stick to widely accepted standards lead to the decision to use SKOS/ RDF [20], a W3C standard, as formal language. Therefore an SKOS/RDF compatible thesaurus editor, which allows collaborative work, is chosen as tool for the establishment. Several tools for that standard are available, but so far the only freeware tool is iQvoc [19].

One benefit of the chosen formal language and tool is that content can also be presented as linked data, thus allowing interconnections with other controlled vocabulary, which will help to establish cross – domain semantic interoperability [18]. Moreover even links to concepts, which are defined for data and metadata transfer, could be established as soon as those models are transformed from UML to OWL.

The guidance and rules for the establishment of the multilingual content is set up in March and the continuous maintenance beyond the end of the project will be topic of the planning of GS SOIL.

Application Schema, Data Harmonization and Interoperability

Data can be exchanged in many different formats and structures. To ensure that the receiver does interpret the data in a proper way, a common or standardised application schema for soil data is needed. Because INSPIRE is determined to use already existing standards, GS SOIL adopted the ideas of the upcoming ISO 28258 Digital Exchange of Soil-related Data (i.e. the working draft available end of July 2010), developed it further and produced a practical implementation in two XML schema files and a set of rules how data providers set up a further, extended XML schema definition and define properties and produce data files in an interoperable way.

ISO 28258 is basically an extension of ISO 19156 Observations and measurements for soil data. The core of the application schema is the feature catalogue. It lists all objects that can be described in the soil universe. The feature types and their relationships have been modeled using the Universal Modelling Language (UML). To ensure the interoperability of the data, this feature catalogue is complete and cannot be extended. The application schema is nonetheless generic in that it leaves the properties that can be described for each feature with the user of the standard (i.e. the data providers).

The application schema has been implemented in XML (Fig. 3). The feature types are defined in the DataFile_core.xsd. In order to have a mechanism to check XML data files against an xsd, the data file definition has to be extended for each use with the properties that shall be exchanged in the data file. In an additional Property-File.xml (that itself can be checked against the PropertyFile.xsd provided with the

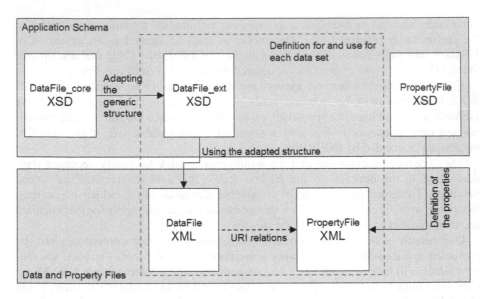

Fig. 3. Implementation of the application schema using XML and XML schema definitions

application schema) further property definitions are given that cannot be put into the DataFile_ext.xsd due to the impossibility to define more than the codes itself in xsd code list definitions. For interoperability, often further information is needed, e.g. the class boundaries of classified numerical values, or the link to the multilingual thesaurus.

The application schema and its implementation serve as reference material for the INSPIRE process of data specification development (e.g. proposal for a soil metadata profile). The GS SOIL amendments to the former ISO 28258 Working Draft were fed back into the ISO process. The application schema is tested with data from the GS SOIL data providing partners using a hands-on testing procedure description. The GS SOIL SoilML is compared with the currently developed INSPIRE application schema for soil data.

Interoperability includes harmonization to varying degrees, depending on domain-specific agreements. A closer look to the descriptions and scope of the INSPIRE Annex Themes shows that soil data include a wide variety of data content. The historic development of soil data, especially high-resolution maps, has caused substantial regional differences in resolution, terminology, and taxonomy. The feasibility to harmonize the content of such products has not yet been systematically investigated. Independently of the agreements under INSPIRE, the array of possible harmonization methodologies is being investigated in detail in GS SOIL test cases. This includes high and low-resolution soil maps, as well as thematic maps, data from soil inventories such as long-term field experiments, and national soil monitoring. Thematic maps are applications of basic soil maps, for example susceptibility maps, very often combined with ancillary data such as climate and land cover. In the future, web processing services will allow such applications on the fly, using data and methodologies shared among distributed information systems. Given these frame conditions and outlook, semantic aspects of harmonization of soil information play an important role to the soil data user community.

Outlook

Until end of May 2012 the best practice network will finalize the self defined work plan. Technically, the GS SOIL Portal is already online and will be further improved. The soil thesaurus with the set of minimum terms will be realized. All data providers in the project and the extended network will make the interoperable data accessible and will also create metadata..

The Best Practice Guidelines for creating and maintaining metadata for soil databases were prepared to answer opened questions that data providers may have. At the same time, it serves as the "cookbook" where the process of metadata creation and management is described step by step to get to INSPIRE valid metadata with added relevant information on soil data. These Guidelines may be used in other application fields as well and in the full scope may be used for metadata according to the Commission Regulation No 1205/2008 (on INSPIRE metadata). Second benefit represents explicit guidelines on data quality including quantitative methodologies on specific measurements that are suitable for soil data. As a result, metadata and data quality information is well defined and contains values that are comparable.

In terms of harmonization GS SOIL first focus on the content framework. Concepts are being exchanged (for example, about map stratification, or about the definition of soil map units), and definitions agreed upon. This will allow focusing test cases on a common vocabulary. Recommendations will be provided as "Best practice guidelines for developing a content framework for interoperable soil data in Europe". Because the World Reference Base for Soil Resources plays an important role in international data exchange, many GS SOIL partners will investigate the possibility of applying this reference system for identifying the taxonomic units of their products as the basic classification system. The next steps will be concentrated on comparing and adapting existing data sets across borders. Further harmonization steps will then look at the soil maps in detail. The geometric data content will be analysed against independent GIS-based criteria for comparing the structure and content of maps. The GS SOIL test cases will thus allow estimating the possibilities and effort to fully harmonize soil data. The results will be provided as "Data Harmonization Best Practice Guidelines".

Acknowledgments. The GS SOIL best practice network "Assessment and strategic development of INSPIRE compliant Geodata-Services for European Soil Data" is co-funded by the European Community programme eContent*plus*. The work presented in this paper is the joint effort of the GS SOIL consortium. The authors are representatives of project partners. They are solely responsible for the content. The text does not represent the opinion of the European Community and the European Community is not responsible for any use that might be made of information contained therein.

For further information on the project please visit the website: http://www.gssoil.eu/.

References

1. Deckers, J.A., Driessen, P.M., Nachtergaele, F.O., Spaargaren, O.C.: World References Base for Soil Resources. Wageningen University and Research Center Publications (2002)
2. European Environment Agency. EIONET. About GEMET,
   http://www.eionet.europa.eu/gemet/about
3. Feiden, K., et al.: Progress of the transnational cooperation in building up a SDI for European soil data (eContentplus-project GS SOIL). In: INSPIRE Conference 2010 – a Framework for Cooperation, Krakow, June 22-25 (2010)
4. Feiden, K., Kruse, F., Epitropou, V., Karatzas, K.: The GS SOIL portal prototype and its integrated network. In: Greve, K. (ed.) 24th International Conference on Informatics for Environmental Protection in cooperation with Intergeo 2010, Integration of Environmental Information in Europe, October 6-8, pp. 420–428 (2010)
5. GS SOIL consortium: D3.1 Metadata profile for soil geographic datasets and dataset series (2010)
6. GS SOIL consortium: D3.2 Metadata profile for soil geographic data services (2010)
7. GS SOIL consortium: D4.1 Theme specific test suite for developing data specifications (2010)
8. GS SOIL consortium: D5.1 Design specifications of the GS SOIL Portal and its network (2010)
9. GS SOIL consortium: D5.2 GS SOIL Portal (Prototype) (2010)
10. GS SOIL consortium: D5.3 First set of open tools and services (2010)
11. GS SOIL consortium: D3.4 Final best practice guidelines for Creating and Maintaining Metadata for Soil Database (2011)
12. GS SOIL consortium: D4.2 Generic application schemes for soil information (2011)
13. INSPIRE DT [Drafting Team] Data Specification. Definition of Annex Themes and Scope. Deliverable D2.3. Version 3.0. (2008a)
14. INSPIRE DT [Drafting Team] Data Specification. Methodology for the development of data specifications. Deliverable D2.6. Version 2.2 (2008b)
15. INSPIRE DT [Drafting Team] Data Specification. Data quality in INSPIRE: from requirements to metadata, discussion paper of the European Commission (2010)
16. International Organization for Standardization. Soil Quality Vocabulary. ISO 11074:2005,
    http://www.iso.org/iso/catalogue_detail.htm?csnumber=38529
17. Kruse, F., Konstantinidis, S.: InGrid® – eine Software zum Aufbau von Umweltinformationssystemen. In: AGIT 2010, Salzburg (July 7-9, 2010)
18. Rüther, M., Fock, J., Bandholtz, T., Schulte-Coerne, T.: Linked Environment Data. Workshop des Arbeitskreises Umweltinformationssysteme der Fachgruppe Informatik im Umweltschutz
19. Bandholtz, T., Schulte-Coerne, T., Glaser, R., Fock, J., Keller, T.: iQvoc – Open Source SKOS(XL) Maintenance and Publishing Tool. In: 6th Workshop on Scripting and Development for the Semantic Web, SWSW 2010, Heraklion, May 31 (2010)
20. W3C: SKOS Simple Knowledge Organization System,
    http://www.w3.org/2004/02/skos/

A Concept of a Virtual Research Environment for Long-Term Ecological Projects with Free and Open Source Software

Mirko Filetti* and Albrecht Gnauck

Brandenburg University of Technology at Cottbus
Dept. of Ecosystems and Environmental Informatics
Konrad-Wachsmann-Allee 1, D-03046 Cottbus, Germany
filetti@tu-cottbus.de

Abstract. The management of data and data resources created by different research activities are heavily influenced by various research philosophies and sampling strategies. Within long-term environmental research (LTER) projects data on flows of individuals, chemical substances and other biotic and abiotic materials are collected by different project partners and institutions. This leads not only to different data bases, but also to incomparable data sets. Therefore, a virtual research environment (VRE) for research projects concerning environmental management should be worked out. The facilities of data sharing, interactive data collaboration and data storage as well as the communication within a project team by metadata are in the focus of a VRE which have to be optimised by WEB 2.0 and other collaboration tools. From this background the FOSS application "GeoNetwork – Opensource" (GNOS) is aimed to be used as a central component for data management in a VRE.

Keywords: Long-term ecological research, data management, virtual research environment, software tools.

1 Introduction

Annually, around ten billion Euros will be invested for information on the public sector by European countries. Approximately 50% of this information consists on spatial data [1]. But much often, wrong data management strategies concerning quantity, quality, actuality and availability of data leads to high redundancies of collected data sets. Therefore, for a good scientific practice the following aspects of data management should be of interest:

1. A data management concept is needed;
2. Primary data must be sorted with the ability to re-find;
3. Data have to be stored in defined standards.
4. Data security, data privacy, copy rights have to be guaranteed;

---

* Corresponding author.

J. Hřebíček, G. Schimak, and R. Denzer (Eds.): ISESS 2011, IFIP AICT 359, pp. 235–244, 2011.

5.   Open access for the public;
6.   All steps of data processing have to be transparent.

According to the Deutsche Forschungsgemeinschaft [2] primary research data should be stored for minimal 10 years on solid storages in the institution that creates the data. Within long-term environmental research (LTER) projects long data sets on flows of individuals, chemical substances and other biotic and abiotic materials are collected by different project partners and institutions. Therefore, an IT-based web 2.0 management concept for the whole project is needed to supply the scientific work with collaboration tools inside and giving representative presentations to the public. The use of free and open source software (FOSS) is an attractive alternative to high cost commercial and often proprietary software solutions because of low cost, short timely software terms, independency and security.

From this background the FOSS application "GeoNetwork – Opensource" [3] is aimed to be used as a central component for data management in a VRE. Based on international standards, GNOS is a data and information management system, which includes interoperability, metadata, data harvesting, and geographical references as well as user groups with different authorisation levels. The development of GNOS has been initiated by the UN in 2001, which has been continued by several partners. In the meanwhile, basic GNOS applications are successfully implemented and modified in many environmental projects of different governmental and non-governmental organisations worldwide.

2   General Working Steps of Long-Term Research Projects

The data resources within a multidisciplinary research project like diagrams, pictures, photographs, measured data curves, visual observations and others should be available for collaboration and permanent long term access. As a first attempt, data sets have to be stored in repositories which should be identified by metadata. The data sets keep their different formats, but they can be searched and collected with their metadata assets by a search engine. For this reason, a modified use of the GNOS application is necessary to guarantee data sharing facilities.

In this context, some questions have to be answered concerning usability of original data, retrieval by metadata and authorised access by specific policies. The following general working steps should be considered:

1.   A general database has to be set up to store the data of subprojects and to record them with metadata. The interoperability is warranted with all external and internal data repositories.
2.   Technical processes have to be adapted and implemented to reference and to maintain research data. Linkages with and references to different data systems and repositories outside of the research project considered are intended as well.
3.   The storage system has to be designed. This will be happen by implementation of interoperability tools and/or interfaces for retrieval and referencing.
4.   Long term storage of data and archiving tools have to be set up within the project under consideration or outside the project to save and to store research data over longer time horizons for further usage.

Thereby, it is not necessary to develop a completely new data storage and retrieval system. Adaptations and modifications of an available GNOS application have to be adapted to the requirements of a specific research project.

3 Virtual Research Environment

A virtual research environment (VRE) can be defined as a set of web applications and tools, systems and processes interoperating to facilitate or enhance any research activity within and outside of institutional boundaries. The key issue of a VRE is the development and implementation of an information and data sharing concept [4] where data sharing can be done by different media [5]. Further technological problems and challenges are given by software and hardware aspects. In practice, for a successful use of a VRE it is necessary to have clear ownerships of data, a confirmed research project plan with data policies among the collaborators, clear research objectives and responsibilities, and an adequate personal resource for the IT management. But, the most important point is that VREs need to be more considered as community building projects than as technology projects. VRE's give benefits scientific disciplines at all levels of research. There is neither an 'out of the box-solution' nor a 'one size fits all realizations' approach that will meet the demands of all research activities. Research results will come out very quickly by using a VRE environment. Also new research directions will be supported as well. The range of applications of VRE is very broad. For long-term research, sustainability is required with the same long-term commitment as other parts of the infrastructure of the project lifecycle.

Most VRE's have an international dimension. Therefore it is necessary to attend legal, ethical and other policies and frameworks that govern the sharing of data and other resources. The VRE's offer benefits not only for the project itself but also for improvements of general co operations and best practice solutions. Arguments for national and international funding schemes of VRE's are formulated by Carusi and Reimer [5]. Research funds should be used to organize general networking procedures and interdisciplinary research. They support expensive research infrastructures and the productivity of researchers. It can be expected that an increasing speed of information and communication lead to a faster dissemination of research results, to a better preservation of research outputs, and to a new quality of research outputs.

4 VRE Services

Depending from the project goals within a VRE environment several services are available. The external view on a VRE should be a unique monolithic system with fast access. But, neither a total self-development of a VRE is possible (because of time, knowledge and resource conflicts) nor is a software tool known, that fits all the requirements for such a VRE. The challenge for an IT-developer is to find best practice FOSS-solutions for all services needed and patch them optionally all together to a "stand alone" VRE-application that is according to all (international) standards and to take care for sustainability (support from the FOSS community).

An overview on some services contained in a VRE is presented in table 1. Between definition of services and selection of applications a lot of work is hidden. For testing and evaluating each software part, several extensions, different versions and the complete VRE system including the web server software and hardware several years have to be spent.

Table 1. Services for a Virtual Research Environment (VRE)

VRE service	Characteristic
Access management	Single sign in for different applications
Communication	Web 2.0 elements like messaging, chat, forum, wiki
Data analysis	Data analysis tools, statistical methods
Data visualization	Visualization of information and datasets
Data warehousing	Complex data storage and data analysis
Decision support	Aggregated data for decision makers
E-Learning	Platform for students with E-Learning procedures
Event calendar	Internal and external community events
Group management	Groups- and rights management, organization for teams
Map and spatial data	Map-server, case area maps
Metadata management	Information about data
Mobile access	Optimized layout of webpages, augmented reality, access control
Monitoring	Real time monitoring of sensor data etc.)
Project management	Project organization tools like tasks, milestones, workflow, reports
Project website	Flexible content management system (CMS)
Repository	Data repository and data storage, compression, indexing
Search engine	Global and local comfortable search engines
Social web	Facebook, Twitter integration, etc.
Search engine optimization	(SEO) ranking in top search engines like Google

In table 2 selected State-of-the-Art of FOSS applications are presented for some core services and their relations to other applications. The CMS Joomla [6] will be recommended as a second core component. It is a very popular CMS with a world-wide developer community and over 7,300 components for all kinds of extensions and hundreds of bridges to third party software.

Table 2. Selected FOSS for VRE Services

Service	FOSS	Relations
Project website, community	Joomla, Typo3, Dupral	LDAP, Shibboleth
Access management	LDAP, Shibolet	
Project collaboration, communication and workflows	BSCW, Joomla components	LDAP, Shibboleth
Repository search with meta data	GNOS, (BExIS, Pangea)	LDAP, Shibboleth
Documentation and best practice	Mediawiki	Bridge for Joomla
Monitoring	Joomla component „Art Data"	LDAP, Shibboleth
Data analysis/Data warehousing	Infobright.org, noSQL, Joomla component „Art Data"	Stand alone on local PC, data Bridge for Joomla
Decision support	Infobright.org, Joomla components,	
E-Learning	Moodle	Bridge for Joomla
Webserver-software	Linux, Apache, MySQL, Tomcat, PHP, XML/XSLT	
Social web	Joomla-Facebook/Twitter integration	Bridge for Joomla
Mobile access	Optimized Homepage	Bridge for Joomla
SEO	Joomla component	

5   GeoNetwork Opensource

The issues of data management, data sharing and data storage are getting more and more important on the different research fields. Only software systems like GeoNetwork Opensource [3] are suitable for an open access onto scientific data within a worldwide net. This software is of low cost, with a worldwide developer scene, independent from commercial dependencies, and follows a unique administrator scheme.

The development of GNOS has been initiated by the UN in 2001, which has been continued by several partners as Food and Agriculture Organisation (FAO), UN Office for the Coordination of Humanitarian Affairs (UNOCHA), Consultative Group on International Agricultural Research (CSICGIAR), The UN Environmental Programme (UNEP) and the European Space Agency (ESA). In the meanwhile, basic GNOS applications are successfully implemented and modified in many

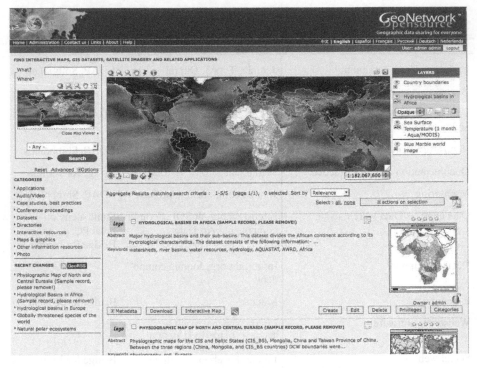

Fig. 1. Start-up page of GeoNetwork Opensource with map-viewer and hit list

environmental projects of national and international governmental and non-governmental organisations worldwide. Figure 1 shows the start-up page of a fresh GNOS installation.

For the facilities of data management, which should be realised in such a project (collaborative processing, aggregation, sharing, publication and long tern archiving) there is obviously no need to initiate a completely new development of GNOS or to create a new application. But it is necessary to modify the available GNOS application, which it fits to the specific requirements of the different sub-projects and work-flows. For this reason, a communication tool should be developed which fulfils the actual data requirements, and connects all long-term data partners within a research project.

5.1 Consideration of Standards

The implementation of a research project on information and storage systems has to be in congruence with national and international standards. Based on GNOS the some international standards for metadata and harvesting which should be introduced in a project work are presented in table 3:

Table 3. Considered metadata standards for GeoNetwork Opensource

Standard	Description
Dublin Core (DC) Metadata (International Organization for Standardization, ISO)	Basic standard for a (minimal) metadata description (not special for spatial data).
Content Standard for Digital Geospatial Metadata (CSDGM) (Federal Geographic Data Committee (FGDC; ESRI FGDC);	Standard for digital geospatial metadata from the leading GIS manufacturer ESRI and the Federal Geographic Data Committee
ISO 19115	Geographic Information Metadata, common base with FGGC, but more detailed
ISO19139	ISO 19139 provides the XML implementation schema for ISO 19115
INSPIRE (Infrastructure for Spatial Information in Europe)	INSPIRE is based on the infrastructures for spatial information established and operated by the 27 Member States of the European Union. The Directive addresses 34 spatial data themes needed for environmental applications, with key components specified through technical implementing rules. This makes INSPIRE a unique example of a legislative "regional" approach [7].
OAI-PMH (Open Archives Initiative Protocol for Metadata Harvesting).	The Open Archives Initiative Protocol for Metadata Harvesting (OAI-PMH) is a low-barrier mechanism for repository interoperability. Data Providers are repositories that expose structured metadata via OAI-PMH. Service Providers then make OAI-PMH service requests to harvest that metadata. OAI-PMH is a set of six verbs or services that are invoked within HTTP' [8].

5.2 Implementation of GNOS

From the statements given above some requirements of an appropriate hardware environment will be derived. Such an environment enables the implementation of the project objectives. GNOS is mainly built on XML/XSLT and offers excellent opportunities for a structured and platform independent programming. Fast processors, large storage devices as well as redundant data provision and back-up services are needed. The system can run on Windows or LINUX including the implementation of an Apache Web-Server, a MySQL database, Tomcat and Java.

Generally a fast multicore server is recommended for GeoNetwork. The running database application and the integrated map-server require sufficient RAM and processing power. LINUX or Windows can be used as operational systems, according to other basic conditions. The hard drive capacity should be calculated by the expected data volume. If only the metadata will be stored, no big capacities are needed. But typically the GNOS-Server is the central storage unit even for the big raw data. The GNOS database can be built with Postgress, MySQL or with a GNOS integrated third party database, which is not so powerful. For different web 2.0 components JAVA and Tomcat needs to be installed on the webserver. As an alternative to the provided third party open source map-server it is possible to use the enterprise ESRI ArcIMS (Map-Server).

For system scaling and reliability of the service cloud computing- and virtualisation technologies can be used. Depending on the last mentioned parameters the following system requirements will be recommended:

- Fast (web)server with multicore processor;
- > 500 GB Hard drive;
- > 4 GB RAM;
- Operation System: Windows Server 2003/2008, Linux;
- Add on: MySQL, PHP, Tomcat, Java SDK;
- ArcIMS (GIS webserver) (optional);
- cloud-server (optional).

5.3 Functions

The core function of GeoNetwork is the metadata referenced search for local and distributed spatial data in a repository by keywords and time- and location filters (what, when where?). The raw data for the repertory can be up-/downloaded in different data types and formats (like maps, PDF, Excel, Word, JPG, etc.) by using of a web interface. An interactive map server provides a fast intuitive search for spatial data with the ability to use layer technology an own or third party (web) maps like Google Maps (see figure 2). Own online composed maps from GNOS can be downloaded as PDF directly.

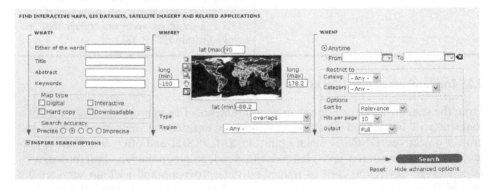

Fig. 2. Search with keyword by location and time

The metadata model is implemented by a template machine with predefined meta-templates according to the international norms and standards. Templates can be new generated or customised to the own requirements. Internal and external thesauri catalogues provides sensitive search functions and suggestions for categorisation while the data input process (controlled vocabulary). A fine granulated user- and group management grants controlled access to each data set. The worldwide exchange of data and the synchronisation of the metadata on distributed (GeoNetwork) server architectures is realised by a standardised harvesting interface. Further core functions of GeoNetwork are given by up- and downloading of data and documents (for instance maps, PDF, Excel-Sheets), by an interactive map-viewer with own maps and layer technology, by map- and layer export procedures as PDF-files, by exchange and synchronization of metadata with standard harvesting technologies, by privacy and access control on each dataset, by an internal/external Thesauri catalogues for keywords, and by international (multilingual) translation procedures.

6 Long-Term Data Management

Water quality management deals with diverse tasks as river basin management, nature conservation, and pollution control. All of these tasks are covered by experts from different scientific, engineering and social-economic disciplines. The resulting statements for water management are based on data sets with different origins and sampling intervals. The management of freshwater ecosystems requires long-term observations of water quantity and water quality indicators like water flow, DO, BOD, algal biomass, nutrients, water plants and others. In table 4 some groups of data for a sustainable water management are given which have to be combined by GNOS to establish a unified research and management information system.

Table 4. Data types of different origin for water management

Origin of data	Types of data
Hydrology	Morphology, water level, water flow
Ecology	Biodiversity, biomass, individuals
Land use	Land cover, patches, farming
Socio economy	Anthropogenic uses, tourism, industry
Energy	Energy production,
Administration	Planning, statistics
Politics	Environmental law, decision support

7 Conclusions

The development of optimal management strategies can only be achieved by using powerful informatic tools like a virtual research environments (VRE), that have a collaborative focus also. The most important point is that VREs need to be more considered as community building projects than as technology projects. To combine data sets from different project partners within a research project is often not only a difficult, but also a complicated task store, to handle and to analyse these data sets. Long-term storage and retrieval of such data is mostly impossible because of the inconsistent spatio-temporal structure of the data sets. The objectives of most research projects don't aim a data warehouse oriented design to evaluate the data sets or the collection of data in a single database and cause the usage of GeoNetwork Opensource. On the base of GNOS an interoperable metadata database will be implemented to aggregate, store, and share datasets from the different projects. In addition a high flexible content management system like Joomla, Dupral or Typo3 or collaboration tool like BSCW is needed to include several enhancements and a single sign in system like LDAP and Shibboleth to build a monolithic VRE in one piece. The exchange of data with harvesting technologies becomes very popular in the last years. Each VRE might have a standard interface for harvesting like the OAI-PMH (Open Archives Initiative Protocol for Metadata Harvesting). The main challenges and problems for the development and success are not only from technical nature but also effected by anthropogenic factors: space, time, funding, isolation, procrastination, poor motivation, trust, commitment, working style, ownership, data access, difficulty of learning software and technology, lack of appropriate skills and ready access to technical support and extensive training needs, rapid advantage of technology. Research activities in the future can be established in the socioeconomic field, in visualisation of data and structures and network structures with harvesting strategies. New useful fields for VREs from the IT-branch are also cloud computing and virtualisation techniques and exploring the semantic web technologies with ontologies.

References

1. Interministerielle Ausschuss für Geoinformationswesen (IMAGI): Geoinformation und moderner Staat, http://www.imagi.de (accessed 10.02.2011)
2. Deutsche Forschungsgemeinschaft (DFG): Sicherung guter wissenschaftlicher Praxis, http://www.dfg.de/download/pdf/dfg_im_profil/reden_stellungnahmen/download/empfehlung_wiss_praxis_0198.pdf (accessed 10.02.2011)
3. GeoNetwork Opensource: Homepage - GeoNetwork Opensource, http://geonetwork-opensource.org (accessed 10.02.2011)
4. Rueppel, U., Gutzke, T., Petersen, M., Seewald, G.: An internet-based spatial decision Support system for Environmerntal data. In: CERN, Sharing. Proc. of EnviroInfo 2004, Geneva, Switzerland, pp. 331–338 (2004)
5. Carusi, A., Reimer, T.: Virtual Research Environment Collaborative Landscape Study; JISC the UK's Joint Information Systems Committee, http://www.jisc.ac.uk/media/documents/publications/vrelandscapereport.pdf (accessed 13.04.2011)
6. Joomla: Homepage, http://www.joomla.org (accessed 13.04.2011)
7. European Commission INSPIRE: Homepage, Inspire Directive on start-up page, http://inspire.jrc.ec.europa.eu/ (accessed 13.04.2011)
8. Open Archives Initiative: Interoperability through Metadata Exchange, http://www.openarchives.org/pmh/ (accessed 13.04.2011)

Corporate Sustainability Reporting
and Measuring Corporate Performance

Zuzana Chvatalová, Alena Kocmanová, and Marie Dočekalová

Brno University of Technology, Faculty of Business and Management,
Kolejni 4, 612 00 Brno, Czech Republic
{chvatalova,kocmanova,docekalova}@fbm.vutbr.cz

Abstract. Corporate sustainability reporting and the measurement of environmental, social, economic and governance performance are discussed in the paper. These are necessary tools of top management for the company strategy
choice of sustainable success. In doing so, the relationship between company
performance and these factors is important, therefore, the need to develop the
modern and advanced methods and metrics to identify them mainly based on
the quantification with the possibility of utilization of information and communication technology. This is discussed in the paper.

Keywords: Corporate Sustainability Reporting; Corporate Performance; GRI;
KPI; Modelling.

1 Introduction

As regards the environmental, economic, social and corporate governance aspects in
relation to measurement of company performance, also the Corporate Sustainability
Reporting is gaining importance. Corporate Sustainability Reporting has become a
mainstream business activity. The *Amsterdam Declaration on Transparency and
Reporting* of the *Board of the Global Reporting Initiative* (GRI)[1] from March 2009
told to global leaders from business, labour and civil society declared their belief that
the lack of transparency in the existing system for corporate reporting has failed its
stakeholders. It brought a new impulse to reporting on environmental, social and
governance (ESG) performance.

The development in the field of corporate sustainability and environmental reporting in the Czech Republic reflect the overall global world trends; see [4]. The available statistics show that through all objective benefits the corporate sustainability
reporting can bring to businesses an appropriate feedback. Existing motivation is not
sufficient to make this a normal business practice as compared to the financial accounting and reporting. On the one hand, some large corporations are actively performing GRI; on the other hand, the relative share of these companies is rather small.
Plenty of companies in the Czech Republic have implemented and certified an Environmental Management System (EMS) as a part of integrated management system
(quality, environment and occupational health and safety management). Therefore,

---

[1] http://www.globalreporting.org/aboutgri/whatisgri/history/amsterdamdeclaration

J. Hřebíček, G. Schimak, and R. Denzer (Eds.): ISESS 2011, IFIP AICT 359, pp. 245–254, 2011.
© IFIP International Federation for Information Processing 2011

the environmental, economical and social data and information are being monitored, codified, registered and aggregated into Key Performance Indicators (KPIs)[2]. This fact indirectly indicates that in the case of such need the company is able to aggregate these data and incorporate it into the corporate sustainability or environmental report, see [4].

Although the GRI has served as an essential and very useful means in improving the standardisation of company reporting, companies continue to have differing degrees of compliance with the GRI and sometimes differing interpretations of the best means to apply the standards to their reporting. To be comparable across all companies, and thus useful for mainstream investment analyses, it is important that economic, environmental, social and governance data is transformed into consistent units and is presented in a balanced and coherent manner in ESG indicators.

2   GRI and UNEP FI Proposals

There the Board of GRI concluded that the root causes of the current economic crisis would have been moderated by a global transparency and accountability system based on the *exercise of due diligence and the public reporting of economic, environmental, social and governance (sustainability) performance*. They called on governments to introduce policies requiring companies to address publicly *sustainability factors*. A revitalized and resilient economic system will only be sustained if it accounts for the full costs and value of sustainability activity. The Board of GRI calls on governments to take leadership by:

- Introducing policy requiring companies to report on sustainability factors or publicly explain why they have not done so;
- Requiring sustainability reporting by their public bodies – in particular: state owned companies, government pension funds and public investment agencies; Integrating sustainability reporting within the emerging global financial regulatory framework being developed by leaders of the G20 (The Group of Twenty)[3].

Investors have been a key driver in promoting the uptake of sustainability reporting – as a result of initiatives such as the United Nations Environment Programme's Finance Initiative (UNEP FI)[4]. They are increasingly asking companies for economic, environmental, social and governance (ESG) information to help them make investment decisions, see [4].

UNEP FI Asset Management Working Group (AMWG) and the Markets & Valuation Work Stream of the Word Business Council for Sustainable Development have jointly published the new report: *"Translating ESG into sustainable business value"*[5]. This report providing key insights for companies and investors on how their business and investment philosophy and practices going forward can better address the why, what and how of communicating corporate economic, environmental, social

---

[2] http://en.wikipedia.org/wiki/Performance_indicator
[3] http://www.g20.org/about_what_is_g20.aspx
[4] http://www.unepfi.org/about/index.html
[5] http://www.unepfi.org/fileadmin/documents/translatingESG.pdf

and governance (ESG) performance to the capital markets. Business leaders and investors can use this report as a tool to advance the integration of ESG factors into corporate and investment decision-making, and to continue discussing the needed evolution towards more holistic and realistic capital market valuation processes.

The AMWG is a global platform of asset managers that collaborate to understand the various ways ESG factors affect investment value and the evolving techniques for the inclusion of ESG criteria and metrics.[6]

From sustainability performance data is necessary to determine KPIs to identify company overall sustainability performance.

Great importance is attributed to the defining of KPIs in the economic, environmental, social and governance areas for a specified economic activities (NACE[7]) with subsequent measurement of sustainable development. The corporate sustainability reporting and overall performance of a company in a specific economic activity would thus be defined by the integrated achievement of economic, social, environmental and corporate governance performance measures. Sustainability performance is, however, often understood as performance in environmental and social terms, thus excluding economic performance [8].

Decision-making is based on a qualified assessment (measurement) of a situation determined at the same time by multiple factors (indicators), primarily in their horizontal development. In pursuit of an outstanding informative force an emphasis is currently placed not only on the absolute data, but in the first place on the change data and analyses of changes of these changes. That is, dynamics of systems is the focus of attention. Appropriately applied vertical analyses then add further dimension to the conditions for decision making. In this conjunction other methods have to be discussed: logical and empirical methods, methods of qualitative and quantitative research such as in particular modelling of statistics.

3   Modelling Tools for Measuring Corporate Performance

"Creating of models of social phenomena is at the heart of economic science. By model we understand here a simplified representation of reality", see [9]. The process of creating models of real situations (in general, not just in economics) may be called real phenomena modelling. The more real situation aspects the model embraces, the more exactly it describes it. Such a model, however, may not be suitable for understanding context and achieving clearness, processing and further manipulation (obtaining results within a reasonable time span, formulation of conclusions; possible uncovering of strengths and weaknesses of facts or inappropriate use of information technology), see [5], [6]. Modelling may be categorized from different points of view. For example if the focus is on description, this may be of verbal, visual, quantitative, qualitative or analytic kinds. If the focus is on character, this encompasses deterministic and stochastic, static, dynamic and other approaches, see [2].

---

[6] http://www.unepfi.org/work_streams/investment/amwg/index.html

[7] NACE is an acronym standing for Statistical Classification of Economic Activities, used by the European Union (or the European Communities) since 1970. NACE provides a framework for statistical data relating to activities in many economic areas (e.g. production, employment, national accounts).

In connection with the currently ever more demanded change analysis, we have to mention Deming's cycle, i.e. application of what is known as Deming's four-component diagram also referred to as Plan-Do-Check-Act (PDCA)[8].

When modelling and employing advanced quantitative methods, optimization, stochastic, dynamic, further mathematic (e.g. disaster theories) and other methods in measuring corporate performance, the level of knowledge may be increased by also considering significant aspects of qualitative character, mainly consisting in capturing facts non-deterministically. For example: by capturing phenomena under conditions of indeterminateness; by means of data extraction; by considering and reflecting upon uncertainties not just by "measuring" empirical data; by considering also inaccuracy of methods, technology and the facts that economic, environmental as well as social experiments are difficult to control; by taking into account degrees of phenomenal ambiguity, delimiting certain balance space etc.

The resulting methods for measuring corporate performance should be modifiable, enabling e.g. local specification which takes into account abnormal or marginal conditions, with a potential of reasonable prediction, deduces historical development, single/multi criteria, capable of further simplification (e.g. comparative statics approach) etc.

Graphical possibilities for results of measuring corporate performance such as visualization, animation, simulation etc. are an important support for their understanding. An indispensable tool is presented by the rapidly developing information and communication technologies (ICTs), see [3], [6]. A great number of ICTs exists at present, e.g. the modelling tools Maple, MuPAD, Mathematica, tailor-made for statisticians are the cutting-edge systems Statgraphics, Statistica and others.

Scientific computing thus plays an ever more important role which is even more accentuated by the rapidly developing ICTs, see [5]. In this way new methods are created, but along with that even some older methods have been re-discovered and transferred from their academic environment into practical use.

Mathematicians found inspiration in the nature and developed new theories such as fuzzy logic (determining "how many" elements belong in a specific set), artificial neuron networks (are sort of imperfect model of the human mind, termed "black box", as it is impossible to thoroughly learn about an internal structure of a system), genetic algorithms (used where exact solutions of practical problems would be almost infinitely long if systematically examined) or chaos (describes behaviour of non-linear systems which though having a hidden order, still appear as systems controlled by chance effects). These methods are considered for measuring ESG performance. E.g. by evaluating the development of a time series of collected enterprise data we are using these theories and we may form an idea of a time series future development ESG performance and carry out a qualified decision making process through applying the fuzzy logic rules based on the findings, see [1].

As regards statistical methods inputs into research of ESG performance, the creation of new fuzzy stochastic models is essential at present for the description and evaluation of sets of collected data of ESG factors with dominating indeterminateness. Furthermore, the creation of unconventional mathematic-statistical methods for fitting discrete distributions of probability aimed at categorical analysis of ESG factor

---

[8] http://en.wikipedia.org/wiki/PDCA

trends including the testing of statistical hypotheses and multicriterial decision-making is crucial. Applied software implementation of these developed methods and their application to real ESG data and information sets is used, see [7].

We also used the conception of managerial functions defined by H. Fayol[9] to the determination of ESG factors. This is five functions that he named administration/governance functions (planning), organizing, directing, coordinating, controlling. The mentioned functions are interrelated and are characterized as "sequential managerial functions" (sequential functions). Decision-making is one of the parallel managerial functions, permeating the sequential managerial functions [1].

The theory of systems[10], i.e. system analysis is another important approach for determination of ESG factors based on gradual decomposition of integrated management system of organisation into its subsystems and elements. It focuses on transformation of system inputs into outputs, i.e. behaviour and features of systems.

The construction of methods for rational while at the same sophisticated use of multi-factor metric, the creation of change methodology of measuring ESG factors, a methodical handbook for an organisations in specific industry considering modifiability and broad spectral application, will be universally applicable in the commercial, institutional and public spheres.

4 Corporate Performance

Corporate sustainability reporting tools designed for the environmental, economic, social and governance corporate performance – Corporate Social Responsibility (CSR), Global Reporting Initiative (GRI) – appear as essential at present. The "Reporting" will thus produce one of the greatest value "products", even if intangible in nature, i.e. information about corporate performance. This, however, needs to be used effectively. The overall corporate performance plays a key role in the general development of a company. The using the reliable method of corporate performance measurement where concurrent acting of multiple ESG factors is in play, can be considered a prerequisite for success not only in decision making, but also with regard to general corporate governance, comparison possibilities, development of healthy competition environment.

4.1 Economic Performance

The Economic Performance is based on Financial Reporting. Sources of financial information are: final accounts, annual reports of a company, company financial analysts and managers information, annual reports, stock exchange news, quantified non-financial information and statistics, unquantified information.

Sustainability Accounting is an important tool which processes, analyzes and evaluates three pillars of sustainable development in their interaction and context for improving the company performance in fields environmental – economic performance, environmental – social performance and economic – social performance.

---

[9] http://www.hrmguide.co.uk/history/classical_organization_theory_modified.htm
[10] http://statpac.org/walonick/systems-theory.htm

There are often used the economic indicators of targeted for selection strategies (maximizing profits, maximizing total costs, company survival, etc.), using new methods of design and measurement is often reflecting the evolution of economic performance lessons from history and look to the future.

Economic performance indicators can be divided in relation to the surveyed area:

- indicators of liquidity (current ratio, quick ratio, cash ratio, etc.);
- indicators of profitability (ROA - return on assets, ROE - return on equity, ROI – return on investment, ROS – return of sales, etc.);
- indicators of indebtedness (debt ratio, self-financing ratio etc.);
- indicators of financial and asset structure;
- indicators of activity and other, e.g.:

  - Benchmarking, EVA (EVA = NOPAT – Capital · WACC, where NOPAT – net operating profit after taxes, Capital – fixed capital in assets, weighted average cost of capital),
  - BSC – Balanced Scorecard and other [10].

We use developed ICT tools with above mentioned modelling tools for measuring corporate performance to facilitate the calculations and the visualizations of models of these economic indicators development and these differences.

4.2 Environmental Performance

The Environmental Performance (EP) of an organisation is defined as results of an organisation's management of its environmental aspects. In the context of EMS these results can be measured against the organization's environmental policy (i.e. overall intentions and direction of an organization related to its environmental performance as formally expressed by top management); environmental objectives (overall environmental goals, consistent with the environmental policy, that an organization sets itself to achieve); environmental targets (i.e. detailed performance requirements, applicable to the whole organization or parts thereof, that arise from the environmental objectives and that need to be set and met in order to achieve those objectives) and other environmental performance requirements.

We propose environmental KPIs to provide businesses with a tool for the measurement of the environmental performance of organizations [11]. They are quantifiable metrics that reflect the EP of a business in the context of achieving its wider goals and objectives. These environmental KPIs will help businesses to implement strategies by linking various levels of an organisation (business units, departments and individuals) with clearly defined targets and benchmarks of selected economic activities. Environmental KPIs are measures by which the performances of organizations, business units, and their division, departments and employees are periodically assessed.

KPIs are summarized in the Table 1.

Table 1. Key Performance Indicators [12]

No.	indicator	unit
Efficiency of material consumption		
EN1	annual mass-flow of different materials used	tonnes
EN2	ratio of the used recycled input materials expressed in units	% of the total input materials
Energy efficiency		
EN3	total direct energy use	MWh or GJ
EN4	total renewable energy use	% of total annual consumption of energy (electricity and heat) produced by the organisation from renewable energy sources
Water management		
EN8	total annual water consumption	m³/ year
Waste management		
EN22	total annual generation of waste	tonnes
EN22a	total annual generation of hazardous waste	kilograms or tonnes
Biodiversity		
EN11a	use of land	m² of built-up area use of land
Emissions into the air		
EN16	total annual emission of greenhouse gases	tonnes of equivalent CO2
EN20a	total annual air emission	kilograms or tonnes
Products and services		
EN26	Initiatives to mitigate environmental impacts of products and services, and extent of impact mitigation expressed	number of initiatives
EN27	sold products sold and their packaging materials that are reclaimed by category	%

4.3 Social and Governance Performance

We have continued in our research from the development of economic and environmental KPIs to "the construction of methods for multifactor measurement of corporate performance in chosen economic (CZ-NACE) activities and the creation of a modifiable and broad-spectrum methodology of their putting into practice."

The main objective of our research is specified by its partial research targets:

1. Analysis of the state-of-art on economic, environmental, social and corporate governance aspects of company performance through targeted research of the world literature and database sources available with using available ICTs tools.
2. Analysis of the current implementation of ESG reporting in chosen economic activities and its justification.
3. Analysis and categorization of contemporary characteristics of the individual pillars: economic, environmental, social and corporate governance (or the attractive sustainability of success) in relation to the measure of progress or dynamics of development of the overall corporate performance.
4. Specification of possibilities for company overall corporate performance measurements in chosen economic activities based on analyses of previous findings.

Identification of the importance and relative roles of ESG factors with using ESG data and KPIs in the company overall performance.

5. Construction of methods of multifactor measurement of complex company overall performance in chosen economic activities through the advanced quantitative and qualitative methods (in detail mentioned above) while using the ICT tools and defining their practical implementation ability, functionality, modifiability and embracing a broad spectrum of factors.

6. Application of methods for multifactor measurement of company overall performance of chosen economic activities in practice with feedback for possible change correction aimed at further improvement.

The first results of our research were determination of additional KPIs following results [12] in Table 2.

Table 2. Additional KPIs [12]

No.	indicator	unit
Compliance with legislation		
EN28	Monetary value of significant fines and total number of non-monetary sanctions for non-compliance with environmental laws and regulations	thousand of CZK
Economic Benefits of Environmental Conservation Activities		
EC1	indicating whether activities in environmental conservation are economically rational f	Economic benefits / Environmental conservation costs.
EC2	indicating whether activities in environmental conservation are economically and social rational	(Economic benefits + social cost reduction) / Environmental conservation costs
EC3	indicating the efficiency of environmental improvements made by the project/investment activity	Environmental impact reduction / Environmental conservation costs.
Environmental Efficiency of Business Activities		
EC4	indicating the environmental impact of business activities and whether those activities respond to public needs and expectations is justifiable	Sales / Total environmental impact.
EC5	indicating whether the business activity generates an appropriate level of profit in relation to its environmental impact	Value-added business activities / Total environmental impact.

5 Conclusion

Environmental, social and governance reporting (ESG reporting) tools designed for the corporate ESG performance appear as essential at present. The overall corporate performance plays a key role in its corporate strategic policy and sustainability of success. The creation of reliable methods of corporate performance measurement where concurrent acting of multiple factors is in play can be considered a prerequisite for success not only in decision making, but also with regard to corporate governance, comparison possibilities, development of healthy competition environment etc.

The planned and already developed applied software components for measuring corporate performance within our research project Nr. P403/11/2085 have great potential to be used in different application contexts. On the one hand selection and configuration of existing plug-ins leads to new software tools which suit special application contexts due to their dedicated functionality. On the other hand the open source platform is a basis for custom developments of plug-in-based software tools, where the existing source code of modelling tools can be extended or customized. If necessary the GUI elements provided by the open source platform can be used to build a low effort user interface with basic core functionalities. Finally the developed prototype of applied software for measuring corporate performance will be used as a prototype application for the involved SME which can be directly used without further development steps.

Acknowledgments. This paper is supported by The Czech Science Foundation. Name of the Project: Construction of Methods for Multifactor Assessment of Company Complex Performance in Selected Sectors. Reg. Nr. P403/11/2085.

References

1. Dostál, P., Rais, K., Sojka, Z.: Pokročilé metody manažerského rozhodování. Grada Publishing, Praha (2005)
2. Fábry, J.: Matematické modelování 1. vyd. Praha VŠE v Praze. Nakladatelství Oeconomia, Praha (2007)
3. Gander, W., Hrebicek, J.: Solving Problems in Scientific Computing Using Maple and Matlab, 4th edn. Springer, Heidelberg (2004)
4. Hrebicek, J., Hajek, M., Chvatalova, Z., Ritschelova, I.: Current Trends in Sustainability Reporting in the Czech Republic. In: EnviroInfo 2009. Environmental Informatics and Industrial Environmental Protection: Concepts, Methods and Tools. 23. International Conference on Informatics for Environmental Protection, pp. 233–240. Shaker Verlag, Aachen (2009)
5. Chvatalova, Z.: Company Sustainable Development and Measuring of its Environmental, Social and Governance Factors. In: Management, Economics and Business Development in European Conditions - VII. International Scientific Conference, pp. 40–49. FBM BUT, Brno (2009)
6. Chvatalova, Z.: The Methods of Quantitative Disciplines in the Environment. In: Sustainability Accounting and Reporting on Micro and Macro-Economical Level - Scientific International Conference, Brno, pp. 116–122. University of Pardubice, Pardubice (2010)
7. Karpisek, Z.: Zadeh-Type Fuzzy Probability with Triangular Norms. In: East West Fuzzy Colloquim 2008, HS Zittau, Gorlitz, pp. 126–133 (2008)
8. Schaltegger, S., Wagner, M.: Integrative Management of Sustainability Performance, Measurement and Reporting. International Journal of Accounting, Auditing and Performance Evaluation 3(1), 1–19 (2006)
9. Varian, H.R.: Microeconomic Analysis, 3rd edn. W. W. Norton and Company, New York (1992)

10. Vecheta, L.: Finanční analýza firmy užitím systému Maple. FBM BUT, Brno. Master´s thesis. Supervisor Zuzana Chvátalová. Brno (2010)
11. Hřebíček, J., Soukopová, J., Kutová, E.: Methodology Guideline. Proposal of Indicators for Environmental Reporting and Annual Reports of EMAS (in Czech), Ministry of Environment of the Czech Republic, Praha (2010)
12. Hřebíček, J., Soukopová, J., Štencl, M., Trenz, O.: Corporate key performance indicators for environmental management and reporting. Acta Universitatis Agriculturae et Silviculturae Mendelianae Brunensis 59(2), 99–108 (2011)

Software Architectures for Distributed Environmental Modeling

Ari Jolma[1] and Kostas Karatzas[2]

[1] Department of Civil Engineering, Aalto University,
Niemenkatu 73, 15140 Lahti, Finland
[2] Department of Mechanical Engineering, Aristotle University of Thessaloniki,
54124 Thessaloniki, Greece
ari.jolma@aalto.fi, kkara@eng.auth.gr

Abstract. Environmental modeling is increasingly more integrative and collaborative work. The Internet and Web hold a promise of a shared environmental information infrastructure, which supports modeling. While the traditional (enterprise) information system architectures have not been much employed in the environmental domain, new standards-based Web technologies create an opportunity. At the same time the modeling workflows are being investigated, and this work may provide a fruitful starting point for new kind of top-down services that support modeling within environmental information infrastructures.

Keywords: Environmental modeling, Distributed information system, Software architecture, Workflow.

1 Introduction

Developing purposeful and credible environmental models that consider all relevant aspects of the problem and integrate heterogeneous information is an acknowledged goal [1], [2]. Environmental modeling is collaborative work involving teams of experts, stakeholders and model users. Interconnecting data and tools in information systems is a traditional method for solving information processing problems. During the last 15 years information systems technology has been embracing the Internet and the Web [3], changing the paradigm of information management to information exchange [4]. Internet is a natural platform for information infrastructures that link information systems. "Shared Environmental Information System" is a concept and initiative put forward by the European Commission and European Environment Agency [5]. Information infrastructure that supports environmental modeling allows interconnecting environmental models with one another and with data. Collaboration that is based on setting up and using information services promises to improve and help modeling.

Attaining the perceived goals of a shared environmental information infrastructure naturally assumes that useful data and services exist on the Web. This is indeed already the case to some degree but often the data and services are still oriented to humans and not programs. To use such services directly in applications is possible but

J. Hřebíček, G. Schimak, and R. Denzer (Eds.): ISESS 2011, IFIP AICT 359, pp. 255–260, 2011.
© IFIP International Federation for Information Processing 2011

error-prone and often includes cumbersome reverse-engineering. Web services are applications, which allow direct interactions with other applications using standards-based protocols and interfaces [3]. Many datasets and real-time data are available or becoming such as web services [6], [7]. Using models in the Web by human users and over the Web by other applications is in production use (our observation) and attempts to more standards-based approaches have been reported since early 2000's [8], [9], [10], [11].

Modeling is much more than just preparing and connecting datasets to various models and running the models. It is very difficult to define modeling and its boundaries to development of model-based information systems and to model-based integrated assessment. For the purposes of this paper we consider modeling to be a process where data is used and processed and various software tools are used and developed to solve problems, answer questions, and provide support for planning and management. Important elements of modeling include objectives, conceptualization, assumptions, validation, consultation, and transparency [1]. A shared information infrastructure for modeling needs to include tools for working and spelling out these.

In this paper we review some key concepts of distributed information system architectures in the light of environmental modeling and cases. Based on the review we discuss possible ways forward in developing shared information infrastructures for environmental modeling.

2 Fundamental Architectural Patterns

Distributed information systems traditionally have a three layer architecture comprising a resource layer, an application logic layer, and a presentation layer. In addition, there may be external components, which request information from or provide data to the system. The three layers can be split in various ways to tiers, which are basically separate systems that communicate in agreed, often standardized, ways. The client – server pattern is used between the tiers and external components, the best-known case being web browser clients requesting information asynchronously and already in presentation form from web servers.

The service-oriented architecture is based on the fundamental concept of a service. Services can be simple, for example obtaining a specific resource from a resource layer, or complex, for example using an application. For using complex services one needs coordination help, which basically means instructions. This is because the same service may need to be contacted several times in order to complete the requested service. Services are described to users based on their interfaces, and a service, which has a very simple interface, may actually trigger a very complex procedure within the information system.

Fundamental architectural patterns are generic designs that employ concepts like services, events, tasks and messages. An event is an occurrence of something at a particular point in time. A task is a set of actions that need to be completed. Order of completing, control flow from one action to another, timing, cancellation of actions and other things make up workflow patterns [12]. A message is an object of communication. Fundamental patterns reflect common or effective ways to deal with situations and they help define generic tools, for example programming languages, event dispatchers, service catalogs, and message parsers. Typically information system designers and developers wish to use generic tools as much as possible in order to develop robust and maintainable systems.

Event-driven architecture is based on the concept of events happening at random. New events are taken up by an event dispatcher, which is responsible for routing the event to an appropriate handler or handlers. Events are handled by services. In some architectures event-handler can be added and removed at will.

The publish–find–bind pattern depicts how service providers publish services, how those needing services find them, and how the services are bound to applications or other services. This patterns implicitly assumes a shared service description language and services for publishing services. Linking of services that publish services is recursively possible by publishing them with each other.

A message broker receives messages, possibly validates and transforms them, and routes them to subscribers. An example of a message is a request for a specific service.

Architectural patterns can be exploited within a single application and they can be used as a model for collaboration among humans.

3 Process and Workflow Management

Environmental modeling is itself a process and it comprises several processes and tasks that deal with new measurements, parameter estimation and other things. These processes and tasks may be very specific and deal with established routines or they may be conceptually high-level considerations of things like what is the appropriate spatial aspect of the problem.

A workflow is a sequence of tasks, which is completed by an orchestrated use of applications or by humans. Workflow management systems originate historically in office automation [3]. A typical workflow application today is an administrative document processing system, for example a business travel procurement system. Programming languages have been developed for workflow systems [12]. The biggest difference between normal programming languages and workflow languages is that workflows may take days or longer to complete [3]. To cope with this workflow languages support complex recovery and exception handling routines. Workflow systems typically store the execution state into persistent storage.

Below we present two architectures, which consider processes and workflows.

3.1 Architecture for Linking Processes and Events

A process can be thought of as anything that produces a result set at a certain point in time. A process may be passive, i.e., it waits for an operator to push data into it and run it, or it may be active, i.e. it listens to events and acts under suitable conditions. The result sets of a processes are stored into a resource layer with appropriate meta data. Each addition of a result set triggers an event, which conveys information about what kind of new information is available.

Consider for example a modeling effort, which considers storm water within a municipality. The modeling proceeds as new data is obtained. The primary processes are measurements and changes to the sensor network, engineering structures and such. Secondary processes are statistical, spatial, data cleaning and such operations, which reduce the amount of data but add to the value of new individual result sets. Tertiary processes may be models, which are run off-line but using data directly from the resource layer. Each model run produces a result set, which may be rather large but also contains appropriate meta data. Another kind of tertiary processes may be specifically designed for detecting anomalies and their results may cause events, which trigger emails or sms's.

This kind of architecture is good in the sense that it can be designed to maintain meta data that allows a high level of provenance for the modeling. The downside is that it would require rather considerable changes to current modeling practices and tools, which are not suited to such information exchange.

3.2 Architecture for Formal Modeling Workflows

The workflow that is described in [1] could possibly be coded into a workflow language. A necessary prerequisite would be an ontology for modeling tasks. The ontology should make it possible for formal treatment of stakeholders, temporal and spatial scope of the model, conceptualization, etc. Formal treatment is make possible for example by having these concepts as classes in the system. The middleware should then make it possible for storing stakeholder, conceptualization, and other such objects into the resource layer. The workflow management system for the modeling should support storing the state of the modeling project. Applications need to exist, which can be used, e.g., to create conceptualizations. The modeling workflow comprises calling such applications as unit operations. Executing the ten step modeling workflow in a specific information system would require a resource layer which can manage rather complete data about the environmental system, stakeholders and other aspects of modeling.

4 Collaboration Support

A shared information infrastructure in the Web implies collaboration among modeling teams, stakeholders, data providers and others. The technical implementation is greatly helped by adhering to technical standards, which also may make it easier for new parties to join. There are several architectural possibilities for developing collaborative information infrastructure, each having its specific model for collaboration. We can distinguish between information management, which in collaborative context implies shared information, and information exchange, which in collaborative context implies shared ontologies. A shared information infrastructure can employ both architectural patterns. In the first case there is a single resource layer in the space into which parties contribute, in the second case each party publishes resources into the infrastructure. Of course mixtures can exist too.

In collaborative modeling parties work on a shared deliverable and bring their own specific contribution into the collaboration. In collaborative software development one common architecture is a revision control system. There are two forms of the revision control system, which reflect the two forms of shared information infrastructure described above. In the first form a single common repository is set up and parties check out versions from that and commit changes into that. In the second form each party has its own repository, where it imports and merges changes from other repositories. Collaborative modeling can mean working on a shared model (source code) in a repository.

Social networks and various toolkit for including, e.g., geospatial applets within them have recently become very popular. The technological platform is JavaScript or other programming language embedded in a web browser. Perhaps the most advanced project employing this technology and paradigm (also called Web 2.0) is iem-HUB.org. IemHUB.org is a website for developing and sharing knowledge and tools for environmental systems analysis [13] started by US EPA.

4.1 An Example of a Collaborative Modeling Website

Within the CLIME project [14] the first author was involved in a collaborative modeling effort, where several teams across Europe were using the same models but each on their own catchment and/or lake. To help this effort an interactive website was developed for uploading parameter sets for comparison. The website was developed upon a rather comprehensive project database, which contains for example used models, modeled catchments and users as classes. In the CLIME database a model object contains (links to) parameters, which are again objects, and a modeled catchment contains (links to) subcatchment objects. Although the database was not formally developed as a resource layer for environmental modeling with a unifying interface more than a standard relational database, the collaborative modeling tool was relatively easy to develop as an interactive tool exploiting the database.

The collaborative modeling web page included, besides the parameter set exchange and comparison tool, a file upload tool to share model configuration files and a simple discussion tool. No web mapping tool was included although other applications based on the modeling database were developed that included one [14].

5 Discussion

In environmental information systems that support modeling, the resource layer contains measurement data, terrain data and data about civil infrastructure, conceptual data about the environmental system, management problem related data, and so on. In the application logic layer there are several applications for managing the data: importing new data, preparing it for analytical tools, various models, visualization tools, etc. In enterprise systems the support for, integration of, and management of these applications is a task for middleware and workflow management systems [3]. Traditionally in the environmental domain integrated modeling systems and geographic information systems (which are increasingly being integrated into modeling systems) have played a dominant role. For example the use of relational databases as independent resource layers in environmental modeling has been very limited.

The workflow language BPEL has received some attention and it has been used in environmental modeling to program a model use [10]. A lot is happening in the standards-based distributed data servicing due to the work carried out within the OGC.

OGC has also defined a standard for a processing service (Web Processing Service, WPS), which has recently gained interest. Mainly the interest is in publishing fundamental geospatial methods as services.

The dangers in blind use of technical solutions in modeling have been said and told in numerous papers and presentations. Our findings as reported in this paper suggest that seeking for ways to publish generic modeling knowledge as services is a possibly rewarding way forward and beneficial for modeling projects. As shortly described above in chapter 3.2 the ten step procedure from [1] is a potential starting point for such an exercise. At the same time possibilities for further developing standards-based interfaces for environmental modeling databases (resource layers) and modeling middleware should be investigated.

References

1. Jakeman, A.J., Letcher, R.A., Norton, J.P.: Ten iterative steps in development and evaluation of environmental models. Environmental Modelling & Software 21, 602–614 (2006)
2. Denzer, R.: Generic integration of environmental decision support systems – state-of-the-art. Environmental Modelling & Software 20, 1217–1223 (2005)
3. Alonso, G., Casati, F., Kuno, H., Machiraju, V.: Web Services: Concepts, Architectures and Applications. Springer, Heidelberg (2004)
4. Aberer, K.: Emergent Semantics. Invited talk at the ICSWN 2004 Conference, Paris (2004), http://lsirpeople.epfl.ch/aberer/Talks/EmergentSemantics%20ICSNW.pdf
5. Shared environmental information system, http://ec.europa.eu/environment/seis/index.htm
6. Doyle, A., Reed, C.: Introduction to OGC Web Services. OGC White Paper (2001)
7. Horsburgh, J.S., Tarboton, D.G., Piasecki, M., Maidment, D.R., Zaslavsky, I., Valentine, D., Whitenack, T.: An integrated system for publishing environmental observations data. Environmental Modelling & Software 24, 879–888 (2009)
8. Kokkonen, T., Jolma, A., Koivusalo, H.: Interfacing environmental simulation models and databases using XML. Environmental Modelling & Software 18, 463–471 (2003)
9. Eder, W.J., Zipf, A.: Towards interoperable atmospheric (air flow) models in Spatial Data Infrastructures using OGC Web Services – state of the art and research questions. In: EnviroInfo 2009 (Berlin) Environmental Informatics and Industrial Environmental Protection: Concepts, Methods and Tools, pp. 403–412. Shaker Verlag (2009)
10. Theisselmann, F., Dransch, D., Haubrock, S.: Service-oriented Architecture for Environmental Modelling – The Case of a Distributed Dike Breach Information System. In: 18th World IMACS / MODSIM Congress, Cairns, Australia, pp. 938–944 (2009)
11. Granell, C., Díaz, L., Gould, M.: Service-oriented applications for environmental models: Reusable geospatial services. Environmental Modelling & Software 25, 182–198 (2010)
12. van Der Aalst, W., Hofstede, A.H.M., Kiepuszewski, B., Barros, A.P.: Workflow Patterns. Distributed and Parallel Databases 14(1), 5–51 (2003)
13. Integrated Environmental Modeling, http://iemhub.org
14. George, G. (ed.): The Impact of Climate Change on European Lakes. Aquatic Ecology Series, vol. 4, p. 507. Springer, Heidelberg (2010)

Supporting the Use of Environmental Information Systems and Services – Experiences with a Course for Postgraduate Professional Education

Roman Lenz, Werner Rolf, and Christian Tilk

University of Applied Sciences, Nürtingen-Geislingen,
Schelmenwasen 4-8, D-72622 Nürtingen

Abstract. At our University we developed a course for further training and professional education in landscape and environmental planning, commenced in 2001 [1]. The main content are Geographical Information Systems (GIS), Data Management Systems, and Visualisation. We introduce relevant software, but apply and teach them from a landscape planning point of view. The course has three weeks of joint training, with partly online-guided self-study phases of four weeks in between. Our clients are mainly professionals from governmental organizations, as well as freelancers. Interestingly, the course helps us to improve our curriculum for Bachelor and Master nowadays [2]. Hence, we believe, the course contains as well as continuously updates somehow the most important digital methods and tools in Landscape Planning, strongly related to current and on-going changes of professional needs. One of those needs is certainly the increasing use of Environmental Information Systems and Services.

Keywords: Environmental Information Systems, further education, Geographical Information Systems, Environmental Informatics.

1 Introduction

In the last years at Nürtingen-Geislingen University a course for further training and professional education in landscape and environmental planning was developed. This course is taught in German and called „Geodatenmanager Umwelt". It's part of the advanced education programme „U3 – Umweltinformatik Unterricht für Umweltplaner" which focuses on the topics of Geographical Information Systems (GIS), Data Management Systems, and Visualisation [1], [3].

The course introduces into relevant software, but apply and teach them from a landscape planning point of view. The course has two weeks of joint training, with partly online-guided self-study phases of four weeks. Clients are mainly professionals from governmental organizations, as well as freelancers. In addition, we often have some graduate students as tutors, who are interested in problem solving approaches of professionals as well as in more sophisticated GIS applications and other digital methods. The professionals not only benefit from updated methods and tools, but also from the skills and knowledge of the students. Interestingly, the course becomes more and more an update of what was offered already during the diploma or bachelor

J. Hřebíček, G. Schimak, and R. Denzer (Eds.): ISESS 2011, IFIP AICT 359, pp. 261–271, 2011.

studies in Landscape Planning at our University, and, vice versa, helps us to improve our curriculum for Bachelor and Master nowadays (e. g. [2]). Hence, we believe, the course contains as well as continuously updates somehow the most important digital methods and tools in Landscape Planning, strongly related to current and on-going changes of professional needs. In other words, courses for professional education, together with academic curricula, support each other's.

In the following we describe the course development over the last 10 years, and the current competence focus as well as different learning methods and tools that can be seen as an selection of the best established methods of the programmes evolution.

After more than a dozen courses we also have had many evaluations, which show the feedback of students and professionals that will be presented besides some, proven applications useful for teaching applied GIS methods.

Because new developments took place in the most recent years this is not an update of a description published earlier [1], but will also lead to new conclusions. Therefore the outlook will contain hints that may inspire other programmes on how digital methods can be taught rather advanced and "with all senses" in universities curricula of landscape planning.

2   Programme Description

2.1   Course Development

This professional education programme evolved as a consequence of a course that was originally developed for students with whom a problem orientated approach was trained.

From 1996 until 2000, within the project "ECCEI – European Canadian Curriculum on Environmental Informatics" international students from Germany, Italy and Canada, coming from faculties of different disciplines (informatics and environmental management) were trained to find IT based solutions for environmental issues [4]. Core element of ECCEI was the so called "Short Alpine Course on Environmental Informatics – SACEI" whereas the Soelk Valley in the central alps (Austria) was the training field for environmentally relevant issues that had to be solved within a one week summer school like workshop.

Although the concept originally was thought to educate students, in the year 2001 the methodological-didactical approach was tested for first time as a training course for professionals named "U3 – Environmental Informatics Education for Environmental Planners". To apply this approach to the needs of professional's further presence modules and online modules for self-study phases and training were developed and combined. The outcome was an in-service training programme of four-month duration. The applied use of GIS, database, visualisation and Internet technologies was the focus.

After 4 courses with 77 participants the programme became "U3plus". The concept changed in the way that now professionals and students were now together course participants. The idea was to offer students the opportunity to learn more about the practical needs and applied IT use and to deepen their interest in environmental informatics beyond the universities curriculum. On the other hand the professionals should benefit from the advanced GIS skills and knowledge of the students, and could fill out a tutor like role. Within the next years three courses with 10 students and 44 professionals took place.

In 2007 the concept was updated again. The complete programme was divided into single specific issues and the modules got a more stringent structure. The training programme "U3" was therefore separated into different parts. The main course is now named "U3-Geodata-Manager Environment". It's an in-service training lasting three month and does have a very strong GIS focus. Other course contents (like database, internet technologies etc.) were extracted into single outlook course modules (each of a weekend duration) called "U3-Extensions". Last ones could be optionally chosen on single topics offered. However the problem orientated approach with a one-week workshop like situation still remains as a characteristic of the methodological-didactical concept in form of a single one-week workshop-like module as part of the "U3-Geodata-Manager Environment" training programme.

Since that time another 77 participants, almost every tenth of them were students, summing the number of participants up to 208 in the past ten years, were visiting the "U3" programme.

2.2 Competence Focus – Learning Goals

Learning goal is the use of Information Technologies (IT) within the field of environmental planning and resource management, with a focus on Geographical Information Systems (GIS). Within the course usually ArcGIS in its most actual version is being used as an example, but other software solutions, especially Open Source GIS, are being used as well.

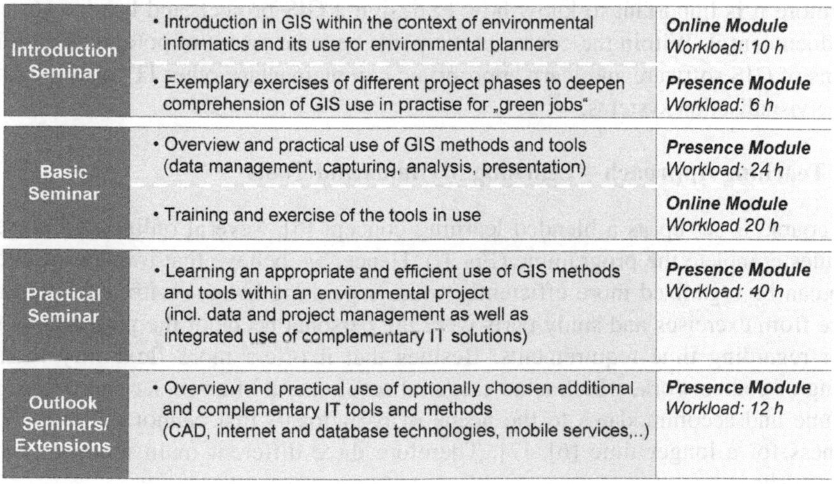

Introduction Seminar	• Introduction in GIS within the context of environmental informatics and its use for environmental planners	*Online Module* Workload: 10 h
	• Exemplary exercises of different project phases to deepen comprehension of GIS use in practise for „green jobs"	*Presence Module* Workload: 6 h
Basic Seminar	• Overview and practical use of GIS methods and tools (data management, capturing, analysis, presentation)	*Presence Module* Workload: 24 h
	• Training and exercise of the tools in use	*Online Module* Workload 20 h
Practical Seminar	• Learning an appropriate and efficient use of GIS methods and tools within an environmental project (incl. data and project management as well as integrated use of complementary IT solutions)	*Presence Module* Workload: 40 h
Outlook Seminars/ Extensions	• Overview and practical use of optionally choosen additional and complementary IT tools and methods (CAD, internet and database technologies, mobile services,..)	*Presence Module* Workload: 12 h

Fig. 1. Different modules with their main learning goals

The participants should get a practice relevant overview of the most important methods and tools and gain ability to break down planning issues for IT based solutions. Herewith participants should be enabled to perform basic applications on their own but also achieve ability to discuss more complex issues with experts. This involves to estimate quality aspects, validity of models as well as management abilities. The relevant issues are split into several different modules (Fig. 1).

The learning goals can be associated to different aspects as follows.

Appropriate and efficient use of GIS tools and methods
Participants get an overview of practice relevant GIS tools and methods for data management, data capturing, data analysis and presentation. The aspect of data capturing includes quality aspects of geo data, quality check and quality improvement. Data analysis contains attribute and spatial analysis of vector and raster data as well as data derivation due to geoprocessing and data modelling. This includes documentation aspects for comprehensibility of manipulated GIS data and to keep transparency of data analysis and modelling for further decision-making processes.

Data Management
This means participants learn how an efficient data management is being organised, taking into account different conditions, i.e. integrated use of geo data server for multiple users etc. Besides that they get introduced into relevant environmental geo data from different sources and in different scales and learn how to handle a combined use. Data documentation with metadata can be associated to this topic as well.

Project Management
This involves learning how to approach and transform environmental planning issues for IT processing and the implementation of the appropriate methods and tools. Therefore it is important to know how to design a GIS project, and how to structure and document it. Within the course participants become aware of potentials and limitations of GIS software and learn appropriate complementary other IT tools like interactive visualisation systems.

2.3   Teaching Approach – Learning Methods and Tools

The course is set up as a blended learning concept [5]. Several online and presence modules complete the programme (Fig 1.). Hence, we believe that transfer of knowledge can be organized more efficiently while separating lessons with teaching attendance from exercises and study parts were the personal needs of the participants may differ regarding time requirements. Besides that it offers more flexibility in time-tabling of course work, which is an essential requirement of an in-service course programme and accommodates to the needs of participants that cannot be absent from business for a longer time [6], [7]. Therefore three different main methods can be distinguished:

1) Teacher-centred lectures with tutor supported exercise blocks

Particularly lessons in which basic knowledge will be introduced are preferred to be taught in teacher-centred lectures [8]. Exemplary, short, tutored exercise blocks usually go along with them. In this way participants learn the principles and get familiar with the software use as well. In this combination this method is used as a key to access prior knowledge. Like a colourful flower bouquet being presented it offers the possibility to negotiate the wide range of methods and tools but the lecturer still has the opportunity to respond on specific interests of the participants, depending on their field of practise.

During the exercise blocks students support the course participants as tutors. As they are usually advanced in the use of GIS tools because of the universities curricula, they can help the professional participants by the software use. In preparation on this the student tutors coincidentally have to self-reflect their knowledge to identify own knowledge gaps and finally to resolve them. In this way this methods helps them as well to enlarge their own knowledge.

2) Problem orientated approach, project work within working groups

This, more or less, is one of the main characteristics of the U3 programme and in particular of the so-called "practical seminar". Here the participants are faced with a real world problem and the task is to "solve this problem" with the help of IT. i.e. GIS [9]. As a first step groups are build perspective the level of profession and/or regarding the interest of deepening certain methods. This will lead to a process that we call an internal differentiation among the heterogeneous participants, as within more homogenous teams learning goals can be achieved more efficient [10], [11]. The only preset is that the groups have to be mixed with students and professional participants together, so they can both learn from each other during the project work.

During the project work the different teams will get individual support by the lecturers, who now have the task of supervisors. Just in case one or more groups end up in a situation where new fundamental knowledge on specific methods or tools are needed theoretical parts are taught with short information blocks as "Lectures on the fly".

After this module of each working group a study is expected that will be presented by the end of the practical seminar. Besides the approach and solution being presented the assignment has to contain as brief description of the used methods and tools as well as possible traps, problems and workarounds.

As case studies several planning tasks are given as choice, that are prepared already in a way that they offer the use of a wide range of methods and tools. Nevertheless the participants usually are developing own project ideas as well.

3) Online-guided self-study phases

Besides the presence modules several online modules are implemented, which are strongly e-learning supported. The main tool for our online modules is the so called

U3-Learning-Management-Platform (U3-lmp), a database once designed for the course needs and realized by programming with PHP and MySQL. The U3-lmp can be accessed via in the Internet. Participants have a personalised user account and will guide after login through a user friendly front-end. An additional mailing list, realised with Majordomo, supports the communication among the participants. Via the backend an administrator is able to organize the participants in different courses and modules, i.e. users, roles and courses can be managed quite easily.

Within the modules different themes can be created where the lecturers assigned to the theme can upload the lessons and tasks. The participants again can upload their results topic associated. The working results can be shared with other co-authors, so that even group work can be done. Furthermore a course blackboard is included besides simple true and false self-tests. Last ones do not have any automated analyses functions integrated, as they are used mainly for self-evaluation through the participants themselves.

Some of the tools can be described similar to common e-learning platform functions of adding, editing, organising resources, learning materials and assignments [12], [13]. Such as discussion forums, chat rooms and web-conferences or grade items are not supported. Even though being aware that other e-learning software packages on the market already offer far more sophisticated options and additional tools, the focus of our work was set on the preparation of suitable learning contents. They exist out of learning materials, tasks, sample data and step-by-step solutions. The material is conceived to prepare course participants to a defined common knowledge background in preparation to an up-coming presence module as well as to recapitulate and exercise lessons learned during the presence modules as a post-process.

Anyhow, because the U3-lmp has, from the technical point of view, not been significantly developed since implementation in 2001 – which is one year before the first Moodle version 1.0 was placed on the marked, in August 2002 [14] – it's most likely to replace it in near future, probably as soon as at our university a university wide e-learning platform is widely accepted and used.

3   Programme Results

3.1   Outcome of Project Work

Within the last years many different projects were worked out. At best, the issue meets the interest of the participant:

- From the thematic point of view (f.i. because of the professional specification).
- From the technical point of view (f.i. because of the intention to learn specific methods and tools)

Table 1 contains a compilation that gives an idea about the thematic spectrum and the used methods as well as being used in the past courses.

Table 1. Overview of different projects and their thematic spectrum
(* VD= Vector Data GIS methods; RD= Raster Data GIS methods; MG= Mobile GIS components; WG= Web-GIS components; 3D=3D-visulisation technologies, DB= with integrated database interface)

Project title/Thematic issue	Used GIS methods and complementary components*					
	VD	RD	MG	WG	3D	DB
Analysis of a biotope connectivity system in for different habitat types	x	x				
Analysis of landscape structures to support habitat connectivity for moor lands	x	x				
Analysis and models to detect potential sites for wind power plants	x	x			x	
Analysis to identify different thematic landscape scenery tours for tourism	x	x			x	
Development of an internet based information system for biking routes	x	x		x	x	
Development of an geo data service for the administration	x	x		x		
Development of a GIS supported field mapping method for a biotope register	x		x			
Development of a mobile touring guide for landscape exploration	x		x			
Development of a hiking information system for different user groups	x					x
Design of an information system for biotope management	x					x

3.2 Evaluation Results

During the years the courses an internal evaluation was done by the end of each course. Around Three aspects of this evaluation will be presented:

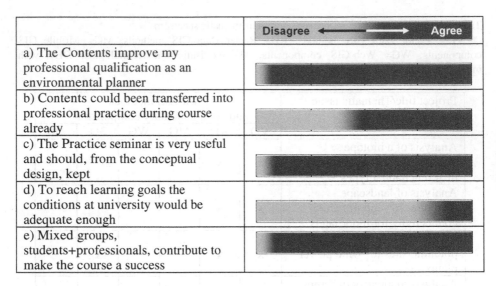

	Disagree ←————→ Agree
a) The Contents improve my professional qualification as an environmental planner	
b) Contents could been transferred into professional practice during course already	
c) The Practice seminar is very useful and should, from the conceptual design, kept	
d) To reach learning goals the conditions at university would be adequate enough	
e) Mixed groups, students+professionals, contribute to make the course a success	

Fig. 2. Evaluation sheets tallied (2a-2d: 123 evaluated participants out of 10 courses; 2e: 69 evaluated participants out of 5 courses)

1. The practical relevance of the course contents

Because the programmes alignment is profession orientated and the target group of environmental planners is clearly defined, it is not very surprising that almost none denied that this course improves the professional qualification as an environmental planner (Fig. 2a). More interesting seems the feedback to the question if the learned topics could contribute to perform tasks in the daily business of profession, while the course is still running (Fig. 2b). More than half of the participants could transfer the lessons learned right away.

2. The methodological-didactic approach of the practical seminar - module 2

More than 90 % of the enumerated questionnaires agree that this module should be kept as it is (Fig. 2c). Furthermore about 70 % doubt that the same learning goals could have been reached with conditions at the university (Fig. 2d). Here the question focused on the situation of working together for one week in teams within a seminar building – away but on site – instead of a regular seminar situation on campus. Here participants often mention that the flexibility of the schedule for the working groups is one practical point to make the learning process productive. Besides that, the intense atmosphere and the option to compare the digital data models with the real world during a field trip also helps to get a better impression of data significance and validity.

Furthermore the working progress was evaluated during the seminars using a mood-barometer, which is supposed to document the atmosphere within the different working groups. Every participant was asked to mark two times a day (around noon and in the evening) his personal satisfaction with a point on a scale. In the context of the working group the supervisors use these marks as an indication about the progress within the different groups. A look at them shows that it is fairly uncommon that there is a steady increasing satisfaction among group members. It's more or less an up and down, which is documenting success and achievement as well as setbacks. In any case, if at the end of the course the line shows up again it's most likely that satisfied project result and therefore learning goals have been achieved (Fig 3).

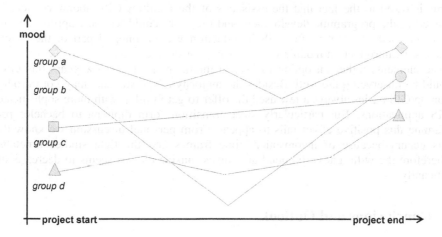

Fig. 3. Schematised figure of evaluated mood-barometers, documented during the practical seminar, may indicate the progress of the working group and achievement of the learning goals.

3. The effect of students and professionals working/learning together

Although just half of the courses could be evaluated from this aspect (see course development at 2.1), the majority of the participants clearly agree to the idea of mixed groups and to the fact that quality of the course would benefit due to this (Fig. 2e). Students often mentioned to appreciate to learn from the structural approach of the professionals and also to get a better impression of practice relevance of GIS. Professionals on the other hand find the time with students not just refreshing for the atmosphere but also benefit from their experience and skills in the use of GIS.

4. The efficiency of the e-learning module

Although this aspect was never structurally evaluated by the questionnaire the results and outcomes as well as the debriefing of the online module allow some conclusions. Therefore professionals appreciate the option to recapitulate lessons from the presence modules and to take time to exercise regarding their personal needs. The contents were evaluated as suitable and effective particularly for post-processed recapitulation of lessons learned and for exercising.

On the other hand the discussions have shown, that it needs a lot of self-discipline and therefore online modules are sometimes neglected, in particular during work intense times, as lots of participants are freelancers. Because of this we discussed with participants again and again if a more compulsory assignments would enforce attendance. But usually those ideas are rejected as being too school-like. One option to increase motivation during online modules is seen in more interactive face-to-face communication tools (like virtual team rooms) and periodic meetings.

5. Benefits to the educational quality for students of the landscape architecture faculty

Especially during the first years synergy effects between the programme development and the development of the faculties GIS curriculum took place and indeed still do. This is owed to the fact that the assistants of the faculties GIS laboratory were involved in the programme development and therefore could test new approaches and teaching methods. Later, after GIS introduction was an integral part of the general studies the introduction module was not being considered as a course to teach students basic elements rather an option to deepen them. In the first view years this effect could be observed quite well. Besides the majority of the students may got introduction on GIS basics always a few used the offer to get familiar with more sophisticated GIS applications. But particularly since transition form diploma to bachelor programme this positive effect fails to appear. From personal discussion we know that this occurs because of inconvenient time frames and the tight studies timetable. Therefore the willingness to attend at courses outside classes seems to decrease significantly.

4 Conclusions and Outlook

Especially the central part of the programme of joint training, the so-called "Practical Seminar", is well appreciated. But this is not just because we run a "real world project" but also because our classroom for this week is on a remote place of the Swabian Alb, where we live and work together – very often until late in the evening. This "summer school like" situation – mainly in the winter season – communicates in an excellent way the various ways of learning, and often brings group members together, who have similar interests and knowledge backgrounds. This so called internal differentiation, combined with the general blended learning concept during the whole course, proved to be quite successful and effective.

10 years of experiences with e-learning methods again and again make us learn that even well evaluated and accepted learning materials are half worth of it, if learning motivation will not constantly raised. This is even more important for an in-service training programme. Therefore interactive tools, like virtual team rooms and regular meetings seem to be essential.

Regarding the students decreasing willingness to attend at courses outside classes due to new time conditions new stimuli needs to be thought about to increase interest again for more sophisticated GIS applications that go beyond the basic GIS curriculum of the faculties. Those can be seen for instance in new corporation forms between the programme and the faculty, i.e. if project and study area of the practical seminar relate to students semester project. Especially in combination with professionals working together at the practical seminars would be mutually beneficial.

References

1. Rolf, W., Lenz, R.: U3-Umweltinformatik-Unterricht für Umweltplaner - Ein Fort- und Weiterbildungskonzept an der Hochschule für Wirtschaft und Umwelt Nürtingen-Geislingen. In: Geoforschungszentrum Potsdam (Hrsg.): Innovationen in der Aus- und Weiterbildung mit GIS, Potsdam, Tagungsband, CD-ROM, Juni 2-3 (2005)

2. Lenz, R.: The IMLA study program: how to strengthen methodology in Landscape Architecture. In: A Critical Light on Landscape Architecture, Proceedings ECLAS Conference 2004, As, Norwegen, September 16-19 (2004)
3. Lenz, R., Rolf, W.: U3 – Umweltinformatikunterricht für Umweltplaner – oder: Lernen mit allen Sinnen. In: Studienkommission Für Hochschuldidaktik An Fachhochschulen In Baden-Württemberg (Hrsg.): Beiträge zum 5. Tag der Lehre, Fachhochschule Nürtingen, Karlsruhe, pp. 174–176 (2003)
4. Lenz, R.J.M.: Project Overview European-Canadian-Curriculum on Environmental Informatics (ECCEI). In: Proceedings International Transdisciplinary Conference, Zürich (2000)
5. Schmidt, I.: Blended E-Learning: Strategie, Konzeption, Praxis. Diploma Thesis. HS Bonn-Rhein-Sieg. Publ.: Examicus, p. 105 (2005)
6. Wiepke, C.: Computergestützte Lernkonzepte und deren Evaluation in der Weiterbildung - Blended Learning zur Förderung von Gender Mainstreaming. Studien zur Erwachsenenbildung, Bd.23, p. 342. Kovac-Verlag, Hamburg (2006)
7. Sauter, A.M., Sauter, W.: Blended Learning. In: Effiziente Integration von E-Learning und Präsenztraining, p. 344. Hermann Luchterhand Verlag, Neuwied (2002)
8. Gudjons, H.: Frontalunterricht - neu entdeckt: Integration in offene Unterrichtsformen, p. 227. UTB, Stuttgart (2007)
9. Blötz, U.: Planspiele in der beruflichen Bildung, p. 271. Bertelsmann, Bielefeld (2008)
10. Schittko, K.: Differenzierung in Schule und Unterricht. Ziele - Konzepte - Beispiele, p. 202. Ehrenwirth Verlag, München (1991)
11. Klein-Landeck, M.: Differenzierung und Individualisierung beim offenen Arbeiten. Beispiel: Englischunterricht. Pädagogik 56(12), 30–33 (2004)
12. Bett, K., Wedekind, J.: Lernplattformen in der Praxis, p. 248. Waxmann Verlag, Münster (2003)
13. Grünwald, S.: Learning Management Systeme im universitären Betrieb, p. 224. Lulu, Deutschland (2008)
14. Hoeksemann, K., Kuhn, M.: Unterrichten mit Moodle. In: Praktische Einführung in das E-Teaching, p. 229. Open Source Press, München (2008)

Envimat.cz – Online Database of Environmental Profiles of Building Materials and Structures

Julie Hodková[1], Antonín Lupíšek[1], Štěpán Mančík[1],
Luděk Vochoc[1], and Tomáš Žďára[2]

[1] Faculty of Civil Engineering, Department of Building Structures, Thákurova 7,
166 29 Praha 6, Czech Republic
[2] Faculty of Electrical Engineering, Department of Computer Graphics and Interaction,
Karlovo náměstí 13, 121 35 Praha 2, Czech Republic
{julie.hodkova,antonin.lupisek,
stepan.mancik,ludek.vochoc}@fsv.cvut.cz, zdaratom@gmail.com

Abstract. Envimat.cz is a new online catalogue of environmental profiles of building materials and structures localized for the Czech Republic. It allows users to compare, model and edit chosen elements. One of the main objectives is to help architects and designers to choose appropriate materials for their building and provide information on its environmental impacts. Information from the catalogue can also play a significant role for developers and their customers. Initial data are derived from the Swiss database Ecoinvent but the goal is to replace them continuously with more accurate, localized data coming from Environmental Product Declarations provided by Czech building industry producers. Envimat.cz brings multiple benefits, especially for the following stakeholders: it gives better information to the building owners; architects can easily choose solutions that are environmentally friendly; efficient producers can make profit from their advantage and Czech construction industry as whole is shifted to higher environmental friendly standard.

Keywords: online database, environmental profiles, building materials, constructions, embodied energy, primary energy, embodied emissions.

1 Introduction

In recent years the technical design of buildings has significantly improved. This led to a sound reduction of environmental impact during the operational stage of their life cycle. So far in the background, however, remained the problem of the construction stage impact. This impact is represented especially by energy consumption, atmospheric emissions and solid waste, but also by depletion of non-renewable sources of raw materials and water consumption during the production phase of materials.

Energy consumption and emissions produced during the life cycle of any structural element are two of the principal parameters used to select environmentally efficient solution. Wider utilization of materials with low values of embodied energy and embodied $CO_{2,eq.}$ or $SO_{2,eq.}$ emissions indicates better environmental quality.

J. Hřebíček, G. Schimak, and R. Denzer (Eds.): ISESS 2011, IFIP AICT 359, pp. 272–279, 2011.

As more low-energy and passive houses are established, the ratio between the construction and operational stage impacts is decreasing, and the consumption of primary energy for construction and related emissions are gaining in importance (see Figure 1).

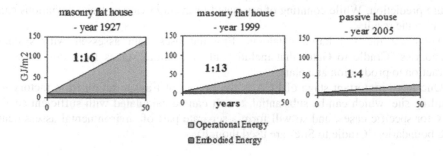

Fig. 1. The ratio between embodied and operational energy consumption [1]

Although the demand for detailed information on products and materials in Czech practice is growing, summary of environmental profiles of materials and structures has not been yet freely available.

With the support of SGS grant of Faculty of Civil Engineering of the Czech Technical University in Prague a web-based catalogue of materials and structures for new buildings and renovations - called Envimat – has been developed. It includes not only their technical but also their environmental parameters.

Fig. 2. Logo of Envimat

Provision of support to compare the environmental quality of several alternatives of proposed structures motivates designer or user of the building to choose the "greener" one and thus could reduce the impact of construction on the environment.

1.1 General Methodology

The basic methodology for evaluation of the environmental impact of buildings is generally Life Cycle Assessment - LCA. The methodology is applicable to any product or process of human activity, including construction materials. All currently used methods for environmental quality assessment of building are based on LCA. They differ primarily by chosen system boundaries, data resources and time of data acquisition.

Correctly, the data from entire life cycle should enter into the assessment of "buildings fabrication" impact. This approach uses the system boundaries "Cradle to Grave", which includes all product life cycle stages from extraction of primary raw materials, through production, transport, application, use and final disposal. More recently, even a "Cradle to Cradle" approach appears, which means a closed life cycle of products including their recycling.

In reality, it is quite difficult to quantify the product life cycle stages between transport to the site and disposal or recycling, because it always means some kind of future prediction. While counting of estimated or average values, large deviations can occur in the results.

Therefore the web-based catalogue Envimat uses data assessed with system boundaries "Cradle to Gate" that include only the initial stages from raw material extraction to production at a plant.

One more important stage of LCA is the impact of transportation from factory to building site, which can be substantial, too. It can be calculated with sufficient accuracy for specific cases, and so will form a separate part of environmental assessment (the boundaries "Cradle to Site" are used though).

1.2 Evaluated Parameters

The substantial parameters of environmental impacts of materials and structures that will be evaluated in Envimat are Primary Energy Input [MJ], Global Warming Potential [$kgCO_{2,eq.}$] and Acidification Potential [$gSO_{2,eq.}$] – i.e. primary energy consumption and related emissions in „Cradle to Gate" system boundaries. The catalogue contains also general building physical characteristics of the constructions as heat transfer coefficient (U [W/m^2K]), weight (m [kg]) or acoustic transmission loss (Rw [dB]).

1.3 Existing Databases

The results of the LCA of materials and structure, with different system boundaries, form the content of many existing databases. The most important of them are listed below:

- Ecoinvent – Swiss Centre for Life Cycle Inventories - up-to-date LCI data
- EPD (Environmental Product Declarations) – www.environdec.com
- INIES – CSTB (Centre Scientifique et Technique du Bâtiment) - French database of EPDs, www.inies.fr
- IBO Baustoffdatenbank – IBO (Austrian Institute for Healthy and Ecological Building) – data of GWP, AP, PEI, EP of materials
- ICE database - Department of Mechanical Engineering, University of Bath - PEI and GWP of a large number of building materials.
- Bauteilkatalog www.bauteilkatalog.ch – SIA (Swiss Society of Engineers and Architects) - data of GWP, PEI, AP of building structures etc., www.bauteilkatalog.ch
- Ökobau.dat - German Institute Bauen und Umwelt (bau-umwelt.de) - German database of EPDs

1.4 Differences among Various Databases

The resulting differences that can occur in assessment of one building while using various databases are shown at the following charts. IBO and ICE databases (see previous paragraph) were used here for a case study.

It is evident especially in the comparison of embodied emissions of CO_2. While IBO assessed the wooden construction as environmentally extremely friendly the ICE methodics presents this construction on similar level with IBO assessment of brick construction. In this case, the difference between two assessments of one building by two different databases is massive.

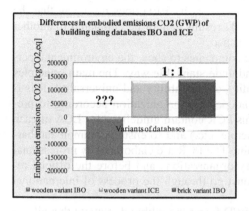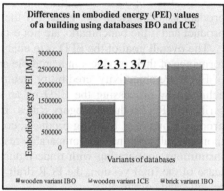

Fig. 3. Differences in embodied energy and carbon of building evaluated with IBO or ICE database [2]

There can be several reasons for such results as different system boundaries in the methodology (what life cycle stages are included, what processes enter the assessment etc.), data sources (from manufacturers or from secondary sources) or age of the data (modern versus older technologies).

2 Methodology of Envimat

The catalogue uses one of the largest international database of building materials Ecoinvent, developed in Switzerland. The database includes pieces of European mean data, but often it offers only Swiss data. To be closer to real conditions, the energy related data were recalculated for the Czech fuel mix in electricity network.

The major aim of Envimat development is to cooperate with local Czech manufacturers to obtain accurate data corresponding to the Czech conditions. Future material database used for Envimat will contain data obtained using EPD - Environmental Product Declaration (see below) or equivalent methodology. It will allow the manufacturers to provide their data and fill them in the database.

2.1 EPD

The Environmental Product Declaration – EPD is defined as "quantified environmental data for a product with pre-set categories of parameters based on the ISO 14040 series of standards, but not excluding additional environmental information"[6]. It measures energy and water consumption, waste production, impact on climate change, eutrophication, destruction of the ozone layer, etc. throughout the life cycle. The EPD document containing this information must be publicly accessible and the data contained therein must be verifiable. It is in fact a detailed "certificate" on the product's environmental impact[3].

In the EPD method every type of material has clearly established the so-called product category rules (PCR), i.e. a set of required parameters with defined system boundaries that must be evaluated in order to maintain the comparability of the results needed. It is important to realize that being labeled by EPD does not mean that the product is "ecological" or "green", if the EPD results cannot be compared to another product and if the benchmarks are not established.

The overall goal of the EPD is to enable companies to show the environmental performance of their products in a credible and understandable way. The main principles of EPDs are objectivity, credibility, neutrality, comparability and universality. This is achieved by processing the EPD by an independent organization according to pre-scribed PCR - Product Category Rules. This PCR contain guidelines for LCA of each product group (e.g. building products, concrete, etc.) and so ensure common and har-monized calculations and comparable results. The PCR are elaborated by professional institutions cooperating with trade industry organizations and before the official re-lease of the final version, the PCR draft must go through the process of international reviews and comments.

For end customers and consumers, the EPD forms a credible document that allows them to choose the most suitable product. As it is elaborated according to unified international methodology, the parameters of the products of the same type from different parts of the world are comparable. This implies also an advantage for pro-ducers and EPD publishers, since the declaration of their products are accepted worldwide [3].

2.2 Goals and Objectives of Envimat

The goal was to create an online tool for evaluating and comparing the building struc-tures and components according to their environmental and physical profiles with regard to the purpose and use of such element.

A missing database of building materials and structures localized for the Czech Republic is prepared. It is focused on embodied energy and CO_2 emissions. It will be available to the professional public and will also be suitable for teaching about these issues at specialized schools.

The tool will allow users to select or edit existing structures, create new structure or the possibility of expanding the database with new structures and materials.

It will be possible to compare, sort and filter the selected structures, using the fuzzy multi-criteria evaluation based on user preferences.

The producers will have an option to import data of their products.

3 Envimat Architecture

The following Figure 3 shows the class model, which serves as a starting point for creating the Envimat database application.

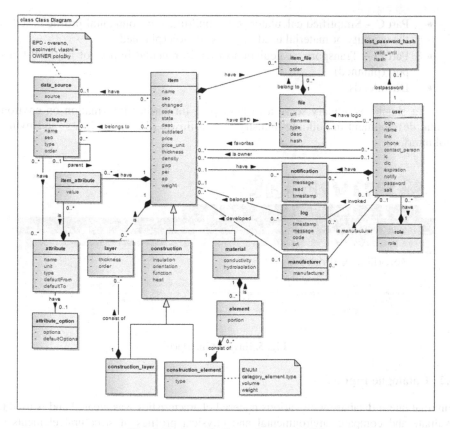

Fig. 4. Envimat database class model [7]

3.1   Envimat Interface

The structure of the web catalogue is as follows:

- Main page with the methodology and links to additional information
- Part A : Catalogue of materials
    - Option 1 – Search in the material database and filtering of the materials according to their paramters and typology
    - Option 2 – Comparison of chosen materials
- Part B : Catalogue of existing structures
    - Option 1 – Structures ranked according to one parameter - Environmental (PEI, GWP...); Technical (U, Rw...)
    - Option 2 – Detailed search according to users criterion preferences – individual weighting of different criteria (under preparation)
    - Option 3 – Comparison of chosen structures
    - Option 4 – Creation of a new structure according to individual parameters and requirements of user – modelling new structure; modification of existing structure; modification of existing historical structure (under preparation)

- Part C – Simplified calculator of the building environmental profile based on the quantity of material used for construction (planned)
- Part D – Transport – calculation of environmental impact of material transport (planned)
- Downloads

Envimat should eventually serve as a guidepost for further information on environmental development in building industry. The following Figure 5 shows the Envimat tool interface.

Fig. 5. Envimat interface

3.2 Catalogue Inputs

Envimat intern database with various material characteristics was created and is used to evaluate and compare environmental and physical profiles of structural elements or building structures. Some of the assessed characteristics are shown at the next Figure 6.

Název	GWP kg CO2 ekv./kg	PEI MJ/kg	AP g SO2ekv./kg	ρ kg/m3	λ W/mK	
antireflexní sklo	1.4913	25.176	0.007702	2600	1.35	
beton chudý	0.055726	0.366257	0.00011	2190	1.3	
beton normální	0.109891	0.608789	0.000185	2380	1.4	

Fig. 6. Envimat interface

As stated above, while working with the tool, user can either use pre-defined materials and structures, or he can create his own structure by filling in the material layers.

As stated in Methodology of Envimat chapter, the manufacturers will be allowed to fill in the data of their products. It is clear that the data entered into the database must be checked and approved before they are officially submitted into the database.

Envimat also provides a possibility of exporting data of a certain material to PDF and comparison of two materials and their environmental profiles.

4 Conclusion

Nowadays the developers, builders, and future users are not enough motivated to address the impact of used construction materials on the environment. They are usually not interested in other solutions that incorporate the same features and technical parameters, but a smaller environmental impact, partly because there is no existing tool that would allow them to do so.

Web-based catalog of materials and structures for new buildings and renovations - Envimat - helps them with environmental assessment and selection of suitable materials or structures. It will also allow producers of building materials to supply the necessary data to include their product into the internal database of the catalogue. In the Czech Republic the catalogue with localized data offers a detailed evaluation and comparison of building structures and components not only based on their physical parameters but also on the impact of their production on the environment.

Acknowledgement. This research has been supported by SGS grant No SGS10/011/OHK1/1T/11.

References

1. Vonka, M.: Hodnocení životního cyklu budov. Doctoral thesis, Prague (2006)
2. Hodkova, J.: Application of environmental characteristics of building materials in construction practice. In: Workshop W2 2010 Proceedings of Workshop/Sborník příspěvků: Workshop Doktorského Grantu GAČR 103/09/H095, Prague (2010).
3. CENIA - Czech Information Agency of the Environment, http://www.cenia.cz/
4. Waltjen, T.: Passivhaus-Bauteilkatalog. Ökologish bewertete Konstruktionen. Springer-Verlag/Wien, Austria (2008)
5. Hammond, G., Jones, C.: Inventory of carbon and energy. University of Bath, UK (2008)
6. The International EPDsystem. Stockholm: Environdec, http://www.environdec.com
7. Žďára, T.: Katalog fyzikálních a environmentálních profilů stavebních konstrukcí. Bachelor thesis, Prague (2011)
8. Catalogue of Environmental Profiles of Building Materials and Constructions, http://www.envimat.cz

The ENVISION Environmental Portal and Services Infrastructure

Patrick Maué[1] and Dumitru Roman[2]

[1] Institute for Geoinformatics (ifgi), University of Münster, Germany
`patrick.maue@uni-muenster.de`
[2] SINTEF, Oslo, Norway
`dumitru.roman@sintef.no`

Abstract. The ENVISION Portal is a Web-enabled infrastructure for the discovery, annotation, and composition of environmental services. It is a tool to create Web sites dedicated to particular domain-specific scenarios such as oil spill drift modeling or landslide risk assessment. The underlying architecture based on pluggable user interface components is briefly discussed, followed by a presentation of the components resulting from the first iteration of the implementation. A walkthrough explains how to create a scenario website and populate it with the user interface components required for one specific scenario. The paper concludes with a discussion of open challenges identified during the implementation.

Keywords: Environmental Services, Environmental Models, Portals, Ontologies.

1 Introduction

Geospatial workflows such as the processing and analysis of environmental data to support decision making are traditionally realized with Geographic Information Systems (GIS). The benefits of distributing tasks into the Web have been acknowledged by the geospatial community. Since the INSPIRE directive entered into force, the number of geospatial Web services embedded in Spatial Data Infrastructures (SDI) has grown considerably. Standards by the Open Geospatial Consortium[1] (OGC) have been specified to enable seamless integration of these Web service into existing geospatial workflows. The standards specify Web service interfaces, data models, and encodings for feature- and raster-based data, or data coming from in-situ environmental sensors. Even though there has been considerable uptake of these Web services in the geographic information community, they are playing only a small role for environmental modeling infrastructures.

Environmental computer models, which, for example, predict future weather conditions or interpolate temperature observations, are still rarely seen on the Web. Migrating existing models into the Web, and the development of Web-based user interfaces for environmental models, is a challenging task. But the

---

[1] Website of the OGC `http://www.opengeospatial.org/`

J. Hřebíček, G. Schimak, and R. Denzer (Eds.): ISESS 2011, IFIP AICT 359, pp. 280–294, 2011.

outcome of this process is of large interest not only for the environmental modeling community [1]. Initiatives such as SEIS ("Shared Environmental Information System") and SISE ("Shared Information Space for Europe") call for a better availability of environmental information for the end users, both public authorities and citizens. Making environmental computer models available on the Web is also the vision of the "Model Web" [2]. The Model Web has been defined within GEOSS ("Global Earth Observation System of Systems") [3] as the potential solution to enhance the interoperability of environmental computer models. It is a vision of a multidisciplinary network of models, data sources, processes, and sensors, which seamlessly interact through the well-defined Web service interfaces specified by the OGC. The interoperable computer models are supposed to be available to researchers, managers, policy makers, and the general public. Environmental service infrastructures are one first step towards the idea of havings Models as services in the Model Web [4].

Several open issues contribute to the lack of environmental services on the Web. The existing models are often complex monolithic systems implemented decades ago in programming languages incompatible with modern distributed architectures. The variability of the input parameters is challenging, and the computer model's graphical user interface required to specify these parameters cannot be simply migrated into the Web. The required data sources are often locked away due to licensing issues and the often proprietary formats impair their reusability for other applications. Another open issue is the modeling expert's fear of losing control over the model execution. In a workshop with geologists working with the modeling infrastructure developed in the research project SWING, the experts were in general convinced about the benefits of migrating existing models into the Web [5]. But they also mentioned the importance of communicating how the model has been executed, e.g. by not also only delivering the resulting maps but also the results of intermediate steps and the input parameter and input data.

The ENVISION ("Environmental Services Infrastructure with ontologies") project[2] started early 2010 as follow-up project to SWING [6]. The research aims to enable the migration of computer models into the Web through the conceptual specification and implementation of an environmental services infrastructure. The results include tools for a semantically enhanced and multilingual discovery of existing environmental services and the adaptive composition of environmental models as services. The Web-enabled creation and publication of scenario Web sites built on these models supports decision making in the environmental domain even for users with little technical skills. The scenario Web sites visualize the results of the environmental models using interactive map viewers, diagrams, and other scenario-dependent components. A pluggable user interface based on *Portal* frameworks ensures a high flexibility for the configuration of these Web sites. This paper introduces the underlying architecture of Portals and the ENVISION user interface components.

---

[2] See http://www.envision-project.eu

The presented research builds on two scenarios to validate the implemented infrastructure for environmental service. Risk assessment for landslide hazards is subject of the first scenario; the focus lies on the integration of real-time data coming from in-situ sensors deployed in the pilot area (the French department Guadeloupe). In the second pilot, the impact of oil spills in the Norwegian Sea on the development of the cod population will be investigated. For both scenarios a set of OGC-compliant Web services coming from various organizations are re-used.

In the ENVISION project, we are following the SEIS principles by enabling end-users to participate in environmental decision making processes through the planned environmental services infrastructure. The provided open source technologies will support the easy creation of new environmental models by coupling existing services to compositions, and to publish these models in domain-specific scenario Web sites which enable both, the general public and the environmental experts, to interact with the models and integrate them into decision-making processes.

This paper gives the reader a first impression about the ENVISION Portal. We start with a short overview of the general architecture, and then walk through the steps required to setup an environmental model and publish it on a scenario Web site. Before we give an outlook in the conclusion, we discuss open challenges which emerged during the first iteration in the development of the platform.

2   Architecture

The primary target of this research has been the specification and implementation of a Web-based portal which supports users in the discovery, annotation, and composition of new environmental models exposed as Web services. The portal enables the creation of domain-specific Web sites. These Web sites enable end users to interact with the models, preferably on maps augmented with interface components suitable for changing and calibrating certain aspects of the model. This approach requires a pluggable user interface, which makes it easy for the scenario Web site designers to select from a library of components useful for one particular computer model.

The user interface is based on Portlets based on the standard "JSR 286: Java Portlet Specification"[7]. The Portlets are the individual building blocks of a Portal. The latter is in its broadest sense an entry point to access certain domain-specific information. The purpose of portal software is similar to other Content Management Systems: it provides a framework for Web sites in need for personalization, authentication, and the management of the presentation layer of information systems [7]. The Portal is provided by the Portal Container, which manages the initialization and rendering of the portlets as well as Inter-Portlet Communication (IPC). Several open source implementations of Portal Containers compliant to JSR 286 exist, with Apache Jetspeed[3] and Liferay[4]

---

[3] See http://portals.apache.org/jetspeed-2
[4] See http://www.liferay.com

being probably the most popular choices. The Portlets are delivered through Portlet Repositories. The portal software linked to these repositories then manages the installation and updating of the deployed portlets. The portal consists of several portal pages, and each page may be composed of multiple Portlets. The Portlets itself communicate with back-end Web services, which perform most of the tasks required in environmental services infrastructures.

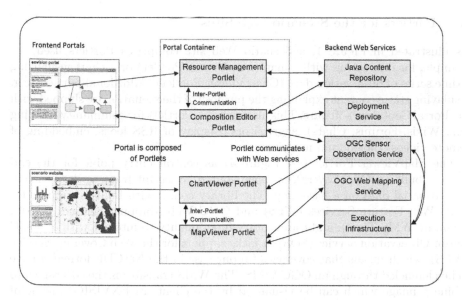

Fig. 1. High-level overview of architecture

Figure 1 illustrates the basic dependencies between the frontend Portals (the scenario Web sites and the ENVISION Portal), the Portlets, and the backend Web Services. The ENVISION Portal is an infrastructure to manage environmental Web services and to configure and publish scenario Web sites. The latter are domain-specific Portals, dedicated to one specific scenario such as showing landslide models for one particular region. The scenario Web sites are implemented as sub-portals, which are conceptually separated from the main Portal, but share the same platform. Creating a scenario Web sites involves the selection of layout, portlets, access rights, and more.

The Portals are composed of Portlets. The communication between portlets is realized through IPC events as defined in the JSR 286 standard. If, for example, a user selects a sensor in a portlet showing a map, another portlet on the same page automatically updates a displayed chart with the data of this specific sensor. A pluggable user interface relies on loosely coupled, but well defined interfaces. It should be easy to switch between different implementations for certain portlets. Loose coupling also decreases the risk of functional dependencies between the components. One portlet has to remain fully functional (but not necessarily useful) if other portlets are not present on the same page. The map's notification for the timeline to update itself therefore has to go through this interface. This technique can potentially work across pages and even different user sessions, making it for example possible to update maps on other users' browsers by the model designer if, for example, the model has been re-computed due to new input data.

2.1 Portlets for the Scenario Web Sites

As illustrated in Figure 1, a Scenario Web site comprises Portlets used, for example, for interacting with a map (MapViewer Portlet) or a chart visualizing a time series of observation data (ChartViewer Portlet). Additional portlets, e.g. displaying static content explaining the purpose of the scenario, are shipped with the Portal Container software. This also includes Portlets for community building (e.g. Wikis, Forums, Chats), aggregators (display of RSS feeds, embedding of remote videos, Blogs), and many more.

The MapViewer Portlet (see Figure 4) as central entry point for the end users is built on OpenLayers[5], an open source javascript framework to visualize geospatial data on a base map. The library comes with built-in support for OGC Web Feature Services (WFS) and OGC Web Mapping Services (WMS, including WMS Time), and rudimentary functionality to interact with an OGC Sensor Observation Service (SOS). It lacks support for the Web Coverage Service (WCS), which means that coverages (in our case in the NetCDF format[6]) have to be channeled through an OGC WMS. The WMS transforms the coverage into a binary image which can be visualized by the client. In ENVISION, some of the services do not necessarily have an OGC-compliant interface. The composed workflows, for example, are at the moment deployed on standard workflow engines which only expose a Web service interface based on the W3C SOAP and WSDL standards. Hence, the Open Layers client had to be extended to also support these service interfaces.

Other crucial portlets for the scenario Web sites include the uncertainty-enabled ChartViewer Portlet (see also Figure 4) and the Notification Portlet. The former expects the sensor data encoded in the OGC Observation&Measurement [8] format to be augmented with uncertainty information. In this case, we rely on the UncertML standard [9]. In-situ sensors produce measurements within a certain confidence interval. If a gaussian distribution for the measurements can be assumed, the observation would include the mean as well as the upper and lower confidence intervals. The chartviewer renders the mean as expected observation value, and the confidence intervals to illustrate the uncertainty of this value. The notification portlet enables users to subscribe to certain events which can be associated to the models and sensor services visualized in the MapViewer Portlet. The nature of the event is modelled in domain ontologies. Complex Event Processing [10] is applied to extract the events from the data streams

---

[5] See http://openlayers.org/

[6] See http://www.unidata.ucar.edu/software/netcdf/

and populate the ontologies with event instances. The underlying architecture is quite complex, and explained in more detail in [11].

2.2 Portlets for the ENVISION Portal

The ENVISION Portal is separated from the scenario Web sites and comes with its own set of portlets required to manage and publish environmental models. The Portal is (for now) composed of three pages for the discovery, annotation, and composition of environmental models. The Resource Management Portlet acts as a bridge between the different pages and manages the user collection of Web services, Ontologies, and Composition Drafts. The user collection is shared across different Portals, the user's email address acts as unique identifier of the collection. The resources are stored in a repository compliant to the Content Repository API for Java [12], which supports the storage and retrieval of arbitrary documents in a tree-like structure.

The annotation consists of a set of portlets enabling the user to link existing Web service with the ontologies. The annotation procedure is based on the methodology developed for the SWING project. We distinguish between the ontology querying tool (using the *Ontology Query Portlet*) and the actual semantic annotation with the visualized ontology. Querying supports natural language queries (expecting the ontologies to be grounded with a rich set of documents) which enables users unaware of the specifics of the ontology to identify the correct concepts. The annotation screen then enables the user to select the entities in the data model (e.g. an attribute of an feature type coming from an OGC WFS) and link them to the discovered ontology concept.

The *Discovery Portlet* is backed by a standard OGC catalogue (in this case we are using the Geonetworks[7] implementation). The Discovery Portlet is a standard catalogue client with support for spatial and keyword-based queries. In the next step, it will be enhanced with semantic query capabilities. The user will be able to browse the ontologies and select the concepts and relations which best reflect the required data. The semantic query is encoded within a standard OGC CSW query. A semantic catalogue adapter is then responsible to forward the standard OGC query constraints to the existing catalogue, and the semantic part to a reasoning engine.

The *Composition Editor Portlet* allows user for coupling OGC Web services via workflows. The core processing of an environmental model (e.g. the interpolation method) are separated from the Web services delivering the input data (e.g. sensor data streams, feature collections, or coverages). With the composition the input data services are linked to the processing services, the result is a workflow document encoded in the Business Process Modelling Execution Language (BPEL) [13] which can be deployed on standard workflow engines such as Apache ODE [8]. The workflows are specified using the Busness Process Modelling Notation (BPMN) [14], and translated to executable BPEL specifications. The

---

[7] See http://geonetwork-opensource.org/
[8] See http://ode.apache.org/

BPMN editor is based on the Oryx Editor[9], a popular Web-based open source BPM diagram editor for the Web [15].

The portlets are all backed up by Web services implementing the processing, execution, and resource management. In particular, the execution of the geospatial workflows can be challenging. The amount of the transported data can be massive, and the processing algorithms can be resource-intensive. A distributed execution infrastructure based on Peer-to-Peer technology is currently implemented in ENVISION to ensure efficient and semantically-aware execution of the workflows [16].

3   Setting Up a Scenario Web Site

The following walkthrough explains the steps required to compose a new environmental model from existing Web services and to publish it with a scenario Web site. The scenario is based on a simple use case developed for the ENVISION project. A WPS has been implemented to model the risk of drought in urbanized areas in France. A range of sensors measuring the current groundwater levels serve as input (via an SOS interface) for the classification. The features representing the urbanized areas come from a WFS loaded with the Corine landcover dataset. The activities described here also illustrated in a video[10].

The targeted user of the ENVISION Portal is the domain expert with knowledge about setting up an environmental model. This does not necessarily include any ICT skills. The Portal is supposed to enable experts with particular expertise in one particular environmental domain (e.g. oil spills) to create a Web site. He might know how to program a model, and has in depth knowledge about the expected outcomes of models and the impact of the input parameter. He most probably has no experience in Web services, OGC standards, data formats, or Ontologies. The end users, which are the target audience of the Scenario Web sites, might have neither experience in environmental models nor ICT. Here, the focus lies on a simple user experience, which enables any user to interact with the models and understand the potential impact of changes in our environment.

3.1   Importing a Resource

In this example we assume that we know the location of the SOS and the WFS. The Resource Manager Portlet allows for directly importing Web services and Ontologies into the user's personal collection. After selecting the service type and version, the importing procedure will request the service capabilities and store a resource descriptor in the user collection. This service itself cannot be used yet for the annotation and composition. The annotation procedure requires RDF-based service models which can be extended with the references pointing to the ontologies. The composition relies on WSDL service descriptions due to the

---

[9] See http://bpt.hpi.uni-potsdam.de/Oryx/
[10] Screencasts are available through the project Web site at
http://www.envision-project.eu

implementation of the workflows in BPEL. Before moving to the next step, we select the "Translate Resource" action in the resource portlet. This triggers three subsequent actions: translation, cross-linking, and proxying. The first results in a set of WSDL and RDF files for each feature type for the WFS, observed property for the SOS, or process for the WPS. Cross-linking injects references to the other representations in each of these files and the original capabilities. Many of the components in the ENVISION architecture require access to the other representations: the semantic-aware optimization of the BPEL compositions has for example only access to the WSDL files, but requires the RDF-based service models to reason on the services. Proxying will register the original capabilities file to the semantic proxy, which ensures that the semantic enhancements are also available to standard OGC clients [17]. The following Figure 2 shows the Annotation Page, which contains the Resource Manager Portlet as well as the annotation portlets.

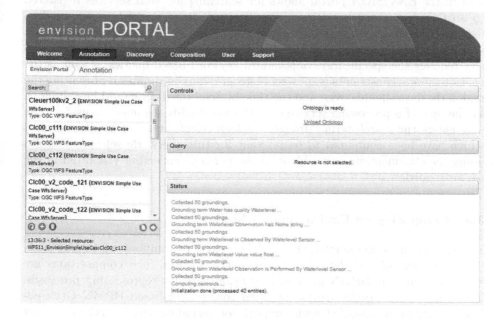

Fig. 2. The Annotation Page with the Resource Portlet

3.2 Annotating a Web Service

In the next step, we semantically annotate the RDF-based service models resulting from the translation. The annotation procedure itself does not put any constraints on the ontologies (besides being encoded in RDF). The ontologies are grounded, which means each concept and relation is automatically enriched with a rich set of textual documents to enable natural language queries. In this example, we are going to annotate the feature type clc00_c112 of the WFS. According to the CORINE documentation, this code represents urbanized areas in Europe. After the ontology has been grounded through the "Prepare Ontology" action in the Resource Manager Portlet, the ontology is loaded into the Annotation Portlet. The user inputs the natural language query "populated areas" to find the appropriate concept in the ontology. Due to the grounding, the Query Portlet is able to infer that the concept `UrbanAreas` matches the user query. The user selects the most relevant result, which results in the next step in an annotation linking the feature type `clc00_c112` to the domain concept `UrbanAreas` through a rule injected into the service description.

3.3   Discovering a Web Service

A WFS and an SOS have been imported in the personal collection, but a Web service capable of processing and reclassifying the input features according the real-time observations is still missing and unknown to the user. The discovery tool in the ENVISION portal allows for searching for Web services registered to an OGC-compliant catalogue. The catalogue itself might be configured to federate queries to other catalogues, making it possible to cover a potentially very large set of relevant Web services. Discovery of geospatial data traditionally requires the specification of standard keyword based queries as well as the spatiotemporal constraints (e.g., a set of geographic coordinates representing the region the data should cover, and the time interval the data should be valid for). In the case of a processing service only the keyword-based query is useful. The user enters the search term "drought", which results in a list of Web services which have been computed to be relevant for this query. He selects the WPS doing the classification, and adds it to the personal collection visualized in the resource portlet.

3.4   Composing an Environmental Model

With the composition portlet, the modeler is able to compose services by specifying the control and data flow between the services. The compositions are specified using the BPMN graphical notation used for representing processes. The composition portlet wraps the open source Web-based BPMN Oryx editor. It has been extended with support for including OGC services as part of process compositions and a module that generates executable BPEL code that can be deployed and executed in a BPEL engine. In combination with the Resource Manager Portlet, the composition portlet offers an integrated modeling environment where the user selects services from the resource module, imports them as tasks in the composition, specifies the necessary control and data flow in BPMN, and generates executable BPEL code from the BPMN composition. The following Figure 3 provides a screenshot of the resource portlet and the composition portlet. The composition portlet depicts the composition of an SOS service (GetElevation) and an WFS service (GetWaterLevel) together with their data and control flows. Once the composition is finished, it is transformed into an executable BPEL composition which is stored in the user collection. As

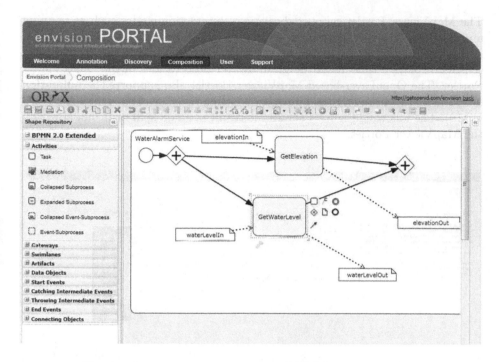

Fig. 3. The Composition Page with the Oryx Workflow Editor

final step, the user deploys the composition to the runtime infrastructure via the Deployment Service.

3.5   Creating the Scenario Web Site

At this stage, a new environmental model has been created and successfully deployed to the runtime infrastructure. The deployment results in a new Web service endpoint, which, if called, returns the result of the model. In the next step, we are setting up a new Web site with the help of the Portal software which is configured to show this result. The functionality required for this task is built into the Portal Container. The user creates a new sub-portal, defines the Portal Pages, and adds the Portlets to the Portal Pages. Some of the Portlets require configuration (e.g. the locations of the Spatial Data Services have to defined for the MapViewer Portlet). Once finished, the user defines who has access to the Scenario Web site (e.g. is authentication required, or is it open to the public).

3.6   Accessing the Environmental Model

The Scenario Web site has been published and consists of the MapViewer Portlet showing the results of a composition computing the risk of water shortage for certain regions in France. The MapViewer Portlet has been configured to show the regions exceeding a certain risk of drought, as well as the groundwater sensors.

The MapViewer Portlet supports basic map interaction modes such as panning and zooming. Besides that the user is able to toggle layers, display a legend, and select the objects presented on the map. Selecting one of the groundwater sensors displays a timeline of the groundwater observations in the ChartViewer Portlet. The OpenLayer-based MapViewer Portlet also supports the animation of spatial data with a temporal dimension (using the time extension of the OGC WMS). The following Figure 4 shows the result of an oil spill drift model within the MapViewer Portlet.

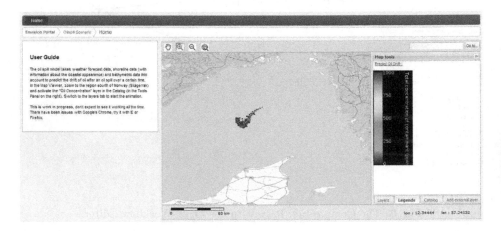

Fig. 4. A Scenario Web site with an Oil Spill Model in the MapViewer

4   Open Challenges

In the following section we highlight some of the open research challenges which came up during the first iteration of the implementation, and which will be further investigated in the following years.

Interacting with environmental models on the Web.   Environmental models are complex software systems whose initial core has been implemented decades ago, and are since then gradually improved and extended. The underlying implementation is based on sometimes ancient software architectures realized with programming languages such as Fortran or Cobolt. This makes it challenging to split up these models into individual reusable software components which can then be migrated to Web services. In addition, invoking models requires rich user interaction. In the oil spill scenario, for example, the domain experts need to be able to constantly adapt the input parameters to calibrate the models. To observe the results, sophisticated data anlyzing tools such as computing and visualizing the cross profile of a submerged oil slick are applied. Making Web-enabled rich user interface components which are generic enough to support different models is an issue which requires a thourough analysis of the end user requirements.

Standardized Web service interfaces for environmental models. The environmental models are transformed either as a whole into Web services or split up into individual and reusable components. These componenets are later coupled again through Web service compositions. In the end, the new Web services have to be made accessible to generic spatial data clients to enable the integration into existing geospatial workflows. Web service standards from the W3C or the OGC (e.g. the Web Processing Service) ensure flexibility regarding the supported operations, but also impair reusability for clients expecting well-defined interfaces. Supporting both - reusability and flexibility - requires a compromise which reflects the best of both worlds.

Integration of generic Web services and domain-specific file formats Even though OGC standards have found wide-spread adaption within some communities, they are rarely seen on a global scale. Talking about Web service usually implies the use of WSDL service descriptions and the SOAP standards for encoding the messages. In contrary to OGC services, these Web service don't have predefined semantics for the operations and the parameters. Finding ways to semantically annotate generic Web services with the methodology described above will be further investigated in the next year. But in the environmental community, even the concept of a generic Web service itself is not common. Here, much data is made available as files, often in unique formats. Making this data available to the BPEL workflows requires the implementation of proxy services which translate the Web service requests and return the appropriate files.

Design-time mediation for the composition. Support for the specification of mappings between data structures is a necessity when one needs to specify data passing in compositions. Being able to map between the output of a task and the input of another task is part of the actual specification of the composition and necessary for the generation of executable code for the composition. Mappings both at the syntactic and semantic layers are needed, as well as techniques to semi-automatically suggest possible mappings to the user.

Efficiency of runtime mediation. The mappings required for linking Web services can range from simply assignments to complex rules including arithmetic or spatial transformations. In the case of environmental data, the number of data entities which have to be processed during the mediation can significantly slow down the execution process. Caching results and the specification of the mediation rules in low-level languages are currently investigated to ensure performant execution.

Inspecting the executed compositions. Severe trust issues still impair the uptake of Web services by environmental modeling experts. The Web services are considered to be black boxes, which produce results hard to understand without knowing the internal processes of the model [5]. The Scenario Web sites will include Portlets allowing for inspecting the provenance of the models, by retracing the individual steps in the workflows and inspecting the intermediate results.

Integration of existing ontologies. Ontologies come in different flavors. Their applicability for annotating the environmental services depends on the chosen ontology language, the invested effort for its engineering, and the authors' experience in the domain. The technical integration of remote ontologies requires a translation into formats which can be processed by the reasoning engines deployed in ENVISION.

Ontology Maintenance. Ontologies usually represent one particular perspective on a domain and have been engineered with one particular application in mind. They hardly ever suit the needs of other domain-specific applications. Integrating existing ontologies relies on techniques to adapt the ontologies for other applications while staying consistent with the original source. Users of the ENVISION Portal will be able to import ontologies into their personal collections. The annotation interface will give them means to dynamically add new concepts or rename existing concepts.

Creating new ontologies. If no suitable ontologies exist, the users have to be able to simply create new ontologies without having to know how to write the actual ontology code. A simple concept suggestion Portlet has been created in the first year, which supports the user through data mining techniques to come up with new ontologies. In the next step, users will align these concepts to a foundational ontology by answering automatically generated questions. The new ontologies are published through the Resource Management Portlet, which enables other users to reuse them for other tasks.

This list only includes practical challenges which have to be addressed to move towards the vision of the Model Web. It is obviously far from complete, other research issues such a handling the uncertainty of environmental data or incorporating the real-time aspects of sensor data are also planned to be investigated.

5   Conclusion

This paper presented the ENVISION Portal, a Web-based infrastructure for the discovery, annotation, and composition of environmental services. We have presented a brief discussion of the underlying architecture, and listed a subset of the user interface components developed in the first iteration of the implementation. The implementation of the Portal is part of the research conducted in the ENVISION project, which is scheduled to end in 2012. The open challenges identified in this paper are part of the project's research agenda.

The targeted user community of the ENVISION Portal are scientists and environmental modeling experts willing to share their models to the public. The Portal supports the publication of Scenario Web sites, which are domain-specific portals making the models accessible to users lacking knowledge about the inner working of environmental computer models. We don't claim that the presented infrastructure will be able to cover all possible environmental models.

In fact, probably only very few will be ever made available as Web services. The inherent complexity of model algorithms, the sophisticated requirements for the user interfaces, and open questions regarding trust and licensing rights are and will be a major obstacle for the distribution of models to the public. Nonetheless we believe that the ENVISION Portal is one important step towards the vision of shared environmental information systems.

Acknowledgements

The presented research has been funded by the European project *ENVISION* (FP7-249120).

References

1. Granell, C., Díaz, L., Gould, M.: Service-oriented applications for environmental models: Reusable geospatial services. Environmental Modelling & Software 25(2), 182–198 (2010)
2. Geller, G.N., Melton, F.: Looking Forward: Applying an Ecological Model Web to assess impacts of climate change. Biodiversity 9(3&4)
3. Christian, E.: Planning for the Global Earth Observation System of Systems (GEOSS). Space Policy 21(2), 105–109 (2005)
4. Roman, D., Schade, S., Berre, A.J., Bodsberg, N.R., Langlois, J.: Model as a Service (MaaS). In: Maué, P., Kiehle, C. (eds.) Proceedings of AGILE Workshop: Grid Technologies for Geospatial Applications, AGILE (2009)
5. Urvois, M., Berre, A. J.: D1.3 - Experience Report, SWING Project Deliverable (July 2009)
6. Andrei, M., Berre, A., Costa, L., Duchesne, P., Fitzner, D., Schade, S., Steinmetz, N., Tertre, F., Vasiliu, L.: SWING: A Geospatial Semantic Web Service Environment. In: Proceedings of AGILE 2008 Workshop "Semantic Web meets Geospatial Applications" (2008)
7. Heppner, S.: JSR 286: Java Portlet Specification 2.0 (2008), http://www.jcp.org/en/jsr/detail?id=286
8. Cox, S.: Observations and Measurements - Part 1 - Observation schema (OGC 07-022r1) (Dezember 2007)
9. Williams, M., Cornford, D., Bastin, L., Ingram, B.: UncertML: an XML schema for exchanging uncertainty. In: Proceedings of GISRUK, Manchester, UK, vol. 44, pp. 0–3 (2008)
10. Luckham, D.: The Power of Events: An Introduction to Complex Event Processing in Distributed Enterprise Systems. Addison-Wesley Professional, Reading (2002)
11. Michels, H., Maué, P.: Semantics for notifying events in the affecting environment. In: Proceedings of Enviroinfo 2010, Bonn, Germany (2010)
12. Nuescheler, D.: JSR 283: Content Repository for JavaTM Technology API Version 2.0 (2009), http://jcp.org/en/jsr/detail?id=283
13. Diane, J., Evdemon, J.: Web Services Business Process Execution Language Version 2.0, OASIS Standard (April 2007)

14. Allweyer, T.: BPMN - Business Process Modeling Notation (German Edition), BoD (2009)
15. Decker, G., Overdick, H., Weske, M.: Oryx – An Open Modeling Platform for the BPM Community. In: Dumas, M., Reichert, M., Shan, M.-C. (eds.) BPM 2008. LNCS, vol. 5240, pp. 382–385. Springer, Heidelberg (2008)
16. Tsalgatidou, A., Athanasopoulos, G., Pantazoglou, M.: Interoperability Among Heterogeneous Services: The Case of Integration of P2P Services with Web Services. International Journal of Web Service Research 5(4), 79–110 (2008)
17. Maué, P., Michels, H., Roth, M.: Injecting semantic annotations into (geospatial) Web service descriptions, Accepted for Semantic Web Journal (SWJ)

Crop Simulation Model Registrator and Polyvariant Analysis

Sergey Medvedev and Alexander Topaj

Agrophysical Research Institute. 14, Grazhdansky Prospect
195220 Saint-Petersburg, Russia
glorguin@yandex.ru, topaj@hotmail.ru

Abstract. Typical use cases of the crop simulation models consist of such operations as parametric identification, yield forecast and optimization, analysis of different technologies etc. All these tasks relate to multiple running of the model with several variants of input parameters and can be automated by means of polyvariant crop simulation framework which allows performing the multiple running in the batch mode. Such framework has been developed in our laboratory. It makes it possible to register any crop simulation model in the database and to perform several typical operations with it. As a result we present the wide-functional computer system for planning and automation of multi-factor computer experiment with arbitrary dynamic crop models.

Keywords: Framework, information system, database, crop simulation model, decision support systems.

1 Introduction

Crop simulation models play sufficient role in computer farming as an intellectual core of computer decision support systems (DSS) in agroecology. Programmatically, crop model is a complex dynamic algorithm allowing to get some kind of output information (yield, maturing date etc.) for the concrete set of input data (weather, technology, cultivar, soil etc.). This elementary procedure of isolated model computation can be called the single- or one-variant model run. However, typical use case of model application in DSS needs the multiple running of the model with different variants of input parameter set in order to analyze and to compare the corresponding outputs. One can enumerate the problems requiring model multiple running or, other words, multi-variant analysis (table 1).

Table 1. Sources of input data variability in typical crop simulation model related tasks

#	Task	Sources of input data variability
1	Parametric identification of the model	Variations of model parameters
2	Operative forecast of crop state during vegetation period	Synthetic scenarios of future weather
3	Optimization of agrotechnology	Variations of technology (rates and termini of human interventions)
4	Investigation of climate change influence into agroecosystem	Synthetic weather scenarios corresponding to future climate
5	Precision agriculture	Crop and soil spatial heterogeneity

J. Hřebíček, G. Schimak, and R. Denzer (Eds.): ISESS 2011, IFIP AICT 359, pp. 295–301, 2011.

It would be sane to perform such multi-variant model running in the batch mode in frames of the special system of polyvariant analysis of crop model. Moreover, taking into account the generic character of corresponding operations (forming input sets, butch running, and statistical analysis of the results) the supplementary challenge for the system is an ability to work with arbitrary crop simulation model. The presented contribution describes the prototype of such a system supporting two basic functionalities — the repository of descriptors of external crop models and generic environment for their polyvariant analysis.

2   Extending Relational Database Meta-information

The system to be developed needs to be versatile i.e. widely customized. It has to permit to registry new models and have functionality for supporting them by all necessary input data in corresponding formats. But neither model execution mode, nor input data format nor output data format has to affect common infrastructure of the polyvariant calculation system. Therefore information model of the system has to consist of two levels of data. The lower one constitutes possible inputs of the registered models and their computed results. All such data sets have a structure and format the model can understand. The higher data level is the information about the models and the data structure required by those models. Such kind of "data about data" is called meta-information. The task of proper data and metadata combined management in the frames of single data storage (relational database, for instance) has a long history and many approaches for possible solution. Fortunately, we don't need to solve the problem in a whole scope, i.e. map into database scheme such abstract concepts as "entity" and "relation". Indeed, any crop model operates with data which can be separated into limited number of information domains. These domains (named "factors" in our system) form the solid ground of the system architecture. We consider the following domains: "location", "weather", "crop", "soil", "initial state" and "technology" for input data and the single domain "results" for output data. The main assumption is that any data for any model can be presented as a data set (with custom columns) linked to the record ("factor level") of one of the root model table, corresponding to one of the predefined factors. This elementary data set may consist of only one record (common cultivar parameters) or many records (soil properties for multiple soil levels, cultivar parameters depending on phenological stage etc.) So, the common problem is to combine domain-specific meta-info and relational data in single data storage.

To solve this problem we appealed to the SQL 92 standard. This standard directs database management systems to provide special views displaying database structure called INFORMATION_SCHEMA. The approach used in the polyvariant analysis system is based on the ability to combine these views with user-defined tables and views of the database in queries. So, We created user-defined views, functions and check constraints based on the views from INFORMATION_SCHEMA. These user-defined views and several tables with such check constraints became database objects of the core of our system. These objects were isolated from the tables to be created by end user via user interface of the system. Such isolation was reached by the set of special technical restrictions (convention about table name prefixes etc.)

This approach is characterized by the following advantages:

- The system works with the physical database tables without performance losses.
- User-defined views with extended metadata are available for database development tools such as Linq2Sql.
- All required constraints, such as foreign keys, can be automatically included into the tables created by the end user.
- User-defined views with extended metadata are based on the efficient standard mechanism.
- The structure of extended metadata is not limited by the abilities of a database-specific tool.
- The system is portable to each database management system supporting INFORMATION_SCHEMA.

3 Model Interaction API

The system provides universal algorithms for arbitrary data formats. Its architecture is like the architecture of the classical gateway with the same fundamental concepts: "schema", "adapter" and "scenario". In our system these concepts have the following meaning:

- Schema is a set of tables and table columns defined by the end user for each factor of the model. Each model can have arbitrary subset of the set of factors predefined in the system. For each table user can select one of the columns as an identifier column. When no such column is selected, only one record of the table can be associated with one level of the factor. When such column is selected, several table rows must have unique values of this column within one level of the factor.
- Adapter is a program component implementing the standard interface declared in the polyvariant analysis system to interact with it. The adapter solves three tasks: transforming input data stored in our database into a model native input data format, launching the model with the prepared input data, and transforming results of the model into intermediate format to be saved in our database.
- Scenario is the data set for a single model running. It contains a single factor level for each factor of the model. Each scenario can be considered as a set of control directives, defining what soil, culture, weather etc. is chosen as input data for the referred variant of model running. After the model running the results are attached to the scenario.

Since we use .NET Framework as the main platform, we have made the intermediate format of data based on ADO.NET dataset [1]. The adapter constitutes an interface defined in our common assembly. The main method of this interface in the current version accepts two parameters: a dictionary with special enumeration FactorType as a key and ADO.NET dataset with data for the corresponding factor type as a value, and a background worker for the progress notification. This method returns single ADO.NET DataTable with model computing results. The structure of these tables is the same as in the model created by the end user in special designer on model registration. The second method is intended to import data from the model native format. It does not return any value and accepts two parameters: the dictionary of factor types and datasets to fill, and a background worker. For the future we are going to provide the full registrator runtime interaction with a model based on OpenMI standard [2].

The system supports plug-ins for working with adapters. All assemblies in the deployment directory are loaded automatically and analyzed for all implementations of this interface. After that all found implementations are presented in menu of the "adapter panel". Additionally, the system provides a few off-the-shelf bricks to build custom adapters without writing any code. Default implementation of model adapter contains three auxiliary interfaces: converting data into model native format, launching model and converting model calculation results into the intermediate format. The system supports Microsoft Excel and CSV data format and launching model via unmanaged function call. We are going to work on the GUICS adapter to support all GUICS-compliant models [3].

4 Automated Computer Experiment with Crop Model

4.1 Operation Principles and Implementation

We describe below the general (not depending on model-specific data) part of information model of our system. It directly relates to main system functionality – planning and performing of multi-variant computer experiment with crop model. The principal concepts of this part are "Project" and "Scenario". The "Project" is the common description of the single experiment we perform. In the current version, we suppose that the experiment takes place with only one crop model, i.e. we can not use different models in frames of one experiment. Project consists of several scenarios; each of them corresponds to one future model running.

So, the procedure of preparing computer experiment or multi-variant crop model analysis contains two steps: forming all interested "factor levels" and their coupling in the project. Consider them by turn.

There are several ways to receive the data composing the "factor level" in order to store it in the system database. Firstly, one can get the data earlier used for model computation from "native" model sources via adapter. Usually, it would be "real" data, i.e. actual field measurements or parameters of real soils or cultures. Secondly, the system provides different mechanisms for data varying in order to generate data sets for "synthetic" levels of this or that factor. The simplest algorithm here is an examination of the parameter values in selected interval with constant step. As a result we can obtain the row of "factor levels" differ each other only in the value of chosen parameters. Additionally, system has built-in generator of weather realizations based on the algorithm proposed by Richardson and Wright [4]. It allows forming synthetic data for the factor "weather" that corresponds to the climate conditions of any selected location. At last, data can be imported from SCV-files or entered manually via the user interface.

The final stage of computer experiment planning is a design of computation variants in terms of project (set of scenarios). This procedure is rather trivial. The set of scenarios is a Cartesian product of all levels chosen for every factor registered for the model. Principle of project forming is demonstrated on screenshots presented in Fig.1.

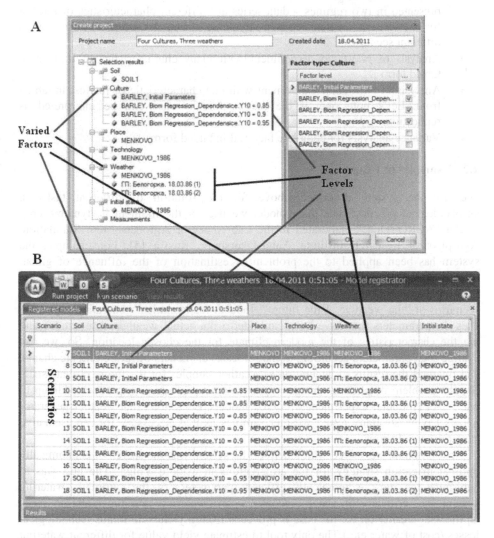

Fig. 1. Principles of multi-variant computer experiment design in "Crop Model Registrator" (A – Project Creation Dialog, B – Project Viewer)

The project being once created as a set of scenarios or running variants can be "calculated" at any time. It means the serial model running (via adapter) with input data sets determined by current scenario in the project and saving the corresponding results to system databases. After project has been calculated its results can be analyzed by means of one of special tools built in the system. For the moment the following tools for analysis of multi-variant computer experiment has been implemented:

- Two-dimensional graphic visualization of model dynamics. Diagrams can be presented in two regimes – data series are different characteristics of interest for one scenario, or data series are dynamic of one characteristic of interest in different scenarios.
- Analysis of one-factor experiment with many characteristics of interest in tabled form
- Analysis of two-factor experiment with one characteristic of interest in tabled from. Let's note one of the factors for the case can be interpreted as replication.
- Variance analysis for complete factorial in tabled form.

4.2 Examples of Usage

We use the system described above for the solution of different tasks in agroecological practice. The main model we use for the moment is dynamic crop model "AGROTOOL" elaborated in the Laboratory of Agroecosystem Simulation, Agrophysical Research Institute, Saint-Petersburg, Russia [5]. For example, the system has been applied to the problem of estimation of the influence of global climate change into agroecosystem stability and productivity in North-West Russian regions. The main idea there was to use the standard weather generator to get the scenarios of "the weather of the future". Indeed, mathematical generation algorithm uses the parameters that have been calibrated from actual weather observations and are the characteristics of the modern climate for the chosen location. So, we can change such parameters according to the forecasts or models of future climate change and interpret the results of generation as weather samples for the future climate state. So, the problem of climate change impact into crop production process adds up to one-factor computer experiment with crop models. Let's note, that weather generator allows having so many tested weather samples as it is necessary for representative statistical conclusions.

Next problem, we solved with a help of the system was the search of economically optimal irrigation strategy for the arid regions in Middle Volga. The task was to determine the most economically efficient parameters of the automatic watering system (i.e. critical soil water content to start watering and the watering rate). Optimization criterion for the case is proceeds from a yield sale minus technological losses (cost of water etc.) The only tool to estimate yield value for different watering strategy under current environment conditions can be dynamic crop model. So, the problem adds up to two-factor computer experiment where first factor would be the watering strategy and the second one (interpreted as replication) is weather. Statistical analysis of corresponding experiment allowed us to give the sound recommendation to the choice of optimal irrigation politics in regional scale.

5 Perspectives

The main challenge of further system development seems to be its evolution to parallel computing. Really, project calculation for the moment is independent but serial runs of the model with different sets of input data. The task is to provide the possibility of parallel model running in several computation threads or processes. It is not the efficiency problem only. One can show that parallel run of several instances of the standard one-dimensional dynamic crop model in synchronized regime with temporal interactions can be sufficient emulation of the processes taking place in spatially heterogeneous ecosystems. So, involving the methods of parallel (and, may be, cloud) computing in the system of multi-variant crop model analysis can increase significantly its possible value for the purposes of precision farming, that is the mainstream of applied researches in modern agriculture [6].

References

1. Microsoft Development Network, http://msdn.microsoft.com/en-us/library/e80y5yhx.aspx
2. Moore, R.V., Tindall, I.: An Overview of the Open Modelling Interface and Environment (the OpenMI). Environmental Science & Policy 8(2005), 279–286 (2005)
3. Acock, B., Pachepsky, Y.A., Mironenko, E.V., Whisler, F.D., Reddy, V.R.: GUICS: A Generic User Interface for On-Farm Crop Simulations. Agronomy Journal 91, 657–665 (1999)
4. Richardson, C.W., Wright, D.A.: WGEN: A Model for Generating Daily Weather Variables. In: U. S. Department of Agriculture, Agricultural Research Service, ARS-8, p. 83 (1984)
5. Poluektov, R.A., Fintushal, S.M., Oparina, I.V., Shatskikh, D.V., Terleev, V.V., Zakharova, E.T.: AGROTOOL – a system of crop simulation. Archives of Agronomy and Soil Science 48, 609–635 (2002)
6. Poluektov, R.A., Topaj, A.G., Kobylanski, S.G.: System of polyvariant computation of dynamic crop model in precision agriculture applications. Reports of Russian Agricultural Academy 6, 58–62 (2005)

Process Methodology for Emergency Management

Tomáš Ludík and Jaroslav Ráček

Faculty of Informatics, Masaryk University, Botanická 68a,
60200 Brno, Czech Republic
{xludik2,racek}@fi.muni.cz

Abstract. Emergency management is represented by managerial functions which aim to reduce vulnerability to hazards and to cope with disasters. Emergencies often have direct impact on the environment. This paper focuses on identification and subsequent software support processes in the emergency management. The paper aims to describe a process methodology for emergency management in details. The methodology describes how to manage an information system development suitable for emergency management, which is built on business processes. The methodology consists of five main phases. Each phase is described in terms of individual activities, work products, and user roles. The next part of the paper recommends the use of particular technologies, tools and resources that have been successfully proved in the analysis of emergency situations in the Czech Republic. The straightforward outcome of the novel process methodology is more effective solution of emergency situations and therefore the reduction of negative environmental impacts.

Keywords: Process Management, Emergency Management, Process Methodology, Recommendations.

1 Introduction

The emergency management requires considerable effort. To manage emergencies, it is necessary to spend human resources and also technical resources. It is useful if there are available some best practices in solving the emergencies, and also specified responsibilities for particular activities. To capture such information it is appropriate to use the process management, which has been approved in the private and public sector [3].

Identification and subsequent automation of the process is a challenging issue. At present, there are primarily two different approaches to the business process deployment. The first approach is based on the business process life-cycle, the second one on the overall architecture which supports the business process deployment. Both of these approaches are supported by the multinational corporation (Object Management Group and Workflow Management Coalition), which enforces standards in this field.

It is convenient to integrate the above mentioned approaches to the process management for effective process deployment and create a common framework for

J. Hřebíček, G. Schimak, and R. Denzer (Eds.): ISESS 2011, IFIP AICT 359, pp. 302–309, 2011.

an unified view of the process deployment. Such a view is defined by Process Framework for Emergent Management that takes into account specific factors relating to the emergency management [4].

The Process Framework for Emergency Management provides a basic view of the process deployment from the methodology and architecture point of view. For this reason, this paper aims to describe the process-oriented methodology in detail, which is an essential part of the framework.

2 Methodologies Based on Business Process

There are many methodologies that lead the user through the process deployment, e.g. *Object Process Methodology, Rational Unified Process, Methodology for Modelling and Analysis of Business Process* or *Business Driven Development*. The business process analysis is the principle of these methodologies, but the process automation of does not follow the process management ideology. The next part of the paper briefly describes the methodologies and also shows their disadvantages.

2.1 Object Process Methodology

Object Process Methodology (OPM) [1] is an approach to designing information systems by depicting them using *object models* and *process models*. OPM combines a minimal set of building blocks with a dual graphic-textual representation in a single diagram type. This makes OPM formal yet accessible to systems engineers and other stakeholders, enabling them to be involved through modelling from the early stages of requirements formulation.

The main disadvantage of this approach is the non-standard diagram notation, which has similar properties to the Data Flow Diagram (DFD). Another disadvantage is a low correlation between modeled process diagrams and their subsequent implementation.

2.2 Rational Unified Process

The Rational Unified Process (RUP) [7] is an iterative software development process framework created by the Rational Software Corporation, a division of IBM since 2003. RUP is not a single concrete prescriptive process, but rather an adaptable process framework, intended to be tailored by the development organizations and software project teams that will select the elements of the process that are appropriate for their needs.

The main disadvantage of RUP methodology is that business process analysis is used only at the beginning in order to create business requirements. The final application reflects the business processes, but there is not created a closer bond with them. Therefore, even a small change of business process leads to a fundamental change of the created information system.

2.3 Methodology for Modelling and Analysis of Business Process

Methodology for Modelling and Analysis of Business Process (MMABP) [6] is based on the fact that a business process model is next to an object model one of the two key assumptions of the information system global model. Both of these models form the basis of a business world general model. The object model is a static model of reality. In contrast, a process model is dynamic, and therefore describes the transition from initial to final states of the process.

The advantage of this approach is the use of BPMN for process diagrams and Class diagram (UML) for describing objects. The disadvantage of this methodology is its focus on process analysis and modelling. The methodology therefore does not cover the entire business process life-cycle.

2.4 Business Driven Development

Services-Oriented Architecture (SOA) provides an IT framework along with a set of principles and guidelines to create IT solutions as a set of reusable, composable, and configurable services that are independent of applications and runtime platforms. Transitioning an enterprise to SOA requires a Business Driven Development (BDD) approach that uses business goals and requirements to drive downstream design, development, and testing [5]. It brings a much needed flexibility in enterprise IT and helps to align IT solutions with business needs.

It is one of the best so far described methodologies from the view of the close interdependence to the business processes. But there is missing the application of a workflow reference model that allows to deploy the modelled process instance directly to the workflow engine.

3   Process Oriented Methodology

The created process-oriented methodology is based on the above mentioned methodologies but also eliminates their disadvantages. This innovative methodology is described in terms of different phases, from which it is composed, as well as in terms of responsible user roles and work products generated by this methodology.

3.1 Phases

The first phase of the methodology is *Identifying*. It tries to define the main strategic objectives of the organization. In accordance with the objectives the processes that bring added value to the organization are identified, directly or indirectly. Accordingly, these processes can be divided into *primary*, *support* and *management* processes [2]. It is also appropriate to assign responsibility for individual processes and particular activities as well. It is appropriate to use the Use Case Diagram to integrate the processes and user roles. The output of the phase is a list of business requirements (more details are in the section 3.3). It is convenient to define the Glossary to better understand the area of interest, which facilitates communication between user roles. The last tasks of the phase are verification and validation of business requirements.

In the *Modelling phase*, the business process is in detail modelled and decomposed into several levels, depending on its complexity. During this phase the emphasis is on the correct data flow in processes. Decision-making in processes are solved by using business rules, which could be changed during the process runtime. Designed process should be simulated in this phase. Simulation can reveal bottlenecks in the process and also visualize the process functions. The outcome of this phase is the system requirements determination that are in accordance with business requirements. System requirements should be approved by the user-validation. One of the key elements in this phase is the appropriate automation level determination.

Configuration is the third phase and deals with a detailed set up of business processes. Processes are transformed from the modelling phase into the configuration phase mostly in BPEL. In this form they are accompanied by the necessary functionality build on service-oriented architecture. Processes consist of already existing services or of the brand new ones that need to be programmed. In this phase are created the key performance indicators that are intended for the process performance control during the runtime. In such way the comprehensive application is built on business process. Its instances can be deployed on the workflow engine. The created system is set to the end customer. The service and process testing, as well as system validation with respect to the system requirements belong to the control mechanisms of this phase.

Execution/Monitoring phase provides primarily two activities. First it is an administration of running process instances in the workflow engine. That allows the end users to effectively work with the processes. Created applications can be set up and configured during the runtime. Business rules enable the configuration of the branching in processes, which enables better response to possible changes in a company. Setting user rights and roles is another option. Roles and rights can be assigned or removed for the current or new users, according to their current responsibilities. This phase is also responsible for process monitoring and for gathering data about process run. Based on this information, it is possible to evaluate the process progress and partly adapt the process on the flow. Defined KPIs have a great impact. They enable overall control of the process and therefore also a rapid response to sudden changes.

The last phase is *Optimization*. This phase is crucial for continuous process improvement. During the monitoring phase the data about process instances are collected, which may result in some gaps in the modelled process. There are some advanced techniques of mathematical statistics or process mining available for the process instances analysis. Based on the results it is possible to choose two different approaches to process improvement. It is a Business Process Reengineering (BPR) or a Total Quality Management (TQM) [6]. TQM is focused on the consequent improvement of processes. On the other hand, BPR focuses on radical changes. According to the chosen approach, new specification of business processes is created.

3.2 Roles

Stakeholder represents interest groups whose needs must be satisfied by the project. It is a role that may be played by anyone who is (or potentially will be) materially affected by the outcome of the project.

Business analyst is a high-level role responsible for the business analysis and BPM work activities. The business analyst performs process modelling and creates functional specifications for process. This high-level role implies that the analyst might also take on more specialized tasks during the project.

Architect is a high-level role responsible for the overall work effort of creating the architecture and design of the system. More specialized roles, such as enterprise architect, application architect, SOA architect, and infrastructure architect, are actually responsible for various architectural work efforts that constitute the design phase of the project.

Developer is a high-level role responsible for the implementation of the solution (services).

Tester is a role responsible for performing activities required to test the application before it is deployed into a production environment.

Line Manager is a person who heads revenue generating departments (manufacturing and selling) and is responsible for achieving an the organization's main objectives by executing functions such as policy making, target setting, decision making.

3.3 Work Products

This section describes the outputs generated by the methodology. Thus outputs are quite a bit through the methodology phases and therefore only main outcomes of the various phases are described.

Business Requirements are requirements based on customer's wishes and their needs. They describe the principles and functioning of a company as a whole, defining its objectives [7]. Identified processes are part of these requirements.

System Requirements are the modeling phase results. These are the requirements for creating an information system built on business processes. Detailed and hierarchically organized process diagrams are part of this output. These requirements also describe the level of process automation.

Information System is a result of the configuration phase. Modeled processes are configured and composed of individual services. Thus created processes are deployed on a process engine, which interprets them. The workflow engine also allows interaction with users and external tools.

Monitoring data is an output of the monitoring phase. It contains information about process instances run, such as duration or cost of individual processes. It also records the passage through the business process, which can be useful in further analysis.

Strategic plans are the optimization phase outputs. The overall technology improvement (TQM, BPR) and strategic plans for further business process improvement are chosen in strategic plans.

4   Recommendations for Emergency Management

In case the methodology is used in the field of emergency management it is appropriate to consider certain features that arise from this specific area. This includes clearly defined organizational structure, legislative and other issues. Some features are illustrated on emergency management in the Czech Republic.

4.1 Organizational Structure

The Integrated Rescue System (IRS) is determined for co-ordination of rescue and clean-up operations in case, where a situation requires operation of forces and means of several bodies, e.g. fire fighters, police, medical rescue service and other bodies, or in case, where the rescue and clean-up operation is necessary to be co-ordinated from the Ministry of Interior or by a leader of region's level, or by mayors of municipalities with extended responsibilities [4]. As the Integrated Rescue System are therefore considered the co-ordinated proceedings of its bodies during preparations for emergencies, and during rescue and clean-up operations.

As permanent authorities for coordination of Integrated Rescue System bodies are considered the operational and information centres of the Integrated Rescue System, i.e. the operational centres of regional Fire Rescue Services and the Operational and Information Centre of the General Directorate of the Czech Fire Rescue Service.

4.2 Legislation and Documentation

There are many laws dealing with emergency management in the Czech Republic. Crisis management elements are codified in the Law No. 240/2000 on crisis management and on modification of certain codes (Crisis Code), in latter wording. Based on this law, state of danger can be proclaimed to overcome unfavourable trends of development. The other important Law is the Law No. 239/2000 on the Integrated Rescue System and on amendment of certain codes, in latter wording, is the basic legal frame describing situation around IRS.

Another feature of the emergency management is the detailed documentation that defines how to proceed in particular situations. The Contingency Plans belong to the basic documents. They contain a set of measures and procedures addressed to crisis situations, i.e. they contain sum of planning, methodological and informational documents used in decision-making, management and coordination of tasks in the emergencies.

4.3 Different Types of Information

To deal successfully with critical situations, it is inevitable for all IRS components to have all the necessary information at their disposal. It is often not trivial because the information used in emergency management can have three basic characteristics or dimensions: *time*, *space* and *aggregation*. The time dimension of the data is important in the crisis situation with dynamic character. It could be contamination spreading or the direction of wind during the fire fighting. This information varies with time so it is a relevant factor in dealing with the crisis situation. Another important aspect of the information is that it is bound to the intervention place. It is only the limited area around the intervention place that is important and it can be defined according to the character of the crisis. The last dimension of information relevant to dealing with a crisis situation is aggregation. The data is provided to the intervention units in aggregated form, for example as specific maps or map layers. However, they contain also specific data sets that could be irrelevant to the character of a particular intervention location or to the crisis itself. The way to avoid unnecessary information is to use adaptive mapping [3].

4.4 Psychological Aspects

There is a new belief that even despite the devastating impact of disasters, substantial lack of resources, and general chaos, there is still a possibility of carrying out some actions that will serve in maintaining at least the basic integrity of the human society and its dignity. Psychological aspects are usually very important for dealing with crises. All activities of crisis management are performed under substantial time and psychological pressure. Intervention commanders work and make decisions in fear of their possible failure. They often have insufficient and inaccurate information at their own disposal during chaotic development of the situation. Other problems arise from lack of necessary resources, like working tools and necessary equipment or integrated rescue system resources. The basic requirements of life may sometimes be restricted under the influence of all these factors.

4.5 Using of Standards

Unified Modelling Language (UML) is a standardized modelling language used in the field of software engineering. Two diagrams are suitable for process modelling. One of them is *Use Case Diagram*, which shows the functionality provided by the system in terms of actors, their goals represented as use cases. Then it depicts all the relations among those use cases. The other is *Activity Diagram*. It represents the business and operational step-by-step workflows of components in a system.

   Business Process Modelling Notation (BPMN) provides a notation that is understandable by all business users, from the business analysts that create the initial drafts of the processes, to the technical developers responsible for implementing the technology that will perform those processes, and finally also the business people who will manage and monitor those processes. This way, BPMN creates a standardized bridge over the gap between the business process design and process implementation.

   Web Services Business Process Execution Language (WS-BPEL) defines a model and a grammar for describing the behaviour of a business process based on interactions between the process and its partners. The WS-BPEL process defines how multiple service interactions with these partners are coordinated to achieve a business goal, as well as the state and the logic necessary for this coordination.

5   Conclusions

The primary contribution of this paper is the innovative, process-oriented methodology. The methodology is described in terms of phases, user roles and work products. The paper also describes the set of recommendations, which should be applied when methodology is used on emergency management processes. Recommendations are based on practical experiences with solving of the research plan called *Dynamic Geovisualisation in Crises Management* [3] [4]. The research plan also illustrates the practical use of the methodology in real situations, for example in accidents with dangerous substances.

   It is appropriate to emphasis on adequate software support during the methodology use. This support is provided by *Business Process Management Suite* (BPMS), where different tools support different methodology phases. In case of a comprehensive emergency management system it is necessary to take the close interoperability to GIS or other operational systems used by the IRS into account. Therefore it is recommended to add the global architecture which will illustrate the overall deployment of the system based on business processes.

The subsequent objective of this research is to define in detail the methodology phases in terms of individual tasks and their links to each other. This is related to the assignment of responsibilities for these tasks. Similarly, detailed description of the role associated with implementing the methodology in terms of ICT and EM is needed. The final aim is to describe in detail the tasks inputs and outputs in terms of work products and determine whether all information is available at the right time.

Acknowledgments. The contribution is a part of the research plan no. MSM0021622418 and the research project no. FRVS/1035/2011, both supported by the Czech Ministry of Education, Youth and Sports.

References

1. Dori, D.: Object-Process Methodology - A Holistic Systems Paradigm. Springer, Heidelberg (2000)
2. Fiala, J., Ministr, J.: The Model of Process Framework in Czech Public Government. In: Proceedings of the 26th International Conference on Organizational Science Development – Creative Organization, University of Maribor, Portorož (2007)
3. Kubíček, P., Ludík, T., Mulíčková, E., et al.: Process Support and Adaptive Geovisualisation in Emergency Management. In: Geographic Information and Cartography for Risk and Crisis Management, Springer, Heidelberg (2010)
4. Ludík, T., Ráček, J.: Process Support for Emergency Management. ECON - Journal of Economics, Management and Business, VŠB-TU Ostrava, 19/2011, 1, Ostrava (2011)
5. Mitra, T.: Business-driven development. Available at URL (2005), http://www.ibm.com/developerworks/webservices/library/ws-bdd/ (20.3.2011)
6. Řepa, V.: Podnikové procesy, procesní řízení a modelování (Business Processes, Process Management and Modelling) Grada. Praha (2007)
7. Shuja, A., Krebs, J.: IBM Rational Unified Process Reference and Certification Guide: Solution Designer. IBM Press (2008)

Architecture of a Pan-European Framework for Integrated Soil Water Erosion Assessment

Daniele de Rigo[1,2] and Claudio Bosco[1]

[1] Joint Research Centre of the European Commission,
Institute for Environment and Sustainability, Via Fermi, 2749, I-21027 Ispra, Italy
{daniele.de-rigo,claudio.bosco}@jrc.ec.europa.eu
[2] Politecnico di Milano, Dipartimento di Elettronica e Informazione,
Via Ponzio 34/5, I-20133 Milano, Italy

Abstract. Soil erosion implications on future food security are gaining global attention because in many areas worldwide there is an imbalance between soil loss and its subsequent deposition. Soil erosion is a complex phenomenon affected by many factors such as climate, topography and land cover (in particular forest resources, natural vegetation and agriculture) while directly influencing water sediment transport, the quality of water resources and water storage loss. A modeling architecture, based on the Revised Universal Soil Loss Equation, is proposed and applied to evaluate and validate at regional scale potential and actual soil water erosion, enabling it to be linked to other involved natural resources. The methodology benefits from the array programming paradigm with semantic constraints (lightweight array behavioural contracts provided by the Mastrave library) to concisely implement models as composition of interoperable modules and to process heterogeneous data.

Keywords: soil erosion, regional scale, environmental modeling, semantic array programming, integrated natural resources management.

1 Introduction

Over the last years, soil erosion is one of the main questions that has attracted considerable attention at a global scale. At geological time-scales there is a balance between erosion and soil formation [1], but in many areas of the world today there is an imbalance with respect to soil loss and its subsequent deposition, mostly caused by anthropogenic activity (mainly as a result of land use change) and climate change.

The EU Thematic Strategy for Soil Protection [2] and the subsequent proposed Soil Framework Directive [3] recognise soil erosion as a major threat to European soil resources and recommend an indicator-based monitoring approach. Given the increasing of soil erosion in Europe and its implications on future food security (Pimentel [4] reports that soil is the basis for 97% of all food production) and water quality, it is important that land managers and decision makers are provided with accurate, timely and appropriate information on the areas more susceptible to erosion phenomena.

J. Hřebíček, G. Schimak, and R. Denzer (Eds.): ISESS 2011, IFIP AICT 359, pp. 310–318, 2011.
© IFIP International Federation for Information Processing 2011

1.1 Setting Soil Erosion in a Wider Context

Soil erosion is a complex phenomenon influenced by very diverse factors such as land cover, climate and topography, and is strictly linked to human practices and activities.

While land cover directly affects soil erosion either positively (i.e. forests cover and good agricultural practices) or negatively (wildfire-degraded cover and bad agricultural practices [5]), climate and climate change affect soil erosion both indirectly by driving land cover changes and directly varying precipitation intensity and duration. Therefore current and long-term analysis frameworks of soil erosion should be suitable to integrate land cover (in particular forest resources and natural vegetation) and wildfire susceptibility as opposite drivers for their influence in mitigating or increasing erosive phenomena.

At the same time, soil erosion influences water sediment transport, water resources quality and water storage loss [6]. These premises make improvement and integration of soil management, in conjunction with other natural resources – forest, water resources – and land use management a high priority which needs to link many aspects, not least those related to renewable energy, in a multicriteria approach [7].

Data modeling and data integration in environmental sciences are actively investigated within ICT [8]. However, this integration is difficult not only from an architectural software perspective but also from a wider scientific point of view: details on how to integrate multiple natural resources "cultures" in the same high level coordination algorithm are quite challenging.

The first step toward a solid and scalable modeling framework to support integrated assessment and management of these resources is the design and development of a reliable modeling architecture which is sufficiently lightweight to be successfully replicated whilst addressing domain-specific peculiarities. An application of the architecture to evaluate and validate at regional scale potential and actual soil erosion is presented. The regional scale allows to properly model the current situation of soil erosion and to link it to other involved resources. Moreover, it enables the possibility to scale the model architecture up to the integrated modeling of natural resources under climate change scenarios.

2 Methods

The proposed approach benefits from the array programming paradigm [9, 10] to concisely implement models as composition of modules while promoting scalable-parallelism idioms to process massive data. At the same time, the architecture pursues the goal to be really suitable to support real world decision-making complexity, up to the continental scale. This also implies the adopted languages, computational environments and technologies have been chosen considering their diffusion, expected durability[1] and suitability to ease the modeling work for the specialized scientific communities.

---

[1] Stroustrup reports [11] "that on the order of 200 new languages are developed each year and that about 200 languages become unsupported each year".

The driving epistemological postulate is to attempt boosting scientific collaboration by building reliable operational bridges between related but distant scientific domains. In order to move from the complexity of modeling natural and man-made resources to the complexity of related decision problems, automatic tools are essential to compare different sub-models and scenarios by also addressing their underlying semantic [12].

Publicly available and improvable free software [13] for supporting EU decision-making can be viewed as a transparency prerequisite to provide involved actors the ability to understand the implications of the technical apparatus on decision-making and to mitigate unwanted technology-driven biases.

2.1 Modeling Architecture

The modeling architecture can be summarized as a non-intrusive, lightweight set of coherent practices to harmonize and strengthen the way information is processed and exchanged between sub-models.

Each sub-model is provided with the ability to autonomously check at run-time its input and output data against a set of semantic constraints which also link together different input and output variables. While the algorithms implemented within sub-models are not constrained to limit their expressiveness, the framework provides a library support to encourage algorithms' implementation to progress in exploiting as much as possible the array programming paradigm.

This lightweight framework has been designed to support regional scale environmental modeling and it has been applied to estimate pan-European soil water erosion by connecting it to climatic and anthropogenic aspects, whose related information is suitable to be provided by existing datasets. On the other hand, updated input information under multiple climatic and anthropogenic scenarios can be in principle estimated using the same modeling approach, within an integrated and multidisciplinary general approach, therefore enabling a future full exploitation of the framework. The framework is mostly based on GRASS GIS [14], MATLAB language [15], GNU Octave [16] and GNU R [17] computing environments and the Mastrave library [18], which supports array-programming oriented environmental modeling with a wide native set of semantic input requirements for models.

Despite it has been designed to enable a future exposition of its main modules as web services, the whole modeling computation is explicitly constrained not to require such exposition, allowing the complete local reproducibility (e.g. within workstation or cluster architectures). The design modularization which can lead to expose web services is also essential to ease future interactions with third-party sub-models.

2.2 Mathematical Notation and Semantic Array Programming

Array programming originated to reduce the gap between mathematical notation and algorithm implementations. Ideally, "the advantages of executability and universality found in programming languages can be effectively combined, in a single coherent language, with the advantages offered by mathematical notation" [9]. It would be quite surprising if a promising algorithm could be transposed from the purely theoretical exposition *on paper* to the application domain, to solve a complex real world problem, without a large set of boundary conditions having a strong influence on the nature of that "naïve" algorithm.

Array programming suggests that an accurate vector-based mathematical description of the model can simplify complex algorithm prototyping while moving mathematical reasoning directly into the source code, where the mathematical description is actually expressed in a completely formalised and reproducible way. To fully benefit from that paradigm in a scientific modeling perspective, we systematically adopted two additional design concepts:

- modularizing sub-models and autonomous tasks with a strong effort toward their *most concise* generalization and reusability in other contexts. It also implies consistently self-documenting the code and engineering module interfaces to provide a uniform predictable convention;
- *semantically* constraining the information entered in and returned by each module instead of relying on external assumptions (e.g. instead of assuming the correctness of input information structured as an object).

Combining these design recommendations, provided with a supporting library, constitute the essence of the Mastrave project [18] approach to semantic array programming. The exposed pan-European soil erosion model applies these recommendations.

Semantic constraints may be contextualized in analogy with behavioural subtyping [19]. For example, let us consider the way a module interacts with external information provided by the module input arguments. The MATLAB language is dynamically and weakly typed so that the concepts of vector, matrix and multidimensional array can all be represented by the native type *double*, which can also represent complex numbers. A variable of type *double* can be an arbitrary array$\in \mathbb{C}^{n_1} \times \cdots \times \mathbb{C}^{n_m}, \forall n_1 \cdots n_m$.

A typical modeling task could consist in manipulating time series of data, e.g. composed by a vertical sequence of time intervals, the corresponding sequence of rainfall values measured within each time interval and a third sequence of weights – from 0 to 1 – representing the reliability of each value. Passing a time series to a module (implemented as a function) can in principle be done using external data containers (structures, classes, nested arrays of cells...) or directly passing time and data sequences. Irrespective of the way information is passed, if for example the module needs to sort by date the time-series elements whose weight is greater than a certain threshold, then a set of run-time preconditions should hold (**::semantic-constraint::** denotes the corresponding Mastrave semantic constraint):

1. the number of time intervals, of values and of weights composing the time series must be the same (**::same_rows::**);
2. the array of values must be a column vector (**::column_vector::**) of real non-negative numbers (**::nonnegative::**);
3. the array of time-intervals must be a two-column matrix whose second-column elements must be not less than to the corresponding elements of the first column (**::interval::**);
4. the weights must be in [0, 1] (**::probability::**);

5. the intervals need to be sortable, so that[2] the intersection of any pair of intervals must be empty (`::sortable_interval::`);
6. the threshold must[3] be a scalar real number (`::scalar_real::`).

Constraints range from trivial syntactic ones to topological relationships among structured data which can only be tested at run-time.

All constraints (except where explicitly states as in `::scalar_real::`) apply to vectors, matrices and in many cases to multi-dimensional arrays, easing their application to complex data, which often require non-trivial networks of semantic constraints used as preconditions, invariants and postconditions. Constraint violations raise exceptions which can be managed enabling model self-healing, or simply can cause a human-readable and self explaining error to abort the computation.

Those errors can be easily exposed in possible future web-interfaces, allowing semantic array-programming filters to wrap pre-existing third-party models and strengthen their robustness in view of their possible integration.

3 The Soil Water Erosion Model

The model and input datasets selection within the integration framework is crucial as they have to offer the most homogeneous and complete pan-European coverage. It must also allow the produced information to be harmonized and easily validated.

Among the different models for soil erosion estimation, the Universal Soil Loss Equation (USLE) [20] is one of the most widely applied empirical models. The USLE is an erosion model designed to predict the soil loss in runoff and it only predicts soil loss from sheet and rill erosion. Either deposition phenomena or concentrated runoff are not considered within the equation. It is one of the least data driven water erosion models which has been developed and it has been applied at different scales. Another advantage in the USLE architecture is related to its flexibility: it is always possible to set this equation to adapt it to the environment to be analysed.

The Revised Universal Soil Loss Equation (RUSLE) [21] retains the structure of its predecessor, the USLE. For all the above mentioned reasons we selected the RUSLE, and also for its intrinsic structure which is suitable to enable integrated analysis of different factors (climate, land cover and human practices).

There are six main factors controlling the soil erosion and considered by the model: the erosivity of the eroding agents (water), the erodibility of the soil, the slope steepness and the slope length of the land, the land cover and the human practices. RUSLE estimates erosion by means of an empirical equation:

$$A_{c,Y} = R_{c,Y} \cdot K_{c,Y} \cdot L_{c,Y} \cdot S_{c,Y} \cdot C_{c,Y} \cdot P_{c,Y}. \tag{1}$$

---

[2] Sortability of intervals can also be otherwise defined, depending on the peculiar task for which an ordering is required. However, an obvious and unambiguously sufficient condition holds when all intervals are disjoint. `::sortable_interval::` enforces this condition.

[3] The framework easily allows more flexibility. For example, instead of a scalar an array can describe a composite threshold (e.g. a range of min and max values to exclude measures below the rain gauge resolution or above an outlier threshold) provided a custom comparison function is passed as optional module's input argument (`::function_handle::`).

where all factors refer to a given spatial grid cell c and are the average within a certain set of years $Y = \{y_1, \cdots, y_i, \cdots, y_{n_Y}\}$ of the corresponding yearly values:

$A_{c,Y}$ = (annual) soil loss (t ha^{-1} yr^{-1}).
$R_{c,Y}$ = rainfall erosivity factor (MJ mm ha^{-1} h^{-1} yr^{-1}).
$K_{c,Y}$ = soil erodibility factor (t ha h ha^{-1} MJ^{-1} mm^{-1}).
$L_{c,Y}$ = slope length factor (dimensionless).
$S_{c,Y}$ = slope steepness factor (dimensionless).
$C_{c,Y}$ = cover management factor (dimensionless).
$P_{c,Y}$ = human practices aimed at erosion control (dimensionless).

Rainfall erosivity factor. The intensity of precipitations is one of the main factors affecting soil water erosion processes. R is a measure of precipitation's erosivity. Wischmeier [22] identified a composite parameter, EI^{30}, as the best indicator of rain erosivity. It is determined, for the k_i-th rain event of the i-th year, by multiplying the kinetic energy of rain by the maximum rainfall intensity occurred within a temporal interval of 30 minutes. The rainfall erosivity factor of the RUSLE model is the average, on a consistent set of data, of n_Y sums of EI^{30} values, each sum being computed for the whole set of $n_{y_i}^{event}$ rainfall events in the i-th year:

$$R_{c,Y} = \frac{1}{n_Y} \cdot \sum_{i=1}^{n_Y} \sum_{k_i=1}^{n_{y_i}^{event}} E_{c,k_i} \cdot I_{c,k_i}^{30} = \sum_{i=1}^{n_Y} \sum_{k_i=1}^{n_{y_i}^{event}} EI_{c,k_i}^{30}. \tag{2}$$

Due to the difficulty to obtain precipitation data with adequate temporal resolution over large areas, the model architecture enables the approximation of R by using one among the many simplified equations available in literature. In the presented application, for the pan-European maps the simplified R equation of [23] has been computed using the E-OBS database as data source [24]. E-OBS is based on the largest available pan-European precipitation data set, and its interpolation methods were chosen after careful evaluation of a number of alternatives. The complete equation has been fully implemented to accurately estimate R where detailed time series of measured precipitation (10 to 15 minutes of time-step) have been made available across Europe.

Soil erodibility factor. The soil erodibility factor "represents the effects of soil properties and soil profile characteristics on soil loss" [21]. The K factor is affected by many different soil properties and therefore quantifying the natural susceptibility of soils is difficult. For this reasons K is usually estimated using the soil-erodibility nomograph [20]. The European soils database (SGDBE) at 1:1.000.000 scale has been used for the calculation (see also [25]).

Cover–Management factor. The cover-management factor represents the influence of terrain cover, cropping and management practices on erosion rate. The calculation of the C factor is very difficult and due to the lack of detailed information in Europe it has been calculated using average values from literature [26, 27, 28] based on the last version of the Corine Land Cover (CLC 2006)[29] database. The impact of natural vegetation (Fig. 1) suggests further analysis with detailed forest types and tree species distribution maps [30, 31, 32] to increase the corresponding C factors accuracy.

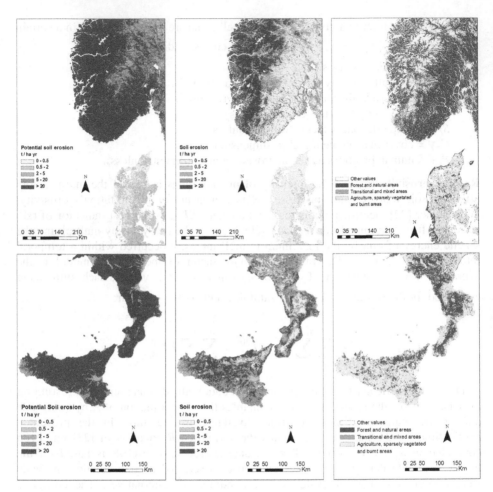

Fig. 1. Effects of land cover on soil erosion rate. The maps (South of Norway and Denmark; South of Italy) show some details of the pan-European potential soil erosion, soil erosion and land cover map. The land cover map has been created aggregating the Corine Land Cover classes in three different categories: forest, grassland and other natural vegetation areas; transitional, mixed natural and agriculture areas; prevalent agriculture, sparsely vegetated areas, burnt areas. Agriculture practices able to reduce soil erosion have not been modeled.

Topographic factors (slope length and slope steepness factors). The effect of topography within the RUSLE model is accounted for by the slope length factor and the slope steepness factor. For the calculation of the *LS* factors we used the DEM obtained from the Shuttle Radar Topography Mission (SRTM) [33] that is the most complete high-resolution digital topographic database of Earth.

Human Practices factor. *P* is the support or land management practice factor. It represents how surface and management practices like terracing, stripcropping or contouring affect erosion phenomenon. For areas where there aren't support practices or without any data the *P* factor is set equal to 1.0.

4 Conclusions

A lightweight framework has been presented to support regional scale environmental modeling within the paradigm of semantic array programming. An application to estimate the pan-European potential soil water erosion and soil water erosion using the Revised Universal Soil Loss Equation (RUSLE) has been exposed by showing its intrinsic integrability with related natural resources models and data (i.e. land cover and forest resources). Accurate estimation of rainfall erosivity factor (R-factor) has been implemented to validate simplified R-factor equations.

The proposed architecture is designed to ease the future integration, within the same lightweight framework, of erosion-related natural resources models and data. The framework will be applied to improve the R-factor modeling, and water erosion estimation in mountainous areas will be progressed by modeling their peculiarities.

Acknowledgments. We acknowledge the E-OBS dataset from the EU-FP6 project ENSEMBLES (http://ensembles-eu.metoffice.com) and the data providers in the ECA&D project (http://eca.knmi.nl).

References

1. Tricart, J., KiewietdeJonge, C.: Ecogeography and Rural Management – a Contribution to the International Geosphere-Biosphere Programme. Longman Group, Harlow (1992)
2. Van-Camp, L., Bujarrabal, B., Gentile, A.R., Jones, R.J.A., Montarella, L., Olazábal, C., Selvaradjou, S.-K.: Reports of the Technical Working Groups Established under the Thematic Strategy for Soil Protection, EUR 21319 EN/1-6, OPOCE, Luxembourg (2004)
3. European Commission: Proposal for a Directive of the European Parliament and of the Council establishing a framework for the protection of soil and amending Directive 2004/35/EC. COM/2006/0232 final Brussels, 22/09/2006; p. 30 (2006)
4. Pimentel, D.: World Soil Erosion and Conservation. Cam. Univ. Press, Cambridge (1993)
5. Foley, J.A., DeFries, R., Asner, G.P., Barford, C., Bonan, G., Carpenter, S.R., Chapin, F.S., et al.: Global consequences of land use. Science 309, 570–574 (2005)
6. Hansen, L., Hellerstein, D.: The Value of the Reservoir Services Gained With Soil Conservation. Land Economics 83(3), 285–301 (2007)
7. Angelis-Dimakis, A., Biberacher, M., Dominguez, J., Fiorese, G., Gadocha, S., Gnansounou, E., Guariso, G., et al.: Methods and tools to evaluate the availability of renewable energy sources. Renewable and Sustainable Energy Reviews 15(2), 1182–1200 (2011)
8. Casagrandi, R., Guariso, G.: Impact of ICT in Environmental Sciences: A citation analysis 1990-2007. Environmental Modelling & Software 24(7), 865–871 (2009)
9. Iverson, K.E.: Notation as a tool of thought. Commun. of the ACM 23, 444–465 (1980)
10. Quarteroni, A., Saleri, F.: Scientific Computing with MATLAB and Octave. Texts in Computational Science and Engineering. Springer, Milan (2006)
11. Stroustrup, B.: A rationale for semantically enhanced library languages. In: ACM LCSD 2005 (2005)
12. Villa, F., Athanasiadis, I.N., Rizzoli, A.E.: Modelling with knowledge: A review of emerging semantic approaches to environmental modelling. Env. Mod. & Software 24(5), 577–587 (2009)

13. Stallman, R.: Viewpoint: Why "open source" misses the point of free software. Commun. ACM 52(6), 31–33 (2009)
14. Neteler, M., Mitasova, H.: Open Source GIS: A GRASS GIS Approach, 3rd edn. The Intern. Series in Engineering and Computer Science, vol. 773. Springer, Heidelberg (2008)
15. The MathWorks: MATLAB, http://www.mathworks.com/help/techdoc/ref/
16. Eaton, J.W.: GNU Octave Manual. Network Theory Limited (2002)
17. R Development Core Team: R: A language and environment for statistical computing. R Foundation for Statistical Computing (2005)
18. de Rigo, D.: the Mastrave project, http://www.mastrave.org
19. Liskov, B.H., Wing, J.M.: Behavioral Subtyping Using Invariants and Constraints, MU CS-99-156, School of Computer Science, Carnegie Mellon University (1999)
20. Wischmeier, W.H., Smith, D.D.: Predicting Rainfall Erosion Losses – A Guide to Conservation Planning. Agriculture Handbook, No. 537, USDA, Washington DC (1978)
21. Renard, K.G., Foster, G.R., Weesies, G.A., McCool, D.K., Yoder, D.C.: Predicting Soil Erosion by Water: A Guide to Conservation Planning with the Revised Universal Soil Loss Equation (RUSLE). US Dept Agric., Agr. Research Service. Agr. Handbook No. 703 (1997)
22. Wischmeier, W.H.: A rainfall erosion index for a universal Soil-Loss Equation. Soil Sci. Soc. Amer. Proc. 23, 246–249 (1959)
23. Loureiro, N.D.S., Coutinho, M.D.A.: A new procedure to estimate the RUSLE EI_30 index, based on monthly rainfall data and applied to the Algarve region, Portugal. J. of Hydr. 250 (2001)
24. Haylock, M.R., Hofstra, N., Klein Tank, A.M.G., Klok, E.J., Jones, P.D., New, M.: A European daily high-resolution gridded dataset of surface temperature and precipitation. J. Geophys. Res (Atmospheres) 113, D20119 (2008)
25. Heineke, H.J., Eckelmann, W., Thomasson, A.J., Jones, R.J.A., Montanarella, L., Buckley, B.: Land Information Systems: Developments for planning the sustainable use of land resources. Office for Official Publ. of the European Communities, EUR 17729 EN (1998)
26. Morgan, R.P.C.: Soil Erosion and Conservation, 3rd edn. Blackwell Publ., Oxford (2005)
27. Šúri, M., Cebecauer, T., Hofierka, J., Fulajtár, E.: Erosion Assessment of Slovakia at regional scale using GIS. Ecology 21(4), 404–422 (2002)
28. Cebecauer, T., Hofierka, J.: The consequences of land-cover changes on soil erosion distribution in Slovakia. Geomorphology 98, 187–198 (2008)
29. Bossard, M., Feranec, J., Otahel, J.: CORINE land cover technical guide - Addendum 2000, Technical report No 40, European Environment Agency (2000)
30. Casalegno, S., Amatulli, G., Bastrup-Birk, A., Houston-Durrant, T., Pekkarinen, A.: Modelling and mapping the suitability of European forest formations at 1km resolution. European Journal of Forest Research (2011), Online First – 16 February
31. Forest Type Map 2006. EC, Joint Research Centre, Inst. for Environ. and Sustainability (2010)
32. Kempeneers, P., Sedano, F., Seebach, L., Strobl, P., San-Miguel-Ayanz, J.: Data fusion of different spatial resolution remote sensing images applied to forest type mapping. Submitted to IEEE Transactions on Geoscience and Remote Sensing (2011)
33. Farr, T., Rosen, P., Caro, E., Crippen, R., Duren, R., Hensley, S., Kobrick, M., et al.: The Shuttle Radar Topography Mission. Reviews of Geophysics 45, 33 (2005)

Towards a Universal Search in Environmental Information Systems

Clemens Düpmeier[1], Werner Geiger[1], Thorsten Schlachter[1],
Rainer Weidemann[1], Renate Ebel[2], and Ulrich Bügel[3]

[1] Karlsruhe Institute of Technology (KIT)
Institute for Applied Computer Science
Hermann-von-Helmholtz-Platz 1, 76344 Eggenstein-Leopoldshafen, Germany
{clemens.duepmeier,werner.geiger,thorsten.schlachter,
rainer.weidemann}@kit.edu
[2] Baden-Wuerttemberg State Institute for Environment, Measurements and Nature
Griesbachstraße 1, 76185 Karlsruhe, Germany
renate.ebel@lubw.bwl.de
[3] Fraunhofer Institute of Optronics, System Technologies and Image Exploitation (IOSB)
Fraunhoferstraße 1, 76131 Karlsruhe, Germany
ulrich.buegel@iosb.fraunhofer.de

Abstract. Full-text search functions in environmental portals make a large amount of environmental data accessible. Many data sources, however, are not suited for indexing by search machines or the data themselves are not suited for access by full-text search. A possibility to make such data of the "dark web" accessible consists in addressing the data sources in the environmental portal directly. The procedure presented here starts with a formal description of data sources (e.g. from the point of view of the portal, these are the target systems). Based on this description, a special component of full-text search, the so-called search broker, can extend and detail a search query, such that all necessary parameters (if possible) are compiled to address these systems and to guide the user directly to the data desired. The presentation component of the environmental portal is responsible for the adequate compilation and display of these data, the so-called result mash-up.

Keywords: Public Search Portals, Semantic Technologies, Result Mash-up, Search Broker, OpenSearch Description, Dark Web.

1 Introduction

Since the adoption of the EU directives on the citizens' access to environmental data in 1990 and 2003 at least, active dissemination of this information has been a duty of environmental administrations [5], [6]. Many authorities provide central environmental portals via which the citizen is given access to data that are often distributed over many individual environmental information systems.

J. Hřebíček, G. Schimak, and R. Denzer (Eds.): ISESS 2011, IFIP AICT 359, pp. 319–326, 2011.
© IFIP International Federation for Information Processing 2011

Unfortunately, these portals often provide links to the start or search pages of the target systems only. While integrated full-text search engines offer access to all text information, other types of data like database tables, geographic information systems, and multi-media files often are not covered by these full-text search engines or they cannot be represented adequately in the list of results.

Huge parts of many environmental information systems have to be connected by specialized adaptors or remain hidden to the users of environmental portals [11].

In practice, very few systems offer a real semantic description or links of data in terms of the semantic web [2]. A "real" semantic search is not yet possible. Analysis of environmental information systems in the state of Baden-Württemberg has even revealed differences in the semantics of individual terms in several systems of a single authority, although this semantics is never expressed explicitly.

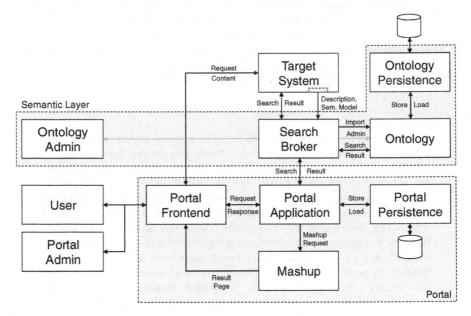

Fig. 1. Architecture of the Environmental Portal with SearchBroker, Semantic Component (Ontology), and Target Systems

The idea of the approach presented here is to deposit some semantics in the description of systems and, thus, to make queries that are as intelligent as possible.

Search requests to environmental web portals typically consist of the following three components:

1. Subject
2. Spatial reference (e.g. coordinate, administrative unit, professional object)
3. Temporal reference (e.g. point or period of time)

Very often, queries refer to one or more topics alone or in combination with a spatial reference. Queries relating to temporal references, also in combination with a subject or spatial reference, are rare.

Mobile end devices, such as smart phones or tablet PCs often allow for a more or less precise determination of the own location (and, hence, of the location of the user) with components like GPS receivers, WLAN, and mobile radio communication devices. This location information is available in principle as a context of the search query, even though these data are not input explicitly by the user.

Within the project "Semantic Search for Environmental Information (SUI)" [1], [3], an architecture was developed (Figure 1), which

— provides and processes descriptions of various target systems,
— delegates preprocessing of search terms to specialized components for environmental issues, spatial, and temporal references, and
— presents multiple data formats in an integrated view (mash-up).

The core of this architecture is the "SearchBroker" that acts as a search engine for the environment portal.

2 Target System Descriptions

By a description, the individual target systems are made known to the SearchBroker (Figure 2). An extension of the OpenSearch description XML format [9] is used as a vehicle for these descriptions.

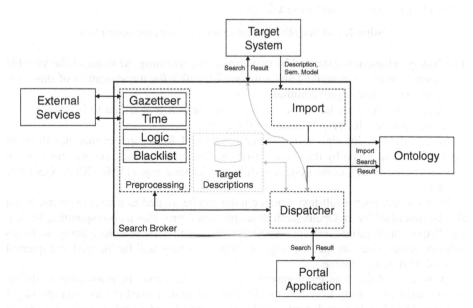

Fig. 2. Architecture of the SearchBroker with Plug-ins and Semantic Component (Ontology)

This format is based on URL patterns[1] which may contain wild cards for all necessary parameters (see Listing 1).

```
<Url type="text/html" template=
"http://foo/?q={searchTerms}&amp;pw={startPage?}"/>

<Url type="application/atom+xml" template=
"http://foo/atom?q={searchTerms}&amp;pw={startPage?}"/>
```

Listing 1. OpenSearch URL templates

Generally, several URL patterns may be contained in an OpenSearch description. The patterns are distinguished by giving the reply format (type). If several reply formats are available, the application may decide which to use and select the corresponding URL pattern.

URL patterns in OpenSearch descriptions normally refer to the addressing of search engines. This mechanism can be extended easily by the admission of any parameters instead of the standard parameter set. While the semantics of standard parameters is set already, the "free" parameters have to be explained more explicitly. Again, the extension of an OpenSearch description element is used, as shown in Listing 2.

```
<Url type="text/html" template=
"http://foo/dienst?repId=biotope&amp;value={commune}"/>
<Query role="substitution" ui:name="commune"
ui:type="geo:commune:id"/>
```

Listing 2. URL template and corresponding semantic description

The "query" element is extended by two attributes containing the name of the variable ("ui: name", here: "commune") and a unique identifier for the semantics of this variable ("ui: type", here: "geo: commune: id").

The unique identifier has to be known to the search broker and to be used by the associated plug-ins for preprocessing of the query.

An OpenSearch description may contain multiple URL templates that may differ in the target format given by the "type" attribute. This enables the environmental portal to retrieve data from a target system in different formats, e.g. HTML, XML, GeoRSS, or Atom.

In this sense, even a full-text search engine can be treated as a target system. It can also be described by an OpenSearch description and provides a corresponding hit list, e.g. "Application/atom+xml" or "application/rss+xml". In practice, many websites will not be described as specific target systems, but they will be indexed and queried by a full-text search engine.

In the case of the state environmental portals [10], it may be reasonable to define certain tasks previously executed by the full-text search machine as separate target systems. The Google Search appliance [8] used as full-text search machine is capable

---

[1] Addressing systems via URL indeed excludes some systems (e.g. such as those based on web services). If required, however, these can be integrated via appropriate adapters.

of submitting queries to other systems parallel to the search in the own index. This mechanism called "OneBox" delegates the search query to other systems. If they reply within a defined period of time, these results are delivered in addition to the search results from full-text index and can be represented near them by the portal (see right column in Figure 3).

If these OneBoxes are addressed by the search broker or the mash-up component of the environmental portal and not by the search machine, many unnecessary queries can be avoided, as it is possible to decide which queries are promising or not after preprocessing the search query already (Section 3).

3 Preprocessing

The search broker knows the descriptions of all systems connected to the environmental portal and, hence, the syntax and semantics of their calls. Upon receipt of a query by a user from the environmental portal, the search broker has to provide for all relevant parameters being available. Otherwise, target systems cannot be called up.

To identify the semantics of a given query, the SearchBroker is assisted by a series of specialized plug-ins. The plug-ins analyze each constituent (e.g. single words or a series of words) of the query and try to allocate an explicit semantics to them.

In this way, one or more gazetteer plug-ins can resolve the spatial reference in a query. Many internet search engines use gazetteer services available online from different vendors. Some environmental agencies also offer specialized gazetteer services which, for example, can resolve field names, names of water bodies or names of natural areas in addition to place names.

In the above example, a gazetteer plug-in can recognize a place name, e.g. "Karlsruhe", and allocate several properties to it, such as:

```
— geo:commune:name = Karlsruhe
— geo:commune:id = 08212000
```

The latter can now serve as a parameter for addressing the target system shown in Listing 2.

Another gazetteer plug-in may supply further information about the same place name "Karlsruhe":

```
— geo:lon = 8.4037563
— geo:lat = 49.0080848
— geo:bbox = 8.2756969,48.9494975 8.5318157,49.0666033
```

Similarly, another plug-in can explain temporal terms. For a search, including "summer 2010", the explicit start and end dates are assigned:

```
— datetime:calendar:day:first = 2010/06/21
— datetime:calendar:day:last = 2010/09/22
```

Apart from spatial and temporal references, resolving of environmental issues is the biggest challenge in the preprocessing of search terms. Resolution aims at mapping search terms onto one or more elements of a well-defined vocabulary, as it is used in the connected target systems. For the purpose of restricting or expanding a query, also the neighborhood of each issue is supplied to the SearchBroker, e.g. synonyms as well as superordinate and subordinate concepts.

The environmental issues are modeled in an ontology. This ontology initially is restricted to the terms of a certain domain (here: "Umwelt" (environment)) that reflects the contents of the portal. The ontology consists of several partial ontologies. The backbone is the GEMET environmental thesaurus [7]. It is extended by a thematic catalog, the entries of which contain further metadata, e.g. frequently used key values. This structure is covered by another partial ontology that contains so-called "life situations". This corresponds to the approach of many portals to meet the citizen in a life situation and to guide him from this situation to the relevant services and data [12]. These partial ontologies are linked by mapping. Due to this mapping, the environmental issues found generally contain entries from all partial ontologies. Hence, a maximum of information is available for queries by target systems. A more detailed description of this semantic approach is given in [4].

4 Presenting Search Results (Mash-up)

After the completion of preprocessing, the SearchBroker can decide which target systems are available and how to request them. The SearchBroker can now query the data by itself or return the full addresses to the environmental portal. Currently, the latter approach is being used.

Within the environmental portal, a mash-up component is responsible for the presentation of search results. Depending on the results supplied, it can decide how these will be presented.

Essentially, the following target formats are distinguished:

— spatial data, e.g. displayed by a web map client
— links, e.g. in the form of link lists
— tabulated data and charts that may be converted into HTML
— multi-media contents, for example in the form of a gallery view
— text messages (e.g. RSS), for example in the form of summary lists
— HTML pages, HTML fragments and microformats displayed at certain points in the layout
— results of a full-text search, for example in the form of hit lists

The target formats are assigned using the MIME types given in the target system descriptions. In case more than one target format are available, the mash-up component can decide how the hits will be displayed. The same data may be displayed at several places, e.g. within a hit list and a map view.

Furthermore, the gathered information may be used to provide the user with additional navigation steps in the portal. These include, for example, the restriction or expansion of the query based on subordinate or superordinate concepts (Figure 3). It is also possible to resolve ambiguities resulting from the preprocessing of place names.

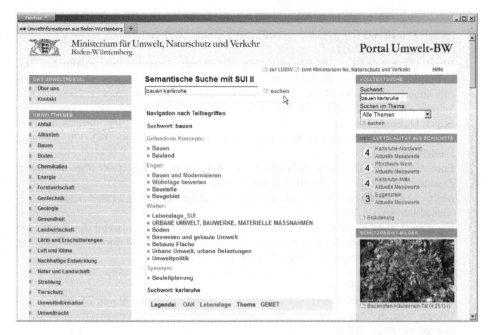

Fig. 3. Screenshot of the SUI II prototype: Subjects gathered from the ontology component for the provision of additional navigation steps within the full-text search results.

5 Conclusion and Outlook

The architecture proposed provides environmental portals with the opportunity to access different target systems with different target formats. The description of the target systems and their addresses are stored in an XML document that is based on and extends the OpenSearch description format.

The parameters necessary for addressing the target systems are obtained from the search query by various specialized plug-ins during preprocessing. An ontology component is included for the resolution and explanation of the thematic reference.

The complete addresses for target system requests are supplied to the environmental portals together with format information. Depending on the formats supplied, the portals display an integrated results page.

Thus, a broad variety of formats can be represented adequately within the search facility of an environmental portal, e.g. map layers with nature reserves, geo-point objects, such as measuring points, full-text search results, tables, or multi-media data.

This "universal search" approach offers a significant value added compared to a conventional full text search.

References

1. Abecker, A., et al.: SUI - Ein Demonstrator zur semantischen Suche im Umweltportal Baden-Württemberg, UIS Baden-Württemberg. In: F+E Vorhaben KEWA, Phase IV 2008/09, Wissenschaftliche Berichte, FZKA-7500, pp. 157–166 (Juli 2009)

2. Berners-Lee, T.: Semantic Web Road Map (1998),
   `http://www.w3.org/DesignIssues/Semantic.html`
   (visited January 19, 2011)
3. Bügel, U., et al.: SUI II - Weiterentwicklung der diensteorientierten Infrastruktur des Umweltinformationssystems Baden-Württemberg für die semantische Suche nach Umweltinformationen, UIS Baden-Württemberg. In: F+E Vorhaben KEWA, Phase V 2009/10, KIT
   Scientific Reports, KIT-SR 7544, August 2010, pp. 43–50 (2010) ISBN 978-3-86644-540-6
4. Bügel, U., et al.: Leveraging Ontologies for Environmental Information Systems. In: Hřebíček, J., Schimak, G., Denzer, R. (eds.) ISESS 2011. IFIP AICT, pp. 372–379. Springer,
   Heidelberg (2011)
5. European Union, Richtlinie 90/313/EWG des Rates vom 7. Juni 1990 über den freien
   Zugang zu Informationen über die Umwelt (1990),
   `http://www.umwelt-online.de/recht/allgemei/90_313gs.htm`
   (visited January 19, 2011)
6. European Union, Richtlinie 2003/4/EG des europäischen Parlaments und des Rates vom
   28. Januar 2003 über den Zugang der Öffentlichkeit zu Umweltinformationen und zur
   Aufhebung der Richtlinie 90/313/EWG des Rates (2003),
   `http://www.umwelt-online.de/recht/eu/00_04/03_4gs.htm`
   (visited January 19, 2011)
7. GEMET, `http://www.eionet.europa.eu/gemet` (visited March 23, 2011)
8. Google Search Appliance, `http://www.google.com/enterprise/search/`
   (visited March 23, 2011)
9. OpenSearch, OpenSearch description document,
   `http://www.opensearch.org/Specifications/OpenSearch/`
   `1.1#OpenSearch_description_document` (visited January 19, 2011)
10. Schlachter, T., et al.: LUPO - Ausbau der Suchfunktionalität der Landesumweltportale und
    Vernetzung mit dem Umweltportal Deutschland, UIS Baden-Württemberg. F+E Vorhaben
    KEWA, Phase V 2009/10, KIT Scientific Reports, KIT-SR 7544, 9–20(August 2010)
    ISBN 978-3-86644-540-6
11. Schlachter, T., et al.: Erschließen von Datenbank-Inhalten durch die Volltextsuche in Lan-
    des-Umweltportalen, Umweltinformationssysteme: Suchmaschinen und Wissensmanage-
    ment - Methoden und Instrumente. In: Workshop 'Umweltdatenbanken/ Umweltinforma-
    tionssysteme', Dessau-Roßlau, June 5-6, Umweltbundesamt, Berlin (2009)
12. Service-BW, `http://www.service-bw.de` (visited March 23, 2011)

Methodology for the Efficiency Evaluation of the Municipal Environmental Protection Expenditure

Jana Soukopová and Michal Struk

Masaryk University, Faculty of Economics and Administration, Department of Public
Economics, Lipová 41a, 602 00 Brno, Czech Republic
soukopova@econ.muni.cz, struk@mail.muni.cz

Abstract. This paper deals with an efficiency of current municipal expenditure
on environmental protection and suggests a methodology for assessing this
efficiency. A proposal of methodological procedure for evaluating efficiency of
municipal environmental protection expenditure uses multi-criteria evaluation,
where a dominant criterion of performance is modified method of Cost-
effectiveness analysis. It was implemented in open source software. The
efficiency in the methodology is intended in terms of 3E methodology –
Economy, Efficiency and Effectiveness, together with the methodology of
sustainable development – social, environmental and economic part of
sustainable development. This procedure is applied to a set of environmental
protection expenditure data that come from the representative sample
of municipalities in areas of waste management which were used in a project of
the Ministry of Environment of the Czech Republic SP/4i1/54/08 "Analysis of
municipal budgets efficiency in relation to the environmental protection".

Keywords: methodology, municipal environmental protection expenditure,
efficiency, effectiveness, economy, sustainable development.

1 Introduction

Environmental protection expenditure is terms for the money that society spends on
the environmental protection. Nowadays, the protection of the environment is
integrated into all fields of policy with the general objective of reaching sustainable
development. Clean air, water and soil, healthy ecosystems and rich biodiversity are
vital for human life, and thus it is not surprising that societies devote large sums of
money to pollution reduction and preservation of healthy environment.

Consequently is the environmental protection expenditure (EPE) one of the
indicators for evaluating the standard of the environmental protection not only at the
level of municipalities and governments, but also for the comparison of
environmental protection in the world.

EPE is the money spent on activities directly aimed at the prevention, reduction
and elimination of pollution resulting from the production or consumption of goods
and services [1]. These are, for example, waste disposal activities and wastewater
treatment activities, as well as activities aimed at noise abatement and air pollution
control. Environmental protection expenditure does not directly take into account the

J. Hřebíček, G. Schimak, and R. Denzer (Eds.): ISESS 2011, IFIP AICT 359, pp. 327–340, 2011.

expenditure for the sustainable management of natural resources. All economic sectors, businesses in agriculture, industry and services as well as the public sector and households spend some money on reducing, preventing and eliminating their pressures on the environment.

For instance, both businesses and households pay for safe waste disposal, spend money on mitigation of the polluting effects of production processes and governments pay for provision of environmental public goods, such as the basic levels of sanitation required to safeguard health.

Governments subsidize environmentally beneficial activities and use public funds in order to make it easier for subjects to borrow money on the financial markets for environmental projects. To be more specific, this is done through measures such as risk sharing, credit enhancement or subsidies that lower the costs of borrowing for communities that cannot afford to carry full costs of investments into environmental projects.

Therefore the main objective of this paper is an evaluation of the efficiency of public expenditure and other financial instruments in the field of environmental protection with focus on particular regions, together with the optimization of incidence of public subsidies for environmental protection on macro and micro-economical level. Further objective is the development of open source software [10] supporting this evaluation.

In the Czech Republic the important part is identification of factors that influence absorption capacity of individual regions and setting of indicators for the evaluation of their effectiveness.

2 Public Environmental Protection Expenditure

Public expenditure in the field of environmental protection represents important part of total public expenditure and, thanks to the active policy of European Union and expenditures from its structural funds, its sum probably won't decrease notably even in the time of financial crisis.

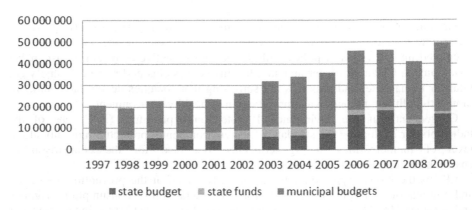

Fig. 1. Environmental expenditures of public budgets in the Czech Republic (in thousands CZK), 1997-2009 [2]

Figure 1 shows the progression of public expenditure since 1997. Apart from legislative and regulatory tasks, the public sector monitors environmental performance, provides grants and subsidies to encourage environmentally sensitive behaviour and funds research and development activities. In the Czech Republic public administrations, for example municipalities, can also provide environmental protection services, such as waste management or wastewater treatment, directly. These services are generally provided by public corporations, whose activities differ from other governmental administrative tasks.

In the Fig. 1 we can see that throughout the time municipal expenditure made always more than 50% of total environmental public expenditure.

Environmental expenditure is divided in the budget structure according to the Classification of Environmental Protection Activities and Expenditure (CEPA 2000) into several categories: protection of ambient air and climate; wastewater management; waste management; protection and remediation of soil, groundwater and surface water; noise and vibration abatement; protection of biodiversity and landscapes; protection against radiation; research and development; and other environmental protection activities [3]. As shown in Fig. 2, largest parts of public environmental protection expenditure are wastewater management expenditure, waste management expenditure and protection of biodiversity landscapes expenditure.

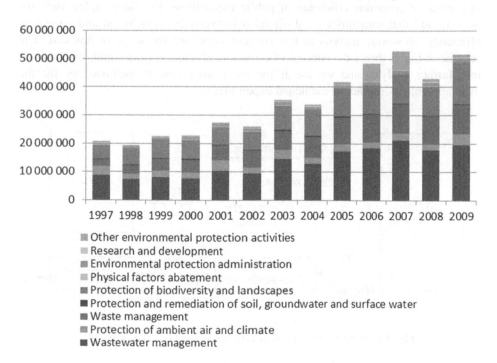

Fig. 2. Municipal environmental expenditures according to CEPA 2000 (in thousands CZK), 1997-2009 [2]

3 Methodology of Efficiency Evaluation

In order to evaluate efficiency of public (environmental) expenditure most authors use the methodology of 3E – economy, efficiency and effectiveness. According to theory, these terms are perceived like this:

1. *Economy* – such use of public expenditures, that leads to provision of given objectives with the least amount of resources spent, while keeping up to the corresponding quality of tasks;
2. *Efficiency* – such use of public expenditures that acquires the greatest possible amount, quality and contribution to the given objectives compared to the amount of resources spent in order to fulfill them[1].
3. *Effectiveness* – such use of public expenditures that leads to the greatest possible output respecting desired outcome, which are prerequisite for optimal fulfillment of goals set in advance. Therefore effectiveness means how the produced goods or services (for example waste disposal) fulfill utility (for example clean municipal environment without waste) [4].

When judging all these criteria (economy, efficiency, effectiveness and quality) we can speak of economic efficiency of public expenditure. For the complex view we need to add that sometimes we distinguish between terms technical and allocation efficiency. However, analysis of this concept is beyond the scope of this text. The scheme in Fig. 3 shows the concept of economic efficiency, from which we move on into further analysis and we use it for the construction of methodology for the evaluation of environmental municipal expenditure.

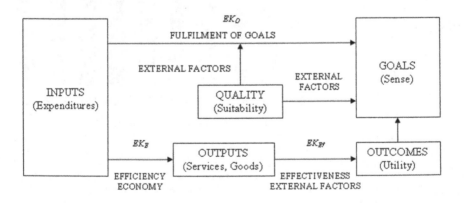

Fig. 3. Conceptual conception of efficiency of public expenditure [4]

---

[1] Economy and efficiency are for purposes of quantification and in respect of usage of methods of economic analysis understood as cost efficiency.

3.1 Environmental Protection Expenditure Efficiency and Effectiveness

One of the contemporary problems is how to allocate public expenditure in the field of environment protection more effectively [5]. When considering efficiency and effectiveness, the methodology is based on multi-criteria evaluation of efficiency and effectiveness that is determined by 3 basic pillars of sustainable development. When the methodology was designed, we came out from the evaluation of efficiency and effectiveness in terms of social, environmental and economic points of view (see scheme in Fig. 4).

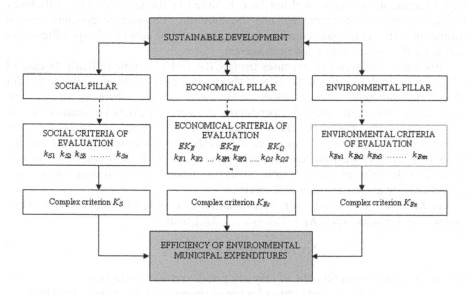

Fig. 4. Scheme of public environmental protection expenditure efficiency evaluation [4]

3.2 Economic Aspect of Evaluation

Economic criteria of evaluation come out from the concept of efficiency explained above and include the economical evaluation of efficiency and economy EK_E, effectiveness EK_{Ef} and economic quality EK_Q, so:

$$K_E = E_E + E_{Ef} + E_Q,\qquad(1)$$

where K_E is the complex criterion of efficiency evaluation,
   E_E is the complex criterion of efficiency and economy evaluation (cost efficiency evaluation),
   E_{Ef} is the complex criterion of effectiveness evaluation,
   E_Q is the complex criterion of economical quality evaluation (quality of environmental goals).

More detailed explanation of evaluation methodology according to the given complex criteria follows.

Efficiency evaluation – E_E

The most commonly used methods for evaluating efficiency of public expenditure are Cost-minimization Analysis (CMA), Cost-effectiveness Analysis (CEA), Cost-utility Analysis (CUA) and Cost-benefit Analysis (CBA). These methods are in general suitable for the evaluation of efficiency of public expenditure for environmental protection. The only exception is CMA, which only compares amount of expenditures, and therefore will not be considered in further evaluation. Efficiency evaluation of current public budgets expenditures, however, encounters several limitations. This is because current expenditures usually consist of expenditures for public services – services of common interest.

This makes evaluation of expenses using CBA or CUA quite difficult. In case of CBA it is difficult to estimate benefits of these services in terms of money and as for CUA, the situation is even more complicated because there is no suitable methodology for environmental expenditures (however, it exists for health-care and several other) [6]. Therefore, choosing the CEA method appears to be the most appropriate [7, 8], when it comes to the evaluation of efficiency. And for the evaluation of C/E we have chosen efficiency indicator E as a complex criterion created with help of multi-criteria analysis depending on factors influencing expenditure on given environmental service.

Let K_E be a set of criteria for the evaluation of quality of environmental public budget expenditures, where $K_E = (k_{E1}, k_{E1}, ..., k_{En})$, then

$$E = f(k_{E1}, k_{E2}, ..., k_{En}),$$ (2)

where k_{Ei} is the criterion of cost efficiency and economy evaluation,
        n is the number of outputs for the environmental protection expenditure.

Then the cost efficiency of given expenditure could be expressed as follows:

$$CEA = \frac{C}{E} \geq 0 \rightarrow \min$$ (3)

where C is the environmental protection expenditure,
        E is the indicator of cost efficiency evaluation.

If $CEA \leq 1$, the expenditure is efficient, if $CEA > 1$, the expenditure is inefficient. Because the criterion is minimizing, it needs to be transformed into maximizing one. Therefore for the construction of EK_E criterion we will use the following formula:

$$E_E = \frac{1}{CEA} = \frac{E}{C} \geq 0,$$ (4)

where if $EK_E > 1$, then the expenditure is efficient and $E_E \rightarrow \max$.

Evaluation of the effectiveness – E_{Ef}

Let K_{Ef} be a set of criteria for the evaluation of effectiveness of environmental municipal expenditures, where $K_{Ef} = (k_{Ef1}, k_{Ef1}, ..., k_{Efn})$, then

$$E_{Ef} = \sum_{i=1}^{n} w_i k_{Efi},$$ (5)

where k_{Efi} is the criterion determining results of given expenditure – percentage fulfillment of the goal No. i (criterion acquires values 0-1),

n is the amount of outcomes (goals) for given environmental expenditure,

w_i is the weight of i-numbered criterion.

It acquires values $0 \leq EK_{Ef} \leq 1 \rightarrow \max$

Evaluation of the quality – EK_Q

Let EK_Q be a set of criteria for the evaluation of the quality of environmental public budget expenditures, where $EK_Q = (k_{Q1}, k_{Q1}, ..., k_{Qn})$, then

$$E_Q = \sum_{i=1}^{n} w_i k_{Qi},$$ (6)

where k_{Qi} is the criterion determining quality – quality of given goal – connection with strategic documents of region or state (in percents) (criterion acquires values 0-1),

n is the amount of outcomes (goals) for given environmental expenditure,

w_i is the standardized weight of criterion No. i.

3.3 Environmental Aspect of Evaluation

Environmental criteria of evaluation come out from indicators of sustainable development in selected field of environmental protection. The complex criterion of the evaluation of efficiency could be from the view of environmental K_{En} constructed as follows [4]:

$$K_{En} = \sum_{i=1}^{n} w_i k_{Eni},$$ (7)

where k_{Eni} is the criterion of environmental efficiency, $k_{Eni} \rightarrow \max$

n is the amount of criteria,

w_i is the standardized weight of criterion No. i.

It acquires values $K_{En} \geq 0$. If $K_{En} = 0$, the expenditure is fully inefficient.

3.4 Social Aspect of Evaluation

Social criteria of evaluation come out from taking the social aspect of existing expenditure into account. The complex criterion for evaluating efficiency from the social point of view K_S could be constructed as follows:

$$K_S = \sum_{i=1}^{n} w_i k_{Si},$$ (8)

Where k_{Si} is the social efficiency criterion (in percents),
n is the number of criteria,
w_i is the weight of criterion No. i.

It acquires values $0 \le K_S \le 1$ and if $K_S = 0$, the expenditure is fully inefficient.

3.5 Summary of the Methodology

The sequence of this methodology for the evaluation of public environmental protection expenditure can be shown in an algorithm with several phases and steps:

1. Phase – the evaluation of the efficiency:

   a. Step 1 – the evaluation of efficiency and economy of expenditure (whether the given goals are being fulfilled with minimal costs, or if the environmental benefits with given costs are maximized). $E_E > 1 \rightarrow$ max;
   b. Step 2 – the evaluation of effectiveness (how municipal environmental expenditure ensures the set goal). $0 \le E_{Ef} \le 1 \rightarrow$ max ;
   c. Step 3 – the evaluation of quality (quality of goals is crucial problem of expenditures, that's why we evaluate it too). $0 \le E_Q \le 1 \rightarrow$ max ;

2. Phase – the evaluation of efficiency from environmental view. $K_{En} \ge 0 \rightarrow$ max .

3. Phase – the evaluation of efficiency from the social view $0 \le K_S \le 1 \rightarrow$ max ;

4. Phase – the evaluation based on importance of individual expenditure in terms of its relation to the whole (each expenditure is multiplied by a weight equal to the proportion of expenditure on total expenditure of the municipality).

This methodology has been programmed as open source software available for all municipalities of the Czech Republic and tested on a sample of 200 South Moravian Region municipalities.

4   Case Study of the Efficiency Evaluation Using the Methodology

In the Czech Republic there are 204 municipalities with extended powers (type III municipalities). To test the developed methodology and software, the South Moravian Region was selected. There are 21 type III municipalities in this region. Table 1 shows the list of them.

Table 1. Municipalities with extended powers in the South Moravian Region

Municipality	Number of citizens
Blansko	21 106
Boskovice	10 965
Brno	370 592
Břeclav	24 242
Bučovice	6 432
Hodonín	25 687
Hustopeče	5 903
Ivančice	9 347
Kuřim	10 492
Kyjov	11 707
Mikulov	7 493
Moravský Krumlov	5 986
Pohořelice	4 521
Rosice	5 504
Slavkov u Brna	6 169
Šlapanice	6 836
Tišnov	8 585
Veselí nad Moravou	11 781
Vyškov	21 875
Znojmo	34 759
Židlochovice	3 472

For the following analysis with using developed software we have chosen the sample of municipalities containing only those over 10 000 citizens (10 municipalities). Year 2008 was chosen for the analysis. Data on the amount of municipal waste were obtained from the Ministry of the Environment Czech Republic, as shown in Table 2.

4.1 Evaluation of Economic Aspect of Efficiency and Effectiveness

Table 2. Information about waste management expenditure and waste amount of type III municipalities in South Moravian Region, year 2008

Type III municipality	Expenditure on waste management, thousands CZK, 2008	Amount of municipal waste, tons, 2008
Blansko	14 962.04	5 417
Boskovice	6 968.61	2 441
Brno	366 459.47	118 663
Břeclav	18 387.23	8 655
Hodonín	19 773.20	9 321
Kuřim	6 410.08	2 662
Kyjov	7 441.25	5 320
Veselí nad Moravou	7 207.84	6 278
Vyškov	13 003.84	9 659
Znojmo	30 575.97	8 694

Economy and efficiency evaluation – E_E

In case of municipal waste collection there are several input parameters of software: waste amount, rate for waste manipulation, rate for waste transportation, transportation vehicle's capacity and distance to the processing facility. Costs of collection are then the following:

$$E = V_E = 2 * v * s_d * \frac{Q}{k_d} + m * Q + p * Q \qquad (9)$$

and

$$E_E = \frac{E}{C} \geq 0$$

where v is distance from the facility (landfill, incinerator) [km] including the distance in the municipality - (k_{E3})

s_d is rate for the transportation [CZK/km], considered 45 CZK/km - (k_{E5})

Q is amount of waste [t] - (k_{E1})

k_d is capacity of waste transportation vehicle [t], considered maximal capacity 25 tons - (k_{E4})

m is rate for waste manipulation, considered average price in the region 150 CZK/ton

p is the price of landfill [CZK/t], considered average price of landfill in the region 1000 CZK/ton

Table 3 contains results of the evaluation of E_E by using software.

Table 3. Efficiency evaluation (economic aspect of evaluation)

Municipality	Distance from the facility	Distance in the municipality	E	$E_E = E/C$	Rank
Blansko	32.1	15	7 286.52	0.49	8.
Boskovice	22.1	9	3 001.36	0.43	9.
Brno	0	35	202 885.25	0.55	6.
Břeclav	16.6	10	11 037.55	0.60	5.
Hodonín	18.2	18	12 058.02	0.61	4.
Kuřim	21.7	8	3 468.59	0.54	7.
Kyjov	20.8	9	6 828.54	0.92	3.
Veselí n. Moravou	16.3	9	7 967.79	1.11	1.
Vyškov	16.8	15	12 161.45	0.94	2.
Znojmo	13.5	20	10 420,63	0.34	10.

According to the results of cost-effectiveness, the best managing municipality in terms of municipal waste expenditure is Veselí nad Moravou followed by municipalities Vyškov, Kyjov and Hodonín.

Effectiveness evaluation – E_{Ef}

Here we have example of effectiveness evaluation of the city of Brno.

City of Brno has in its Waste Management Plan the following objectives and performance criteria of expenditure effectiveness:

1. Increase material utilization of municipal waste to 50% by 2010 compared to year 2000 - $k_{Enf\,1}$;
2. Material utilization of municipal waste in relation to the whole Czech Republic (ensure the collection and subsequent use or alternatively controlled disposal of hazardous components of municipal waste (50% in 2005 and 75% in 2010)) - $k_{Ef\,2}$;
3. Ensure recycling of construction and demolition waste (utilize 50% of the weight of emerging construction and demolition waste before end of 2005 and 75% before end of 2012) - $k_{Ef\,3}$;
4. Prefer incineration of mixed municipal waste with energy recovery over landfill storage - $k_{Ef\,4}$;
5. Reduce the weight ratio of landfilled waste with perspective of further reduction by 20% in 2010 compared to year 2000 - $k_{Ef\,5}$;
6. Decrease the ratio of landfilled waste with potential of energy utilization (35% in 2010) - $k_{Ef\,6}$;
7. Decrease ratio of landfilled biodegradable municipal waste (75% of what the production was in 1995 compared to 2010) - $k_{Ef\,7}$;
8. Increase utilization of waste through recycling up to 55% in 2012 - $k_{Ef\,8}$.

For simplification, all the criteria implemented in software were assigned the same weight $w_i = 0.125$. The expert panel gave each criterion the values in Table 3.

Table 4. Evaluation of effectiveness (city of Brno)

Criterion	k_{Ef1}	k_{Ef2}	k_{Ef3}	k_{Ef4}	k_{Ef5}	k_{Ef6}	k_{Ef7}	k_{Ef8}
Criterion value	0.95	1	0.86	1	0.85	0.95	0.65	1

Then $EK_{Ef} = 0.9075$.

Evaluation of the quality – E_Q.

The South Moravian Region has in its strategic document called Waste Management Plan (WMP) 25 goals related to waste management. The city of Brno put in its own Waste Management Plan 8 goals, all of which are all included in the South Moravian Region's WMP. Therefore, these criteria take value of 1 (100% associated with the strategic documents). Considering the evaluation of quality of expenditure, it is possible to use criteria of effectiveness evaluation and build E_Q, when $E_Q = 1$.

For the city of Brno the complex criterion for evaluation of economic efficiency comes out as follows:

$$K_E = E_E + E_{Ef} + E_Q = 0.55 + 0.9075 + 1 = 2.4575$$

4.2 Evaluation of Environmental Aspect

Considering waste management expenditure, criteria for evaluation of environmental efficiency could be determined as follows (all of them are maximizing):

k_{En1} Amount of municipal solid waste per capita in comparison with Czech national average (national average proportion of the municipality value);

k_{En2} Waste management expenditure per capita compared to the Czech average (ratio of Czech average to the to the actual municipality value);

In this analysis we have chosen to evaluate only sample of South Moravian Region municipalities over 10 000 citizens. Experts assigned these criteria by similar weight of wi = 0.5. Table 5 contains values calculated by software that the expert panel assigned to each criterion:

Table 5. Evaluation of environmental aspect (South Moravian Region's municipalities over 10 000 citizens), year 2008

Criterion/ Municipality	k_{En1}	k_{En2}	Weight Sum	Rank
Blansko	1.033	1.054	1.044	3.
Boskovice	1.192	1.081	1.137	1.
Brno	1.099	0.741	0.920	5.
Břeclav	0.851	0.979	0.915	6.
Hodonín	0.870	0.844	0.857	9.
Kuřim	1.152	0.636	0.894	7.
Kyjov	0.705	0.997	0.851	10.
Veselí n. Moravou	0.880	1.108	0.994	4
Vyškov	1.090	1.139	1.115	2.
Znojmo	1.061	0.698	0.880	8.

According to the results in Table 5, Boskovice is the best municipality in terms of environmental efficiency, followed by Vyškov, Blansko, Veselí nad Moravou and Brno.

4.3 Evaluation of Social Aspect

When it comes to municipal waste management expenditure, suitable criteria for social efficiency evaluation of given calculated expenditure could be the following:

k_{S1} Willingness to sort municipal waste (in percents)

k_{S2} Employment – Influence on employment (is given service carried out by local company or external one, and so on) (in percents)

k_{S3} Living standard of citizens – does the expenditure have positive impact on living standard of citizens of municipality (in percents)

When evaluating municipal waste management expenditure in Brno, experts gave these weights to the given criteria: w_1 = 0.4, w_2 = 0.3, w_3 = 0.3. Table 6 contains calculated values assigned by experts to each criterion.

Table 6. Evaluation of social aspect (city of Brno)

Criterion	k_{S1}	k_{S2}	k_{S3}
Criterion value	0.58	0.85	0.86

Then $K_S = 0.748$.

5 Summary and Outlook

Evaluation of the effectiveness of public environmental protection expenditure is already very complex matter [9, 10, 11]. There are many factors and indicators that affect the level of expenditure [11]. This paper discusses why the most appropriate tool seems to be the Cost-effectiveness Analysis with its application as a part of multi-criteria analysis depending on factors influencing expenditure on given environmental service. The open source software was developed to implement this tool. Determination of all these factors, as shown in the case study of South Moravia Region municipalities, is a necessary prerequisite for establishing an indicator of efficiency.

We believe that this is one of the ways to evaluate the efficiency of public spending on environmental protection with the use of developed software. At the same time we realize that the described problem is much more complicated in practice because the amount of public spending is influenced by a variety of external factors, such as performance orientation, organizational aspects, human resources, the use of information technology, political decisions, interest groups, etc. Some of these factors cannot be quantified, they can only be described.

Methodology for the efficiency evaluation of municipal environmental protection expenditure is primarily meant for municipalities and faces the following criteria:

1. *the utilization of sustainable development concept*;
2. *the utilization of existing methodologies and analyses*;
3. *data availability*;
4. *multi-criteria evaluation with weight sums utilization*;
5. *simplicity together with complexity of outcome*.

This methodology was implemented in open soursce application software and it has been tested on sample of 200 South Moravian Region Municipalities together with all Czech municipalities with extended powers. It has been approved and certified by Ministry of Environment of the Czech Republic in November 2010 [12]. A software [13] as a tool for evaluation has been also connected with the methodology and it is available for all municipalities of the Czech Republic.

Acknowledgements. We thank the Ministry of Environment (MoE) of the Czech Republic for the support. Paper is one of the results of the MoE of the Czech Republic project SP/4i1/54/08 „Analysis of municipal budgets efficiency in relation to the environmental protection", where we have identified that efficiency evaluation of municipal environmental expenditure is very complex and extraordinary difficult task. This paper is based on our common findings.

References

1. EPA, An Introduction to Environmental Accounting As a Business Management Tool: Key Concepts And Terms. EPA 742-R-95-001 (1995)
2. Automated budget information system / automatizovaný rozpočtový informační systém ARIS, http://wwwinfo.mfcr.cz/aris/
3. Eurostat, Classification of Environmental Protection Activities and Expenditure (CEPA 2000) (2000), http://ec.europa.eu/eurostat/ramon/nomenclatures/index.cfm?TargetUrl=LST_NOM_DTL&StrNom=CEPA_2000&StrLanguageCode=EN&IntPcKey=&StrLayoutCode=HIERARCHIC
4. Soukopova, J., Bakos, E.: Assessing the efficiency of municipal expenditures regarding environmental protection. In: Environmental Economics and Investment Assessment III, pp. 107–111. WIT Press, Cyprus (2010)
5. Farrell, J.: The Measurement of productive efficiency. Journal of the Royal Statistical Society, Part III 1957 120(3), 253–290 (1957)
6. Boardman, A., Cost-benefit, E.: analysis: concepts and practice, 2nd edn. Prentice Hall, Upper Saddle River (2001)
7. Levin, H., McEwan, M., Cost-effectiveness, P.J.: analysis: Methods and applications, 2nd edn. Sage Publications, Inc., Thousand Oaks (2000)
8. Raszka, J.: The CEA – a superior alternative to the cost-benefit Analysis of environmental infrastructure investments. Paper Presented at the Fifth European Conference on Evaluation of the Structural Funds, Challenge for Evaluation in an Enlarged Europe, Budapest (June 26/27, 2003)
9. García-Sánchez, I.: Efficiency measurement in Spanish local government: The case of municipal water services. Review of Policy Research 23(2), 355–371 (2006)
10. Lokkainen, H., Susiluoto, I.: Cost efficiency of Finnish municipalities 1994-2002. An application of DEA and Tobit methods. In: Paper Presented at the 44th Congress of the European Regional Science Association, Porto, Portugal, August 25-29 (2004)
11. Mandl, U., Dierx, A., Ilkowitz, F.: The effectiveness and efficiency of public spending, European Commission, Economic paper 301 (2008)
12. Soukopova, J., Neshybova, J., Bakos, E., Hrebicek, J.: Methodology for the efficiency evaluation of the municipal environmental protection expenditure no. 2437/320/109398/ENV/10 (Metodika hodnocení efektivnosti výdajů obcí na ŽP), Ministry of Environment of the Czech Republic, Praha (2010)
13. Soukopova, J., Neshybova, J.: Software for Methodology for the efficiency evaluation of the municipal environmental protection expenditure (2010), http://cms.amr.webnode.cz/metodika-hodnoceni-vydaju-obci/software-pro-hodnoceni

CryoLand – GMES Service Snow and Land Ice – Interoperability, Service Integration and User Access

Gerhard Triebnig[1], Andrei Diamandi[2], Richard Hall[3], Eirik Malnes[4],
Lars Marklund[5], Sari Metsämäki[6], Thomas Nagler[7], Jouni Pulliainen[8], Helmut Rott[7],
Christian Schiller[1], Rune Solberg[9], and Andreas Wiesmann[10]

[1] EOX IT Services GmbH, Thurngasse 8/4, 1090 Wien, Austria
{gerhard.triebnig,christian.schiller}@eox.at
[2] Administratia Nationala de Meteorologie R.A., Sos Buchuresti-Ploiesti 97,
Buchuresti Sectorul 1, 013686, Romania
diamandi@meteoromania.ro
[3] Kongsberg Satellite Services AS, Prestvannveien 38, 9011 Tromsoe, Norway
richard@ksat.no
[4] Northern Research Institute, Sykehusveien 21, Forskningsparken I, Tromsoe AS, Norway
eirik@norut.no
[5] Swedish Meteorological and Hydrological Institute, Folksborgsvaegen 1,
Norrkoeping, 60176 Sweden
lars.marklund@smhi.se
[6] Suomen Ymparistokeskus, Mechelininkatu 34a, 00251 Helsinki, Finland
sari.metsamaki@ymparisto.fi
[7] ENVEO Environmental Earth Observation IT GmbH, Technikerstrasse 21a, 6020
Innsbruck, Austria
{thomas.nagler,helmut.rott}@enveo.at
[8] Ilmatieteen Laitos, Erik Palmenin aukio 1, 99600 Sodankylä, Finland
jouni.pulliainen@fmi.fi
[9] Norwegian Computing Center,
Gaustadalleen 23, 0371 Oslo, Norway
rune.solberg@nr.no
[10] GAMMA Remote Sensing Research and Consulting AG, Worbstrasse 225,
3073 Gumlingen, Switzerland
wiesmann@gamma-rs.ch

Abstract. The CryoLand project implements and validates a standardized and sustainable service on snow and land ice monitoring as a Downstream Service of GMES. It will provide geospatial product coverages of seasonal snow (snow extent, snow mass, melt state), glaciers (area, snow / ice extent, ice velocities, glacier dammed lakes), and lake / river ice (extent, temporal variations, snow burden) derived from Earth observation (EO) satellite data. Processing lines and a service infrastructure will be developed on top of existing Web service environments supporting the publication, provision and chaining of involved geospatial data services. The CryoLand service architecture commits INSPIRE, OGC, and OASIS standards specifically respecting HMA and GENESIS frameworks. User information services offering discovery, view and download functions will be provided.

Keywords: snow, glacier, ice, spatial data infrastructure, service architecture.

J. Hřebíček, G. Schimak, and R. Denzer (Eds.): ISESS 2011, IFIP AICT 359, pp. 341–348, 2011.
© IFIP International Federation for Information Processing 2011

1 Introduction

The CryoLand project [1] is expected to establish new snow and land ice service capacities targeting its specified user communities. It will provide geospatial products on snow extent and snow pack physical properties, maps of glacier area and other glacier parameters, and on fresh water ice from EO data. Significant uptake of these products and suitable business models for long-term operational supply will have to be supported.

This paper describes preliminary results of the service requirements and system architecture definition activities aiming at setting-up the spatial data infrastructure of CryoLand including the interfaces for interoperability with neighbouring systems and to end-users.

2 Infrastructure Requirements

2.1 High-Level Requirements

The CryoLand Infrastructure will be designed to support advancements of product generation chains (e.g. for automatic integration of space and in-situ data into hydrological process models) including tools for Sentinel-based snow and ice products as well as chains for product delivery in near-real-time after (satellite) observation. It will be the platform for testing and validation of snow and ice products tailored to user needs and the associated product generation and access services. It will also serve for demonstration, training and service up-take activities by identified external customers.

A GMES-embedded, pre-operational, Internet-based service infrastructure shall be designed such as to be transferrable at the end of the project into sustainably operational multi-provider environments.

2.2 Neighbouring Systems

Fig. 1 shows how the CryoLand system will conceptually be surrounded by other infrastructures.

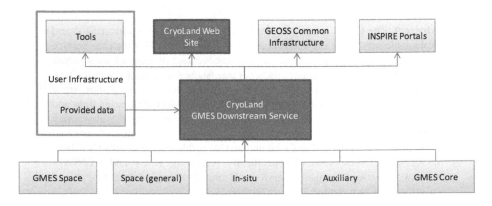

Fig. 1. CryoLand and its neighbouring systems

A significant number of external interfaces will have to be dealt with in order to integrate CryoLand's snow and ice services into the wider geospatial infrastructure. A heterogeneous set of input data sources will have to be connected. Furthermore, the CryoLand services must be prepared for being consumed by a (yet unknown) number of client-side systems supporting virtual and real users. There is also the requirement to establish native access via the CryoLand's own Web site.

3 CryoLand Architecture

3.1 Architecture Definition Approach

The CryoLand architecture elements for (1) user access, (2) service integration, and (3) data storage management are being defined, designed, implemented and documented in alignment with the definition and design of the thematic snow and ice processing and product generation services. The architecture definition methodology applied is based on RM-ODP (ISO 10746) which essentially requests to look at the architecture from the interrelated "five viewpoints" as further explained in sections 3.3 through 3.7.

3.2 Architecture Baseline and Good Practice

CryoLand attempts to build on the state-of-the-art for geospatial data systems with particular considerations on good practice in EO satellite payload data ground segment infrastructures. The following is a summary of the areas impacting the design of the CryoLand infrastructure:

- INSPIRE geodata infrastructure standards framework and implementing rules
- OGC geospatial standards/tools framework and best practices
- OASIS security standards
- FP7 GENESIS environmental service concepts and software re-use
- Heterogeneous Missions Accessibility (HMA) framework and GMES Coordinated Data access Service
- FP7 geoland2 concepts, interoperability requirements and service interfaces
- Other GMES Core and Downstream Infrastructures (PASODOBLE, ENDORSE, etc.)
- ESA algorithm development, processing, service support environments and user service interfaces (KEO, G-POD, SSE, ngEO)
- GEOSS Common Infrastructure integration

Legacy snow mapping infrastructures provided by CryoLand project partners (who themselves are involved in a range of national and international thematically related projects) are, naturally, the starting points of the good practice analysis. The CryoLand project is performing a thorough assessment of this legacy and heritage in order to define re-use and evolution strategies from existing and available infrastructure solutions.

3.3 Enterprise Viewpoint

This RM-ODP (see section 3.1) viewpoint asks for the definition of CryoLand's purpose, scope, policies, and related business which altogether are impacting infrastructure implementation decisions. In addition to the high-level requirements stated in section 2.1 the infrastructure shall support:

- Higher automation degree of processing lines, workflows and logistics
- Coordinated data storage management
- Standard interfaces of network services and for user access (INSPIRE and GEOSS compliant)
- Services operations in multi-provider environment
- Validation of Sentinel-1 utility and service lines
- Production facilities for European Climate Change Initiative (probably)

The implementing organizations (i.e. the FP7 consortium partners – see affiliation list of paper authors) and some 40 formally committed user organizations are in the process of formulating their different operational mandates, commitments and business expectations related to the future sustained operations of the CryoLand provided services.

3.4 Information Viewpoint

This viewpoint is concerned with the semantics of information or products as well as of the information processing to be implemented by CryoLand. The CryoLand Information Model - aligned with OGC geospatial information model – will define in all details the complete sets of (1) Applications and Output Products – see Table 1, (2) Input Data/Products, and (3) System Management Data/Information. Building on results from [2], [3], [4] and [5] it will also describe the algorithms of choice which will generate information and knowledge from data. This will be the data processing recipes for e.g. improving the quality of the snow cover products, in particular in forested regions and in areas of complex land use; for capitalizing on the enhanced sensor characteristics and coverage of the GMES Sentinel satellite series; for the integration of systematic in-situ measurements and remote sensing data; and the like.

Table 1. CryoLand applications and output product groups (preliminary)

Topic	Main Parameters
Seasonal Snow	Snow extent, snow mass, melt state of snow (wet / dry)
Glaciers	Glacier outline (area), snow / ice extent, ice velocity, glacier dammed lakes
Lake / River Ice	Ice extent, temporal changes of ice extent, snow burden

The extensive list of Input Data/Products corresponding to the input data interfaces indicated in Fig. 1 will include optical EO data (including when available: Seninel-2 & -3), radar feeds (Sentinel-1), in-situ/reference data (e.g. topography models), and GMES Core Service products (e.g. Pan-European Degree of Soil Sealing).

In Table 2 a preliminary list of System Management Data types is shown which will be essential for the functioning of the CryoLand services. Very relevant in the definition of these data will be the OGC Geospatial Information Model [1] since it standardizes geographic features (and mark-up language), spatial referencing, geometry and topology, and provides OGC Schema Repositories and many more important elements.

Table 2. CryoLand system management data/information (non-comprehensive)

Use	Data / Information
Security & User Management	Authentication and Authorization Data, Access Policies
Discovery Service & Annotations Service	Metadata
Portrayal Service	Geo Data Visualizations
Archive & Resource Management Service	EO Datatsets, EO Dataset Metadata, In-situ Datatsets
Workflow Services	Service Registration Data, Process Metadata

3.5 Computational (Service) Viewpoint

This viewpoint is concerned with the functional decomposition of the overall CryoLand system into a set of services that interact at interfaces. The design activites will fully draw upon the OGC Service Model [7] which establishes the principles for the service oriented architecture and points to the extensive set of specifications related to the OGC Web Services. A number of those will be essential to implement interoperable CryoLand service interfaces.

Table 3. Abstract service types to be implemented by CryoLand based on OWS specifications

OGC Web Service (OWS)	Abstract service / Use
CSW	Catalogue
WFS (-T)	Download Feature
WMS & EO AP	View/Portrayal
WCS (-T) & EO AP	Download Coverage
SOS	Sensor Observation
SPS	Sensor Planning
WPS	Processing Invocation
-T = Transactional (Upload)	AP = Application Profile

For the implementation of raster data flows (up- und downloads) between CryoLand system components the Web Coverage Service and its transactional extension (WCS-T) is considered a capable mechanism. In particular the recent developments of the EO Application Profile of WCS 2.0 [8] demonstrate the usefulness of this protocol in the distributed facility organization of CryoLand (see section 3.7).

3.6 Technology Viewpoint

This viewpoint will address the specific software to be used for the implementation of the CryoLand service components and make decisions on the hardware platforms which are needed for deployment and hosting of the software instances. The project has an orientation towards Free and Open Source Software (FOSS) but not made any decisions so far on the specific software platforms for the system at the various stages of evolution.

3.7 Engineering Viewpoint

This viewpoint defines a set of components that provide the basis for deployment of the CryoLand system in a distributed environment as shown in Fig. 2. These engineering components are accessed by services (see section 3.5).

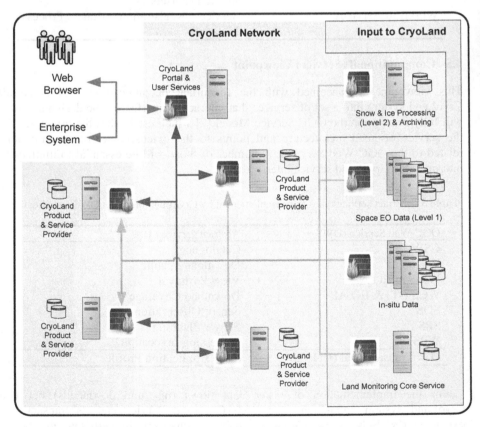

Fig. 2. CryoLand multi-provider & distributed network

The CryoLand Engineering Model - aligned with OGC model of reusable patterns for deployment – foresees a multi-tier architectures with a number of distributed nodes representing CryoLand service partners each acting as processing and service provider. The Spatial Data Infrastructures will link these nodes with the input data providers. These include space EO data acquisition and archiving centres providing Level-1 data (calibrated, swath-based satellite data), e.g. ESA processing and archiving centres (PAFs), the KSAT PAF, etc. Another important link is with the GMES Land Monitoring Core Service (LMCS) centre, as LMCS products will be integrated with satellite data for producing enhanced satellite snow products of CryoLand. Links to in-situ data providers (archives) will be set up according to user needs. Additionally, the CryoLand service concept foresees to maintain a Level-2 product archive (swath-based geophysical product, e.g. snow area extent) if required. This facilitates the production of customized (Level-3) satellite-based products that are derived from the same basic input data. Each node will be protected under a jointly organized security scheme. The interface for the users to the individual CryoLand nodes will be through a portal, providing virtual centralized access to the decentralized, chained services and the generated products.

4 Status of Development

The starting points of the CryoLand project are offerings of legacy snow and ice services available at project partner organizations. Based on user requirements assessed within the early project phase the services and products will be harmonized and tailored to match the customer needs. The infrastructure is already and will remain - by principle - distributed to designated service operators with a unique reference Web location [1] providing a logical entry point to these services. Currently a number of WMS-based viewing services to snow products are shown for demonstration purposes. Furthermore, a collection of example products is put online to indicate the future CryoLand product portfolio by showing early results.

5 Conclusion and Outlook

A GMES-embedded, pre-operational, Internet-based service infrastructure supporting the generation and provision of seasonal snow, glaciers, and lake / river ice information products is designed and will be implemented by the CryoLand project such as to be transferrable into sustainably operational multi-provider environments at project end. The overall project time span is February 2011 to January 2015 with service pre-operations and consolidation during 2013 - 2014. Services and products making use of data from the first GMES satellite Sentinel-1 (currently planned for launch in the first quarter of 2013) are expected during 2014.

Acknowledgements

The work described in this paper is partly supported by funding from the European Community's Seventh Framework Programme ([FP7/2007-2013]) under Grant Agreement n° 262925.

References

1. CryoLand Project Web Page, http://www.cryoland.eu/
2. Malnes, E., Storvold, R., Lauknes, I., Solbø, S., Solberg, R., Amlien, J., Koren, H.: Multi-sensor monitoring of snow parameters in Nordic mountainous areas. In: Proc. IGARSS 2005, Seoul, South Korea, July 25-29 (2005)
3. Nagler, T., Rott, H.: Retrieval of wet snow by means of multitemporal SAR data. IEEE Trans. Geosci. Remote Sensing 38(2), 754–765 (2000)
4. Nagler, T., Rott, H.: Snow classification algorithm for Envisat ASAR. In: Proc. of Envisat & ERS Symposium, Salzburg, Austria, p. 8 (September 2005), ESA SP-572
5. Solberg, R., Amlien, J., Koren, H., Eikvil, L., Malnes, E., Storvold, R.: Multi-sensor and time-series approaches for monitoring of snow parameters. In: Proc. of IGARSS 2004, Anchorage, Alaska, USA, September 20-24 (2004a)
6. OGC Geospatial Information Model, http://www.opengeospatial.org/standards/orm#_Toc87953568
7. Geospatial Services Model, http://www.opengeospatial.org/standards/orm#_Toc87953580
8. OGC 10-140 WCS Earth Observation Application Profile, https://portal.opengeospatial.org/files/?artifact_id=42579 as an OGC Standard

RBIS – An Environmental Information System for Integrated Landscape Management

Franziska Zander[1], Sven Kralisch[1], Carsten Busch[2], and Wolfgang-Albert Flügel[1]

[1] Department of Geoinformatics, Hydrology and Modelling,
School of Chemical and Earth Sciences, Friedrich-Schiller-University, Jena, Germany
[2] Codematix GmbH, Felsbachstraße 5/7, 07745 Jena, Germany
{Franziska.Zander,Sven.Kralisch,
Wolfgang.Albert.Fluegel}@uni-jena.de,
Carsten.Busch@codematix.de

Abstract. In this paper we present the web-based River Basin Information System (RBIS) for data management, analysis and exchange as an integral standalone part of the Integrated Landscape Management System (ILMS). Its architectural layout will be outlined together with the underlying software platform. Selected RBIS modules will be characterized in more detail to emphasize the benefits of integrated data management as a basis of the holistic environmental planning workflow covered by ILMS.

Keywords: environmental information systems, integrated landscape management, hydrological modeling.

1 Introduction

The need for a detailed understanding of environmental systems and strategies for their adequate management is gaining more and more importance as we face complex problems arising from global climate change, population growth and socio-economic development. In order to create strategies for the sustainable use and management of such systems and to assess the complex interactions of their underlying processes, the integration of data from different sources and disciplines is unavoidable, e.g. from remote sensing, hydrology, biology, soil science or socio-economic sciences. To transfer these data into well-presented and meaningful information for decision makers, they usually have to run through a workflow of different processing steps. This may include data preparation and storage, integrated data analysis by means of methods from various scientific disciplines, the development of future development scenarios and the application of environmental simulation models. Therefore, integrated environmental management systems are needed to address all parts of this workflow as well as a strategy to handle the needed input and produced output data.

2 Integrated Landscape Management System (ILMS)

The Integrated Landscape Management System (ILMS) developed at the Department of Geoinformatics, Hydrology and Modelling at the Friedrich Schiller University of

J. Hřebíček, G. Schimak, and R. Denzer (Eds.): ISESS 2011, IFIP AICT 359, pp. 349–356, 2011.

Jena provides an integrated, modular software platform to address the above mentioned needs and covers different steps of environmental system analysis and planning in a flexible and user-friendly workflow (http://ilms.uni-jena.de). This includes the following integrated but also standalone and mainly open-source platform components:

- **ILMS*info*:** the River Basin Information System (RBIS) for the management, analysis, visualization and presentation of different types of data.
- **ILMS*image*:** a software for the identification and classification of real-world objects from satellite imagery using methods of object based image analysis [3].
- **ILMS*gis*:** a software (GRASS-HRU) for the derivation of modelling entities using a Web Processing Service based on GRASS GIS and following the Hydrological Response Unit (HRU) approach (http://www.geogr.uni-jena.de/jamswiki /index.php/GRASS-HRU_en) [4].
- **ILMS*model*:** an environmental modelling framework (Jena Adaptable Modelling System - JAMS) for building, running and analyzing environmental simulation models (http://jams.uni-jena.de) [2].

3 River Basin Information System (RBIS)

Providing sophisticated data storage, management and interface functionality, RBIS is one of the core components of ILMS. RBIS is a modular structured web-based information system that offers user-friendly interfaces for the management, analysis, visualization and presentation of different types of data in the context of multidisciplinary environmental assessment and planning. This includes besides metadata (RBISmeta) and datasets of certain content types (e.g. soil (RBISsoil) and vegetation (RBISbio)) also the support for measured or simulated time series data (RBISts), documents (RBISdoc), remote sensing data (RBISrs) and spatial data in raster or vector format (RBISmap). The system was designed to fit the requirements arising from integrated research projects as well as to offer a platform to preserve knowledge beyond their end. Since RBIS is accessible via the web it features a fine grained permission management based on data types (e.g. time series data, soil, geodata, ...) and types of access (e.g. view, edit, delete, ...) to ensure data security and quality control. In addition to the permission management, transparency is ensured by an access logging mechanism which is responsible for recording data manipulations.

The common layout of RBIS follows a standard 3-tier architecture design (figure 1) using the database management system *PostgreSQL* (http://www.postgresql.org) as storage engine and the extension *PostGIS* (http://www.postgis.org) to add support for spatial data to PostgreSQL. The whole system is built based on open source software, ensuring a cost-effective deployment and operation. The following sections will shortly explain the underlying software architecture, give an overview of selected RBIS modules and outline some RBIS application examples.

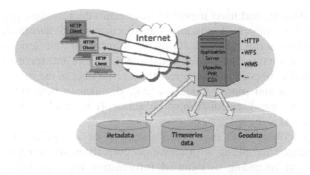

Fig. 1. RBIS technical layout [1]

3.1 System Architecture

The development of RBIS was guided by the objective of offering a flexible and modular database and application design that meets emerging demands for new data types and their relationships. This is realized by a data description layer that provides all information needed to manage both, read and writes access to the undelying database as well as the automated creation of web-based user interfaces (figure 2). A XML document describes database relations and attributes that define a certain data type, e.g. a person or a measurement station. The XML document is then evaluated by RBIS in order to create SQL statements and user interfaces needed to perform different actions on these data, e.g. search, browse, edit, add or delete datasets. New data types can easily be added by (i) adopting the database design (e.g. by adding new relations and attributes), and (ii) defining how RBIS shall access these data by means of a new XML document.

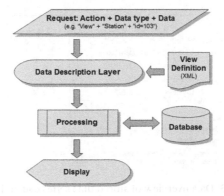

Fig. 2. RBIS information access via data description layer [1]

3.2 Time Series Data Management (RBISts)

The module RBISts provides several functions to manage measured or simulated time series data with a special focus on environmental modelling (figure 3). The main functions are:

- manual, automatic and mass import of time series data (including e.g. automatic adding of new values of ongoing measurements and automatic creation of station and time series metadata during mass import of time series data)
- gap detection, quality and format consistency checks and recording of detailed metadata during import and storage of time series data in the database
- spatial analysis and search functions (e.g. distance to next station with same measured parameter), calculation of indicators (e.g. trend) and visualization of time series data and gaps
- gap filling toolbox with rule based selection of interpolation methods (e.g. inverse distance weighting with elevation correction, linear regression, nearest neighbor) and recording of detailed information on used methods and time series data for each gap
- export of data in original temporal resolution or aggregated export to specific time steps including maximum and minimum values
- API for direct data access from external tools.

Simulated and measured time series data usually have a spatial reference, e.g. a point that they have been measured at or a representative area. These virtual or real measurement stations are stored as separate datasets with name, coordinates, elevation and more information (e.g. year of establishment and closing, picture of the station). Regarding to the given spatial position and type of station the station will be automatically linked and displayed in a map (see figure 4).

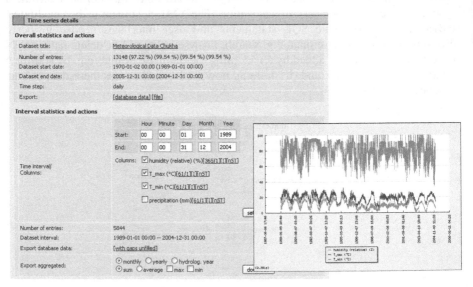

Fig. 3. Data overview of stored time series data in RBIS

3.3 Geodate Management and Visualization (RBISmap)

In order to manage and visualize spatial data the module RBISmap was developed. RBISmap also uses open source software like the *UMN MapServer* to create maps and *OpenLayers* with Ajax techniques for a user friendly display of map data in a web browser. RBISmap can handle vector data (ESRI Shapefile) and raster data

(GeoTIFF, JPEG, …). Each uploaded dataset has to be described by metadata following the ISO 19115 standard for geographic information metadata before the data can be used elsewhere (e.g. as a layer in maps). The user is demanded to fill in all information required according to the standard that cannot be automatically extracted from the dataset itself. The newly created metadata dataset is automatically linked to all maps, in which the layer is used. The linkage allows an easy switching between metadata and associated maps.

Maps are visualized in a user friendly, feature-rich frontend, including zooming/moving the map, changing the order of the displayed layers, searching for geometry objects and displaying their attribute values (figure 4). Stations and all datasets with given coordinates (e.g. soil, vegetation) can be automatically linked to a map and back which opens the possibility to search for datasets not only by metadata but also by their spatial location in a map.

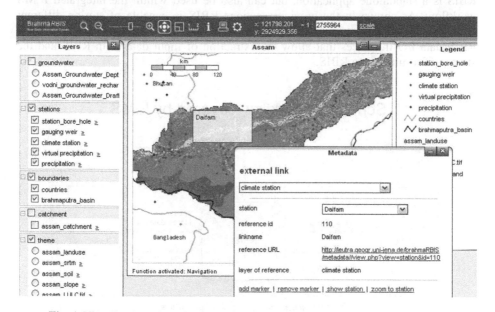

Fig. 4. Visualization of geodata and linkage between station and station metadata

3.4   Further RBIS Modules

In order to meet the rising demands in multidisciplinary research projects RBIS is continually extended by additional modules which can be easily added or modified as described in section 3.1. An important one is RBISdoc which allows adding an unlimited number of files (e.g. documents, images) to other RBIS datasets independent from the described data. RBISdoc furthermore offers a possibility to describe uploaded or linked documents (e.g. project proposal, master theses, paper, web links). The module RBISobserv has been developed to describe field observations (e.g. field trip, site inspection, water and soil sample) by a short description together with their spatial relation and related documents or files (e.g. pictures). Another module (RBISsoil) was developed to store soil profile and horizon data with a special focus is on hydrologically important parameters. Vegetation information (e.g. canopy height or leaf area index) can be stored in the RBIS module RBISbio.

For the description of future development scenarios and the management of related environmental indicators along with their values the module RBISind provides various functionalities. Indicator values (e.g. single value, time series data, diagrams, maps) can be associated to scenarios and optional to regions (e.g. hydrological catchment). New RBIS modules are under development to cover additional data types emerging from ongoing research projects.

4   RBIS Role in the ILMS Workflow

RBIS is a standalone application, but can also be used within the integrated ILMS workflow. As shown in the previous sections RBIS is capable of storing different types of data. In order to maximize interoperability, each ILMS component features RBIS data I/O interfaces that allow the extraction of input data from RBIS and the storage of result data to RBIS.

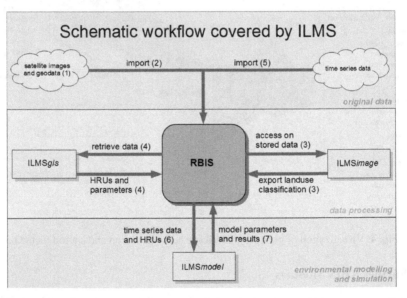

Fig. 5. Schematic workflow covered by ILMS showing the role of RBIS and the data flow between different ILMS components

Figure 5 sketches the following example workflow, using RBIS as a central data store and providing flexible and easy data exchange between ILMS components:

1. Collection of satellite images and available geodata of a defined region, including re-projection of data to a defined Spatial Reference System.
2. Import of the data into RBIS together with detailed meta-information.

3. Direct access of stored satellite images by ILMS*image* and export of a produced land use classification to RBIS.
4. Import of RBIS data to ILMS*gis* (i.e. DEM, land use classification, soil and geology data) and export of derived HRUs and parameter files.
5. Collection of measured time series data and import to RBIS. Preprocessing of data by filling gaps in RBIS.
6. Export of stored time series data and HRUs to ILMS*model* (for further information see [1]).
7. Model application and storage of model results in RBIS.
8. Preparations of final results and upload to RBIS for presentation.

As described in the above workflow RBIS is able to support the complete data flow starting at the original data from several sources via different processing steps to intermediate and final results consisting of simulated time series data or generated maps as base for subsequent decision making processes. The maintenance of metadata at each step also ensures transparency of data origin, change and processing as well as the reproducibility of results.

5 Use of RBIS in Research Projects

RBIS is used in many national and international research projects with different combinations of RBIS modules. Most of the RBIS instances are hosted at the Department of Geoinformatics, Hydrology and Modelling at the Friedrich Schiller University of Jena, but a few also in other institutions like the Institute for Technology and Resources Management in the Tropics and Subtropics at the Cologne University of Applied Sciences. Examples are the BrahmaRBIS created during the EU-Project BRAHMATWINN (twinning European and South Asian river basins to enhance capacity and implement adaptive integrated water resources management approaches - www.brahmatwinn.uni-jena.de) and instances created during other national funded projects, e.g. the BMBF projects ILMS (Integrated Landscape Management System - http://ilms.uni-jena.de), DINARIO (Climate change, landscape dynamics, land use and natural resources in the Atlantic Forest of Rio de Janeiro - http://dinario.fh-koeln.de) and LUCCI (Land Use and Climate Change interactions in the Vu Gia Thu Bon River Basin/Central Vietnam - http://www.lucci-vietnam.info).

6 Summary and Outlook

Due to its modular structure and interfaces RBIS is a flexible environmental information system that can be used in a wide range of applications related to integrated landscape management. On the one hand RBIS is designed as standalone modular application to provide support for sophisticated data management and data sharing in multidisciplinary research projects independent of tools used in the different disciplines. On the other hand the example of ILMS shows its ability to work as a central data store by providing flexible data exchange functionalities and services, allowing related tools and application to easily access the stored data and metadata.

Further work will focus on the development of additional RBIS modules and the implementation of various OGC standards like Catalog Web Service (CSW) or Sensor Observation Service (SOS) to provide standardized interfaces for data access and exchange that further enhance the RBIS flexibility and open it as a central data management system to an even broader range of applications.

Acknowledgments

We would like to thank the German Federal Ministry of Education and Research for funding the development of ILMS and RBIS in the course of the program "Entrepreneurial Regions – the BMBF Innovation Initiative for the New German Länder".

References

1. Kralisch, S., Zander, F., Krause, P.: Coupling the RBIS Environmental Information System and the JAMS Modelling Framework. In: Anderssen, R., Braddock, R., Newham, L. (eds.) Proceedings of the 18th World IMACS Congress and MODSIM 2009 International Congress on Modelling and Simulation, Cairns, Australia, pp. 902–908 (2009)
2. Kralisch, S., Krause, P.: JAMS - A Framework for Natural Resource Model Development and Application. In: Voinov, A., Jakeman, A., Rizzoli, A. (eds.) Proceedings of the iEMSs Third Biannual Meeting "Summit on Environmental Modelling and Software", Burlington, USA (2006)
3. Matejka, E., Reinhold, M., Selsam, P.: IMALYS - an automated and database-integrated object-oriented classification system. In: GEOBIA 2008 - Pixels, Objects, Intelligence: Geographic Object Based Image Analysis for the 21st Century, Proceedings GEOBIA 2008, Calgary, Kanada (2008)
4. Schwartze, C.: Deriving Hydrological Response Units (HRUs) using a Web Processing Service implementation based on GRASS GIS. In: Geoinformatics FCE CTU 2008, Workshop Proceedings, Prag, vol. 3 (2008)

User-Friendly Access to Structured Environmental Data

Andreas Abecker[1,2], Veli Bicer[2], Wassilios Kazakos[1],
Gabor Nagypal[1], Radoslav Nedkov[2,1], and Aleksei Valikov[1]

[1] disy Informationssysteme GmbH,
Erbprinzenstr. 4-12, D-76133 Karlsruhe, Germany
{Andreas.Abecker,Wassilios.Kazakos,Gabor.Nagycal,
Radoslav.Nedkov,Aleksei.Valikov}@disy.net
[2] FZI Forschungszentrum Informatik,
Haid-und-Neu-Str 10-14, D-76131 Karlsruhe, Germany
Veli.Bicer@fzi.de

Abstract. We sketch the HIPPOLYTOS and the KOIOS system prototypes for simple, keyword-based search in structured environmental data. Built on top of a commercial Spatial Data Warehouse software, the prototypes apply lightweight Semantic Web techniques to facilitate search in complex environmental information systems.

Keywords: Semantic Search, Semantics and Environment.

1 Motivation

With the increasing uptake of INSPIRE, the amount of publicly available environmental data is continuously growing. Nevertheless, the commercial and societal impact of open environmental data is still very limited. This has a number of reasons, but one of them is certainly the largely intransparent access to complex and distributed databases. This obviously holds true for interested citizen and companies, but even for employees of public authorities in a different domain, the heterogeneity and distribution of environmental data is often overwhelming. Hence, user-friendly and powerful search interfaces are a must-have in this area.

On the other hand, Semantic Web technologies promise advanced functionalities for intelligent search, integration, and processing of Web-accessible data, documents, and services [1]. Based on the annotation of complex machine-readable *metadata* to Web-based information resources, these resources can better be found and interpreted. Semantic metadata instantiate and refer to *ontologies*, rich conceptual domain models, agreed within a certain user community and represented in expressive, logic-based languages, which are standardized by the World Wide Web Consortium (W3C) [2]. The power of semantic technologies relies on several factors – the specific importance of each depending on the specific use case – like standardization of representation languages, metadata or knowledge models; like automation of some reasoning services because of the logic-based semantics; or like empowering user or systems by the domain-specific background knowledge represented in ontologies. Ontologies for knowledge organization and human search and navigation, often comprise a so-called *lexical layer*, which describes how the concepts are referred to by natural-language

J. Hřebíček, G. Schimak, and R. Denzer (Eds.): ISESS 2011, IFIP AICT 359, pp. 357–363, 2011.

expressions; such a lexical layer allows to cover the variability of human language, addressing phenomena like synonymy, or enabling multilingual knowledge access.

Although comprehensive metadata and extensive background knowledge for knowledge organization (in the form of thesauri) are widespread in environmental information systems, there are not many industrial-strength applications of semantic technologies in this area. This paper sketches the GUI approach of the HIPPOLYTOS project which aims at a practicable combination of semantic technologies and a commercial tool for geodata management and spatial reporting. Very generally spoken, the project goals of HIPPOLYTOS were:

- to map an intuitive text-based search interface at the front-end
- to complex data structures and relationships in the back-end (environmental information system/ spatial data warehouse)
- by exploiting existing expert knowledge (in form of domain ontologies and in predefined selectors and selector metadata),
- taking into account real-world constraints and requirements.

The presentation of the HIPPOLYTOS search interface is completed by a short description of the KOIOS schema-agnostic search, another prototype which has complementary characteristics.

The paper is structured as follows: in Section 2, we sketch the look-and-feel of the HIPPOLYTOS prototype; in Section 3, the same is done for KOIOS; in Section 4, we summarize and discuss current status and some future work.

2 Look-and-Feel of the HIPPOLYTOS Semantic-Metadata Search

In contrast to other semantic search projects, HIPPOLYTOS and KOIOS do not focus on text, documents or multimedia information (as we do in complementary research [3,4]), but on **structured data** in relational databases or a Data Warehouse. We develop a search layer on top of such data repositories realized, e.g., by disy GmbH's Cadenza software.[1]

Fig. 1 below illustrates the current prototype of the HIPPOLYTOS system: Assume the user types in "Eisenschrott Ballungsraum Stuttgart" ("iron junk city region Stuttgart") at a Google-like query interface. The system reasons as follows:

- "Iron junk" is not a technical term in environmental information systems, but "recyclable fraction FE scrap" is – which is represented in the ontology, with "iron junk" as a synonymous wording.

---

[1] disy Cadenza (http://www.disy.net/produkte/cadenza.html) is a system for building search, analysis, and visualization solutions for spatial data. At its core stands a re¬po¬si¬to¬ry system, which manages the back-end data sources. An important Cadenza concept are so-called Selectors, pre-defined query templates for the back-end systems which are designed by domain experts for specific query and analysis tasks. Selectors can be described with text metadata. They stand at the heart of many special applications that disy has built for environmental agencies and other public authorities.

- The ontology also contains the taxonomic knowledge that "potential recyclables" is a super-concept of FE scrap and that "metal" is a super-concept of iron/FE whereas "waste" is a super-concept of scrap.

- It also contains in its taxonomy the knowledge that "recyclable fraction Aluminium scrap" and "recyclable fraction glass" may be siblings to "recyclable fraction FE scrap" in the taxonomy.

- Furthermore, the lexical part of the ontology knows that "city region" is a synonym for "metropolitan region" or for "urban agglomeration", which is an informal term that can be mapped to several spatial interpretations, such as the city of Stuttgart, the Stuttgart region constituted by 6 neighboring administrative districts, or the geographic area within a certain radius around Stuttgart city center.

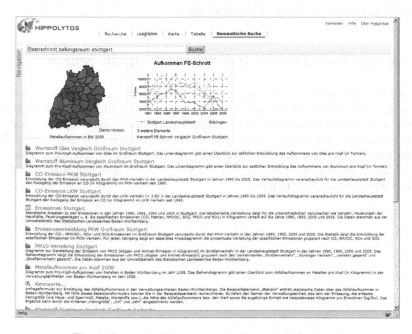

Fig. 1. Query for "Eisenschrott Ballungsraum Stuttgart"

Using the lexical and conceptual background knowledge, the system can identify a number of stored, semantically indexed *selectors* – parameterized, predefined query templates, accessing the data sources in the back-end. The match between query concepts and annotation concepts of stored selectors can be based on:

- The *subject matter* of the selector (e.g., there may be a selector querying for the amount of certain recyclable <u>materials</u> [which is a parameter of this selector] in sorted waste of a given <u>region</u> [2nd parameter] in a given <u>timeframe</u> [3rd parameter] – here a proximity match could be made with the "potential recyclables" concept in the set of super-concepts of the query concepts.

- The co-domain of the selector **parameters** (e.g., "FE" could be a parameter value for the 1st parameter of the example selector above, and "Stuttgart" for the 2nd parameter).
- The **visualization** or presentation type (data value, data series, data table, map-based visualization, specific diagram type, ...) for the results. For instance, if the query would contain terms like "comparison", "trend", or "distribution", this could give hints to the expected kind of presentation.[2]

Then – for the given query – the most appropriate selectors and parameter settings can be identified and sent to the back-end system. The result screen in Fig. 1 shows a ranked list of potential result selectors as well as previews of the visualized results of the two top-ranked ones.

3 Look-and-Feel of the KOIOS Schema-Agnostic Search

The KOIOS approach is fundamentally different (see Fig. 2). It applies a so-called **schema-agnostic search**, which takes a set of keywords and heuristically creates a number of potential SQL-queries which *might* have been meant by the user when launching his keyword query. These hypotheses are based on the given DB-schema and the statistical distribution of DB-values occuring in the concrete, actual DB-content. Based on that hypothetical SQL-queries, we can then select those Cadenza Selectors which come close to them.

Fig. 2. KOIOS Faceted-Search Interface for Query "Karlsruhe CO Emissionen"

---

[2] This kind of "query hints" for the visualization type is not yet implemented.

In practice, with large DB-schema and often occurring data values, normally many different hypotheses will be possible. In order to quickly deliver probably highly relevant hypotheses to the user, ranking mechanisms are of utmost importance for such approaches (cp. [5]). Furthermore, we can offer to the user a very structured interface to navigate through the hypotheses, which is done by a *faceted-search GUI* (see Fig. 2): If different potential query interpretations differ in several dimensions, each dimension will be represented by one tab in the left-hand part of the search GUI in Fig. 2. There, a search for "CO emissions in the city of Karlsruhe" yields a number of possible selectors which can be differentiated according to:

- The year for which information is sought (only years for which we have actual DB content will be offered).

- The administrative region which is examined by the selection (concretely, Karlsruhe city versus Karlsruhe county).

- The actual measured value considered (e.g., CO emissions from motor-bikes, CO emissions from passenger cars, CO emissions from trucks, ...).

A selection on this left-hand side will immediately refresh the list of possible resulting queries shown at the right-hand side of Fig. 2. As shown before in Section 2, clicking one of these results on the right-hand side will then evaluate this selector and deliver the actual query results from the back-end database.

4 Summary and Future Work

Summary. We have sketched functionality and realization of two prototypes for semantic search over geo-referenced environmental data. The goal is a "third kind of information access" for disy's Spatial Reporting products, which currently offer map- and form-based access to geodata. This third kind of access shall be a Google-like, simple text query interface, which automatically finds and instantiates available selectors and thus automatically configures appropriate structured queries to the back-end data sources.

Following the HIPPOLYTOS approach, repository elements and their textual descriptions are semantically annotated (by hand, by the public servants who create the Selectors and attach already metadata for human reading, in the current installations) with ontology concepts. The ontological background knowledge about taxonomic and non-taxonomic relationships between concepts and about lexical variations of concept references allows to build a semantic index – such that also vague, too abstract, too specific, or wrongly expressed queries can be resolved. In order to provide a solution suitable for real-world usage, we aim at largely automated ontology creation and annotation processes.

KOIOS is a second prototype, which does not require any pre-modeled extra knowledge in form of ontologies or metadata, but instead exploits existing schema information and value distributions of database content in order to find possible query interpretations. The results are offered to the user in a faceted-search GUI which facilitates orientation in the space of possible query interpretations.

Obviously, both approaches, HIPPOLYTOS and KOIOS, exhibit different strengths and have different prerequisites and basic assumptions. This makes it an interesting idea to think about their synergetic integration.

Status. Both presented prototypes still have some "hardwired" aspects. But they show that, also for realistic data volumes and ontology sizes, it is possible to deliver reasonable results with acceptable performance. The evaluation of the retrieval *quality* still has to be evaluated in long-term experiments. Obviously, the quality of the HIPPOLYTOS retrieval depends on the used ontologies and annotations. Here, the practicability of *fully*-automated ontology creation and semantic annotation still has to be verified – and, probably, user-friendly editors for manual corrections must be implemented. Regarding KOIOS, the ranking heuristics are the most important critical aspect to evaluate in practice. From the HCI points of view, both prototypes must be seen as design studies which explore technical feasibility, but still lack evaluation from the usability point of view. However, one thing seems to be clear: that mask-based, browsing-based, or also clumsy map-based search interfaces will hardly be accepted in the near future, by the members of the "Google generation" of end users. Regarding KOIOS, there are also positive prior results about the usability of faceted-search in Semantic Web search approaches.

Future work. There are still many areas for potential future work, to mention only two: (1) In the SUI and SUI II projects [3, 4], more usage and design studies for ontology-based access to environmental information have been performed, including *unstructured* information and the *links* between information sources, as well as *navigational* support for end users through ontological knowledge. A combination with HIPPOLYTOS/KOIOS could make sense. (2) The current approach mainly employs background knowledge about the domain of geo-referenced *environmental information*. It does not yet go very deeply into the semantic analysis of the *spatial concepts* themselves in the query. Though the use of ontologies is a longstanding research topic in GIS (see, e.g., [6,7]), it has not yet found its way very far into OGC or W3C standardization. Pragmatic steps into this direction may be a thrilling long-term goal.

Acknowledgment. HIPPOLYTOS has partially been funded by the German Federal Ministry of Economics and Technology (BMWi) in the project HIPPOLYTOS which runs within the "SME sub-programme" of the BMWi research programme THESEUS; KOIOS has been developed within the CTC-WP3 sub-project of THESEUS. Both have been supported by the Ministry of Environment, Nature Conservation and Transport of the Federal State of Baden-Württemberg and by the "Landesanstalt für Umwelt, Messungen und Naturschutz Baden-Württemberg (LUBW)", as part of the KEWA cooperation for environmental informatics research. Both have been supported by the Ministry of Economics of Baden-Württemberg which gives a base funding for FZI.

References

1. Domingue, J., Fensel, D., Hendler, J.A. (eds.): Handbook of Semantic Technologies. Springer, Heidelberg (2011)
2. Staab, S., Studer, R. (eds.): Handbook on Ontologies, 2nd edn. Springer, Heidelberg (2009)
3. Abecker, A., et al.: SUI – Ein Demonstrator zur semantischen Suche im Umweltportal Baden-Württemberg. In: Mayer-Föll, R., Keitel, A., Geiger, W. (eds.) Kooperative Entwicklung wirtschaftlicher Anwendungen für Umwelt, Verkehr und benachbarte Bereiche in neuen Verwaltungsstrukturen, Phase IV 2008/2009, Forschungszentrum Karlsruhe, Wissenschaftliche Berichte, FZKA 7500, pp. 157–166 (2009) (in Gernan)
4. Bügel, U., et al.: SUI II – Weiterentwicklung der diensteorientierten Infrastruktur des Umweltinformationssystems Baden-Württemberg für die semantische Suche nach Umweltinformationen. In: Mayer-Föll, R., Ebel, R., Geiger, W. (eds.) Kooperative Entwicklung wirtschaftlicher Anwendungen für Umwelt, Verkehr und benachbarte Bereiche in neuen Verwaltungsstrukturen, Phase V 2009/2010, Karlsruher Institut für Technologie, KIT Science Reports, FZKA 7544, pp. 43–50 (2010) (in Gernan)
5. Nedkov, R.: Schlüsselwortsuche über relationalen Datenbanken, Diploma thesis, KIT Karlsruhe Institute of Technology (May 2011) (in German)
6. Fonseca, F., Egenhofer, M., Agouris, P., Camara, G.: Using Ontologies for Integrated Geographic Information Systems. Transactions in GIS 6, 231–257 (2002)
7. Bittner, T., Donnelly, M., Smith, B.: A Spatio-Temporal Ontology for Geographic Information Integration. International Journal of Geographical Information Science 23(6), 765–798 (2009)

Leveraging Ontologies for Environmental Information Systems

Ulrich Bügel[1], Martin Schmieder[1], Boris Schnebel[1],
Thorsten Schlachter[2], and Renate Ebel[3]

[1] Fraunhofer Institute of Optronics, System Technologies and Image Exploitation (IOSB),
Fraunhoferstraße 1, 76131 Karlsruhe, Germany
`{Ulrich.Buegel,Martin.Schmieder,`
`Boris.Schnebel}@iosb.fraunhofer.de`
[2] Karlsruhe Institute of Technology (KIT), Institute for Applied Computer Science,
Hermann-von-Helmholtz-Platz 1, 76344 Eggenstein-Leopoldshafen, Germany
`Thorsten.Schlacher@kit.edu`
[3] Baden-Württemberg State Institute for the Environment, Measurements and Nature
Conservation (LUBW), Grießbachstraße 1-3, 76185 Karlsruhe, Germany
`Renate.Ebel@lubw.bwl.de`

Abstract. The provision of accurate, comprehensive and condensed information contained in distributed environmental information systems via public search interfaces raises several technological challenges. Our approach to tackle these challenges is based on a consequent use of ontologies. Starting with an analysis of requirements resulting from semantic search scenarios, we explain the advantages of using ontologies based on standards and aim to reuse and transform terminological systems available in the environmental domain into ontologies. We develop an architecture guided by the premise of exerting a minimum of influence on existing search infrastructures. As a consequence of using a (possibly large) number of ontologies, tools for ontology management are needed. A key argument for using ontologies is that nowadays – as an outcome of the Semantic Web initiative - very powerful processing tools are available. We elaborate ontology mapping as an example and outline how a comprehensive ontology management can be achieved.

Keywords: Public Search Portals, Environmental Terminology, Semantic Technologies, Ontology Management, Ontology Mapping, Life Circumstance Ontology.

1 Introduction

Guided by environmental directives at the regional, national and international levels, many environmental agencies nowadays offer free access to distributed environmental information by means of public portals. Typically the underlying Environmental Information Systems (EIS) were primarily designed to provide highly detailed information and sophisticated user interfaces to thematic experts. They have to be re-focused to provide information in a more restricted and aggregated form to a new user

J. Hřebíček, G. Schimak, and R. Denzer (Eds.): ISESS 2011, IFIP AICT 359, pp. 364–371, 2011.

community: the public user, e.g. the citizen who wants environmental information about his surroundings. The provision of accurate, comprehensive and condensed information contained in EIS via public search interfaces is a technological challenge for several reasons:

- EIS usually comprise many sub-systems which hold information in different representation forms and may have dedicated built-in search functions. When retrieving environmental information, it is helpful to link structured information in databases with unstructured information contained in documents.
- For public users, keyword-based search is the most favoured method for information search. In order to integrate responses of query-based subsystems into the search results, text-to-query approaches need to be integrated.
- Public users often do not know the correct search keywords that exactly match stored information which may result in a poor recall.

Our approach to tackle these challenges is based on the utilization of available environmental terminologies as a basic asset. The development of terminologies has been influenced by technological progress and observed trends. The most advanced specification techniques for describing a knowledge domain are developed in the context of the Semantic Web initiative. The World Wide Web Consortium (W3C) has approved standards by which ontologies can be specified in terms of formal logic with high expressivity. In the following sections, we suggest a consequent use of ontologies and explain why this yields considerable advantages. Moreover, nowadays very powerful processing and management tools are available.

2 Enhancing Search Facilities – How Ontologies Can Help

2.1 Semantic Search Scenarios – Why Are Full-Text Engines Not Enough?

Nowadays, full-text search engines provide access to various types of information and exhibit excellent performance. However, they still have deficits as soon as an intelligent combination of different information types and information content is required. Users of environmental portals often search for topics with a concrete location reference, e.g. "air quality in the Upper Rhine Valley" or "measurement values for respirable dust in my environment". Moreover, users with a concrete objective in mind generally need to submit a series of requests to (one or several) EIS and collect and select "manually" the retrieved information which is relevant to take a decision. Consider a citizen who looks for "building land" where he would like to build a house. He is interested in getting an overview about environmental conditions (e.g. transport connections, noise disturbance, air quality, land contamination) in a given geographical area. An ontology describing life circumstances may define a concept structure "build house"/"find location"/"living conditions"/"environmental conditions" that helps to provide links to all content of interest as the result of a single search. The idea is to use keywords entered by a user to identify corresponding concepts defined in an uploaded ontology. Starting from a concept, other concepts that reside in a "semantic bounding box" determined by ontological relationships (parent, children and property relationships) are additionally looked up in the ontology. This context can be used to provide automatic query expansion and context-based navigation through domain knowledge before submission of the final query.

2.2   Architectural Aspects – Spicing Up the Established Search Infrastructure

Technologies emerging in the Semantic Web area still have some academic flavour and their integration into established infrastructures for conventional information retrieval is a challenge. In order to achieve acceptance by organisations that operate an EIS, we favour an approach by which components of the deployed IT infrastructure (e.g. catalogues, search engines) do not need to be replaced. Hence, we propose an architecture which foresees semantic add-ons in terms of pre-processing of user queries before their execution through the deployed EIS search facilities, and post-processing of search results before their final presentation to the user.

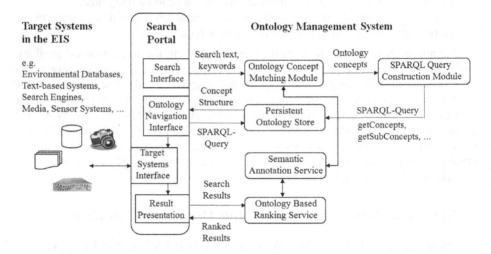

Fig. 1. Pre- and post-processing of keyword based queries via public portals by an Ontology Management System

The architectural approach is outlined in Fig. 1. We distinguish three main architectural components: the search portal, the target systems in the EIS and the Ontology Management System providing the semantic add-on functionality.

In the first step, search strings entered via the portal are processed by a text-to-query system. In order to resolve relationships between the input text in natural language with ontological concepts, we suggest to use automatic semantic annotation tools as described in [6]. Once corresponding concepts have been identified, queries to the ontology store (e.g. SPARQL queries) can be composed automatically. These queries return the "semantic bounding box" of the identified concepts. The portal software transforms this ontological structure into a navigation structure which allows the user to explore the semantic context of his query and then issue his request more precisely, e.g. by narrowing or widening his initial request.

In the next step, the portal software constructs requests to the various EIS target systems. As the ontological elements have been defined independently from the interfaces of the target systems, we face another matching problem here; this can be resolved by attaching target system information to the ontological elements. This crucial issue is not further elaborated here; a generic approach based on OpenSearch descriptions is described in a further contribution to ISESS 2011 [18].

Once the results from the target systems have been received by the portal, ontology based post-processing can be applied before the results are finally presented to the user. One way to improve the quality of the search results is to exert influence on the ranking of the results by means of the ontology, i.e. the results are ordered according to their semantic closeness to the search item. For instance, if a user searches for "environmental conditions", entries about "air quality" are ranked higher despite the fact that the terms "air" and "quality" were not search terms [15].

Finally, the search results from target systems with various forms of information representation (e.g. text-based systems, databases) can be presented uniformly and combined by means of relationships defined in the ontology.

2.3   Ontologies – Where Do They Come From?

We have validated the developed architecture in various projects, e.g. as frontend/ backend of conventional OGC Catalogue Systems [12] and in a project "Semantische Suche nach Umweltinformation (SUI)" of the German environmental cooperation network KEWA [16] for an integrated semantic search over environmental systems in Baden-Württemberg [1][5][18]. Here, we have made two important observations:

- We usually have to deal with a number of ontologies from different sources, rather than a single ontology covering all aspects.
- As ontology development is costly and time consuming, whenever possible ontologies should not be developed from scratch. Especially in the area of EIS, the information to be covered in many cases is available in terms of terminological systems which have formerly been developed under huge effort. Thus, we favour to reuse these systems and spend new effort mainly for development of methods and tools which transform these systems into ontologies and which help to automate the process of updating.

In SUI, we use the following ontologies:

- Environmental thesauri: We use GEMET (GEneral Multilingual Environmental Thesaurus [9]) because it covers a comprehensive base of search terms. GEMET is available as SKOS ontology (Simple Knowledge Organisation Systems [22]).
- Feature Type Catalogues: In order to facilitate data exchange in integrated EIS such as WIBAS [13], so-called feature type catalogues are being defined for all domain areas represented by features that describe real word phenomena. This information is often available as structured data in environmental databases. Although not originally designed for the task of keyword based search, such catalogues provide valuable information, especially for accessing structured information (e.g. object type codes). We have transformed the WIBAS feature type catalogue into a SKOS ontology such that it can be used in the search and navigation interface.
- Life circumstance ontologies: We have referred to this in the "build house" scenario in section 2.1. Portals of various federal state authorities in Germany offer a navigation through their web pages according to a structure of defined life circumstances, e.g. "Service-BW" operated by the Ministry of Interior of Baden-

Württemberg [19] or the "Directory to Administrations" operated by the Bavarian Ministry of Interior [2]. We have extended the structure of Service-BW with concepts that specialise on environmental information issues and made it applicable to semantic search.

The list is open, i.e. there are plans to transform further terminological systems into ontologies in order to feed the semantic search interface. A candidate is the GSBL (Gemeinsamer Stoffdatenpool Bund/Länder), a database of substances operated by the German Federal Government and the Federal States [8].

3   Fostering Integrated Domain Knowledge - Ontology Mapping

Up to now, we have explained that ontologies can guide users to explore available domain knowledge. Naturally, each of the deployed ontologies offers specialised knowledge focussed on the common view of a particular domain. Cross references between domains are not explicated and the terms used to express similar concepts in different domains may differ. However, the ontology system should provide means to make these relationships transparent to the user.

The necessity for ontology mapping arises because query expansions computed for search terms should have a range across multiple ontologies. Consider for instance a search for "building land": the corresponding concept is found in GEMET and a bounding box will be constructed only from ontological elements contained in GEMET. If we relate the concept "building land" in GEMET to the concept "build house" as described above, the bounding box will additionally contain ontological elements from the life circumstance ontology.

Such mappings can be constructed by means of automatic ontology mapping tools. In the SUI project, we use a tool developed in the German Research Program THESEUS [21] which utilizes Particle Swarm Optimization (PSO) to search for the optimal alignment of ontologies [4]. It was specially designed for parallel execution in distributed systems and exhibits excellent performance especially for large ontologies.

While tools for automatic ontology mappings are available (e.g. in the form of console programs) and can be selected according to specific needs, integration of these tools into a concrete application environment requires additional functionality and customization. Bilateral mappings between ontologies have to be developed and deployed. Moreover, it is important to provide means for manual post-processing of automatically generated mappings; although they can be very helpful and some tools exhibit excellent precision/recall, we do not recommend uncritical confidence in these automatic findings and we recommend to check the consequences in the context of the entire application.

Fig. 2 illustrates a workflow for the management of mappings as applied in the SUI project. Via the administration GUI of the SUI ontology system mapping contexts for bilateral mappings can be defined and stored. For a stored context, a run of the automatic mapping process can be configured and started. It produces an alignment, i.e. a number of correspondences between entities of two ontologies in the format of the Alignment API [7]. Dependent on the size of the ontologies, this process may consume a considerable amount of time. The computed alignment is treated as an initial suggestion of correspondences which can be manually post-processed via the GUI: correspondences can be accepted, rejected, added and changed. Finally, the alignment can be activated. Activated alignments are involved in the execution of the SPARQL queries: the resulting semantic bounding is spawned across ontologies.

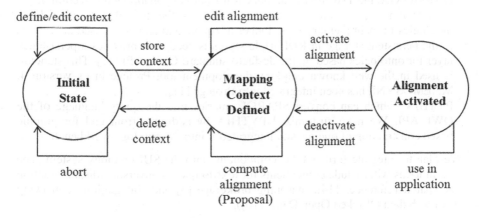

Fig. 2. State Transition Diagram for a Mapping Workflow

4   Driving the Change – A Comprehensive Ontology Management

We have elaborated the aspect of ontology mapping as we conceive it as a key component to support semantic search scenarios. Beyond that, ontologies can provide excellent support for further applications needed in EIS, e.g. navigation in content, interpretation and analysis of content, visualization of relationships or combination/orchestration of environmental information services. The effective utilization of the expressive power of ontologies can be further extended by consecutive incorporation of ongoing developments of domain ontologies, geo-ontologies, top level ontologies and ontologies constructed from any available representation format. This can open up outstanding opportunities to excavate treasures of information hidden deeply in a distributed EIS.

However, there are no benefits without costs: the boosting impact of ontologies can only be leveraged if we can provide the means for a comprehensive ontology management. One important motivation to favour ontologies as the unique representation form is that the Semantic Web is a driving force not only for standardization, but also for the development of the needed management tools. Ontology management covers a wide range of tools, namely for ontology design, evolution, persistent storage, querying, mapping, reasoning, visualization and provenance management. Moreover, there is a growing number of available tools to extract instance data from various sources such as databases, text-based systems, web pages, media, sensors systems or maps.

In the SUI project we mainly integrate tools developed in the context of the THESEUS program. The THESEUS Core Technology Cluster (CTC) focuses on the development of generic components to be used in several defined use cases.

Especially CTC-WP3 is concerned with all aspects of ontology management. At Fraunhofer IOSB we integrate tools developed in WP3 (and other WPs) into our development platform WebGenesis® [22]. We apply it in the shape of an Internet ontology workbench in several projects in the area of EIS. In SUI, we have reused and customized the following components:

- HARMONIA, the THESEUS component for ontology mapping (cf. section 3).
- MNEMOSYNE, a component which addresses the fact that keeping large ontologies in main memory is no longer adequate and an OWL based alternative to the persistent storage in RDF triple stores is needed. It provides a persistency layer for ontologies based on the de-facto standard OWL-API [17]. This standard is used in the well known ontology development tool Protégé in its version 4. MNEMOSYNE has been integrated into Protégé [11].
- PYTHIA, which can convert SPARQL queries into the query language of the OWL-API. We have customized PYTHIA by adding a front end for graphic based construction of queries and integrated it into the ontology workbench.

We plan to integrate further CTC components into the SUI ontology system. The near-term focus will include components for text-to-query conversion, disambiguation of geo-spatial references [14], reasoning brokerage [3] and integration of growing pools of web data ("Linked Open Data" [10]).

5 Conclusions

Finally, it can be stated that semantic search technologies and ontology management tools can help to "open-up the door" for public users to information contained in EIS which was originally designed for domain experts. For implementation purposes we recommend to use technologies, tools and standards (e.g. OWL-API, Alignment API, SPARQL) developed in the context of the Semantic Web initiative. Deployment of innovative tools within an existing EIS infrastructure, even when being state-of-the-art and easily available, requires careful selection, adaptation and operation in order for them to be accepted by the EIS community.

Acknowledgements. The presented work has been funded by the German Federal Ministry of Economics (BMWi) in the THESEUS research programme under grant 01MQ07019 and by the environmental research network KEWA led by the Ministry of the Environment, Nature Conservation and Transport of Baden-Württemberg, Germany.

References

1. Abecker, A., et al.: SUI – Ein Demonstrator zur semantischen Suche im Umweltportal Baden-Württemberg. In: Mayer-Föll, et al. (eds.) F+E Vorhaben KEWA, Phase IV 2008/2009, Forschungszentrum Karlsruhe, Wissenschaftliche Berichte FZKA 7500, pp. S.157–S.166 (2009)
2. Behördenwegweiser Bayern, http://www.behoerdenwegweiser.bayern.de/
3. Bock, J., Tserendorj, T., Xu, Y., Wissmann, J., Grimm, S.: A Reasoning Broker Framework for OWL. In: 5th Int. Workshop on OWL: Experiences and Directions (OWLED 2009), Chantilly, Virginia, USA (October 2009)

4. Bock, J., Hettenhausen, J.: Discrete particle swarm optimization for ontology alignment. Information Sciences (2010), doi:10.1016/j.ins.2010.08.013
5. Bügel, U., et al.: SUI –Weiterentwicklung der diensteorientierten UIS Infrastruktur für die semantische Suche. In: Mayer-Föll, et al. (eds.) F+E Vorhaben KEWA, Phase V 2009/2010, Karlsruhe Institute of Technology, KIT Scientific Reports 7544, pp. 43–50 (2010)
6. Bügel, U., Usländer, T.: Discovery and analysis of environmental information based on formalised terminology. Towards eEnvironment. In: European Conference of the Czech Presidency of the Council of the EU 2009: Opportunities of SEIS and SISE: Integrating Environmental Knowledge in Europe, Prague, Czech Republic, March 25-27 (2009)
7. Euzenat, J.: An API for ontology alignment. In: McIlraith, S.A., Plexousakis, D., van Harmelen, F. (eds.) ISWC 2004. LNCS, vol. 3298, pp. 698–712. Springer, Heidelberg (2004)
8. Gemeinsamer zentraler Stoffdatenpool Bund/Länder (GSBL), http://www.umweltbundesamt.de/chemikalien/gefahrstoffe/gsbl.htm
9. GEMET, http://www.eionet.europa.eu/gemet
10. Haase, P., Eberhart, A., Godelet, S., Mathäß, T., Tran, T., Ladwig, G., Wagner, A.: The Information Workbench – Interacting with the Web of Data. Forschungsbericht KIT (2009)
11. Henß, J., Kleb, J., Grimm, S., Bock, J.: A Database Backend for OWL. In: 5th Int. Workshop on OWL: Experiences and Directions (OWLED 2009), Chantilly, Virginia, USA (2009)
12. Hilbring, D., Usländer, T.: Ontology-Based Discovery of Geoscientific Information and Services. In: Session on Semantic Interoperability, Knowledge and Ontologies in the European Geosciences Union General Assembly in Vienna, April 13-18 (2008)
13. Informationssystem Wasser, Immissionsschutz, Boden, Abfall, Arbeitsschutz (WIBAS), http://www.lubw.baden-wuerttemberg.de/servlet/is/23889/
14. Kleb, J., Volz, R.: Ontology based Entity Disambiguation with Natural Language Patterns. In: Grosky, B., Andres, F., Pichappan, P. (eds.) Proceedings of Fourth IEEE International Conference on Digital Information Management, ICDIM 2009, November 1-4, pp. 19–26. University of Michigan, Ann Arbor (2009)
15. Madlener, A.: Entwurf und Implementierung eines Verfahrens für Ontologie-basiertes Ranking von Suchergebnissen. Master Thesis, Karlsruhe Institute of Technology / Fraunhofer IOSB, Karlsruhe (2010)
16. Mayer-Föll, R., Keitel, A., Geiger, W. (eds.): F+E Vorhaben KEWA Phase V 2009/2010 (2010), http://www.fachdokumente.lubw.baden-wuerttemberg.de/servlet/is/5121/2009
17. OWL API, http://owlapi.sourceforge.net/
18. Schlachter, T., et al.: Towards a Universal Search in EIS. In: Hřebíček, J., Schimak, G., Denzer, R. (eds.) ISESS 2011. IFIP AICT, vol. 359, pp. 326–333. Springer, Heidelberg (2011)
19. Service-BW, http://www.service-bw.de/
20. SKOS Simple Knowledge Organisation Systems, http://www.w3.org/2004/02/skos/
21. The THESEUS Programme, http://theseus-programm.de/home/default.aspx
22. WebGenesis®, http://www.iosb.fraunhofer.de/servlet/is/2223/

An Architecture for the Semantic Enhancement of Environmental Resources

P. Dihé[1], S. Frysinger[2,3], R. Güttler[2], S. Schlobinski[1], L. Petronzio[4], R. Denzer[2],
S. Nešić[5], T. Lobo[6], G. Schimak[7], J. Hřebíček[8], and M. Donatelli[9]

[1] cismet GmbH, Altenkesseler Strasse 17 D2, 66115 Saarbrücken
[2] Environmental Informatics Group (EIG),
Goebenstrasse 40, 66117 Saarbrücken, Germany
[3] James Madison University, Harrisonburg, Virginia, USA 22807
[4] Telespazio S.p.A, Via Tiburtina, 965 - 00156 Rome - Italy
[5] IDSIA - USI/SUPSI, Galleria 2, 6928 Manno, Switzerland
[6] Atos Research and Innovation, C/Albarracín 25, 28037 Madrid, Spain
[7] AIT Austrian Institute of Technology GmbH, A-2444 Seibersdorf, Austria
[8] Masaryk University, Kamenice 126/3, 625 00 Brno, Czech Republic
[9] Joint Research Centre of the European Commission, Ispra, Italy
pascal.dihe@cismet.de

Abstract. The vision of a Single Information Space in Europe for the Environment (SISE) requires seamless access to environmental resources, including data, models and services. Standardization organizations like OGC and OASIS have laid the foundations for interoperability on a syntactic level for many aspects of distributed environmental information systems (e.g. OGC SWE for sensor information). At the same time, the EC has undertaken a considerable effort to commit European stakeholders to offering their environmental information in such a way that it is accessible by interested parties, both on the scientific level by supporting research projects, like ORCHESTRA and SANY, and on the legal level by introducing directives (such as the INSPIRE directive). This development, amongst others, has led to the present situation in which a large number of environmental information sources are available. However, to implement the vision of the SISE it is not enough to publish resources. Environmental information must be discoverable, and it must be 'understandable' in different contexts in order to be used effectively by parties of various thematic domains. Therefore, in order to foster the implementation of SISE, semantic interoperability is a necessary element. Key to semantic interoperability is the presence of meta-information which describes the concepts of the environmental resources. Producing this meta-information puts a heavy technological burden on the individual resource providers such that it seems unlikely that enough semantic meta-information will ever be made available to reach semantic interoperability and thus accomplish the vision of SISE unless other ways to provide this essential meta-information are found. In this paper we introduce an architecture, developed in the FP7 project TaToo (247893), which tries to overcome the aforementioned obstacles by providing the possibility to easily annotate and rate environmental information resources, even by parties which do not own the resource, and transparently equipping this information with domain knowledge and thus enhancing discoverability and

J. Hřebíček, G. Schimak, and R. Denzer (Eds.): ISESS 2011, IFIP AICT 359, pp. 372–384, 2011.
© IFIP International Federation for Information Processing 2011

usability of resources with semantic technologies. The objective of the architecture is to seamlessly blend in with existing infrastructures by making use of *de facto* standards while offering support for discovery, annotation and validation of environmental resources through open interfaces.

Keywords: SISE, semantics, search, discovery, annotation, tagging, resources.

1 Introduction

Search and discovery have been staples of the modern Internet culture since the release of the first practical browser. But these were followed in short order by the need to save discovered information through "bookmarking." This allowed an individual user to keep track of web-based resources that were interesting to them, and it added value to the information in that the facts of its prior discovery and selection constituted some additional information: acceptance. That is, the individual had already searched for, discovered, and somehow approved of the resource, and creating a bookmark captured this additional information.

But is that the limit of the possibilities of web-based information enrichment? Could a user attach more detailed semantic content to a discovered resource to help them use it in the future? Could the attachment of such information be independent of the particular computer on which they were working? Could they share such semantic enhancements with others? Would such capabilities facilitate the use of highly distributed web-based resources – such as environmental data and services – in the solution of complex problems being addressed by many individuals and organizations distributed across many organizations and nations?

These questions are critical to the notion of a Single Information Space in Europe for the Environment (SISE), an important effort on the part of the European Commission to harmonize and facilitate environmental decision-making. The vision of SISE requires seamless access to environmental resources, including data, models and services. But these resources themselves also have the potential for semantic content that is related to the viewer of the resource.

Consider a simple example. A restaurant aficionado might find a reference to a particular Italian restaurant and, having been pleased by the chef's generous use of garlic, might annotate this restaurant favourably. This will be useful when this particular customer is choosing a restaurant for a future dinner. But it might also be useful for another user who, sensitive to garlic, would choose to avoid this restaurant because of this very same characteristic.

One could imagine a very similar situation occurring within the context of environmental data and services. A particular data set, for example, may be valuable for some applications because of a characteristic that, for other applications, renders it inappropriate.

Environmental data and models are generally very dependent on the conditions of their capture or generation, respectively. Rarely would an astute environmental manager base a decision on a data set without understanding the conditions under which the data were obtained, in order to ensure that those conditions were consonant with the decision problem at hand. Similarly, the use of modelling results must be conditioned on the consistency between the assumptions made in the model with those in the question being decided.

In order to achieve the objectives of SISE, it will be necessary to find a way to capture and report "auxiliary semantics" associated with data and services discoverable on the web. These auxiliary semantics would, in general, be independent of the original author of the data or service, and would be understood to be subjective, at least to the extent that they represent the interpretation of a viewer of the resource, as opposed to the generator of the resource.

2   Requirements of SISE

As described by Hřebíček and Pillmann [1] and the Inspire Forum [2], the concept of the **Single Information Space in Europe for the Environment (SISE) was introduced in the European Commission's Framework Programme 7 (FP7) in association with objective** ICT-2007.6.3: ICT for Environmental Management and Energy Efficiency. The central idea is to support real-time connectivity to and seamless search of multiple environmental resources, across borders and disciplines, with facilitated data acquisition and sharing, along with service chaining on the web. Several workshops were conducted.

As reported by O'Flaherty [3], following an Expert Consultation Workshop in Brussels in February of 2008, "[t]he central requirement of the SISE will be to enable technical interoperability, driven by two key trends:

1. Complexity Management: requiring a holistic approach, multi-disciplinary research, and an infrastructure accessible to all disciplines, communities and actors.
2. Environmental Legislation in Europe: driving higher requirements for common environmental monitoring and reporting."

Six dimensions of SISE were identified at this workshop:

1. User Dimension: Actor centric and adaptable to the expectations and needs of many types of users.
2. Content Dimension: A global information space including models, knowledge, services and tools.
3. Data Dimension: Fusing multiple heterogeneous sources, sensors, platforms, networks and visualisations.
4. Modelling & Decision Support Dimension: Involving distributed virtual teams and communities
5. Information and Service Dimension: Stable and secure multilingual services, using semantically enhanced, *ad hoc* on-demand service chaining on the web.
6. Other SISE Dimensions: Including standardisation, ethics/privacy, data policy, IPR and liability

The assembled experts agreed about the following prioritisation of topics for future research and innovation actions on the SISE:

These dimensions and priorities lead naturally to some high-level requirements of SISE, which may be briefly summarised as follows:

- Support the discovery of relevant resources
- Facilitate integration of and seamless access to data sources residing on a standard based infrastructure (such as those provided by SANY or ORCHESTRA)
- Support repositories (e.g. databases, caches, inventories) for quality controlled and securely managed resources and their results
- Incorporate integrated security in order to control access to resources (e.g. data sources, catalogues, whether one's own or third party resources)
- Preserve the possibility to publish results on the web for public access
- Provide easy to use tools and user-friendly services and interfaces, e.g. access control, workflow management, delivery management, visualisation, data extraction, and administration, embedded in the users' semantic context.

The deployment of a Single Information Space for the Environment in Europe is inhibited by the lack of a mechanism allowing data and service users to provide annotations that would add value to these resources. A middleware infrastructure is needed to fill this gap between environmental resources and end users. This framework needs to facilitate the life-cycle utility of environmental information from its collection and persistent storage to its discovery and purpose-oriented exploitation. Such a goal can be achieved through coherent, transparent, efficient and context dependent (e.g. semantically enhanced) discovery mechanisms, pre-processing services that translate meaning and structure of information, accompanied by services or information items (e.g. data) tailored to end-user needs, and explanatory facilities.

TaToo's open approach to this need allows it to contribute not only to a single European Information Space for Europe, but also to the requirements of sharing information as expressed in the requirements of the SEIS (Shared Environmental Information System).

3 Needs, Gaps and Objectives of TaToo

Given the objectives and requirements of SISE, as described in Section 2, the TaToo project targets one major objective:

To contribute to the elimination of obstacles in discovery as well as the context-sensitive interpretation and use of environmental resources within SISE by developing easy to use tools within a semantic framework for discovery, access, and interpretation in a multilingual and multi-domain context.

This objective was approached first by conducting two needs & gaps analyses to identify the most pressing issues regarding the enhancement of the annotation and discovery process of environmental resources (i.e. data and services). Users were asked which types of environmental resources are important to them (e.g. geospatial data, structured raw data, time series, etc.); for which purposes the user needs the discovered resources (e.g. input data for models); how the user currently searches for relevant resources (e.g. search engines, data catalogues, etc.); and how discovered resources can currently be accessed (downloads, web services, etc.).

Users are mostly interested in various types of data ranging from time series data to data aggregated in reports or documents, as well as software and mathematical models. Common to most types of data requested is that they should be related to a specific geographical location. Users particularly want additional meta-information that helps them to assess whether a resource is usable for their clearly defined purpose. This includes, for example,

- information about the quality of the data,
- how data were collected, and by whom,
- whether and which interpolation methods were applied, and
- the applicability of models and algorithms to a certain domain.

Thus, one of the crucial features of TaToo is the ability to provide appropriate and rich semantic meta-information about a resource during the discovery process.

Regarding the discovery of environmental resources, most users rely on classical search engines but would prefer a solution that combines the usability and simplicity of search engines with the power and advanced features of semantic discovery. The most common problems that need to be addressed are related to low precision of the results, because the search results are often cluttered with too many irrelevant or unsuitable resources. Another issue is that resources exposed through services (in particular OGC services) often cannot be found by classical search engines. Users would also like to be able to perform discovery that takes their context (e.g. user profiles, user relationships, user location, search history, etc.) into account in order to improve results or to discover new relevant resources. Furthermore, they want to be able to search for links between related topics, e.g. for data that are available for the same spatio-temporal scope and pertain to two different thematic domains (e.g. distribution of persistent organic pollutants and cancer incidence statistics).

Regarding the different means to tag resources, or to view, alter and evaluate tags attached with resources, users raised the concern that multiple tags for the same meaning could emerge. They recommended that TaToo take standardised thesauri and dictionaries into account and provide a mechanism to propose new tags that can be added to existing ontologies.

Most users would use a portal as the main system entry point, but integration of TaToo functionality with their current systems is also a topic of great interest. Therefore, they appreciated the possibility of accessing the TaToo framework through public service interfaces in order to create their own custom clients.

Concerning the question of whether and how the users would be willing to use and contribute to TaToo, the vast majority indicated that they would like to use TaToo to search for and interpret environmental resources. Users also requested tools to enable them to tag resources in a manner specifically related to their field of expertise in order to improve the discovery of environmental resources in general. Furthermore, the ability to easily register their own resources and to harvest an initial set of meta-information during a (semi-) automatic registration process is a highly desired feature.

4 The TaToo Architecture

TaToo's primary aim is to provide the functionality to discover and tag resources with metadata in order to improve future discovery through the information enrichment process described above. In order to offer this kind of functionality, the TaToo framework has to include a set of system components (on the server side) providing the implementation of the functionality, and a set of user components (on the client side) helping the end users interact with the core components through graphical user interfaces (GUI) [4].

In the context of the TaToo objectives stated previously, the TaToo architecture must incorporate a number of properties and principles, such as the re-use of existing software wherever possible, in order to avoid wasted development effort, and the use of data- and interface-related standards from the relevant communities, where appropriate, to assure seamless integration into existing infrastructures. Moreover, TaToo must provide easy to use GUI clients for all TaToo functions to a wide range of users, and provide well-defined interfaces (e.g. APIs and standardised web service interfaces) allowing third parties to embed TaToo functionality in their own applications.

The TaToo Framework Architecture has to consider the facilities for data and information discovery, visualisation, and evaluation/validation, as well as tagging/annotation by humans and the harvesting of meta-information about resources by (semi-) automated processes.

A coherent architectural design approach, especially in the context of SISE and the TaToo objectives stated in Section 2, demands careful consideration of crucial functional requirements as well as the adoption of well-proven architectural design procedures which result in service oriented architectures that meet essential architectural properties like openness, interoperability, extensibility, flexibility and loose coupling. For this reason, the conceptual foundations of the TaToo architecture follow an evolutionary approach based on experience from former infrastructure projects and sound procedures already established in ORCHESTRA [5] and SANY [6]. Among the predominant procedures which are applied in the architectural design and specification of the TaToo framework are the separation of concerns, the logical grouping of functionalities, the specification of open and standards based interfaces, the introduction of an implementation independent layer, and the establishment of a domain-independent generic infrastructure. This ultimately leads to a multi-tier architecture composed of interacting components, which is not influenced by implementation specific restrictions, technological choices, or a specific thematic domain.

When talking about conceptual foundations of the architecture, one has to also consider supporting elements like guidelines, templates and tools that help architects and developers to specify and develop their components and domain ontologies in a structured, methodical and consistent manner. In this spirit, the TaToo architecture doesn't only specify the TaToo framework, but it also provides both the methodology and the tools to effectively facilitate the initial architectural specification as well as the further extensibility of the TaToo framework, including the support for arbitrary thematic domains. Extensibility is a key feature for TaToo, since it allows third parties to register their own resources for semantic annotation, to plug in their own domain ontologies and to contribute to the TaToo framework itself with their own specialised client applications and semantic tagging and discovery services. Thus, the TaToo community will greatly benefit from the framework's open nature.

The TaToo architecture consists of an implementation independent Functional Purview and an Implementation Purview (Figure 1). Implementation independence at the architecture level leads to a more sustainable architecture that is not vulnerable to technology changes in the future, and it is thus able to accommodate changes in technology without changing the architecture itself. This is especially important because TaToo intends to make use of existing solutions, such as widely adopted semantic frameworks like Sesame and Jena.

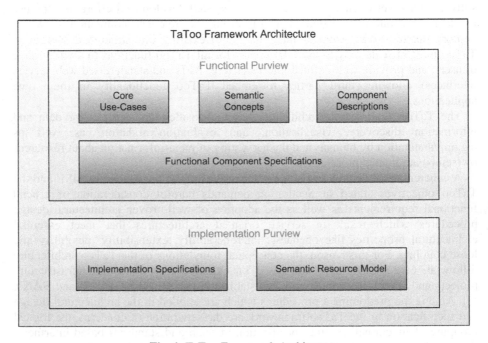

Fig. 1. TaToo Framework Architecture

The Functional Purview therefore introduces an implementation independent layer that is mapped to a concrete implementation platform, resulting in a reference implementation of the TaToo framework. At first, the Functional Purview specifies the conceptual foundations of the architecture, including the definition of the architectural design process followed by its objectives and structural elements (Tiers and Building Blocks). It also explains the considerations and decisions that resulted in the chosen architectural definition process, which follows widely accepted principles of software architecture. Additionally, it establishes the conceptual principles for discovery and tagging in TaToo as well as an ontology framework that allows the production of formal, semantically enhanced resource descriptions. Finally, it provides the actual implementation independent specification of the TaToo framework consisting of the descriptions and functional specifications of all TaToo components, and an illustration of their basic interactions with the help of a set of core use-cases.

The Implementation Purview complements the Functional Purview in the areas of implementation and technology. The focus of the Implementation Purview lies on how a certain component is realised in detail, the formal specification of the component's interfaces and information exchanged, and the specification of a Minimum Environmental Resource Model (MERM).

The elements of architectural design that define the overall structure of the TaToo Framework are Tiers and Building Blocks. Tiers logically separate general concerns, like presentation and business logic, while Building Blocks and the components defined therein share a common set of properties and organise and group more concrete functionalities.

The specification process in service-oriented architectures often stops at the service interface level. The TaToo architecture goes one step further by specifying the functionalities of client components and underlying business logic components in addition to the publicly visible functionality of the system exposed through the interfaces and operations of services.

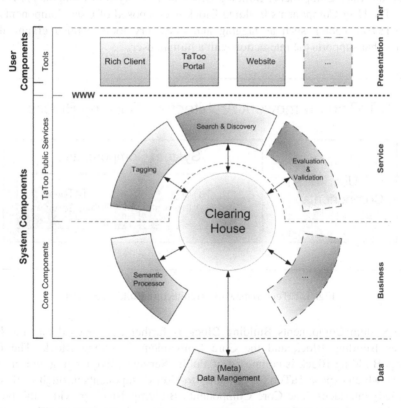

Fig. 2. TaToo Framework Architecture Tiers and Building Blocks

Therefore, Figure 2, which shows only Building Blocks, illustrates some essential components and the most important information flows. The TaToo framework architecture is designed as an n-tier architecture that currently consists of the following 4 tiers:

1. The Presentation Tier, which is concerned with user interaction and the presentation and aggregation of information.
2. The Service Tier decoupling the Business Tier and Presentation Tier, as well as serving as a layer to enforce interoperability through the provision of well defined and self-describing service interfaces.
3. The Business Tier, which is responsible for the core functionality (business logic) of the TaToo System.
4. The Data Tier, which is concerned with the storage of semantically enriched information, and other data (registered resources to be harvested, user's information, etc.).

Besides the tiers, the second elements of architectural design are the Building Blocks (Figure 3). The architecture is composed of two main high level Building Blocks: the User Components Building Block and the System Components Building Block. The User Components Building Block is composed of User Components (also called TaToo Tools), such as tagging and discovery tools, with a graphical user interface that supports the interaction with a human user.

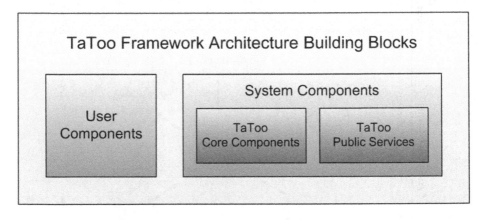

Fig. 3. TaToo Framework Architecture Building Blocks

The System Components Building Block is further decomposed into the Public Services Building Block and the Core Components Building Block. The Public Services Building Block is composed of Public Services, like tagging and discovery services, which expose TaToo functionality to User Components through well defined (specified) interfaces. The Core Components Building Block provides the business logic, data and meta-information management, thus insulating complex semantic procedures from the rest of the system. These components are only accessed by other System Components and by the TaToo Public Services. Consequently, interoperability is less of a concern and the System Components may, but need not, be accessible over standardised web service interface.

5 TaToo Architecture – Added Value for SISE

TaToo is very ambitious in its goal of providing added value to the domain of discovery and annotation of environmental resources. TaToo provides the appropriate means to create easy to use discovery mechanisms and tools, and facilitates discovery with each iterative tagging cycle. Discovery becomes more precise and information quality and value are increased.

TaToo mitigates the burden of creating 'meaningful' - i.e. semantically enhanced - meta-information by preparing the ground for information enrichment of the discovered resources. One of TaToo's benefits is that when handling a resource with a known semantic context TaToo supports users in their effort to add annotations and ranking information (e.g. according to importance, quality, uncertainty, etc.).

More concretely, TaToo delivers tools facilitating discovery of environmental resources through the use of underlying semantic structures. It provides open specifications of semantic discovery frameworks and tools and substantially contributes to the fulfilment of the requirements of SISE. TaToo provides a public Service tier to deal with arbitrary resources and in particular with resources that are based on open standards. TaToo's ability to deal with a variety of ontologies in a multilingual context, depending on the current discovery strategy, strives to overcome well-known problems in this area.

Due to the iterative improvement and enhancement of descriptive information through TaToo's tagging cycles, supported by an intelligent tagging process, decision support quality increases significantly.

Going back to the SISE imperatives identified in Section 2, we can explicitly state the manner in which TaToo supports fulfilment of each of these imperatives.

Regarding the six dimensions of SISE:

1. User Dimension: Actor centric and adaptable to the expectations and needs of many types of users.

The TaToo architecture deals with this dimension on technical as well as functional levels. On the technical level the TaToo architecture foresees user components including a portal that can be tailored to different user types, and specific user-centric client applications that can use the public service interface of the public services (such as tagging and discovery). On the functional level the TaToo architecture establishes no restrictions on the type of resources for which TaToo functionality is offered, thus supporting the needs of many types of users.

2. Content Dimension: A global information space including models, knowledge, services and tools.

The TaToo architecture is open to easy integration of new services, tools, knowledge, or any kind of resources.

3. Data Dimension: Fusing multiple heterogeneous sources, sensors, platforms, networks and visualisations.

Any kind of resource coming from any kind of source can be the object of TaToo functionality (tagging, discovery, evaluation, etc.).

4. Modelling & Decision Support Dimension: Involving distributed virtual teams and communities

TaToo supports decision-making by offering the decision maker valuable meta-information of different kinds (e.g. "rating information", evaluation information about resources of different types) introduced by other users, thus supporting community building.

5. Information and Service Dimension: Stable and secure multilingual services, using semantically enhanced, *ad hoc* on-demand service chaining on the web.

The TaToo architecture anticipates a set of public services designed according to standards or best practises with standardized security measures. Semantic meta-information supports the use of these services.

6. Other SISE Dimensions: Including standardisation, ethics/privacy, data policy, IPR and liability

The TaToo architecture calls for the use of standard approaches wherever possible. Regarding the technical requirements of SISE:

- Support the discovery of relevant resources

The TaToo architecture offers a public discovery service making use of different kind of semantic meta-information.

- Facilitate integration of and seamless access to data sources residing on a standard based infrastructure (such as those provided by SANY or ORCHESTRA)

TaToo offers meta-information about resources like data sources, including information about access procedures and semantic meta-information about suitability of the use of a data source in a given situation.

- Support repositories (e.g. databases, caches, inventories) for quality controlled and securely managed resources and their results

TaToo doesn't directly support repositories, but it supports the discoverability and usability of repositories by offering corresponding meta-information.

- Incorporate integrated security in order to control access to resources (e.g. data sources, catalogues, whether one's own or third party resources)

The TaToo architecture provides security measures for access by the public to meta-information about resources and TaToo services, but TaToo does not directly support security concerning the resources themselves. Nevertheless, meta-information about a resource offered by TaToo can include meta-information concerning access control for a resource.

- Preserve the possibility to publish results on the web for public access

The TaToo architecture supports the discoverability of published results as well as meta-information about them (e.g. concerning their usability for a given purpose).

- Provide easy to use tools and user-friendly services and interfaces, e.g. access control, workflow management, delivery management, visualisation, data extraction, and administration, embedded in the users' semantic context.

The TaToo architecture foresees different kinds of user components offering user-friendly access to TaToo functionality, such as a portal, or public services to be accessed by user-centric client applications.

6 Generalization and Future Research

In this paper we have introduced an architecture for the semantic enhancement of web-based environmental resources that serves to enhance the discoverability and usability of these resources with semantic technologies in the context of the vision of a Single Information Space in Europe for the Environment (SISE). The architecture is built upon widely accepted architectural design principles and addresses in its first iteration the core functionalities, tools and concepts necessary to leverage semantic discovery and annotation of resources in a multi-domain context.

Future work on this architecture will take into account further research and innovation on SISE and will be engaged in activities to

- continuously enhance existing services and tools and identify new services and tools according to user needs
- develop an integrated user context management and access control concept incorporating the Friend of a Friend FOAF vocabulary and the OpenID standard for decentralized authentication.
- update TaToo's environmental resource model and the adjacent ontology framework in order to leverage domain ontologies development and provide support for cross-domain mappings
- invent new discovery strategies to improve context-aware and domain-oriented discovery
- develop a common model that allows inference with ontologies in different languages, in order to support multilingual tagging and discovery
- adopt the so-called linked data approach for the semantic web [7] in order to enable TaToo to join the ever-growing linked data community, and thus to access and discover semantically annotated resources on a global scale

Acknowledgments

TaToo is a Collaborative Project (contract number 247893) co-funded by the Information Society and Media DG of the European Commission within the RTD activities of the Thematic Priority Information Society Technologies.

References

1. Hřebíček, J., Pillmann, W.: Shared Environmental Information System and Single Information Space in Europe for the Environment: Antipodes or Associates? In: Hřebíček, J., Hradec, J., Pelikán, E., Mírovský, O., Pillmann, W., Holoubek, I., Bandholtz, T. (eds.) European conference of the Czech Presidency of the Council of the EU TOWARDS eENVIRONMENT. Masaryk University, Brno (2009)

2. Inspire Forum, Single Information Space in Europe for the Environment (SISE) (April 4, 2011), `http://inspire-forum.jrc.ec.europa.eu/pg/groups/10035/single-information-space-in-europe-for-environment-sise/`
3. O'Flaherty, J.J.: Towards a Single Information Space for the Environment in Europe. In: Experts Consultation Workshop – ICT for Sustainable Growth – Brussels, February 15 (2008), `ftp://ftp.cordis.europa.eu/pub/fp7/ict/docs/sustainable-growth/sise-workshop-report-08_en.pdf`
4. Schimak, G., Rizzoli, A.E., Avellino, G., Pariente Lobo, T., Fuentes, J.M., Athanasiadis, I.N.: Information enrichment using TaToo's semantic framework. In: Sanchez-Alonso, S., Athanasiadis, I.N., García-Barriocanal, E., Palavitsinis, N. (eds.) Proceedings of Metadata and Semantics Research (MTSR) Conference 2010, Alcala de Henares, Spain (2010), `http://www.ieru.org/org/mtsr2010/`
5. Usländer, T. (ed.) Reference Model for the ORCHESTRA Architecture v.2.1, OGC "Best Practices" paper No. 07-097 (2007), `http://www.opengeospatial.org/standards/bp`
6. Usländer, T. (ed.): Specification of the Sensor Service Architecture v3.2, OGC discussion paper No. 09-132r1 (November 15, 2009), `http://sany-ip.eu/filemanager/active?fid=333`
7. Bizer, C., Heath, T., Berners-Lee, T.: Linked Data - The Story So Far. International Journal on Semantic Web and Information Systems, Special Issue on Linked Data (2009), `http://tomheath.com/papers/bizer-heath-berners-lee-ijswis-linked-data.pdf`

Building Environmental Semantic Web Applications with Drupal

Denis Havlik

Austrian Institute of Technology - AIT,
Donau-City-Straße 1, A-1220 Vienna, Austria
denis.havlik@ait.ac.at
http://www.ait.ac.at

Abstract. Efforts required for publishing information as Linked Data often appears too high compared to obvious and immediate benefits. Consequently, only a tiny fraction of the web can be easily used as a semantic "database" today. Drupal 7 changes the rules of the game by integrating the functionality required for structuring and semantically annotating arbitrary content types in the Drupal "core", as well as encouraging the module authors to use this functionality in their Drupal extensions. This paper presents the authors recent experiences with strengths and shortcomings of the Drupal 6 and Drupal 7 semantic web extensions, and discusses feasibility of the future semantic web environmental applications based on a Drupal platform. The intention of the paper is (1) to analyse the state of the art in semantic web support, as well as the potentials for further development in Drupal today; (2) to prove the feasibility of Drupal based semantic web applications for environmental usage area; and (3) to introduce the idea of Drupal as a rapid prototyping development environment.

Keywords: Drupal; Semantic Web; Linked Data; web services; rapid prototyping; environmental usage area.

1 Introduction

A huge and growing number of environmental observations are collected on a daily bases, and a large part of these observations are published on the web today. Many of these observations are unfortunately published in a form unsuitable for further processing, for instance as a human readable text or as color-coded maps. Finding and binding the available observations, even if they have been published e.g. as structured XML [5] and annotated by appropriate ontology terms, for the value added application one wants to develop can often be a challenge of its own, since major search engines often ignore the existence of such data.

Linked Data [12] provides an alternative approach for publishing of arbitrary data in a form that is both suitable for automated processing, and easily discovered on the web: rather, or in addition to publication of the data through some form of a web service, the actual human-readable information published

J. Hřebíček, G. Schimak, and R. Denzer (Eds.): ISESS 2011, IFIP AICT 359, pp. 385–397, 2011.

on the web site is annotated by ontology terms embedded in eXtensible Hyper-Text Markup Language (XHTML, [3]). The resulting combination is described in "Resource Description Framework in attributes (RDFa)in XHTML" W3C Recommendation [6]. Unfortunately, the effort required for publishing the Linked Data can often be quite high compared with the effort required to publish a human readable content on the Web. The seventh release of the Drupal Content Management System (CMS) promises to drastically lower this barrier: Drupal 7, which has been realised in January 2011 is the first major CMS platform with full integration of the key semantic web technologies [10]. Consequently, the additional effort and knowledge required to semantically enable a web site build upon a Drupal platform is expected to drastically lower within the next year or two. This may in turn positon Drupal as a primary platform for all stakeholders interested in painless transition from classical CMS to semantic web enabled applications.

This paper takes a critical look at the support for "Resource Description Framework" (RDF, [4]), SPARQL Query Language for RDF [8], and RDFa [7] in Drupal, from the point of view of a stakeholder interested in developing a lightweight semantic-web enabled applications, while at the same time keeping all advantages of modern CMS-es.

It starts by introducing the Drupal platform and the state of the art of semantic web support in Drupal 6 and Drupal 7 releases in Q1 2011 (section 2). This section is mainly intended as overview for the readers considering the use of semantic web Drupal extensions in their own projects.

Section 3 "Proof of Concept Application" presents a simple application which takes advantage of the Drupal's semantic web extensions. Due to Drupal's popularity in the biodiversity community, the use cases are pertinent to biodiversity usage area. This information is provided as a base for discussion, and in the hope it may be of some use for readers with little or no experience in semantic web and interested in building similar applications for other usage areas.

Finally, the section 4 "Conclusions and Outlook" section summarises the lessons learned in preparing this paper, and presents a vision of Drupal as a rapid prototyping development environment for building web services and semantic web applications.

2   Drupal and Semantic Web

Drupal is one of the most sucesfull open Source CMS platforms today. By the end of February 2011 there were almost 400k active Drupal installations [15]. Out of these, 25k sites already used the Drupal 7 release, which was published only two months earlier, in January 2011.

Drupal code is highly modular. "Drupal core" provides the functionality used by a great majority of the web sites and the large number of third party modules [9] providing more specialised functionality (e.g. "project management", "visualisation on the map", or "e-commerce"). In early February 2011, 5264 open source modules for Drupal 6, and 1069 Drupal 7 modules were available for download on the Drupal web site. Two weeks later, there were already 1119 modules for Drupal 7. In the same period, the number of Drupal 6 modules also grew to 5311, indicating that the Drupal 6 is still considered as a main development target by many developers [15].

Drupal 6 already provides a number of possibilities for structuring and implicitly associating of meaning to information, but it does not associate this implicit knowledge with explicit machine readable representation. The development of third party semantic extensions for Drupal 6 resulted in a heterogeneous set of add-on modules that never reached maturity. Therefore only a small fraction of the Drupal 6 sites and of the Drupal 6 add-on modules ever made use of these semantic extensions. Table 1 summarises the development status of the key Drupal modules used in the preparation of this paper, and Table 2 lists some additional modules pertinent to the papers topic.

Core functionality required by semantic web Drupal applications is provided by CCK, Feeds, Views, RDF and RDF CCK modules. CCK allows site administrators to structure the data, Feeds module allows them to import the data from various sources and Views module provides a mechanism to define how the result will be published. RDF module provides RDF data type and an API for Drupal, while the RDF CCK (RDF in Drupal 7) allows us to annotate the node types and fields with ontology terms. It is therefore interesting to note that the Drupal 7 integrates most of the functionality offered by CCK, Views and RDF modules in the "core" Drupal code base.

Remaining modules provide functions for importing, exporting, annotating and manipulating structured data, as well as semantically annotated data, in Drupal. For example:

- SPARQL and VARQL modules provide support for SPARQL queries;
- Calais module illustrates the feasibility of automated semantic annotation of the texts associated with Drupal nodes;
- Semantic Markup Editor does the same for manual annotations;
- Finally, the modules such as Feeds and its plugins (e.g. Feeds XPath Parser, Feeds View Parser, Feeds QueryPath Parser), RDF SPARQL Proxy, VARQL and the Lin Clark's SPARQL_Views provide ways to both integrate external data into Drupal and transform between various Drupal's data representations (e.g. nodes, views, taxonomies).

The information presented in tables 1 and 2 clearly indicate that semantic functionality in Drupal hasn't reached maturity yet, in spite of the excellent support for RDF and RDFa in Drupal 7. Development of Drupal 6 RDF-related modules in most cases stopped at "proof of concept" level, and the Drupal 7 versions of these modules may not be even available yet. Consequently, most of the experiments presented in this paper have nevertheless been conducted using experimental Drupal 6 implementations.

Development of Drupal 7 semantic web modules is an on-going activity and many of the modules are expected to issue stable releases within next 12 months.

Table 1. Key Drupal modules used in this paper and their development status (GIT= only available through Github; dev=development snapshot, alpha, beta, or stable; core=integrated in Drupal core; RDF=provided by Drupal 7 RDF module)

Module name	Summary	D6 status	D7 status	No. sites
Views	Smart query builder that, given enough information, can build the proper query, execute it, and display the results in various ways.	stable	core, alpha	>280k
Content Construction Kit (CCK)	Web interface allowing the administrator to add custom fields to nodes using a web browser.	stable	core, dev	>260k
Feeds	Import or aggregate data as nodes, users, taxonomy terms or simple database records.	beta	alpha	>12k
Resource Description Framework (RDF)	Provides comprehensive RDF functionality and interoperability for the Drupal 6.x platform.	alpha, dev	core, dev	>10k
Feeds XPath Parser	Feeds plugin for parsing XML and HTML documents. It enables site builders to leverage the power of Feeds to easily import data from complex, external data sources.	stable	beta	1k
SPARQL	enables the use of SPARQL queries with the RDF API for Drupal 6.x.	alpha	dev	0,3k
RDF external vocabulary importer (Evoc)	Evoc caches any external RDF vocabulary in Drupal, and exposes its classes and properties to other modules. RDF CCK relies on Evoc to offer classes and properties to be mapped to CCK fields, node title and body.	alpha	RDF	0,2k
RDF CCK	Allows site administrators to map each content type, node title, node body and CCK field to an RDF term (class or property).	dev	RDF	0,2k
Feeds View Parser	This module enables Feeds to take in data from a view output (i.e. from Views module). Combined with pluggable query backend in Views 3.x, this will enable Drupal to import data from practically anywhere from the web	dev	-	20
SPARQL_Views	Allows to query RDF data in SPARQL endpoints and RDFa on Web pages, and bring the data into Views.	alpha, GIT	GIT	2

Table 2. Additional Drupal modules related to semantic web and their development status (GIT= only available through Github; dev=development snapshot, alpha, beta, or stable; core=integrated in Drupal core; RDF=provided by Drupal 7 RDF module)

Module name	Summary	D6 status	D7 status	No. sites
Calais	Integrates Drupal with Thomson Reuters Calais service (http://www.opencalais.com/). Calais analyses the text, and finds the entities, facts and events related with the text.	stable	-	>5k
Taxonomy import/export	Import and export vocabularies and taxonomy terms via XML, Comma Separated Values, RDF and other formats.	stable	-	>2,5k
QueryPath	Integrates the QueryPath library (PHP equivalent of jQuery) for searching and manipulating HTML and XML documents into Drupal	stable	stable	>1k
Feeds QueryPath Parser	A plugin for the Feeds module that allows to run CSS queries against an XML, or HTML document (requires QueryPath)	beta	beta	0,1k
RDF SPARQL Proxy	Allows to instantiate RDF resources on demand (lazy loading) via SPARQL CONSTRUCT queries.	dev	-	12
VARQL	Provides SPARQL Query backend for Views in Drupal 7	-	dev	9
Semantic Markup Editor	Allows users to add semantic (RDFa) annotations tags to arbitrary texts.	dev	-	6

3   Proof of Concept Application

In order to develop a proof of concept for the abstract use case of building a semantic web application capable of discovering, binding, processing and visualisation of the environmental observations, I first had to choose a concrete instance related to one of the environmental domains. For this paper, the choice fell to "biodiversity", in anticipation of the biodiversity-related developments that are planned in the ENVIROFI project [17].

The idea was to find some data sets with geo-temporal context which can be visualised on a map and on the time scale and then to mash this data with additional information from another source and present the results in several ways. Obvious candidates for such initial data are for instance "species occurrence", "species sightings", or "habitat extent". Good candidates for additional data could be for instance "species/habitat descriptions", illustrations and translations to various languages.

In order to narrow down the problem at hand even further, I decided to concentrate only on the cats and their relatives (family: Felidae; genus: *).

3.1 Retrieving Biodiversity Data from GBIF and DBpedia

All the data used in this application originates either from DBpedia (http://dbpedia.org), or from the the experimental "GBIF data" site (http://data.gbif.net). DBpedia data can be directly retrieved through DPpedia sparql endpoint at http://dbpedia.org/sparql, while the GBIF site only allows querying by humans using the web interface and downloading of the resulting data sets[1]. Searching for a "cat" on either of the sites does not lead to satisfactory results, but the search for "Felidae" on GBIF data site quickly leads us to the web page featuring the map shown in the figure 1.

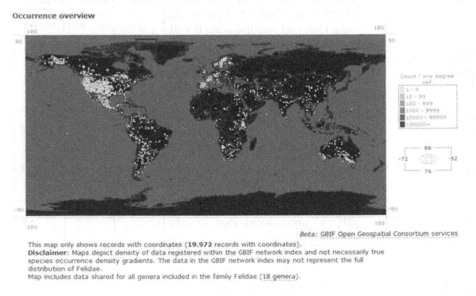

Occurrence overview

This map only shows records with coordinates (**19.972** records with coordinates).
Disclaimer: Maps depict density of data registered within the GBIF network index and not necessarily true species occurrence density gradients. The data in the GBIF network index may not represent the full distribution of Felidae.
Map includes data shared for all genera included in the family Felidae (18 genera).

Fig. 1. GBIF occurency overview for felidea family (detail from data.gbif.org web site)

The "Actions" box (not shown in figure 1 provides a link to "Occurences", which in fact offers a comfortable query builder. The final query consisted of: (1) "Classification includes Family: Felidae"; (2) "Coordinate status is Includes coordinates"; (3) "Coordinate issues is No issues detected"; (4) "Basis of record is Observation"; (5) "Year range is between 1900 and 2011"; and (6) Data originating from Argentina, South Africa or Spain. This returned 2.419 occurence records; 1.766 thereof in Spain [16].

---

[1] In fact, GBIF data site also provides a RESTful service interface, but I did not realise this on time.

GBIF data can be downloaded in several formats, including the semantically annotated "Darwin Core" format. The first occurrence record from the downloaded GBIF file is shown below.

```
<dataProviders>
  <dataProvider gbifKey="326" rdf:about="326">
    <name>Administracion de Parques Nacionales, Argentina</name>
    <dataResource gbifKey="10868" rdf:about="10868">
      <name>VERTEBRADOS DE VALOR ESPECIAL EN REAS PROTEGIDAS DE LA ARGENTINA</name>
      <occurrenceRecords>
      <tax:TaxonOccurrence gbifKey="233877940"
          rdf:about="http://data.gbif.org/ws/rest/occurrence/get?key=233877940">
          tax:catalogNumber>APN-ML-21</tax:catalogNumber>
        <tax:country>AR</tax:country>
        <tax:decimalLatitude>-50.428</tax:decimalLatitude>
        <tax:decimalLongitude>-69.066</tax:decimalLongitude>
        <tax:earliestDateCollected>2006-05-03 00:00:00.0</tax:earliestDateCollected>
        <tax:identifiedTo>
          <tax:Identification>
            <tax:taxon>
              <tax1:TaxonConcept gbifKey="13815711" rdf:about="13815711">
                <tax1:hasName>
                  <tax2:TaxonName>
                    <tax2:nameComplete>Puma concolor</tax2:nameComplete>
                    <tax2:genusPart>Puma</tax2:genusPart>
                    <tax2:specificEpithet>concolor</tax2:specificEpithet>
                    <tax2:scientific>true</tax2:scientific>
                  </tax2:TaxonName>
                </tax1:hasName>
              </tax1:TaxonConcept>
            </tax:taxon>
            <tax:taxonName>Puma concolor</tax:taxonName>
          </tax:Identification>
        </tax:identifiedTo>
        <tax:latestDateCollected>2006-05-03 00:00:00.0</tax:latestDateCollected>
      </tax:TaxonOccurrence>
```

The next step was to find some complementary information on various Felidae species from DBpedia. A search for "Felideae" using the DBpedia's "faceted search" interface (http://dbpedia.org/fct/) returned over 200 matches and the quick analysis of the results shows that the entries we are interested in, share the "Family is dbpedia:Felidae" relationship. Furthermore, the search results included a wealth of highly structured information consisting of names and descriptions of the Felidae members in various languages, photos, links to external resources and many other properties including the "genus", "species" and "binomial". For Iberian Lynx, the DBpedia genus is "Lynx", species "L. pardinus" and binomial "Lynx pardinus" which perfectly maps to "genus Lynx; species pardinus" in the GBIF data sets.

DBpedia faceted search results provide all information needed to build SPARQL queries and to retrieve the data. For example, the following SPARQL query returns some basic information on Iberian Lynx (Lynx pardinus).

```
PREFIX rdfs: <http://www.w3.org/2000/01/rdf-schema#>
PREFIX db-owl: <http://dbpedia.org/ontology/>
PREFIX db-prop:<http://dbpedia.org/property/>
PREFIX db-res:<http://dbpedia.org/resource/>
PREFIX foaf: <http://xmlns.com/foaf/0.1/>
SELECT DISTINCT ?species ?label ?abstract ?thumbnail ?depiction WHERE {
?feline db-owl:family db-res:Felidae;
```

```
db-owl:abstract ?abstract;
rdfs:label ?label;
db-prop:binomial ?species;
db-owl:thumbnail ?thumbnail.
FILTER (
    langMatches(lang(?abstract), 'en') &&
    langMatches(lang(?label), 'en') &&
    regex(str(?species), ".*pardinus")
).
OPTIONAL {?feline foaf:depiction ?depiction}
}
```

3.2   Defining the Data Model and Semantic Annotations

The basic unit of data in Drupal is called a "node". In most cases, each node corresponds with a single web page, but for our purpose it is convenient to see a node as Drupal equivalent of an SQL table entry. Each node is structured according to a node type and new node types can be easily defined by Drupal users possessing adequate rights (administrator, web-developer). For this application, I defined two node types: "animal description" and "animal occurrence". Definition of the animal description node type is illustrated in figure 2.

LABEL	NAME	FIELD	WIDGET	OPERATIONS	
✛ Title	title	Node module element			
✛ Identification	group_ad_name	Fieldset	fieldset collapsible classes	⚙	delete
✛ English Name	field_ad_name_en	Text	Text field	edit	delete
✛ Scientific Name	field_ad_name_sci	Text	Text field	edit	delete
✛ Abstract	field_ad_abstract	Long text	Text area (multiple rows)	edit	delete
✛ Thumbnail	field_ad_thumbnail	Text	Text field	edit	delete
✛ Depiction	field_ad_depiction	Text	Text field	edit	delete
✛ **Add new field**	field_	- Select a field type -	- Select a widget -		
Label	Field name (a-z, 0-9, _)	Type of data to store.	Form element to edit the data.		

Fig. 2. Field definitions of the "animal description" node type

The simplest "animal occurrence" node type needs to contain a Latin name, observation time and georeference. In addition, a node reference field is required in order to mash up occurrence and description data later and an unique ID helps to keep the data synchronized with the original source.

Next, is to decide upon semantic annotations for each of the node types and for each of the fields. In Drupal 7, all data is automatically annotated with a site ontology, but users can define additional annotations if they want. For this application, I choose to re-use the original annotations used by DBpedia and GBIF data site respectively. Detailed description of the process has been described in "Produce and Consume Linked Data with Drupal" paper by Stéphane Corlosquet et. al. [14]. Probably the most appropriate way to proceed here is to (1) decide which ontologies will be used; (2) use Evoc module to upload them; and (3) use the classes and terms from these ontologies to annotate the data.

Once the RDF annotations have been defined, Drupal will automatically add RDFa annotations to all data of this type, as illustrated below.

```
<!DOCTYPE html PUBLIC "-//W3C//DTD XHTML+RDFa 1.0//EN"
  "http://www.w3.org/MarkUp/DTD/xhtml-rdfa-1.dtd">
<html xmlns="http://www.w3.org/1999/xhtml" xml:lang="en" lang="en" dir="ltr"
  xmlns:Animal_description="http://www.havlik.org/d6/?q=rdf/schema/Animal_description#"
  xmlns:db-owl="http://dbpedia.org/ontology/"
  xmlns:db-prop="http://dbpedia.org/property/"
  xmlns:db-res="http://dbpedia.org/resource/"

...

    <div class="field-label">Scientific Name: </div>
    <div class="field-items">
      <div class="field-item even"
        property="db-prop:binomial" datatype="">Puma concolor</div>
    </div>
...
```

Defining the data model and semantic annotations is straightforward and works "out of the box" in Drupal 7. This is not the case for Drupal 6, where RDFa support can only be introduced by installing the CCK, RDF, RDF CKK, Evoc and Evoc reference modules, and requires patching of the CCK module.

3.3 Binding Data into Drupal

In section 3.1 and 3.2, I introduced two biodiversity-related data sources and explained how to prepare Drupal data models. Next critical step is to assure that the Drupal site can actually use the GBIF and DBpedia data. In order to avoid latencies, I opted for pre-fetching of the data to the Drupal site. Feeds module provides an elegant way to pre-fetch the data, cache it in a suitable node type and synchronize it as needed. Feeds parsers allow "feeding" of data from various sources, including for example local and remote HTML, XML, CSV and Excel files, Atom and JSON feeds, as well as the services such as Youtube, Flickr and Slideshare. XPath Parser provides a way to import data from XML files by specifying the XPath expressions[1] for each of the fields. Part of the XPath Parser configuration for GBIF occurrence data is shown in figure 3.

No SPARQL Parser for Feeds exists, but Lin Clark's SPARQL_Views module can be used to fetch the data from a SPARQL server and temporary store it in a Drupal feed. Furthermore, Lin explained how to store the data from a view into nodes using the Feeds View Parser in her blog [13]. The proposed solution is highly experimental and breaks XPath Parser. Similar functionality could be probably achieved in other ways, for instance by exporting the view as XML and parsing it with XPath parser. However, the direct feeding of the content from Drupal views to nodes is likely to be more efficient.

Context: *
```
//tax:TaxonOccurrence
```
This is the base query, all other queries will run in this context.

title:
```
@gbifKey
```
The XPath query to run.

field_animal_name:
```
tax:identifiedTo/tax:Identification/tax:taxonName
```
The XPath query to run.
The variables $title are availliable for replacement.

field_genus:
```
tax:identifiedTo/tax:Identification/tax:taxon/tax1:TaxonConcept/tax1:hasName/ta
```
The XPath query to run.
The variables $title, $field_animal_name are availliable for replacement.

field_genus_spec:
```
tax:identifiedTo/tax:Identification/tax:taxon/tax1:TaxonConcept/tax1:hasName/ta
```
The XPath query to run.
The variables $title, $field_animal_name, $field_genus are availliable for replacement.

field_obs_lat:
```
tax:decimalLatitude
```
The XPath query to run.
The variables $title, $field_animal_name, $field_genus, $field_genus_spec are availliable for replacement.

Fig. 3. First part of the XPath Parser configuration for GBIF occurrence data

3.4 Mashups and Visualization

The views module provides a rich set of functions for mashing data. However, the Drupal 6 version of the Views module relies on the foreign key relationship between two nodes for this task. Drupal Node Reference CCK module provides a way to establish this relationship, but these references can not be automatically computed within the Drupal framework. Inability to generate node references may be the biggest shortcoming of the Feeds module today, but fortunately quite easy to work around.

Extending the Drupal functionality with ad-hoc PHP code snipsets is quite easy, and the Computed Field CCK extension allows the administrators to define computed values in custom content types. As a workaround, I therefore defined a custom node field that calculates the reference at node generation time. Unfortunately, I did not succeed in persuading the system to use this field as a node reference. So, eventually I decided to fill-in the node references at SQL database level, which worked without any advert effects. Once the node reference was in place, mashing of two datasets with Views was straightforward, resulting in the table shown in figure 4.

Similarly to Feeds, the Views module is itself providing a pluggable environment for add-on modules. One such modules (SPARQL_Views) has already been introduced in this paper. Due to its immense popularity (see table 1), the Drupal site features a separate "Views" section with over 400 Views related modules. On

Observation period   **Items per page:**

From date: | 5 ∨ | | Apply |
| 2000 ∨ |
To date:
| 2002 ∨ |

Animal Name	English Name	Genus	Specific Epithet	GBIF Occurence Key	Observation Latitude	Observation Longitude	Observation Start	Observation End
Leopardus wiedii	Margay	Leopardus	wiedii	233874278	-25.68	-54.17	2000-04-10 (All day)	2000-04-10 (All day)
Puma concolor	Cougar	Puma	concolor	233877622	-25.71	-54.44	2002-05-05 (All day)	2002-05-05 (All day)
Puma concolor	Cougar	Puma	concolor	233877721	-25.68	-54.50	2002-05-15 (All day)	2002-05-15 (All day)
Puma concolor	Cougar	Puma	concolor	233878400	-25.79	-54.04	2002-11-14 (All day)	2002-11-14 (All day)
Puma concolor	Cougar	Puma	concolor	233878402	-25.80	-54.08	2002-12-13 (All day)	2002-12-13 (All day)

1   2   next ›   last »

Fig. 4. Table illustrating the mash-up of "animal sightings" and "animal description" content types

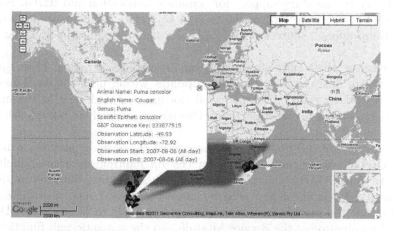

Fig. 5. Representation of the mashed data on a map

top of this, a huge number of modules exist which can take the result from views and present it in various ways. Figure 5 illustrates the feasibility of presenting the mashed data on a map.

This map was generated using the gmap module which integrates the google maps into Drupal. Far more complex maps can be generated using the Open Layers module, which integrates the OpenLayers javascript library into Drupal [11], but gmap module is easier to set up and provides sufficient functionality for this experiment.

4   Conclusions and Outlook

This paper explores the possibilities of semantically enabled Drupal sites by building a simple application that:

- uses SPARQL query and XPath parsing to bind data from two external sources;
- semantically annotates the imported data and presents is as RDFa;
- produces new data by mashing the two sources; and
- presents the results as a table and on a map.

Drupal 7 release excels at basic semantic web functionality. It provides a possibility to define complex data (node) types, semantically annotate the data and publish the results as RDFa out of the box. Unfortunately, it is currently not possible to import external data to a Drupal 7 site using SPARQL query. Therefore, the final application has been built using Drupal 6.

Following the excellent documentation provided by Lin Clark, I was able to successfully test SPARQL import under Drupal 6, but the proposed solution breaks the XPath Parser module. As a result, the site was able to either import data from a SPARQL source, or from the XML file, but not both at the same time. Other shortcomings of the Drupal 6 solution included unreliable Evoc module and very rudimentary support for semantic annotation and RDFa. Further unsolved issue is establishing of the foreign key relationships between data imported from different sources, which currently has to be done at SQL database level.

Nevertheless, the results obtained so far are very encouraging. Most module developers are likely to issue Drupal 7 updates within next couple of months, so that a working solution (stable, well documented and easy to set up) for applications, similar to one presented in this paper, are likely to become available within next 1-2 years.

While preparing this paper, I also discovered the Services module, which allows a Drupal site to provide web services via multiple interfaces (including REST [18] and SOAP[2]). I did not test its functionality, but this module is under active development and used by more than 10k Drupal instances. This indicates that the module is of high quality and likely to be ported to Drupal 7 soon. Combination of the Service Module and the semantic web functionality outlined in this paper may transform Drupal from a CMS into rapid prototyping environment for all types of web services and semantic web services.

Acknowledgments

The work leading to the results presented in this paper has been partially funded by European Commission through FP7 *Tagging Tool based on a Semantic Discovery Framework* project (TaToo; EC grant agreement nr. 247893; http://www.tatoo-fp7.eu/tatooweb/).

Furthermore, I would like to thank: (1) Lin Clark and Stéphane Corlosquet for their visionary Drupal developments and excellent publications explaining how to use the Drupal's semantic extensions; (2) Fuada Havlik and Gerald Schimak, for encouraging me in this work and proofreading the manuscript; and (3) Linux, Apache, MySQL and Drupal developers, for developing the immensely valuable Open Source software.

References

1. Xml path language (xpath) (November 1999), http://www.w3.org/TR/xpath/
2. Simple object access protocol (soap) 1.1 (May 2000),
   http://www.w3.org/TR/2000/NOTE-SOAP-20000508/
3. Xhtml 1.0 the extensible hypertext markup language (second edition) a reformulation of html 4 in xml 1.0 (August 2002), http://www.w3.org/TR/xhtml1/
4. Rdf primer (February 2004), http://www.w3.org/TR/rdf-primer/
5. Extensible markup language (xml) 1.0, 5th edn. (November 2008),
   http://www.w3.org/TR/xml/
6. Rdfa in xhtml: Syntax and processing a collection of attributes and processing rules for extending xhtml to support rdf (October 2008),
   http://www.w3.org/TR/rdfa-syntax/
7. Rdfa primer bridging the human and data webs (October 2008),
   http://www.w3.org/TR/xhtml-rdfa-primer/
8. Sparql query language for rdf (January 2008),
   http://www.w3.org/TR/rdf-sparql-query/
9. Drupal modules (February 2011), http://drupal.org/project/modules
10. Drupal web site (February 2011), http://drupal.org/
11. Openlayers: Free maps for the web (February 2011), http://openlayers.org/
12. Berners-Lee, T.: Linked data. International Journal on Semantic Web and Information Systems 4 (2006), http://www.w3.org/DesignIssues/LinkedData.html
13. Clark, L.: Importing / syncing content from external sites like wikipedia. Blog entry (November 2010), http://lin-clark.com/blog/
    importing-syncing-content-external-sites-wikipedia
14. Corlosquet, S., Delbru, R., Clark, T., Polleres, A., Decker, S.: Produce and consume linked data with drupal! In: Bernstein, A., Karger, D.R., Heath, T., Feigenbaum, L., Maynard, D., Motta, E., Thirunarayan, K. (eds.) ISWC 2009. LNCS, vol. 5823, pp. 763–778. Springer, Heidelberg (2009), http://openspring.net/
    sites/openspring.net/files/corl-etal-2009iswc.pdf
15. Drupal: Drupal module usage statistics (February 2011),
    http://drupal.org/project/usage
16. GBIF: Biodiversity occurrence data. Provided by: Administracin de Parques Nacionales, Argentina, Borror Laboratory of Bioacoustics, GBIF-Spain, and University of Helsinki, Department of Applied Biology (February 2011), http://data.gbif.org, accessed through GBIF Data Portal
17. Havlik, D., Schade, S., Sabeur, Z.A., Mazzetti, P., Watson, K., Berre, A.J., Mon, J.L.: From sensor to observation web with environmental enablers in the future internet. Sensors 11(3) (2011)
18. Rodriguez, A.: Restful web services: The basics. developerWorks (2008),
    https://www.ibm.com/developerworks/webservices/library/ws-restful/

Semantics Annotations of Ontology for Scenario: Anthropogenic Impact and Climate Change Issues

Miroslav Kubásek[1], Jiří Hřebíček[1], Jiří Kalina[1],
Ladislav Dušek[1], and Ivan Holoubek[2]

[1] IBA, Masaryk University, Kamenice 126/3, 625 00 Brno, Czech Republic
{kubasek,hrebicek,urbanek,dusek}@iba.muni.cz
[2] RECETOX, Masaryk University, Kamenice 126/3, 625 00 Brno, Czech Republic
holoubek@recetox.muni.cz

Abstract. The synthesis of existing Persistent Organic Pollutants (POPs) pollution monitoring databases with epidemiological data is considered for identifying some impacts of POPs on human health. This task requires new, rich, data, services and models discovery capabilities from a multitude of monitoring networks and web resources. The FP7 project TaToo (Tagging Tool based on a Semantic Discovery Framework) is setting up a semantic web solution to close the discovery gap that prevents a full and easy access to web resources. The use of TaToo tools together with software GENASIS and SVOD is discussed as TaToo validation scenario for anthropogenic impact and global climate change influence on POPs trajectory. This paper contains the first propose of POPs and cancer domain ontology intended for TaToo framework.

Keywords: TaToo, semantic web, POPs, Stockholm Convention, GENASIS, SVOD, anthropogenic impact, global climate change.

1 Introduction

The FP7 project TaToo (Tagging Tool based on a Semantic Discovery Framework) aims to set up a semantic web solution to close the discovery gap that prevents a full and easy access to environmental resources on the web [9]. The core of the project will focus on the development of tools allowing third parties to easily discover environmental resources (data and/or services residing on different information nodes) on the web and to add valuable information in the form of semantic annotations to these resources, thus facilitating future usage and discovery, and kicking off a beneficial cycle of information enrichment.

TaToo validates the usability of its developments through the implementation of three different validation scenarios. All three scenarios are embedded in highly complex environmental domains and are therefore mainly addressed to domain expert groups and communities as well as to technically skilled users.

This paper contains the detailed framework of the Masaryk university[1] validation scenario (MU scenario), which is the anthropogenic impact and the influence of

---

[1] http://www.muni.cz

J. Hřebíček, G. Schimak, and R. Denzer (Eds.): ISESS 2011, IFIP AICT 359, pp. 398–406, 2011.

global climate change on this impact [5], [6]. The purpose of the paper is to give the overview of the MU scenario (background, objectives, and available tools), the definition of users who will use the TaToo tools, describe the possible use cases, and to provide with the mock ups.

2 Description of the Scenario

The MU scenario of TaToo project named *Anthropogenic impact and global climate change* is managed by Masaryk University (MU). This scenario is dealing with the correlation of environmental pollutants and their health impact on the population and the correlation of transport of environmental pollutants with global climate change [5], [6]. The aim is to create a central place for researchers, domain experts and decision makers to discover and access interdisciplinary knowledge in more efficient and usable way that is the currently state of the art. Due to the fact that there is an enormous amount of information resources in scientific fields, which is steadily growing, available search mechanisms like search engines, scientific networks and similar technologies are not sufficient to meet the complex requirements of today's researchers and scientists. The result of conventional discovery processes are often not matching the domain context of the users and obligate them the tedious task of filtering large result sets to obtain the original object of the interest of the researcher intended to find with the search. Therefore the need arises for an improving discovery method, which will incorporate the domain knowledge and additional semantic information into the search in order to obtain a more fitting result for the specific context of the user.

The MU scenario not only aims to improve the discovery of scientific resources for one particular domain, but also tries to discover and create new relationships among different domains. The correlation of environmental pollutants including their transport due to global climate change and their health impact on the population is only one significant example of creating new relationships among different domains. These dependencies could represent new scientific insights for already available resources and connect the knowledge of the single domains. These relationships should facilitate further discovery process to deliver matching resources of multiple domains.

The MU scenario represents the close cooperation and joint venture of two university institutes: the *Research Centre for Toxic Compounds in the Environment*[2] (RECETOX) and *Institute of Biostatistics and Analyses*[3] (IBA).

RECETOX is an independent institute of the MU. RECETOX performs research, development, education and expertise in the field of environmental contamination by toxic compounds with specific focus on persistent organic pollutants (POPs), polar organic compounds, toxic metals and their species and natural toxins - cyanotoxins. It is also Stockholm Convention Regional centre[4] for capacity building and transfer of technology in Central and Eastern European countries. The *Stockholm Convention on*

---

[2] http://www.recetox.muni.cz
[3] http://www.iba.muni.cz
[4] http://www.recetox.muni.cz/index-en.php?pg=regional-pops-center

Persistent Organic Pollutants[5] (*Stockholm convention*) is a global treaty to protect human health and the environment from chemicals that remain intact in the environment for long periods, become widely distributed geographically and accumulate in the fatty tissue of humans and wildlife. RECETOX is formed by several research divisions, service laboratories and technology-transfer centres: Environmental chemistry and modelling, Ecotoxicology and risk assessment, Trace laboratory, and Laboratory of data analyses. Research and development of the centre include monitoring of environmental matrices, studies of environmental fate and effects (ecotoxicology) of toxic compounds, ecological and human risk assessment as well as the development of informational and expert systems.

RECETOX launched the first version of the *Global Environmental Assessment and Information System* (GENASIS)[6] in January 2010 [1]. GENASIS provides information support for implementation of the *Stockholm convention* at an international level [7]. The initial phase of the GENASIS project is focused on data from regular monitoring programmes of POPs, providing a general overview of spatial patterns and temporal trends of pollutants concentrations [10].

IBA is a research institute of the MU, which is focused on delivering solutions to research problems arising in the environment and human health and it is providing related services, especially in the field of biological and clinical data analysis, organization and management of clinical trials, software development and Information and Communication Technology (ICT) applications. IBA research activities are primarily focused on organizational and expert services for large scientific projects. IBA is formed by four divisions: Division of Data Analysis, Division of Clinical Trials, Division of Information and Communication Technologies, and Division of Environmental Informatics and Modelling. For example, IBA created the first web portal for epidemiology of malignant tumours in the Czech Republic, the *System for Visualizing of Oncological Data* (SVOD)[7], based on the data from the Czech National Oncology Registry [3].

Dušek [2] pointed in 2009:"*A full-area monitoring of the environmental risk factors in all main environmental components is performed in the Czech Republic. The main objective of this functional monitoring network is the estimation of exposure to xenobiotic substances, and the evaluation of subsequent risks to human health. The system provides information for health risks management and also serves for public education, which is a prerequisite for active care of one's own health. The outputs from monitoring systems may also be used for assessing human risks associated with cancer epidemiology. Data about POPs are of key importance, since these compounds are known to have a wide spectrum of carcinogenic effects, a tendency to bioaccumulation, and are subject to long-distance transport.*"

The objective of the MU scenario is to use and validate the resulting tagging and discovery framework of the TaToo project. Since the primary scope of the TaToo project is to facilitate the discovery of environmental resources, this scenario delivers the perfect opportunity to validate the resulting solution against challenging real word problems. There are numerous scientific domains available and actively researched at

---

[5] http://www.pops.int
[6] http://www.genasis.cz
[7] http://www.svod.cz

the MU, but two important domains have been carefully chosen to demonstrate and validate the envisioned functionality of the TaToo project. The vision of the MU scenario is that other scientific domains could follow the initial institutes to further spin a new kind of knowledge network to deliver a new generation of tools and methods to effectively and conveniently support the scientific user in their daily work.

2 Align Ontology for POP's and Cancer Domain

The MU case study ontology is aligned to the TaToo ontology framework through the TaToo Bridge ontology. Importing the bridge ontology enable to have all of the class, property and individual definitions from the Bridge ontology available for use in our proposed ontology. Figure 1 shows classes from the first version of the bridge ontology which are important in proposed align ontology.

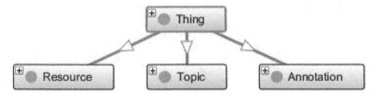

Fig. 1. TaToo Bridge ontology

2.1 Analyze of POP's and Cancer Interests

By analyzing of both domains, i.e. environmental and human risk assessment areas we identify four levels of proposed ontology system.

The first one named **nomenclature** contains a set of nominal descriptors identifying key objects (variables) which should be mostly identified in investigation or in research searching for information (POPs – chemical compounds and diseases – cancer diagnoses). This level is highly standardized adopting internationally unified, extensively translated nomenclature systems. The proposed framework works with key (major) nomenclature system and additional (supporting) sub-systems. Proposed ontology architecture is relatively rigid in this dimension as the used nomenclature systems are based of widely accepted international consensus. In proposed version of ontology we used ICD-10 class hierarchy (International Classification of Diseases) and recommended POPs and Matrix taxonomy based on Stockholm Convention.

The second level is **classifiers** which present a attributes determining some key properties of the examined objects (chemical compounds, diseases). Only classifiers highly relevant for exposure environmental studies and risk assessment studies are adopted. In result, the classifiers represent binary codes or multiple categories, typically derived on the basis of some external information reachable from standardized database, evidence-based literature, thesaurus or encyclopedia (properties of given chemical compounds, properties of disease at the time of diagnosis, etc.). The set of attributes is flexible according of used classifiers; e.g. In case of studies focusing on some special topics etc. This level is included in the proposed ontology.

Next level is **information source identifiers** - necessary descriptors of the source of information which is processed or needed. These attributes also refer to some type of validity scoring because they describe type of studies and other information sources which can be regarded as relevant. Furthermore, this set of attributes allows the users to specify studied problem or scientific field to be inspected. Representative from this level in proposed ontology is *ProjectType* showed in Fig. 2.

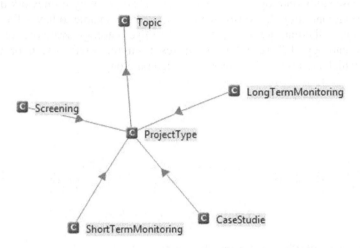

Fig. 2. Example of information source identifiers - *ProjectType*

Last level contains **obligatory descriptors** which represent family of variables describing the lowest level of the information processed or searched for. It means set of variables which are obligatory to understand numerical values reached in searching engines (units, sampled, matrices, epidemiological measures, time and site specification, etc.). These descriptors are strictly obligatory and represent valid information, i.e. only information, numerical value supplied with these descriptors can be regarded as valid and trustworthy.

2.2 Identification of Basic Concepts

By analyzing of our two domains (POPs contamination and cancer epidemiology) we identified number of concepts. Below we describe several of them, which are necessary for understanding of proposed concept and proposed connections with MERM (Minimal Environmental Resource Model) concept [8]. The MERM concept has been developed following the NeOn methodology [4]. The MERM describes the structure of resources and annotations in TaToo, being a reference data model for both services and user interfaces.

CancerTopic - defined as sub-concept of the MERM *Topic* concept and represent the possible keywords belonging into cancer risk domain.

POPsTopic - defined as sub-concept of the MERM *Topic* concept and represent the possible keywords belonging into POPs domain.

CancerAnnotation - defined as sub-concept of the MERM *Annotation* concept and represent the group of annotations connected with cancer risk domain.

POPsAnnotation - defined as sub-concept of the MERM *Annotation* concept and represent the group of annotations connected with POPs domain.

Matrix - define the taxonomy of possible matrixes and this concept is connected with *POPsTopic* sub-concept.

Disease - define the taxonomy of possible diseases. Because our domain is restricted to cancer epidemiology, we also define sub-concept *Cancer* and example class *BreastCancer*. These sub-concepts are also connected with ICD10 taxonomy of diseases. This taxonomy is used through connection with *Diagnose* class (sub class of *CancerTopic*).

In proposed ontology are also others concepts, but they have similar structure as classes mentioned above. We plan later extend these concepts with all aspects mentioned in chapter 2.1.

2.3 Alignment Domain Ontology to the TaToo Ontology Framework

The TaToo Ontology framework comprises the bridge ontology, a number of domain ontologies, and a number of alignment ontologies. The framework is not limited by a number of different domain ontologies, that is, by a number of different environmental sub-domains whose resources are managed by the TaToo system. However, in order to be able to plug-in a domain ontology in the TaToo ontology framework, the domain ontology needs to be accompanied by an appropriate mapping interface. This mapping interface is identified in the framework as an alignment ontology.

There are two possible alignment strategies for mapping these ontologies. The first mapping strategy, uses the *rdfs:subClassOf* construct defined in the *RDFS* to map concepts of the domain ontology to the concepts of the MERM and bridge ontology. The second mapping strategy, assumes the usage of the *owl:equivalentClass* and *owl:sameAs* constructs defined in OWL.

For mapping of our domains to the TaToo ontology framework we used the first strategy. Mapping is based on four ontology concepts: CancerAnnotat, POPsAnnotat, CancerTopic and POPsTopic. Fig. 3 illustrates these mappings and connections between them.

Fig. 3. Mappings domain concepts to the TaToo ontology framework

2.4   Description of Basic Concepts

We describe in this section some of identified concepts in more detail. These examples are not trivial and show an interesting perspective of described domains from the ontology design point of view.

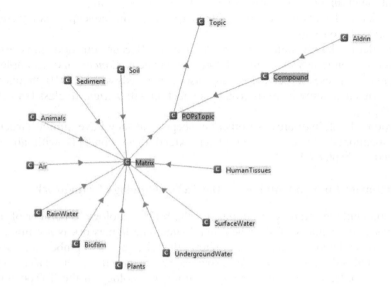

Fig. 4. Definition of *POPsTopic* class

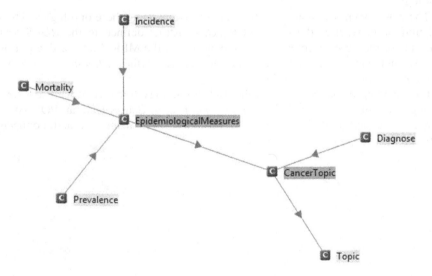

Fig. 5. Definition of *CancerTopic* class

First one is illustrated at Fig. 4, where is presented *POPsTopic* class, which is the super class of *Topic* from the MERM ontology. It has sub classes *Matrix,* and *Compound* which are connected with POPs domain and enable to classify annotated resource. First contain information about used matrix and the second information about monitored compound.

The next one describes the definition of *CancerTopic* class. We can see on Fig. 5 that this class has a super class *Diagnose* and a sub class *EpidemiologicalMeasures.* The class *Diagnose* is equal with the *Cancer* class which is sub class of *Diseases.* The *Diagnose* class is equal with *C00_D48* sub class form ICD10 ontology (taxonomy of diseases).

4 Conclusions

This paper contains the first initial proposal of align domain ontology for POPs contamination and cancer epidemiology domains. The development of domain ontologies in the TaToo Ontology framework is an evolutionary process, so we plan to extend them by adding new specific concepts and relationships that are currently not provided.

Acknowledgments

The research leading to these results has received funding from the European Community's Seventh Framework Programme (FP7/2007-2013) under grant agreement nr. 247893.

References

1. Brabec, K., Jarkovský, J., Dušek, L., Kubásek, M., Hřebíček, J., Holoubek, I., Čupr, P., Klánová, J.: GENASIS: System for the Assessment of Environmental Contamination by Persistent Organic Pollutants. In: EnviroInfo 2009. Environmental Informatics and Industrial Environmental Protection: Concepts, Methods and Tools. 23. International Conference on Informatics for Environmental Protection, pp. 369–376. Shaker Verlag, Aachen (2009)
2. Dušek, L., Mužík, J., Koptíková, J., Brabec, P., Žaloudík, J., Vyzula, R., Kubásek, M.: The national web portal for cancer epidemiology in the Czech Republic. In: Enviroinfo 2005. 19th International Conference Informatics for Environmental Protection, pp. 434–439. Masaryk University Press, Brno (2005)
3. Dušek, L.: Czech Cancer Care in Numbers 2008–2009. Grada Publishing, Praha (2009)
4. Gómez-Pérez, A., Motta, E., Suárez-Figueroa, M.C.: NeOn Methodology in a Nutshell (2010), http://www.neon-project.org/nw/NeOn_Book
5. Hřebíček, J., Dušek, L., Kubásek, M., Jarkovský, J., Brabec, K., Holoubek, I., Kohút, L., Urbánek, J.: Anthropogenic Impact and Global Climate Change. Description of Validation Scenario in TaToo Project. In: 7. letní škola aplikované informatiky. Indikátory účinnosti EMS podle odvětví, pp. 6–23. nakladatelství Littera, Brno (2010)

6. Hřebíček, J., Dušek, L., Kubásek, M., Jarkovský, J., Brabec, K., Holoubek, I., Kohút, L., Urbánek, J.: Validation Scenario for Anthropogenic Impact and Global Climate Change for Tatoo. In: Proceedings of the Workshop "Environmental Information Systems and Services - Infrastructures and Platforms", Aachen. CEUR-WS (2010)

7. Klánová, J., Čupr, P., Holoubek, I., Borůvková, J., Přibylová, P., Kareš, R., Kohoutek, J., Dvorská, A., Komprda, J.: Towards the Global Monitoring of POPs - Contribution of the MONET Networks. RECETOX. Masaryk University, Brno (2009)

8. Pariente, T., et al.: A Model for Semantic Annotation of Environmental Resources: The TaToo Semantic Framework. In: Hřebíček, J., Schimak, G., Denzer, R. (eds.) ISESS 2011. IFIP AICT, vol. 359, pp. 429–437. Springer, Heidelberg (2011)

9. Rizzoli, A., Schimak, G., Donatelli, M., Hřebíček, J., Avellino, G., Mon, J.: TaToo: tagging environmental resources on the web by semantic annotations. In: iEMSS 2010. International Congress on Environmental Modelling and Software. Modelling for Environment's Sake, pp. 1192–1199. iEMSS, Ottawa (2010)

10. Urbánek, J., Brabec, K., Dušek, L., Holoubek, I., Hřebíček, J., Kubásek, M.: Monitoring and assessment of environmental impact by persistent organic pollutants. In: Diamantaras, K., Duch, W., Iliadis, L.S. (eds.) ICANN 2010. LNCS, vol. 6354, pp. 483–488. Springer, Heidelberg (2010)

Towards a Semantically Unified Environmental Information Space

Saša Nešić[1], Andrea Emilio Rizzoli[1], and Ioannis N. Athanasiadis[2]

[1] IDSIA, Manno, Switzerland
{sasa,andrea}@idsia.ch
[2] Democritus University of Thrace, Xanthi, Greece
ioannis@athanasiadis.info

Abstract. In recent years we have witnessed a proliferation of environmental information on the Web thanks to advances in automated data acquisition and to the widespread use of computer based models and decision support systems processing environmental data. The number of environmental data providers has been also increasing. However, each provider manages its own data sets encoded into specific data formats and unaware of related and relevant data managed by other providers. Also, most of the environmental data providers store their data into huge, centralized repositories, which makes the access and discovery of desired data difficult. The Linked Data principles along with the Semantic Web technologies have been recognized as a promising solution to both environmental data integration and discovery. Unique identification of environmental data by HTTP dereferencable URIs, semantic annotation of environmental data by shared domain conceptualizations (ontologies), and interlinking of related environmental data by typed (semantic) links will enable the integration of disconnected environmental data sets into the semantically unified environmental information space. Semantic annotations and semantic links will then enable semantic discovery of environmental data over such unified information space. In this paper, we try to identify a number of requirements that environmental data providers should satisfy in order to make their data fully contribute to this vision. In particular, we are focused on requirements regarding environmental data identification, representation, annotation and linking.

Keywords: environmental data identification, semantic annotation, semantic linking.

1 Introduction

Over recent years, the adoption of the Linked Data best practices for publishing and collecting structured data on the Web [6] has opened the possibility of creating a unified information space, connecting data from different sources and domains such as weather forecasts, music stores, television and radio programs, on-line communities and business records. This information space is commonly

J. Hřebíček, G. Schimak, and R. Denzer (Eds.): ISESS 2011, IFIP AICT 359, pp. 407–418, 2011.

refereed as a Linked Open Data (LOD) Cloud and is considered as an incubator for the envisioned Web of Data. The main idea of the Web of Data is linking data instead of linking documents, which should enabling fine-grained integration of cross-domain information into a globally unified information space [3]. Moreover, the Web of Data has also been recognized as a foundation for the Semantic Web, which in spite of a number of different interpretations, has been recognized as a global Web of machine-readable data. Humans are the current Web's semantic component. They are required to process the information available on the Web to ultimately determine their meaning and relevance for the task at hand. The Semantic Web intends to move some of that processing to software agents [7]. In order to discover and map data more precisely, software agents require machine-readable data and machine-understandable data semantics (metadata). What the Semantic Web brings to the situation are the new data representation model (the predicate-based structures to express meaningful assertions) and the ontologies and rules to enable intelligent software agents to parse meaning from these assertions (sentences). Intelligent software agents will not be able to 'think' like their human counterparts, but they will be able to reason logically around the encoded explicit assertions, infer new ones, and assist humans in committing their tasks.

The Linked Data and the Semantic Web principles are universal; they are not restricted to any particular domain. As such, they represent promising solution for semantic integration of currently disconnected environmental data sets present on the Web. Traditionally, environmental data has been published on the Web as chunks of digital content, more frequently as text files, in some cases either stored as XML or marked up as HTML tables. Some HTML documents containing related environmental data are interlinked but the meaning of the relationships between the linked documents can only be implicitly distinguished. Hyperlinks indicate that two documents are related in some way, but it mostly left up to the human user to infer the nature of the relationship. HTML initially did not provide neither elements enabling typed links between documents nor between individual entities described in particular documents. Advances towards this direction, as microformats[1] has not been widely adopted either. Environmental data are no exception to this situation, while complexity, spatiotemporal reference, and uncertainty, make things even worse. Common practice has proven that environmental data are usually stored in non-reusable raw formats, situated in sparse locations and managed by different authorities, which ultimately raise obstacles in making environmental information accessible [1]. As a result of that, environmental data published on the Web looks like sets of disconnected data islands that are unaware of each other. Having environmental data published in accordance with the Linked Data and the Semantic Web principles would enable building of the *semantically unified environmental information space*, where environmental information becomes a common asset that is shared among peers, instead of a resource in scarcity that peers strive for [1].

---

[1] http://microformats.org/about

In this paper we discuss and analyze a set of requirements/principles that environmental data providers should respect in order to publish their data to the semantically unified environmental information space. We start the discussion by providing a brief overview of the use of the Semantic Web technologies in the environmental domain so far (Section 2). Then, we discuss and analyze requirements for environmental data identification and representation (Section 3). After that we continue with requirements for semantic annotation (Section 4) and linking (Section 5) of environmental data. Finally, in Section 6 we discuss and analyze requirements for semantic discovery (i.e., search and navigation) of the environmental data that are part of the unified environmental information space. Section 7 concludes the paper and outlines future work.

2 Application of the Semantic Web Technologies in the Environmental Domain

Environmental modeling and software are challenged to deal with complexity, uncertainty, scaling and integration issues, qualities inherited from the physical world, and thus comprise a challenging testbed for Semantic Web technologies. Environmental software embody sophisticated statements of environmental knowledge. Yet, the knowledge they incorporate is rarely self-contained enough for them to be understood and used by humans or machines without the modelers mediation [18]. Research efforts, so far has concentrated in three lines of work:

- **Semantics for environmental data annotation** through the development of domain vocabularies, thesauri and ontologies. There are several ongoing efforts on defining standards for sharing environmental data, and contribute to the Semantic Web vision, including these published by the US Environmental Data Standards Council (EDSC 2006), the standards developed gradually since 1994 by the European Environment Information and Observation Network[2] and the guidelines on vegetation plots and classifications of the Ecological Society of America (VEGBANK[3]). Also, the Ecological Metadata Language (EML)[4] provides with a metadata specification for describing data relevant to ecology. Food and Agriculture Organization (FAO) of the United Nations has made its thesaurus of food and agricultural terms, publicly available through the AGROVOC web services[5]. Towards the same direction contributes the OpenGIS specifications by the Open Geospatial Consortium[6] for the standardization of geo-referenced data, which are very common in environmental applications. The above are selected only as an indication of the parallel efforts for organizing and naming environmental

---

[2] http://www.eionet.europa.eu/
[3] http://www.vegbank.org
[4] http://knb.ecoinformatics.org/software/eml/
[5] http://www.fao.org/agrovoc/
[6] http://www.opengeospatial.org

data units using standard vocabularies and URIs for sharing them on the Semantic Web.

- **Semantics for environmental software annotation**: Environmental Modeling Frameworks typically offer though an API a collection of technical solutions for environmental scientists to program and deploy their models, and include facilities for data management and visualization, mathematical integration and scaling across time and space, among others. However, Environmental Modeling Frameworks are often invasive and heavyweight [11], thus software reuse comes with a high price. Integrating rich semantics in environmental model interfaces has a great potential to both maximize interoperability [16] and ensure sound integration [2]. For example, in the SEAMLESS project domain ontologies were adopted for the annotation of model interfaces, and used them for generating software code to facilitate software integration through a semantic-rich development methodology [1,10,9]

- **Semantically-aware environmental modelling** is a way of designing, implementing and deploying environmental datasets and models based on the independent, standardized formalization of the underlying environmental science [18]. It can be seen as the result of merging the rationale of declarative modelling with modern knowledge representation theory, through the mediation of the integrative vision of a Semantic Web. In this knowledge-driven approach, where the knowledge is the key not only to integration, but also to overcoming scale and paradigm differences and to novel potentials for model design and automated knowledge discovery [18]. Despite the clear potential offered by semantic modeling applied to environmental problems, only limited case studies are available, i.e IMA [17], ESD [19], SEEK [12], and ARIES [18]. The feasibility of wide adoption of the approach remains to be seen in the coming years.

While the visions of the Semantic Web and Linked Open Data have not come into life yet, there is a growing interest from the Environmental community on the field, and the semantically unified environmental information space is an era to come. In the following sections we preview how this will be achieved.

3   Environmental Data Identification and Representation

Before considering how environmental data should be identified we first need to define what kind of data is meaningful to be identified. We distinguish between the following concepts: *content unit, information unit* and *data unit*. Content units are units of raw digital content (e.g., text, graphics, audio, and video). Information units are pieces of information that can be understood when provided as standalone. Data units are content units which have one of more information units encoded inside themselves. In the envisioned semantically unified environmental information space, environmental data will be organized in data units, each one of which being characterized by a set of machine-processable descriptions and a set of relationships. The relationships can be established among

related environmental data units but also between them and other web entities
as well as real-world entities and abstract concepts.

Linked Data vision builds directly on the Web architecture [8], thus environmental data units should be identified by unique resource identifiers (URIs).
There has been a lot of confusion about URIs and URLs (Uniform Resource
Locators) so far. The two concepts share the same meaning up to some extent,
but are not equivalent. URIs identify resources either by location, or a name, or
both. Accordingly, they can be classified as locators, or as names, or as both. A
URI that identifies a resource by name in a given namespace, without defining
how the resource could be obtained, is called unique resource name or URN.
Unlike a URI, a URL identifies a resource by specifying a network location from
where the resource can be obtained. Linked Data principles suggest using only
HTTP URIs and avoiding other URI schemes such as URNs [13] and DOIs [15].
Two essential reasons for this are that HTTP URIs provide a simple way to
create globally unique names in a decentralized fashion and that HTTP URIs
serve not just as a name but also as a means of accessing the identified entity.
In order to achieve not only global uniqueness but also good arrangement of the
HTTP URIs within the environmental information space it is recommended that
environmental data providers agree on using a standardized HTTP URI schema.
One proposal for such an HTTP URI schema for the environmental could be as
follows:

```
http://[domain name]/[provider OpenID]/[resource ID]
```

The parts of the schema are:

- **domain name** - a reserved DNS name for the environmental domain, it
  might be a sponsored top level domain .envi such as .mobi or .edu;
- **provider OpenID** - an OpenID identifier identifying the environmental
  data provider; OpenID is an open, decentralized standard for the authentication of online users;
- **resource ID** - a local resource identifier which is unique among the data
  units published by the data provider;

Having environmental data units uniquely identified by HTTP dereferencable
URIs, the next principle that the environmental data providers should adhere to
in order to make their data be seamlessly integrated to the semantically unified
environmental information space is a universal data representation model. On
the Web of Data, data is represented by the Resource Description Framework
(RDF) data model. RDF is the data representation model especially designed
towards the Web architecture and aiming at providing integrated representation
of information that originates from multiple sources. Any resource published on
the Web of Data is represented by unique RDF node and described by a number
of RDF triples (sentences of a basic structure): *subject*, *predicate*, and *object*.
The *subject* is the URI of the resource, the *predicate* indicates the relationship
between the *subject* and the *object* and is identified by a URI of the property that
models the predicate, and the object which can either be a simple *literal value*

(e.g., string or number) or a URI of another resource. The two possible object types determine two types of RDF triples: *Literal Triples* and *RDF Links*. While literal triples are used to describe properties of a resource, RDF Links describe relationships between two resources. A collection of RDF triples can be also seen as an RDF graph. Since resources on the Web of Data are identified by globally unique URIs it is possible to imagine all Linked Data as one "giant global graph" [5].

There is a tendency that people conceive RDF as a data format which is wrong. It is only a data representation model. In order to publish a collection of RDF triplets (i.e., an RDF graph) on the Web of Data, they must first be serialized into an RDF serialization format. There exist several RDF serialization formats, two of which have been standardized by W3C: RDF/XML and RDFa. So far, the RDF/XML syntax [4] has been the most often used RDF serialization format in spite of the fact that it is difficult for humans to read and write it. One of the main reasons for that is a large number of available XML parsers. RDFa is the RDF serialization format that mixes RDF triples and HTML. It is applicable in contexts where data providers are allowed to modify HTML contents to which they intend to add RDF triples. RDFa embeds RDF triples into HTML as values of a set of attribute level extensions to XHTML. RDFa has risen its popularity mostly on the fact that it enables both human-readable and machine-processable data representations to coexist in the same Web document. Besides RDF/XML and RDFa, other RDF serialization formats include Turtle, N-Triples and RDF/JSON.

4   Semantic Annotation of Environmental Data

RDF is a generic, abstract data representation model for describing Web resources. It does not provide any domain-specific terms (concepts) for describing a group of resources from a certain domain. This task is delegated to *taxonomies*, *thesaurii* and *ontologies* which are usually expressed in languages such as RDFS (the RDF Vocabulary Description Language, also known as RDF Schema) and OWL (the Web Ontology Language). All three *taxonomies, thesaurii,* and *ontologies* represent collections of controlled vocabulary terms, each term representing a particular name of one domain concept. They differ in the way the terms are organized as well as the expressivity of relationships between them. A taxonomy organizes terms into a hierarchical structure applying parent-child relationships. A thesaurus is a collection of controlled vocabulary terms that uses associative relationships in addition to the parent-child relationships. An ontology is far more expressive than a taxonomy and thesauri, providing a set of terms, properties (relationships) and property restrictions necessary for the conceptualization of a given domain.

Semantic annotation of linked data refers to the process of linking concepts defined in domain ontologies to RDF nodes that represent the data units to be linked. Semantic annotations, that is annotating by using ontological concepts, represent the conceptualization of information held by the annotated data units.

However, in reality, it is rare that the annotated data units contain exact instance of the annotating ontological concepts unless they belong to the ontology's documentation. It is more realistic that annotated data units model only some aspects of the ontological concepts. Therefore, besides linking the ontological concepts, it would be useful if the annotations also provide information on the relevance (relatedness) of the ontological concepts for the data units they annotate.

The quality of semantic annotation strongly depends on the quality of the domain ontology. Some domains are described by better ontologies than others, but still there is a major shortcoming of standardized domain ontologies. In most cases domain ontologies cover only a specific part of a domain, so that it is very unlikely that data providers can literally reuse an existing ontology. In a more realistic scenario data providers will have to extend some of the existing ontologies by adding new terms that serve their purposes.

4.1 A Short "howto" Guide for Environmental Data Providers

When choosing the ontology, the environmental data provider should first check the usage of the ontology in the domain. That is, how much the ontology has been used in the domain and whether is has been standardized by an ontology standardization body. Second, they should check if the ontology is actively maintained and updated according to a well-established governance process. Third, does the ontology cover substantial part of the data that the environmental data provider intends to annotate? Finally, they should check if the ontology delivers enough expressivity for their data sets and for the intended application scenarios. After choosing the ontology, if the environmental data providers still need to extend it, here are the aspects that should be considered:

- Identify subsets of concepts and properties of your interest from the ontology;
- Identify missing concepts and properties;
- Define a new namespace that you can control;
- Define new concepts and properties under the defined namespace;
- Document the new concepts with human-friendly labels and comments;
- Relate the new concepts to the existing, related concepts from the ontology;

New concepts can be defined completely from scratch or derived from the existing ones. If derived from the existing concepts, the `rdfs:subClassOf` property should be used to relate new concepts to the parent ones. When relating the new concepts to to some existing and related concepts, an arbitrary number of mappings can be established. The better connected ontology is, the better integrated data that it annotates will be [14]. In case new hierarchical and associative relationships need to be defined, it is recommended to rely on reusing properties from existing well established vocabularies such as SKOS (Simple Knowledge Organization System) rather than defining new ones. For example, the `skos:broader` and `skos:narrower` properties can be used to assert a direct hierarchical link between two concepts, while the `skos:related` property can be used to assert an associative relationship between two concepts. Since both research on a given environmental domain and the ontologies describing it evolve over time, there is a high probability that at a later point in time the environmental data providers discover that another environmental domain ontology contains the same concepts they have already defined. In that case the owl:equivalentClass property can be used to state that the concepts in the two ontologies are equivalent.

Besides choosing and extending the domain ontology, the environmental data providers should also decide on the way ontological concepts are being linked to their data units. This actually means that the environmental data providers should decide on an annotation interface that will provide structures for linking ontological concepts to the data units. We distinguish between two general approaches in designing the annotation interface, each of which having comparative advantages and drawbacks.

The first approach assumes linking concepts from domain ontologies directly to RDF nodes of the data units. This approach enables a very flexible annotation approach and does not require a complex annotation interface. The annotation interface is composed of predefined properties whose domain comprises data units to be annotated and range comprises concepts from domain ontologies. Most commonly used property for this purpose is dc:subject which is defined in the Dublin Core (DC) vocabulary. The advantage of this approach is the simplicity of adding/linking annotating ontological concepts to data units. The drawback is limited expressively, which is reflected in the fact that annotating concepts are left without any contextual information such as who added them, when they were added, and how relevant they are.

The second approach assumes the existence of an intermediate annotation concept in the annotation interface, over which domain concepts are linked to the RDF nodes of the data units. This concept is usually named as "Annotation" and provides an arbitrary number of properties that model additional information about the annotating domain concept. Figure 1 shows an example of the annotation interface that conforms to this annotation approach. As it can be seen from the figure, besides the annotating domain concept that determines the annotation, the annotation interface also holds information about the annotation's author, the date and time when the annotation was created, and the relevance (weight) of the annotating domain concept. The last information actually depicts up to what extent the annotating domain concept conceptualizes semantics of the data unit it annotates.

By applying the second annotation approach we have annotations loosely coupled with the data unit, which gives flexibility to add additional information about the annotating domain concept. The main drawback of this approach is that software applications that intend to consume the annotations will need to be aware of the complexity of the annotation interface. Moreover, retrieving the annotations will require the execution of more complex queries, which in case of large collections of interlinked data can cause significant lose of the applications' performance.

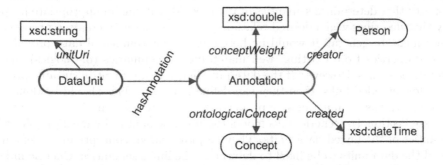

Fig. 1. An example of the annotation interface

5   Semantic Linking of Environmental Data

Having environmental data uniquely identified and semantically annotated, the next step in building the semantically unified environmental information space is to create links between related data units. Links should be established both internally, among data units belonging to the same data set (i.e., the data units from the same data provider), and externally between data units belonging to different data sets. Both internal and external links are important in ensuring that the data set is well integrated into the semantically unified environmental information space and further into the global Web of Data. While establishing the internal links is mainly responsibility of the environmental data provider, external links can be established by other environmental data providers and a general Web audience as well. There are two types of external links: *outgoing links* pointing from data units inside the data set to data units from other data sets and *incoming links* pointing in the opposite direction. Both types are equally important in ensuring that each data unit can be discovered and accessed by software applications consuming the data through link traversal.

External links can be established only after the data set is published on the Web. What is important for us is how environmental data providers can contribute to this process. At first glance it might appear that the data providers can only create outgoings links from their data sets. However, when using the RDF data representation model, there is no difference in creating outgoing and incoming links. In both cases, creating links between data units is about generating and publishing RDF triples that describe the links. A good practice would be that the environmental data providers, once they publish their data sets, try to identify related data within other data sets available on the Web and create an initial set of links. Moreover, they should also well document their data sets in order to convince third parties of the value of linking to their data sets.

Considering semantics of a relationship between two linked data units, we distinguish between two types of links: property-based (predefined) and generic links. Property-based links are described by RDF triples in which the subject and object are URIs of the data units to be linked and the predicate is a predefined property that determines semantics of the link. Identifying an appropriate property that describes well a desired relationship is a key issue in creating property-based links. In general, it would be better if the environmental data providers reuse properties from existing, well maintained vocabularies (ontologies) than defining new ones. However, if the data providers can not identify suitable properties for intended links, then they can define new ones. This should be done in the same way as defining missing properties in the environmental domain ontology (see Section 4). Generic links model the link's semantics by means of shared semantics of the linked data units. They employ shared, conceptualized semantics of the data units to be liked to determine the link's semantics. Generic links are especially useful in case of automatic link generation as we explain later.

Creating generic links is more complex than creating property-based links. While a property-based link is described by one RDF triple, a generic link is described by a number of RDF triplets that represent an instance of a generic link specification. Figure 2 exhibits an example of the generic link specification. As we can see from the figure, the generic link in this case is specified by the SemanticLink class and the following properties: unitA and unitB, which hold references to the data units linked by the generic semantic link; linkingConcept that holds the reference to the ontological concept that conceptualizes shared semantics between the linked data units and determines the semantic relation between them; and the linkStrength property whose value determines the strength of the semantic relation, that is, semantic relatedness between the data units.

Both property-based and generic links can be set manually or automatically. Manual interlinking is more appropriate for small, static data sets, while larger data sets generally require an automated or semi-automated approach. The main idea of the automated approaches is to measure semantic relatedness between the data units and if it is above a given threshold then they generate the links. Generic links appear to be more applicable for the automated link generation than property-based links since they are not constrained to a set of predefined properties. In principle, possible semantics of the relationships between data

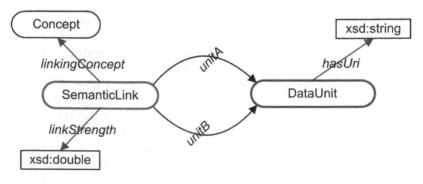

Fig. 2. An example of the generic link specification

units are unbounded so that it is difficult to cover all of them by a predefined set of properties.

6 Conclusions

In this paper we have analyzed the requirements that environmental data providers should satisfy when publish their data, so that the data becomes seamlessly integrated into LOD cloud and the Semantic Web. The requirements consider environmental data identification, representation, annotation and linking. Publishing environmental data according to the proposed requirements will lead towards creation of the semantically unified environmental information space. Search engines and intelligent software agents will take advantage of such unified information space to enhance discovery of environmental data and to assist humans in improving their research and understanding of the environment we live in.

Acknowledgements. The research leading to these results has received funding from the European Community's Seventh Framework Programme (FP7/2007-2013) under Grant Agreement Number 247893.

References

1. Athanasiadis, I.N., Janssen, S.: Semantic mediation for environmental model components integration. Information Technologies in Environmental Engineering 1(3-11) (2008)
2. Athanasiadis, I.N., Rizzoli, A.E., Donatelli, M., Carlini, L.: Enriching environmental software model interfaces through ontology-based tools. International Journal of Applied Systemic Studies (in press, 2011)
3. Becker, C., Bizer, C.: Exploring the geospatial semantic web with dbpedia mobile. Journal of Web Semantics 7(4), 278–286 (2009)
4. Beckett, D.: RDF/XML Syntax Specification (Revised) - W3C Recommendation (2004), http://www.w3.org/TR/rdf-syntax-grammar/
5. Berners-Lee, T.: A Framework for Web Science. Fondation and Trends in Web Science 1(1), 1–130 (2006)
6. Bizer, C., Heath, T., Berners-Lee, T.: Linked Data - The story so far. Int. Journal on Semantic Web and Information Systems 5(3), 1–22 (2009)
7. Hendler, J.: Agents and the Semantic Web. IEEE Intelligent Systems 16(2), 30–37 (2001)
8. Jacobs, I., Walsh, N.: Architecture of the World Wide Web (2004), http://www.w3.org/TR/webarch/
9. Janssen, S., Athanasiadis, I.N., Bezlepkina, I., Knapen, R., Li, H., Dominguez, I.P., Rizzoli, A.E.: Linking models for assessing agricultural land use change. Computers and Electronics in Agriculture (2010)
10. Janssen, S., Ewert, F., Li, H., Athanasiadis, I.N., Wien, J., Thérond, O., Knapen, M., Bezlepkina, I., Alkan-Olsson, J., Rizzoli, A., Belhouchette, H., Svensson, M.: Defining assessment projects and scenarios for policy support: use of ontology in integrated assessment and modelling. Environmental Modelling and Software 24, 1491 (2009)

11. Lloyd, W., David, O., Ascough, J., Rojas, K., Carlson, J., Leavesley, G., Krause, P., Green, T., Ahuja, L.: Environmental modeling framework invasiveness: Analysis and implications. In: International Congress on Environmental Modelling and Software (iEMSs 2010), pp. 1073–1080 (2010)
12. Madin, J., Bowers, S., Schildhauer, M., Krivov, S., Pennington, D., Villa, F.: An ontology for describing and synthesizing ecological observation data. Ecological Informatics 2(3), 279 (2007)
13. Moats, R.: Rfc 2141: Urn syntax (1997), http://tools.ietf.org/html/rfc2141
14. Nešić, S., Crestani, F., Gašević, D., Jazayeri, M.: Search and Navigation in Semantically Integrated Document Collections. In: Proceedings of the 4th International Conference on Advances in Semantic Processing, SEMAPRO, Florence, Italy, pp. 55–60 (2010)
15. Page, L., Brin, S., Motwani, R., Winograd, T.: The pagerank citation ranking: Bringing order to the web. Technical report, Stanford Digital Library Technologies Project (1998)
16. Rizzoli, A.E., Donatelli, M., Athanasiadis, I.N., Villa, F., Huber, D.: Semantic links in integrated modelling frameworks. Mathematics and Computers in Simulation 78(2-3), 412 (2008)
17. Villa, F.: Integrating modelling architecture: a declarative framework for multiparadigm, multi-scale ecological modeling. Ecological Modelling 137, 23–42 (2001)
18. Villa, F., Ceroni, M., Bagstad, K., Johnson, G., Krivov, S.: Aries (artificial intelligence for ecosystem services): a new tool for ecosystem services assessment, planning, and valuation. In: 11th International BIOECON Conference (2009)
19. Villa, F., Ceroni, M., Krivov, S.: Intelligent databases assist transparent and sound economic valuation of ecosystem services. Environmental Management 39, 887–899 (2007)

A Model for Semantic Annotation of Environmental Resources: The TaToo Semantic Framework

Tomás Pariente[1], José María Fuentes[1], María Angeles Sanguino[1], Sinan Yurtsever[1], Giuseppe Avellino[2], Andrea E. Rizzoli[3], and Saša Nešić[3]

[1]ATOS Origin, Madrid, Spain
{tomas.parientelobo,jose.fuentesl,maria.sanguino,
sinan.yurtsever}@atosresearch.eu
[2]Telespazio, Rome, Italy
giuseppe.avellino@telespazio.com
[3]IDSIA, Lugano, Switzerland
{andrea,sasa}@idsia.ch

Abstract. During the past years huge amounts of resources in the environmental domain have been published on the internet. To facilitate search and discovery of relevant data among an ever increasing mass, the use of tags has been suggested. Yet, the use of non-formal tags for annotating resources allows simple categorization and search capabilities, but it does not provide the means to create cross-domain annotations. On the other hand, ontologies are a shared and formal conceptualization of a given domain and they can be used to formalise tags. The use of formal semantics for tagging allows taking advantage of the reasoning and inference power of the ontologies to create richer resource annotations enhancing the discovery process. In the environmental domain there is a clear need of frameworks and tools allowing formal tagging and discovery. In this paper we discuss about the definition of a Semantic Framework helping the tagging and discovery process of environmental resources. Moreover, we also report on the definition of a model to describe environmental resources allowing cross-domain annotation and search.

Keywords: environment, discovery, annotation, ontology, cross-domain, search, tagging, semantics.

1 Introduction

Since its inception, the Web has brought a revolution on how to publish, transmit and consume information. While at first the number of information publishers on the Web was limited, now almost everyone publishes personal and / or professional information on the Web. Much of this growth is due to the fact that the expertise needed to publish information on the Web is quite small. Basically, publishers only need to own information and organize it in a way that makes it possible to be accessed by consumers. However, the ease of publication, which originally facilitated the growth of the Web, is not necessarily matching the ease of discovery and access to data. In professional environments, where information needs are highly complex, it is

J. Hřebíček, G. Schimak, and R. Denzer (Eds.): ISESS 2011, IFIP AICT 359, pp. 419–427, 2011.

necessary that machines, and not just humans, understand the published information to improve its exploitation capabilities. Meta-information and semantics associated with meta-information are the concepts we need to introduce in order to allow for automated machine-processing of information. And such concepts are at the foundations of the TaToo project.

The TaToo project, which started in 2010, aims at improving the discovery and exploitation capabilities of the published environmental information by providing a way to semantically enrich environmental resources. TaToo is built on top of three fundamental pillars:

- A framework to create complex and formal annotations. Informal annotations are relatively good for human interpretation, but fail to help machines to understand the meaning and perform more advanced tasks based on those annotations. Annotations should be then formal and shared across the domain.
- Usage of ontologies to enhance discovery capabilities and to prevent interoperability issues. TaToo provides an ontology framework that allows cross-domain and cross-language tagging and search. Producing annotations is a time consuming task. TaToo offers both the automatic harvesting of meta-information from existing resources, and a manual interface for humans; both approaches are based on the above mentioned ontology framework.
- A community driven approach. TaToo pays special care in providing easy-to-use and effective tagging interfaces to enable and facilitate the tagging process. TaToo is strongly inspired by existing social bookmarking initiatives, such as reddit, StumbleUpon, Digg, etc. In this sense, TaToo allows the user producing their own annotations, and share them with the community, starting an information enrichment cycle. On the other hand, TaToo differs from the aforementioned social approaches in the use of formal semantic annotations.

This paper focuses on the TaToo ontology framework. The first objective of TaToo is the establishment of an ontology framework that allows the production of formal resource descriptions. Subsequently, the TaToo system is taking advantage of domain ontologies and formal resource descriptions to improve the exploitation of environmental resources by improving the discovery processes, enhancing the resource presentation and providing interoperability between different fields of the environmental domain with the aim of allowing cross-domain search.

Much of the functionality provided by TaToo relies on ontologies. Ontology development is a complex, time-consuming task involving different roles (ontology developers and domain experts) and activities (requirements acquisition, design, etc.). Therefore, from the ontological point of view, one of the biggest challenges of TaToo is to use or produce a formal description of the environmental domain that is at the same time good enough to cover the project objectives, and on the other hand simple enough to avoid unnecessary complexity and gruesome maintenance. The environmental domain is actually a very broad domain that includes several sub-domains dealing with such diverse areas as climatology, toxic compounds fate assessment, crop management, and so on.

Although there are ontologies dealing with environmental issues, presently there is no encompassing ontology detailing such a broad domain that fits the needs of TaToo. Therefore, a realistic objective of TaToo in this regard is to allow experts to model their own sub-domain and at the same time provide the maximum degree of integration between such sub-domain models. Because of this, the ontology framework should ensure semantic interoperability between different domain ontologies while ensuring their modular nature.

2 Ontology Framework

There are several approaches to achieve semantic interoperability when dealing with different ontologies. Watche [2] defined three ways to integrate ontologies by using single ontology, multiple ontology or hybrid ontology approaches.

The single ontology approach uses one global ontology that provides a shared vocabulary for the specification of the semantics. Thus, all information sources are related to one ontology, which usually is a combination of several specialized ontologies. This approach is suitable for solving integration problems where all information sources to be integrated provide nearly the same view on a domain.

In the multiple ontology approach each information source is described by its own ontology. The main advantage of this approach is that no common and minimal ontology commitment about a global ontology is needed. To achieve a common understanding of the information sources, defined ontologies must be related. To relate several "source describing" ontologies, several inter-ontology mappings must be introduced. In practice, these inter-ontology mappings are very difficult to define because of the many semantic heterogeneity problems, which may occur, and the situation is aggravated when there are many domain ontologies to map.

The hybrid approach is based on using a common shared ontology and a set of local or application ontologies that are mapped uniquely to the shared vocabulary. In this case the local ontologies would extend the vocabulary to the needs of a given domain and the interoperability is achieved based on the shared ontology. TaToo follows the hybrid approach as shown in Fig. 1.

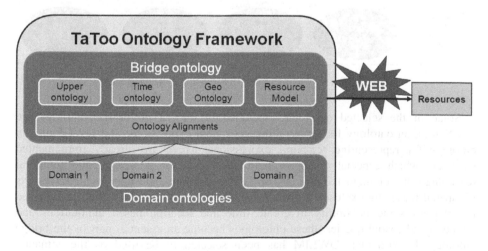

Fig. 1. TaToo high-level ontology framework

In order to apply the hybrid approach, a bridge ontology that will become the upper layer of the integrated ontology framework has to be developed. Our bridge ontology includes concept and property definitions from widely adopted ontologies and necessary concept definitions in order to ensure the mappings between domain ontologies. Any domain ontology should be mapped properly to the bridge ontology in order to be usable by the integrated ontology framework. So the system interacts with the domain ontologies via the bridge ontology.

The mapping process is done manually by defining equivalency and subsumption relationships between concepts, object properties, data properties and individuals of bridge ontology and the domain ontology. From the point of view of the bridge ontology, the entire ontology framework is seen as one big knowledge base. In Fig. 2, where the current version of the TaToo ontology framework is shown, some example mappings between ontology elements from the bridge ontology (crossed-out circles in green) and the domain ontologies (crossed-out circles in gray) are depicted to represent the cross-domain alignment process.

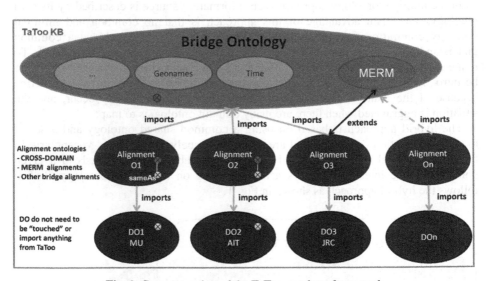

Fig. 2. Current version of the TaToo ontology framework

Some of the selected ontologies included in the TaToo bridge ontology are GeoNames, an ontology for representing geospatial expressions, and OWLTime, an ontology for representing temporal expressions. There are already implemented reasoners which especially support both ontologies for geospatial and temporal reasoning. One of them is OWLIM, an OWL semantic repository, which supports geospatial reasoning exclusively for the GeoNames ontology. As TaToo is expected to offer users the possibility to create time and location based annotations and temporal and spatial queries, these ontologies become an essential part of the bridge ontology. In particular, OWLIM has been selected to be used as the semantic repository and the availability geospatial reasoning has been one of the reasons for this choice. OWLIM supports OWL2-RL, a web ontology language profile inspired by rule-based languages. OWL2-RL is much more efficient and scalable compared to OWL2-DL but less expressive. This is the reason why OWL2-RL has been chosen. Because of the constant incremental annotated data that will be manipulated, a need for more efficient reasoning arose and OWL2-RL is aimed to cover these kinds of needs.

In TaToo, there is also the need to uniformly describe environmental information resources. We think of an environmental resource as a web resource (being a web page, a document, a model, a service, etc.), which is identified by a URI. For future releases, the usage of an upper-level ontology to perform more elaborate cross-domain mappings will be investigated. The Semantic Web for Earth and Environmental Terminology (SWEET) [1], a widely-used set of ontologies providing semantic descriptions of Earth system science, is a good candidate for the TaToo ontology framework.

3   The Minimal Environmental Resource Model

A minimum resource model is defined as the largest common denominator between a set of heterogeneous description formalisms related to a common resource. Minimum resource models have been applied in other research areas with satisfactory results. In [4] a description of an open system for web services publication and discovery based on a description of a minimal service model resulting in an ontology for service modelling called POSM is presented. Functionally, the minimum resource model aims at a similar objective as the bridge ontology: providing a common framework between different domain ontologies. However, conceptually, the minimum resource model is an effort to identify a minimal model that, without limiting the expression of specific domains, acts as a reference for past and future applications in a specific area. This minimisation effort and referencing aim is what differentiates the bridge ontology from a minimum resource model and it is what makes it a valuable resource.

One of the most relevant parts of the TaToo bridge ontology is the Minimal Environmental Resource Model (MERM). MERM describes the structure of resources and annotations in TaToo, being a reference data model for both services and user interfaces. As any other ontology developed in the scope of TaToo, MERM has been developed following the NeOn methodology [3]. The NeOn methodology encourages reusing as much as possible. To that extent, MERM contains, besides the already mentioned POSM ontology, concepts from several other ontologies like SIOC[1], FOAF[2], Dublin Core[3] and O&M[4]. Fig. 3 presents the main classes of MERM: *Resource, Annotation*, and *ResourceAccessInfo*.

---

[1] The SIOC initiative (Semantically-Interlinked Online Communities), http://www.sioc-project.org/
[2] The Friend of a Friend (FOAF) project, http://www.foaf-project.org/
[3] Dublin Core metadata iniciative, http://dublincore.org/
[4] Observations and Measurements ontology, http://seres.uni-muenster.de/o&m/O&M_discussion_paper.pdf

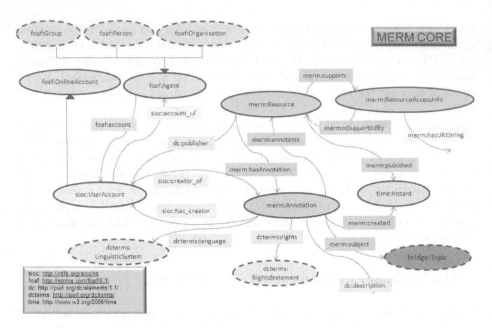

Fig. 3. MERM core classes and relations

The *Resource* class represents a resource in the TaToo system. It includes resource management information as author, owner, provider, date of creation, etc. A *Resource* usually has access information presented in the *ResourceAccessInfo* class. The *ResourceAccessInfo* class contains all information needed to access a resource. This information is very heterogeneous ranging from a simple URL to a complex WSDL depending on the nature of the resource. Finally, a resource presents a set of annotations, represented by the *Annotation* class. An annotation describes what a resource is about. Except for some management information, the content of an annotation depends on the type of the annotated resource. An annotation for a web document would be different from an annotation for a web service, being the "some resource is related to some domain concepts" the simplest kind of annotation. Resources in TaToo are retrieved taking their annotations as basis. In the current version, MERM distinguishes between three kinds of annotations:

- *TimeSeriesAnnotation* that describes time series following the model proposed by the Observations and Measurements Ontology.
- *WebServiceAnnotation* that describes web services following the model proposed by POSM.
- *WebAnnotation* that describes web resources following the model proposed by SIOC.

MERM is still work in progress so the addition of new models for several resources is expected. Fig. 4 shows in details the model adopted for *TimeSeriesAnnotation*.

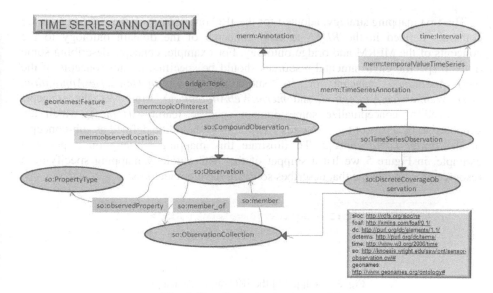

Fig. 4. TimeSeriesAnnotation model

Finally, there is also a special kind of annotations, the evaluations, which are annotations that relates to another annotation instead to a resource. Evaluations are created by users in order to evaluate how accurate or useful a resource annotation is. This information is used during the discovery process to improve discovery results and accuracy.

4 Integrating Domains

The TaToo Ontology framework, as it was described in Section 2, comprises the bridge ontology, a number of domain ontologies, and a number of alignment ontologies (see Fig. 2). The framework is not limited by a number of different domain ontologies, that is, by a number of different environmental sub-domains whose resources are managed by the TaToo system. However, in order to be able to plug-in a domain ontology in the TaToo ontology framework, the domain ontology needs to be accompanied by an appropriate mapping interface. This mapping interface is identified in the framework as an alignment ontology. In this section we describe two possible alignment/mapping strategies on the example of three domains ontologies, specific to the validation scenarios of the TaToo project, namely the JRC, MU, and AIT ontologies. The JRC ontology describes the agro-environmental domain, the MU ontology describes the anthropogenic impacts of global climate change, and finally the AIT ontology contains concepts related to the comparison of climatic conditions in different regions. These three domain ontologies are considered to be an integral part of the TaToo ontology framework, thus justifying the proposed ontology integration approach. Moreover, we also plan to use them in the evaluation of the semantic tagging and discovery capabilities of the TaToo system.

The first mapping strategy, adopted for the JRC ontology, uses the *rdfs:subClassOf* construct defined in the *RDFS* to map concepts of the domain ontology to the concepts of the MERM and bridge ontology. For example, concepts describing some domain specific environmental resources should be specified as sub-concepts of the *merm:Annotation* concept or its sub-concepts (*merm:TimeSeriesAnnotation*, *merm:WebService-Annotation*, and *merm:WebAnnotation*). Moreover, the concepts introduced to conceptualize some domain specific features (topics), which are supposed to be a part of the resources' annotations, should be defined as sub-concepts of the *bridge:Topic* concept. To illustrate this mapping strategy on a practical example, in Figure 5 we list a snippet of the JRC ontology mapping specifying a resource annotation type that describes software development kits:

```
<owl:Class rdf:ID="SoftwareDevelopmentKit">
      <rdfs:subClassOf rdf:resource="merm:Annotation"/>
</owl:Class>
```

Fig. 5. A snippet of the JRC ontology mapping

The second mapping strategy, used for the AIT and MU ontologies, assumes the usage of the *owl:equivalentClass* and *owl:sameAs* constructs defined in OWL, plus the *skos:broadMatch* and *skos:narrowMatch* constructs defined in the SKOS[5] (Simple Knowledge Organization System) vocabulary to map concepts and properties of a domain ontology to the concepts and properties of the MERM and bridge ontology. The difference between the OWL and the SKOS constructs is that the latter ones provide a looser mapping. There is also a slight difference between the two OWL constructs regarding the strength of the mapping they provide. The meaning of the *owl:equivalentClass* is that the two concepts have the same set of individuals. However, the *owl:equivalentClass* does not imply the concept equality. Concept equality means that the concepts have the same intentional meaning. Real concept equality can be expresses by the *owl:sameAs* construct. In Figure 6 we show a snippet of the MU ontology mapping that specifies the mapping of the "*Diagnose*" concept from the MU domain to the *merm:Annotation* concept of the MERM ontology.

```
<owl:Class rdf:about="Diagnose">
    <owl:equivalentClass rdf:resource="merm:Annotation"/>
</owl:Class>
```

Fig. 6. A snippet of the MU ontology mapping

The development of both bridge ontology (including MERM) and domain ontologies (i.e., JRC, AIT, and MU) in the TaToo Ontology framework is an evolutionary process. In case of domain ontologies we plan to extend them in future by adding new domain specific concepts and relationships that are currently not

---

[5]http://www.w3.org/TR/skos-reference/

provided. In case of the bridge ontology we want to identify which of the concepts from the domain ontologies can be generalized and potentially become members of the MERM ontology.

5 Conclusions

In this paper we have presented the approach of the TaToo project to the development of an ontology framework for the semantic annotation of environmental resources. As the environmental domain is composed by a wide number of sub-domains, we chose a hybrid approach to be able to integrate ontologies for the various sub-domains. Such an approach required the development of a bridge ontology and a series of alignment ontologies to map concepts from domain specific ontologies to the bridge ontology. A minimum environmental resource model has also been developed to be included in the bridge ontology in order to provide a minimal set of common concept to be shared across the different domains and facilitate alignments.

The TaToo ontology framework is functional to the declared objectives of the TaToo project that is to allow for the semantic annotation of environmental resources in order to enhance and facilitate search and discovery.

Acknowledgements. The research leading to these results has received funding from the European Community's Seventh Framework Programme (FP7/2007-2013) under Grant Agreement Number 247893.

References

1. Raskin, R.G., Pan, M.J.: Knowledge representation in the semantic web for earth and environmental terminology (SWEET). Computers & Geosciences 31, 1119–1125 (2005)
2. Wache, H., Vogele, T., Visser, U., Stuckenschmidt, H., Schuster, G., Neumann, H., Hubner, S.: Ontology based integration of information: a survey of existing approaches. In: Proceedings of the IJCAI 2001:17th International Joint Conferences on Artificial Intelligence, Seattle, WA, USA, pp. 108–117 (2001)
3. Gómez-Pérez, A., Motta, E., Suárez-Figueroa, M.C.: NeOn Methodology in a Nutshell (2010), http://www.neon-project.org/nw/NeOn_Book
4. Klusch, M., Kapahnke, P.: iSeM: Approximated reasoning for adaptive hybrid selection of semantic services. In: Aroyo, L., Antoniou, G., Hyvönen, E., ten Teije, A., Stuckenschmidt, H., Cabral, L., Tudorache, T. (eds.) ESWC 2010. LNCS, vol. 6089, pp. 30–44. Springer, Heidelberg (2010)

Climate Twins – An Attempt to Quantify Climatological Similarities

Joachim Ungar, Jan Peters-Anders, and Wolfgang Loibl

AIT - Austrian Institute of Technology,
Department of Foresight and Policy Development
Tech Gate Vienna, Donau-City-Str. 1, 1220 Vienna, Austria
joachim.ungar@gmail.com

Abstract. As climate change appears, strategies and actions will be necessary to cope with its effects on environment and society in the coming decades. Current climate conditions can be observed everywhere in the world but future climate conditions can only be estimated through climate simulations which produce huge amounts of quantitative data. This data leads to statements like "temperature increase is expected to exceed 2.6°C" or similar and remain fuzzy to non-experts in climate research. The Climate Twins application is designed to communicate climate changes in an intuitive and understandable way by showing regions which have now similar climate conditions according to a given Point of Interest (POI) in the future. This paper explains how the application seeks for locations with similar climatological patterns according to the POI. To achieve this goal a method has been developed to quantify similarity between two locations' climate data.

Keywords: Climate Change, Similarity Measures, Web Mapping.

1 Introduction

To allow "real world insights" about future climate impact and appropriate adaptation, one can look at model regions, where the current climate appears similar to an expected future climate of a POI. We call such region pairs with similar climate conditions (at different times) "Climate Twins". From these (remote) current Climate Twin region parts we can learn "hands on" how future climate impacts may be experienced in the POI and how to adapt there to the changing climate conditions, expected in the future.

The idea of Climate Twins is to identify regions whose current climate conditions show high similarity to the expected future climate in the POI. The Climate Twins search tool is a web-based graphical user interface (GUI) allowing to explore climate change effects based on maps of current and future climate.

To identify climatological similarity seems to be a simple exercise but the accuracy and validity of the result strongly depends on the indicators used and the similarity thresholds defined. A huge number of indicators in combination with

J. Hřebíček, G. Schimak, and R. Denzer (Eds.): ISESS 2011, IFIP AICT 359, pp. 428–436, 2011.

narrow threshold ranges will reduce the number of matching regions significantly as well as few indicators combined with wide thresholds will show a big number of matching regions.

The climate indicators used here are daily mean temperatures and daily precipitation because they are seen as the most important ones and provide sufficient input for proving the concept's applicability. The most important part was to find a suitable matching method which strongly depends on the quantification of similarity between any two data vectors.

This matching method now provides

- a "unit-less" similarity value able to be combined with similarity values of other indicators,
- information of the degree of similarity to derive statements like "more similar than" or "less similar than", and
- a consideration of many statistical properties because whole statistical distributions are being compared.

2   Theory and Methodology

2.1   Climate Data

Climate can be seen as a statistical collection of various climate variables. These variables are either measured or modeled in various time steps and therefore come as a list of values. A statistical distribution of these values can be described by three main attributes: dispersion (measure of variability), skewness (measure of asymmetry) and kurtosis (measure of peakedness) or by aggregations like mean, median or range.

There are various ways to quantify these properties but especially measuring skewness and kurtosis is challenging and the results are not always satisfactory. By using conventional methods major problems have to be faced as climate data is rather not normally distributed. Furthermore the results have to be combined to a single attribute afterwards which also leads to problems in weighting them in an appropriate manner.

Figure 1 shows frequency distributions of modelled daily temperature means. A quick visual interpretation shows that the more values are located on the right hand side, the warmer the location (e.g. Rome). The annual temperature amplitude equals the value range. As Vienna and Munich have a higher value range, the annual temperature range is wider due to their rather continental location. On the other hand Rome and Copenhagen, wich are located in maritime locations, show a narrow value range. Bipolar distributions indicate strong and distinct seasons like winter and summer with short and alternating changeovers in spring and autumn (Rome) whereas Gauss-like distributions indicate a more homogeneous climate (Vienna, Copenhagen, Munich) and so on.

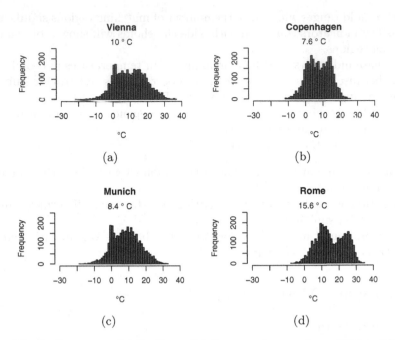

Fig. 1. Frequency distributions of daily mean temperatures 2001 to 2010

2.2 Similarity Measures

A similarity measure in this context should define and quantify the similarity between two statistical distributions—i.e. the numerical attributes we used to describe climate. Vegelius et al. [6] did a comparative analysis on various similarity measures. His research group tested measures according to predefined criteria. The three main criteria being:

1. The result of the measurement (r) has to be a value between 0 and 1,
2. between two identical distributions r has to be 1 and
3. r has to be equal when measuring in both directions.

After the analysis the group pointed out two measures which fit to all criterias given. These two were the *Proportional Similarity* (*PD*, 1) and the *Hellinger Coefficient* (r_{H}, 2).

$$PD(U,V) = \sum_{i=1}^{C} min(f_{\mathrm{U}i}, f_{\mathrm{V}i}) \tag{1}$$

$$r_{\mathrm{H}}(U,V) = \sum_{i=1}^{C} \sqrt{f_{\mathrm{U}i} * f_{\mathrm{V}i}} \tag{2}$$

U, V are two distributions, r similarity value, C being "category". Both measures use relative frequencies to measure similarity. Having data on a categorical or ordinal scale these categories are already defined. Given for examples two farms with cattle, chickens and sheep it is possible to quantify the relative similarity by using the frequencies of the three species living in each farm. In this example each species is a category.

2.3   Application

Problem: Climate data though occurs on an interval (temperature) or ratio (precipitation) scale where the borders—value ranges—that enclose the categories have to be defined manually in order to use these similarity measures.

Solution: The number of categories a distribution is split into determines the resolution of the measure (and therefore the accuracy of the measurement). If there is only one category describing each distribution, this category contains 100% of the values which leads to a r value of 1. The more categories are introduced, the more convincing the similarity measurement gets but for the Climate Twins application a meaningful number of categories had to be found where on the one hand the r value provides a valid similarity indicator and computer ressources are used effectively on the other hand.

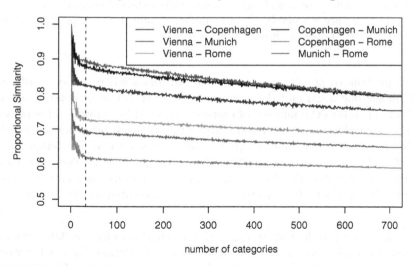

Fig. 2. Influence of category number on similarity measures (daily mean temperatures 2001-2010)

In Figure 2 the behaviour of Proportional Similarity values when increasing the category number is shown. Visually the resulting curve can be divided into three parts: (1) when having one category the r values have—as expected—a value of 1. When increasing the number the curve shows major fluctuations until it (2) stabilizes after approximately 30 categories. The r values stay (3) constant when having approximately 700 categories and more.

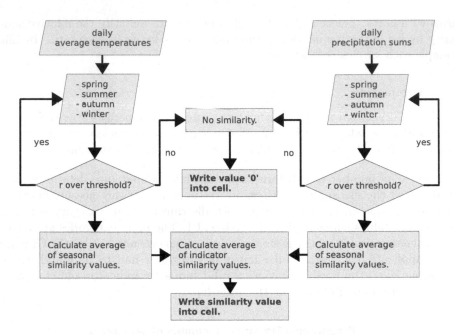

Fig. 3. Logical structure of combining r-values while define similarity between two locations. The structure is scalable, i.e. any number of indicators can be implemented as long as respective similarity thresholds are applied.

It is important to specify an amount of categories where valid results are possible on the one hand and the computing effort is as low as possible on the other hand. Therefore the number of categories should be a lower value of part two of the curve. Due to other reasons like the total possible value range, the categories for the Climate Twins application were set to 37 for temperature (every 2°C between −30°C and 40°C and one category each below and above that range) and 29 categories for precipitation (1 mm width each category from 0 to 10 mm, 5 mm width from 10 to 100 mm and one category for 100 mm and more).

Problem: A major problem in applying this method on climate data was losing all temporal information. A pure frequency distribution does not contain the chronological information of the distribution values anymore. Therefore two locations where the precipitation peaks occur at location A in spring and at location B in autumn will show erroniously high similarity.

Solution: The data is split up in seasonal data by aggregating to spring (MAM), summer (JJA), autumn (SON) and winter (DJF). After computing the respective seasonal r values they are recombined by averaging to an annual value.

Recombination can be done easily at least in combining seasonal r values to an annual value as the r value is "unit-less". To asses the problem in combining the similarity values of two different indicators a slider was implemented in the web application to interactively change the weighting. However, the results showed no significant change in Climate Twin result regions whilst variing the indicator weighting.

Figure 3 shows the logic behind the combination of single r values to an overall simlarity value. The most important part is that every single seasonal r value has to exeed a certain similarity threshold so that every overall similarity is mapped. If two locations match perfectly in three of four seasons but not in the fourth season, there is no point in declaring the two locations similar to each other.

Problem: As the declaration of similarity is a subjective one and up to some point an arbitrary process, so is the definition of the similarity thresholds. The thresholds should of course be tight eneough to provide a reliable result but on the other hand wide enough so that an acceptable amount of Climate Twin regions can be found. Furthermore an applicable threshold also depends on the indicator used and the category number as it can be seen in Figure 2.

Solution: Until now no satisfying validation method or data could be found to compare the Climate Twin results with. Therefore the fictive line between "good" and "bad" results can only be drawn subjectively by visual interpretations of result maps while variing the thresholds. In the web application the user is enabled and encouraged to influence this parameter interactively through a slider. The problem of thresholds has to be faced in order to further development of this method.

3   Technical Infrastructure

3.1   Input Data

The input data is from the COSMO-CLM (COnsortium for Small-scale MOdelling - Climate Local Model) model 2.4.11 which is embedded into the ECHAM5/MPIOM global model. The model results are climate data on an hourly basis from 1960 to 2100 in a raster with a resolution of 0.165° (approx. 18 to 20 km)[2].

The input data for the Climate Twins exploration have to be prepared and "condensed" in advance for fast data retrieval and comparison. The data actually stored in the data base are the absolute frequencies of daily data aggregated seasonally and in fourteen blocks of ten years each.

3.2   Interactive Map Application

The Climate Twins map functions have been built on open source software making use of UMN map server's [11] capabilities of displaying file based geographical data and spatially enabled data through PostGIS [9] layers stored in a PostGreSQL [10] database while using JSP (Java Server Pages) technology to conduct the grid cell queries. On the client side the highly configurable Flamingo Viewer [8] is used to display the maps served by the map server and to communicate with the Climate Twins data cube.

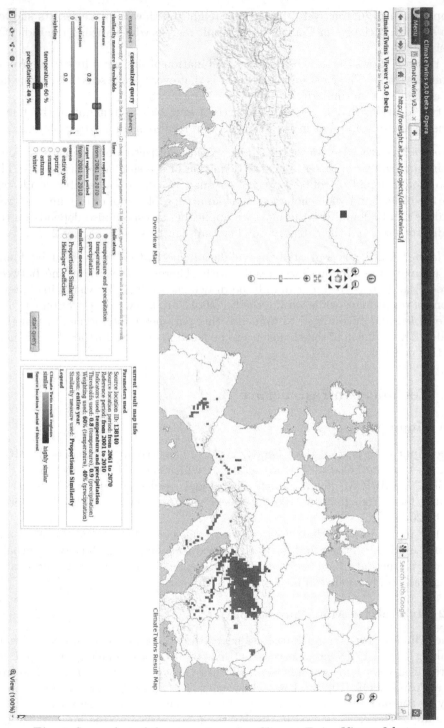

Fig. 4. Screenshot of the current version Climate Twins Viewer 3 beta

Each click on a location in the interactive map triggers a database query and array comparison of future with current climate indicators from the selected grid cell related to the respective municipality. The comparison results of the query are stored in a 2nd map view of the database, displayed in the application's second window.

4 Summary and Outlook

This paper showed the advanced matching method of Climate Twins v3 to identify locations or regions with similar climate conditions. By applying a similarity measure and configuring it for a use on interval and ratio scaled data, it was possible to build this prototype with a completely new matching method. The main advantages of this method is its scalability towards adding any number of further climate indicators and the representation of similarity's spatial fuzziness. The definition and quantification of similarity thresholds still is a challenge and not solved, yet.

The current Climate Twins application's climate data is based on the "business as usual" green house gas (GHG) increase scenario IS92b [1]. For the future, a set of climate scenarios of different GHG increase rates will be applied in order to show the "movement" of the Climate Twins areas over Europe (to be expected in south and southeast direction) with respect to larger time steps into future climate.

Semantic web technologies (developed in the EU FP7 project TaToo) may allow direct access to web sites related to Climate Twins areas in order to identify adaptation measures to cope better with further climate conditions.

References

1. IPCC. Climate Change 2007: The Physical Science Basis. Final Report Working Group 1, Intergovernmental Panel on Climate Change, Assessment Report 4, Geneva, Swiss (2007),
   http://ipcc-wg1.ucar.edu/wg1/Report/AR4WG1_Print_SPM.pdf
2. Lautenschlager, M., Keuler, K., Wunram, C., Keup-Thiel, E., Schubert, M., Will, A., Rockel, B., Boehm, U.: Climate simulation with CLM, scenario A1B run no.1, data stream 3: European region MPI-M/MaD (2009)
3. Loibl, W., Beck, A., Dorninger, M., Formayer, H., Gobiet, A., Schner, W. (eds.) reclip:more - research for climate protection: model run, evaluation, Executive summary, ARCsys, Vienna (2009),
   http://systemsresearch.ac.at/projects/climate
4. Roeckner, E., et al.: The Atmospheric General Circulation Model ECHAM5. Part 1: Model Description, Report 349, Max Planck Institute for Meteorology (MPI), Hamburg (2003)
5. Ungar, J.: A Comparative Analysis of Region Pairs Matching Current and Future Climate Conditions. Diploma Thesis, University of Vienna, Department for Geography and Regional Research, Vienna (2011)
6. Vegelius, J., Janson, S., Johansson, F.: Measures of similarity between distributions. Quality and Quantity 20(4), 437–441 (1986)

7. Climate Twins Viewer 3, http://foresight.ait.ac.at/projects/climatetwins3
8. Flamingo Mapcomponents, http://www.flamingo-mc.org
9. PostGIS, http://postgis.refractions.net
10. PostGreSQL, http://www.postgresql.org
11. UMN Mapserver, http://mapserver.org

Semantic Wiki in Environmental Project Management

Jakub Talaš, Tomáš Gregar, and Tomáš Pitner

Masaryk University, Faculty of Informatics,
Research Lab Software Architectures and Information Systems
Botanická 68a, 60200 Brno, Czech Republic
173016@mail.muni.cz, {xgregar,tomp}@fi.muni.cz
http://lasaris.fi.muni.cz

Abstract. Advanced management of environmental data requires appropriate metadata and tooling. Moreover, contemporary environmental data is heterogenous, encompassing also data about people, environmentaly-related projects, and documents. Also geographical- and time-related information are vital for any environmental data and should be supported. To satisfy these requirements, "semantic wikis" represent suitable tools but usually requiring knowledge management skills. In this paper, we present a semantic extension to project-management tool Trac, enabling advanced but user-friendly querying in semantic data stored in the system and its visualization. As it builds upon the general concept of RDF-based semantic data, it can be freely extended into other contexts and deployed in various environmental management applications. We also discuss automatic formal visualization of semantic data. Such process significantly lowers the requirements on users in preparing the visualization in domains like environmental studies – and also helps to build *Linked Data*-aware and better human-readable interfaces of semantic data repositories.

Keywords: environmental project management, semantic wiki, RDF.

1   Semantic wiki in Real Project Management

Since many (if not a majority) of modern systems for computer-aided environmental project management require not only the baseline, generic functionality and collaborative content creation but also its sharing and publication. The idea of Semantic Web builds upon the assumption that the data should be accessible, reusable and even re-purposable. So they should be accompanied by rich metadata sets based on standardized (or commonly-agreed) ontologies wherever applicable. However, their key users are usually not experts in knowledge management, they are not capable of operating advanced semantic tools like ontology editors. They like to work with really simple tools, editing a wiki is the most "technical" activity that can be expected in this terms. On the other hand, we might need at least some support of complex functionality like semantic querying. It enables to automatically present selected data about projects, people,

J. Hřebíček, G. Schimak, and R. Denzer (Eds.): ISESS 2011, IFIP AICT 359, pp. 437–444, 2011.

their participation and progress on wiki pages. The wiki is no more a tool for fast collaborative creation of static textual content by end-users and starts to be a powerful instrument to present anything stored in a *semantic repository*.

In an environment targeted to *software projects*, these requirements are even amplified, cf.[1]. The members of a project team must share a common environment, see all relevant analytical documents, and contribute to discussions with the clients. All these activities intensively deal with content. For instant content creation, wiki systems became a de-facto "golden standard" as a mean to share, present and exchange information, and are present in nearly all project hosting and management platforms such as Sourceforge.net, Google Code, Codeplex.com, or github.org, among others. They are less demanding than online office-like suites like *Google Docs* though they still allow user to create and edit web content without a need to know languages like HTML/CSS or to have physical access to the web server.

There exist many implementations of such interface, based on different languages and storage databases[1] — like *MediaWiki* (PHP and MySQL), *Dokuwiki* (PHP), *Twiki* (Perl) etc. An integrated Wiki is also an inevitable part of the (installed) open-source project management system *Trac*[2] being used by many open-source projects as referred later.

2   Semantic Support in Existing wiki Systems

However, the vast majority of systems run without support for semantics. Only few wikis are built with semantic capabilities [2]. Most of current semantic wiki engines are developed in academic environment. Such conditions bring some advantages (they are almost all open source and freely distributed), as well as some drawbacks (lots of them is currently abandoned, not developed at all; sometimes, they even do not ever reach a usable milestone)[3]. Existing semantic wikis can stand as the functionality model. Actively developed semantic wikis are in alphabetical order:

ACE wiki works with an interesting concept of syntax definition in natural language (definitions like "every country is an area"). It is easy and well-arranged wiki with wide capabilities in building the semantics. The statements are checked for potential semantic collisions like *"Country has one capital"* vs. *"The capital of Germany is Berlin"* and *"The capital of Germany is Bonn"*.

KiWi stands for *Knowledge In Wiki*. This system is intended for sharing and managing the knowledge.

KnowWE this system has a technique for annotating content of wiki pages similar to techniques used in our developed *Trac Semantic Extension*. It also recommends pages with semantically related topics or topics with similar

---

[1] http://www.wiki.org/wiki.cgi?WhatIsWiki
[2] http://trac.edgewall.org/
[3] http://semanticweb.org/wiki/Tools

attributes. It features an easy-to-use semantic search functionality ("Select sports where Flexibility = spontanious").

OntoWiki very advanced and user friendly wiki-engine.

Semantic MediaWiki is an extension of the popular *MediaWiki*. It adds possibility to add properties to pages and semantic searching.

TaOPis easy wiki system for project and contributors' listing.

Wikidsmart communicates with project management system *Jira*. Wiki authoring can create bug/feature/feature document in Jira (or other connected management system).

3   Projects Presentation in a Broader Context

Typically, a particular environmental project is a part of a broader activity, being led by a public body (agency, office), an academic institution, or a commercial subject. So, relationships to other activities should be taken into account. In order to satisfy this aspect, an appropriate project management tool has to be found and deployed. Another important factor determining the selection of a right project management system are its semantic capabilities related to project management tasks [3]. The system selected to satisfy these needs, *Trac*, includes an integrated wiki for project presentation, allows synchronization with a Subversion repository, contains modules for bug tracking and issue reporting, a module for browsing the source code, and the like. It can be enhanced with the support of multiple projects and localization which is still vital, particularly in the highly international context.

Our experimental installation implemented in the research lab of the authors is called *Deep Thought* (DT), cf. [4]. A fundamental advantage of Trac/Deep Thought is a wide support for extensions. Trac is based on the *Python component architecture* — a basic module, and also each plug-in are components distributed as .egg packages. There exist two types of extensions — *plugins* and *macros*. Plugins can, thanks to their low-level interface to other Trac modules, extend whole system functionality. Macros are direct components of the Trac wiki-subsystem. They allow to dynamize wiki pages.

4   Semantic Extension in the wiki

4.1   Key Requirements

The key ideas how to combine the wiki ease of use with semantic information are:

1. Connect the wiki with a semantic repository containing info on categories like projects, people, or documents.
2. Provide instruments to easily annotate/link the wiki content with references to pieces of semantic information from the repository.
3. Offer enhancements to insert even complex semantic queries into wiki pages in order to dynamize the content.

Fig. 1. Popups with semantic information from the wiki

4. Facilitate the querying with visual appliances like context-aware drop-down menus and stored queries for repeating tasks.

Our recent project, *Semex* (Semantic extension) experimentally implements the above ideas, see also [5]. Semex allows annotations of wiki content according to ontological definitions in the knowledge database *Sesame 2*. It also enables visual highlighting of the tagged parts of text and viewing their context. This added functionality brings the possibility of browsing pages via semantic relations; e.g. *person* — his/her *projects*; or *"show all people contributing to this project, who are older than 18 years"*. It can integrate the content with other services (e-mail), mine concept definitions from the repository or other web-service, or list other instances of the same concept [6]. It is composed of a Trac plugin assuring the administrative functions and communication with the knowledge repository and a set of wiki macros. Macros visualize semantic data instantly on the wiki pages and interact with the users; they are capable to wrap the authoring of semantic statements directly in the user interface, cf. Fig. 1.

4.2 Technology

As the Trac environment is Python-based, the extensions must also satisfy its non-functional requirements: at least to be written in Python. There exists library *RDFLib*[4] for work with RDF triples (i.e. inner representation of sources, statements, relations, ontologies) in Python. Python interface with Sesame 2 (via its REST protocol interface) could be offered by *RDF Alchemy*[5]; Sesame is just one of triple-stores the library can communicate with.

The important part of the Semex development was also the selection – to prevent reinventing the wheel – of prepared ontologies (see [7]) to work with. DT, as multi-project management system cope with information about persons (foaf, http://xmlns.com/foaf/0.1/, see [8]), projects (doap, http://usefulinc.com/ns/doap#, see [9]), documents (dc, http://purl.org/dc/elements/1.1/), wiki pages (wiki, http://sw.deri.org/2005/04/wikipedia/wikiont.owl#), in project management also with temporal events (event, http://purl.org/NET/c4dm/event.owl#), or places (geo, http://www.w3.org/2003/01/geo/wgs84_pos#). This ontological structure allows describing semantics of the wiki documents — define developers, deadlines, meetings, used literature etc. A very important feature of our approach is *generality* and *universality*. The ontologies used in the system can be extended, replaced, or combined with others which enables seamless employment of environmental ontologies like [10] as well together with the more general ones.

4.3 Functionality

The solution covers all basic use-cases required for a computer-aided project management and presentation using wiki. The administrative section allows creating, editing and deleting persons, projects, events, places and documents via a form-based web interface. The module also automatically creates wiki pages for the respective objects — names of these wiki pages start with prefix Semex:, therefore they are easy recognizable and can be quickly deleted in the administrative section. In the prototype, access to the sections is authenticated and authorized via *Kerberos* and the users can use their Faculty accounts credentials and do not have to bother with maintaining separate access data, namely passwords.

Wiki macros are the "visible" part of the module, cf. Fig. 2. A common visitor of Deep Thought sees only them. General Trac macros could be written in wiki page as short tag enclosed in doubled square brackets (with optional parameters in parentheses).

The following "bootstrap" macros have been developed for Semex so far:

Info it shows popup menu with options and information about selected object. It also allows user to see all statements of this object.

Query returns a list of RDF sources according to entered SPARQL query. Suitable for automatic lists.

Calendar prints out simple calendar with upcoming events.

Allabout prints out all information about a source and similar ones.

---

[4] http://www.rdflib.net/

[5] http://www.openvest.com/trac/wiki/RDFAlchemy

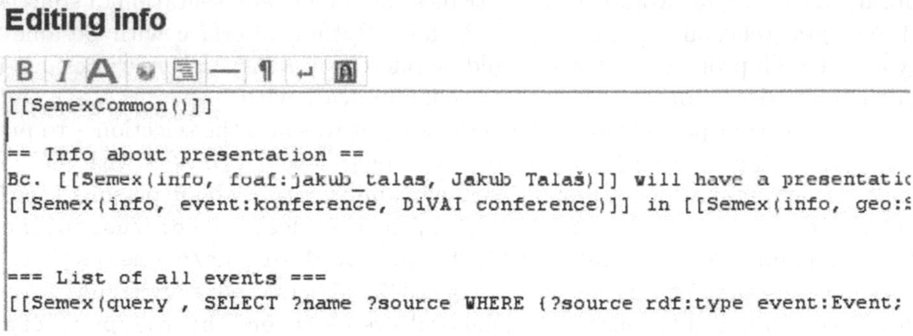

Editing info

```
B  I  A  ⬦  ▤ — ¶  ↵  ▣
[[SemexCommon()]]

== Info about presentation ==
Bc. [[Semex(info, foaf:jakub_talas, Jakub Talaš)]] will have a presentatic
[[Semex(info, event:konference, DiVAI conference)]] in [[Semex(info, geo:£


=== List of all events ===
[[Semex(query , SELECT ?name ?source WHERE {?source rdf:type event:Event;
```

Fig. 2. Writing complex queries in wiki

SemexCommon this macro is the prerequisition for other semantic macros (includes semantic methods, defines GUI forms used in macros), and hence has to be included in every wiki page.

The GUI of macros is created via the *jQuery 1.3* library. It creates popup menus, and also user-centered simple wizards helping common user to incorporate macros which makes them accessible even for users with only a minimal notion of the formal semantic. However, the semantics in the wiki can be explored to its full power using queries in fully-fledged languages like *SPARQL*, as depicted on the last figure.

5   System Integration

One of the usage patterns of the semantically enhanced project management system Deep Though is the university teaching. Choosing the right pattern of integration into the whole study process and administration is crucial, it was necessary to integrate the extension module and the whole system with the *University's study administration information system* (IS) in order to ensure smooth application in software development oriented courses. Students in these courses have to *build a team*, sign up for some *project assignment* and then *work on it*. This integration allows to get needed data from the IS, automatically create an environment for student projects defined in IS containing basic wiki pages, bug-tracker module, or source-code browser. Metadata about project is also imported into the semantic repository and utilized via the semantic module of Deep Thought.

The most visible features and contributions of this semantically-enhanced project management system in comparison with tradition PM systems is a common knowledge base consisting of concepts (entities) maintained centrally and reusable in all projects wherever it is relevant, see Fig. 3. A clear advantage of this approach is in its flexibility — once the DOAP ontology schema is replaced by a newer standard for project description, the transition will be significantly

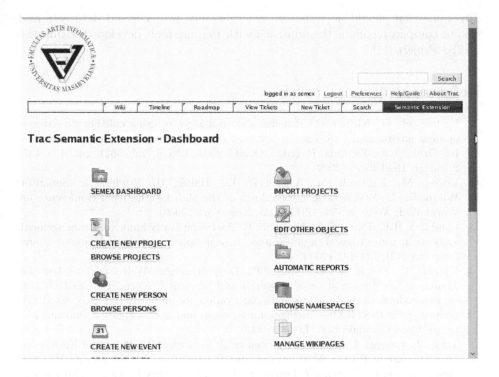

Fig. 3. Entities common for all projects in Deep Though

easier that in a classical database system where the relational or object/class schema must be modified — with all the undesired consequences it might have.

6 Conclusion and Further Work

Let us summarize the achievements reached so far. The key requirements showed to be realistic and implementable. The presented semantic extension to a project management tool Trac has proven as a working combination of

- Advanced, popular project management system for hosting public-, community-, or internal projects including commercial ones;
- Integrated semantic repository containing semantically precise and well-treatable data about environmental projects, people, places, events, and documents that represent a substantial part of all data typically processed;
- Tools for advanced semantic querying and dynamic wiki content;
- Visualization facility to user-centered query formulation and content browsing.

So, all the main ideas have resulted in a succesfully implemented working prototype. Further development will include both general and domain-specific directions that should be tested on a larger-scale projects and data sets and also to compare/combine the approach with tagging tools developed within the *TaToo Project* [11].

References

1. Kadenbach, D., Kleiner, C.: Benefits and challenges of using collaborative development environments with social software in higher computer science education. In: Ozok, A.A., Zaphiris, P. (eds.) OCSC 2009. LNCS, vol. 5621, pp. 479–487. Springer, Heidelberg (2009)
2. Völkel, M., Krötzsch, M., Vrandecic, D., Haller, H., Studer, R.: Semantic Wikipedia. In: WWW 2006: Proceedings of the 15th International Conference on World Wide Web, pp. 585–594. ACM, New York (2006)
3. Landaeta, R.E., Pinto, C.A., Kotnour, T.: Assessing faulty knowledge management systems in project-based organisations. International Journal of Knowledge and Learning 5(2), 122–143 (2009)
4. Gregar, T., Pospilová, R., Pitner, T.: Deep Thought: Web based System for Managing and Presentation of Research and Student Projects. In: CSEDU 2009 — Proceedings of the first International Conference on Computer Supported Education, p. 5. INSTICC — Institute for Systems and Technologies of Information, Control and Comunication, Lisboa (2009)
5. Talaš, J., Gregar, T., Pitner, T.: Semantically Enriched Tools for the Knowledge Society: Case of Project Management and Presentation. In: Knowledge Management, Information Systems, E-Learning, and Sustainability Research. Third World Summit on the Knowledge Society, Springer, Heidelberg (2010)
6. Geurts, J., et al.: Towards Ontology-driven Discourse: From Semantic Graphs to Multimedia Presentations. In: 2nd International Semantic Web Conference, Sundial Resort, Sanibel Island, Florida, USA, vol. 1, p. 16 (2003)
7. Gómez-Pérez, A., Corcho, O.: Ontology Languages for the Semantic Web. IEEE Inteligent Systems 17, 54–60 (2002)
8. Brickley, D., Miller, L.: FOAF vocabulary specification (2007), http://xmlns.com/foaf/spec/
9. Dumbill, E.: Description of a Project (DOAP) (2004), http://trac.usefulinc.com/doap
10. Morrison, N.: The Environment Ontology – Linking Environmental Data. In: Proceedings of the Towards the eEnvironment, Prague, Czech Republic (2009)
11. Rizzoli, A.E., Schimak, G., Donatelli, M., Hřebíček, J., Avellino, G., Mon, J.L., et al.: TaToo: tagging environmental resources on the web by semantic annotations. In: Proceedings of the International Congress on Environmental Modelling and Software Modelling for Environments Sake (2010)

The Relevance of Measurement Data in Environmental Ontology Learning

Markus Stocker[1], Mauno Rönkkö[1],
Ferdinando Villa[2], and Mikko Kolehmainen[1]

[1] University of Eastern Finland,
P.O. Box 1627, Kuopio, Finland
{markus.stocker,mauno.ronkko,mikko.kolehmainen}@uef.fi
[2] Basque Centre for Climate Change [BC3],
Alameda Urquijo 4-4, 48008 Bilbao, Spain
ferdinando.villa@bc3research.org

Abstract. Ontology has become increasingly important to software systems. The aim of ontology learning is to ease one of the major problems in ontology engineering, i.e. the cost of ontology construction. Much of the effort within the ontology learning community has focused on learning from text collections. However, environmental domains often deal with numerical measurement data and, therefore, rely on methods and tools for learning beyond text. We discuss this characteristic using two relations of an ontology for lakes. Specifically, we learn a threshold value from numerical measurement data for ontological rules that classify lakes according to nutrient status. We describe our methodology, highlight the cyclical interaction between data mining and ontologies, and note that the numerical value for lake nutrient status is specific to a spatial and temporal context. The use case suggests that learning from numerical measurement data is a research area relevant to environmental software systems.

Keywords: Ontology, learning, rule-based reasoning, environmental data.

1 Introduction

Ontology, defined as an explicit specification of a conceptualization [4], is a means to formally represent knowledge of a domain, meaning the concepts of some area of interest and relations that hold among them. Domains such as bioinformatics have used ontologies for over a decade [2,1]. More recently ontologies have found applications in ecoinformatics [17] and environmental modelling [16]. With the development of ontologies it became clear that one of the major problems in ontology engineering is the often labour-intensive and time-consuming construction [19]. Therefore, efforts have been on-going to automate the ontology acquisition, construction and maintenance processes [13].

Much of the effort within the ontology learning community has focused on learning from text collections, lexical databases, structural data, and usage data

J. Hřebíček, G. Schimak, and R. Denzer (Eds.): ISESS 2011, IFIP AICT 359, pp. 445–453, 2011.
© IFIP International Federation for Information Processing 2011

[19]. To the best of our knowledge, the state of the art in ontology learning mainly consists of several methods and tools to learn text entities such as words, concepts, relations, and noun hierarchies using machine learning and natural language processing [19,13]. Learning beyond text is an open issue [19].

We investigate *environmental* ontology learning. Specifically, for the rule $p \rightarrow q$, meaning the implication between the antecedent p and the consequent q, we demonstrate the learning of a data value for an atom of p from sets of tuples with *numerical* elements obtained by measurement. Measurement is taken here to be the "process of empirical, objective assignment of numbers to the properties of objects and events of the real world in such a way as to describe them" [14].

Measurement is fundamental to environmental science: hence the relevance of numerical measurement data in environmental ontology learning. In environmental informatics, computational methods developed within disciplines such as data mining, machine learning and pattern recognition are routinely used to learn from data obtained by measurement, e.g. a linear regression model to forecast ambient ozone concentration. We demonstrate the application of such methods to environmental ontology learning. Further, we show that ontological knowledge can serve as a heuristic to guide the parametrization of data mining algorithms. Hence, we highlight an example of a data mining with ontology cycle [11] whereby ontological knowledge is used in data mining and the knowledge discovered from the resulting models is formalized and added to the ontology.

2   Materials and Methods

The environmental ontology used here is based on a taxonomy of lakes [18]. According to the trophic system for the classification of lakes, there are three main types of lakes, i.e. oligotrophic, eutrophic and heterotrophic [10,15]. Several modifications have been proposed to this basic classification to account for our increased understanding of the lake ecosystem. The taxonomy of lakes adopted here extends the basic trophic system in that it evolves the naming convention to include the physico-chemical nature of water, the climatic zone, the type of lake basin, and the dominant class of organisms [18].

For the purpose here, we focus our attention on two properties for the physico-chemical nature of water, specifically the two ontology relations `richIn` and `poorIn` for the nutrient status of a lake with respect to nitrogen, phosphorus, and humus. Naturally, the question arises what being rich and poor in a nutrient for a lake exactly means and, thus, how to tell a lake is rich or poor in a given nutrient. We can refine the two relations with the suitable ranges for the concentrations [18].

In our implementation, we define two rules and use rule-based reasoning to infer the knowledge on whether an individual lake is rich or poor in a nutrient, more accurately the nutrient status as measured by an individual lake monitoring station. Specifically, we consider the mean annual total nitrogen concentration. Thus, we learn the data (threshold) value `?y` of the atoms `lessThanOrEqual(?x, ?y)` and `greaterThan(?x, ?y)` for the rules

$$\text{totalNitrogen(?i, ?x)} \land \text{lessThanOrEqual(?x, ?y)}$$
$$\rightarrow \text{poorIn(?i, Nitrogen)}$$

$$\text{totalNitrogen(?i, ?x)} \land \text{greaterThan(?x, ?y)}$$
$$\rightarrow \text{richIn(?i, Nitrogen)}$$

where ?i, ?x, ?y are variables. Informally, the rules state that an individual (lake monitoring station) ?i with measured total nitrogen concentration ?x $\leq$?y is poorIn nitrogen. Conversely, an individual ?i with measured total nitrogen concentration ?x > ?y is richIn nitrogen. The rules are encoded in Jena[1] [3] (version 2.6.4) and the Jena general purpose rule engine is used for rule-based reasoning. Jena is a Java framework for building Semantic Web [7] applications.

Our aim is to learn the threshold value ?y. For this purpose we use the k-means clustering algorithm [8] as implemented in WEKA[2] [5] (version 3.6.4) using data on the nutrient concentration of European lakes[3] (version 10) compiled by the European Environmental Agency (EEA). The two ontological relations poorIn and richIn suggest a binary classification of lakes with respect to nutrient status. This knowledge is used as a heuristic for the number of k-means clusters. Thus, we perform k-means clustering such that the unsupervised algorithm learns *two* centroids for the two-cluster separation of data on the mean annual total nitrogen concentration of lakes, typically for the lakes of a specific country as measured for a year. The values of the resulting k-means centroids represent a central tendency for the value of a lake poorIn and richIn, respectively. We define the threshold value ?y to be the mean value for the two centroids. This modelling result is added as new knowledge to the ontology, specifically as knowledge about the two rules. Given an ontology for individual lakes we can, hence, use rule-based reasoning to infer new knowledge on lakes that are poorIn and those that are richIn nitrogen. Note that the choice of the mean for the two centroids as threshold value is for simplicity and may not be the most sensible as it may fall into one of the two clusters. Naturally, a different computation may be used.

For better data handling, we imported the EEA datasets for lake monitoring stations (3201 records) and for nutrients and organic matter in water (mean annual concentration for both total nitrogen and total phosphorus, 30866 records) into a PostgreSQL[4] database. We use the Resource Description Framework[5] (RDF) [9] language to represent information about lake monitoring stations, in particular the corresponding lake name and the measured mean annual total nitrogen concentration. The Jena general purpose rule engine, customized with the learned rules, is used for rule-based reasoning. The SPARQL[6] [12] query language for RDF is used to query the resulting inference model for lakes richIn and lakes poorIn nitrogen.

---

[1] http://jena.sourceforge.net/
[2] http://www.cs.waikato.ac.nz/ml/weka/
[3] http://www.eea.europa.eu/data-and-maps/data/waterbase-lakes-6
[4] http://www.postgresql.org/
[5] http://www.w3.org/TR/rdf-primer/
[6] http://www.w3.org/TR/rdf-sparql-query/

Table 1. Centroid values (mg L^{-1}), threshold values ?y (mg L^{-1}) and number of lake monitoring stations for lakes `poorIn` and `richIn` mean annual nitrogen concentration for 7 European countries in 2008

Country	poorIn		richIn		
	Centroid	# stations	Centroid	# stations	?y
Denmark	0.57	15	1.52	4	1.04
Finland	0.39	150	0.88	53	0.63
Germany	0.72	24	3.84	4	2.28
Great Britain	0.36	53	4.51	3	2.43
Italy	0.82	127	2.46	9	1.64
Spain	0.78	137	8.36	12	4.57
Switzerland	0.66	6	1.76	4	1.20

3   Results

We learn the threshold value ?y for the `poorIn` and `richIn` rules for the mean annual total nitrogen concentration (mg L^{-1}) as measured by 203 lake monitoring stations for Finnish lakes in 2008. There are a total of 203 measurements. The values of the two centroids as learned by WEKA using k-means are 0.39 and 0.88. They represent the central tendency for the value of `poorIn` and `richIn` mean annual nitrogen concentration for Finnish lakes in 2008, respectively. Thus, the threshold value ?y is 0.63. SPARQL queries on a corresponding inference model return 150 lake monitoring stations for lakes `poorIn` and 53 `richIn` total nitrogen.

We perform a similar experiment for the threshold value for the mean annual nitrogen concentration as measured by 149 lake monitoring stations for Spanish lakes in 2008. There are a total of 149 measurements. The values of the two centroids are 0.78 and 8.36 for `poorIn` and `richIn`, respectively. Thus, the threshold value ?y is 4.57. For Spain in 2008, there are 137 lake monitoring stations for lakes `poorIn` and 12 `richIn` total nitrogen.

Table 1 summarizes the central tendency for the value of a lake `poorIn` and `richIn` mean annual total nitrogen concentration for 7 European countries, in 2008. We also add the threshold value ?y used in the corresponding rules. Further, the table shows the number of lake monitoring stations of lakes `poorIn` and lakes `richIn` total nitrogen. As the table highlights, the value of a lake `poorIn` and `richIn` total nitrogen greatly varies between countries. In fact, for the listed countries the mean and standard deviation of the two centroids are 0.61 ± 0.18 and 3.33 ± 2.56, respectively.

Next, we analyse the variation of the value of a lake poor and rich in a nutrient over time. Table 2 summarizes the centroid mean and standard deviation for the central tendency and variation over time for lakes `poorIn` and `richIn` mean annual total nitrogen concentration for 7 European countries. For instance, for Finland Table 2 shows the mean and standard deviation for the centroids corresponding to `poorIn` (0.41 ± 0.02) and `richIn` (0.95 ± 0.14), for 33 years between 1976 and 2008. Figure 1 shows the variation for Finland over 33 years between

Table 2. Centroid mean and standard deviation ($mg\,L^{-1}$) for lakes `poorIn` and `richIn` mean annual nitrogen concentration on data for the total number of years for 7 European countries. The table includes the number of years and the first year for which data is available for each country. The last year is 2008. Note that not all countries have data for all years.

Country	# years	First	Centroid mean	
			poorIn	richIn
Denmark	20	1989	0.65 ± 0.09	1.71 ± 0.36
Finland	33	1976	0.41 ± 0.02	0.95 ± 0.14
Germany	17	1991	0.69 ± 0.64	2.28 ± 1.91
Great Britain	14	1995	0.62 ± 0.24	3.87 ± 1.37
Italy	6	2003	0.53 ± 0.13	3.21 ± 3.88
Spain	1	2008	0.78 ± 0.00	8.36 ± 0.00
Switzerland	16	1993	0.78 ± 0.14	2.10 ± 0.48

1976 and 2008. As expected from Table 2, there is considerable variation, in particular for the value of a lake `richIn` total nitrogen, for Finnish lakes over the time period.

4 Discussion

Given the rule $p \rightarrow q$, the main aim of this paper is to demonstrate the learning of a data value for an atom of the antecedent p from sets of tuples with *numerical* elements obtained by measurement. We have shown this using an environmental ontology for a taxonomy of lakes with the mean annual total nitrogen concentration, as measured by lake monitoring stations. We learned a threshold value for lakes poor and rich in total nitrogen as the data value for an atom of p. Given p with the rule atom `totalNitrogen(?i, ?x)` for the total nitrogen as measured by a lake monitoring station and the inequality rule atom, e.g. `lessThanOrEqual(?x, ?y)`, with the learned threshold value ?y, we can apply rule-based reasoning to infer new knowledge on the two consequent q, `poorIn` and `richIn`. Hence, we demonstrate the relevance of numerical measurement data in environmental ontology learning.

Further, we have used ontological knowledge about the two-classes separation of lakes with respect to nutrient status as a heuristic to guide k-means in learning the centroids of the two classes. Thus, we describe an example of a cyclical interaction between data mining and ontologies [11].

Our results show that whether a lake is poor (or rich) in total nitrogen is dependent on spatial context. As summarized in Table 1, the value for a lake poor or rich in total nitrogen clearly varies between countries. For instance, the central tendency of a Finnish lake rich in total nitrogen (0.88) is closer to the central tendency of a Spanish lake *poor* in total nitrogen (0.78) than to a Spanish lake rich in total nitrogen (8.36). Given the Finnish threshold value (0.63) for a Spanish lake with a mean annual total nitrogen concentration of $2.0\,mg\,L^{-1}$

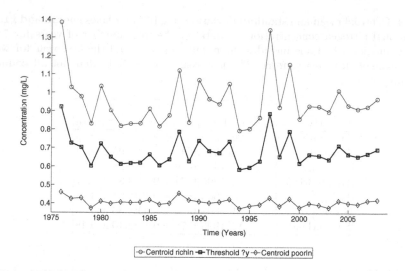

Fig. 1. Centroid values as central tendencies for lakes `poorIn` and `richIn` mean annual total nitrogen concentration and threshold value `?y` for Finland over 33 years between 1976 and 2008

a rule-based reasoner would wrongly classify the Spanish lake as rich in total nitrogen.

Similarly, the results show that whether a lake is poor (or rich) in total nitrogen is dependent on temporal context. As summarized in Table 2, in particular by standard deviation, and shown in Figure 1, the value for a lake poor or rich in total nitrogen clearly varies over time. Thus, the threshold value for Finnish lakes for the year 1994 (0.58) is considerably different from the threshold value for the year 1997 (0.89).

Hence, environmental ontologies may be specific to spatial and temporal contexts. While this is unlikely to surprise the limnologist, we argue that environmental ontologies should reflect such spatial and temporal variation, and environmental ontology learning may provide methods and tools to automatically adapt ontologies to spatial and temporal context using appropriate measurement data.

Moreover, the spatial and temporal variability raises the question why the value of a lake rich in nitrogen is significantly different between, say, Finland and Spain. Ontologies may provide a foundation for explanation services, in particular if ontological knowledge about the sources of nitrogen for lakes is available. For instance, a service may conclude that the spatial variability is (partially) explained by a different application of inorganic nitrogen fertilizers, properties of soil surrounding lakes that may affect the leaching of nitrogen, nitrogen fixation by cyanobacteria, or atmospheric deposition of nitrogen.

The use case discussed here is relatively straightforward, in particular with respect to the method used to learn the central tendency for the value of a lake poor or rich in a nutrient. While other clustering algorithms may be used for our aim of learning a threshold value, the chosen method reflects the rather simple, univariate, data. We may think of a use case whereby a decision tree for multivariate data is used to learn ontological rules, or to learn datatype restrictions for axioms of a knowledge base,[7] or to couple a trained neural network with an ontology, to classify a lake. Moreover, data-driven methods may help to uncover altogether new ontological classes or relations. For instance, cluster analysis may identify a set of lake classes different from that of the basic, or more advanced, trophic system and, therefore, affect the knowledge encoded in a corresponding ontology more profoundly.

Some of the techniques presented in this paper have been suggested elsewhere. Henson *et al.* [6] use a rule for high winds that states that a wind observation measurement greater or equal to 35 miles per hour is considered to be a high winds observation. Similarly to our example for the nutrient concentration of a lake, the authors use the rule for wind speed to infer new knowledge on high winds observations. Contrary to their example on wind, where the speed is known a priori, in our example we learn the meaning of richIn (and poorIn) from lake measurement data, i.e. from measurement of properties of real-world objects that exist in the domain modelled by the ontology.

5   Conclusions

We aimed at demonstrating the learning of ontological rules using numerical measurement data and clustering methods, specifically for an environmental ontology of lakes using k-means and the mean annual concentration of total nitrogen as measured by lake monitoring stations. Given the learned rules, we applied rule-based reasoning to infer new knowledge on the nutrient status of lakes. We described an example that shows the relevance of numerical measurement data in environmental ontology learning and the interaction between data mining and ontology engineering. The results of our experiments using the presented methodology on data for the lakes of a number of European countries highlight the expected spatial and temporal dependency of the numerical meaning of lake nutrient status, a characteristic that may justify further attention in the field of environmental ontology learning.

In our future work, we intend to develop a software prototype that implements the core ideas of the methodology presented in this paper. In particular, we envision the development of an ontology to describe learning tasks for the software to perform. Such an ontology may integrate the source and description of numerical data, the target ontology and what ought to be learned about it, as well as the method used for learning. We think such a software may support the learning of more complex environmental ontologies and, ultimately, lead to methodological generalizations.

---

[7] For instance, we may learn the interval for the basic ratio [18] datatype restriction basicRatio some double[>= 0.0, < 1.2] which is a property restriction in the terminological axiom that defines the ontological concept of *eutrophic lake*.

Acknowledgements. We wish to thank Dr. Eila Torvinen, Ph.D., university researcher in the Environmental Microbiology Research Group at the University of Eastern Finland, and Dr. Bijan Parsia, lecturer in the School of Computer Science at the University of Manchester (UK), for their expertise, critique, and suggestions in numerous discussions. Further, we wish to thank the European Environmental Agency for providing open access to data, a service without which this work would not have been possible.

References

1. Ashburner, M., Ball, C., Blake, J., Botstein, D., Butler, H., Cherry, J., Davis, A., Dolinski, K., Dwight, S., Eppig, J., Harris, M., Hill, D., Issel-Tarver, L., Kasarskis, A., Lewis, S., Matese, J., Richardson, J., Ringwald, M., Rubin, G., Sherlock, G.: Gene ontology: Tool for the unification of biology. Nature Genetics 25(1), 25–29 (2000)
2. Boeckmann, B., Bairoch, A., Apweiler, R., Blatter, M.C., Estreicher, A., Gasteiger, E., Martin, M., Michoud, K., O'Donovan, C., Phan, I., Pilbout, S., Schneider, M.: The Swiss-Prot Protein Knowledgebase and its supplement TrEMBL. Nucleic Acids Res. 31, 365–370 (2003)
3. Carroll, J.J., Dickinson, I., Dollin, C., Reynolds, D., Seaborne, A., Wilkinson, K.: Jena: Implementing the Semantic Web Recommendations. Tech. Rep. HPL-2003-146, HP Laboratories, Bristol, UK (2003)
4. Gruber, T.: A translation approach to portable ontology specifications. Knowledge Acquisition 5(2), 199–220 (1993)
5. Hall, M., Frank, E., Holmes, G., Pfahringer, B., Reutemann, P., Witten, I.H.: The WEKA Data Mining Software: An Update. SIGKDD Explorations 11 (2009)
6. Henson, C.A., Pschorr, J.K., Sheth, A.P., Thirunarayan, K.: SemSOS: Semantic Sensor Observation Service. In: Proc. of the 2009 International Symposium on Collaborative Technologies and Systems (CTS 2009), Baltimore, MD (May 2009)
7. Lee, T., Hendler, J., Lassila, O.: The Semantic Web. Scientific American (2001)
8. MacQueen, J.: Some methods for classification and analysis of multivariate observations. In: Proceedings of 5th Berkeley Symposium on Mathematical Statistics and Probability, vol. 1, pp. 281–297. University of California Press (1967)
9. Manola, F., Miller, E.: RDF Primer. Tech. Rep. W3C Recommendation, W3C (2004)
10. Naumann, E.: Nagra synpunker angaende planktons okologi. Med sarskild hansyn till fytoplankton. Svensk Bot. Tidskr. 13, 129–158 (1919)
11. Nigro, H.O., Císaro, S.E.G., Xodo, D.H.: Data mining with ontologies: Implementations, findings, and frameworks. Information Science Reference (an imprint of IGI Global) (2008)
12. Prud'hommeaux, E., Seaborne, A.: SPARQL Query Language for RDF. Tech. Rep. W3C Recommendation, W3C (2008)
13. Shamsfard, M., Barforoush, A.: The state of the art in ontology learning: A framework for comparison. Knowledge Engineering Review 18(4), 293–316 (2003)
14. Sydenham, P.H.: Handbook of Measurement Science: Volume 1 Theoretical Fundamentals. John Wiley & Sons, Chichester (1982)
15. Thienemann, A.: Physikalische und chemische Untersuchungen in den Maaren der Eifel. Verh. Naturh. Ver. preuss. Rheinl. u. Westfalens 71, 281–389 (1915)

16. Villa, F., Athanasiadis, I., Rizzoli, A.: Modelling with knowledge: A review of emerging semantic approaches to environmental modelling. Environmental Modelling and Software 24(5), 577–587 (2009)
17. Williams, R., Martinez, N., Golbeck, J.: Ontologies for ecoinformatics. Web Semantics 4(4), 237–242 (2006)
18. Zafar, A.: Taxonomy of lakes. Hydrobiologia 13(3), 287–299 (1959)
19. Zhou, L.: Ontology learning: State of the art and open issues. Information Technology and Management 8(3), 241–252 (2007)

Using Semantic Search as a Means of Support for Research Projects

Michael Stencl, Oldrich Trenz, Ondřej Popelka, and Jiří Hřebíček

Mendel university in Brno, Faculty of Business and Economics,
Department of Informatics, Zemedelska 1, 613 00 Brno, Czech Republic
{michael.stencl,oldrich.trenz,
ondrej.popelka,jiri.hrebicek}@mendelu.cz
http://ui.pefka.mendelu.cz/en/gacr403

Abstract. The present contribution deals with analyzing the issue of semantic searching and the possibilities of its integration as a part of the portal for scientific projects support. The difficulties of integration of the semantic principles into the solution itself, the software support of the portal creation, i.e., solutions that are accessible, and possibilities of further development are discussed here. A part of the solution is the integration and support of XBRL documents being a fundamental part of inter-company communication and information exchange. Last but not least, the contribution discusses the possibilities of employing the principles of semantic searching in portal discussions which are treated on the levels of social networks, and the integration of these discussions as supporting the management of team projects.

Keywords: Searching, semantic search, XBRL, CMS, social networking.

1 Introduction

Semantic search and its principles is very often joined with the principles of semantic web and often also Web 2.0 [2], potentially Web 3.0 [5]. Garca-Crespo (2010) then clearly defines the Web 3.0 *"[. . .] as a new version of Web 2.0 in which web has advanced to become what Tim Berners-Lee (2007) has termed the Giant Global Grap."* Development of the Semantic research is connected with the basic needs of information, no data, in actual Web era/age. The amount of actual date accessible for free on the Internet is huge and to get the right information in the right time means to have advantage on all levels including business and research. Retrieving information from heterogeneous data stores give power to development or reincarnation of several machine-learning methods to use them in newly defined hybrid expert systems [6] and not only in experts systems. The Semantic Web its impacting traditional sciences, such as chemical, physical [2], sciences.

The Aim of the article consists in state-of-the-art analysis of semantic search applications as background for the Research project and integration of the Semantic search in the research project phases. The integration will be shown

J. Hřebíček, G. Schimak, and R. Denzer (Eds.): ISESS 2011, IFIP AICT 359, pp. 454–460, 2011.

on application of the approach in the Czech Science Foundation GACR project P403/11/1103 - Construction of Methods for Multi-factorial Assessment of Company Complex Performance in Selected Sectors. The Semantic Web[1] offers another communication channel for the research team at different phases of the project. Integration of the Semantic Search, its tools and approaches aid to reliable re-use of data. It also has potential to bring more efficiency to the resources library productivity. Modern digital libraries offers huge amount of information, but the problem is data retrieval. An actual tool includes traditional browsing or keyword-based search strategies. However current approaches still results in enormous numbers of pages without affecting the right topic. This leads to time-consuming manual browsing/filtering while deciding which of the filtered data is relevant to the topic. The manual browsing hand-in-hand with the diversity of file format used in the resource data store has impact on productivity of retrieving the information and on used information system [7] too.

2   Materials and Methods

2.1   The Semantic Web and Web 2.0

The fundamental of the semantic web is searching based on the semantic analysis of source data. We are dealing here with amplifying the concept of web pages by supplementary metadata which describes the semantic information of websources; and this in such a way that the data are written in a form that can be machine-processed. The metadata subsequently contain a given vocabulary and enable the creation of an adequate relationship between concepts. For in the environment of the common web, it is not possible to establish a single descriptive language containing an established vocabulary (also bearing in mind the specialization of the concrete web), and for this reason we are at present witnessing an overlapping of several descriptive languages (Fig.1). In general, we can call this approach decentralized, i.e., it contains in its core all the areas of knowledge.

One competitor or even a successor to the semantic web is the web 2.0, or its successor web 3.0, which enables the centralized treatment of individual services, i.e., processing in one place. This approach greatly improves the capacities of unified administration and the unified application response. In view of the support of community networks and projects (semantic wiki, semantic blogging, semantic desktop), the web 2.0 is, at present, considered to be a suitable extension of the semantic web.

2.2   Semantic Searching and Search Engines

The search engines designed for the semantic and for the classical web are, on the highest application level, very similar i.e., the documents search, data mining from documents, identification of users requests, agents, sequencing and

---
[1] http://www.w3.org/2001/sw/

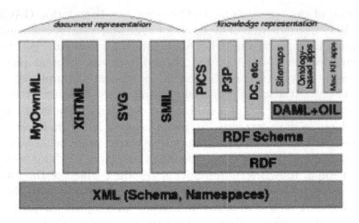

Fig. 1. Descriptive languages [8]

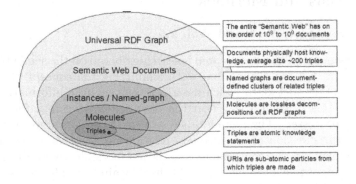

Fig. 2. Search machine [8]

storing results. There is a different configuration, however, on the level of the search core. Here, there is the support of the machine processing on the level of the marked content. If the data is stored using RDF, the support of effective indexing and searching is necessary. In a single document, there are more facts, knowledge and complementing metadata, and all this creates great requirements for the search machine this is shown in Fig.2. If we compare the search chart of the semantic web with the chart created from hypertext links of common web documents, at first glance the two charts are structurally very different. This fact greatly influences the strategy for acquiring and searching documents, and also influences the creation of metrics for their final allocation.

When searching, the search engine compares the identified users requests with the data which have appeared in the indexing already performed. The results of the search engines come as particularly composed documents which, as opposed to ordinary documents, can aggregate data on more levels, and this starting at the level of all RDF data located on the given web, all the way to individual RDF triplets.

3   Results

Good review of Semantic Web applications in, and not only in, digital libraries bring Garca-Crespo (2010). They comment several applications of Semantic Web that provides a complementary vision as a knowledge management environment. The typical research life cycle involves 4 phases:

1. **Planning**; defining the project, involving literature analysis, discussions with a range of experts, arranging funding and resources;
2. **Data preparation**; processing, collecting and describing data;
3. **Analysis**; commenting results, data access, data dissemination, preparation of the knowledge transfer and undertaking the necessary analysis, publications of results over the undertaken experiments;
4. **Research Outcomes**; publications of obtained results, generalizing of the results according to the methods used.

Semantic Web as a research tool could be used across all the phases. Our approach combines several technologies and tools to create qualitatively strong resources for several projects phases.

All the present projects have their own web presentation with basic information about the topic, research team, etc. Our project GACR P403/11/1103 is

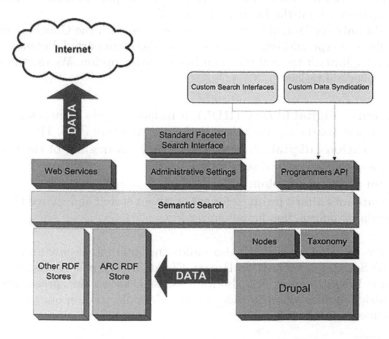

Fig. 3. Drupal Semantic Search module [4]

Table 1. Resource Digital Library (RDL) and Publications digital library (PDL) structure

PID	Authors	Year of Publication	Publisher	Citation (in text)	Key words	Source DBS	Processed by	DOI /URL

focused on the construction of methods for multifactor measurement of company performance in chosen economic (CZ-NACE) activities and the creation of a modifiable and broad-spectrum methodology of their putting into practice. Presently we are in the first phase, where the literature analysis takes place.

As a web project presentation tool we chose the Drupal CMS for the project team background. Outside the standard project annotation and description, Drupal includes the module for Web 3.0[2] that implements the Semantic Search architecture. The module logic of the Drupal is shown on Fig. 3. CMS Drupal uses an RDF store as a search index. The built in store is easy to use. Other RDF stores require Java and configuration. Also dynamically creates default search interfaces, for many searches per site, configurable via admin interfaces. [4] Other possibility to be used as search engine is the Yahoo! SearchMonkey Apps.

Yahoo! SearchMonkey share structured data with Yahoo! Search to display a standard enhanced result (available for certain content types) or the Search-Monkey developer tool could be used to extract data and build apps to display custom enhanced results. [9] For Drupal also speaks presentation of his creator, Dries Buytaert, about the Drupal solution. [3]

But not only the Drupal is involved. Is combined with the Google Docs tools, especially with spreadsheets. The selection where supported because of easy usage and it support the real time multi-user editing option. We use the spreadsheets for several tasks:

1. **Resource digital library (RDL)** it includes results of literature analysis of the state-of-the-art analysis with defined structure (Tab. 1);
2. **Publications digital library (PDL)** key information of the team own publication with defined structure;
3. **Team publication plan**;
4. **Documents share point** information about stored and shared documents containing information for/about project.

First two, the RDL and PDL, also builds the internal resource layer for the Semantic Search engine in CMS Drupal. Google Docs spreadsheets allow usage of standard SQL to query and also its possible to access the spreadsheets data from outside application. The Semantic Search application in our project could be described as on figure 4.

---

[2] http://semanticsearch.org/

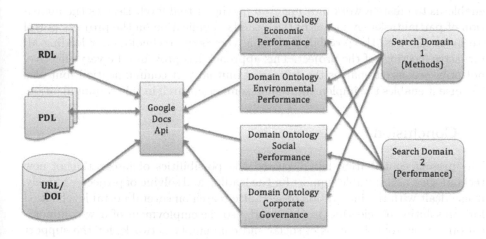

Fig. 4. Project Semantic Search with Google Docs

3.1 XBRL

The XBRL format (eXtensible Business Reporting Language) was chosen as s suitable means of information exchange and inter-company communication. It is a worldwide standard for the exchange of commercial information with the support of searching on the level of semantic meaning. An advantage of this standard is the possibility of its simple processing at the level of important world institutions in the state, as well as private sector. This fact is a necessary prerequisite for the integration into the company environment and the willingness to make use of this means of communication for inter-company data exchange.

In our case, the XBRL will be used for acquiring financial documents from individual monitored company subjects. Because the communication will be periodical, the chosen standardized framework appears to be a good choice. The acquired data will subsequently enable us to calculate the indicators describing the present situation of the company, and, based on historical connections, balance sheets about its future aims can be created. The integration will be done on the level of incorporation of the XBRL conversion module into the already existing system; a similar approach to database connection has been applied in the following source. [1]

3.2 Using the Social Communication Means as Support of the Project Solution

Regular meetings are necessary support for the project. The basis is not only the recapitulation of individual steps resolution, but also the coordination of subsequent steps inside each workgroup, because the individual participants are not always available temporally, as well as spatially (teaching, internships, vacations, etc.). It is therefore necessary to select a suitable framework that would enable us to create a work meeting even on the virtual level. Besides the allocation of partial tasks by means of the calendar application on the projects portal we have discussed the possibility of using the Skype technology for leading alternative meetings of the project. This approach has proven to be very effective, not only because it enables the storage of mutual text communication, but also because it enables the implementation of semantic search in this communication.

4 Conclusion

The present contribution has discussed the possibilities of integration of new technologies, as a suitable support for the leading and solving of projects. Namely, it has dealt with the integration of semantic search on several portal levels, used for the solution of scientific projects, and also the employment of new communication means from the areas of social and community networks for the support and leading of projects, and the execution of work meetings. It has been shown that the use of these technologies brings about the simplification of communication among the group of solvers, and above all, it increases the effectiveness of the project solution.

Acknowledgments. This work has been supported by the project No P403/11/1103 Construction of Methods for Multi-factorial Assessment of Company Complex Performance in Selected Sectors. The Grant Agency of the Czech Republic (GACR).

References

1. Altova, XBRL Mapping, http://www.altova.com/mapforce/xbrl-mapping.html
2. Burzagli, L., Como, A., Gabbanini, F.: Towards the convergence of web 2.0 and semantic web for E-inclusion. In: Miesenberger, K., Klaus, J., Zagler, W., Karshmer, A. (eds.) ICCHP 2010. LNCS, vol. 6179, pp. 343–350. Springer, Heidelberg (2010) ISSN 0302-9743
3. Buytaert, D.: Drupal, the semantic web and search, http://buytaert.net/drupal-the-semantic-web-and-search
4. Drupal Semantic Search Group, http://drupal.org/project/semantic_search
5. Garca-Crespo, A. Gmez-Berbs, J. M. Colomo-Palacios, R.: Digital libraries and Web 3.0. The CallimachusDL approach. Computers in Human Behavior 1 (2010) ISSN 0747-5632, http://www.sciencedirect.com/science/article/B6VDC-50T94B0-7/2/d0dbc819f8781a98d1c09074eab38800
6. IBM Watson, http://www-03.ibm.com/innovation/us/watson/index.html
7. Trenz, O.: The impact of document format on productivity of information systems. Acta of Mendel University of Agriculture and Forestry 6, 177–186 (2007)
8. Sklenár, V.: Web 2.0 vs. sémantický web. [In Czech] In Inforum 2007 : Sborník z konference INFORUM 2007 [online]. Praha : Inforum (2007) (cit. 2011-04-1), http://www.inforum.cz/pdf/2007/sklenak-vilem.pdf
9. Yahoo! SearchMonkey Definition, http://developer.yahoo.com/searchmonkey/

Conceptual Model Enhancing Accessibility of Data from Cancer–Related Environmental Risk Assessment Studies

Ladislav Dušek[1,2], Jiří Hřebíček[1], Miroslav Kubásek[1], Jiří Jarkovský[1],
Jiří Kalina[1], Roman Baroš[2], Zdeňka Bednářová[2], Jana Klánová[2], and Ivan Holoubek[2]

[1] Institute of Biostatistics and Analyses, Masaryk University,
Kamenice 128/3, 625 00 Brno, Czech Republic
[2] Research Centre for Toxic Compounds in the Environment, Masaryk University,
Kamenice 128/3, 625 00 Brno, Czech Republic
{dusek,hrebicek,kubasek,jarkovsky,kalina}@iba.muni.cz,
{baros,bednarova,klanova,holoubek}@recetox.muni.cz

Abstract. This paper proposes conceptual model which can be used to facilitate the discovery, integration and analysis of environmental data in cancer-related risk studies. Persistent organic pollutants were chosen as a model because of their persistence, bioaccumulation potential and genotoxicity. Part dealing with cancer risk is primarily focused on population-based observations encompassing a wide range of epidemiologic studies, from local investigations to national cancer registries. The proposed model adopted multilayer hierarchy working with characteristics of given entities (POPs, cancer diseases as *nomenclature classes*) and couples *"observation – measurement"* as content defining classes. The proposal extends formally used taxonomy applying multidimensional set of descriptors including scores of measurement validity and precision. This solution has the potential to aid multidisciplinary data discovery and knowledge mining. The same structure of descriptors used for environmental and cancer part enables the users to integrate different data sources recognizing their methodical origin, time & space coordinates and validity.

Keywords: Persistent organic pollutants, cancer risk, data model, data discovery.

1 Introducing Problems with Data Accessibility

"Data rich – information poor" is becoming obligatory phrase or accepted "professional dialect" associated with environmental monitoring. It also extends to the cancer risk assessment which has recently attracted increasing attention. Most problems can be explained by the heterogeneity of input data ranging from laboratory bio-tests to multilevel epidemiologic observations. Progress increasingly requires standardized access to multi-disciplinary information resources, including chemical, geological, meteorological, epidemiologic and demographic data. Each broadly ranged ecological or human risk study must adopt both following scenarios [1,2]:

J. Hřebíček, G. Schimak, and R. Denzer (Eds.): ISESS 2011, IFIP AICT 359, pp. 461–479, 2011.
© IFIP International Federation for Information Processing 2011

1. retrospective exploitation of data sources and their description in discovery process
2. prospective arrangement enabling effective electronic data capture in future

From the viewpoint of informatics, environmental risk assessment can be characterized as processing of heterogeneous data leading to probabilistic estimation of some uncertain (prospective approach) or on the other hand relatively certain (retrospective approach) risk event. Main complications that hamper progress in this field are highlighted in the following list:

1. Extremely wide range of data types and structures in environmental studies
2. Insufficient metadata description and standardization
3. Lack of well established repositories based on standardized protocols which is in strong contrast to methodical progress in environmental and medical sciences
4. Variability of technologies, coding and reporting systems used by different research groups
5. Growing number of small and not adequately published and described studies, which however produce valuable and important data.

Especially last point deserves special attention. Growing number of studies is not accompanied with adequate progress in information technologies and in practical implementations of SW tools [3,4]. It inevitably results in publishing of non-consistent outcomes with ad hoc data management support. To discover such broadly heterogeneous data we need consensus on data and metadata standardization, but it itself is not enough. We need sufficiently complex conceptual models, advancing development of formal ontologies over environmental and epidemiological data capture systems.

Although there are some usable standardizing concepts already published (Ecological Metadata Language)[1] [5,6], they are not extensively used in practice or there is a lack in support in data capture systems. Environmental data collection is still subjected to research in the informatics field [7,8]. In cancer research, we can take the advantage of accessible nomenclature standards like Clinical Terms (SNOMED-CT)[2], the Unified Medical Language System (UMLS)[3], and the National Cancer Institute Thesaurus (NCIT)[4]. Several consistent attempts to design ontologies functional for cancer treatment and management have also been published recently [9].

Nevertheless, widespread support for ontology-based approaches is not implemented in the field ecological risk assessment [10]. However, interest in developing ontologies is growing, because new synthetic environmental analyses increasingly rely on access to a broad range of cross-disciplinary data sources and monitoring studies. The effective system should encompass not only structure and content of such data repositories, but also hierarchical architecture and mutual relationships among components [11].

---

[1] http://knb.ecoinformatics.org/software/eml/
[2] http://www.nlm.nih.gov/research/umls/Snomed/snomed_main.html
[3] http://www.nlm.nih.gov/research/umls/
[4] http://www.mindswap.org/2003/CancerOntology/

That is why we try to propose multidisciplinary conceptual model with ambition to discover and process data on environmental pollution and cancer risk using the same methodical template. Our principal aim is to support data integration across the geographical borders, disciplines and professional terminologies; as well as integration of newly gathered data with data already collected and archived.

2 Persistent Organic Pollutants as Model for Cancer Risk Studies

Nowadays, many environmental factors, both chemical and physical, are proved to be involved in causing cancer. In our proposal of conceptual data model for cancer risk studies, we took persistent organic pollutants (POPs) as a proper model namely due to the following reasons:

- POPs have become recently intensively studied due to their properties which represent remarkable risk for ecosystems and human population (persistence, bioaccumulation, carcinogenicity, genotoxicity). The ability to accumulate in human tissues together with persistence enable long term exposure of an individual, the effect of which is further enhanced by genotoxic impact.
- Clear nomenclature of POPs which facilitates development of formal concepts based on well defined entities.
- There are important international initiatives to control distribution and associated impacts of POPs; participating countries and institutions form growing family of potential users of developed informatics solutions. The decisions by the Conferences of the Parties to the Basel, Rotterdam and Stockholm conventions on enhancing cooperation and coordination among the three conventions invite Parties to coordinate their efforts when implementing the three conventions to ensure close cooperation among relevant ministries and programmes at the national levels [12].

Not all POPs are proved as direct carcinogens or co-carcinogens. There are several widely accepted systems reporting data on carcinogenicity (IARC: International Agency for Research on Cancer; US EPA: United States Environmental Protection Agency; ACGIH: American Conference of Governmental Industrial Hygienists, see also Table 1). Therefore, this property is an important classifier extending information content given by nomenclature itself.

3 Cancer Epidemiology as Endpoint in Risk Studies

Growing cancer burden affects visible proportion of worldwide population and logically attracts research interest. Furthermore, the era of personalized medicine put the cancer diseases to the position of primary target of IT support [13,14]. Studies focused on cancer epidemiology address the virtual top of the system of cancer research. Cancer is however entirely multifactorial problem with its roots in molecular mechanisms inside the cells. Therefore, the main added value of IT is to facilitate integration of data acquired from multiple levels of investigation. The knowledge of mechanisms explaining cancer origin can mostly explain changes observed in the population level, or at least minimize the bias in interpretation.

Cancer–related environmental risk studies require very comprehensive data background. We typically evaluate probability of increased risk for a given population, typically exposed to some dangerous factor. Prospective studies work namely with laboratory data and estimate intensity of probable exposure pathways. Retrospective studies utilize accessible epidemiologic observations performed in a target area. Estimates of incidence, mortality or prevalence are employed as frequent en-points.

Most of the investigations studying harmful effect of chemicals on population cancer burden are designed as case control studies, which often determine their frequently inconclusive results. We can mention problems with mutual variations in outcomes of similar studies, insufficient power of accessible retrospective records on individual environmental exposures, lack of biomarkers reflecting stages of the carcinogenic process or problems with sufficiently long time series of observation [15,16]. Origin of analyzed data, precision and validity of measurements are therefore very important attributes to be followed in these studies.

4 Proposed Conceptual Model and Reasoning of Its Structure

Here we proposed simplified conceptual model that should broaden our capability for understanding the validity, content and relevance of the data coming from environmental and epidemiologic monitoring (Table 1). The adopted concept should support scientists in mapping of cancer-risk. The proposed model is based on hierarchically layered architecture providing different levels of classifiers or properties of homologous entities as well as scoring of data origin. The model works with three principle layers:

1. **Entities** (POPs or cancer diagnoses) defined on the basis of internationally standardized nomenclature systems. The level is linked with classifiers, i.e. given properties extending the nomenclature and filtering homologous groups of entities.
2. **Observation – measurement** level and its descriptors, focused namely on time & space coordinates, methodical attributes, measured endpoints, reference benchmarking of their value and validity scoring.
3. **Content** identification describing employed measures, units and precision estimates.

Important principles applied in conceptual model construction are further summarized here:

1. Reduction of the number of object properties is important and practical; when necessary, the set of attributes can be expanded before specifically designed data discovery. Too many object properties cannot be utilized efficiently in retrospective exploitation of the resources.
2. Any relevant data discovery must reflect heterogeneity of experimental and methodical approaches at ecosystem and population level. That is why type of the study or data resource is obligatory attribute among the observation descriptors.
3. A measured value cannot be interpreted without reference to a defined/known measurement standard or reference benchmarks. Both internal

reference norms (e.g. self-benchmarking of time series data) and external benchmarks (e.g. background concentration levels or limits, hygienic norms, detection limit of applied method, international epidemiologic burden) are used.

4. Descriptors of measures must fulfill obligatory Measurement Standard, i.e. the units, scales and lists of attributes defining origin of the measures (e.g. examined matrix, sampling methods, investigated population, cohort, demographic selection etc.)

We proposed the same discovery template for POPs and cancer resources as it is summarized in Table 1. From the first step, we must categorize the key subjects, i.e. POPs and cancer diagnoses. At this obligatory tier, internationally validated nomenclature is recommended and summarized in Tables 2 and 3. The subsequent tiers gradually unravel attributes important for interpretation of cancer risk studies (e.g. carcinogenicity of POPs, malignant/benign classification of cancers, data origin in terms of study design, etc.). These layers form multidimensional descriptive space which is significantly more robust than any single formal classification. This minimizes the probability of missing or omitting of some important facts and protects the solution against selection bias or misinterpretation.

The same template used for POPs and cancer risk enables the IT tools to integrate these data resources. The relevance of the integration process relies on the ability to determine if two values (studies) are compatible, not only in time and space coordinates. Description of model levels in table 1 implies interdisciplinary interactions of classifiers extending the nomenclature (e.g. "carcinogenic compound x malignant neoplasm"), observation – measurement validity identifiers (e.g. long-term national monitoring of POPs x national cancer registry) and mutually related observation-measurement (e.g. trend in POPs concentration in food chains vs. disease specific mortality due to GIT cancers). The most important added value of the model is the capability to determine if two data sets can be either fully or partially merged or mutually related once they are discovered. To decide it, the system undertakes important steps in all levels of proposed architecture:

1. The system must control relevance and compatibility at the taxonomic level (nomenclature) and in space & time localization of data resources
2. Identified data resources must be assessed if, and at what semantic resolution, the data are compatible (level of classifiers and/or extending descriptors like type of the study, etc.)
3. Finally, the measurement standards for the mutually related environmental and epidemiologic endpoints have to be controlled for compatibility (units, scales, reference benchmarking, methodical origin).

Obviously, not all descriptors must be necessarily fulfilled in all data discovery sessions, sometimes the uncertainty is too high. Different situations give to different tiers different weights. For example, the situation is thoroughly different if someone needs well designed retrospective or prospective assessment than if it is sudden catastrophic situation like exposure due to industrial accident where we must in first line mitigate the immediate effects. Moreover environmental factors cannot necessarily impact upon human population is some isolated system, highly probably they interact with other harmful effects associated with life style, occupational factors and relating exposures causing probable carcinogenic synergies. It complicates the interpretation of population risk studies where precise and standardized description of input data is becoming a key step limiting the relevance of reached outcome.

5 Projection of Proposed Conceptual Model to Data Standards

The quality of conceptual model determines its utility for assisting in data discovery and information searching. However, the applicability of any such model strongly depends on quality of description and content of processed data sets. That is why, we should insist on minimized, but obligatory database components, i.e. limited number of entities and their descriptors. Minimized data model as standard can be used both retrospectively (scoring of validity and usefulness of discovered resources) and prospectively (when designing new data capture systems). Proposed conceptual model intrinsically encompasses these obligatory items:

1. POPs data resources
    - institution (origin of data), time & space coordinates, type of resource (study design), examined entities (compounds), measures and methodical descriptors (experimental units, values & units, matrices, methods)
2. Cancer risk data resources
    - institution (origin of data), time & space coordinates, type of resource (study design, examined effects), examined entities (tumors, cancer diseases), measures and methodical descriptors (experimental units, values & units, cohorts, methods)

The system allows any type of reasonable extension; additional properties may be added on demand. However, minimized data standard ensures accessibility of key information namely in Measurement level of the model; i.e. when and where measurements were recorded, who recorded each measurement, the methodology of measurements, study design and aim. In this way the model can improve data visibility to search engines and enables greater levels of automation of common data transformation, summarization and integration.

Proposed conceptual model also contributes to widely recommended discovery of data based on the concepts they really represent [10,17,18]. In contrast to formal frameworks usually published with focus on one discipline [11,19] our model presumes search which exploits relationships between classes within environmental and human data sets as well as interdisciplinary relationships between the two areas. The concept supports development and formalization of ontologies, relevant for both environmental sciences and cancer epidemiology.

Ontology should represent the knowledge in a domain of interest, defined via the terminology (concepts, nomenclature) used within the domain and the properties and relationships among domain objects [20]. This concept is fully implemented in the model proposed here; the nomenclature baseline is extended by selected descriptors with defined dependencies. It is a formal framework for observational studies where we adopted structured approach recognizing key entities (nomenclature classes) in the 1st level and their characteristics (classifiers) important for the cancer risk studies. Second level consists of measurements and their characteristics, i.e. validity criteria, origin of data, etc.. Third level covers content identification, namely values and units, scales.

6 Impact of Proposed Data Model on Data Processing and Analysis

Population studies focused on cancer risk are complex and require processing of highly diverse data. Even if we can get adequate data sources accessible for analyses, it is often difficult to select the best approach how to mutually relate measured factors; mostly our later analytic steps assume some specific input or data aggregation from the preceding measurements. That is why the data structure must be well defined but at the same time, flexible enough to reflect a wide range of possible hypotheses. Regarding heterogeneity of environmental problems, no unique, definitely the best model can be recommended. Of course, such system cannot be constructed retrospectively, on demand of running analyses. Baseline standardization proposed here in conceptual data model positively impacts upon analytical procedures, namely in the following three fields.

- **Hierarchical structure advances the data analysis.** The proposed conceptual model intrinsically distinguishes hierarchy of levels and descriptors which facilitates implementation of tools focused on data analysis and knowledge mining. The position of nomenclature entities and measurements can be used to denote a wide range of entity characteristics (nominal or ordinal measures of existence, prevalence). Using the hierarchy of descriptors we can easily decide whether the data are useful for a particular analysis.
- **Conceptual model supports robust reference comparison of values.** Regarding data analysis, very important attribute of the proposed model is incorporation of measurement level and its characteristics. Validity criteria reflect some precision measures as well as reference values or protocol standards. A measured value cannot be interpreted and analyzed without reference to a defined measurement standard.
- **Stratified analyses and integration of different data sources.** Hierarchical relationships among nomenclature classes and descriptors also potentiate development of automated SW tools for comparison of values using different strata. For example we can summarize prevalence of some cancer according to site locations because the sites and their population provide context for observation of cancer load. Similarly, the sites and matrices provide a context for measurement of POPs exposure. Both summaries can be then interlinked using various time frames. The concept thus facilitates evidence-based data integration, reasoned by compatibility of interlinked values.

7 Examples of Practical Implementation

Proposed model has already been used and implemented in SW toolkit focused on data discovery over Czech National Cancer Registry (system SVOD[5], [21]) and on processing of data from various POPs monitoring networks (system GENASIS[6]). Both information systems distinguish object entities (nomenclature items) and enable users to stratify accessible measures (content of resources) across a set o classifiers and methodically important attributes.

8 Conclusions and Future Challenges

In this study we proposed interdisciplinary conceptual model as a support of cancer-related environmental risk studies. The model can be useful in basic characterization of data standards and context of observations, as well as for information search. The model intrinsically defines dependency of obligatory descriptors and hierarchy in nomenclature attributes and supports establishment of data repositories with respect to other meaningful dimensions like cancer-related properties of chemical compounds, origin of data, coding of extreme or unusual values, etc. Such repositories allow the scientists to work with functional properties of nomenclature entities and related measurements. Moreover, measurements are linked to internal and external reference benchmarks which subsequently facilitate data integration or summaries.

Of course, many barriers that limit interdisciplinary data discovery still remain. The problems refer intrinsically to the information reachable in observation studies and cannot be easily solved by informatics. In cancer risk assessment, it is hard to collect representative data in relatively short period of time. Timescales here are long and the ability to switch a system to more complex level is limited by cost and organizational constraints. It is mostly not possible to carry out adequate assessment of the large scale systems with techniques that have been successful in smaller systems with limited heterogeneity.

Therefore, completely new methodical and experimental approaches are needed, especially those introducing novel, more sensitive and specific indicators. Population monitoring using methods of molecular epidemiology combined with reliable data on exposure offers such new powerful approach to determine the effect of genotoxic agents on human populations [16]. Study on the genetic polymorphism that can be a risk indicator for cancer development is a newly occurring stream in environmental sciences [22]. This methodical progress is making possible the collection and organization of biological informatics at an unprecedented level of detail and in extremely large quantities.

Acknowledgements. This research received financial support from the CETOCOEN project of the European Structural Funds (CZ.1.05/2.1.00/01.0001) and project FP7 No. 247893 TaToo – Tagging Tool based on a Semantic Discovery Framework) granted by European Commission.

---

[5] http://www.svod.cz
[6] http://www.genasis.cz

References

1. Michener, W.K., Brunt, J.W.: Ecological Data: Design, Management and Processing. Blackwell Science, Oxford (2000)
2. Jones, M.B., Schildhauer, M., Reichman, O.J., Bowers, S.: The New Bioinformatics: integrating ecological data from the gene to the biosphere. Ann. Rev. Ecol. Evol. Syst. 37, 519–544 (2006)
3. Elmagarmid, A., Rusinkiewicz, M., Sheth, A.: Management of Heterogeneous and Autonomous Database Systems, vol. 4. Morgan Kaufmann, San Francisco (1999)
4. Grossman, D.A., Frieder, O.: Information Retrieval: Algorithms and Heuristics. Springer, Heidelberg (2004)
5. Darwin Core: Darwin Core Schema (version 1.3), a draft standard of the Taxonomic Database Working Group (TDWG), http://wiki.tdwg.org/DarwinCore
6. DCMI. DCMI Metadata Terms, http://www.dublincore.org/documents/dcmi-terms
7. Athanasiadis, I.N., Mitkas, P.A.: A methodology for developing environmental information systems with software agents. In: Cortés, U., Poch, M. (eds.) Whitestein Series in Software Agent Technologies and Autonomic Computing: Advanced Agent-Based Environmental Management Systems, pp. 119–137. Springer, Heidelberg (2009)
8. Huang, P.S., Shih, L.H.: Effective environmental management through environmental knowledge management. Int. J. Environ. Sci. Tech. 6, 35–50 (2009)
9. Brochhausen, M., Spear, A.D., Cocos, C., et al.: The ACGT Master Ontology and its applications – Towards an ontology-driven cancer research and management system. J. Biomed. Inform. 44, 8–25 (2011)
10. Madin, J., Bowers, S., Schildhauera, M., et al.: An ontology for describing and synthesizing ecological observation data. Int. J. Ecol. Informatics 2, 279–296 (2007)
11. Williams, R.J., Martinez, N.D., Golbeck, J.: Ontologies for ecoinformatics. J. Web Semant. 4, 237–242 (2006)
12. UNEP Report of the First Expert Meeting to update the Guidance on the Global Monitoring Plan for Persistent Organic Pollutants (2010), http://chm.pops.int/Programmes/GlobalMonitoringPlan/Meetings/GMP1stExpertMeeting2010/tabid/760/ctl/Download/mid/3261/language/en-US/Default.aspx
13. Sotiriou, C., Pickard, M.J.: Taking gene-expression profiling to the clinic: when will molecular signatures become relevant to patient care? Nat. Rev. 7, 545–553 (2007)
14. Tsiknakis, M., Brochhausen, M., Nabrzyski, J., et al.: A semantic grid infrastructure enabling integrated access and analysis of multilevel biomedical data in support of postgenomic clinical trials on Cancer. IEEE Trans. Inform. Technol. Biomed., Special issue on Bio-Grids 12, 191–204 (2008)
15. Sram, R.J.: Future research directions to characterize environmental mutagens in highly polluted area. Environ. Health Perspect. 104(suppl. 3), 603–607 (1996)
16. Kyrtopoulos, S.A., Georgiadis, P., Autrup, H., et al.: Biomarkers of genotoxicity of urban air pollution. Overview and descriptive data from a molecular epidemiology study on populations exposed to moderate-to-low levels of polycyclic aromatic hydrocarbons: the AULIS project. Mutat. Res. 496, 207–228 (2001)
17. Berkley, C., Jones, M.B., Bojilova, J., Higgins, D.: Metacat: a schema-independent XML database system. In: Proc. of the 13th Intl. Conf. on Scientific and Statistical Database Management. IEEE Computer Society, Los Alamitos (2001)
18. Borgida, A.: Description logics in data management. IEEE Trans. Knowl. Data Eng. 7, 671–682 (1995)

19. Bard, J.R.L., Rhee, S.Y.: Ontologies in biology: design, applications and future challenges. Nat. Rev. Genet. 5, 213–222 (2004)
20. Baader, F., Calvanese, D., McGuinness, D., Nardi, D., Patel-Schneider, P.: The Description Logic Handbook: Theory, Implementation, and Applications. Cambridge University Press, Cambridge (2003)
21. Dušek, L., Mužík, J., Kubásek, M., Koptíková, J., Žaloudík, J., Vyzula, R.: Epidemiology of malignant tumours in the Czech Republic, http://www.svod.cz
22. Knudsen, L.E., Loft, S.H., Autrup, H.: Risk assessment: the importance of genetic polymorphisms in man. Mutat. Res. 482, 83–88 (2001)

Appendix

Table 1. Conceptual model proposed for environmental cancer-related data management

1a. Resources of persistent organic pollutants (POPs)

CONCEPTUAL MODEL - LEVELS	DEFINITION & COMMENT
RESOURCE IDENTIFICATORS	Obligatory descriptors identifying institution (project) which guarantees the data (mostly also as owner of the resource content). In already closed resources, the identification is supplied with overall time/ space description.
OBJECTS – KEY ENTITIES	
NOMENCLATURE	Internationally used nomenclature of POP compounds (UNEP, 2010) – see Table 2. System allows selection of individual compounds and their groups.
OBJECT CLASSIFIERS	Categorized classifiers derived from external (encyclopedic) sources of information. Classifiers define groups but can be used also for scoring of individuals. Classifying criterion is linked to the individual compounds and/or to their groups.
Carcinogenicity	Attribute extending recognition of nomenclature classes, coded as no/yes/suspected. Code is directly interlinked with individual compounds. There are several international database sources of this information (IARC/US EPA/ACGIH) – see table 1.
Reference concentration values	Internal (time series analysis, background values) and/or external reference benchmarks. The classifier is coupled with given entity (compound), typically with direct link to matrix sampled and method used.
OBSERVATION – MEASUREMENT (OM)	
TIME & SPACE COORDINATES	Obligatory attributes, also proposed as inescapable items of any data standard.
STUDY TYPE (design)	Study type (list): Long-term environmental monitoring / Short-term environmental monitoring / Case studies / Screening.
PROBLEM STUDIED (exposure)	Problem studied (list): Accident, short-term exposure / Long-term exposure / Random inspection (survey of some area) / Examination of background (reference) site

METHODICAL ATTRIBUTES Measured entities Matrix Experimental unit Sampling methods Analytical methods	Obligatory identification of observation – measurement, necessary for interpretation of measured values. Measured entities select nomenclature items which are examined in given environmental matrix (soil, sediment, water, air, biota). Experimental unit identifies context of measured values (micro-samples within site, site – single sample, site – mixed sample, sample mixed across sites). Sampling and analytical methods fulfill minimized list of items which follows standardized norms and guidelines.
CONTENT Measures Units Precision measures	Content of the resource, in case of POPs mostly concentration levels in internationally standardized unit scales. Precision measures include sample variability (in concentration units) or detection limits of performed analytical methods.

1b. Resources of cancer epidemiology and risk

CONCEPTUAL MODEL - LEVELS	DEFINITION & COMMENT
RESOURCE IDENTIFICATORS	Obligatory descriptors identifying institution (project) which guarantees the data (mostly also as owner of the resource content). In already closed resources, the identification is supplied with overall time/ space /population description.

OBJECTS – KEY ENTITIES

NOMENCLATURE	Internationally guaranteed system of classification of diseases – see Table 3. "Cancer" is used in many synonymous terms: tumor, neoplasm, metastasis.
OBJECT CLASSIFIERS	Categorized classifiers derived from external (encyclopedic) sources of information. Classifying criterion is linked to the individual cancer diagnosis and extent its information value
Nomenclature subsystems (TNM classification)	Internationally standardized nomenclature of cancer diseases, based on ICD-O-3 as key system and ICD-10 as multi-component subsystem for identification of malignant neoplasms.
Tumor type	Classifier important for risk studies focused on some type of harmful exposure (list): malignant / benign / unknown behavior
Reference values	Internal (time series analysis, background values) and/or external reference benchmarks (internationally reported values; reference epidemiological characteristics). The classifier is coupled with given entity (cancer type) and epidemiological measure, typically with relation to type of population observed.

OBSERVATION – MEASUREMENT (OM)

TIME & SPACE COOR-DINATES	Obligatory attributes, also proposed as inescapable items of any data standard.
STUDY TYPE (design)	Study type (list): National epidemiological registry / Local (regional) registry / Hospital-based project / Cancer screening /

PROBLEM STUDIED (exposure)	Clinical trial / Cohort study / Case-control study / Descriptive epidemiologic observation
	Problem studied (list): Genetic factors, hereditary syndromes / Life style factors / Demography, ageing, gender studies / Occupational factors / Environmental factors / toxic exposures
METHODICAL ATTRIBUTES Measured entities Matrix Experimental unit Sampling/measurement methods	Obligatory identification of observation – measurement, necessary for interpretation of measured values. Measured entities select nomenclature items which are examined in given population. Experimental unit identifies context of measured values (representative population, selected cohort). Sampling/measurement methods fulfill minimized list of items which follows standardized guidelines for epidemiologic observation studies.

CONTENT Measures Units Precision measures	Content of the resource, typically recognized epidemiological measure (incidence, mortality, prevalence) in internationally standardized unit scales (crude estimate, ASR, etc.). Precision measures include population representativeness (coverage) of the data resource.

Table 2. List of POPs from annexes A, B and C of the Stockholm convention and their congeners according to recommendation for monitoring from the first workshop that considered the 2nd revision of the Guidance document for the GMP, held 12-14 April 2010 in Geneva (UNEP 2010)

CAS	ES	name	level	state	carcinogenity[1]
309-00-2	**206-215-8**	**aldrin**	**1**	**substance**	3/B2/A3
57-74-9	**200-349-0**	**chlordane**	**1**	**group**	2B/B2/A3
5103-71-9	225-825-5	*cis*-chlordan	2	substance	-/-/-
5103-74-2	225-826-0	*trans*-chlordan	2	substance	-/-/-
5103-73-1		*cis*-nonachlor	2	substance	-/-/-
39765-80-5		*trans*-nonachlor	2	substance	-/-/-
26880-48-8		oxychlordane	2	mixture	-/-/-
8017-34-3		**DDT**	**1**	**group**	2B/B2/A3
50-29-3	200-024-3	4,4'-DDT	2	substance	2B/B2/A3
789-02-6	212-332-5	2,4'-DDT	2	substance	-/-/-
72-55-9	200-784-6	4,4'-DDE	2	substance	2B/B2/-
3424-82-6	222-318-0	2,4'-DDE	2	substance	-/-/-
72-54-8	200-783-0	4,4'-DDD	2	substance	2B/B2/-
53-19-0	200-166-6	2,4'-DDD (mitotane)	2	substance	-/-/-

Table 2. (*continued*)

60-57-1	**200-484-5**	**dieldrin**	**1**	**substance**	3/B2/A4
72-20-8	**200-775-7**	**endrine**	**1**	**substance**	3/D/A4
118-74-1	**204-273-9**	**hexachlorbenzene (HCB)**	**1**	**substance**	2B/B2/A3
76-44-8	**200-962-3**	**heptachlor**	**1**	**substance**	2B/B2/A3
1024-57-3	213-831-0	heptachlor epoxide	2	substance	3/B2/A3
2385-85-5	**219-196-6**	**mirex**	**1**	**substance**	2B/-/-
1336-36-3	**215-648-1**	**polychlorinated biphenyls (PCB)**	**1**	**group**	2A/B2/
7012-37-5	230-293-2	2,4,4'-trichlorobiphenyl (PCB 28)	2	substance	-/-/-
35693-99-3		2,2',5,5'-tetrachlorobiphenyl (PCB 52)	2	substance	-/-/-
37680-73-2		2,2',4,5,5'-pentachlorobiphenyl (PCB 101)	2	substance	-/-/-
31508-00-6		2,3',4,4',5-pentachlorobiphenyl (PCB 118)	2	substance	-/-/-
35065-28-2		2,2',3,4,4',5'-hexachlorobiphenyl (PCB 138)	2	substance	-/-/-
35065-27-1		2,2',4,4',5,5'-hexachlorobiphenyl (PCB 153)	2	substance	-/-/-
35065-29-3		2,2',3,4,4',5,5'-heptachlorobiphenyl (PCB 180)	2	substance	-/-/-
32598-13-3		3,3',4,4'-tetrachlorobiphenyl (PCB 77)	2	substance	-/-/-
70362-50-4		3,4,4',5-tetrachlorobiphenyl (PCB 81)	2	substance	-/-/-
32598-14-4		2,3,3',4,4'-pentachlorobiphenyl (PCB 105)	2	substance	3/-/-
74472-37-0		2,3,4,4',5-pentachlorobiphenyl (PCB 114)	2	substance	-/-/-
31508-00-6		2,3',4,4',5-pentachlorobiphenyl (PCB 118)	2	substance	-/-/-
65510-44-3		2,3',4,4',5'-pentachlorobiphenyl (PCB 123)	2	substance	-/-/-
57465-28-8		3,3',4,4',5-pentachlorobiphenyl (PCB 126)	2	substance	-/-/-
38380-08-4		2,3,3',4,4'-hexachlorobiphenyl (PCB 156)	2	substance	-/-/-
69782-90-7		2,3,3',4,4',5'-hexachlorobiphenyl (PCB 157)	2	substance	-/-/-
52663-72-6		2,3',4,4',5,5'-hexachlorobiphenyl (PCB 167)	2	substance	-/-/-
32774-16-6		3,3',4,4',5,5'-hexachlorobiphenyl (PCB 169)	2	substance	-/-/-
39635-31-9		2,3,3',4,4',5,5'-heptachlorobiphenyl (PCB 189)	2	substance	-/-/-
		polychlorinated dibenzo-p-dioxins (PCDD)	**1**	**group**	-/-/-
1746-01-6	217-122-7	2,3,7,8-tetrachlorodibenzo[b,e][1,4]dioxin (2378 TCDD)	2	substance	1/-/-
40321-76-4		1,2,3,7,8-Pentachlorodibenzo-p-dioxin (12378-PeCDD)	2	substance	3/-/-

Table 2. (*continued*)

39227-28-6		1,2,3,4,7,8-Hexachlorodibenzo-p-dioxin (123478-HxCDD)	2	substance	3/-/-
57653-85-7		1,2,3,6,7,8-Hexachlorodibenzo-p-dioxin (123678-HxCDD)	2	substance	3/-/-
19408-74-3		1,2,3,7,8,9-Hexachlorodibenzo-p-dioxin (123789-HxCDD)	2	substance	3/B2/-
35822-46-9		1,2,3,4,6,7,8-Heptachlorodibenzo-p-dioxin (1234678-HpCDD)	2	substance	3/-/-
3268-87-9		Octachlorodibenzo-p-dioxin (OCDD)	2	substance	3/-/-
		polychlorinated dibenzofurans (PCDF)	**1**	**group**	**-/-/-**
51207-31-9		2,3,7,8-tetrachlorodibenzofuran (2378-TCDF)	2	substance	3/-/-
57117-41-6		1,2,3,7,8-pentachlorodibenzofuran (12378-PeCDF)	2	substance	3/-/-
57117-31-4		2,3,4,7,8-pentachlorodibenzofuran (23478-PeCDF)	2	substance	3/-/-
70648-26-9		1,2,3,4,7,8-hexachlorodibenzofuran (123478-HxCDF)	2	substance	3/-/-
57117-44-9		1,2,3,6,7,8-hexachlorodibenzofuran (123678-HxCDF)	2	substance	3/-/-
72918-21-9		1,2,3,7,8,9-hexachlorodibenzofuran (1,2,3,7,8,9-HxCDF)	2	substance	3/-/-
60851-34-5		2,3,4,6,7,8-hexachlorodibenzofuran (234678-HxCDF)	2	substance	3/-/-
67562-39-4		1,2,3,4,6,7,8-heptachlorodibenzofuran (1234678-HpCDF)	2	substance	3/-/-
55673-89-7		1,2,3,4,7,8,9-heptachlorodibenzofuran (1234789-HpCDF)	2	substance	3/-/-
39001-02-0		Octachlorodibenzofuran (OCDF)	2	substance	3/-/-
8001-35-2	**232-283-3**	**toxaphene**	**1**	**mixture**	**2B/B2/A3**
142534-71-2		2-endo,3-exo,5-endo,6-exo,8,8,10,10-octachlorobornan (P26)	2	substance	-/-/-
6680-80-8		2-endo,3-exo,5-endo,6-exo,8,8,9,10,10-nonachlorobornan (P50)	2	substance	-/-/-
154159-06-5		2,2,5,5,8,9,9,10,10-nonachlorobornan (P62)	2	substance	-/-/-
143-50-0	**205-601-3**	**chlordecone**	**1**	**substance**	**2B/-/-**
319-84-6	**206-270-8**	**α-hexachlorcyclohexane**	**1**	**substance**	**-/B2/-**
319-85-7	**206-271-3**	**β-hexachlorcyclohexane**	**1**	**substance**	**-/C/-**
58-89-9	**200-401-2**	**γ-hexachlorcyclohexane**	**1**	**substance**	**-/-/A3**
36355-01-8	**252-994-2**	**hexabromobiphenyl (HBB)**	**1**	**group**	**-/-/-**
59080-40-9		PBB153	2	substance	-/-/-
67888-98-6		PBB138	2	substance	-/-/-
608-93-5	**210-172-0**	**pentachlorbenzene (PeCBz)**	**1**	**substance**	**-/D/-**
40088-47-9		**tetrabromodiphenyl ethers (TBDE)**	**1**	**group**	**-/-/-**

Table 2. (*continued*)

147217-75-2		2,2',4 (BDE 17)	2	substance	-/-/-
41318-75-6		2,4,4' (BDE 28)	2	substance	-/-/-
5436-43-1		2,2',4,4'-tetrabromdiphenylether (BDE 47)	2	substance	-/-/-
32534-81-9		**pentabromodiphenyl ethers (PeBDE)**	**1**	**group**	*-/-/-*
60348-60-9		2,2',4,4',5-pentabromodiphenyl ether (BDE 99)	2	substance	-/-/-
189084-64-8		2,2',4,4',6-pentabromodiphenyl ether (BDE 100)	2	substance	-/-/-
36483-60-0		**hexabromodiphenyl ethers (HxBDE)**	**1**	**group**	*-/-/-*
68631-49-2		2,2',4,4',5,5'-hexabromodiphenyl ether (BDE 153)	2	substance	-/-/-
207122-15-4		2,2',4,4',5,6'-hexabromodiphenyl ether (BDE 154)	2	substance	-/-/-
68928-80-3		**heptabromodiphenyl ethers (HpBDE)**	**1**	**group**	*-/-/-*
446255-22-7		2,2',3,3',4,5',6-heptabromodiphenyl ether (BDE 175)	2	substance	-/-/-
207122-16-5		2,2',3,4,4',5',6-heptabromodiphenyl ether (BDE183)	2	substance	-/-/-
32536-52-0		**oktabromodiphenyl ether (OBDE)**	**1**	**group**	*-/-/-*
1763-23-1	**217-179-8**	**perfluorooctane sulfonic acid (PFOS) and derivates**	**1**	**group**	*-/-/-*
31506-32-8		N-methyl heptadecafluorooctane sulfonamide (NMeFOSA)	2	substance	-/-/-
4151-50-2		N-ethyl heptadecafluorooctane sulfonamide (NEtFOSA)	2	substance	-/-/-
24448-09-7		N-methyl heptadecafluorooctane sulfonamidoethanol (NMeFOSE)	2	substance	-/-/-
1691-99-2		N-ethyl heptadecafluorooctane sulfonamidoethanol (NEtFOSE)	2	substance	-/-/-

[1] Carcinogenity groups IARC/US EPA/ACGIH, - means, that the substance is not listed. Toxned database was used: http://toxnet.nlm.nih.gov/cgi-bin/sis/search.

IARC: International Agency for Research on Cancer (http://monographs.iarc.fr/index.php)

Group 1	Carcinogenic to humans (107 agents)
Group 2A	Probably carcinogenic to humans (59 agents)
Group 2B	Possibly carcinogenic to humans (266 agents)
Group 3	Not classifiable as to its carcinogenicity to humans (508 agents)
Group 4	Probably not carcinogenic to humans (1 agent)

US EPA: United States Environmental Protection Agency (http://www.epa.gov/iris/)

Group A	Human carcinogen
Group B1	Probable human carcinogen (limited evidence of carcinogenity from epidemiological studies)
Group B2	Probable human carcinogen (sufficient evidence of carcinogenicity in animals and others)
Group C	Possible human carcinogen
Group D	Not classifiable as to human carcinogenity
Group E	Evidence of non-carcinogenity for humans

ACGIH: American Conference of Governmental Industrial Hygienists (http://www.acgih.org/SiteSearch/index.cfm)

Group A1	Confirmed human carcinogen
Group A2	Suspected human carcinogen
Group A3	Confirmed animal carcinogen with unknown relevance to humans
Group A4	Not classifiable as a human carcinogen
Group A5	Not suspected as a human carcinogen

Table 3. International classification systems of cancer diagnoses[7]

International Classification of Diseases, 10th edition (ICD-10)

(C00–C14) Malignant neoplasms, lip, oral cavity and pharynx

(C15–C26) Malignant neoplasms, digestive organs

(C30–C39) Malignant neoplasms, respiratory system and intrathoracic organs

(C40–C41) Malignant neoplasms, bone and articular cartilage

(C43–C44) Malignant neoplasms, skin

(C45–C49) Malignant neoplasms, connective and soft tissue

(C50–C58) Malignant neoplasms, breast and female genital organs

(C60–C63) Malignant neoplasms, male genital organs

(C64–C68) Malignant neoplasms, urinary organs

(C69–C72) Malignant neoplasms, eye, brain and central nervous system

(C73–C75) Malignant neoplasms, endocrine glands and related structures

(C76–C80) Malignant neoplasms, secondary and ill-defined

(C81–C96) Malignant neoplasms, stated or presumed to be primary, of lymphoid, haematopoietic and related tissue

(C97) Malignant neoplasms of independent (primary) multiple sites

(D00–D09) In situ neoplasms

(D10–D36) Benign neoplasms

(D37–D48) Neoplasms of uncertain or unknown behavior

International Classification of Diseases for Oncology, 3rd Edition (ICD-O-3) - overview

Topography. The topography of the tumor is described by topographical code. Topographical code corresponds to the C section of ICD-10 (exceptions are listed in ICD-O-3).

Morphology. The morphology provides five-digit codes ranging from M-8000/0 to M-9989/3. The first four digits indicate the specific histological term. The fifth digit after the slash (/) is the code, which indicates whether a tumor is malignant, benign, in situ, or uncertain.

Grade. A separate one-digit code is also provided for histological grading (differentiation).

(8000–8009) Not otherwise specified

(8000–8004) Neoplasms, NOS

(8010–8790) Epithelial

(8010–8040) Epithelial neoplasms, NOS

(8050–8080) Squamous cell neoplasms

(8090–8110) Basal cell neoplasms

(8120–8130) Transitional cell Papillomas And Carcinomas

(8140–8380) Adenomas And Adenocarcinomas (glands)

(8390–8420) Adnexal And Skin appendage Neoplasms

(8430–8439) Mucoepidermoid Neoplasms

(8440–8490) Cystic, Mucinous And Serous Neoplasms

---

[7] WHO, International Classification of Diseases (ICD); http://www.who.int/classifications; U.S. National Institute of Health, National Cancer Institute, http://www.seer.cancer.gov/iccc

Table 3. (*continued*)

(8500–8540) Ductal, Lobular And Medullary Neoplasms

(8550–8559) Acinar cell neoplasms

(8560–8580) Complex epithelial neoplasms

(8590–8670) Specialized gonadal neoplasms

(8680–8710) Paragangliomas And Glomus tumors

(8720–8790) Nevi And Melanomas

(8800–9370) Connective tissue

(8800–8809) Soft tissue Tumors And Sarcomas, Nos

(8810–8830) Fibromatous neoplasms

(8840–8849) Myxomatous neoplasms

(8850–8880) Lipomatous neoplasms

(8890–8920) Myomatous neoplasms

(8930–8990) Complex Mixed And Stromal Neoplasms

(9000–9030) Fibroepithelial Neoplasms

(9040–9049) Synovial-Like Neoplasms

(9050–9059) Mesothelial Neoplasms

(9060–9090) Germ cell Neoplasms

(9100–9109) Trophoblastic neoplasms

(9110–9119) Mesonephromas

(9120–9160) Blood vessel tumors

(9170–9179) Lymphatic vessel tumors

(9180–9240) Osseous And Chondromatous neoplasms

(9250–9259) Giant cell tumors

(9260–9269) Miscellaneous bone tumors

(9270–9340) Odontogenic tumors

(9350–9370) Miscellaneous tumors

(9380–9589) Nervous system

(9380–9480) Gliomas

(9421/3) Pilocytic astrocytoma

(9440/3) Glioblastoma multiforme

(9490–9520) Neuroepitheliomatous neoplasms

(9530–9539) Meningiomas

(9540–9570) Nerve sheath tumors

(9580–9589) Granular cell tumors and Alveolar soft part sarcoma

(9590–9999) Hematologic (Leukemias, Lymphomas and related disorders)

ICD-O-3 classification of Hematologic malignances according to WHO Classification of Tumors of Haematopoietic and Lymphoid Tissues (ICD-10 diagnoses C81–C96) - simplified

Lymphomas and related disorders

(9590–9599) Malignant lymphoma, NOS, Or diffuse

(9650–9660) Hodgkin's disease

(9670–9680) Malignant lymphoma Specified Type, Diffuse Or Nos

(9690–9699) Malignant lymphoma, Follicular Or Nodular, With Or Without diffuse areas

Table 3. (*continued*)

(9700–9709) Specified Cutaneous And Peripheral T-Cell Lymphomas

(9710–9719) Other Specified Non-Hodgkin's lymphomas

(9720–9729) Other Lymphoreticular neoplasms

(9730–9739) Plasma cell tumors

(9740–9749) Mast cell Tumors

(9760–9769) Immunoproliferative diseases

Lymphoid leukemias, and related conditions

(9800–9809) Leukemias, NOS

(9820–9829) Lymphoid leukemias

(9830–9839) Plasma cell leukemia

Myeloid leukemias, and related conditions

(9840-9849) Erythroleukemias (FAB-M6)

(9850–9859) Lymphosarcoma cell leukemia

(9860–9869) Myeloid (Granulocytic) Leukemias

(9870–9889) Basophilic leukemia and Eosinophilic leukemia

(9890–9899) Monocytic leukemias

(9900–9948) Other Leukemias

Other

(9950–9970) Miscellaneous Myeloproliferative And Lymphoproliferative disorders

(9980–9989) Myelodysplastic syndrome

International Classification of Childhood Cancer (ICCC) based on International Classification of Diseases for Oncology, 3rd Edition (ICD-O-3)

I Leukemias, myeloproliferative diseases, and myelodysplastic diseases

[011] (a) Lymphoid leukemias

[012] (b) Acute myeloid leukemias

[013] (c) Chronic myeloproliferative diseases

[014] (d) Myelodysplastic syndrome and other myeloproliferative diseases

[015] (e) Unspecified and other specified leukemias

II Lymphomas and reticuloendothelial neoplazma

[021] (a) Hodgkin lymphomas

[022] (b) Non-Hodgkin lymphomas (except Burkitt lymphoma)

[023] (c) Burkitt lymphoma

[024] (d) Miscellaneous lymphoreticular neoplasms

[025] (e) Unspecified lymphomas

III CNS and miscellaneous intracranial and intraspinal neoplazma

[031] (a) Ependymomas and choroid plexus tumor

[032] (b) Astrocytomas

[033] (c) Intracranial and intraspinal embryonal tumors

[034] (d) Other gliomas

[035] (e) Other specified intracranial and intraspinal neoplasms

[036] (f) Unspecified intracranial and intraspinal neoplasms

Table 3. (*continued*)

IV Neuroblastoma and other peripheral nervous cell tumors

[041] (a) Neuroblastoma and ganglioneuroblastoma

[042] (b) Other peripheral nervous cell tumors

[050] V Retinoblastoma

VI Renal tumors

[061] (a) Nephroblastoma and other nonepithelial renal tumors

[062] (b) Renal carcinomas

[063] (c) Unspecified malignant renal tumors

VII Hepatic tumors

[071] (a) Hepatoblastoma

[072] (b) Hepatic carcinomas

[073] (c) Unspecified malignant hepatic tumors

VIII Malignant bone tumors

[081] (a) Osteosarcomas

[082] (b) Chondrosarcomas

[083] (c) Ewing tumor and related sarcomas of bone

[084] (d) Other specified malignant bone tumors

[085] (e) Unspecified malignant bone tumors

IX Soft tissue and other extraosseous sarcomas

[091] (a)Rhabdomyosarcomas

[092] (b) Fibrosarcomas, peripheral nerve sheath tumors, and other fibrous neoplasms

[093] (c) Kaposi sarcoma

[094] (d) Other specified soft tissue sarcomas

[095] (e) Unspecified soft tissue sarcomas

X Germ cell tumors, trophoblastic tumors, and neoplasms of gonads

[101] (a) Intracranial and intraspinal germ cell tumors

[102] (b) Malignant extracranial and extragonadal germ cell tumors

[103] (c) Malignant gonadal germ cell tumors

[104] (d) Gonadal carcinomas

[105] (e) Other and unspecified malignant gonadal tumors

XI Other malignant epithelial neoplasms and malignant melanomas

[111] (a) Adrenocortical carcinomas

[112] (b) Thyroid carcinomas

[113] (c) Nasopharyngeal carcinomas

[114] (d) Malignant melanomas

[115] (e) Skin carcinomas

[116] (f) Other and unspecified carcinomas

XII Other and unspecified malignant neoplasms

[121] (a) Other specified malignant tumors

[122] (b) Other unspecified malignant tumors

[999] Not Classified by ICCC or in situ

GENASIS Information System: A Global Environmental Assessment of Persistent Organic Pollutants

Ivan Holoubek[1], Ladislav Dušek[1,2], Jana Klánová[1], Miroslav Kubásek[2], Jiří Jarkovský[2], Roman Baroš[1], Klára Komprdová[1], Zdeňka Bednářová[1], Richard Hůlek[2], and Jiří Hřebíček[2]

[1] Research Centre for Toxic Compounds in the Environment, Masaryk University, Kamenice 126/3, 625 00 Brno, Czech Republic
[2] Institute for Biostatistics and Analyses, Masaryk University, Kamenice 126/3, 625 00 Brno, Czech Republic

Abstract. Global ENvironmental ASsessment and Information System (GENASIS) is a tool developed by expert teams of the Research Centre for Toxic Compounds in the Environment (RECETOX) and the Institute for Bio-statistics and Analyses (IBA) of the Masaryk University in Brno. The aim of GENASIS is to compile validated data on persistent organic pollutants, including their properties, sources, long-term levels, life times, transport mechanisms, effects and risks, scattered throughout various institutions and ministries, and to provide tools for their visualization, analyses, interpretation, assessment of environmental and human risks or modelling of fate. Such a tool should significantly enhance comprehensive understanding of the fate of POPs in the environment, their impacts on ecosystem and the human population.

1 Introduction

Supporting the sustainable development and management of natural environment means among others prevention of risks and stresses connected to the global changes of climate and pollution. Protection of the environment and biodiversity, as well as prevention of environmentally induced diseases requires implementation of the international measures based on the comprehensive analysis of global trends in environmental as well as epidemiological data.

2 Background

Although protection of the environment and human health is an objective of several international conventions on toxic chemicals and wastes (namely Stockholm, Basel, and Rotterdam Conventions), the concept of evaluation of effectiveness of their measures have been developed only recently. Global monitoring plan (GMP) as one of the effectiveness evaluation mechanisms under the Stockholm Convention (SC) was designed to addresses the trends in ambient air and human milk levels of persistent organic pollutants and invited the countries to establish the long-term monitoring

J. Hřebíček, G. Schimak, and R. Denzer (Eds.): ISESS 2011, IFIP AICT 359, pp. 480–485, 2011.
© IFIP International Federation for Information Processing 2011

programmes. Mechanism of evaluation of data collected under the GMP, however, has not been developed yet.

Lack of widely applicable and publicly available environmental databases was identified as a problem also in the SWOT analyses on the national (strategic documents as Long-term directions in research and development in the Czech Republic) as well as European (reports of thematic working group on Environmental sciences of the European Strategic Forum on Research Infrastructures) levels.

3 Initiation of the GENASIS Project

The decisions adopted by the Conferences of the Parties to the Basel, Rotterdam and Stockholm Conventions on enhancing cooperation and coordination among the three conventions (the so-called synergies decisions) invited Parties to coordinate their efforts when implementing the three conventions to ensure close cooperation among relevant ministries and programmes at the national levels. The Research centre for toxic compounds in the environment (RECETOX) together with the Institute for biostatistics and analyses (IBA) answered this call by activating the GENASIS project (www.genasis.cz).

As recommended by the synergies decisions, the GENASIS system provides a national information database available to experts as well as to the general public, useful for preparation of national positions for meetings of the conferences of the Parties and other bodies of the Basel, Rotterdam and Stockholm Conventions, but also for the development of regional policies and measures protecting human health and the environment from the harmful impacts or adverse effects of hazardous chemicals and wastes.

4 Information Database

The GENASIS system is built as a modular structure providing complex services to a wide range of potential users. The initial version of the database launched in 2010 contains data from the long-term integrated monitoring at the Košetice observatory which is a part of the European Monitoring and Evaluation Programme (EMEP) [1-2], and long-term data from the ambient air MOnitoring NETworks (MONET) in the Czech Republic, Central and Eastern Europe, Africa, Central Asia and Pacific Islands [3-7]. All available data are stored in the intranet database linked to an ArcGIS server enabling spatial interpretation of all results. The user has an access to the maps of the sampling sites, their description, as well as to the POPs concentration values at all sites. Descriptive summary statistics and basic analyses of time series (seasonal and long-term patterns, robust trend estimates) is also available for selected data.

Data from the large-scale monitoring of soil, sediment, and surface water [8-9] will be included in a new version the GENASIS system, which is currently under development and will be launched in 2011. Enhanced analytical tools allowing implementation of algorithms for spatial analyses, and modules enabling comparative analyses of multiple substances or matrices will be also introduced [10-11]. Based on the contract signed between RECETOX and the Czech Ministry of Environment, an import of data from external sources will also be initiated in 2011. Compatibility of the GENASIS system with existing databases is crucial in order to assess the environmental patterns, calibrate the indicator systems, and implement the legislation requirements. The fully developed system will serve as an interactive, on-line national POPs inventory of the Czech Republic.

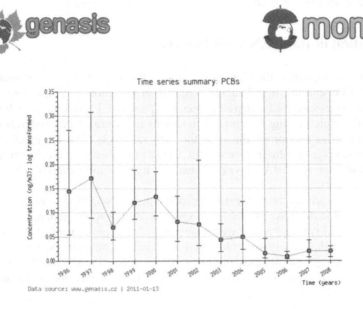

Fig. 1. Temporal trend in PCBs concentration in active air sampling at Košetice station (median and 5-95th percentile; 1996-2008)

5 Analytical and Interpretation Tools

Development of the information system includes accumulation of environmental data from various sources, their validation, followed by the advanced data analyses, interpretation, visualization, and spatial presentation supported by the geographic information systems (GIS).

Available interpretation tools include the POPspedia database providing information on chemicals of interest, detailed description of the sampling sites and sampling techniques, summary description of contamination, analyses of the time series and seasonal variability, comparison of sites, regions, time periods, and analytes, correlation analysis, and model calculators.

E-learning modules focused on the assessment of ecological risks provide the additional support to variety of users. A methodology of the ecological risk assessment starts with the problem formulation, continues with the assessments of exposure, effects, and risks, and is completed by the risk communication and management

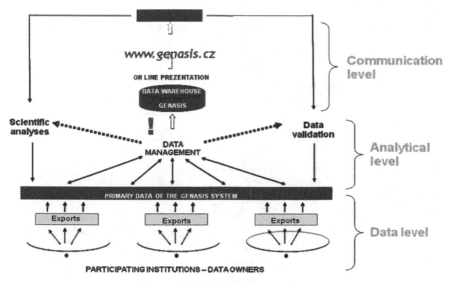

Fig. 2. GENASIS system architecture

6   Deliverables and Impacts of the GENASIS Project

RECETOX acting as the National POPs Centre of the Czech Republic became a documentation centre gathering available national information on environmental risks and impacts on human health relevant to the three conventions. However, in the role of the SC Regional Centre, RECETOX also offers GENASIS as a global system for information exchange and a clearing-house mechanism for all three conventions. Such a system is very valuable for the evaluation of the effectiveness of the Stockholm Convention measures. Currently, GENASIS hosts all available data from the international MONET project monitoring POPs in ambient air of Europe, Africa, Asia and Pacific.

The international dimension of both, the MONET and GENASIS programmes, provides an opportunity for strengthening technical assistance and capacity building in the field of data collection, interpretation and visualization on the regional and global levels. Special attention is being paid to the needs of developing countries and countries with economies in transition.

By providing access to necessary information, the GENASIS system supports decision-making on the sound management of chemicals throughout their life cycles as well as the sound management of hazardous wastes. It is also an important tool for the development of policies and measures protecting the environment and human health, and supporting sustainable development.

Last but not least, it is a tool for the joint outreach and enhancement of public awareness as an important means of prevention and environmental protection. As such, the GENASIS provided a model of coordination mechanism and example of good coordination practice, and it was selected for publication in the book of Synergies success stories jointly prepared by the Division for Sustainable Development, United Nations Department of Economic and Social Affairs (UNDESA), and Secretariats of the Stockholm, Basel, and Rotterdam Conventions in 2011.

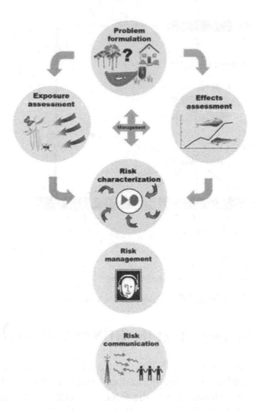

Fig. 3. A scheme of the e-learning module focused on ecological risk assessment

Acknowledgments. Development of the GENASIS system is supported by the CETOCOEN project (CZ.1.05/2.1.00/01.0001) of the European Structural Funds, and the INCHEMBIOL project (MSM 0021622412) of the Ministry of Education of the Czech Republic.

References

1. Holoubek, I., Klánová, J., Jarkovský, J., Kohoutek, J.: Trends in background levels of persistent organic pollutants at Kosetice observatory, Czech Republic. Part I. Ambient air and wet deposition 1988-2005. J. Environ. Monit. 9(6), 557–563 (2007)
2. Dvorska, A., Lammel, G., Klanova, J., Holoubek, I.: Košetice, Czech Republic – ten years of air pollution monitoring and four years of evaluating the origin of persistent organic pollutants. Environ. Pollut. 156(2), 403–408 (2008)
3. Harner, T., Bartkow, M., Holoubek, I., Klanova, J., Sweetman, A.J., Wania, F., Jones, K.C.: Passive air sampling for persistent organic pollutants: introductory remarks to the Special Issue. Environ. Pollut. 144(2), 361–364 (2006)
4. Klánová, J., Kohoutek, J., Hamplová, L., Urbanová, P., Holoubek, I.: Passive air sampler as a tool for long-term air pollution monitoring: Part 1. Performance assessment for seasonal and spatial variations. Environmental Pollution 144(2), 393–405 (2006)

5. Čupr, P., Klánová, J., Bartoš, T., Flégrová, Z., Kohoutek, J., Holoubek, I.: Passive air sampler as a tool for long-term air pollution monitoring: Part 2. Air genotoxic potency screening assessment. Environ. Pollut. 144(2), 406–413 (2006)

6. Klánová, J., Čupr, P., Holoubek, I., Borůvková, J., Kareš, R., Tomšej, T., Ocelka, T.: Monitoring of persistent organic pollutants in Africa. Part 1: Passive air sampling across the continent in 2008. J. Environ. Monit. 11, 1952–1963 (2009)

7. Klánová, J., Čupr, P., Kohoutek, J., Harner, T.: Assessing meteorological parameters on the performance of PUF disks passive air samplers for POPs. Environ. Sci. Technol. 42(2), 550–555 (2008)

8. Holoubek, I., Klánová, J., Jarkovský, J., Kubík, V., Helešic, J.: Trends in background levels of persistent organic pollutants at Kosetice observatory, Czech Republic. Part II. Aquatic and terrestrial environments 1988-2005. J. Environ. Monit. 9(6), 564–571 (2007)

9. Růžičková, P., Klánová, J., Čupr, P., Lammel, G., Holoubek, I.: An assessment of air-soil exchange of polychlorinated biphenyls and organochlorine pesticides across Central and Southern Europe. Environ. Sci. Technol. 42(1), 179–185 (2008)

10. Komprda, J., Kubošová, K., Dvorská, A., Scheringer, M., Klánová, J., Holoubek, I.: Application of an unsteady state environmental distribution model to a decadal time series of PAH concentrations in the Central Europe. J. Environ. Monit. 11, 269–276 (2009)

11. Kubošová, K., Komprda, J., Jarkovský, J., Sánka, M., Hájek, O., Dušek, L., Holoubek, I., Klánová, J.: Spatially resolved distribution models of POP concentrations in soil: A stochastic approach using regression trees. Environ. Sci. Technol. 43(24), 9230–9236 (2009)

Is On-Line Data Analysis Safety? Pitfalls Steaming from Automated Processing of Heterogeneous Environmental Data and Possible Solutions

Jiří Jarkovský, Ladislav Dušek, and Eva Janoušová

Institute of Biostatistics and Analyses, Masaryk University,
Kamenice 3, Brno, Czech Republic

Abstract. The current situation in environmental monitoring is characterized by increasing amount of data from monitoring networks together with increasing requirements on joining of these data from various sources in comprehensive databases and their usage for decision support in environmental protection and management. The automated analysis of such a heterogeneous datasets is a complicated process, rich in statistical pitfalls. There is a number of methods for multivariate classification of objects, e.g. logistic regression, discriminant analysis or neural networks; however, most commonly used classification techniques have prerequisites about distribution of data, are computationally demanding or their model can be considered as "black box". Keeping these facts in mind, we attempted to develop a robust multivariate method suitable for classification of unknown cases with minimum sensitivity to data distribution problems; and thus, suitable for routine use in practice.

Keywords: classification, nonparametric, multivariate analysis, heterogeneous data.

1 Introduction

The current situation in environmental monitoring is characterized by increasing amount of data from monitoring networks together with increasing requirements on joining of these data from various sources in comprehensive databases and their usage for decision support in environmental protection and management. The important part of these requirements is demand on automated on-line analysis of data with immediate delivery of results.

The automated analysis of such a heterogeneous datasets is a complicated process, especially in case of multivariate analysis. The common tasks and their pitfalls in automated analysis are as follows.

Descriptive statistics of measured concentrations and sampling sites characteristics: i) Pitfalls: unfulfilled prerequisites of parametric descriptive statistics can easily lead to unrealistic results and automated testing and taking these prerequisites into account is extremely problematic; ii) Solutions: there is a well-accepted alternative of parametric descriptive statistics , i.e. nonparametric statistics.

Statistical tests of differences in measured values between/among groups of sampling sites or relationships between measurements: i) Pitfalls: unfulfilled prerequisites

J. Hřebíček, G. Schimak, and R. Denzer (Eds.): ISESS 2011, IFIP AICT 359, pp. 486–490, 2011.

of parametric tests lead to biased or incorrect results; ii) Solutions: nonparametric tests can be computed instead of parametric testing.

Classification of newly added samples or sampling sites into defined classes of environmental quality based on multivariate analysis of reference dataset: i) Pitfalls: most of commonly used classification techniques have prerequisites about distribution of data, are computationally demanding or their model can be considered as "black box"; Solutions: nonparametric models can be the solution but they are not common and well developed.

There are a number of methods for multivariate classification of objects, e.g. logistic regression, discriminant analysis or neural networks; however, these also have their problems, e.g. prerequisites of normality and absence of outliers for discriminant analysis [1]. Moreover, the methods should be used in a routine way in monitoring, i.e. without proper analysis of problems concerning the data. Keeping these facts in mind, we attempted to develop a robust multivariate method suitable for classification of unknown cases with minimum sensitivity to data distribution problems; and thus, suitable for routine use in practice.

2 Suggested Methodology

The suggested methodology of the classification of unknown cases into categories of reference data for automated procedure should be as simple and robust as possible.
The simplest and the most objective measure of object association in multivariate space is their distance; thus, we decided to build our method on an analysis of a distance matrix among objects.

Now, selection of proper distance metrics is the first task in designing the method. We have adopted Gower distance metrics [2]; however, any multivariate distance metrics suitable for given data could be used. Concerning environmental monitoring data, there are some advantages in Gower metrics:

Continuous, binary or categorical parameters may be incorporated in computation: binary data is computed by coefficient – agreement and disagreement of values forming distance 0 or 1 respectively; categorical data is computed in the same way. Distance of objects according to continuous data is weighted to i) a parameter range in the data file or ii) an externally provided parameter range, i.e. difference in parameter values of objects is divided by parameter range to obtain partial metrics ranging from 0 to 1.

As noted above, parameters are weighted to their range, i.e. the influence of parameter absolute value is removed.

The final distance metrics ranges from 0 to 1 and could be interpreted easily.

Parameters in computation could be weighted according to expert knowledge or results of preliminary analysis. The final metrics takes the following form:

$$D\left(x_1, x_2\right) = \frac{\sum_{j=1}^{p} w_j d_{12j}}{\sum_{j=1}^{p} w_j} \tag{1}$$

where D is a distance between objects x_1 and x_2, d_{12j} is a partial distance of objects x_1 and x_2 associated with parameter j (there are 1..p parameters; partial metrics associated with parameter ranges from 0 to 1) and w_j is a weight of parameter j ranging from 0 to 1.

Every homogeneous category of reference data could be characterised by its position in the multivariate space; and also, by its multivariate variability. Position of the reference category centroid (based on the median of continuous data and modus of binary/categorical data) exhibits representative of this group; multivariate radius of group provides the measure of its variability (in fact 95% percentile of radius is used in our computation to remove the influence of outliers). The distance of an unknown case to the centroid (**D**) is compared to the percentile of the reference category range (**R**). This ratio measures the extent to which an unknown case differs from objects incorporated in the reference category – see figure 1. Due to the fact that reference categories are not probably multivariate spheres we had to add a safety measure reflecting the real multivariate shape of the reference data. There are two parameters incorporated in the computation: the distance of an unknown case to the nearest neighbour in the reference group (**N**) and the measure of intragroup distances (**I**) within the reference group. The measure of intragroup distances is taken as median length of the MST branches (minimal spanning tree, [3]) of objects in the reference group. The following formula gives the measure of distance of an unknown case to the reference group x (U_x) in multiplies of the reference group x radius weighted for multivariate shape of this group.

$$U_x = \frac{abs(D+N-I)}{R}$$

(2)

This computation could be also expressed as a probability of case U belongs to group x:

$$P(U_x) = \frac{1}{U_x} \times 100$$

(3)

Where values over 100 % (i.e. objects inside the reference group) are truncated to 100 %. In the first step of the analysis, $P(U_x)$ is computed for all reference groups x=1..n and probability of unknown case belongs to a particular group is weighted as follows:

$$PW(U_x) = \frac{P(U_x)}{P(U_1) + P(U_2) + \cdots + P(U_n)}$$

(4)

In the second step of the analysis, U_x or $P(U_x)$ based on case characteristics is adopted for assessing distance/similarity of an unknown case from/to a particular reference group. The main output is the probability of assigning a locality into the reference category based on case characteristics, i.e. to which reference category the evaluated case belongs.

**1) Simple classification of
unknown case**

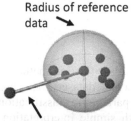

Radius of reference
data

Distance from centroid of
reference category

**2) Real situation of
heteregeneous multivariate data**

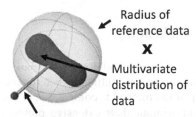

Radius of
reference data

X

Multivariate
distribution of
data

Distance from centroid of
reference category

3) Centroid distance as classification method

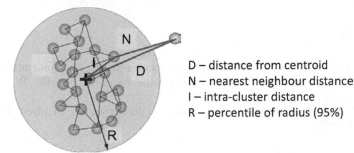

D – distance from centroid
N – nearest neighbour distance
I – intra-cluster distance
R – percentile of radius (95%)

Fig. 1. Centroid distance method classification

3 Results of Methodology Testing

The presented methodology was tested on real datasets of 300 reference localities on river network thorough the whole Czech Republic. First, the localities were divided into 8 homogeneous clusters using k-means clustering. The clusters were based on parameters of natural heterogeneity (ecoregion, Strahler order, main river basin, width and depth of the stream, distance from well and altitude), the importance of factors and mutual clusters position was validated using principal component analysis. The analyses were performed using Statistica for Windows (StatSoft, Inc., 2005).

The classification methods applied on data were: i) The novel method ("centroid distance") mentioned above; ii) Discriminant analysis; iii) Classification tree and iv) Neural network.

The dataset with the given groups of localities was divided into two files which were used for cross validation in these analyses. The following results of application of the models on independent cross validation datasets were obtained: i) Centroid distance: correct classification 91.3%; ii) Discriminant analysis: 87.6%; iii) Classification tree: 94.7%; iv) Neural network: 93.7%.

The results suggest that the developed methodology has similar predictive power as the commonly used methods or even better than some of them (discriminant analysis).

4 Conclusion

The presented methodology is a robust nonparametric classification method suitable for automated computing in heterogeneous environmental datasets. The predictive power of the method is comparable to commonly used parametric classification methods but without their extensive prerequisites and with simple interpretation of the classification model based on multivariate distances of objects.

Acknowledgments. This study was supported by FP7 project TaToo "Tagging Tool based on a Semantic Discovery Framework".

References

1. Legendre, P., Legendre, L.: Numerical ecology. Elseviere Science BV, Amsterdam (1998)
2. Gower, J.C.: A general coefficient of similarity and some of its properties. Biometrics 27, 857–871 (1971)
3. Prim, R.C.: Shortest connection networks and some generalizations. Bell Syst. Tech. J. 36, 1389–1401 (1957)

CETOCOEN Project: From the Laboratory to the Field and Beyond

Jana Klánová[1], Luděk Bláha[1], Jiří Damborský[1,2], Petr Klán[1,3], Ladislav Dušek[1,4], and Ivan Holoubek[1]

[1] Research Centre for Toxic Compounds in the Environment, Faculty of Science, Masaryk University, Kamenice 126/3, 625 00 Brno, Czech Republic
[2] Department of Experimental Biology, Faculty of Science, Masaryk University, Kamenice 753/5, 625 00 Brno, Czech Republic
[3] Department of Chemistry, Faculty of Science, Masaryk University, Kamenice 753/5, 625 00 Brno, Czech Republic
[4] Institute of Biostatistics and Analyses, Masaryk University, Kamenice 126/3, 625 00 Brno, Czech Republic
{klanova,blaha,holoubek}@recetox.muni.cz,
jiri@chemi.muni, klan@sci.muni.cz, dusek@iba.muni.cz

Abstract. Growing demand for data on the environmental impacts of persistent organic pollutants coming from legal and regional authorities as well as from private subjects, professionals and public resulted in initiation of the CETOCOEN project. This project is coordinated by the Research centre for toxic compounds in the environment of the Masaryk University in Brno and provides complex information supporting decision making and development of strategies related to protection of natural environment and human health.

Keywords: Persistent organic pollutants, POPs, ambient air, monitoring, Stockholm Convention, Global Monitoring Plan, CETOCOEN, MONET.

1 Introduction

Environmental problems including their social and economical impacts have to be set into the context of the overall development of society, as a good management of natural resources is one of the key aspects of sustainable development. Such management requires sufficient information on the key factors affecting environment, data on occurrence, fate, persistence and long-range transport of various chemicals, their accumulation in biota and food chains as well as on mechanisms of their toxicity, and related ecological and human health risks. Only such complex information can provide sufficient support for decision making and development of strategies related to protection of natural environment and human health. International cooperation in this field is crucial as the environmental pollution goes beyond the boundaries.

Growing demand for such information coming from legal and regional authorities as well as from private subjects, professionals and public resulted in initiation of the

J. Hřebíček, G. Schimak, and R. Denzer (Eds.): ISESS 2011, IFIP AICT 359, pp. 491–499, 2011.

CETOCOEN (CEntre for TOxic COmpounds in the ENvironment)[1] project of Operational Program Research and Development for Innovations[2] supported from European Union (EU) Structural funds. The CETOCOEN project is coordinated by the *Research centre for toxic compounds in the environment* (RECETOX)[3] of the Masaryk University in Brno.

2 Background

The centre addressing problems related to persistent organic pollutants (POPs) was established in 1996 and from the beginning it has been involved in a number of international networks and projects. In cooperation with the Czech Hydrometeorological Institute, the centre established the programme of integrated monitoring of POPs in all environmental matrices at the central European background station in Košetice in 1996.

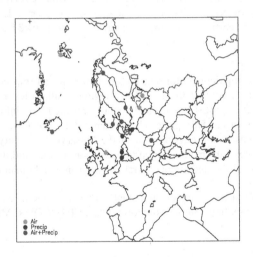

Fig. 1. Network of EMEP stations monitoring POPs

Unique data on long-term trends in environmental levels of polycyclic aromatic hydrocarbons (PAHs), polychlorinated biphenyls (PCBs) and organochlorine pesticides (OCPs) at European background are reported to the *European Monitoring and Evaluation Programme* (EMEP)[4], a collaborative project addressing long-range transport of the air-born pollutants in Europe and supporting international *Convention on Long-range Transboundary Air Pollution* (CLRTAP)[5] [1], [2], [3].

---

[1] http://www.cetocoen.cz/
[2] http://www.strukturalni-fondy.cz/getdoc/977e2e36-937e-4432-afe7-165afd87e676/
   OP-Vyzkum-a-vyvoj-pro-inovace
[3] http://www.recetox.muni.cz/index-en.php
[4] http://www.emep.int/
[5] http://www.unece.org/env/lrtap/

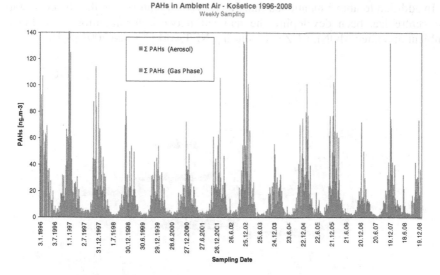

Fig. 2. Long-term trends of PAHs at the Košetice EMEP station

In the last decade, interactions among chemicals, environment and biological systems and their consequences at local, regional and global levels were the main focus of the centre. New approaches and experimental techniques were developed in photochemistry, toxicology, risk assessment, biostatistics, modelling and environmental informatics. Interdisciplinary links were established when addressing effects of the climate change on the contaminant cycling in the atmosphere [4 – 7].

In 2001-4, the centre coordinated the project funded by United Nations Industrial Development Organization (UNIDO)[6] focused on implementation of the Stockholm Convention on Persistent Organic Pollutants (SC)[7] in the Czech Republic. Consequently, a *National centre for POPs*[8], was established as a part of RECETOX, an expert body focused on chemical and toxicological assessments of the chemicals being a subject of the international conventions ratified by the Czech Republic.

The centre serves the needs of government, ministries, regional authorities and industry, and provides new information on levels and fate of these chemicals, their toxicological properties and risks, and developing new methods of sampling, chemical analyses and effective toxicological testing.

In 2009, the Conference of the Parties of the Stockholm Convention of United Nations Environmental Programme (UNEP)[9] officially endorsed RECETOX as a *Regional Centre of the Stockholm Convention for capacity building and technology transfer in the region of Central and Eastern Europe*[10].

---

[6] http://www.unido.org/
[7] http://chm.pops.int/default.aspx
[8] http://www.recetox.muni.cz/index-en.php?pg=national-pops-centre
[9] http://hqweb.unep.org/
[10] http://www.recetox.muni.cz/index-en.php?pg=regional-pops-center

In addition to above mentioned integrated POPs monitoring at the Košetice station, the centre has been developing the national network for monitoring of POPs in ambient air called MONET CZ (MOnitoring NETwork)[11] since 2003 [8-10].

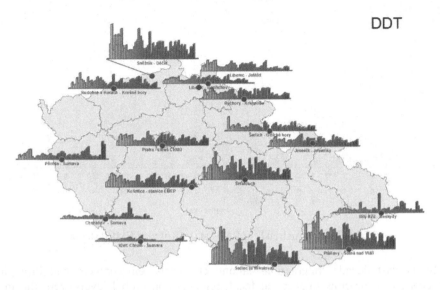

Fig. 3. Long term measurement of DDT and metabolites in ambient air at background stations of MONET network

Since 2004, MONET CZ has expanded to all Central and Eastern European (CEE) countries as MONET CEE[12] and became a successful example of know-how and technology transfer in the region [11-15]. Passive air sampling technique was selected as an official tool for global monitoring of POPs, and RECETOX became a strategic partner for many world regions (CEE, Africa, Asia and Pacific) [16].

Currently, the centre operates the long-term air monitoring programme (MONET EU) at the EMEP stations in all European countries and executes the air monitoring programme in Africa (MONET AFRICA) supported from the EU . With a help of the Global Environmental Facility (GEF)[13] the centre also contributes to the development of analytical capacities in participating countries.

Vast number of samples collected in frames of such long-term monitoring programs introduced a problem of efficient data management. Robust environmental database was urgently needed as well as interactive tools permitting the user to validate, aggregate, analyze, and visualize data.

Due to the international and multilateral character of the MONET project, the centre faced a task to develop a web portal allowing professionals as well as general

---

[11] http://www.monet-cz.cz/
[12] http://www.recetox.muni.cz/index-en.php?pg=regional-pops-center--scope-of-sc-rc-activities--monitoring-of-pops-in-the-cee-countries-and-other-regions
[13] http://www.thegef.org/gef/home

public to assess available environmental data providing them at the same time with the advanced analytical and modelling tools based on the Geographical information system (GIS).

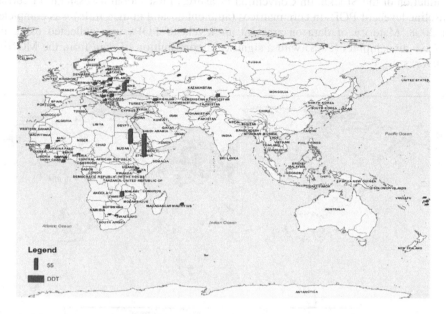

Fig. 4. Measurement of DDT and metabolites at the background stations of the MONET networks in Europe, Asia and Africa

3   CETOCOEN Project and Its Goals

In 2009, the research team of the centre prepared a successful project for the EU Structural funds, Operational programme Research and Development for Innovations, in the priority axis 2, Regional centres of applied research. The CETOCOEN project stemmed from the previous successful history of the centre and set new and ambitious goals. Following substantial enhancement of the laboratory capacities and human resources, the centre is expanding from the original fields of research to new directions including development of sampling and analytical methods for emerging environmental pollutants, laboratory and field studies of processes affecting the fate of chemical substances in the environment, development of biosensors and natural biocatalyzers, and assessment of toxic effects of chemical compounds and natural toxins on organisms.

Major contribution of the CETOCOEN project is improved understanding to the environmental fate of toxic compounds, their distribution among matrices, long range transport and bioaccumulation, degradation mechanisms of pollutants in various climatic regions with respect to increasing risks of their re-release due to the climate change, responsible assessment of toxic effects, and quantification of ecological and human health risks. The project will help to identify new classes of toxic chemicals suspected of persistence, bioaccumulation and long-range transport, which are major criteria for their listing in the global conventions on chemical safety. The centre is also involved in the *Global monitoring plan* (GMP)[14]. GMP is an activity developed under the Stockholm Convention with a purpose of providing a tool for effectiveness evaluation of the Stockholm Convention measures. First global assessment of current baseline levels of POPs in core matrices (ambient air and human milk) was completed in 2008. Majority of data on ambient air levels of POPs was collected using the passive air samplers (PAS) with a significant contribution of data from the MONET networks.

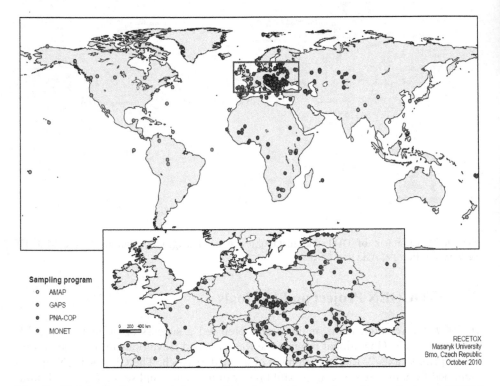

Fig. 5. Global distribution of the sampling sites with on-going air monitoring. MONET sampling sites are coloured blue.

In 2009, the Conference of the Parties of the SC decided that levels of POPs in core matrices will be assessed every six years assuming that such period will be sufficient for establishment of the temporal trends. As the Košetice station is the only site worldwide where active and passive samplers have been co-employed for full six years so far, results from this station have an important role in the intercalibration of both techniques, comparison of trends derived from both datasets, and development of future global monitoring programmes [17-19]. Long-term sustainability of such

---

[14] http://chm.pops.int/Programmes/Global%20Monitoring%20Plan/Overview/tabid/83/language/en-GB/Default.aspx

monitoring programmes is of a great importance for a success of the Global monitoring plan.

To integrate available monitoring data reporting environmental levels of toxic chemicals with newly acquired knowledge on their behaviour and effects in a single database available to public and widely utilized requires a new type of software for simultaneous visualization and analyses of various types of data. Development of the mathematical models for quantification of mass transfers from primary and secondary sources, exposure of ecosystems and human, model simulations of distribution, transformation, and long range transport of POPs, as well as designing the software tools allowing the use of the whole database as expert system, is the most important task of the CETOCOEN project.

This unique environmental data system should be further linked to existing epidemiological databases in order to enhance our understanding to environmentally induced diseases and their triggering mechanisms. While epidemiological data are currently well organized, data from the environmental monitoring programmes are rather fractionated. This problem has been also recognized on the international level.

4 Project Deliverables and Impacts

Successful implementation of the CETOCOEN project, namely development of Global environmental assessment and information system (GENASIS)[15] would provide professional platform and decision making tool supporting implementation of European legislation and international conventions on environment protection. At the same time, the GENASIS should function as a clearing house mechanism transferring know-how between experts, institutions, countries and regions.

The outcomes of the CETOCOEN project will serve to the government and national ministries by providing information services necessary to control compliance with international conventions, to update inventories, toxicological databases and risk profiles, to develop of monitoring networks and expert systems for interpretation of environmental data. They will support the regional state authorities coordinating studies of environmental quality, toxicological investigations and risk assessments. Impact assessments of industrial technologies, data on contamination of the working environment and assessment of related risks will be useful for industrial partners. Availability of such data may trigger transfer of environment-friendly technologies, development of new remediation methods and better education of experts.

The project reduces a problem of insufficient links between scientific and applied sector and, at the same time, it establishes the links between the applied research and higher education. It is closely related to the capacity building and technology transfer, supports development of the human resources and training of interdisciplinary educated experts for industrial innovations as well as public authorities.

Beside a scientific quality, the CETOCOEN project has also an important social-economical impact on the local and regional levels. It increases attractiveness of the region for the scientists and in so doing prevents a brain drain of young scientists, supports underdeveloped congress tourism, and enhances environmental education and public awareness in the region.

---

[15] http://www.genasis.cz/main-index/en/

Acknowledgments. This research received financial support from the CETOCOEN project of the European Structural Funds (CZ.1.05/2.1.00/01.0001), the Ministry of Education (MSM 0021622412) and the Ministry of Environment (SP1a3/29/07) of the Czech Republic.

References

1. Dvorska, A., Lammel, G., Klanova, J., Holoubek, I.: Košetice, Czech Republic – ten years of air pollution monitoring and four years of evaluating the origin of persistent organic pollutants. Environ. Pollut. 156(2), 403–408 (2008)
2. Holoubek, I., Klánová, J., Jarkovský, J., Kohoutek, J.: Trends in background levels of persistent organic pollutants at Kosetice observatory, Czech Republic. Part I. Ambient air and wet deposition 1988-2005. J. Environ. Monit. 9(6), 557–563 (2007)
3. Holoubek, I., Klánová, J., Jarkovský, J., Kubík, V., Helešic, J.: Trends in background levels of persistent organic pollutants at Kosetice observatory, Czech Republic. Part II. Aquatic and terrestric environments 1988-2005. J. Environ. Monit. 9(6), 564–571 (2007)
4. Lammel, G., Klánová, J., Kohoutek, J., Prokeš, R., Ries, L., Stohl, A.: Observation and origin of organochlorine pesticides, polychlorinated biphenyls and polycyclic aromatic hydrocarbons in the free troposphere over central Europe. Environ. Pollut. 157, 3264–3271 (2009)
5. Lammel, G., Klánová, J., Ilić, P., Kohoutek, J., Gasić, B., Kovacić, I., Lakić, N., Radić, R.: Polycyclic aromatic hydrocarbons on small spatial and temporal scales – I. Levels and variabilities. Atmos. Environ. 44, 5015–5021 (2010)
6. Lammel, G., Klánová, J., Ilić, P., Kohoutek, J., Gasić, B., Kovacić, I., Škrdlíková, L.: Polycyclic aromatic hydrocarbons on small spatial and temporal scales – II. Mass size distributions and gas-particle partitioning. Atmos. Environ. 44, 5022–5027 (2010)
7. Gasić, B., MacLeod, M., Klánová, J., Scheringer, M., Ilić, P., Lammel, G., Pajović, A., Breivik, K., Holoubek, I., Hungerbühler, K.: Quantification of sources of PCBs to the atmosphere in urban areas: A comparison of cities in North America, Western Europe and former Yugoslavia. Environ. Pollut. 158, 3230–3235 (2010)
8. Harner, T., Bartkow, M., Holoubek, I., Klanova, J., Sweetman, A.J., Wania, F., Jones, K.C.: *: Passive air sampling for persistent organic pollutants: introductory remarks to the Special Issue. Environ. Pollut. 144(2), 361–364 (2006)
9. Klánová, J., Kohoutek, J., Hamplová, L., Urbanová, P., Holoubek, I.: Passive air sampler as a tool for long-term air pollution monitoring: Part 1. Performance assessment for seasonal and spatial variations. Environmental Pollution 144(2), 393–405 (2006)
10. Čupr, P., Klánová, J., Bartoš, T., Flégrová, Z., Kohoutek, J., Holoubek, I.: Passive air sampler as a tool for long-term air pollution monitoring: Part 2. Air genotoxic potency screening assessment. Environ. Pollut. 144(2), 406–413 (2006)
11. Klánová, J., Kohoutek, J., Kostrhounová, R., Holoubek, I.: Are the residents of former Yugoslavia still exposed to elevated PCB levels due to the Balkan wars? Part 1: Air sampling in Croatia, Serbia, Bosnia & Hercegovina. Environ. Int. 33(6), 719–726 (2007)
12. Klánová, J., Kohoutek, J., Čupr, P., Holoubek, I.: Are the residents of former Yugoslavia still exposed to elevated PCB levels due to the Balkan wars? Part 2: Passive air sampling network. Environ. Int. 33(6), 727–735 (2007)
13. Škarek, M., Čupr, P., Bartoš, T., Kohoutek, J., Klánová, J., Holoubek: A combined approach to the evaluation of organic air pollution – A case study of urban air in Sarajevo and Tuzla (Bosnia and Herzegovina). Sci. Tot. Environ. 384(1-3), 182–193 (2007)

14. Růžičková, P., Klánová, J., Čupr, P., Lammel, G., Holoubek, I.: An assessment of air-soil exchange of polychlorinated biphenyls and organochlorine pesticides across Central and Southern Europe. Environ. Sci. Technol. 42(1), 179–185 (2008)

15. Bartoš, T., Čupr, P., Klánová, J., Holoubek, I.: Which compounds are most responsible for elevated human health risks in the Western Balkans? Environ. Int 35, 1066–1071 (2009)

16. Klánová, J., Čupr, P., Holoubek, I., Borůvková, J., Kareš, R., Tomšej, T., Ocelka, T.: Monitoring of persistent organic pollutants in Africa. Part 1: Passive air sampling across the continent in 2008. J. Environ. Monit. 11, 1952–1963 (2009)

17. Klánová, J., Čupr, P., Kohoutek, J., Harner, T.: Assessing meteorological parameters on the performance of PUF disks passive air samplers for POPs. Environ. Sci. Technol. 42(2), 550–555 (2008)

18. Chaemfa, C., Barber, J.L., Gocht, T., Harner, T., Holoubek, I., Klanova, J., Jones, K.C.: Field calibration of polyurethane foam (PUF) disk passive air samplers for PCBs and OC Pesticides. Environ. Pollut. 156(3), 1290–1297 (2008)

19. Chaemfa, C., Barber, J.L., Moeckel, C., Gocht, T., Harner, T., Holoubek, I., Klanova, J., Jones, K.C.: Field calibration of polyurethane foam (PUF) disk passive air samplers for PBDEs. J. Environ. Monit. 11, 1859–1865 (2009)

Spatial Soil Modeling of Organochlorine Pesticides, Their Pools and Volatilization Fluxes

Klára Komprdová[1], Jiří Komprda[1], Milan Sáňka[1], and Ondřej Hájek[2]

[1] RECETOX (Research Centre for Toxic Compounds in the Environment), Kamenice 126/3,
CZ–625 00 Brno, Czech Republic
[2] Department of Botany and Zoology, Masaryk University, Kotlářská 2,
CZ-611 37 Brno, Czech Republic
komprdova@recetox.muni.cz

Abstract. The goal of this study was to use the modeling tools for prediction of environmental concentrations and pools of pesticides (HCB and DDT) in soil. The characterization and quantification of secondary background sources of HCB, were computed using fugacity based deterministic model. Areas with a high potential for deposition and volatilization of HCB were identified. Results of modeling were maps showing spatial distribution of HCB and DDT in the Czech Republic which have been visualized on the web portal GENASIS (Global Environmental Assessment Information System) to provide information on environment contamination.

Keywords: pesticides, pool, modeling, fugacity, POPs.

1 Introduction

HCB and DDT were produced during last decades for various agricultural and industrial purposes. They are widely distributed in all environmental compartments including air, soil, water, sediment and biota because of their physical-chemical properties. The considerable amount of these compounds is still presented mainly in the soil. Sources of HCB in the environment in the mid 1990s were considered to be the manufacture of chlorinated solvents, the manufacture and application of HCB containing pesticides [1], metal production and the residential sector [2]. DDT was widely used in the second half of the 20th century and Czechoslovakia was an important producer and consumer of DDT [3].

In addition to the long-range transport, HCB and DDT are also re-mobilized from primary and secondary sources such as contaminated sites and soils, which may strongly influence their concentration in air on shorter spatial scales e.g., in areas of former heavy HCB application elevated soil concentrations of HCB are commonly found [4]. DDT is very persistent in soil, too.

One of important properties of those compounds is semivolatility. When atmospheric concentrations of POPs (persistent organic pollutants) declined as a

J. Hřebíček, G. Schimak, and R. Denzer (Eds.): ISESS 2011, IFIP AICT 359, pp. 500–506, 2011.

result of restrictions to low level volatilization from soil become their significant or even dominant emission source in the environment. Spatially resolved deterministic model based on fugacity approach was created for calculation of volatilization fluxes and total amount of HCB being volatilized was predicted. Influence of environmental temperature changes and variation of organic carbon content in soil was included in the model.

1.1 Data Sources

In central Europe, unique continuous monitoring of POPs is conducted at the background sampling site Košetice, Czech Republic, since 1988. This dataset allow analyzing pollution level and temporal trend in various environmental matrices and study the environmental fate of POPs more deeply. Input concentrations for the soil model were collected from several projects. The most important sources of data came from two nation-wide soil monitoring systems: Basal monitoring of agricultural soils conducted by CISTA (Central Institute for Supervising and Testing in Agriculture) and Basal monitoring of soils in protected areas conducted by ANLP (Agency for Nature and Landscape Protection). Other data sources were projects conducted by RECETOX (Research Centre for Toxic Compounds in the Environment) for various purposes and at various spatial scales. Altogether, comprehensive data from about 600 sites around the country formed the basic database used for further evaluation and modeling. The collected data covered not only soil concentrations of POPs but also other important parameters measured at individual sites, e.g. geographical coordinates, soil organic carbon content, soil type, land use.

2 Methodology

2.1 Determination of the Spatial and Quantitative Distribution of POPs in Soil

Concentration maps for each substance in soil at a 1x1 km grid resolution were constructed using the GIS approach. The prediction model was based on the dependency of POP concentration levels on environmental parameters. Only parameters which were supposed to influence the concentration were used. Four groups of predictor variables were used: 1. markers of anthropogenic activity such as distance from industry, distance from populated areas and road classes, NO_x, SO_2, particulate matter content in air, old dumps, size of populated area 2. climatic factors such as altitude, mean annual temperature, annual precipitation 3. soil properties such as soil type, character of soil and organic carbon content and 4. land cover [5]. Prior to modeling, a square grid was generated for the Czech Republic using ArcGIS 9.2 (in total 80 033 squares of 1x1 km).

Non-parametric methods, CART [6] and Random Forest [7], were used for the prediction of POP soil concentrations in CZ. The reason is the character of data (categorial variables with many categories, assumption of nonlinear relationships, non-normal distribution of variables and multicolinearity). The concentrations' maps of HCB and DDT were used from previous study on RECETOX [8]. A pool of POPs in the top soil layer was calculated for each cell of the grid using concentration of pesticides and a bulk density and thickness of soil horizons. The values were specific for each grid square [9].

2.2 Construction of a Fugacity Model for Determining the Volatilization of POPs from Czech Soils

Land cover, soil type, temperature gradient and organic carbon content in soil form the basis of the applied fugacity model. It was necessary to construct temperature maps for the whole area of the Czech Republic. Results were evaluated according to the potential of individual areas to volatilization and deposition of HCB. The fugacity model [10] was based on a dynamic box model, based on previous experience with the construction and use of a similar model type comprising both soil and air [11]. Input parameters were both physical-chemical properties of the studied substances and properties of the environment, e.g. temperature and organic carbon content in soil. Three resistance concept based on fugacity approach was used (Fig. 1).

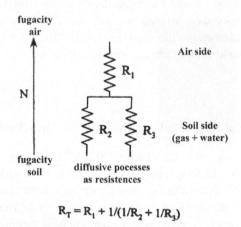

$$R_T = R_1 + 1/(1/R_2 + 1/R_3)$$

Fig. 1. Three resistance concept based on fugacity approach [10]

Volatilization flux is proportional to difference of fugacities between air and soil. Fugacity as criterion of equilibrium is a "pressure" of POPs in compartments. The model contains mass transfer coefficients describing transfer over the air-soil interphase (air and soil compartments are homogenous boxes). Temperature dependence was included through partitioning coefficients (K_{ow} n-octanol/water, K_{aw} air/water, K_{oc} organic carbon/water, K_{sw} soil/water).

Correction of partitioning coefficients to the specific environmental temperature (van´t Hoff's equation):

$$K_{aw} = K_{aw0} * e^{(dH/R*(1/T0 - 1/T))} \tag{1}$$

Evaluation of partitioning coefficients soil-water (K_{sw}):

$$K_{oc} = K_{ow} * 0.41 \tag{2}$$

$$K'_{sw} = K_{oc} * f_{oc} \tag{3}$$

$$K_{sw} = K'_{sw} / (1000 * \rho) \tag{4}$$

Evaluation of fugacity capacities Z [mol· (m³·Pa)⁻¹]:

$$Z_a = 1 / (R * T) \tag{5}$$

$$Z_l = 1 / (K_{awt} * R * T) \tag{6}$$

$$Z_s = K_{sw} * Z_l \tag{7}$$

$$Z_{sbulk} = f_s * Z_s + f_a * Z_a + f_l * Z_l \tag{8}$$

Evaluation of transport coefficients D [mol· (h·Pa)⁻¹]:

$$D_a = MTC_a * Z_a \tag{9}$$

$$D_{sa} = MTC_{sa} * Z_a \tag{10}$$

$$D_{sl} = MTC_{sw} * Z_l \tag{11}$$

$$D_s = 1 / (1/D_a + 1/(D_{sa} + D_{sl})) \tag{12}$$

Evaluation of total flux of pollutant between air and soil:

$$F = F_{sa} - F_{as} \tag{13}$$

$$F = D_s * f_s - D_s * f_a \tag{14}$$

When s–soil, a-air, l-liquid, w-water, R- gas constant 8.314 [J·(mol·K)⁻¹], MTC- mass transport coefficient [m·h⁻¹], f_s, f_a f_l– solid, liquid and air fractions in soil, f_s, f_a – fugacities of pollutant in soil and air [Pa], F- flux of pollutant over air/soil interphase [mol·h⁻¹], f_a – fugacity of pollutant in air was set to average fugacity from regular monitoring in Kosetice., f_s – fugacity of pollutant in soil was calculated from predicted concentration maps using Z_{sbulk} (grid specific values). For detail see [12]. The median of HCB concentration in air from background side (Kosetice) was used. The evaluation was performed in MATLAB.

4 Results and Conclusions

Concentration maps of DDT and HCB were constructed with a high accuracy of prediction and their pools were computed (Fig. 2 and 3). Based on these results, the total POPs pool in soils was determined in grassland, forests soil and arable land (Fig. 4)

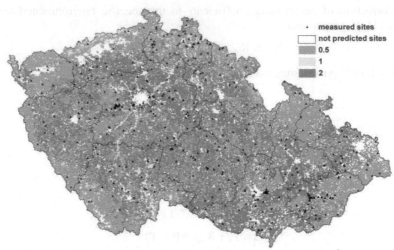

Fig. 2. Spatially resolved (grid of 1×1 km) pools of HCB (kg·km^{-1})

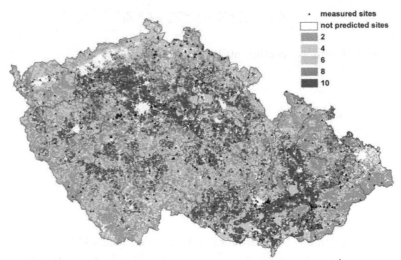

Fig. 3. Spatially resolved (grid of 1×1 km) pools of DDT (kg·km^{-1})

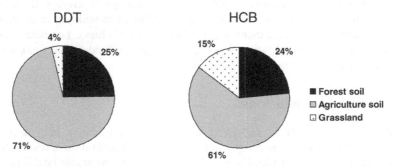

Fig. 4. Percentage of the total DDT and HCB pool in grassland, forests soil and arable land

HCB and DDT maps clearly show higher pools in lowlands when compared to mountain soils. It is a result of using these compounds as pesticides for several decades. Volatilization maps show that pools are active source of these pollutants during warm part of year. This is in contrast to colder regions in mountains which are target places of air transport e.g. cold condensation nearly during whole year (Fig. 5 and 6).

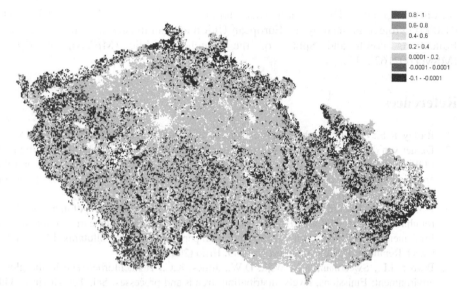

Fig. 5. Volatilization flux of HCB from soil in January (ng·m^{-2}·h^{-1})

Fig. 6. Volatilization flux of HCB from soil in July (ng·m^{-2}·h^{-1})

This approach was proved to be very suitable. The total amount of a substance volatilized into air was determined. The areas with a high potential for deposition and volatilization and areas with potential for fast pesticides concentration changes in soil were identified during the analysis. Maps have been visualized on the web portal GENASIS (Global Environmental Assessment Information System) to provide information on environment contamination.

Acknowledgments. The research was supported by CETOCOEN (CZ.1.05/2.1.00/01.0001) project, granted by the European Union and administered by the Ministry of Education, Youth and Sports of the Czech Republic (MEYS), by MEYS (MSMT0021622412).

References

1. Bailey, R.E.: Global hexachlorobenzene emissions. Chemosphere 43, 167–182 (2001)
2. Denier van der Gon, H., van het Bolscher, M., Visschedijk, A., Zandveld, P.: Emissions of POPs and eight candidate POPs from UNECE-Europe in 2000, 2010 and 2020 and the emission reduction resulting from the implementation of the UNECE POP protocol. Atmos. Environ. 41, 9245–9261 (2007)
3. Holoubek, I.: Úvodní národní inventura persistentních organických polutantů v České republice. Project GF/CEH/01/003: Enabling activites to facilitate early action on the implementation of the Stockholm convention on persistent organic pollutants (POPs) in the Czech Republic. TOCOEN Report No. 249, Brno (2005)
4. Barber, J.L., Sweetman, A.J., Wijk, D.W., Jones, K.C.: Hexachlorbenzene in the global environment: Emissions, levels, distribution, trends and processes. Sci. Tot. Environ. 349, 1–44 (2005)
5. Bossard, M., Feranec, J., Otahel, J.: CORINE land cover technical guide– Addendum 2000, Technical report No 40 European Environment Agency, Copenhagen (2000)
6. Breiman, L.: Random forests. Machine Learning J. 45, 5–32 (2001)
7. Breiman, L., Friedman, J., Stone, C.J., Olshen, R.A.: Classification and Regression Trees. Chapman and Hall, New York (1984)
8. Kubosova, K., Komprda, J., Jarkovsky, J., Sanka, M., Hajek, O., Dusek, L., Holoubek, I., Klanova, J.: Spatially resolved distribution models of POP moncentrations in moil: A stochastic approach using regression trees. Environ. Sci. Technol. 43, 9230–9236 (2009)
9. Cupr, P., Bartos, T., Sanka, M., Klanova, J., Mikes, O., Holoubek, I.: Soil burdens of persistent organic pollutants — Their levels, fate and risks Part III. Quantification of the soil burdens and related health risks in the Czech Republic. Sci. Tot. Environ. 408, 486–494 (2010)
10. Mackay, D.: Multimedia Environmental Models: The Fugacity Approach, 2nd edn. Lewis Publishers, Boca Raton (2001)
11. Komprda, J., Kubosova, K., Dvorska, A., Scheringer, M., Klanova, J., Holoubek, I.: Application of an unsteady state environmental distribution model to a decadal time series of PAH concentrations in Central Europe. J. Env. Monit. 11, 269–276 (2009)
12. Koblizkova, M., Ruzickova, P., Cupr, P., Komprda, J., Holoubek, I., Klanova, J.: Soil Burdens of Persistent Organic Pollutants: Their Levels, Fate, and Risks. Part IV. Quantification of Volatilization Fluxes of Organochlorine Pesticides and Polychlorinated Biphenyls from Contaminated Soil Surfaces. Environ. Sci. Technol. 43, 10–18 (2009)

Global Environmental Assessment Requires Global Functional Searching Engines: Robust Application of TaToo Tools

Miroslav Kubásek[1], Jiří Hřebíček[1], Jiří Kalina[1], Ladislav Dušek[1], Jaroslav Urbánek[2], and Ivan Holoubek[2]

[1] IBA, Masaryk University, Kamenice 126/3, 625 00 Brno, Czech Republic
[2] RECETOX, Masaryk University, Kamenice 126/3, 625 00 Brno, Czech Republic
{kubasek,hrebicek,kalina,dusek}@iba.muni.cz,
{urbanek,holoubek}@recetox.muni.cz

Abstract. The synthesis of existing Persistent Organic Pollutants (POPs) pollution monitoring databases with epidemiological data is considered for identifying some impacts of POPs on human health. This task requires new, rich, data, services and models discovery capabilities from a multitude of monitoring networks and web resources. The FP7 project TaToo (Tagging Tool based on a Semantic Discovery Framework) is setting up a semantic web solution to close the discovery gap that prevents a full and easy access to web resources. The use of TaToo tools together with software GENASIS and SVOD is discussed as TaToo validation scenario for anthropogenic impact and global climate change influence on POPs trajectory.

Keywords: TaToo, semantic web, POPs, Stockholm Convention, GENASIS, SVOD, anthropogenic impact, global climate change.

1 Introduction

The FP7 project TaToo (Tagging Tool based on a Semantic Discovery Framework) aims to set up a semantic web solution to close the discovery gap that prevents a full and easy access to environmental resources on the web [8]. The core of the project will focus on the development of tools allowing third parties to easily discover environmental resources (data and/or services residing on different information nodes) on the web and to add valuable information in the form of semantic annotations to these resources, thus facilitating future usage and discovery, and kicking off a beneficial cycle of information enrichment.

TaToo validates the usability of its developments through the implementation of three different scenarios. All three scenarios are embedded in highly complex environmental domains and are therefore mainly addressed to domain expert groups and communities as well as to technically skilled users.

This paper contains the detailed framework of Masaryk university scenario, which is the anthropogenic impact and the influence of global climate change on this impact [4], [5]. The purpose of the paper is to give the overview of the scenario (background,

J. Hřebíček, G. Schimak, and R. Denzer (Eds.): ISESS 2011, IFIP AICT 359, pp. 507–518, 2011.

objectives, and available tools), the definition of users who will use the TaToo tools, describe the possible use cases, and to provide with the mock ups.

2 Description of the Scenario

The third validation scenario of TaToo project named *Anthropogenic impact and global climate change* is managed by Masaryk University[1] (MU). MU validation scenario is dealing with the correlation of environmental pollutants and their health impact on the population and the correlation of transport of environmental pollutants with global climate change [4], [5]. The aim is to create a central place for researchers, domain experts and decision makers to discover and access interdisciplinary knowledge in more efficient and usable way that is the currently state of the art. Due to the fact that there is an enormous amount of information resources in scientific fields, which is steadily growing, available search mechanisms like search engines, scientific networks and similar technologies are not sufficient to meet the complex requirements of today's researchers and scientists. The result of conventional discovery processes are often not matching the domain context of the users and obligate them the tedious task of filtering large result sets to obtain the original object of the interest of the researcher intended to find with the search. Therefore the need arises for an improving discovery method, which will incorporate the domain knowledge and additional semantic information into the search in order to obtain a more fitting result for the specific context of the user.

This validation scenario not only aims to improve the discovery of scientific resources for one particular domain, but also tries to discover and create new relationships among different domains. The correlation of environmental pollutants including their transport due to global climate change and their health impact on the population is only one significant example of creating new relationships among different domains. These dependencies could represent new scientific insights for already available resources and connect the knowledge of the single domains. These relationships should facilitate further discovery process to deliver matching resources of multiple domains.

This validation scenario represents the close cooperation and joint venture of two university institutes: the *Research Centre for Toxic Compounds in the Environment*[2] (RECETOX) and *Institute of Biostatistics and Analyses*[3] (IBA).

RECETOX is an independent institute of the Masaryk University. RECETOX performs research, development, education and expertise in the field of environmental contamination by toxic compounds with specific focus on persistent organic pollutants (POPs), polar organic compounds, toxic metals and their species and natural toxins - cyanotoxins. It is also Stockholm Convention Regional centre[4] for capacity building and transfer of technology in Central and Eastern European countries. The *Stockholm Convention on Persistent Organic Pollutants*[5] (*Stockholm*

---

[1] http://www.muni.cz
[2] http://www.recetox.muni.cz
[3] http://www.iba.muni.cz
[4] http://www.recetox.muni.cz/index-en.php?pg=regional-pops-center
[5] http://www.pops.int

convention) is a global treaty to protect human health and the environment from chemicals that remain intact in the environment for long periods, become widely distributed geographically and accumulate in the fatty tissue of humans and wildlife. RECETOX is formed by several research divisions, service laboratories and technology-transfer centres: Environmental chemistry and modelling, Ecotoxicology and risk assessment, Trace laboratory, and Laboratory of data analyses. Research and development of the centre include monitoring of environmental matrices, studies of environmental fate and effects (ecotoxicology) of toxic compounds, ecological and human risk assessment as well as the development of informational and expert systems. In January 2010 RECETOX launched the first version of the *Global Environmental Assessment and Information System* (GENASIS)[6], which provides information support for implementation of the *Stockholm convention* at an international level. The initial phase of the GENASIS project is focused on data from regular monitoring programmes of POPs, providing a general overview of spatial patterns and temporal trends of pollutants concentrations [1].

IBA is a research institute focused on delivering solutions to questions arising in scientific projects and providing related services, especially in the field of biological and clinical data analysis, organization and management of clinical trials, software development and Information and Communication Technology (ICT) applications. IBA activities are primarily focused on organizational and expert services for large scientific projects and clinical research projects. IBA is formed by four divisions: Division of Data Analysis, Division of Clinical Trials, Division of Information and Communication Technologies, and Division of Environmental Informatics and Modelling. For example, IBA created the web portal for epidemiology of malignant tumours in the Czech Republic, the *System for Visualizing of Oncological Data* (SVOD)[7], based on the data from the Czech National Oncology Registry [3].

Dušek [2] pointed in 2009:*"A full-area monitoring of the environmental risk factors in all main environmental components is performed in the Czech Republic. The main objective of this functional monitoring network is the estimation of exposure to xenobiotic substances, and the evaluation of subsequent risks to human health. The system provides information for health risks management and also serves for public education, which is a prerequisite for active care of one's own health. The outputs from monitoring systems may also be used for assessing human risks associated with cancer epidemiology. Data about POPs are of key importance, since these compounds are known to have a wide spectrum of carcinogenic effects, a tendency to bioaccumulation, and are subject to long-distance transport."*

The objective of the MU validation scenario is to use and validate the resulting tagging and discovery framework of the TaToo project. Since the primary scope of the TaToo project is to facilitate the discovery of environmental resources, this scenario delivers the perfect opportunity to validate the resulting solution against challenging real word problems. There are numerous scientific domains available and actively researched at the MU, but two important domains have been carefully chosen to demonstrate and validate the envisioned functionality of the TaToo project. The vision of the MU validation scenario is that other scientific domains could follow the

---

[6] http://www.genasis.cz
[7] http://www.svod.cz

initial institutes to further spin a new kind of knowledge network to deliver a new generation of tools and methods to effectively and conveniently support the scientific user in their daily work.

2.1 System for Visualizing of Oncological Data

Creating the SVOD web portal about tumour epidemiology in the Czech Republic was primarily motivated by the effort to make this representative and valuable data available to wide spectrum of users. We anticipated that general epidemiology data about these serious diseases and related population risks should be freely available to everybody in the Czech Republic. Another ambition of the SVOD web portal was to provide relevant information about tumor epidemiology in the Czech Republic abroad.

The SVOD web portal information services can be divided into three sections:

1) *Current news*: regularly updated information about population risk assessment and tumor epidemiology;
2) *Interactive analyses* that allow the user to investigate directly epidemiological trends of selected oncological diagnoses;
3) *Predefined presentations of important topics* (Authorised information service).

These services are available free to all users. All analyses contain only safe and publicable data of tumour epidemiology, without any personal data of patients.

The project of creating the SVOD web portal for tumour epidemiology in the Czech Republic was tied with longstanding development of analytical software for data from National Oncology Registry (NOR) of the Czech Republic. The SVOD portal was created in the years 1999-2003. Currently is used its sixth version. The SVOD web portal solves all these problems and provides an effective way of access to epidemiological analyses to unlimited number of users. It makes accessible all NOR data via wide range of automated analyses. Although the SVOD was finalized successfully, there are severe limits with its distribution and availability, [3].

2.2 Global Environmental Assessment Information System

The GENASIS web portal provides information support for the implementation of the Stockholm Convention at the international level. This environmental information system was developed as a subsystem of the *Single Information System of the Environment*[8] (JISŽP) of the Ministry of Environment of the Czech Republic, which will be connected to *Share Environmental Information System*[9] (SEIS) of European Union [7]. GENASIS connection with other accessible information sources creates the potential for a comprehensive assessment of anthropogenic impact on the environment and the associated ecological and health risks. The GENASIS portal contains data collected by RECETOX and its partners since 1988 in various monitoring types (long-term, short-term, research studies ...).

---

[8] http://www.mzp.cz/cz/jednotny_informacni_system_zivotni_prostredi
[9] http://www.eea.europa.eu/about-us/what/shared-environmental-information-system

The GENASIS portal also offers analytical tools, one of the most important parts of the web portal. These tools allow basic processing of measured environmental data by "statistical" application programs. The user of GENASIS web portal can determine in the introductory screen what kind of data will enter to the analysis by the selection of various parameters (e.g. project name, sampling time, matrix, chemical compound, etc.). It will obtain by this way core set of data. The GENASIS system is able to visualize location of each sampled site where data are monitored or measured by the means of synoptic maps and examine general and / or detailed information about sampling frequency. It is also possible to sort and select / deselect monitored localities and view measured concentrations of selected compounds at these localities.

However, mere visualization is not the main objective of the development od analytical tools. Using additional GENASIS modules it is possible to obtain descriptive statistics for selected data set, observe changes in concentration of the user-selected chemicals during time period and easily depict seasonal and long-term trends (Fig. 1).

Fig. 1. GENASIS Analytical Tools

Each module includes an option to use additional criteria that restrict entry data (e.g. selection of explicit altitudes). Another integral part of the analytical modules is stratification of localities according to various parameters (land use, altitude, distance to roads, sources of pollution, inhabited areas), which enables more detailed view and localities discrimination. More complex analyses and models are currently and continuously being prepared.

The pilot version of GENASIS uses data from monitoring network MONET [6], [9], which is focused on occurrence of POPs in an ambient air of the Central and Eastern European region (CEEC), Central Asia, Africa and Pacific Islands driven by RECETOX as the Regional Center of the Stockholm Convention for the CEEC region. For many of the participating countries these activities generated first data on the atmospheric levels of POPs. But the primary motivation for GENASIS project is to make all representative and very valuable data about presence and distribution of these dangerous substances in the environment accessible for wide forum of users and interested public.

GENASIS project uses data collected both within the National Implementation Plan for the Implementation of the Stockholm Convention in the Czech Republic (NIP)[10] and international projects to reach its goals. The Czech Republic has had a long-term tradition in POPs monitoring in the environment and its monitoring networks cover all environmental components. A basic description supplemented by outputs used within the frame of the NIP is available for each monitoring network.

3   Relevance of the Scenario

The synthesis of existing (air) pollution monitoring databases (e.g. EEA Datasets[11], AirBase[12] etc.), with epidemiological databases (e.g. Virtual Library: Medicine and Health: Epidemiology[13], NOR etc.) is required for identifying the effects of pollution on human health (anthropogenic impact). This task requires new, rich, data discovery capabilities within the bodies of available knowledge. IBA and RECETOX customers pose requests for new anthropogenic impact studies and influence of global climate change (e.g. a contamination of all environmental components by POPs through their changed transport due to global climate change) requiring data discovery from a multitude of monitoring networks and resources. Proper use of such data requires contextual information, which TaToo will deliver through tagging and enhanced information description (meta-data) provided by an appropriate semantic environment. In this context, MU intends to employ TaToo tools and validate their performance for tagging and semantic rich discovery of anthropogenic impact and global climate change resources. TaToo aims to set up a semantic web solution to close the discovery gap that prevents a full and easy access to environmental resources on the web.

TaToo developments will be demonstrated in the domain of anthropogenic impact and global climate change analysis. To achieve such a goal, it is necessary to use data from national and international monitoring networks, and to discover and obtain as-complete-as-possible data sets representing environmental anthropogenic impact.

---

[10] http://www.recetox.muni.cz/pops-centrum/index.php?pg=pops--nip
[11] http://www.eea.europa.eu/
    data-and-maps/data#c5=all&b_start=0&c9=air%2520emissions&c11=air
[12] http://acm.eionet.europa.eu/databases/airbase/index_html
[13] http://www.epibiostat.ucsf.edu/epidem/epidem.html

Discovery, use, and reuse of these data require enhancements of meta-information descriptions, which can be achieved through TaToo's semantic rich environment (Fig.2).

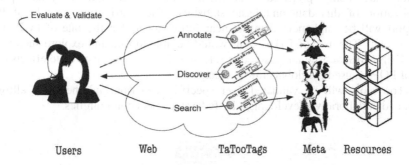

Fig. 2. TaToo's semantic rich environment of information resources

In this context, MU intends to employ TaToo tools and validate their performance for tagging and semantic rich discovery of resources of anthropogenic impact and the influence of global climate change on the transport of pollutants.

Climate is a factor strongly interacting with transport, transformation and effects of POPs in the environment. They are emitted into ambient air from various primary and secondary sources and atmosphere plays a key role in their transport both around their source surroundings and on long distances. Atmospheric transport is also main pathway of POPs transport into aquatic and terrestrial ecosystems. Current research of POPs global fate searches new information on sources, but also on other factors that affect pollutants concentration in ambient air, because climate, processes at the interface of air and soil or water surface, and atmospheric transport significantly affect spatial and time variability of POPs in ambient air. From this point of view, regular measurements of pollutants concentration in ambient air at various localities and monitoring studies at various levels from immediate vicinity of local point sources up to continental level are of key importance. Important components of these measurements are monitoring design, selection of monitored chemicals, selection of sampling and analytical methods, processing method, and data interpretation.

Scenarios of climate changes predict decreasing temperature contrast between poles and equator, drier continental interiors, wetter arctic and sub polar regions, modification of wind and precipitation patterns, sea level rise and others. All these environmental changes can influence the level of POPs in the environment, their partitioning among environmental compartments (air, soil, water), long-range transport, degradation rates, and toxic effects. Also, the release of POPs can be higher, for example due to pesticides usage to stop potential increase of malaria disease. Higher concentrations of POPs in the environment would then probably have more serious effects on living organisms.

The GENASIS information system is based on database and linked analytical tools providing information base available on the web portal [1]. Visualization of temporal and spatial patterns linked to characteristics of chemical compounds involved in

Stockholm Convention support development of scenarios for individual environmental compartments.

Initial version of GENASIS system contains air pollution data and data from other matrices are being prepared. Analytical tools of GENASIS system provide visualization of this data and basic statistics. The distribution models of POPS transport will be implemented in the near future to predict the fate of POPs in the environment. The user of TaToo tools would be able to find and explore such models from GENASIS website and also other relevant resources to investigate effects on the fate of POPs caused by global climate change.

TaToo tools will be validated over specific scenarios and they will allow for continued collaborative development by federated users communities.

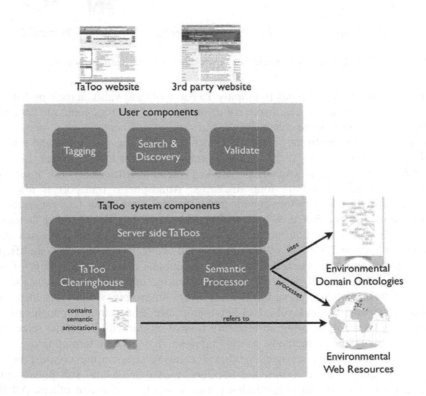

Fig. 3. TaToo architecture[14]

4   TaToo Architecture

TaToo aims to deliver a web based system centred on a three main elements:

- *a clearinghouse*, which plays the role of organising the semantic information on environmental resources. The clearinghouse contains a list of semantic

---

[14] http://www.tatoo-fp7.eu/tatooweb/?q=node/20

annotations of environmental resources, referring to the original content as available on the world wide web.

- *a semantic processor*, a core component of the TaToo system, since it uses a set of (pluggable) environmental ontologies to provide semantic services to the tagging tools of TaToo.

- *a set of tagging tools* (TaToos), which offer services such as tagging new environmental resources, including quality and uncertainty information, searching for and discovering tagged environmental resources, validating the results of a search.

The server side interacts with web based client components. These components can be interactively combined in order to enable human users to create, modify, delete and update TaToos. The composition is open, so that third party will be able to exploit the components to deliver their specifically targeted services.

The TaToo Web Portal represents the main entry point for the TaToo Semantic Framework and its functionality.

Due to the nature of a Web Portal the user has access independently of his location to all the Tagging, Discovery and Evaluation/Validation functionality. The TaToo Web Portal implements user first level authentication and authorization for access control and offers a customisable portal content.

The TaToo Web portal is in principle composed of a set of portlets that match with the set of services provided by the TaToo Semantic Framework: *Tagging Portlets, Discovery Portlets, Evaluation and Validation Portlets*. If a functionality requires a complex design, it can be provided throw the means of a set of the portlets..

The TaToo Web Portal interacts mainly with the portlets that make up the portal. The information exchanged between the portal and the portlets is not relevant at the specification level and depends on the specific portlet server / container.

4.1 Tagging Portlet

The Tagging Portlet interacts with the Tagging Service. It exchanges the following information with the Tagging Service:

- *Domain selected by the user;*
- *Ontologies (in simplified representation) matching the domain;*
- *Tags (selected terms from an ontology);*
- *User context information (to associate a tag with a user).*

The user accesses the TaToo Web Portal in tagging process and selects the Tagging Portlet user interface. The Tagging Portlet presents to the user one or more resources that were just discovered, or already known and stored. The user can add a new tag (meta-information). Once the user fills, for example, an input text box or chooses a term from a selection box on the Tagging Portlet, the meta-information entered is then sent to the Tagging Service associated with the selected resource(s). It will be then up to the TaToo Clearinghouse to manage storage of the meta-information associated with the resource(s).

4.2 Discovery Portlets

There are three discovery portlets: *Simple Search Portlet; Hierarchical Search Portlet; Result Presentation Portlet*:

*   *Simple Search Portlet* acts as a Web Client of the TaToo Discovery Service. To display the retrieved information, the Simple Search Portlet redirects the results to a TaToo User Component able to show results. This is the component responsible for the search and discovery of tagged environmental resources. It provides a GUI suitable for expressing the most relevant queries for a given domain. This component provides functionality to search and discover through the key concepts and relations chosen from the corresponding ontology domain. The user accesses the TaToo Web Portal in discovery process looking for search and discovery functionality. On the TaToo Web Portal the user can access the related Search and Discovery user interface. The Search and Discovery Portlet will contact the TaToo Service tier and in particular will access the Discovery Service, which will be responsible for forwarding the required operation to the Clearinghouse. The Simple Search Portlet asks the Discovery Service for Ontologies matching a domain selected by the user and sends the search terms (chosen from the ontology) to the Discovery Service. It receives search results from the Discovery Service in the form of URIs of matching resources along with some meta-information describing the resource.
*   *Hierarchical Search Portlet* acts as a Web Client of the TaToo Discovery Service. To display the retrieved information, the Hierarchical Search Portlet redirects the search results to a TaToo User Component (e.g. the Result Presentation Portlet) able to show results. This is the component responsible for the search and discovery of tagged environmental resources. The Hierarchical Search Portlet provides a GUI suitable for the discovery strategy called navigation. It can be accessed by the user through its GUI which allows formulating the search query via a category tree. The user retrieves the resources belonging to a category (previously selected on the tree) and its related meta-information. The Hierarchical Search Portlet interacts with the TaToo Web Portal and the Discovery Service. It asks the Discovery Service for Ontologies matching a domain selected by the user and sends the search terms (chosen from the category tree) to the Discovery Service. It receives search results back in the form of URIs of matching resources along with some meta-information describing the resource.
*   *Result Presentation Portlet* interacts with Search Portlets to present search results. It allows users to view, in a user-friendly manner, the results of a query, and to interact with them. To this end, the component will show different elements in different areas such as performed query, found resources, annotation related to those resources, and so on.

4.3 TaToo Evaluate and Validate Portlet

The TaToo Evaluate and Validate Portlet is a component responsible for the evaluation and validation of search results and tags associated with resources. It is part of the TaToo Presentation tier on the TaToo Web Portal providing evaluation and validation functionality to the user, communicating with the Evaluate and Validate Service.

It shows all available tags of a previously discovered resource including potentially attached validation meta-information. Validation meta-information, or validation tags, are special tags for the purpose of evaluation and validation. They are used, for example, to rate the quality, uncertainty, reliability, etc. of resources as well as tags (including Validation Tags). The portlet should also provide an indicator for overall level of quality, uncertainty, reliability, etc., of the resource computed from all available Validation Tags.

This Portlet interacts with the TaToo Web Portal, the Discovery Portlet, the Tagging Service and the Evaluate and Validate Service. It receives the URI of a resource from the Search Portlet receives associated Validation Tags from the Evaluate and Validate Service and sends new Validation Tags to the Evaluate and Validate Service.

5 Conclusions

In this paper we have introduced the aims and the vision of the MU scenario of FP7 project TaToo, which aims at providing a collaborative platform for the semantic enrichment of environmental information resources on the web. The main challenges of the TaToo project are the provision of an appealing user interface for the semantic annotation of environmental resources, more specifically environmental data, information, web services and models, and the development of a set of TaToo tools to provide a preliminary semantic analysis of the content of web resources, with the ability to access different published ontologies that describe the available knowledge basis.

Acknowledgments. The research leading to these results has received funding from the European Community's Seventh Framework Programme (FP7/2007-2013) under grant agreement nr. 247893.

References

1. Brabec, K., Jarkovský, J., Dušek, L., Kubásek, M., Hřebíček, J., Holoubek, I., Čupr, P., Klánová, J.: GENASIS: System for the Assessment of Environmental Contamination by Persistent Organic Pollutants. In: EnviroInfo 2009. Environmental Informatics and Industrial Environmental Protection: Concepts, Methods and Tools. 23. International Conference on Informatics for Environmental Protection, pp. 369–376. Shaker Verlag, Aachen (2009)
2. Dušek, L., Mužík, J., Koptíková, J., Brabec, P., Žaloudík, J., Vyzula, R., Kubásek, M.: The national web portal for cancer epidemiology in the Czech Republic. In: Enviroinfo 2005. 19th International Conference Informatics for Environmental Protection, pp. 434–439. Masaryk University Press, Brno (2005)
3. Dušek, L.: Czech Cancer Care in Numbers 2008-2009. Grada Publishing, Praha (2009)

4. Hřebíček, J., Dušek, L., Kubásek, M., Jarkovský, J., Brabec, K., Holoubek, I., Kohút, L., Urbánek, J.: Anthropogenic Impact and Global Climate Change. Description of Validation Scenario in TaToo Project. In: 7. letní škola aplikované informatiky. Indikátory účinnosti EMS podle odvětví, pp. 6–23. nakladatelství Littera, Brno (2010)
5. Hřebíček, J., Dušek, L., Kubásek, M., Jarkovský, J., Brabec, K., Holoubek, I., Kohút, L., Urbánek, J.: Validation Scenario for Anthropogenic Impact and Global Climate Change for Tatoo. In: Proceedings of the Workshop "Environmental Information Systems and Services - Infrastructures and Platforms", Aachen. CEUR-WS (2010)
6. Klánová, J., Čupr, P., Holoubek, I., Borůvková, J., Přibylová, P., Kareš, R., Kohoutek, J., Dvorská, A., Komprda, J.: Towards the Global Monitoring of POPs - Contribution of the MONET Networks. In: RECETOX. Masaryk University, Brno (2009)
7. Pillmann, W., Hřebíček, J.: Information Sources for a European Integrated Environmental Information Space. In: EnviroInfo 2009. Environmental Informatics and Industrial Environmental Protection: Concepts, Methods and Tools. 23. International Conference on Informatics for Environmental Protection, pp. 341–352. Shaker Verlag, Aachen (2009)
8. Rizzoli, A., Schimak, G., Donatelli, M., Hřebíček, J., Avellino, G., Mon, J.: TaToo: tagging environmental resources on the web by semantic annotations. In: iEMSS 2010. International Congress on Environmental Modelling and Software. Modelling for Environment's Sake, pp. 1192–1199. iEMSS, Ottawa (2010)
9. Urbánek, J., Brabec, K., Dušek, L., Holoubek, I., Hřebíček, J., Kubásek, M.: Monitoring and assessment of environmental impact by persistent organic pollutants. In: Diamantaras, K., Duch, W., Iliadis, L.S. (eds.) ICANN 2010. LNCS, vol. 6354, pp. 483–488. Springer, Heidelberg (2010)

Temporal Changes in Biological Communities Affecting Models for Evaluating of Ecological Status

Simona Littnerová and Jiří Jarkovský

Institute of Biostatistics and Analyses, Masaryk University, Kamenice 3, Brno

Abstract. Temporal changes in the structure of biological communities are one of the factors affecting water quality assessment systems. The aim of our work was to analyze the temporal variability of benthic macroinvertebrates and its consequences for the established streams typology. The data analyzed come from a biomonitoring of streams of the Czech Republic during 2002-2005. Changes of the structure of macroinvertebrates communities were observed using diversity indices (Shannon index) and biotic indices (saprobic index) and using actual changes in community structure. The time related shift in indices and the community composition was found, but the correlation of the locality typologies and the change was not found.

1 Introduction

The most important process in communities we can rate is variation in species caused by extinction and colonization [1]. Dynamics of extinction and colonization can also affect the response of communities to environmental change, potentially leading to weakly predictable patterns of communities structure [2]. Therefore, understanding the influence of temporal variation on community structure and community-environment relationships is very important for predicting community distribution along environmental gradients. Current predictive models used in bioassessment mostly rely on single-surveys. We assume that results from single-surveys are representative of local community. The next assumption is that communities were stable in time [3]. However, in reality, the temporal dynamics of local community may swamp any general patterns [4].

The stability of habitat and interactions between species in community are the main factor, which have influence on temporal variability in community structure [5]. From this viewpoint the stream communities should be more studied, because they are highly variable in response to changes in environments. However, the relatively few studies are interested in temporal variability in streams. Their results are very controversial. Some studies have shown community structure to be relatively stable, especially if environmental conditions do not vary over time [6], [7], [8], whereas others have reported considerable temporal changes in community structure [9], [10], [11], [12].

In [6] were observed stable communities in 19 locations for 5 years. The authors have created for their data classification and ordination for each of the years and found that they are consistent in different years. They also created a model

J. Hřebíček, G. Schimak, and R. Denzer (Eds.): ISESS 2011, IFIP AICT 359, pp. 519–527, 2011.

discriminating observations in the first year. This model predicted a correct group of invertebrates. Only for localities with riffles there was evidence of changes of communities that were subject to diminishing vegetation cover of banks.

Community of macroinvertebrates in the reference sites in remote areas of Idaho followed the authors in [7] for six years (1990-1995). Temporal changes of community environmental parameters were observed simultaneously. The authors stated that, despite changes in environmental conditions, caused mainly by climate change, there were only small changes in community structure, and thus could be regarded as stable community.

Also in [8] monitored community could be considered stable. The authors had 6-year time series for 26 sites. Changes in environmental conditions were indeed statistically significant, but the link between changing environmental conditions and changing communities was very weak. Although communities were very different in different places, the overall change in community structure between years was not statistically significant. The authors also stated that it was followed by inter-season changes in communities.

On the other hand, other studies showed considerable change in communities over time. [9] watched the 27 rivers in southern England, whether they differ between year 1976 and 1984 in terms of macroinvertebrates and if this change is related to the variation of environmental conditions. The study examined whether the 15 most abundant species in 1976 occurred in 1984. The authors stated that among the surveyed year is great variability in temperature, pH and flow. With these changes also explained the structure of communities. Nevertheless the study reported that despite explanation the change in community structure with environmental parameters, community composition is hardly predictable.

Also in [10] there were significant community changes. In this study, the authors had available a very long time series (20 years). The 17 sites on two rivers in Australia were monitored. The authors focused on the structure of communities at the family and species level. At the family level the authors did not observed statistically significant changes over time, while at a more detailed level of species the change of community structure was significant. The authors discuss which units of biological classification to use, family or more detailed species. There was found that at the family level the temporal change may not always be detectable. Also, the author argues that it is not clear that the variability of community structure is related to changes of climate. Therefore a change in the community may not directly respond to climate change.

The study [11] observed influence of changes in environmental conditions on the change of macroinvertebrates in the river Rhone in France. It observed temporal change at the nine sites that were sampled from 1985 to 2004. During this period dry season (2003) occurred in the monitored area, caused by climate change. In this study, the authors used Procrustean analysis. The method discovered to what extent the environmental conditions are associated with the communities. The result was that the environmental conditions and macroinvertebrates communities change over time and changing community is strongly associated with variation of environmental conditions.

A very comprehensive study, which studied the temporal change of community and due to this change in the typology, is [12]. The study examined how much the general models were based on sampling from one year. In the work were used 34 localities in the north of Finland, which have been studied for three years (2001-2003). In this study, three tasks have been solved. First, what was the temporal variability in the community classification? For each year was established typology of communities. By the method Meansim was given the value of the classification strength (CS) for each year. The second task was to determine changes in temporal variability of relationships community-environment. Here the authors used discriminant analysis to determine the significance of environmental parameters for classification. A third task was to detect changes among communities in different years. Here Procrustean analysis was used and the related ProTest, which calculates the statistical significance of the compliance in community. It was found that communities in different years are different. The result of this study was that the classification of the different years is statistically significantly different and that during the monitored period, the composition of the groups formed by the classification changed. In terms of the relationships community-environment the change of community was penalized by vegetation cover of banks.

For conservation and bioassessment of streams is important to know temporal variability in community structure. Predictive models use biological and environmental data to model community-environmental relationships, with the aim predicting of biodiversity patterns. In streams, benthic macroinvertebrates are often used.

The aim of our work was to analyze the temporal variability of macroinvertebrates and its consequences for the established typology of streams.

2 Study Area

The data analyzed come from a biomonitoring of streams of the Czech Republic during 1996-2007. The data consists of two parts: reference and non-reference localities. On the basis of reference localities classifications were defined, abiotic and biotic. These were used in further analyses. To obtain the time series we selected localities with the complete record of the time period 2002-2005, 261 sites were selected. Changes in the structure of communities were observed between 2002-2003, 2002-2004 and 2002-2005 (Figure 1.). These were non-reference AWMA (Agricultural Water Management Authority) localities, mostly found in middle altitude with the rivers order 3-4. Predominant areas were from central Bohemia and in the nearest surroundings of the selected streams were the agriculture areas.

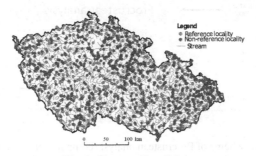

Fig. 1. Observed localities

3 Statistical Methods

Standard descriptive statistics was used for the analysis. Several multivariate statistical methods were used too.

Changes were observed in terms of both diversity indices and biotic indices describing the community and in the terms of actual changes in community composition.

The first were created univariate categorizations based on environmental parameters. Next cluster analysis was used to create abiotic and biotic typologies. Both were produced on reference localities. Cluster analysis for abiotic classification was run on ln-transformed data of environmental parameters. The clustering algorithm Complete linkage was used for abiotic classification; biotic classification was computed using association matrix based on Jaccard coefficient of species distribution on sites. Optimal numbers of clusters were assessed by combination of Silhouette validation method, Meansim (Analysis of Similarity; [13]) and discrimination analysis. Non-reference localities were put into clusters by using discriminant analysis. Changes were observed in terms of both diversity and biotic indices and describing the community in terms of actual changes in community composition. Subsequently was tested whether the typologies of sites has an impact beyond this change; tested was the typology used in various types of assessment models of ecological status. To determine the indices changes over time and within types of sites was used RM ANOVA, for change in community Procrustean analysis [12], [14], [15], [16] followed by detailed analysis of temporal changes of individual taxa.

The Procrustean analysis is prior ordination methods. The aim of Procrustean analysis is measure of association between two ordinations. The method of Procrustean fitting is based on least-square criterion, which minimizes the sum of squared residuals between these two configurations. The results of Procrustean analysis is that every locality have two representations, from every matrix one. The simplified scheme used in this study is in Figure 2.

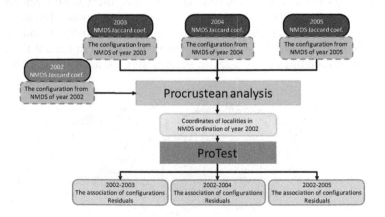

Fig. 2. The scheme of Procrustean analysis computation used in this study

Computationally, the Procrustean fit can be achieved in two steps: (1) centering and scaling:

$$\mathbf{X}_{scl} = \frac{(\mathbf{I} - \mathbf{P})\mathbf{X}}{\sqrt{tr((\mathbf{I} - \mathbf{P})\mathbf{X}^T(\mathbf{I} - \mathbf{P}))}} \qquad (1)$$

$\mathbf{X}$ is reference configuration, $\mathbf{I}$ is (n × n) identical matrix, $\mathbf{P}$ is (n × n) matrix with all elements =1/n. Repeated this step for configuration $\mathbf{Y}$ we obtain $\mathbf{Y}_{scl}$. Note that the scaling process do not change variance of variables, so that variables with have high variances originally will have more importance in the overall fit. This problem can be eliminated by standardization of variables; (2) Reflection, rotation and the residual sum-of-squares statistics:

$$m_{12}^2 = 2(1 - Tr\mathbf{W}) \qquad (2)$$

$\mathbf{W}$ is obtained by the singular value decomposition

$$(\mathbf{X}_{scl}^T \mathbf{Y}_{scl}) = \mathbf{VWU}^T \qquad (3)$$

The value of m_{12}^2 vary between the range of 0 and 1.

The optimal rotation matrix (that providing the best fit) can be calculated as

$$\mathbf{H} = \mathbf{UV}^T. \qquad (4)$$

The m_{12}^2 can also be calculated by first rotating the matrix $\mathbf{Y}$

$$\mathbf{Y}_{rot} = \mathbf{Y}_{scl}\mathbf{H}. \qquad (5)$$

and then finding the sum of the squared distances between $\mathbf{X}_{scl}$ and $\mathbf{Y}_{rot}$. Note that where X and Y have only one variable each, $\mathbf{W}$ is equal to the Pearson correlation index and therefore.

$$m_{12} = 1 - r^2. \qquad (6)$$

The superimposition process requires that matrices have same dimension, where this is not, the matrix with smaller number of variables can be filled with vectors of zeros until it has the same dimension as the larger matrix.

Statistical significance of Procrustean fit (m_{12}^2) was assumed by a permutation test - ProTest.

Prior procrustean analysis was used non-metric multidimensional scaling (NMDS) ordination based on Jaccard coefficient to summarize communities structure in each study year.

ProTest provides vector of residuals for every sample. These residuals present difference in the position of individual sample between superimposed ordinations. The length of residuals is lack of fit for an individual sample in between ordinations. It corresponds to change of community structure on each locality between time points. To determinate the influence of categorizations and typologies on residuals was used one-way ANOVA.

Afterwards were observed if vectors of residuals were related to change of chemical parameters. The associations between residuals and change of chemical parameters were assessed by Spearmans correlation coefficient. This analysis was only supplementary, because time series of chemical parameters had incomplete records (190 localities).

PASW Statistics 18 for Windows (Release 18.0.0, © SPSS Inc. 2009) was used for descriptive data analysis. Procrustean analysis was computed by software R (R version 2.10.1 (2009-12-14),Copyright © 2009 The R Foundation for Statistical Computing). For Meansim analysis was used software MEANSIM MEANSIM, Version 6.0 (http://www.epa.gov)

The map was created by ArcMap 9.2 (build 1324, © 1999-2006 ESRI Inc).

4 Results

The changes of indices were found in years and season (Table 1). Both of indices (Shannon and saprobic) changed in years, under seasons was observed statistically significant difference only in saprobic index, the change in Shannon index not. The influence of the typology on this change was found in years, but in interaction of time and typologies was not found.

Table 1. Value of Shannon and saprobic index for spring and fall

		2002	2003	2004	2005
Spring	**Shannon index**	2.09/2.13	1.70/1.76	1.73/1.73	2.1/2.14
		(0.98;3.06)[1]	(0.71;2.72)	(0.53;2.76)	(0.95;3.16)
	Saprobic index	2.21/2.22	2.32/2.30	2.37/2.42	2.34/2.30
		(1.32;3.33)	(1.43;3.34)	(1.34;3.44)	(1.48;3.49)
Fall	**Shannon index**	1.93/1.98	1.90/1.99	1.83/1.93	2.11/2.18
		(0.50;2.90)	(0.74;2.81)	(0.41;2.76)	(1.03;3.00)
	Saprobic index	2.25/2.18	2.45/2.32	2.42/2.28	2.38/2.31
		(1.50;3.54)	(1.55;3.76)	(1.54;3.70)	(1.60;3.60)

[1] mean/median (5th percentile; 95th percentile).

Table 2. Conclusion of ProTest. Statistical significance of Procrustean fit

Comparison	m	m^2	Sig.
2002 and 2003	0.512	0.262	<0.01*
2002 and 2004	0.518	0.268	<0.01*
2002 and 2005	0.447	0.200	<0.01*

Afterward was observed change of community structure by Procrustean analysis. It was compared structure of community from year 2002 with years 2003-2005. The ProTest, with 999 permutations, assessed statistical significance of ordination fit, from Table 2. It is obvious that associations for each individual pair of ordination are statistically significant. But the associations were not significant, therefore the changes between ordinations in time were observed. The considerable change was recorded between 2002 and 2003 (Table 2). This change is a possible consequence of high precipitation in 2002. The effect of this change on typology was not found.

The result of Procrustean analysis was positions of localities from ordinations from years 2003-2005 in ordinations from year 2002 (Figure 3). The distances between localities in different years in Figure 3 can be understood as measure of community change.

Thanks to gained values of chemical parameters for several localities was possible to assess relationships between change of chemical parameters and Procrustean residuals. Complementary calculations it was found that the change is linked to the biological oxygen demand.

In conclusion temporal changes of biotic indices and community structure were observed, but relationship between the change and typology was not established. Changes in community structure could be related to biological oxygen demand and change of nutrients volume.

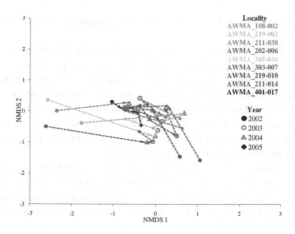

Fig. 3. Positions of nine the most changing localities. In ordination from year 2002 there were represented positions of localities from other years.

5 Conclusion

Predictive models of ecological status are based on relationship community-environment. Therefore understanding of variability in these relationships is a critical aspect of the utility of these models. Yet models assume that communities are stable over time.

First time were monitored indices describing the communities, saprobic and Shannon index. Here it was found that the indices changes over time, but the typology does not follow the changes in these indices, except groups of altitude for saprobic index and type of hydroecoregion for saprobic and Shannon index. Nevertheless, we can say that time changes in indices are consistent in each categorization of localities.

Temporal variability of community structure was also studied by Procrustean analysis and ProTest. It was observed that the communities of the years 2003, 2004 and 2005 differ from the community from the initial 2002. Here it was found that the change from the initial year is considerable. Communities of individual sites in different years were compared using Jaccard index, this confirmed a considerable change among the communities in surveyed years. The Procrustean analysis made a vector of residuals, which represent the distance from the site one year-another year, which means similarity between sites in two time points. The analysis of these residuals was used to determine whether classifications were influenced by the magnitude of the change. The result was that the classification does not affect the levels of residuals. Therefore, the community has changed over time, but in all the categorization by analogy. The complementary calculation, available for several localities, found that the change is linked to the biological oxygen demand.

References

1. Lomolino, M.V., Riddle, B.R., Brown, J.H.: Biogeography, 3rd edn. Sinauer asociates, Sunderland (2006)
2. Ozinga, W.A., Schaminee, J.H.J., Bekker, R.M., Bonn, S., Poschlod, P., Tackenberg, O., Bakker, J., van Groenendael, J.M.: Predictability of plant species composition from environmental conditions is constrained by dispersal limitation. Oikos 108, 555–561
3. Bunn, S.E., Davies, P.M.: Biological processes in running waters and their implications for the assessment of ecological integrity. Hydrobiologia 422, 61–70 (2000)
4. Olden, J.D., Jensen, O.P., Vander Zanden, M.J.: Implications of long-term dynamics of fish and zooplankton communities for among-lake comparisons. Canadian Journal of Fisheries and Aquatic Sciences 63, 1812–1821 (2006)
5. Oberdorff, T., Hugueny, B., Vigneron, T.: Is assemblage variability related to environmental variability? An answer for riverine fis. Oikos 93, 419–428 (2001)
6. Weatherley, N.S., Ormerod, S.J.: The constancy of invertebrate assemblages in soft-water streams: implications for the prediction and detection of environmental change. Journal of Applied Ecology 27, 952–964 (1990)
7. Robinson, C.T., Minshall, G.W., Royer, T.V.: Inter-annual patterns in macroinvertebrate communities of wilderness streams in Idaho, USA. Hydrobiologia 421, 187–198 (2000)
8. Scarsbrook, M.R.: Persistence and stability of lotic invertebrate communities in New Zealand. Freshwater Biology 47, 417–431 (2002)
9. Townsend, C.R., Hidrew, A.G., Schofield, K.: Persistence of stream invertebrate communities in relation to environmental variability. Journal of Animal Ecology 56, 597–613 (1987)
10. Metzeling, L., Robinson, D., Perriss, S., Marchant, R.: Temporal persistence of benthic invertebrate communities in south-eastern Australian streams: taxonomic resolution and implications for the use of predictive models. Marine and Freshwater Research 53, 1223–1234 (2002)
11. Daufresne, M., Bady, P., Fruget, J.F.: Impacts of global changes and extreme hydroclimatic events on macroinvertebrate community structures in the French Rhone River. Oecologia 151, 544–559 (2007)

12. Mykrä, H., Heino, J., Muotka, T.: Concordance of stream macroinvertebrate assemblage classifications: How general are patterns from single-year surveys? Biological conservation (2008), doi:10.1016/j.biocon.2008.02.017

13. Van Sickle, J., Hughes, R.M.: Classification strengths of ecoregions, catchments, and geographic clusters for aquatic vertebrates in Oregon. Journal of The North American Benthological Society 19, 370–384 (2000); Smith, T.F., Waterman, M.S.: Identification of Common Molecular Subsequences. J. Mol. Biol. 147, 195–197 (1981)

14. Peres-Neto, P.R., Jackson, D.A.: How well do multivariate data sets match? Evaluating the association of multivariate biological data sets: comparing the robustness of Mantel test and a Procrustean superimposition approach. Oecologia 129, 169–178 (2001)

15. Jackson, D.A.: ProTest: a Procrustean randomization test of community environment concordance. Ecoscience 2, 297–303 (1995)

16. Legendre, P., Legendre, L.: Numerical Ecology, 2nd Engl. edn. Elsevier, Amsterdam (1998) ISBN 0444892494

Autocalibration of Environmental Process Models Using a PAC Learning Hypothesis

Markiyan Sloboda and David Swayne

University of Guelph, Guelph N1G2W1, Canada
dswayne@uoguelph.ca

Abstract. Using the probably approximately correct (PAC) learning hypothesis, we have conducted experiments using clustered computers, high-performance workstations and ad-hoc grids of personal computers, to develop an analytical model for, and demonstrate asymptotic convergence of simple parallel search in the parameter space of complex environmental models such as the Soil and Water Assessment Tool (SWAT). SWAT calibration for hydrological flow, N and P is, for our test cases, superior to current genetic algorithms, as well as to SWAT-CUP, a multi-paradigm calibration solver and to its components. With more complex models, there is no current alternative to our approach in a realizable wall-clock time.

Keywords: SWAT, autocalibration, high performance computing, distributed computing.

1 Introduction

Environmental models are widely used for analyzing and predicting physical systems. Typically, models require many variables to simulate real world scenarios, thus leading to increasingly complex computations and as the result to dramatic increase in running time.

In order for the model to predict correct results, it has to be adjusted to the specific region of interest. The most common way to calibrate environmental models is a manual approach. The process is monotonous, slow and requires a lot of expertise in the modeled region as well as considerable expertise. Recently, some automatic calibration tools have been developed, such as genetic algorithms (GA) and stochastic algorithms. Most of these approaches, however, require a complex initial set up, and they typically run in sequential mode, which leads to long running times.

This paper examines some aspects of autocalibration adapted to high-performance computing (HPC), using machine learning, specifically the notion of Probably Approximately Correct (PAC) learning [4]. Our HPC resource is available from the Shared Hierarchical Academic Research Computing NETwork, located in Ontario, Canada. Our experiments with the Soil and Water Assessment Tool (SWAT) [6] for rainfall / runoff estimation in watersheds, and with complex interconnected hydrological and pollutant transport models such as PolTra and OneLay [5] have led us to the conclusion that an embarrassingly parallel search strategy is an effective way to harness the power of HPC in fitting models to existing observations. Furthermore,

J. Hřebíček, G. Schimak, and R. Denzer (Eds.): ISESS 2011, IFIP AICT 359, pp. 528–534, 2011.

a naïve multiobjective fitting strategy for the combination of runoff and water chemistry in SWAT gives acceptable results so long as all of the components (runoff and chemistry) are fitted simulataneously.

2 "Goodness of Fit" Measure for Hydrological Models

We use both the Coefficient of Determination (CoD or r^2) and the Nash-Sutcliffe Coefficient of Efficiency (NSE) given respectively by:

$$r^2 = \frac{\sum_{i=1}^{N}(O_i - \overline{O})(P_i - \overline{P})}{\sqrt{\sum_{i=1}^{N}(O_i - \overline{O})^2}\sqrt{\sum_{i=1}^{N}(P_i - \overline{P})^2}}, \tag{1}$$

and

$$NSE = 1.0 - \frac{\sum_i(O_i - P_i)^2}{\sum_i(O_i - \overline{O})^2}, \tag{2}$$

where O_i and P_i are observed and model simulated data at time stamp i respectively and the overbar denotes the observed mean of the entire time period of the evaluation. The CoD ranges from 0 to 1 and NSE ranges from minus infinity to 1 (from poor to perfect). NSE represents an improvement over CoD since it is responsive to differences in observed and model-simulated means and variances [3].

3 The Method

Russell and Norvig [4] state that the main PAC principle is based on the following: "any hypothesis that is seriously wrong will almost certainly be "found out" with high probability after a small number of examples, because it will make an incorrect prediction. Thus, any hypothesis that is consistent with a sufficiently large set of training examples is unlikely to be seriously wrong: that is, it must be probably approximately correct".

The main question answered by a PAC-learning algorithm is the determination of the minimum number of examples required.

$$N \geq \frac{1}{\varepsilon}(\ln(H) - \ln(\delta)) \tag{3}$$

where H is the space of all possible hypotheses, and if a learning algorithm returns a hypothesis that is consistent with N examples, then with probability at least $1-\delta$, it has error at most ε. We typically run the PAC learning approach with δ and ε set at 5% or 1%..

With this in mind, we grid the set of tuneable parameters, and select from the set of all possible configurations a number of parameter sets at least as large as the estimate of N in equation 3. We run those simulations and store in a database for possible future use, and choose on the basis of equation 1 or 2 the best candidate or set of candidates. The process is embarrassingly parallel and, with the aid of a high performance workstation or a cluster of computers it is faster and (in our experience) more accurate than other methods we have tried, including Shuffled Complex Evolution, and the calibration tools known as GLUE [2] and SUFI-2 [1].which form a major part of SWAT-CUP [7].

4 Data Used in Experiments

For calibrating SWAT model data for Raisin River watershed in Southeastern Ontario, Canada was used. Data was available from three Water Survey of Canada (WGC) stream gauging (hydrometric) stations, which are located within the Raisin watershed. Flow values from the station 02MC001 nearest to the outlet from the watershed was used.

Observed data was provided by the Ontario Ministry of Environment, Raisin River Conservation Authority and Water Survey of Canada for research purposes only. Monthly averages for 1985-1994 were used for calibration and for 1995-2004 for validation

5 SWAT Manual Calibration

SWAT model actuators that were varied included: SFTMP, SMTMP, SMFMX, SMFMN, TIMP, SNOCOVMX, ESCO and SURLAG. We used monthly average values for calibration and validation. The manual calibration was conducted by colleagues at Environment Canada. The r^2 and NSE for the monthly calibration were 0.86 and 0.84, respectively. These values are greater than 0.5 and confirm reasonable model results. Validation for TN and TP produced slightly lower, but acceptable, values for NSE.

6 SWAT-CUP

SWAT-CUP is a freely available computer program which calibrates the SWAT model by linking it to several calibration algorithms, such as the Generalized Likelihood Uncertainty Estimation (GLUE), Sequential Uncertainty Fitting (SUFI-2) among others. It provides a user friendly interface for sensitivity analysis, calibration, validation, and uncertainty analysis of SWAT using only one approach at a time. The following results were obtained for GLUE and SUFI-2.

Table 1. GLUE calibration results for flow, TP and TN Loads

r^2 Flow	NSE Flow	r^2 TP Load	NSE TP Load	r^2 TN Load	NSE TN Load
0.87	0.85	0.66	-0.06	0.79	0.67

Table 2. GLUE validation results for flow, TP and TN Loads

r^2 Flow	NSE Flow	r^2 TP Load	NSE TP Load	r^2 TN Load	NSE TN Load
0.81	0.81	0.61	-0.13	0.69	0.59

Table 3. SUFI-2 calibration results for flow, TP and TN loads

r^2 Flow	NSE Flow	r^2 TP Load	NSE TP Load	r^2 TN Load	NSE TN Load
0.87	0.85	0.55	0.29	0.79	0.67

Table 4. SUFI-2 validation results for flow, TP and TN loads

r^2 Flow	NSE Flow	r^2 TP Load	NSE TP Load	r^2 TN Load	NSE TN Load
0.85	0.85	0.47	-0.05	0.76	0.67

Flow results and TN load are acceptable and consistent for both calibration and validation and results are very close to manual or GLUE calibrated results. TP load values for calibration time period can be acceptable, since r^2 is greater than 0.5 but NSE = 0.29. However, validation results for TP load are poor, since NSE is negative, generally considered unacceptable.

7 SWAT PAC Learning

In this Section, we show that a so-called *gridded calibration*, at least for this watershed, is capable of producing an equivalent answer.

The first step in gridded calibration was to create a grid of actuators, define range and step values for them. Next, for each separate calculation of the SWAT model, actuators are randomly selected from the grid. Actuators are independent of each other and their values are selected only from the grid points using the uniform distribution. After a certain number of simulations dictated by the PAC learning hypothesis, calibration sensors are sorted in increasing value of the objective function defined, and the set of actuators which satisfy the objective function the best are calibrated values.

Since, calibration evaluations for flow, TP and TN loads were calculated at the same time, it was necessary to use a rule to know if the database contains the best result, and if no other improvements can be made to it. Therefore, a simple weighting process was used. All comparison was done based on the NSE values. The weighted NSE adopted was 50% flow, 25% TN and 25% TP. Lower values for the flow CoD and NSE are obtained, but all three measures are acceptable, particularly the NSE for TN and TP. Results displayed in the Tables 5 and 6 show high NSE values for flow, TP and TN loads. All these values are above 0.5 and therefore the calibration is successful.

Table 5. Calibration of flow, TP and TN loads, 1% error (3223 simulations)

r^2 Flow	NSE Flow	r^2 TP Load	NSE TP Load	r^2 TN Load	NSE TN Load
0.86	0.82	0.68	0.62	0.75	0.69

Table 6. Validation results for flow, TP and TN loads with 1% error

r^2 Flow	NSE Flow	r^2 TP Load	NSE TP Load	r^2 TN Load	NSE TN Load
0.87	0.85	0.58	0.27	0.69	0.61

To run each SWAT simulation without any modifications using Raisin River watershed dataset, it requires about 4.5 minutes on the average desktop computer and about 30 seconds on most clusters on the SHARCNET, with our parallelized (MPI) SWAT version. Even, with such a short run time it would take a long time to generate the 10^{12} possible values. Therefore, the space was scaled down to 2 million distinct actuator sets. The simulations corresponding to this space were generated, when processors on the SHARCNET clusters were available. It took a week, using 200 processors.

Since, the new space $\overline{H}$ is the sub-space of H, there is a need to calculate a *shift* in the number of required simulations, which we derived as:

$$N - \overline{N} \geq \frac{1}{\varepsilon}\left(\frac{10^{12}}{2*10^6}\right) = \frac{1}{\varepsilon} * 13.12 \qquad (4)$$

where N – total number of simulations required, when the whole space $H = 10^{12}$ is used

$\overline{N}$ – total number of simulations, when the sub space $\overline{H} = 2*10^6$ is used

ε – the upper error value

For the original 10^{12} simulations, 5% error would require 613 iterations and 1% error would require 3223 simulations. The minimum number of simulations required to satisfy the PAC learning theorem for the subspace space $\overline{H}$ is, for 1% error at least 1912 calls to the SWAT model and for 5% error at least 350 simulations.

Since, calibration evaluations for flow, TP and TN loads were calculated at the same time, a simple weighting process was used. All comparison was done based on the NSE values, since the NSE represents the best measure of the closeness of the simulated results to the observed data. The weighted NSE adopted was 50% flow, 25% TN and 25% TP. The highest *Weighted Total NSE* from all three components within the 2 million records in the database was equal to 0.77.

To analyze how results are correlated to the number of simulations and to confirm that a PAC learning theorem is acceptable it was decided to run different number of simulations 1000 times each. The number of simulations being tested were from 500 to 5000 with the 500 iterations interval, i.e. 500, 1000, 1500,..., 4500, 5000. The highest *Weighted Total NSE* from all three components within the 2 million records in the database was equal to 0.77. We approximated this experiment by building a database containing 2 million records, we did not re-run SWAT simulations, but instead actuators and corresponding results were randomly chosen from the database of 2 million simulations, using the best NSE for flow only.

The best flow-only result over all 2 million simulations (NSE = .986011) is already stored in the database. This value was taken as a benchmark to which all the other results were compared. Q1 is the lower quartile (25th percentile), Q3 is the upper quartile (75th percentile) and IQRange is the interquartile range.

Table 7. Box plot statistics of NSE for percent accuracy (flow only)

Sample size	Q1	Median	Q3	IQRange	Whiskers (from, to)
315 (95%)	0.866952	0.883709	0.905719	0.0387668	(0.809034, 0.961108)
500	0.873536	0.891648	0.914876	0.0413396	(0.823719, 0.963922)
1912 (99%)	0.908964	0.924717	0.938933	0.0299687	(0.865485, 0.982025)
4000	0.926839	0.938907	0.951072	0.0242329	(0.891142, 0.986011)
4500	0.928043	0.941754	0.954204	0.0261607	(0.891745, 0.986011)
5000	0.930305	0.942234	0.953604	0.0232990	(0.897061, 0.986011)

The (IQR) interquartile narrows as the sample sizes increase, and the full range of NSE values at and above 99% is significantly higher than from the other methods as calculated

In a further analysis, we derived a tighter approximation to the actual ε and δ in the PAC theorem and we developed a relationship between the δ^* for each of the calculated N^* values in Table 7, as a ratio of the baseline δ value for $N = 315$:

$$\delta/_{\delta^*} = e^{\varepsilon(N^*-N)}, \text{ and } \varepsilon = \frac{\ln((1-NSE)/(1-NSE^*))}{N^*-N}.$$

Experimentally, we find that, as N increases, the value of ε stabilizes (*Figure 1*).

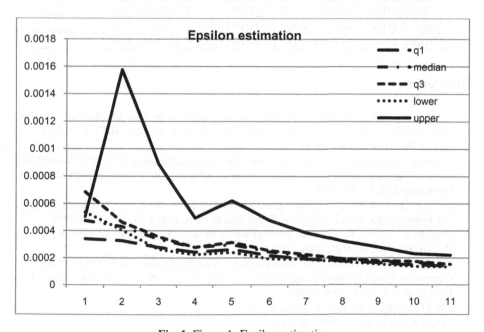

Fig. 1. Figure 1: Epsilon estimation

8 Conclusions

This paper has examined some aspects of autocalibration adapted to high-performance computing (HPC), using machine learning, specifically the notion of Probably Approximately Correct (PAC) learning. Our experiments with the Soil and Water Assessment Tool (SWAT) for rainfall / runoff estimation in watersheds, and with complex interconnected hydrological and pollutant transport models have led us to the conclusion that an embarrassingly parallel search strategy is an effective way to harness the power of HPC in fitting models to existing observations. Furthermore, a naïve multiobjective fitting strategy for the combination of runoff and water chemistry in SWAT gives acceptable results so long as all of the components (runoff and chemistry) are fitted simultaneously. Calibration times are reduced from days or weeks, to hours, depending on the availability of high performance computing resource (multi-core server or computer cluster such as SHARCNET), as shown in Table 8.

Table 8. Comparative run-time for all tested techniques

Technique	Computation	Run time
GLUE	Server	15 days, 11 hours, 35 min
SUFI-2	Server	3days 2 hours, 30 min
Explicit gridded with 1% error	Laptop	4 days 20 hours 26 min
Explicit gridded with 5% error	Laptop	22 hours 11 min
Explicit gridded with 1% error	Server	8 hours 9 min
Explicit gridded with 5% error	Server	1 hour 32 min
Explicit gridded with 1% error	SHARCNET	1 hour 6 min
Explicit gridded with 5% error	SHARCNET	10 min 24 sec

References

1. Abbaspour, K.C., Johnson, A., van Genuchten, M.T.: Estimation of uncertain flow and transport parameters by a sequential uncertainty fitting procedure: SUFI-2. Vadose Zone Journal 3(4), 1340–1352 (2004)
2. Beven, K., Freer, J.: Equifinality, data assimilation, and uncertainty estimation in mechanistic modelling of complex environmental systems using the GLUE methodology. Journal of Hydrology 249, 11–29 (2001)
3. Legates, D., McCabe, J.: Evaluating the use of Goodness of Fit measures in hydrological and hydroclimatic model validation. Water Resources Research 35, 233–241 (1999)
4. Russell, S., Norvig, P.: Artificial Intelligence: a Modern Approach by Russell, S., Norvig, P., 2nd edn. Prentice-Hall, USA (2003)
5. Simons, T.J., Lam, D.C.L.: Documentation of a Two-Dimensional X-Y Model Package for Computing Lake Circulations and Pollutant Transports, pp. 258–267. American Society of Civil Engineers, New York (1986)
6. SWAT, http://www.brc.tamus.edu/swat
7. SWAT-CUP, http://www.eawag.ch

Modeling Heterogeneous Experts' Preference Ratings for Environmental Impact Assessment through a Fuzzy Decision Making System

Ivan Vrana[1] and Shady Aly[2]

[1] Czech University of Life Sciences Prague, Faculty of Economics and Management, Department of Information Engineering, Kamycka 129, 16521 Prague, Czech Republic
vrana@pef.czu.cz
[2] Faculty of Engineering at Helwan, Sherif St., 1, Helwan, Egypt
shady.aly@helwan.edu.eg

Abstract. Currently, there is an increasing demand for more efficient and practical environmental impact assessment (EIA) tools due to the emerging climate change challenges and need to better evaluate and control impacts of industrial technologies and activities. However, due to the inherent uncertainties, vagueness's of assessment data, traditional EIA methods are unable to handle efficiently and properly such decision making process, and consequently more efficient method resorts to the opinions of group of relevant experts in order to enhance the reliability of the assessment decision. However, experts' assessments are usually in heterogeneous forms, multi-metric or multi-criterion and usually conflicting. This article presents a fuzzy decision making systems (FDMS) that enables heterogeneous experts' preference ratings assessment and provides for aggregation of those opinions over multi-metric scales. Experts can provide their opinion in form of crisp, linguistic or fuzzy values.

Keywords: Environmental Impact Assessment (EIA), Fuzzy Logics, Heterogeneous Experts Preferences, Multi-metric Evaluation.

1 Introduction

Recently major climate changes occurred in the environment have led to a greater government's awareness of environmental problems and their prevention, on both local and global levels. Consequently, there has therefore been a proliferation of environmental impact assessment (EIA) tools which enable this impact on the environment to be measured.

The environmental impact assessment (EIA) of industrial technologies and projects requires the evaluation of the effects of very diverse actions on a number of different environmental factors, the uncertainty and inaccuracy being inherent in the process of allocating values to environmental impacts—carried out by a panel of experts, stakeholders and affected population—and for these reasons, fuzzy logic is a suitable and useful tool with which to carry out EIAs [1]. All industrial and development projects affect their surroundings. If they produce

J. Hřebíček, G. Schimak, and R. Denzer (Eds.): ISESS 2011, IFIP AICT 359, pp. 535–549, 2011.

a benefit like less pollution and more wildlife, then they are said to have 'a positive environmental impact'. If their affect on the environment is harmful, then they are said to have 'a negative environmental impact'. An EIA is an assessment of the likely positive and/or negative influence a project may have on the environment. The purpose of the assessment is to ensure that decision-makers consider environmental impacts before deciding whether to proceed with new or existing projects. The problem typically involves: huge quantities of data to manipulate, low quality of data (uncertainty, measurement errors, missing data), different spatial and temporal scales (from seconds to years, from local to global), dynamic and stochastic behavior, and being at the crossroad among many disciplines/domains, and so many qualitative or subjective factors [2].

The processes of environmental impact assessment (EIA) are based on a series of mathematical techniques which attempt to localize, describe and assess the positive and negative effects that any human activity has on our environment, generally causing it to deteriorate. The main purpose of EIA is to predict and as far as possible minimize the negative impacts suffered by the environment as a result of sustaining all human activity. The main problem which appears in EIA models is that they are unable to handle information of a qualitative nature. In order to avoid this problem, qualitative information has traditionally been converted to a numerical scale. We believe that there are now techniques and developments with promising results, which allow us to handle, add and compare linguistic information, which is a reason to continue working in this direction. On account of this, the application of fuzzy techniques to traditional environmental impact assessment models avoids the previously mentioned problem [3].

Rodrigues et al. in 2003 [4] presented definition of the scale, delimitation of the scope, establishment of the objective, and outline of the norm for the formulation of an EIA system for agricultural technology innovations in the institutional context of R&D:

1. Scale – the adoption of an agricultural technology innovation may affect the immediate environment where the activity modified by the technology is carried-out (the near environment), the neighboring area (proximate environment), and the surrounding environment, mainly due to residue emissions. These are, thus, the scales to be addressed by the assessment system.
2. Scope – although the social, economic and ecological dimensions are equally essential for sustainability, the EIA system proposed here is restricted to the ecological aspects.
3. Objective – to promote rural sustainable development by the adoption of technological innovations that contribute to improve environmental quality as well as ecosystem conservation and restoration.
4. Norm – recommendation of agricultural technology is conditioned to improvement of the environmental performance of the activity to which technology is applied, as measured by designed environmental impact indicators.

On the other hand, attributed to its capability to handle inexactness and vague qualitative values, fuzzy set theory has been used extensively in manipulating the data and processing of the EIA decision problem. During the last years several approaches based on fuzzy logic have been developed to assess environmental impacts, indicating the potential of fuzzy logic in this field. Anile et al. [5] developed an approach based on fuzzy logic, which was applied to assess the impact of the use of a river on social and economic environmental factors. Parashar et al. [6] designed a fuzzy procedure of cross-impact simulation to carry out EIAs, which was applied to a textile industry. Silvert [7] proposed a method based on fuzzy logic to analyze ecological impacts in complex cases, in which there were conflicts between the results obtained by different indicators or when the information was non-quantitative. Enea and Salemi [8] developed an EIA procedure based on the extension principle by using parameters defined by means of fuzzy numbers, which was applied to assess the environmental impact of an incineration plant. De Siqueira and De Mello [9] developed a decision-making method to assess environmental impacts by means of fuzzy logic, which was applied to compare different options of a high-speed rail project in Santa Catalina (Brazil). Szczepaniak et al. [10] assessed the environmental impact of a phosphatic fertilizer plant by means of fuzzy logic. Liu and Lai [11] combined fuzzy logic and a fuzzy analytic network process to assess the environmental impact of the deposition of minerals in Punta Gorda (Cuba). Blanco et al. [3] developed an EIA computational application based on fuzzy logic, which takes into account either the quantitative or the qualitative assessments of each environmental impact.

In fact, the surveyed literature has indicated that little or even no researches have considered addressing the heterogeneity of EIA data for a multi-metric variables. As the EIA process involves huge amount of quantitative and qualitative factors that influence the outcomes of the assessment process, vagueness, uncertainty and heterogeneity makes the problem more complex, that demands an adequate solution approach to treat such complexity. Consequently one efficient method is to resort to the opinions of group of relevant experts in order to enhance the reliability of the intended assessment outcome decision. But, because these experts' assessments can usually be in heterogeneous forms, multi-metric or multi-criterion and usually conflicting, a new EIA approach is needed. This research is mainly intended to address the issue of heterogeneity of experts EIA data typically confronted in most EIA situations. This is through developing a fuzzy decision making system (FDMS) that make use of the fuzzy logics the main tool for handling inherent assessment vagueness, uncertainty and heterogeneity.

The paper is organized as follows. Section 2 describes how heterogeneous experts' data can be comfortably dealt with. Section 3 introduces the architecture of a proposed FDMS for EIA. Section 4 finally states the conclusion.

2 Handling Heterogeneous Experts EIA Data Using Fuzzy Numbers

Zadeh [12] pioneered the use of fuzzy set theory (FST) to address problems involving uncertainty, inexactness and vagueness. In a universe of discourse X, a fuzzy subset $\tilde{A}$ of X is defined with a membership function $\mu_{\tilde{A}}(x)$ that maps each element x in X to a real number in the interval $[0, 1]$. The function value of $\mu_{\widetilde{A}}(x)$ signifies the grade of membership of x in $\widetilde{A}$. When $\mu_{\widetilde{A}}(x)$ is large, its grade of membership of x in $\widetilde{A}$ is strong [13].

All elements in the judgment matrix and weight vectors can be represented by triangular fuzzy numbers (TFN). A fuzzy number $\widetilde{A}$ expresses the meaning 'about A'. For fuzzy numbers we use triangular fuzzy numbers (that is, fuzzy numbers with lower (l), modal (m), and upper (u) values), because they are simpler than trapezoidal fuzzy numbers. A fuzzy triangular number is defined as follows:

Definition 1. *A fuzzy number M on R is defined to be a fuzzy triangular number if its membership function $\mu_m : R \to [0, 1]$ is equal to:*

$$\mu_m = \begin{cases} \frac{1}{m-l}x - \frac{l}{m-l} & x \in [l, m], \\ \frac{1}{m-u}x - \frac{l}{m-u} & x \in [m, u], \\ 0 & otherwise \end{cases} \tag{1}$$

Where $l \leq m \leq u$, and l and u stand for the lower and upper values of the support of the fuzzy number M, respectively, and m for the modal value. A fuzzy triangular number, as expressed by Equation (1), will be denoted by (l, m, u). Fuzzy membership function and the definition of a fuzzy number are shown in Figure 1.

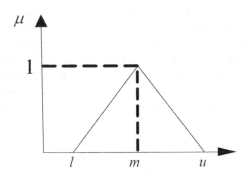

Fig. 1. The membership of a fuzzy triangular number

Some basic relevant operations on fuzzy triangular numbers which were developed and used in [14] are defined as follows. For any two fuzzy triangular numbers $\widetilde{A} = (a_1, a_2, a_3)$, $\widetilde{B} = (b_1, b_2, b_3)$:

$$\widetilde{A} \oplus \widetilde{B} = (a_1 + b_1, a_2 + b_2, a_3 + b_3) \qquad \textit{for addition}$$
$$\widetilde{A} \otimes \widetilde{B} = (a_1 \cdot b_1, a_2 \cdot b_2, a_3 \cdot b_3) \qquad \textit{for multiplication}$$
$$\widetilde{A}/\widetilde{B} = (a_1/b_1, a_2/b_2, a_3/b_3) \qquad \textit{for division}$$
$$\frac{1}{\widetilde{A}} = (\frac{1}{a_1}, \frac{1}{a_2}, \frac{1}{a_3}) \qquad \textit{for reciprocal}$$
$$\widetilde{A}^n = (a_1^n, a_2^n, a_3^n) \qquad \textit{for power}$$

Therefore, using fuzzy triangular numbers, the decision-maker when faces a complex, uncertain problem, he can conveniently express his/her judgments as a range of values around a fuzzy value instead of exact number, and can as well express it using linguistic values (i.e., "High", "Low", etc.) corresponding to some fuzzy numbers.

This article is concerned about considering fuzzy numbers as a tool to enable treating heterogeneous experts' opinions in assessing environmental impacts. Before explaining how, let us first state the basic variables of EIA, upon which the underlying EIA will be explained later in this article. Figure 2 below depicts the hierarchical nature of the EIA problem.

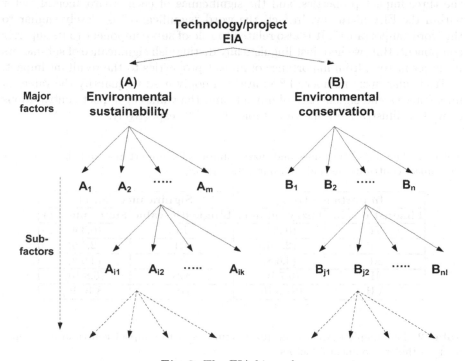

Fig. 2. The EIA hierarchy

In figure 2, the impact of an industrial technology or a project activity is usually assessed hierarchically based on a number of quantitative and qualitative environmental factors. Two major factors are most often and generally considered: environmental conservation and environmental sustainability. These two factors collect the majority of other sub-factors that are always affected by any industrial project or activity.

It is important to state how impact characteristics and magnitudes of various environmental factors can be computed. In fact this article is partially inspired, but in some slightly different form, on the EIA method based on fuzzy logic proposed by the authors in [1]. The impact has three properties: (1) intensity, (2) extent, (3) persistence. They used respective assessment functions to define the relationship between these impact characteristics and their contribution, which has proven a vague issue. The values of the three impact properties were estimated for each of them by means of triangular fuzzy numbers. Then, the impact contribution are combined into either negative or positive impact values. The authors in [1] estimated other properties for impact like confidence intervals on impacts.

However, in this article, we propose simpler and more logical approach that enables reliance on experts' judgments in estimating directly the contribution of impacts for various environmental factors. In addition, experts participate in judging the importance's (called pondering coefficients [1]) of each one of the three impact properties, and the significance of each environmental factor within the EIA hierarchy. In fact, the word "significance" is closely similar to the word "importance". It is also related to role of sub-component to its superior component. But, we here just linguistically distinguish significance of sub-factors to major factors, from importance of impact properties to the resultant impact.

Triangular fuzzy number (TFN) are commonly used to quantify the values of importance's and significance of impacts and the values of impact contributions as well, as illustratively shown in tables 1 and 2 respectively.

Table 1. The linguistic values and fuzzy numbers for importance and significance of the impact contributions and environmental factors

Importance ($\tilde{I}_{tijk}$)		Significance ($\tilde{S}_{tijk}$)	
Linguistic value	Fuzzy number	Linguistic value	Fuzzy number
VL	(0,2,4)	IS	(0,3,4)
L	(2,4,6)	MI	(2,4,6)
M	(4,6,8)	N	(4,6,8)
H	(6,7,10)	MS	(6,8,10)
VH	(8,10,10)	HS	(8,10,10)

Table 2. The linguistic values and fuzzy numbers of the impact contribution components of the environmental factors

Impact contribution				
Impact component contribution ($\tilde{v}_{tijk}$)				
Linguistic value	VL	VL–L	L	L–M	M
Fuzzy number	(0,10,20)	(10,20,30)	(20,30,40)	(30,40,50)	(40,50,60)
Linguistic Value	M–H	H	H–VH	VH	
Fuzzy number	(50,60,70)	(60,70,80)	(70,80,90)	(80,90,100)	

In table 1, the linguistic labels VL, L, M, H, VH stand for "very low", "low", "medium", "high", "very high" options, respectively and are used as pondering coefficient for the values of the three impact contributions corresponding to three impact properties mentioned above. Also, the linguistic labels IS, MI, N, MS, and HS stands for "insignificant", "moderately insignificant", "neutral", "moderately significant", "highly significance" options. Both the two psychometric scales range from 0 up to 10.

In table 2, nine linguistic labels can be used to quantify the magnitude of the environmental impact contribution of the environmental factors. These are: VL, VL-L, L, L-M, M, M-H, H, H-VH, VH stand for "very low", "between very low and low", "low", "between low and medium", "medium", "between medium and high", "high", "between high and very high", "very high" decision options, respectively. These linguistic values of impact contribution range from 0 up to 100 (the range is arbitrarily chosen, and may be: 0 to 10 or even 0 to 1000, or any other convenient range) as a psychometric, dimensionless, unified quantification of the impact contribution of any environmental factors regardless of its physical scale. So, every contribution of each component is assessed from 0 to 100. Naturally, if the intensity component reaches 100, then this means maximum intensity and 0 value means lowest level of intensity, and the same applies for other impact components. Each impact contribution can be either negative or positive, applying the same scale.

It should be noted that the adoption of the above psychometric numerical scales could be arbitrary altered by the decision making analysts based on their views of how usefully and adequately the assessment decision making can be controlled.

Here, based on the above adopted judgment scales, the heterogeneity of assessment data are efficiently treated through giving experts three options for evaluation, or in other meaning, enabling manipulating these three assessment choices of data format. These data formats are as follows:

- Linguistic judgments (e.g., VL, IS, etc.)
- Crisp judgments (i.e., crisp 2 is taken as (2,2,2))
- Fuzzy judgments (e.g., FTN : (2,4,6), (8,10,10))

In fact, the above options cover almost all possible cases or situations of EAI assessment data, and this constitutes the major concern of this article, besides being able to logically handle these values through a well-defined decision making procedure.

Next section, the architecture of the proposed FDMS is presented.

3   FDMS for EIA

This section presents the proposed FDMS (see Fig. 3) for carrying out EIA. Actually, the proposed system is specially intended to be utilized in one of two possibly different cases. The intended case is the need to conduct the EIA of an individual industrial technology or activity, without having to compare it with other offered technology or project alternative. The other case involves the comparison of several alternatives against group of impact assessment criteria. The first case is not common and very few or even scarce approaches exist for

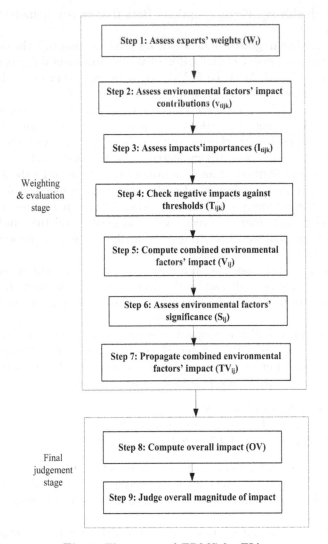

Fig. 3. The proposed FDMS for EIA

handling single alternative (Yes-or-No). Usually most of the existing approaches apply multi-criterion decision making, for which there exist wide spectra of solution methodologies. This represents the novelty of the proposed approach, the capability to solely conduct judge a single offered technological alternative.

In fact, the proposed procedure suites for the both cases; multiple and single alternatives. It can be used to score individual technological alternative, with the ability to judge its acceptance or rejection, based on either some preliminary benchmarking information or through using estimation and rules of thumbs. It transparently tackles the hierarchical nature of the EIA, its uncertainty, vagueness, subjectivity in a simple procedure.

The proposed systems mathematics are typically and collectively synthesized from the work previously conducted in [1] and [15], where triangular fuzzy numbers and fuzzy numbers arithmetic are used to simply combine and aggregate preference ratings guided by levels of importance and significance of impact contributions and environmental factors, respectively. A summary of the logical sequence of computations for the proposed FDMS for EIA is as follows.

1. Weighting & evaluation stage

Step 1: Assess experts' weights (Wt):

A team of relevant experts to the EIA process at each assessment sub-area are formed by the decision making analysts responsible for managing the decision support. Then, triangular fuzzy numbers for importance of each tth expert are judged by the decision analysts or other stakeholder, based on their relevance, experience, and knowledge. These importances guide the influence of each experts on the whole assessment process. This can be also done alternatively using Fuzzy-AHP [16]. Expert importances are then defuzzified for simpler use thereafter. Then, expert weights are defuzzified as explained in [15]. Defuzzification of expert weights could be accomplished through utilizing the Best Non-fuzzy Performance (BNP) values defuzzification method [17]. The COA method's BNP value for triangular fuzzy performance score can be calculated as follows:

$$BNP = l + \frac{(u - l) + (m - l)}{3} \qquad (2)$$

Then, the defuzzified weight $d(\widetilde{W}_t) = BNP(\widetilde{W}_t)$. Expert weights are then normalized using the following formula:

$$W_t = \frac{d(\widetilde{W}_t)}{\sum_{t=1}^{T} d(\widetilde{W}_t)} \qquad (3)$$

Step 2: Assess environmental factors' impact contributions ($\widetilde{v}_{tijk}$):

Let t: the index of tth expert, $t= 1,2,\ldots T$.

i: the ith level in the EIA hierarchy, $i = 1,2,\ldots n$.

j: the jth environmental factor in the EIA hierarchy, $j = 1,2,\ldots m$.

k: the kth impact contribution component in the EIA hierarchy (i.e., intensity, extent and persistance), $k = 1,2,3$.

$\widetilde{v}_{tijk}$: the kth contribution component of the jth environmental factors's at i^{th} level in the EIA hierarchy, and assigned by the tth expert.

Now, using the linguistic scale (table 2), and for the jth environmental factor within the ith level, each relevant t^{th} expert assigns a value for each kth impact contribution.

Positive and negative impacts are identified.

Step 3: Assess impacts' importances ($\tilde{I}_{tijk}$):

Now, the importance I_{tijk} for each kth impact component of the jth environmental factor at the ith level is assigned by the tth expert, utilizing the linguistic values and the corresponding fuzzy number of the table 1.

Step 4: Check critically negative impacts against thresholds (H_{ijk}):

It is common that for each environmental factor, expert scientists usually agree on the values of threshold for each component of critical impact. This means that, before hand, the values of thresholds corresponding to the: H_{ij1}, H_{ij2}, H_{ij3}. Any negative impact contribution is assessed against a pre-established threshold values defined by the stakeholder experts. Generally, the technology should be discarded when the threshold for negative impact is exceeded. Practically, the upper value of the fuzzy number impact component assigned by the experts is compared to the crisp value of the impact threshold. For instance, the technology should be discarded, as long as 75% agreement or 75% sum of weights (arbitrarily can be chosen utilizing common western democracy majority) exists on that the experts' assigned values of impact contribution exceeds thresholds. Otherwise, weighted average of experts' assignment decides for acceptance, in comparing impact values with their corresponding thresholds.

Example: suppose that we have four experts ($t = 4$) assessing the values of a negative impact contributions of a given j^{th} environmental factor on a ith level of the EIA hierarchy. Their assignments (v_{tijk}) and their computed defuzzified weights (W_t) are as follows:

Expert 1: $W_1 = 0.35$, $\tilde{v}_{1ij1}= (10,20,30)$, $\tilde{v}_{1ij2}= (40,50,60)$, $\tilde{v}_{1ij3}= (80,90,90)$
Expert 2: $W_2= 0.15$, $\tilde{v}_{2ij1}= (0,10,20)$, $\tilde{v}_{2ij2}= (60,70,80)$, $\tilde{v}_{2ij3}= (50,60,70)$
Expert 3: $W_3= 0.25$, $\tilde{v}_{3ij1}= (10,20,30)$, $\tilde{v}_{3ij2}= (80,90,90)$, $\tilde{v}_{3ij3}= (40,50,60)$
Expert 4: $W_4= 0.25$, $\tilde{v}_{4ij1}= (10,20,30)$, $\tilde{v}_{4ij2}= (40,50,60)$, $\tilde{v}_{4ij3}= (20,30,40)$

Now, applying the above decision making principle to the following case of impacts thresholds: $H_{ij1} = 40$, $H_{ij2} = 80$, $H_{ij3} = 60$.

Comparing the three thresholds with the corresponding upper values of the impact contributions, the upper values of the first components (i.e., intensity) do not exceed 40 across all experts. Concerning the second component (i.e., extent), assessments of expert 1 and expert 2 exceed $H_{ij2} = 80$, but they constitute 50 % of the experts group, and their sum of weights makes only $40 < 75\%$, so we resort to the average value of upper values $(60+80+90+60)/4 = 72$ which is $< H_{ij2} = 80$. Regarding the third component (i.e., persistence), we find that three experts (1,2,3), constituting 75% of the four experts, agree on the exceed of impact values over the threshold. In this case, the technology or project must be rejected, and we must stop assessment of the corresponding j^{th} environmental factor if it was preliminarily designated as "critical". Other decision making schemes in dealing with threshold could be designed.

Step 5: Compute combined environmental factors' impact ($\tilde{V}_{tij}$):

Now, given the experts' assigned values of the impact contributions, $\tilde{v}_{tijk}$, together with their assessment of the corresponding importances, $\tilde{I}_{tijk}$, then, the combined impact of the jth environmental factor, $\widetilde{V}_{tij}$, for each tth expert is computed using the following mathematical formula:

$$\widetilde{V}_{tij} = \sum_{k=1}^{3} \widetilde{v}_{tijk} \cdot \widetilde{I}_{tijk} \tag{4}$$

Then, the total combined environmental factors' impact for all experts are computed and defuzzified as follows:

$$\widetilde{TV}_{ij} = \sum_{t=1}^{T} W_t \cdot \widetilde{V}_{tij} \tag{5}$$

$$TV_{ij} = d(\widetilde{TV}_{ij}) = BNP(\widetilde{TV}_{ij}) \tag{6}$$

Now, the value of the combined environmental factors' impact, TV_{ij}, is assigned a positive or negative sign depending on the known characteristic of the jth environmental factor.

Step 6: Assess environmental factors' significance ($\widetilde{S}_{tij}$):

Each ith environmental factors at the ith level of the EIA hierarchy is assessed by the relevant experts using the linguistic scale in table 1, expressing the environmental sub-factors influence the impact of their main factor up the hierarchy of EIA assessment. Then, the significance at each ith level is defuzzified and normalized as follows:

$$S_{ij} = d(\widetilde{S}_{ij}) = BNP(\widetilde{S}_{ij}) \tag{7}$$

$$S_{ij} = \frac{d(\widetilde{S}_{ij})}{\sum_{j=1}^{m} d(\widetilde{S}_{ij})} \tag{8}$$

Sub-factors are related by their significance on their common main factors. This logical interpreted as the sum of significances of sub-factors at the ith level is equal 1 ($\sum S_{ij} = 1$).

Step 7: Propagate combined environmental factors' impact (TV_{ij}):

The combined environmental impacts are transferred up the hierarchy toward first level (0th level). Figure 4 below describes the idea of propagating impacts.

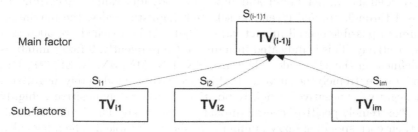

Fig. 4. Propagating impacts up to the main factors of the EIA hierarchy

The formula (equation 9) used to compute the combined impact of the main $(i-1)^{th}$ environmental factor $(TV_{(i-1)j})$, using the impacts (TV_{ij}) weighted by the normalized sub-factors' significances at the ith level (positive and negative signs are used), is as follows:

$$TV_{(i-1)j} = \sum_{j=1}^{m} TV_{ij} \cdot S_{ij} \tag{9}$$

2. Final judgement stage

Step 8: Compute overall impact (OV):

Now, at the top level of the hierarchy (0th level), the positive and negative combined impacts, TV^{+} and TV^{-}, respectively, are subtracted from each other to determine the signed resultant impact:

$$OV = TV^{+} - TV^{-} \tag{10}$$

Step 9: Judge overall magnitude of impact:

The overall impact can be judged based on fuzzified dimensionless scale of impact levels, guided by transformed (parallel and dimensionless) benchmarking values, to either accept or refuse the proposed technology or the project. Figure 5 and table 3 illustrate how judgment could be made, which is explained below.

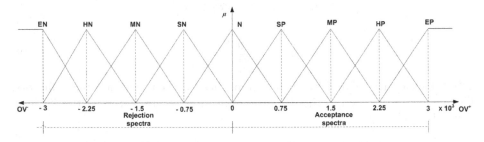

Fig. 5. The fuzzified judgmental scale for the overall impact (OV)

First of all, before fuzzifying the values of the overall impact (OV), it is important to identify its maximum and minimum possible values. According to equations 4 through 10, and given the selected linguistic scales, the maximum and minimum possible overall impact values that can be reached are 3000 and -3000, respectively. This is indicated in figure 6. Consequently, 9 fuzzy numbers can be defined on the OV scale. They are; EN, HN, MN, SN, N, SP, NP, HP, EP stand for "extremely negative", "highly negative", "moderately negative", "slightly negative", "negative", "slightly positive", "moderately positive", "highly positive", "extremely positive" overall impacts, respectively. These linguistic values and their corresponding fuzzy numbers are shown in table 3. Then, logically, and based on the experts and decision analysts involved and their decision control policy, an acceptance and rejection spectra or ranges could be located on

Table 3. The linguistic values and corresponding fuzzy numbers of the fuzzified environmental impacts

Overall impact (OV)	
Linguistic value	Fuzzy number
EN	(-3,-3,-2.25)
HN	(-3,-2.25,-1.5)
MN	(2.25,-1.5,-0.75)
SN	(-1.5,-0.75,0)
N	(-0.75,0,0.75)
SP	(0,0.75,1.5)
MP	(0.75,1.5,2.25)
HP	(1.5,2.25,3)
EP	(2.25,3,3)

the fuzzified scale. Based on the computation the resultant value of the OV are matched with this scale and using the maximum membership operator it is then assigned to some linguistic value on such scale, and the final judgment can be taken. Also, benchmarking values for previously assessed technologies can be helpful in tuning the established linguistic values and their corresponding fuzzy numbers.

4   Conclusion

EIA is a very complex decision making problem that besides its inherent ambiguity and uncertainty, usually involves heterogeneous assessment data associated with multi-metric parameters and assessment scales as a result of diverse or heterogeneous experts and decision maker's background and tools.

This article has outlined a method for how heterogeneous experts' opinions under fuzzy environment can be addressed, and presented a new approach for EIA that takes into account the natural properties of impacts besides their uncertainty and vagueness's, and makes extensive use of human expert efficient control. The proposed methodology is advantageous in that it can solely assess the EIA of an individually offered technological alternative, without a need to compare it or consider multiple several alternatives. It also can implicitly make use of benchmark assessment cases through adjusting the acceptance and rejection zones on the fuzzified scale of the overall impact.

Finally, it should be noted that the transformation of the various impact values of various quantitative environmental factor across the levels of EIA hierarchy obviously promote homogeneity and alleviate heterogeneity through the suggested judgmental scales, based on the utilized linguistic values and their corresponding fuzzy numbers. This also enables considering and blending together impacts of both quantitative and qualitative environmental factors. Still, there are several opportunities for further improving the proposed approach through fine-tuning the fuzzy number scales and impacts combination methods.

Acknowledgement

This work was supported by the Ministry of Education, Youth and Sports of the Czech Republic (Grant No. MSM 604070904 – Information and knowledge support of strategic management and 2C06004 – Intelligent instruments for assessment of relevance of content of data and knowledge resources.

References

1. Peche, R., Rodríguez, E.: Environmental impact assessment by means of a procedure based on fuzzy logic: A practical application. Environmental Impact Assessment Review 31, 87–96 (2011)
2. Aly, S., Vrana, I.: An Intelligent Decision Support System for Environmental Impact Assessment of Industrial Projects International Congress on Environmental Modelling and Software (iEMSs), Barcelona, Spain (July 2008)
3. Blanco, A., Delgado, M., Martín-Ramos, J.M., Polo, M.: AIEIA: software for fuzzy environmental impact assessment. Expert Syst. Appl. 36, 9135–9149 (2009)
4. Rodrigues, G.S., Campanhola, C., Kitamura, P.C.: An environmental impact assessment system for agricultural R&D. Environmental Impact Assessment Review 23, 219–244 (2003)
5. Anile, A.M., Deodato, S., Privitera, G.: Implementing fuzzy arithmetic. Fuzzy Sets Syst. 72, 239–250 (1995)
6. Parashar, A., Paliwal, R., Rambabu, P.: Utility of fuzzy cross-impact simulation in environmental assessment. Env. Impact Asses. Rev. 17, 427–447 (1997)
7. Silvert, W.: Ecological impact classification with fuzzy sets. Ecol. Model 96, 1–10 (1997)
8. Enea, M., Salemi, G.: Fuzzy approach to the environmental impact evaluation. Ecol Model 135, 131–147 (2001)
9. Szczepaniak, K., Sarbu, C., Astel, A., Rainska, E., Biziuk, M., Culicov, O., Frontasyeva, M.V., Bode, P.: Assessment of the impact of a phosphatic fertilizer plant on the adjacent environment using fuzzy logic. Cent. Eur. J. Chem. 4, 29–55 (2006)
10. De Siqueira, A., De Mello, R.: A decision support method for environmental impact assessment using a fuzzy logic approach. Ecol. Econ. 58, 170–181 (2006)
11. Liu, K.F., Lai, J.: Decision-support for environmental impact assessment: a hybrid approach using fuzzy logic and fuzzy analytic network process. Expert Syst. Appl. 36, 5119–5136 (2009)
12. Zadeh, L.A.: Fuzzy sets. Information and Control 8, 338–353 (1965)
13. Keufmann, A., Gupta, M.M.: Introduction to Fuzzy Arithmetic: Theory and Application. Van Nostrand Reinhold, New York (1991)
14. Triantaphyllou, E., Lin, C.T.: Development and evaluation of five fuzzy multi-attribute decision-making methods. International Journal of Approximate Reasoning 14, 281–310 (1996)
15. Chou, S.Y., Chang, Y.H., Shen, C.Y.: A fuzzy simple additive weighting system under group decision-making for facility location selection with objective/subjective attributes, Decision Support. European Journal of Operational Research 189, 132–145 (2008)

16. Aly, S., Vrana, I.: Evaluating the knowledge, relevance and experience of expert decision makers utilizing the Fuzzy-AHP. Agric. Econ. Czech. 54(11), 529–535 (2008)
17. Chen, M.F., Tzeng, G.H., Ding, C.G.: Combining fuzzy AHP with MDS in identifying the preference similarity of alternatives. Applied Soft Computing 8(1), 110–117 (2008)

New Methods of Flash Flood Forecasting in the Czech Republic

Lucie Březková[1], Milan Šálek[1], Petr Novák[2], Hana Kyznarová[2], and Martin Jonov[3]

[1] Czech Hydrometeorological Institute, Regional Office Brno, Kroftova 43,
616 67 Brno, Czech Republic
[2] Czech Hydrometeorological Institute, Na Šabatce 17,
143 06 Prague, Czech Republic
[3] Czech Hydrometeorological Institute, K myslivně 3,
708 00 Ostrava, Czech Republic

Abstract. In June/July 2009 the weather in the Czech Republic was influenced by a 12 days lasting baric low located over Mediterranean, which resulted in a sequence of many flash foods. The total damage was estimated to be about 200 mil. EUR and 15 people died. Although the flash flood is considered as hardly predictable phenomena, first efforts in flash floods forecasting have been already done [1]. Some flash floods can be predicted several tens of minutes in advance. Nowadays, new methods of nowcasting are being developed and they promise a new progress in predicting of these events. The paper shows a detail case study of a flash flood - from the point of view of flash flood forecasting. Based on the results, the prediction system consisting of several nowcasting tools (COTREC, CELLTRACK, etc.) combined with the HYDROG rainfall-runoff model will be set up for testing in operation.

Keywords: flash flood, hydrological forecast, hydrological model.

1 Introduction

Flash floods are usually considered as almost unpredictible phenomena. However, the development of precipitation monitoring, quantitative precipitation estimates and precipitation nowcasting enable the progress in flash flood forecasting as well. Flash floods caused by localized local heavy precipitations are from the point of view of current meteorological and hydrological forecasting rather "small" phenomena. Thus, the precipitation data used for the prediction of flash floods must be of very high temporal and spatial resolution. In spite of these limitation, the rainfall-runoff process can be simulated and the danger of rapid discharge increase predicted with the hydrological model set up on the particular catchment.

The Czech Hydrometeorological Institute (CHMI) is responsible for following tasks:

- Real-time precipitation monitoring – CHMI operates two weather radars, the radar reflectivities are available in 5 minute step [2], the spatial resolution is 1 square kilometer.

J. Hřebíček, G. Schimak, and R. Denzer (Eds.): ISESS 2011, IFIP AICT 359, pp. 550–557, 2011.

- Quantitative precipitation estimates (QPE) – rainfall intensities derived from radar reflectivities are combined with the precipitation sums obtained by raingauges to get the most accurate precipitation field, which is calculated operationally in 1 hour step [2], [12].
- Quantitative precipitation forecast (QPF) - several methods of precipitation nowcast (i.e. forecasts up to several hours) are calculated operationally in 5 or 10 minute step.
- Flood forecasting service – the discharge forecast is calculated by hydrological models for more than 100 significant river profiles daily, in case of flood emergency several times a day.

The above mentioned tools were used for the first efforts in flash flood forecasting. The case studies of flash floods, which hit Hodonínka river and Sloup creek, proved that some of flash floods can be predicted several dozens of minutes in advance [1].

It is necessary to stress that the flash flood forecasting deals with great uncertainties, those with major influence are mentioned below:

- The uncertainty of QPE – since radar measurement has many problems, the proper adjustment methods are necessary. Without a raingauge station situated inside or nearby the catchment the QPE is accompanied by significant errors.
- The uncertainty of QPF – the precipitation nowcasting methods are based on extrapolation of radar echo, the development of new storm cells (often crucial) is not considered. So the error of the QPF can be really very high.

It is obvious that the deterministic forecast of a flash flood based on one precipitation scenario can give us only very simplified information about the expected development of the flood. Thus the probabilistic aproach which takes into account all available precipitation scenarios is preferred.

In the paper the detail study of a flash flood which hit Luha catchment on 24th June 2009 is presented. The example shows possibilities but also limitations of the flash flood forecasting. Luha is one of the catchments which have been selected for the flash flood forecasting tested in operation in coming convective season.

2 The Method

The method is based on detail analysis of the state in the catchment. As mentioned above, the flash floods hit usually small catchments (the size of the analyzed catchment should be less than approx. 100 km^2). Since the flash floods are very quick the analysis must be performed repeatedly in small time steps (usually 5 or 10 minutes).

The repeated analysis can be described by so called "evaluation circle" (see Fig. 1), which consists of several steps:

1. **Inputs.** In this step the QPE and QPF data for the particular catchment are computed. The precipitation forecasts are obtained by various nowcasting methods, for Luha flash flood the following methods were considered:

- **COTREC** is radar echo extrapolation technique, which uses two consecutive (10-minute or 5-minute step) maximum reflectivity image of Czech Weather Radar Network (CZRAD) for calculation of motion vector fields; the QPFs are being obtained by calculation of the "nowcast" PseudoCAPPI 2km reflectivity in the area of CZRAD domain [3].
- **COTREC ext** is COTREC applied to the CZRAD extended domain that include radar data from neighboring countries [4].
- **Celltrack** is an algorithm initially used in the CHMI for identification of cells exhibiting high radar reflectivity, and for their tracking and extrapolation. Cells in the Celltrack algorithm are approximately defined as continuous areas of radar reflectivity equal to 44 dBZ or higher. Extrapolation forecast is made using movement vectors defining cell shift between the last two radar measurements. [5].
- **Celltrack ext (history).** This method is the same as Celltrack mentioned above but the extrapolation forecast is made using movement vectors that are derived by identification of the cell movement from 1 hour history with the weight decreasing for older movement vectors [5].
- **INCA cz.** INCA is a software package developed by ZAMG, which combines different inputs such as station data, radar information or Numerical Weather Prediction model (NWP) outputs and uses its own algorithms to process the inputs and provide nowcasts and forecasts of various meteorological quantities; for more detail description see [6]. In this case no NWP data were used since the maximum forecast time was 3 hours.
- **INCA ext** is the same method as INCA cz, but incorporating also measurement of Polish weather radars.
- **COSMO1** The COSMO NWP model [7], version 4.11, with a horizontal resolution of 2.8 km, is applied, and radar reflectivity data are assimilated using a water vapour correction method. The assimilation uses observed radar reflectivity and extrapolated radar reflectivity. The extrapolation is performed by the COTREC method, the length of the extrapolation is 1 hour [8]. COSMO1 utilized the standard one-moment microphysics, a Lin-Farley-Orville type [9], which considers five classes of hydrometeors (rain water, cloud water, snow, ice, and graupel).
- **COSMO2** uses two-moment microphysics developed by Seifert and Beheng [10], in this case the set of hydrometeors is complemented by hail.
- **Persistence** repeats the precipitation intensity derived from the last available radar measurement for the following hour. This procedure can simulate the backbuilding of the storm cells or the quasistationarity of the precipitation system.

As the "bottom" level of the precipitation forecast also the variant "**no precipitation forecast**" were taken into account. The simulation of discharge forecast based only on measured precipitation input data (assuming that no other precipitation will occur in the catchment) shows the probable **minimum discharge increase** that can be expected.

2. **Hydrological simulations.** Rainfall-runoff simulations are based on all available precipitation scenarios. Thus we obtain the set of various discharge scenarios, which is evaluated in the form of peak discharge exceedance curve.

3. **Decision point.** The probability of exceedance of the limit water level is the final output of the hydrological simulation. The forecaster must decide whether he/she should issue a warning to the threatened areas. The rule for this decision-making is a subject of a long time testing, because due to the high uncertainty of the whole process there can be a great amount of the false alarms.

4. **Proceeding to the next time step.**

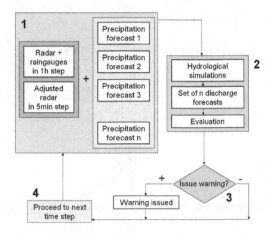

Fig. 1. Evaluation circle – the principle of flash flood forecasting. 1) Preparation of precipitation inputs 2) Hydrological simulations based on various precipitation forecasts (nowcasts). 3) Final decision whether to issue warning 4) Proceeding to the next time step. The evaluation circle should be run in 5 or 10 minute step for every catchment.

3   Results and Dicussion

On 24th June 2009 the Luha river catchments was hit by extreme flash flood, the peak discharge exceeded 100 year return time period. The radar based QPEs were strongly affected by attenuation. The Polish radars viewing the squall line from north showed remarkably better performance, probably due to less pronounced attenuation.

Following the process described as "evaluation circle" the simulation of the flood development in 5 min step has been done. The discharge forecasts were calculated with the use of HYDROG rainfall-runoff model [11]. The discharge in of Jeseník nad Odrou river station was calculated. The particular emphasis was put on the simulation of **real operation**, that means - the real data availability in the particular time were considered. The examples of the discharge simulations are given on Fig. 2. For every term of the forecast the peak discharge exceedance curves were calculated (see example on Fig. 2). The probability of the discharge exceeding the limits according to the forecast time is given on Fig. 3 and Fig. 4.

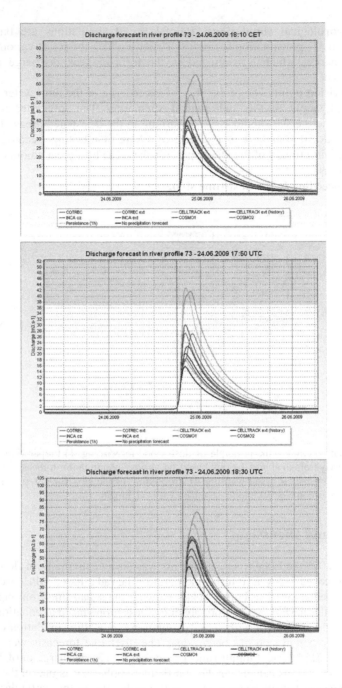

Fig. 2. The simulation of operative discharge forecast at 17:50, 18:10 and 18:30 UTC in the Jeseník nad Odrou river profile according to the various precipitation inputs. The red colour depicts the limit discharge.

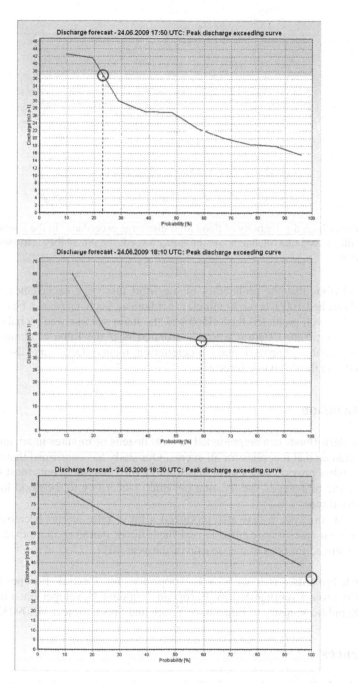

Fig. 3. The simulation of operative discharge forecast at 17:50, 18:10 and 18:30 UTC in the Jeseník nad Odrou river profile – **peak discharge exceedance curves**. The red colour depicts the flood discharge limit; the probability of the exceedance of the limit is signed by the circle.

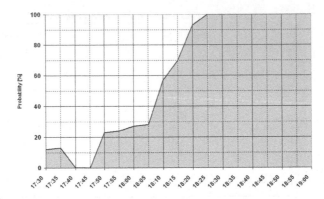

Fig. 4. The estimated probability of flood limit discharge exceedance in the Jeseník nad Odrou river profile in the Luha catchment. As the time proceeds the probability increases and reaches 100 procent.

It is obvious that the probability of the limit discharge exceedance increased in time and reached 100% level 30 minutes in advance. Such a case can be considered as a reasonably well predicted flash flood and the main success was probably caused by the Bělotín raingauge station which is situated near the Luha catchment. The data from this station improved main precipitation inputs (QPE and also QPF), thus improved also the discharge forecast.

4 Conclusion

Some of flash floods can be predicted several dozens of minutes in advance but there is no guarantee that it applies for all events. Our study has confirmed that although the weather radars provide very useful information, their measurements must be corrected by telemetric raingauges, the location of which (according to the flood location) play often crucial role.

However, the system may also produced a lot of false alarms because it has been tested only on cases that resulted in real flash flood; therefore more extensive testing is being planned for the summer season of the year 2011.

Acknowledgments. The work was supported by Central Europe Programme, INCA-CE project (cofinanced by European Regional Developement Fund) and the Czech Republic Ministry of Education, Youth and Sport, project ME09033.

References

1. Šálek, M., Březková, L., Novák, P.: The use of radar in hydrological modelling in the Czech Republic - case studies of flash floods. NHESS 6, 229–236 (2006)
2. Šálek, M., Novák, P., Seo, D.-J.: Operational application of combined radar and rain-gauges precipitation estimation at the CHMI. In: ERAD 2004 Proceedings. ERAD publication series, vol. 2, pp. 16–20 (2004)

3. Novák, P.: The Czech Hydrometeorological Institute's Severe Storm Nowcasting System. Atmospheric Research 83, 450–457 (2007)
4. Novák, P., Frolík, P., Březková, L., Janál, P.: Improvements of Czech Precipitation Nowcasting System. In: ERAD 2010, Sibiu, September 6-10 (2010)
5. Kyznarová, H., Novák, P.: CELLTRACK – Convective Cell Tracking Algorithm and Its Use for Deriving of Life Cycle Characteristics. Atmospheric Research 93, 317–327 (2009)
6. Haiden, T., Kann, A., Wittmann, C., Pistotnik, G., Bica, B., Gruber, C.: The Integrated Nowcasting through Comprehensive Analysis (INCA) system and its validation over the Eastern Alpine region. Wea. Forecasting 26 (2011)
7. Doms, G., Schattler, U.: A Description of the Nonhydrostatic Regional Model LM. Deutscher Wetterdienst (2002)
8. Sokol, Z.: Assimilation of extrapolated radar reflectivity into a NWP model and its impact on a precipitation forecast at high resolution. Atmos. Res, (2011), doi:10.1016/j.atmosres.2010.09.008.
9. Lin, Y.L., Farley, R.D., Orville, H.D.: Bulk parameterization of the snow field in a cloud model. J. Clim. Appl. Meteorol. 22, 1065–1092 (1983)
10. Noppel, H., Blahak, U., Seifert, A., Beheng, K.D.: Simulations of a hailstorm and the impact of CCN using an advanced two-moment cloud microphysical scheme. Atmos. Res. 96, 286–301 (2010)
11. Starý, M., Tureček, B.: Operative control and prediction of floods in the River Odra basin. In: Flood Issues in Contemporary Water Management. NATO Science Series, 2. Environmental Security, vol. 71, pp. s.229–s.236. Kluwer Academic Publishers, Dordrecht (2000) ISBN 0-7923-6452-X
12. Šálek, M.: Operational application of the precipitation estimate by radar and raingauges using local bias correction and regression kriging. In: ERAD, Proceedings. National Meteorological Administration of Romania, Sibiu (2010)

Web Services for Incorporation of Air Quality and Climate Change in Long-Term Urban Planning for Europe

Magnuz Engardt[1], Christer Johansson[2,3], and Lars Gidhagen[1]

[1] Swedish Meteorological and Hydrological Institute, SE-601 76 Norrköping, Sweden
{magnuz.engardt,lars.gidhagen}@smhi.se
[2] Stockholm Environment and Health Administration, Box 8136,
SE-104 20 Stockholm, Sweden
[3] Department of Applied Environmental Science, Stockholm University,
SE-10691 Stockholm, Sweden
christer.johansson@itm.su.se

Abstract. Planning for sustainable cities requires the inclusion of environmental aspects like air quality. Within a planning perspective of 20-30 years, there are various factors influencing future air quality:

Worldwide: Climate change may change global background pollution levels and it will affect the atmospheric chemistry.

Europe: Many efforts are taken to reduce emissions of air pollutants and climate forcing agents. These efforts will contribute to changes in the levels of air pollution reaching European cities.

Locally: City populations will grow. The population growth, together with the design of transportation and energy production systems, influence the city's own contribution to air pollution.

The web-service presented allows end-users in an arbitrary European city to consider these factors impact on air quality. It also includes tools for visualization and standards for easy connection to existing local model systems in the cities.

Keywords: climate change, climate services, climate scenario, air quality modeling, urban planning.

1 Introduction

The FP7 ICT-2009-6.4 project SUDPLAN [1],[2] includes the development of a web-based ICT tool that will assist urban planners to incorporate future environment factors in the decision process. Due to its strong impact on citizens' health, comfort, safety and quality life it is important to also consider air quality in urban planning. For European cities, the future urban air quality will be determined by processes and decisions on very different scales.

J. Hřebíček, G. Schimak, and R. Denzer (Eds.): ISESS 2011, IFIP AICT 359, pp. 558–565, 2011.

Climate change will alter the global background of pollutants and it will also affect the way the atmosphere reacts to air pollution emissions over Europe. Actions taken – e.g. in form of emission ceilings for EU member states – may reduce emissions of both air pollutants and climate forcing agents. These efforts will, over decadal periods, contribute to changes in the levels of long range transported air pollution reaching European cities. On the local scale, city populations will grow and planners may opt for spatial expansion or for concentration. This, together with the design and technical developments of transportation and energy production systems, will determine how much local emissions will influence the future air quality.

Through the SUDPLAN web based user interface, named Scenario Management System (SMS), end-users in an arbitrary European city will be able to use a service for climate and environmental information: the Common Services (CS). CS offers as one component the visualization of how temperature and precipitation will evolve over Europe during the coming decades. The information consists of gridded 10-year-averages for a certain period, currently the years of 1960-2100 output from SMHI's regional climate model RCA3 [3]. Available for SUDPLAN visualization is currently RCA3 downscaled results using the Global Climate Models (GCMs) ECHAM5 A1B [4],[5] and HADLEY A1B [6] as boundary conditions. An important aspect in SUDPLAN use of climate scenarios is an ensemble approach, i.e. to use various scenario results to illustrate the uncertainty in future climate.

SUDPLAN visualization on the European scale also includes scenarios of the evolution of NOx, NO_2, O_3 and PM10. These air quality results stem from simulations with the regional dispersion model MATCH [7], forced by meteorological data from RCA3 simulating different climate change realizations. In order to include a realistic temporal evolution of European primary and precursor emissions, the MATCH model has used the RCP4.5 emission scenario [8] to assess air quality impact of the ECHAM5 A1B and HADLEY A1B climate scenarios. SUDPLAN will, in the near future, replace the current GCM and RCA3 results from the IPPC fourth assessment's A1B scenario with the new results based on RCP emissions also on the global scale.

SUDPLAN offer European cities downscaling of future rainfall, hydrological conditions and air quality. The focus of this paper is the urban air quality downscaling that can be performed with the European scale climate and air pollution as input. In what follows the downscaling procedure is described, how this is performed by the end-user and how the results can be presented. We will also evaluate the downscaling model results against measured air quality. All results are taken from Stockholm, one of four SUDPLAN pilot cities.

2   Methods

The following sections describe the chemistry transport model MATCH used for the downscaling and how it is used in the SUDPLAN tool.

2.1 Air Quality Downscaling Model

To determine future air quality over a city we use a dedicated version of the three-dimensional off-line CTM MATCH [7], operated over the city of concern. The domain is flexible and set by the user – typically 100×100 km^2 with 50-100 grids in each horizontal direction. This model is driven by high-resolution tracer emissions from a local emission inventory and interpolated meteorology from a regional climate model. Local emission scenarios should represent both present (reference) and future conditions, the latter based on assumptions about traffic solutions and future population densities, etc. In the SMS it will be possible to operate the urban-scale model with different local emission scenarios, thus executing the model a number of times. As outlined in the introduction, the meteorology from the regional climate model is also driving a version of MATCH operating on courser resolution to calculate concentrations of tracers in Europe, following climate change and variations of tracer emissions.

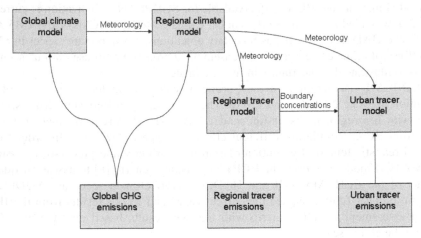

Fig. 1. SUDPLAN models. Linking global climate change to future air quality. A sequential approach.

The SUDPLAN SMS user interface lists an ensemble of climate simulations and European-scale air quality simulations representing different climate change realizations and different European tracer emission scenarios. These results are available as boundary conditions to the urban air quality downscaling.

2.2 Air Quality Downscaling in Common Services

The basic principle for SUDPLAN Common Services (CS) is that the end-user provides local data to improve the downscaling of environmental information reflecting a future climate change. This means that the end-user operating the SUDPLAN user interface, the Scenario Management System (SMS), will transfer data both to and from CS, and they will also operate models inside CS. For air quality downscaling the transfer of time series or gridded data is through Sensor Observation Services (SOS) and the model execution takes place through the Sensor Planning Services (SPS), see Table 1. The use of these two standard interfaces will allow also external users to access CS information, without using the SMS user interface.

Table 1. Overview of standardized interfaces (OGC) used to access Common Services

Model	SOS	SPS	WMS	WFS
European scale visualisation	X		X	
Rainfall downscaling	X	X		
Hydrological downscaling	X	X		X
Air quality downscaling	X	X		

Fig. 2 illustrates the data flows and user options while doing an air quality downscaling. Local emissions may be uploaded to CS as spatial grids of annual averaged emissions for NOx, SOx, CO, VOC, NH3 and PM10. Temporal variations for each grid are described as tables for monthly and daily variations. Uploaded emissions are stored in a CS emission database, so that upload of a specific emission scenario is only made once.

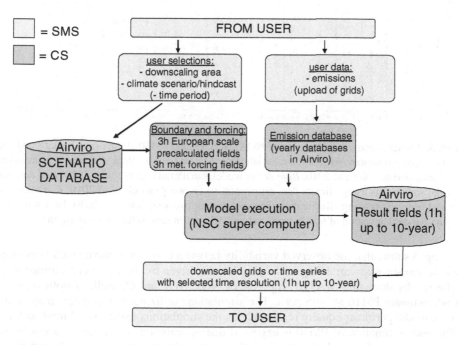

Fig. 2. Work flows in Common Services

Other options for the end-user is defining grid size and simulation area, emission database, simulation period and which European scale result to use as forcing and boundary conditions (see preceding section of details). During model execution there will be status messages sent to the SMS user interface, notifying when the simulation is completed. Downscaled results are available as 10-year, yearly, monthly and daily averaged grids. For shorter simulation periods up to one year, also hourly grids will be available (allowing extreme values to be visualized statistically compared to relevant limit values).

3   Air Quality Downscaling Results

To demonstrate the performance of the urban downscaling Fig. 3 shows observed concentrations of NOX, NO₂, O₃ and PM10 at Torkel Knutssonsgatan and Norr Malma during 2009 and 2010 together with calculated concentrations of these species. The calculations were all done on the same domain covering Stockholm and its surroundings, utilizing identical emission inventory but meteorology and tracer boundaries concentrations from different sources.

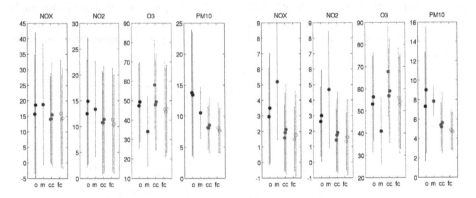

Fig. 3. Annual average concentration of NOX, NO₂, O₃ and PM10 at the urban background site Torkel Knutssonsgatan (*left*), and a rural site Norr Malma (*right*). *Black dots* are measurements collected during 2009 and 2010. *Blue dot* is model simulations for the year 2010. *Red dots* are model simulations using climate data representative of two years close to 2010. *Red rings* are model simulations using climate data representative of two years close to 2030. Bars represent ± one standard deviation of hourly mean values. All concentrations are given in $\mu g\ m^{-3}$.

Fig. 3 shows that the observed variability between two consecutive years is as large as the year-to-year variability of the simulations driven by the European climate data. The results show that MATCH reproduces NOx, NO₂ and O₃ well, at both sites but underestimate PM10 at both sites. The simulations utilizing meteorology from a climate model performs equally reasonable as the simulations using "real" meteorology. The underestimation of PM10 is expected due to omissions of certain sources in the present set-up. Omitted sources include non-tailpipe emissions, which contribute significantly to PM10 in the Stockholm region [9], [10], [11].

Fig. 4 and 5 show 3-year averaged concentrations of NO₂ and O₃ centered in 2010 and 2030. In this example, the change between the two periods is only brought about by changes in European tracer emissions and changes in climate. Note that the data is the result of a chain of three-dimensional meteorological and air quality models, operating with hourly resolution over multi-year periods. The figures demonstrate that the background concentration of NO_2 and O_3 will decrease in the future – mainly as a result of reduced precursor emissions in Europe. Other studies have shown that climate change may, to some extent and in particular in continental Europe, counteract the positive effects on ozone levels achieved by reduced precursor emissions [12]. In Stockholm it seems that the effect of reduced precursor emissions in Europe will have a dominating positive effect on average ozone levels.

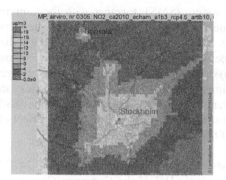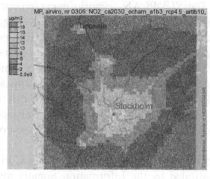

Fig. 4. 3-year average NO_2 concentration (*ca. 2010 left, ca. 2030 right*). The simulations depict a situation where the local emissions were kept at the levels of 2010, but meteorology and climate were changing according to the ECHAM A1B scenario and European tracer emissions following RCP4.5.

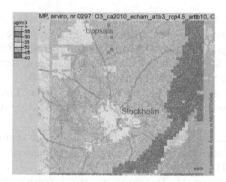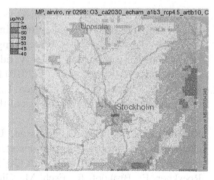

Fig. 5. 3-year average O_3 concentration (*ca. 2010 left, ca. 2030 right*). The simulations depict a situation where the local emissions were kept at the levels of 2010, but meteorology and climate were changing according to the ECHAM A1B scenario and European tracer emissions following RCP4.5.

4 Conclusions

The SUDPLAN air quality downscaling model system has been executed over the Stockholm region and reproduces observed concentration of NOx, NO_2, and O_3 well. The average concentration and variability of PM10 is underestimated, however this is expected since all sources of PM10 are not included in the simulations. From comparisons between simulations with "observed" meteorology and simulations with meteorology from a climate model represented "current climate" it is deduced that the climate data is well suited for describing current climate. Using one particular climate realization (ECHAM5 A1B) together with one tracer emission scenario (RCP4.5) result in decreasing concentrations of air pollutants NO2 and O3 in Stockholm from 2010 to 2030 – mostly a result of decreasing precursor emissions. Other studies have shown that climate change may counteract the positive impact resulting from emission reductions over Europe.

The SUDPLAN scenario management system (SMS), together with the Common Services (CS), are developed to investigate the effect of different climate scenarios and different tracer emissions over Europe. The Sudplan tool also permits the utilization of different emissions scenarios in specific cities. In the present study we investigated the result of changing tracer emissions in Europe together with changing climate, but maintaining local city emissions at a fix (today's) level. The next step will be to include also the effect of different political decisions taken in a particular city, decisions that will alter local emissions. For example, what will be the effect of a certain city bypass, or a general increase of the vehicle fleet.

Acknowledgments. SUDPLAN is a Collaborative Project (contract number 247708) co-funded by the Information Society and Media DG of the European Commission within the RTD activities of the Thematic Priority Information Society Technologies.

References

1. Gidhagen, L., Denzer, R., Schlobinski, S., Michel, F., Kutschera, P., Havlik, D.: Sustainable Urban Development Planner for Climate Change Adaptation (SUDPLAN). In: Berre, A., Roman, D., Maué, P. (eds.) Proceedings of ENVIP 2010 Workshop at EnviroInfo2010, "Environmental Information Systems and Services - Infrastructures and Platforms, Bonn, October 6-8. CEUR-WS, vol. 679 (2010) ISSN 1613-0073, urn:nbn:de:0074-679-9
2. Denzer, R., Schlobinski, S., Gidhagen, L.: A Decision Support System for Urban Climate Change Adapatation. In: Proceedings of the 44th Hawaii International Conference on System Sciences (2011)
3. Kjellström, E., Nikulin, G., Hansson, U., Strandberg, G., Ullerstig, A.: 21st century changes in the European climate: uncertainties derived from an ensemble of regional climate model simulations. Tellus, 63A (2011)
4. Roeckner, E., Brokopf, R., Esch, M., Giorgetta, M., Hagemann, S., et al.: Sensitivity of simulated climated to horizontal and vertical resolution in the ECHAM5 atmosphere model. J. Clim. 19 (2006)
5. Jungclaus, J.H., Botzet, M., Haak, H., Keenlyside, N., Luo, J.-J., et al.: Ocean circulation and tropical variability in the coupled ECHAM5/MPI-OM. J. Clim., 19 (2006)
6. Gordon, C., Cooper, C., Senior, C.A., Banks, H., Gregory, J.M., et al.: The simulation of SST, sea ice extents and ocean heat transports in a version of the Hadley Centre coupled model without flux adjustments. Clim. Dyn., 16 (2000)
7. Robertson, L., Langner, J., Engardt, M.: An Eulerian limited-area atmospheric transport model. J. Appl. Meteorol. 38 (1999)

8. Moss, R.H., Edmonds, J.A., Hibbard, K.A., Manning, M.R., Rose, S.K., van Vuuren, D.P., Carter, T.R., Emori, S., Kainuma, M., Kram, T., Meehl, G.a., Mitchell, J.F.B., Nakicenovic, N., Riahi, K., Smith, S.J., Stouffer, R.J., Thomson, A.M., Weaynt, J.P., Wilbanks, T.J.: The next generation of scenarios for climate change research and assessment. Nature 463 (2010)

9. Norman, M., Johansson, C.: Studies of some measures to reduce road dust emissions from paved roads in Scandinavia. Atmos. Environ. 40, 6154–6164 (2006)

10. Johansson, C., Norman, M., Gidhagen, L.: Spatial & temporal variations of PM10 and particle number concentrations in urban air. Environ. Monit. Assess. 127, 477–487 (2007), doi:10.1007/s10661-006-9296-4

11. Omstedt, G., Johansson, C., Bringfelt, B.: A Model for vehicle Induced Non-tailpipe Emissions of Particles Along Swedish Roads. Atmos. Environ. 39, 6088–6097 (2005)

12. Engardt, M., Bergström, R., Andersson, C.: Climate and Emission Changes Contributing to Changes in Near-surface Ozone in Europe over the Coming Decades: Results from Model Studies. Ambio. 38(8), 452–458 (2009)

The Global Warming, Sustainability, and Environmental Tax: Dynamic General Equilibrium Model

Toshitaka Fukiharu

School of Social Informatics, Aoyamagakuin University
fukiharu@si.aoyama.ac.jp

Abstract. A primitive economic model with classical population theory is constructed in order to examine the greenhouse effect on the sustainability of human population as well as the environmental tax when the sustainability is in danger. The conclusion of this paper is that when the negative effect is small, the tax can guarantee the sustainability, where the effective tax rate interval for the sustainability shrinks as the negative effect rises. When the negative effect exceeds the critical level, however, the environmental tax cannot guarantee the sustainability of human population. Thus, the remedial measure to reduce the greenhouse effect other than the environmental tax is needed for the sustainability.

Keywords: general equilibrium, simulation, population, sustainability, environmental tax.

1 Introduction

The argument on the global warming through greenhouse effect gained momentum in the 1980s. Brown [1] warned the decline of food production due to the greenhouse effect. One of the main concerns of The Earth Summit in Rio de Janeiro in 1992 was whether the participants could agree to adopt the environmental tax on CO_2 emission globally. The agreement was not reached. In 1995 the IPCC concluded that global warming is taking place due to human activity: greenhouse effect. The main aim of the 1997 Kyoto Protocol was to reach agreement for each country to reduce the global warming gases. Stern [7] still warned the decline of food production due to the greenhouse effect, while CO_2 has the carbon fertilization effect.

In this paper, a primitive economic model is constructed in order to examine this greenhouse effect on the sustainability of human population, as well as the economic policies when the sustainability is in danger. This model is constructed in terms of dynamic general equilibrium (GE) approach.

2 Economic Model and Short-Run Equilibrium

In this model, there are two industries: food industry and energy industry. For simplicity the capital accumulation is omitted from the model. The food industry

J. Hřebíček, G. Schimak, and R. Denzer (Eds.): ISESS 2011, IFIP AICT 359, pp. 566–573, 2011.

produces output (food), using labor and energy. The energy industry produces output (energy), using only labor. Two industries maximize profit. The aggregate household maximizes utility subject to income constraint, where the utility is a function of food and energy.

In the short run, the population (working hours) and the CO_2 level are assumed to be constant. Given the population and CO_2 level, it is guaranteed that general equilibrium prices exist which equate demand and supply in food and energy markets. Under these prices, energy is consumed, expanding CO_2 level in the atmosphere. In the long run, the expanded CO_2 level affects food production. Furthermore, population varies in the long run according to classical population theory, propounded by Malthus and Verhulst. We start with the formal model and the short run equilibrium.

2.1 Formal Model

A primitive general equilibrium (GE) model is constructed, for the purpose of examining the greenhouse effect. Suppose that there are two industries (firms). The first firm is a farm which produces food; Z_f. Whereas food is produced by labor: L_1, and energy: H_{f1}, the output is affected by CO_2 level: Y, in the atmosphere. Thus, this firm has the production function:

$$Z_f = g_1 [L_1, H_{f1}, Y] \quad g_{11} > 0, \ g_{12} > 0$$

where g_{ij} is the partial derivative of g_i with respect to the jth variable. It aims at the profit maximization:

$$\max \pi_1 = pZ_f - wL_1 - p_H H_{f1}$$

where p is the wheat price, w is the wage rate, and p_H is the energy price.

The second firm is the energy industry which produces energy: H_{f2}, using only labor: L_2. It has the production function

$$H_{f2} = g_2 [L_2] \quad g_{21} > 0 .$$

It aims at the profit maximization:

$$\max \pi_2 = p_H H_{f2} - wL_2$$

There is only one (representative) household, which consumes food: Z_h, and energy: H_h. Household maximizes utility subject to budget constraint:

$$\max u[Z_h, H_h] \text{ s.t. } pZ_h + p_H H_h = wN + \pi_1 + \pi_2$$

where $u[Z_h, H_h]$ is the utility function, and N is the initial leisure hours (population), and π_i is the profit from the ith firm ($i=1, 2$). For the sake of simplification, in this model, leisure consumption is excluded from the utility function.

2.2 Short-Run GE and Specification of Functions

Given CO_2 level: Y, and N, the short-run General Equilibrium (SGE) is defined, which satisfies

$$H_{f1}{}^d + H_h{}^d = H_{f2}{}^s \quad \text{(energy market)}$$
$$Z_h{}^d = Z_f{}^s \quad \text{(wheat market)}$$
$$L_1{}^d + L_2{}^d = N \quad \text{(labor market)}$$

where superscript $d(s)$ implies "demand" ("supply").

We assume that the production and utility functions are stipulated by the following.

$$g_1[L_1, H_{f1}, Y] = L_1{}^{\alpha 1} H_{f1}{}^{\alpha 2} A[Y, x_0]^{\alpha 3}, \quad \alpha_1 + \alpha_2 + \alpha_3 \leq 1, \; 0 \leq x_0 \leq 1$$
$$g_2[L_2] = L_2$$
$$u[Z_h, H_h] = Z_h{}^{\gamma} H_h{}^{1-\gamma}, \quad 0 < \gamma < 1$$

The function, $A[Y, x_0]$, is a negative factor from the greenhouse effect. Suppose that $Y[0]=1000$ is the present level of CO_2 in the atmosphere. We specify that

$$A[Y, x_0] = \text{Min} \, [1, \; 1 - (1 - e^{-Y/1000})^5 x_0]$$

When $x_0 = 1/10$, for example, $A[Y, 1/10]$ is depicted as in Figure 1.

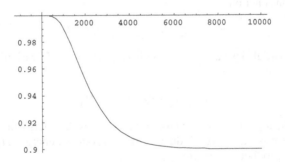

Fig. 1. $A[Y, 1/10]$: Greenhouse Effect Factor

In this formulation, the *relative price of energy*, p_H/p^*, is determined at SGE, as in what follows.

$$p_H/p^* = ((1-\gamma(1-\alpha_1-\alpha_2))/\gamma N)^{1-\alpha 1 - \alpha 2} \alpha_1{}^{\alpha 1} \alpha_2{}^{\alpha 2} A[Y\text{-}1000, x_0]^{\alpha 3}$$

The SGE *labor input for wheat*, L_1^*, is given as in what follows.

$$L_1^* = \alpha_1 \gamma N / (1 - \gamma(1 - \alpha_1 - \alpha_2)) \tag{1}$$

The SGE *energy input for wheat*, H_{f1}^*, is given as in what follows.

$$H_{f1}^* = \alpha_2 \gamma N / (1 - \gamma(1 - \alpha_1 - \alpha_2)) \tag{2}$$

The SGE *energy consumption of household*, H_h^*, is given as in what follows.

$$H_h^* = (1 - \gamma) N / (1 - \gamma(1 - \alpha_1 - \alpha_2)) \tag{3}$$

Also for the later use, the SGE *wheat output*, g_1*, is computed as in what follows.

$$g_1 *= \alpha_1^{\alpha1}(\alpha_1+\alpha_2)^{\alpha2}(\gamma N)^{\alpha1+\alpha2} A[Y\text{-}1000, x_0]^{\alpha3}/((1-\gamma(1-\alpha_1-\alpha_2))^{\alpha1+\alpha2}. \tag{4}$$

3 Long-Run General Equilibrium Dynamics

The analysis in the previous section is called *the short-run general equilibrium model*, SGE, since two variables were fixed by the assumption. First, CO_2 in the atmosphere: *Y*, was fixed. In fact, CO_2 in the atmosphere increases through the use of energy in the household's direct consumption and farm's use of energy in the wheat production, while it decreases thanks to the absorption by the working of sea and the photosynthetic function of food. The variation of CO_2 in the atmosphere, in turn, causes the variation of food output. Thus, the economic analysis of greenhouse effect must be constructed in terms of dynamic system.

Second, population was assumed to be constant in the previous section. In this section this assumption is relaxed. In "On Population", T.R.Malthus argued that population growth is expressed as the geometric progression; 1, 2^2, 3^2, ..., n^2, ..., while food production as the natural progression; 1, 2, 3, ..., *n*, ..., since the latter is under diminishing marginal productivity. It was asserted that in *the long run*, a society's population growth is restricted by food production. In this section, this assertion is incorporated. However, the population cannot become infinite due to the capacity limit of the earth. Considering this limit, P.f. Verhulst proposed a different type of population growth model. In this section, population growth has two factors, the first of which is the one stemming from the Verhulst model, while the second is the one stemming from the Malthus model.

If we admit the variation of two variables, the previous model must be reformulated in terms of dynamic system, which is called *the long-run general equilibrium dynamics* (LGED). In this section, an extension of this sort is attempted.

3.1 The Variation of CO_2 in the Atmosphere

Formally, as energy is produced, *Y*: a in the atmosphere, increases by the amount of $F_1[H]$ where $H=H_{f1}+H_h$, while *Y* decreases, first, by the amount of $F_2[Y]$, thanks to the activity of the sea and forest, second, $F_3[g_1]$, thanks to the photosynthetic function of wheat. Thus, we have a dynamic system

$$dY[t]/dt = \mu_1 H[t] - \mu_2 Y[t] - \mu_3 g_1[t] \tag{5}$$

where *t* stands for time and μ_i s are all positive constant (*i*=1,2 3).

3.2 The Variation of Population

P.f. Verhulst assumed that the variation of population follows the differential equation: $dN[t]/dt = \varepsilon N[t](1-N[t]/K)$ where $N[t]$ is the population at time *t*, *K* is the capacity limit for the population, and ε is a positive parameter. In view of the Malthus' argument it is assumed that *K* depends on the per-capita consumption of food when we reach *K*. In this process, $N[t]$ monotonically converges to *K*. Taking account of the Malthus argument, we assume the variation of population as in what follows where β is a positive parameter.

$$dN[t]/dt = \varepsilon N[t](1-N[t]/K) + \beta(d(g_1[L_1[t], H_{f1}[t], Y[t]]/N[t])/dt)N[t] \qquad (6)$$

It is assumed that if the per capita consumption of wheat decreases the population growth decreases: *growth adjustment*, and vice versa. The dynamic analysis in terms of differential equations, derived from (1), (2), (3), (4), (5), and (6), is called *the long-run general equilibrium dynamics*.

4 Simulations

In this section, simulations are attempted by specifying parameters. When $x_0=0$ or $\alpha_3=0$, the greenhouse effect is zero, which is the starting point of the present section. As the greenhouse effect is intensified, x_0 rises. Assuming $\alpha_3>0$, we conduct the simulations by raising x_0 from zero. In this simulation, the parameters are specified as in what follows.

$$\alpha_1=1/4, \ \alpha_2=1/4, \ \varepsilon=1/1000, \ \gamma=1/2, \ \mu_1=1/5, \ \mu_2=1/100, \ \mu_3=1/100, \ K=1000000, \ \beta=1$$

4.1 Zero Greenhouse Effect Case

When $x_0=0$ or $\alpha_3=0$ (the case of no greenhouse effect), the trajectory path of $\{N[t], Y[t]\}$ on LGED, starting from the initial position, $\{N[0], Y[0]\}=\{1000, 1000\}$, converges to $\{N^*, Y^*\}$, where $N^*=1000000$ and $Y^*= 832573.39699090708710$. The trajectory path of per capita food production, $g_1[t]/N[t]$ on LGED, starting from the initial position, $\{N[0]), Y[0]\}=\{1000, 1000\}$ is depicted in Figure 2. It converges to $(g_1/N)^*= 0.000408248$.

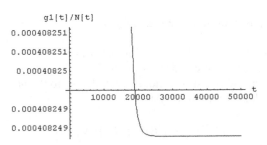

Fig. 2. Trajectory of Per Capita Consumption: $x_0=0$

It must be noted that population capacity, $K=1000000$, is sustainable only when the per capita consumption of wheat is at least $(g_1/N)^*$

4.2 Active Greenhouse Effect Case: $\alpha_3=1/4$ and $x_0=1/10$

We examine what happen to the convergence on LGED when the greenhouse effect is positive. Suppose that $\alpha_3=1/4$ and $x_0=1/10$. The trajectory path of $\{N[t], Y[t]\}$ on

LGED, starting from the initial position, $\{N[0], Y[0]\}=\{1000, 1000\}$, converges to $\{N^*, Y^*[1/10]\}$, where $N^*=1000000$ and $Y^*[1/10]=16666269.0313023>Y^*$. The trajectory path of per capita food production, $g_1[t]/N[t]$ on LGED, starting from the initial position, $\{N[0]), Y[0]\}=\{1000, 1000\}$ converges to $(g_1/N)^*[1/10]=0.000397635364383525<(g_1/N)^*$. Thus, in the long run, K is *not* sustainable when the greenhouse effect is active.

Traditionally, Pigou proposed the Pigouvian tax in order to alleviate pollutions. In the present days, this *tax on the consumption of energy* is called the environmental tax. In this subsection we examine the effect of environmental tax. Let τ be the tax rate on the consumption of energy. In other words, for the demanders of energy, they must pay $p_H(1+\tau)$, although the tax receipt, $p_H \tau$, is distributed to the (aggregate) household. Depending on τ, the convergent per capita food production, $(g_1/N)^*[1/10, \tau]$, can be computed utilizing the simulation for LGED. By definition we have $(g_1/N)^*[1/10, 0]= (g_1/N)^*[1/10]$.

In Figure 3, $(g_1/N)^*[1/10, \tau]$ is depicted as a function of τ. It is ascertained that $(g_1/N)^*[1/10, \tau]\geq(g_1/N)^*$ for τ belonging to the interval [0.18, 22.21], $T[1/10]$, which is called the *sustainability tax range*. Note that too high tax rate cannot guarantee the sustainability, whereas too low tax rate cannot either.

4.3 Active Greenhouse Effect Case: $\alpha_3=1/4$ and $x_0>1/10$

As in 4.2, when $\alpha_3=1/4$ and $1/10<x_0<5/10$, in the long run, K is *not* sustainable when the greenhouse effect is active without remedial measures.

As one of the remedial measures, the environmental tax is required to guarantee the sustainability. For $x_0=1/10$, 2/10, 3/10, and 4/10, corresponding $(g_1/N)^*[x_0]$ and sustainable tax range $T[x_0]$ are shown in Table 1.

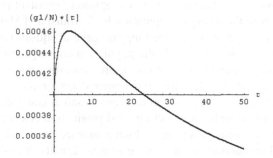

Fig. 3. The Effect of Tax: $x_0=1/10$

Table 1. The Sustainable Tax Range

x_0	$(g_1/N)^*[x_0]$	$T[x_0]$
0	0.000408248	
1/10	0.000397635364383525	[0.18, 22.21]
2/10	0.000386097395096089	[0.45, 16.35]
3/10	0.000373421126552421	[0.88, 12.32]
4/10	0.000359304111963084	[1.87, 7.73]

4.4   Active Greenhouse Effect Case: $\alpha_3=1/4$ and $x_0=5/10$

As in the previous subsections, in the long run, K is *not* sustainable when the greenhouse effect is active without remedial measures. In Figure 4, $(g_1/N)*[5/10, \tau]$ is depicted as a function of τ. It is ascertained that $(g_1/N)*[5/10, \tau]<(g_1/N)*$ for all $\tau>0$. Thus, when $x_0=5/10$, it is shown that the environmental tax cannot guarantee the sustainability

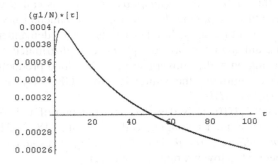

Fig. 4. The Effect of Tax: $x_0=5/10$

5   Conclusions

The aim of this paper is to examine the economic consequences of greenhouse effect, constructing a primitive general equilibrium model by simulation approach. In Section 2, short-run general equilibrium model is constructed, with population and CO_2 level assumed constant. In Section 3, the assumption of constant population and CO_2 level is relaxed, where the theory of population by Verhulst and Malthus is utilized. In Section 4 by simulation approach on the long run general equilibrium dynamics it was shown that CO_2 level converges, while the population converges to the capacity limit, K. The converging per capita food consumption, however, might not allow the sustainability of K. It is shown that the environmental tax on the energy consumption raises the converging per capita food consumption and it can guarantee the sustainability of K when the greenhouse effect on food production is small. It is shown, furthermore, that the sustainable tax range, which guarantee the sustainability, shrinks as the effect on food production becomes more serious. Finally, it is shown that the sustainable tax range disappears when the effect exceeds a critical level. Thus, we may conclude that the remedial measure to reduce the greenhouse effect other than the environmental tax is needed for the sustainability.

Acknowledgements

The author appreciates the financial support provided by the Grants-in-Aid for Science Research (Contract Number: 22530181).

References

1. Brown, L.R.: State of the World. W.W. Norton & Company, New York (1987)
2. Fukiharu, T.: A General Equilibrium Approach to Environmental Problems-Enlarged Version. Kobe University Economic Review 37, 13–44 (1991)
3. Fukiharu, T.: Dynamic System Analysis and Environmental Problems. In: Rizzoli, A.E., Jakeman, A.J. (eds.) Proceedings of iEMSs 2002, vol. 2, pp. 586–591 (2002)
4. Fukiharu, T.. The Global Warming, Sustainability and Environmental Tax: A Dynamic General Equilibrium Model (2010),
   http://home.hiroshima-u.ac.jp/fukito/index.htm
5. Malthus, T.R.: An Essay on the Principle of Population, as It affects the Future Improvement of Society, with Remarks on the Speculation of Mr. Godwin, M. Condorcet, and Other Writers, London (1798)
6. Pigou, A.C.: The Economics of Welfare. Macmillan, London (1920)
7. Stern, N.: The Economics of Climate Change: The Stern Review. Cambridge University Press, Cambridge (2007)
8. Verhulst, P.F.: Notice sur la Loi que la Population Poursuit dans son Accroissement. Correspondance Mathématique et Physique 10, 113–121 (1838)
9. Verhulst, P.F.: Recherches Mathematiques sur La Loi D'Accroissement de la Population", Nouveaux Memoires de l'Academie References (1845)

Going Public with Advanced Simulations

Niclas Hjerdt, Berit Arheimer, Göran Lindström, Ylva Westman,
Esa Falkenroth, and Martin Hultman

Swedish Meteorological and Hydrological Institute, Folkborgsvägen 1,
SE-60176 Norrköping, Sweden
niclas.hjerdt@smhi.se

Abstract. Web technology provides public access to advanced simulation models and efficiently distributes vast volumes of data in an unprecedented way. The traditional boundary between the producers and the users of data has become less distinct. Users now download data generated by themselves or by others. The role of the hydrologist has therefore shifted towards the management of systems and tools that are publicly available. A recent example of this development is the SMHI VattenWeb, a web application that makes available different databases and modelling tools managed by the Swedish Meteorological and Hydrological Institute. Since VattenWeb was primarily developed to meet the demands of the EU Water Framework Directive, one of the key elements is a database of simulated discharge and nutrient transport generated by the SMHI HYPE model. These data consist of daily, monthly and annual hydrologic simulations for all Swedish water bodies reported within the WFD. We show the present status of SMHI VattenWeb and highlight the strategies that have made this application successful among users seeking to characterize the quantity and quality of water at high spatial resolution across Sweden.

Keywords. Large scale, High-resolution, WFD, public access, web interface.

1   The New Challenges of Water Management

Hydrologic modelling has traditionally been an exclusive activity for trained hydrologists, but this has begun to change rapidly as a result of recent development in technology and legislation. The implementation of the European Union Water Framework Directive (WFD) has created a need for hydrologic information at high resolution in both time and space. In addition, web technology now provides tools to efficiently share vast volumes of data. Other recent legislation at the EU level, such as the INSPIRE Directive, has created a framework for sharing geographic information with the public in a standardized manner.

At 450,295 square kilometres, Sweden is the third largest country in the European Union by area, and Sweden's 23,418 reported water bodies make up a relatively large proportion of all European water bodies. Since Sweden is a country with vast water resources and a relatively small population, it is impossible to maintain a monitoring program that covers all water bodies. Therefore, models offer a cost-efficient option for many steps in the six-year water management cycle. Therefore, the implementation

J. Hřebíček, G. Schimak, and R. Denzer (Eds.): ISESS 2011, IFIP AICT 359, pp. 574–580, 2011.
© IFIP International Federation for Information Processing 2011

of the WFD and subsequent delineation of water bodies has created a need for models that can operate at a much finer resolution than previously needed. This could not be achieved with, for instance, the hydrological model used in the international reporting of nutrient loads to the Baltic, i.e., the HELCOM Pollution Load Compilation. The model used for this is the HBV-NP model which only divides Sweden in around 1,100 subbasins, as compared to the 23,418 water bodies reported to the EU (Figure 1).

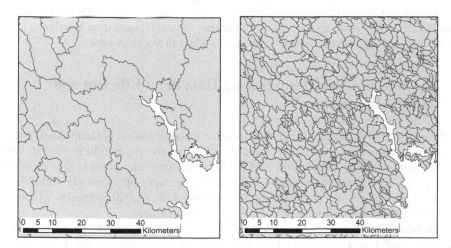

Fig. 1. The resolution of models used in the HELCOM pollution load compilation reports (left) and for the EU Water Framework Directive reports (right)

2   The Solution, Part One: A New, Large-Scale Hydrologic Model with High Resolution

The challenges of the WFD clearly created a need for a new type of hydrologic models. One such model is the hydrological catchment model HYPE (HYdrological Predictions for the Environment), which simulates water flow and substances on their way from precipitation through soil, river and lakes to the river outlet [1, 2]. The catchment is divided into subbasins which in turn are divided into classes (calculation units) depending on land use, soil type and elevation.

An important feature of HYPE is that classes can not be coupled to a geographic location within the subbasin but are given as part of its area. Typical land uses are forest, lake, open land, but also different crops, e.g. cereal and potatoes, are common. Elevation can be used to get temperature variations within a subbasin to influence the snow conditions.

In contrast to the earlier type of models, such as the HBV-NP model, HYPE simulates the water flow paths and nutrient transformations in soil. The soil is modelled as several layers which may have different thickness for each class. Agricultural land classes commonly use three soil layers to simulate nutrient transformation more accurate. Model parameters may be associated with land use (e.g. evapotranspiration), soil type (e.g. water content in soil), or be common for the whole catchment. This way to couple the parameters to geographic information makes the model better suited for simulations in ungauged catchments.

HYPE simulates the nutrients nitrogen and phosphorus divided into the following fractions: inorganic nitrogen, organic nitrogen, soluble reactive phosphorus and particulate phosphorus. In addition, organic material and conservative substances like ^{18}O can be simulated. The calculations are made with a daily time step for water and concentrations, but result can also be delivered as mean values over a longer period and in the form of transported amount of nutrients and source apportioned transport. The HYPE model is set up for a growing number of basins, including Sweden [2], the Baltic Sea drainage basin, Europe [2,3], and La Plata in South America.

3 The Solution, Part Two: Storing Data in an Efficient and Flexible Database

Running the HYPE model at high resolution for a country or a continent quickly generates vast volumes of data. For Sweden only, the present S-HYPE version with 17,313 subbasins and calculations of discharge, nitrogen- and phosphorous transport with a daily time step for the period 1990-2010 generates approximately 400 million values. For Europe, the present E-HYPE version with 47,000 subbasins generates approximately half a billion values of daily discharge values.

The best solution in our opinion was to follow standard procedure. As a first step, a database model was developed to characterise the dependencies and relationships between different attributes to be stored in the database. After the structure of the database had been determined, a Postgres 8.4 database was generated. A database loading program in Java was developed to read model output files into the SQL database.

It was crucial already at this point to assure that the database would be highly accessible through a web-based interface. Achieving short response times was a priority. Different accessibility solutions were developed for the Swedish database and the European database. For the Swedish database, data were cached in main memory (currently 68 GB main memory) for rapid delivery. For the European database, we chose to partition the database per subbasin, which resulted in a good throughput as long as you retrieve data from a limited number of subbasins. The partitioning require much less main memory on the database server but the disadvantage is sacrificed flexibility of retrieval, i.e., retrieve all subbasins for a single point in time is not practical.

4 The Solution, Part Three: A Web-Based User Interface

Developing a web-based user interface was a strong requirement to assure public accessibility. We have developed two services that satisfy a range of data accessibility needs.

The first service is a simple but functional map interface which allows users to first identify and select subbasins of interest. After subbasins have been selected the user fills out a short form to identify the data period, temporal resolution and variables to download. Finally, after the "download" button has been pressed, data series will be delivered in a spreadsheet that can be opened or saved to a local hard drive.

The second service is a web service that delivers data in xml-format following a REST call. This solution is suitable for machine-to-machine communication and when downloading data for a large number of subbasins. Due to network security reasons, the web service has so far been restricted to registered users, but there are plans to turn this into an open API in the near future. Technically, we have identified a series of components that together meet the requirements of effective, web-based, data-sharing (Table 1):

Table 1. List of reliable components that have been used to construct the technical basis of SMHI VattenWeb

Purpose	Component
Web-application framework	Google Web Toolkit
Client side map viewer	Openlayers
Database solution	Postgres 8.4
Coupling to database	JDBC
Log	log4j
Map server	Geoserver and GeoWebCache with cached images for different zoom levels
Web server	Apache
Run web applications in Java	Tomcat
Web service call	Jersey
Spread sheet generation	Apache POI

The web-based user interface is constructed with the framework Google Web Toolkit (GWT) together with Openlayers as a map viewer. With the help of GWT both client and server side can be written in java-code. On the server side, JDBC is used to communicate with a Postgres database and Apache POI generates spread sheets from returned data. The web services REST interface is built with the help of Jersey. Both the web-application and web services is hosted within a Tomcat web server that runs under Apache. Geoserver and GeoWebCache is used to host to the Openlayers client with geographical metadata and pre cached maps through standard protocols WFS and WMS.

5 The Solution, Part Four: An Operational Production Line for WFD Support Services

In most cases, piecing together models, databases and web pages is carried out in project form with financial resources restricted to a limited time period. However, to meet the challenges of European water management, information must be updated and accessible more or less continuously. One solution is to incorporate supporting systems into an operational production line, but this requires a solid technical infrastructure.

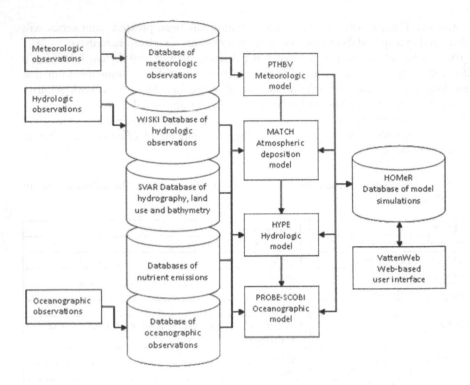

Fig. 2. A simplified illustration of the operational production line for WFD supporting services at the Swedish Meteorological and Hydrological Institute. Parts of this production line is also utilized for our pan-European services, such as E-HypeWeb [4].

This technical infrastructure is already in place at SMHI. As a government agency with national responsibility for meteorology, hydrology and oceanography, SMHI already operates a number of services on a daily basis. There is a strong IT department with high computational capacity and around-the-clock technical support. Data security issues are dealt with in a professional manner.

The production line for WFD supporting services has now been established at SMHI but is still in its infancy and subject to improvements (Figure 2). Due to Sweden's late implementation of the WFD (2004), and even later involvement of WFD at SMHI (2008), many WFD supporting services were initially developed as individual projects with minimum overlap. As a result, these systems became very expensive to keep updated and operational. Therefore, many first-generation systems are now being merged to maximize cost-effectivness.

The establishment of a production line is critical also for handling system and information updates efficiently. For data on river discharge and nutrient transport, both products of multiple data sets and calculation steps, it is critical to keep track of the exact combination of model versions and data sets used in the calculation. Nevertheless, new observations, or changes in the delineation of water bodies, require databases and models to be updated frequently. Thus, data sets must be carefully associated with metadata to ensure that data can be traced and reproduced at a later stage. In our opinion, it is very difficult to sustain the handling of data versions and reproducibility without a firm production line in place.

6 Conclusions

The first web application that gave public access to large-scale hydrologic simulations with high resolution was SMHI VattenWeb [5], a web interface that offers time series of river discharge and nutrient transport from 17,313 subbasins in Sweden. Since the launch in April 2010, the number of unique visitors has steadily increased and approach 3000 at the end of March 2011 (Figure 3).

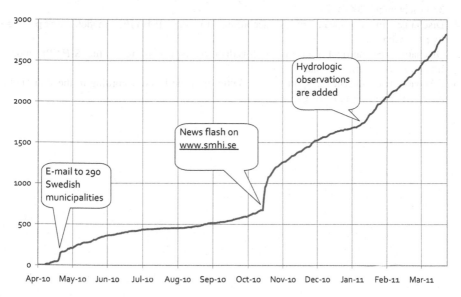

Fig. 3. Number of unique visitors at SMHI VattenWeb [5] from the start in April 2010 to March 31, 2011, according to statistics from Google Analytics

Later during 2010 a pan-European HYPE model, E-HYPE, was set up and launched as a demonstration tool [4]. The E-HYPE model has a resolution of approximately 47,000 subbasins across the European continent. Other publicly available web services include Balt-HYPE, a HYPE model for the Baltic drainage basin [6].

We believe that strong hydrologic research and development must be placed in an operational production line to satisfy the needs of the WFD. We have demonstrated how a production line has been set up at the SMHI and described the different components. It is clear that public interest for these services is very high and we see many benefits of such systems at the European scale, not only for fresh water management related to the WFD, but also in other sectors. In the near future we will probably see the emergence of a large variety of downstream services that utilize data from publicly available core services.

References

1. Arheimer, B., Lindström, G., Pers, C., Rosberg, J., Strömqvist, J.: Development and test of a new Swedish water quality model for small-scale and large-scale applications. In: XXV Nordic Hydrological Conference, Reykjavik, August 11-13, NHP Report No. 50, pp. 483–492 (2008)
2. Donnelly, C., Dahne, J., Lindström, G., Rosberg, J., Strömqvist, J., Pers, C., Yang, W., Arheimer, B.: An evaluation of multi-basin hydrological modelling for predictions in ungauged basins. In: Proc. of Symposium HS.2 at the Joint IAHS & IAH Convention, Hyderabad, India. IAHS Publ. 333 (September 2009)
3. Strömqvist, J., Dahne, J., Donnelly, C., Lindström, G., Rosberg, J., Pers, C., Yang, W., Arheimer, B.: Using recently developed global data sets for hydrological predictions. In: Proc. of Symposium HS.2 at the Joint IAHS & IAH Convention, Hyderabad, India. IAHS Publ. 333 (September 2009)
4. Discharge in European rivers according to the E-HYPE model, http://e-hype.smhi.se
5. Discharge and nutrient transport in Swedish rivers according to the S-HYPE model, http://vattenweb.smhi.se
6. Discharge and nutrient transport for the Baltic drainage basin according to the Balt-HYPE model, http://balt-hype.smhi.se

Design and Development of Web Services for Accessing Free Hydrological Data from the Czech Republic

Jiří Kadlec and Daniel P. Ames

Idaho State University, 995 University Blvd, Idaho Falls, ID, 83402, USA
Kadljiri@isu.edu, dan.ames@isu.edu

Abstract. The target of the open source hydrodata.cz web application and web services is to bridge the gap between modelers and field hydrologists by providing free, publicly accessible precipitation, snow, temperature, and discharge data series from multiple organizations in the Czech Republic using the standardized the CUAHSI WaterML data format and search services. Data providers contributing to this effort include the CUAHSI, NOAA, Charles University experimental watershed network, Czech watershed authorities, and networks of volunteer observers. Time period covered includes the floods of 2006, 2009, 2010 and 2011 as well as the 2007 drought. Adopting the WaterML standard also allows the use of other free third party client side web based and desktop data discovery software tools – which has the added benefit of making the Czech Republic hydrological data more readily accessible to the international community.

Keywords: Hydrology, web services, interoperability, information system.

1 Introduction

Hydrologic simulation models are used extensively by scientists and water management authorities for evaluating the response of water ecosystems to land use and climate changes. A large number of open source simulation models are available, including SWAT [1],WASIM-ETH [2], HSPF [3] and AGNPS [4]. Using open source tools for rainfall-runoff simulation (as opposed to proprietary software) can give the researcher better understanding of the approximations used in the model because of access to source code and hence inherent model assumptions and implementation. It also encourages improvement of the model by the user community [5]. The obstacle in implementing either open source or proprietary models by researchers in the Czech Republic is limited availability of precipitation, discharge and soil data for model parameter setup, calibration and validation. Similar to other European countries, the Czech Republic has a long record of systematic meteorological observation and soil mapping. These observations are rarely accessible to the general public. Fig. 1 shows an example of obtaining hourly precipitation data for a recent flash flood event for a small catchment in south-west Bohemia. The process includes contacting several organizations, finding the responsible data managers, signing the data agreement, and transferring the data fee. In each organization contacted by the user, the data manager

J. Hřebíček, G. Schimak, and R. Denzer (Eds.): ISESS 2011, IFIP AICT 359, pp. 581–588, 2011.

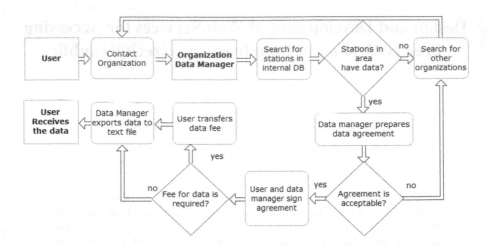

Fig. 1. Obtaining Precipitation data from Blšanka watershed, Czech Republic

must connect to an internal database, find any available observation sites, export database query results to text file and deliver the text file to the user.

Some free data sources already exist in the Czech Republic. Indeed, as required by the information access law of the Czech Republic and emergency early warning system, many government organizations are required by law to publish real-time records of streamflow on the voda.gov.cz [6] internet server. A user with programming experience may set up a method of automated, scheduled data retrieval from this server (Fig. 2). This approach has already been used by the raft.cz white water rafting information web site [7] for the Czech rivers and streams to determine the best time of the year for river navigation. A problem with this approach is large amount of HTML parsing code that requires ongoing maintenance when the structure of the original HTML page changes.

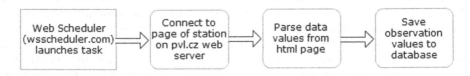

Fig. 2. Getting stream stage data – automated method used by raft.cz

1.1 CUAHSI Hydrologic Information System

The Consortium of Universities for Advanced Hydrologic Science Hydrologic Information System (CUAHSI HIS) is a distributed internet system for sharing hydrologic time series field and derived observations from international and U.S agencies, universities, experimental watersheds and other organizations [8]. The system consists of three main components: *HydroServer*, *HydroCatalog* and *HydroDesktop* (Fig. 3). This configuration follows the well-established "publish-find-bind" model used throughout the Internet for web services [9].

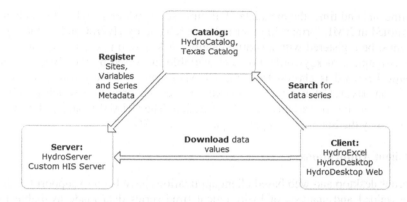

Fig. 3. Main components of the CUAHSI hydrologic information system

1.2 HydroServer

A "HydroServer" is any server connected to the Internet which exposes a standard web service defined by CUAHSI [10]. Primary web methods of the web service include GetSites, GetSiteInfo and GetValues. The GetSites method returns all sites with available data. GetSiteInfo returns the list of variables available for a specific site. GetValues returns the time series for the specified site, variable and time interval. The results of the web methods are returned in the standardized WaterML format [11]. WaterML is an extended variant of the XML language and includes specific elements for defining attributes of hydrologic time series. WaterML requires the data publisher to include complete metadata about the time series. Each HydroServer web service method response is a fully self-describing WaterML document which contains metadata for units, data source, method, quality control level, site location and variable data type. CUAHSI is working together with the Open GIS Consortium (OGC) and World Meteorological Organization (WMO) to estabilish WaterML 2.0 which will be fully compliant with the widely used WFS (Web Feature Service) and SOS (Sensor Observation Service) standards. The adoption of services oriented architecture exposes a platform – independent interface which may be implemented by any server based web application technology. A default implementation (HydroServer) is provided by CUAHSI as open source software [12]. The core of the HydroServer is a Microsoft SQL Server database using the Observations Data Model (ODM) schema [13]. The comprehensive schema of the ODM database is designed for efficiently storing climate, hydrology and water quality time series observations. The official release of CUAHSI HydroServer requires a virtual private or dedicated server with the Microsoft Windows Server operating system. A simplified implementation of HydroServer on a commercial web hosting provider is described later in this paper.

1.3 HydroCatalog

HydroCatalog provides a centralized registry of publicly accessible HydroServers. It exposes a catalog web service with a set of web methods that allow searching for sites and time series across multiple servers. The main web method of the web service is *GetSeriesCatalogForBox*. Given a latitude and longitude bounding box, keyword, start time and end time, the metadata of all time series which match the search criteria are returned in XML format. In order to be searchable by HydroCatalog, the HydroServer must be registered with a central catalog. A key step in the registration process is the assignment of keywords. For each variable measured by the HydroServer, the matching keyword is chosen from the CUAHSI Ontology Keyword list [8]. After registration, HydroCatalog runs a periodic harvesting operation which ensures that any additional sites or variables may be searched. The CUAHSI catalog, HIS Central, is operated by the San Diego Supercomputer Center (SDSC).

1.4 Client Applications

Numerous desktop and web based client applications have been to support the discovery, download and analysis of hydrological time series data made available by the CUAHSI HIS. The desktop applications include HydroExcel and HydroDesktop. HydroExcel [8] supports the download and descriptive statistical analysis of time series from a user specified HydroServer web service. HydroDesktop is an open source geographic information system (GIS) – based tool with special features for hydrological data visualization and analysis [14]. The map component of HydroDesktop enables detailed spatial analysis of the observation sites. Recently a web based client similar to HydroDesktop has been developed [15] with the same core functionality as HydroDesktop (search, map, graph and data export). It is expected that additional client applications will be developed in the near future, customized for specific regions or research domains.

2   Software Design and Implementation

2.1   Analysis of Requirements

For a more detailed analysis of data and software requirements we have selected precipitation, air temperature, water stage, discharge and snow cover data requirements. As a first step, the potential data providers with existing meteorological and hydrological observations covering the Czech Republic were examined.

2.2   Evaluation of Data Sources

Hourly **precipitation** time series are published by the Czech Hydrometeorological Institute (CHMI) flood warning service (HPPS) for previous 7 days from automated rain gauge stations. The CHMI radar network provides images of radar reflectivity for previous day in 2 km, 15 minute resolution. A series of combined 24-hour radar / ground station precipitation maps is also available starting January 2007. In these maps, precipitation for each pixel is represented showing discrete color interval. Some parts of the Czech Republic have coverage of radar networks in Germany, Poland and Slovakia. For the southern part of the country, the global satellite derived precipitation data products (PERSIANN) are available [16]. Precipitation is also published from automated sites of the Czech watershed authorities on the government water portal [6] and by university experimental watershed networks. Precipitation data are susceptible to large measurement errors. By combining multiple systems, automated quality control can be enhanced. **Air temperature** hourly time series are available from the Czech watershed authorities and from university experimental watersheds. The existing NCDC Hourly data web service in the CUAHSI HIS system also provides long term temperature time series from several locations in the Czech Republic. Water **stage** and **discharge** observations are publicly available on the government water portal [6]. Additional observations are published by municipality owned early warning systems [17] and by university experimental watershed networks. **Snow cover** is an important input parameter for rainfall-runoff modeling during the winter period. Daily observations of snow depth are publicly accessible on the web sites of CHMI and watershed authorities. Several volunteer groups also measure snow depth. This includes HS Brdy (Brdy mountain guard) whose cross country skier observers provide detailed coverage of snow conditions in Brdy, the largest forested mountain are in inland Bohemia [18]. Table 1 shows the list of data providers contributing to this system, including the current status.

Table 1. Organizations from the Czech Republic contributing to CUAHSI web services

Organization	Type of observations
CHMI	Snow depth, precipitation, stage, discharge
Povodí Ohře	Snow depth, precipitation, air temperature, stage, discharge
Povodí Vltavy	Precipitation, stage, discharge
Charles University Prague	Water stage, precipitation, temperature, solar radiation, conductivity, dissolved oxygen
HS Brdy	Snow depth

2.3 Implementation of HydroServer for Small Organizations

For smaller data providers, including volunteer observer groups, the main obstacle for providing data in the form of HydroServer web services are associated with hardware and software requirements of the default CUAHSI HydroServer software. These organizations frequently use third-party webhosting services. However, the original HydroServer software was designed to work on large dedicated university servers. Initial testing has shown that third party webhosting providers do not allow running applications under full trust and restrict the usage of some software libraries which were required by the original HydroServer. To address such limitations, the source code of HydroServer was modified, creating a customized product: HydroServer Lite specifically to meet the needs of a Czech HIS implementation. HydroServer Lite may be deployed on any ASP.NET webhosting service, reducing maintenance costs for the organization.

2.4 Overcoming Data Security Concerns

The large Czech government supported organizations (CHMI, watershed authorities) were initially reluctant to make any changes on their servers in support of the hydrodata.cz web services and the CUAHSI HIS system. As a result, an alternative strategy has been implemented (Fig. 4). The hydrodata.cz web server has been set up on a large third party webhosting service. Each day, an automatic scheduled task is launched. This program sends a request to the CHMI web pages, parses the HTML code using regular expression template, extracts time series observations and stores these to the hydrodata.cz database. The standard HydroServer web service is built on top of this database. In case the formatting of the CHMI web page changes significantly, a message is sent by the system, notifying the hydrodata.cz manager that a change in the html parser template is required. With increasing future awareness of the CUAHSI HIS system and more emerging applications, it is expected that the CHMI and other organizations will gradually implement the HydroServer web services directly on their own servers as HIS becomes more widely adopted.

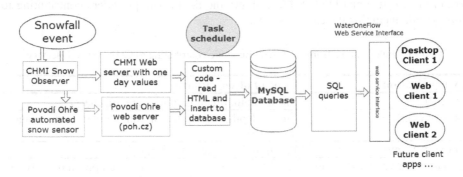

Fig. 4. Adaptation of HydroServer for Czech Republic Snow HydroServer web service

3 Conclusion

The Czech Republic has become one of first regions in the world outside North America full, countrywide coverage of snow and precipitation data made publicly accessible through the CUAHSI HIS (Fig. 5). After fully integrating discharge records, this will allow to re-calculate the surface water balance of any watershed in the country. Other potential applications include hydrology education and agricultural management and planning. The hydrodata.cz web services and application are in the prototype testing stage. By developing the services as an open source system, the authors are convinced that contributions from new users will lead to improvement in system usability. Major developments planned in near future include: (1) Integration of satellite and radar estimates of precipitation, which requires more efficient handling of gridded datasets, (2) Integration of downscaled global climate model outputs, (3) Addition of publicly accessible services providing soil and land use maps using the WMS / WCS standards, (3) Inclusion of more volunteer meteorological observer networks in the system, and (4) Implementation of pay-per-access method to enable access to data sets from institutions which require the purchase fee. By implementing an automated internet payment system, more users will be able to promptly access data sets which require additional financial support. Adopting the WaterML standard also allows the use of other free third party client side web based and desktop data discovery software tools – which has the added benefit of making the Czech Republic hydrological data more readily accessible to the international community.

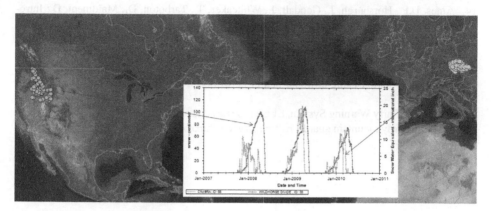

Fig. 5. Map of snow cover sites in Idaho Rocky mountains (USA) and Czech Republic with a comparison of snow depth time series graph in HydroDesktop

References

1. Arnold, J.G., Srinavasan, R., Muttiah, S., Williams, J.R.: Large Area Hydrologic Model-ling and Assessment Part I: Model Development. J. Am. Water Resour. As. 34, 73–89 (1998)
2. Schulla, J., Jasper, K.: Model Description WaSiM-ETH. IAC ETH Zürich, p. 166 (2001)
3. Donigian, A.S., Bicknell, B.R., Imhoff, J.C.: Hydrological Simulation Program – Fortran (HSPF). In: Singh, V.P. (ed.) Computer Models of Watershed Hydrology, pp. 395–442 (1995)
4. Young, R.A., Onstad, C.A., Bosch, D.D., Anderson, W.P.: AGNPS: A nonpoint-source pollution model for evaluating agricultural watersheds. J. Soil Water Conserv. 44(2), 168–173 (1989)
5. Gregersen, J.B., Gijsbers, P.J.A., Westen, S.J.P.: OpenMI: open modelling interface. J. Hydroinform 9, 175–191 (2007)
6. Water Management Information Portal, http://voda.gov.cz
7. Raft.cz Water Sport Portal, http://rivers.raft.cz
8. Maidment, D.R.: Bringing water data together. J. Water Res. Pl. 134(2), 95–96 (2008)
9. OGC Reference Model. Open Geospatial Consortium, 2008-11-11. OGC 08-062r4, http://www.opengeospatial.org/standards/orm
10. Tarboton, D.G., Horsburgh, J.S., Schreuders, K., Maidment, D.R., Zaslavsky, I., Valentine, D.W.: The HydroServer Platform for Sharing Hydrologic Data, American Geophysical Union, fall Meeting 2010, abstract #H53H-03 (2010)
11. Zaslavsky, I., Valentine, D., Whiteaker, T.: CUAHSI WaterML. OGC 07-041r1, Open Geospatial Consortium Discussion Paper (2007)

12. Horsburgh, J.S., Tarboton, D.G., Piasecki, M., Maidment, D.R., Zaslavsky, I., Valentine, D., Whitenack, T.: An integrated system for publishing environmental observations data. Environ. Modell. Softw. 24, 879–888 (2009)
13. Horsburg, J., Tarboton, D.G., Maidment, D.R., Zaslavsky, I.: A relational model for environmental and water resources data. Water Resour. Res. 44 (2008)
14. Ames, D.P., Horsburgh, J., Goodall, J., Whiteaker, T., Tarboton, D., Maidment, D.: Introducing the Open Source CUAHSI Hydrologic Information System DesktopApplication (HIS Desktop). In: 18th World IMACS/MODSIM Congress, Australia (2009)
15. HydroDesktop Web Map Application, http://www.hydromap.info
16. Hsu, K.L., Gao, X.G., Sorooshian, S., Gupta, H.V.: Precipitation estimation from remotely sensed information using artificial neural networks. J. Appl. Meteorol 36(9), 1176–1190 (1997)
17. Hladiny.cz Early Warning System, http://www.hladiny.cz
18. HS Brdy (Brdy mountain guard), http://www.hsbrdy.com

SUDPLAN's Experiences with the OGC-Based Model Web Services for the Climate Change Usage Area

P. Kutschera, M. Bartha, and D. Havlik

Austrian Institute of Technology - AIT,
Donau-City-Straße 1, A-1220 Vienna, Austria
{peter.kutschera,mihai.bartha,denis.havlik}@ait.ac.at
http://www.ait.ac.at

Abstract. SUDPLAN is currently developing a technical solution for Model Web/Observation Web in the Climate Change usage area. Proposed solution is based on the Open Geospatial Consortium standards, and follows the ideas expressed in SANY Sensor Service Architecture (SensorSA). SUDPLAN also continued the development of the SANY software, resulting in native SOS, SPS and 2D coverage support in "Time Series Toolbox" framework for building sensor web applications. SUDPLAN re-uses much of the OGC SWE and SANY SensorSA functionality to: (1) configure and run the models; (2) provide the data (observations) required for model execution; (3) inform the user on model run progress and (4) access the model results. In this paper, we shall describe the SUDPLAN's experiences with implementing of the interoperable Model Web using OGC standards, and discuss the advantages of various services from the OGC SWE suite as compared to non-SWE alternatives in the Climate Change context.

Keywords: Environmental modelling; Open Geospatial Consortium; Sensor Web enablement; OGC SWE; Model Web; Observation Web; Time Series Toolbox; Sensor Service Architecture; SensorSA.

1 Introduction

SUDPLAN is an EU FP7 project under the Information Communication Technology programme (ICT-2009-6.4), running 2010-2012. The project responds to the calls target "ICT for a better adaptation to climate change" which asks for solutions that combine advanced environmental modelling and visualization, in support to EU initiatives like The "Shared Environmental Information System" (SEIS) [22] and The "Single Information Space in Europe for the Environment" (SISE) [28].

The on-going implementation of the *Infrastructure for Spatial Information in Europe* directive (INSPIRE) [21], the transition from research to operations of the *Global Monitoring for Environment and Security* (GMES) initiative[23], the development of a *Shared Environmental Information System* (SEIS), and the

J. Hřebíček, G. Schimak, and R. Denzer (Eds.): ISESS 2011, IFIP AICT 359, pp. 589–604, 2011.

combination of all three as a European contribution to the *Global Earth Observation System of Systems* (GEOSS) initiative [25], are profoundly changing the design of environmental applications. In order to allow re-using of investments across usage areas, organisations and applications, the researchers and application developers are required to provide access to "their" data and other functional building blocks (e.g. processing, visualization) through standardized web service interfaces.

Sensor Web Enablement suite of standards developed by *Open Geospatial Consortium* (OGC SWE) [20] already provides much of the required functionality for sensors and sensor observation archives; the SANY *Sensor Service Architecture* (SensorSA) [11] and the "Model Web" [24] envision the similar functionality for environmental models, and the newly coined "observation web" [26] extends these ideas to observations provided by humans.

2   Data, Transport, and Model Runs in Service Oriented Architecture

Service-oriented architecture (SOA) is widely accepted as the paradigm of choice to loosely couple software components in distributed applications [29,10].

Applied to numerical models, the SOA paradigm leads to idea of "Model Web", where model engines, as well as the resources required by these models are consequently encapsulated behind service interfaces and re-usable across a range of applications.

This section summarizes some of the key SOA requirements. A more detailed discussion of this topic is given in ORCHESTRA RM-OA [10] and SANY fusion architecture documents [12]

1. Discovery of data and models With a notable exceptions of the RESTfull web services[33] and the LinkedData approach [19], the web services remain invisible for end users and web crawlers.

   Model Web resource discovery therefore requires special-purpose catalogs offering structured information on available resources. At the time of writing this paper, no fully functional generic solution for data and model discovery exists, but the future INSPIRE and GMES catalogues are expected to provide much of the required functionality. Comprehensive knowledge archive network (CKAN, http://ckan.net) search engine provides an interesting alternative to both Google and specialised catalogues for the Linked Data cloud.

   Data and service discovery is not on the SUDPLANs' research agenda, and therefore will not be further considered in this paper.

2. Formal definition of the model, required input data, parameters and output values (not shown in Fig. 1).

   SOA paradigm foresees re-using services and resources in applications they were not initially designed for. Consequently, each service needs provide formal self-description of its methods, as well as of the specific functionality provided by the service. Model web services should also provide the estimates about input- and output- data sizes and expected runtimes.

3. Handling of the large data sets

Model web services consume data from one or more sources on input side, process it and produce new data set(s) on the output side. Furthermore, the processing is controlled by parameters.

Examples of input- and output- data relevant to SUDPLAN include climate-relevant sensor observations, pollution and rainfall patterns. Both the input data consumed by models, and their output can be large compared to the network throughput and the capacity of data services to deliver the required data. Consequently, the architecture must provide a way to replicate the data required for the model runs and to keep the local copy synchronised. An interesting discussion of the data replication and syncronization in OGC SWE networks has been given by Havlik et al. [27].

4. Model execution

SOA services are typically idle unless explicitly triggered to perform some action. Model web services are often trigered by providing a set of parameters, but the model execution may be also performed separately from model configuration. Model parameters define the temporal and spatial constraints, as well as the initial conditions for the model run. In the model web context, the parameters may also allow the users to choose one of the available processing algorithms, decide which input data to use, or to schedule the delayed model execution.

5. Progress monitoring and control

Some models are capable of calculating the results almost imediately. Other, including the SUDPLANs' downscalling services may require weeks to complete the task.

This results in the need for monitoring the model progress and notifying the users of model status changes.

6. Download the results, which are also potential large datasets

The type and size of the model result differes in a wide range. From just a few numbers to a timeseries of 3D grids in the scale of 100GB.

So it makes no sense to return each result to the client. Instead it is stored on the server site and the client gets informed of when and where (parts of) the results can be downloaded.

3   Selection of Standards to be Used by SUDPLAN

All data need to be self describing [30] which means that there is information about the values like unit of measurement, description of phenomena (e.g. a URN of a ontology), precision and uncertainty and methods of measurement in the form of sensor descriptions. The same is true for models as we expect to get more models over time and they should be usable without prior knowledge of any details. There is a lot of standards for data transport and remote service invocation. SANY SensorSA[31] and Fusion Architecture[12] documents already foresee most of this.

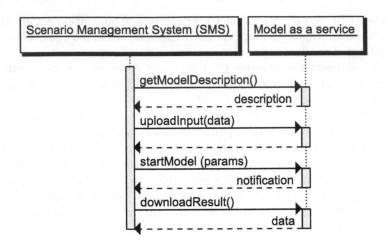

Fig. 1. The overall picture of a model invocation

Within SUDPLAN we concentrated to the OGC service interfaces. The main reasons where:

- The OGC service interfaces are an accepted standard in the GIS comunity, and cover a large number of use-cases relevant to environmental usage area
- All OGC specifications are freely available to everyone
- All OGC service specifications share common data encodings (O&M - Observation and Measurement[6]) and descriptions (GML - Geography Markup Language[2], SensorML - Sensor Model Language[8]).
- There is a lot of service interfaces to select from
- Implementations of libraries and some ready to use services are already available as open source

Now we will discuss which of the OGC interfaces are used in SUDPLAN and why we decided to use them.

3.1   Data Transport: SOS, WCS, WFS, WMS?

Most of the data used in SUDPLAN fall into one of the following two categories:

- timeseries of scalar values like e.g. rain data from one measurement station, and
- timeseries of field data, e.g. mean temperature changes over whole europe for the next 100 years, one field every 10 years, one value in the field representing a 100x100 km sqare over Europe.

As discussed in the previous section, the associated meta-information such as units, spatial and temporal references hs to be provided together with the data. Consequently, most of the SUDPLAN data can be thought of as timeseries of observations [31].

We needed to find a service interface that is generic enough to transport all out data but as specific as possible. Following OGC services were considered in SUDPLAN:

WMS - Web Map Server. The main goal of the WMS[1] is to deliver maps to be visualized by a client. There is a lot of clients available ranging from browser-based interfaces to complete GIS systems.

The focus of the maps is the visualization, so the information is rendered and deliverd as images. In SUDPLAN the results from one model is often the input to the next model so images are not the data format of our choice. Also images are not the best data representation when comparing different climate or planning scenarios or when doing some more sophisticated visualizations.

Therefore the use of WMS in SUDPLAN is limited to background maps and quick overviews of the model results. The best candidate for this are the precalculated Climate Scenario data, which are used to show SUDPLAN users what climate changes to expect.

WFS - Web Feature Service. A WFS[3] provides GML-encoded data with geographic reference.

This is a very powerfull service and many GIS systems can access a WFS to get data to render on a map.

WMS is often used to access shape files. While it would be possible to use WMS for accessing data in SUDPLAN, this standard is not optimised for handling timeseries of observations.

WCS - Web Coverage Service. The WCS[5] is in many aspects similar to WMS.

Unlike WMS, the WCS return a grid of values suitable for further processing.

The usage of WCS as a way to access coverages was discussed within SUDPLAN. However, WCS is not optimised for timeseries of simple observations (unlike SOS). WCS remains an option for later extensions as at this early project state we tried to reduce complexity and implementation overhead.

SOS - Sensor Observation Service. SOS[4] has been designed to provide access to sensor observations. Many sensors repeatedly observe the same phenomenon, so the result is typically a timeseries of observations, each associated to a time stamp. A model, or other processing entity, can be treated similarly to a sensor. Same is valid for the model input, output, parameters and identification information[12,?].

Although SOS appears to be the obvious service interface for data access in SUDPLAN, the encoding of continuous coverages has not been well-defined in OGC SWE version 1.0. SOS relies on O&M information model, and the SUDPLAN approach for encoding continuous coverages, within limitations of the SOS 1.0 and O&M 1.0, is discussed in 3.3 section of this paper.

3.2   Model Invocation: SPS, WPS?

Two of the OGC service specifications are suitable for initiation of remote program runs: Web Processing Service (WPS) and Sensor Planning Service (SPS).

WPS - Web Processing Service. The WPS, initially named "Geoprocessing Service", was first introduced 2005. The WPS v1.0 (2007)[9] defines the web service interface and the mechanisms necessary to execute processes (analisys of georeferenced data) as well as to publish process dectiptions. The three WPS operations (GetCapabilities, DescribeProcess and Execute), providr enough flexibility to easily handle most processing use cases. Unfortunately, the WPS's flexibility of defining provider and domain specific input and output formats comes at the cost of the client which must support these formats.

SPS - Sensor Planning Service. The more capable and complex SPS v1.0 was introduced in 2007[8] with the goal to describe sensor platforms and to allow the planning and scheduling of complex tasks in the context of earth observation satellites. While the initial goal of SPS seems somewhat distant from our goal of runing models subsequent research has shown that SPS can be sucesfully used as a general purpose interface for models and data fusion services.

In comparison to the WPS the SPS standard is more structured, and provides pre-defined mechanisms for client notification (status and result availability). The GetFeasibility operation in the SPS standard allows for client feedback, on the viability of a processing operation, before committing to execution. The SUDPLAN requirements on model description with formal specifications of parameters, input data and results, can be fulfilled by both WPS and SPS. However, the requirements on scheduling, cancelling, and monitoring the progress of the model runs can only be fulfilled by SPS. Further advantage of the SPS over WPS lies in the built-in notification handling.

Usage of OGC services for model invocation SUDPLAN

3.3   O&M Encoding of Timeseries of Fields

As mentioned earlier, based on the size of the data, a distinction is made between parameters for a model run and input data. While the parameters are of simple type and small in size the input data for a model is complex in nature and quite common of several GB in size. Because the model needs a fast access to the input data this data has to be uploaded to the model site. The user of the model does this (sometimes over institutional boundaries) through an implementation of the SOS interface. This interface is also used to enumerate and retrieve the model results. Model result data transfered through the SOS interface is encoded using the O&M [6] information model.

The O&M encoding is straight forward for timeseries of scalar values and used by many SOS implementations (52North[16], OOSTethys[17]). The encoding of timeseries of coverages is not that well defined. Observations and Measurements

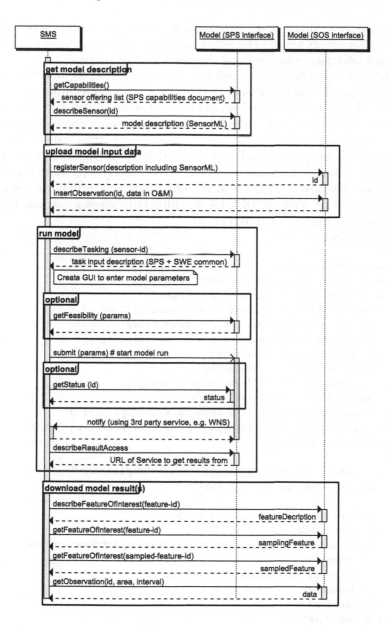

Fig. 2. Model invocation details showing OGC interface usage

- Sampling Features (O&M-SF)[7] specification provides means to encode discrete coverages and provides dedicated elements to do so, but it lacks dedicated elements necessary to describe continuous coverages.

SANY "Fusion and Modelling Architectural Design"[12] document describes two methods for encoding coverages in O&M. Both are using the O&M-SF sa:SamplingSurface element. While there is no dedicated element in O&M-SF

v1.0 to specify a grid on which the sampling takes place, both methodes describe the sampling points and grid by embeding its description in sub-elements of the sa:SamplingSurface, which was not designed for this purpose.

In SUDPLAN a further method has been considered for describing continuous coverages. The optional SOS method DescribeFeatureOfInterest allows for retrieval of the feature type description (xml schema) for a given feature of interrest. This allows us to introduce a new namespace containing additional Sampling Feature types. The new SamplingGrid type inherits from the sa:SpatiallyExtensiveSamplingFeatureType defined in O&M-SF and contains a gml:RectifiedGrid element that describes the rectified grid on which the sampling takes place. The advantage of the mentioned inheritance is that the sampledFeature relation is retained. SUDPLAN SamplingGrid schema and one Sampling-Grid instance example are shown below.

SamplingGrid schema:

```
<schema xmlns="http://www.w3.org/2001/XMLSchema"
     xmlns:xlink="http://www.w3.org/1999/xlink"
     xmlns:gml="http://www.opengis.net/gml"
     xmlns:sa="http://www.opengis.net/sampling/1.0"
     xmlns:aitsa="http://www.ait.ac.at/sampling"
     targetNamespace="http://www.ait.ac.at/sampling"
     elementFormDefault="qualified"
     attributeFormDefault="unqualified">
  <import namespace="http://www.opengis.net/gml"
     schemaLocation="./gml4sos.xsd"/>
  <import namespace="http://www.opengis.net/sampling/1.0"
     schemaLocation="http://schemas.opengis.net/sampling/1.0.0/
samplingManifold.xsd"/>

  <element name="SamplingGrid" type="aitsa:SamplingGridType"
     substitutionGroup="gml:_Feature"/>

  <complexType name="SamplingGridType">
    <complexContent>
      <extension base="sa:SpatiallyExtensiveSamplingFeatureType">
        <sequence>
          <element ref="gml:RectifiedGrid"/>
        </sequence>
      </extension>
    </complexContent>
  </complexType>
</schema>
```

SamplingGrid instance example:

```
<?xml version="1.0" encoding="UTF-8"?>
<SamplingGrid xmlns="http://www.ait.ac.at/sampling"
   xmlns:gml="http://www.opengis.net/gml"
   xmlns:xlink="http://www.w3.org/1999/xlink"
```

```
  xmlns:sa="http://www.opengis.net/sampling/1.0"
  xmlns:xsi="http://www.w3.org/2001/XMLSchema-instance"
  xsi:schemaLocation="http://www.opengis.net/gml
     http://schemas.opengis.net/gml/3.1.1/base/gml.xsd
     http://www.ait.ac.at/sampling
     ./SamplingGridSchema.xsd ">
<gml:description>Sweden grid</gml:description>
<gml:name>Swenden Grid</gml:name>
<gml:location />
<sa:sampledFeature xlink:href="urn:MyOrg:feature:sthlm_1"/>
<gml:RectifiedGrid dimension="2">
  <gml:limits>
    <gml:GridEnvelope>
      <gml:low>0 0</gml:low>
      <gml:high>50 60</gml:high>
    </gml:GridEnvelope>
  </gml:limits>
  <gml:axisName>x</gml:axisName>
  <gml:axisName>y</gml:axisName>
  <gml:origin>
    <gml:Point srsName="urn:x-ogc:def:crs:EPSG:3021">
      <gml:pos>6546000.0 1580000.0</gml:pos>
    </gml:Point>
  </gml:origin>
  <gml:offsetVector srsName="urn:x-ogc:def:crs:EPSG:3021">
  0 2e-005</gml:offsetVector>
  <gml:offsetVector srsName="urn:x-ogc:def:crs:EPSG:3021">
  2e-005 0</gml:offsetVector>
  </gml:RectifiedGrid>
</SamplingGrid>
```

3.4   Using UncertML to Describe Statistical Data

The descriptive model language Uncertainty Markup Language - UncertML[32]
developed by the INTAMAP project can be used to encode the accuracy of the
observation collection. SUDPLAN rainfall downscaling service generates a 2D
table of the predicted precipitation values for the total seasonal accumulation
(TOT), maximum 30-min intensity (MAX) and frequency of occurrence (FRQ).
Because of the statistical characteristics of this data, UncertML could be used
to encode it, similar to the way uncertainities in sensor data and model outputs
were encoded in SANY.

This would mean treating this data as description of the timeseries of rainfall,
not as an independent result. At the same time this data has the characteristics
of a time series, meaning that it provides the above mentioned statistical information for every season. At this point no decission has been taken on wether
in SUDPLAN this data should be encoded as observations (using O&M), or as
observation uncertainities (using UncertML).

3.5   Using SensorML to Describe Models and Required Parameters

The SOS and SPS interfaces provide process descriptions encoded in in SensorML, through describeSensor operation. In SUDPLAN, the process is a models and can be described as Non-Physical (pure) process. The information provided in the form of a SensorML document can be quite extensive encompassing model inputs, parameters, outputs, the model algorithm itself and details of the implementation module. Currently, our use-cases require descriptions of constant model parameters necessary for the human interpretation of the model results. This includes: model identification, responsible party, input and output model. Our processing services act as clients to several Sensor Observation Services.

The following simplified SensorML document shows basic model identification as well the inputs and outputs of the rain downscaling model used in SUDPLAN. The model takes as input a SOS offering name containing the historical rain measurements as well as a future timestamp around which the downscaling results are generated. The model outputs a timeseries of coverages with the result model described in the Downscaled_rain named element.

```
<sml:SensorML xmlns:sml="http://www.opengis.net/sensorML/1.0.1"
   xmlns:swe="http://www.opengis.net/swe/1.0.1"
   xmlns:gml="http://www.opengis.net/gml"
   xmlns:xlink="http://www.w3.org/1999/xlink" version="1.0.1"
   xmlns:xsi="http://www.w3.org/2001/XMLSchema-instance"
   xsi:schemaLocation="http://www.opengis.net/sensorML/1.0.1
   http://schemas.opengis.net/sensorML/1.0.1/sensorML.xsd ">
 <sml:member>
  <sml:System gml:id="SUDPLAN_A1B3">
   <gml:description>Simple rain downscaling model</gml:description>
   <sml:identification>
    <sml:IdentifierList>
     <sml:identifier name="UID">
      <sml:Term definition="urn:x-ogc:def:identifier:OGC:uuid">
       <sml:value>urn:x-ogc:object:model:SUDPLAN:prec:A1B3</sml:value>
      </sml:Term>
     </sml:identifier>
     <sml:identifier>
      <sml:Term definition="urn:x-ogc:def:identifier:OGC:shortName">
       <sml:value>SUDPLAN A1B3</sml:value>
      </sml:Term>
     </sml:identifier>
    </sml:IdentifierList>
   </sml:identification>
   <sml:inputs>
    <sml:InputList>
     <sml:input name="ObservationOfferingName">
      <swe:Text />
     </sml:input>
     <sml:input name="centerTime">
      <swe:Time />
```

```
    </sml:input>
   </sml:InputList>
  </sml:inputs>
  <sml:outputs>
   <sml:OutputList>
    <sml:output name="Downscaled_rain">
     <swe:DataArray>
      <swe:elementCount>
       <swe:Count />
      </swe:elementCount>
      <swe:elementType name="CoverageType">
       <swe:DataRecord>
        <swe:field name="Timestamp">
         <swe:Time definition="urn:ogc:data:time:iso8601"/>
        </swe:field>
        <swe:field name="Grid">
         <swe:DataArray>
          <swe:elementCount>
           <swe:Count />
          </swe:elementCount>
          <swe:elementType name="value">
           <swe:Quantity
             definition="urn:ogc:def:property:OGC:1.0:precipitation">
            <swe:uom code="mm"/>
           </swe:Quantity>
          </swe:elementType>
         </swe:DataArray>
        </swe:field>
       </swe:DataRecord>
      </swe:elementType>
     </swe:DataArray>
    </sml:output>
   </sml:OutputList>
  </sml:outputs>
 </sml:System>
 </sml:member>
</sml:SensorML>
```

4 Different Model Types Used in SUDPLAN

This section provides three examples of the SUDPLAN Common Services[13] illustrating the bandwith of the model characteristics. We concentrate on:

1. Required input data type and size
2. Need of parameters,
3. Expected runtime,
4. Type and size of result

4.1   Climate Scenario Data

Climate Scenario Common Service provides access to precalculated results of the climate change model. The result are timeseries of fields, typically about 51x51 values, one grid per 10 years over a time period of 140 years. Each field can contain some values (e.g. Temp, NO2). The entire dataset is about (51 * 51 * 13 decades * 7 different observed properties) 250000 values.

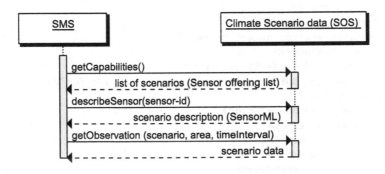

Fig. 3. Access Climate Scenario data

From the model invocation point of view the Climate Scenario Common Service is merely a data access service, as it does not provide any interface for model execution and control.

4.2   Rain Timeseries Downscaling

SUDPLAN rain timeseries Downscaling Service provides information on the local rainfall patterns for the next 100 years.

The input data is a historical timeseries of scalars, typically ten years of measured precipitation, one value every 5 minutes. This gives about one million values. Three parameters have to be provided by user for each model run: the name of the uploaded timeseries, the climate scenario to use, and the date for which a new timeseries shall be calculated[1].

The runtime of the model is short, just some minutes. The result is a timeseries with the same characteristics as the input timeseries, just moved into a possible future. Additional results are aggregated timeseries (e.g. one value every 30 minutes) and statistical information on the created data.

4.3   Air Quality Downscaling

Air quality Downscaling Service is the most important of the SUDPLAN Common Services. The model behind this service is able to perform local air quality downscaling based on local emission data.

---

[1] The location for which the future timeseries should be calculated is taken from the input timeseries.

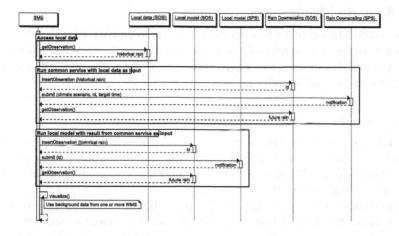

Fig. 4. Using downscaled rain timeseries as input to a local model

The input is a field of expected emissions of greenhouse gases over an area of interest, typically a city. The parameters for this service are the climate scenario to use, the time interval and the area for which the air quality has to be calculated.

The runtime on a background supercomputer is expected to be around 10 days for a typical model run, and the result size is about 100GBytes. The model user has the possibility to download some result subsets, e.g. timeseries of grids, one value every 10 years or a timeseries for one location with higher temporal resolution. Available phenomena include temperature, precipitation, NO2 and more.

5 Software Used

SUDPLANS aims to provide affordable downscaling services with standardised interfaces, and usable by every city in Europe. The main software components developed in SUDPLAN are:

5.1 Common Services

Most of the SUDPLAN Common Services already existed before the SUDPLAN project. These services are propriatery and executed on specialised supercomputers.

These services are accessed through standardized interfaces implemented by AIT using the open source TimeSeries Toolbox[18]. This implementation provides a wrapper around the models providing SOS interfaces for the transfer of data and SPS interfaces for executing and monitoring the models.

In addition, the WMS provides quick overviews of the model results. SUDPLAN uses the GeoServer[15] open source WMS implementation.

5.2 Scenario Management System

The Scenario Management System (SMS) is the main SUDPLAN user interface providing means to control models, retrieve and visualise results. SMS is based on cismet's CIDS system[14]. Both, CIDS as well an the SUDPLAN specific extensions are available under an open source licence.

5.3 Local Models

SUDPLAN foresees two ways to extend the functionality of the system with additional local models: through SMS extensions, and through exposing of the local models through an SPS interface implementation analogously to the Common Services implementations described above.

Depending on the data type, a WFS (e.g. digital elevation model), a WMS (Aerial photos for visualisation) or a SOS (Sensor data) can be used. Open source implementations for all of these services are available from various sources.

6 Conclusion and Outlook

This paper describes the current status of the SUDPLAN Model Web Implementation. SUDPLAN implementation bases of the OGC SWE 1.0 standards and on the SANY SensorSA idea of interfacing the models with SOS and SPS service interfaces. Our results confirm the suitability of the OGC SOS and OGC SPS services and related data encodings from the OGC SWE 1.0 standard suite for Climate Change related models and model results. SUDPLAN software related to interfacing of models and accessing the model results is avaliable as open source on ts-toolbox.ait.ac.at web site.

Some of the shortcomings mentioned in the paper have been adressed in SWE 2.0 development, in particular, the O&M 2.0 specification of the SamplingFeature. The SamplingGrid introduced in SUDPLAN provides an alternative method for describing the SamplingFeature (grid) of a continuous coverage. This method is superior to grid-encoding methods proposed in SANY, as it both retains the SampledFeature relation to the FeatureOfInterest and avoids the need of explicitly specifying all points of the grid. Furthermore, we believe that SamplingGrid is better aligned with O&M 2.0 specifications and provides a valid altenative to WCS encoding of continuous coverages.

SUDPLAN consortium is discussing the feasibility of using UncertML to describe statistic features of the downscaling results, and welcomes input on this topic.

Acknowledgments

The work leading to the results presented in this paper has been partially funded through FP6 Integrated Project *Sensors Anywhere* (SANY; FP6 Contract number 033564; http://sany-ip.eu/) as well as through the FP7 *Sustainable Urban Development Planner for Climate Change Adaptation* project (SUDPLAN; EC grant agreement nr. 247708; http://sudplan.eu).

References

1. Ogc web map service interface (January 2004),
   http://portal.opengeospatial.org/files/?artifact_id=4756
2. Opengis geography markup language (gml) implementation specification (February 2004), http://portal.opengeospatial.org/files/?artifact_id=4700
3. Web feature service implementation specification (May 2005),
   http://portal.opengeospatial.org/files/?artifact_id=39967
4. Opengis sensor observation service - implementation specification (February 2006),
   http://portal.opengeospatial.org/files/?artifact_id=26667
5. Web coverage service (wcs) implementation specification (October 2006),
   http://portal.opengeospatial.org/files/?artifact_id=18153
6. Opengis observations and measurements part 1 - observation schema (December 2007), http://portal.opengeospatial.org/files/?artifact_id=22466
7. Opengis observations and measurements part 2 - sampling features (December 2007), http://portal.opengeospatial.org/files/?artifact_id=22467
8. Opengis sensor model language (sensorml) implementation specification (July 2007), http://portal.opengeospatial.org/files/?artifact_id=21273
9. Opengis web processing service (June 2007),
   http://portal.opengeospatial.org/files/?artifact_id=24151
10. Reference model for the orchestra architecture (rm-oa) v2 (rev 2.1). Best Practice OGC 07-024, D3.2.3 of the European Integrated Project ORCHESTRA FP6-IST-511678 OGC 07-024, Open Geospatial Consortium (2007),
    http://portal.opengeospatial.org/files/?artifact_id=23286
11. Specification of the sensor service architecture v3 (rev. 3.1). Discussion Paper OGC 09-132r. Deliverable D2.3.4 of the European Integrated Project SANY FP6-IST-033564 OGC 09-132r, Open Geospatial Consortium (2009),
    http://portal.opengeospatial.org/files/?artifact_id=35888
12. Sany fusion and modelling architecture. Discussion Paper OGC 10-001, Deliverable D3.3.2.3 of the European Integrated Project SANY FP6-IST-033564 OGC 10-001, Open Geospatial Consortium (2010),
    http://portal.opengeospatial.org/files/?artifact_id=37139
13. Common services (March 2011), http://www.smhi.se/sudplan/About-SUDPLAN/About-SUDPLAN/common-services-1.10161
14. Geoinformationsplattform (March 2011),
    http://www.cismet.de/en/cidsfacts.pdf
15. Geoserver web map service documentation (March 2011),
    http://docs.geoserver.org/stable/en/user/services/wms/index.html
16. Sensor observation service (March 2011),
    http://52north.org/communities/sensorweb/sos/index.html
17. Sensor observation service (March 2011), http://www.oostethys.org
18. The time series toolbox overview (March 2011),
    http://ts-toolbox.ait.ac.at/TS-Toolbox/pdf/TS-Toolbox_Summary.pdf
19. Berners-Lee, T.: Linked data. International Journal on Semantic Web and Information Systems 4 (2006), http://www.w3.org/DesignIssues/LinkedData.html
20. Botts, M., Percivall, G., Reed, C., Davidson, J.: Ogc sensor web enablement: Overview and high level architecture (July 2007),
    http://portal.opengeospatial.org/files/?artifact_id=25562

21. EC: Directive 2007/2/ec of the european parliament and of the council of 14 march 2007 establishing an infrastructure for spatial information in the european community (inspire). EU Directive 2007/2/EC, European Community (March 2007), http://eur-lex.europa.eu/LexUriServ/
LexUriServ.do?uri=OJ:L:2007:108:0001:0014:EN:PDF

22. EC: Communication from the commission to the council, the european parliament, the european economic and social committee and the committee of the regions - towards a shared environmental information system (seis) SEC(2008) 111SEC(2008) 112 . Tech. Rep. COM(2008) 46 final, European Commision (February 2008), http://eur-lex.europa.eu/LexUriServ/
LexUriServ.do?uri=CELEX:52008DC0046:EN:NOT

23. EP, Council: Regulation (eu) no 911/2010 of the european parliament and of the council of 22 september 2010 on the european earth monitoring programme (gmes) and its initial operations (2011 to 2013). Regulation 911/2010, European Parliament and Council (September 2010), http://eur-lex.europa.eu/LexUriServ/
LexUriServ.do?uri=OJ:L:2010:276:0001:0010:EN:PDF

24. Geller, G.N., Melton, F.: Looking forward: Applying an ecological model web to assess impacts of climate change. Biodiversity 9(3&4), 79–83 (2008)

25. GEO: Geo 2009-2011 work plan. Tech. rep., Group on Earth Observations (December 2010), http://www.earthobservations.org/documents/work
%20plan/geo_wp0911_rev3_101208.pdf

26. Havlik, D., Schade, S., Sabeur, Z.A., Mazzetti, P., Watson, K., Berre, A.J., Mon, J.L.: From sensor to observation web with environmental enablers in the future internet. Sensors 11(3) (2011)

27. Havlik, D., Schimak, G., Bleier, T.: Cascading and replicating the ogc sensor observation service. In: Anderssen, R.S., Braddock, R.D., Newham, L.T.H. (eds.) Proceedings of the 18th World IMACS / MODSIM Congress, Modelling and Simulation Society of Australia and New Zealand and International Association for Mathematics and Computers in Simulation, Cairns, Australia, pp. 966–972 (July 2009), http://www.mssanz.org.au/modsim09/C4/havlik.pdf

28. Hebek, J., Pillmann, W.: Shared environmental information system and single information space in europe for the environment: Antipodes or associates? In: Hebek, J., Hradec, J., Pelikn, E., Mrovsk, O., Pillmann, W. (eds.) Proceedings of the European conference of the Czech Presidency of the Council of the European Union, TOWARDS eENVIRONMENT, pp. 447–458. Masaryk University, Prague (2009), http://www.epractice.eu/files/SEIS%20and%20SISE%20for%20the
%20Environment_Antipodes%20or%20Associates.pdf

29. ISO: Iso 19119 geographic information – services (2005)

30. Klopfer, M., Kanellopoulos, I. (eds.): orchestra - an open source architecture for risk management. In: The ORCHESTRA Consortium (2008), http://www.eu-orchestra.org/, ©2008 by the ORCHESTRA Consortium

31. Klopfer, M., Simonis, I. (eds.): SANY - an open service architecture for sensor networks. SANY Consortium (2009), http://www.sany-ip.eu/publications/3317

32. Williams, M., Cornford, D., Bastin, L., Pebesma, E.: Uncertainty markup language, uncertml (2007), http://www.intamap.org/uncertml/uncertml.php

33. Rodriguez, A.: Restful web services: The basics. developerWorks (2008), https://www.ibm.com/developerworks/webservices/library/ws-restful/

Modelling Micro-climate Characteristics for Urban Planning and Building Design

Wolfgang Loibl, Tanja Tötzer, Mario Köstl, Hans Züger, and Markus Knoflacher

AIT Austrian Institute of Technology GmbH, Foresight and Policy Development Department,
A-1220 Donau-City-Strasse 1, Vienna, Austria
{Wolfgang.Loibl,Tanja.Toetzer,Mario.Koestl,Johann.Zueger,
Markus.Knoflacher}@ait.ac.at

Abstract. Climate sensitive urban planning and building design require detailed information on effects of a changing climate. To simulate thermal building performance appropriate data are required as "standardized weather files". But as historic weather records cannot be used to model building performance for future climate, synthetic "future weather" data are necessary. Here we present the steps to derive such data for the urban development project "Seestadt Aspern" in Vienna. We start with regional climate simulations with 10x10 km grid spacing, where hourly data for years of current and future climate have been extracted for the Aspern area. Micro-scale simulations at 5m-resolution have been carried out to consider local influences on urban micro-climate, taking regional simulation results as framework condition. As micro-simulation results are delivered only for single days, transfer functions have been developed to generate synthetic weather records, turning hourly regional climate simulation results into local climate characteristics.

Keywords: future climate, urban climate, regional climate simulation, micro-climate simulation, transfer function, synthetic weather records, Seestadt Aspern, Vienna.

1 Introduction

Climate conditions in urban environments - today and in the future – may differ distinctively from general climate conditions, depending on certain local properties which have effects on the urban microclimate – e.g. street orientation, building height and orientation, open space distribution and surface properties, either influencing irradiance, reflection and absorption, which accelerates heating, and influence shading, ventilation and evaporation, which supports cooling.

The "Seestadt Aspern" is the test case to examine the approach providing information on the expected future climate conditions. The Aspern area is a former airfield in the East of Vienna, which shall be developed as a new urban sub-centre in the coming years, providing a mix of residential, commercial and recreational areas for 20,000 inhabitants and 26,000 employees [3]. Fig. 1 shows the general layout as planned by Tovard Architects & Planners. Sustainability criteria are a key issue to ensure high levels of energy efficiency for buildings, as well as the general adaptability of buildings and open space to a changing climate [2].

J. Hřebíček, G. Schimak, and R. Denzer (Eds.): ISESS 2011, IFIP AICT 359, pp. 605–617, 2011.
© IFIP International Federation for Information Processing 2011

Fig. 1. The planned Aspern development, viewing north (Rendering: AIT)

Two different kinds of climate simulations are applied to provide the data for building performance simulation.

The first input comes from regional climate simulations. Regional climate model results are extracted from AIT's reclip:century project [5] applying COSMO CLM, a numerical regional climate model (RCM) delivering data on atmospheric dynamics for a century for the Greater Alpine Region with 10km grid-spacing as best possible spatial resolution. Urban microclimate simulations are the second input for the Aspern area. These are modelled applying ENVI-met 3.0 - a numerical model which calculates atmospheric dynamics at city block level, considering the influence of block layout and open space pattern on irradiance, ventilation, heat flux, heat storage, humidity and transpiration etc., based on the fundamental laws of fluid dynamics and thermodynamics [1].

While regional climate simulations can be carried out for years, with a rather coarse resolution, the local climate simulations are conducted with a resolution of centimetres to meters, but only for single days. To deliver synthetic future weather records for years on an hourly basis, it is necessary to transfer the regional climate simulation results to micro-climate conditions with the help of the micro-scale simulations. This will be carried out for selected receptor points inside the Aspern area considering specific urban environment characteristics, leading to a specific microclimate which deviates distinctly from regional climate characteristics as simulated for the more rural east of Vienna.

To estimate the local deviations for the certain receptor points, transfer functions for these locations must be generated with the help of the microclimate simulation results, calculated for typical reference days. The applied weather records for building performance simulations contain temperature, wind speed and direction, solar radiation and humidity. While (horizontal) solar radiation and humidity show no or little changes within such small distances as observed in the Aspern region, temperature and wind characteristics data have to be transferred from regional scale to urban micro-scale to show the potential microclimate.

2 Applied Regional Climate Simulations

A broad variety of climate simulations, following different assumptions, have been carried out by various institutions. As we need data with a high resolution and with hourly intervals we use our own simulations. AIT's reclip:century simulations, applied here, have been carried out with the COSMO CLM regional climate model, delivering data with the best available spatial resolution (10x10km grid spacing) for the entire Greater Alpine Area [5]. The simulations have been carried out for the years 1961-2050 using ERA40 global climate re-analysis data as forcing for hindcast runs and 2 global climate simulations runs (GCMs) of current climate and of future climate using ECHAM5- and HADCM3-GCM results as forcing data based on two IPCC SRES greenhouse gas scenarios (A1B, B2) [4].

The current results have been compared, e.g. regarding temperature variation, in order to examine effects of RCM forcing from different GCMs and from different SRES scenarios. Within the decades till 2050 there are no significant differences between the examined SRES scenarios. The two RCM results based on A1B forcing show also nearly the same annual mean temperatures, with some deviations during the seasons.

2.1 Uncertainty Assessment of Regional Climate Simulations

Modelling climate dynamics at regional scale let expect some uncertainties. To explore the uncertainty range climate scenarios have been carried out for current climate to compare the results with measurements. Regional climate simulations have been extracted from control runs for 3 current climate years (1998-2000) and compared with monitoring data. The following Fig. 2 shows this uncertainty exploration by comparing model results for climate model's raster cells where eastern Vienna (and the Aspern area) is embedded, with observation data. As the area is rather flat, the neighbouring raster cells show quite the same simulation results. This indicates that the raster cell's model results, covering Aspern, can be compared with weather records from the monitoring site Gross-Enzersdorf (located in near distance of 3 km to Aspern).

In general the diagram (Fig. 2) shows a high coincidence of both data sets: the correlation coefficient ($R^2 = 0.84$) lets expect little unexplained variance of around 15% between observations and model results. As the simulation results show high coincidence with the observations it can be expected that the simulations of the future climate with increasing greenhouse gas concentrations deliver similar plausible results for the decades till 2050.

The wind speed and wind direction of model results and observations turn out to be rather similar. The diagram below (Fig. 3) depicts that the model under-estimates to some extend the number of hours with wind speed <1.5 m/s (500 hours less) und slightly over-estimates the number of hours with higher wind speed (<3 m/s, <5m/s: 200 hours more, <7m/s: 100 hours more). Such deviations can be observed in many

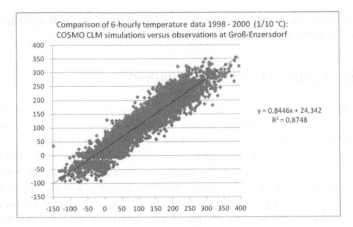

Fig. 2. Comparison of modelled and observed temperature (in 1/10°C) in 6-hourly intervals for the years 1998-2000: COSMO-CLM simulation runs based on ERA40 forcing data for the 10x10km model cell "Vienna South-East" (Source: AIT) and Gross-Enzersdorf monitoring records (Source: ZAMG – Central Agency for Meteorology and Geodynamics, Vienna-Austria)

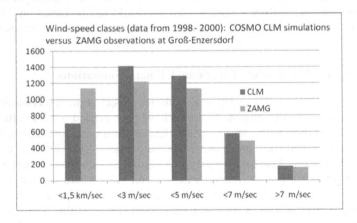

Fig. 3. Comparison of modelled and observed wind speed - hours by wind speed classes (years 1998 – 2000): COSMO-CLM simulation results for the 10x10km model cell „Vienna South-East"(Source: AIT) versus observations from the Gross-Enzersdorf monitoring site (Source: ZAMG)

climate simulations, because the surface roughness often turns out to be smooth, because of the climate model's coarse resolution land use model. In our simulations they are relatively small.

2.2 Future Climate Year Selection

Regional climate simulation results of certain reference years have to be selected, which shall serve as basis for the generation of synthetic weather records representing the local weather characteristics. Objective is to select a hot and an average year, which makes it necessary to examine the occurrence of hot, cool and average years of prior and coming decades. The following Fig. 4 shows the range of the highest and lowest mean temperature of the years in each decade between 1991 and 2050 for the "Vienna South-East" grid cell as carried out through the COSMO CLM simulations: the highest yearly mean temperatures increase from around 10.5°C to 13.3°C, while the lowest yearly mean temperatures increase from 8.1°C to 10.6°C.

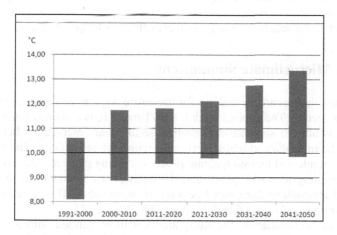

Fig. 4. Yearly temperature means of cool and hot years per decade – the range of the yearly temperature means between 1991 and 2050 for the eastern Vienna area

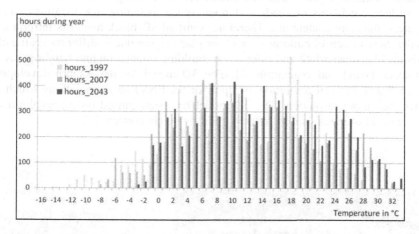

Fig. 5. Number of hours by temperature for 1997, 2007 and 2043 for the eastern Vienna area (hot reference years) (AIT)

For further simulations and investigations we take those years of the current decade and of the "last" decade 2041-2050 with highest mean temperatures as reference years to produce synthetic weather records. Fig. 5 depicts the temperature simulation results of the hottest years during the decades 1991-2000, 2001-2010 and 2041-2050 as number of hours with identical temperature. The hottest years 2007 and 2043 will be also compared with the hottest year of the initial simulation decade – which is 1997. Distinct shifts of the number of hours by temperature can be observed: the yellow bars start with hours of -12°C and range till hours of 28°C, the orange bars of the year 2007 start with hours of -8°C and range till hours of 32°C, while the red bars (of year 2043) start with hours of -3°C and range till hours of 34°C and above.

The shifts show the distinct changes of the temperature regime to be expected during certain episodes of the coming years which will have much effect on the local microclimate which really requires quantifying these effects with appropriate accuracy.

3   Urban Microclimate Simulations

The micro-simulations are carried out for the entire Aspern area with a spatial resolution of a few meters. The applied model, ENVI-met 3.0, is a micro-climate modelling tool, which is able to simulate and analyse small scale interactions between urban design and the immediate climatic surrounds, with high resolutions. The model simulates fluid dynamic and thermodynamic processes taking place at walls, roofs, ground surface, interacting with soil, plants and the atmospheric boundary conditions which deliver local atmosphere dynamics like wind flow, radiation, fluxes, temperature and humidity during one day or a few days at city block scale [1].

To conduct the simulation, the study area has to be defined with its 2D- and 3D conditions by several input data sets using identical grid spacing: building shapes and heights, as well as properties of these structures such as heat storage capacity and irradiance reflection; plant sizes and characteristics relating to shading/wind protection; surface conditions of roads and open space including tree locations, surface roughness, moisture content etc. Therefore a virtual 3D-block model is introduced to consider these effects of building-, street- or plaza layout due to different spatial characteristics like street width and orientation, building orientation and height as well as open space layout and vegetation [6]. The 3D model for the Aspern development shows a 5 and 7 m cell resolution as input for the ENVI-met simulations which also defines the output resolution. The 3D-model has been carried out by exploring the preliminary Master plan and the related building height concept [2].

Fig. 6. Block volumes and building heights transferred into a 7m resolution 3D-model compatible with ENVI-met formats. (Rendering of the central Aspern area and a detail of the ENVI-met 3D-model edit environment (AIT)

Initial atmospheric framework conditions are integrated at the beginning of the model runs, requiring also data like geographical positioning, date and time (to calculate the solar angle), wind speed and wind direction at ground level, the initial temperature at ground level, the specific humidity at 2500m and the relative humidity at ground level. Meteorological information comes from a nearby monitoring site or is derived from climate model-outputs for the grid-cells covering the study area.

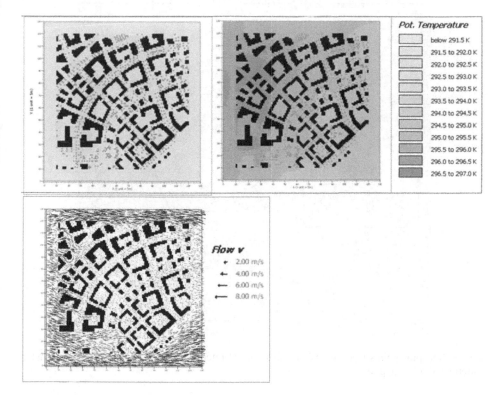

Fig. 7. Potential air temperature at 8h (top-left) and 12h (top-right) and initial windfield pattern (bottom) at 21st of June in the Aspern North-West quadrant (AIT)

A wide range of data is simulated by ENVI-met, and stored as 3D-fields which can be extracted and visualized for any section and direction (beside temperature indicators and wind, humidity, surface conditions, soil conditions, plant conditions and several others) [1]. Fig. 7 shows some results for a detail of the Aspern development – the North-West quadrant: the increase of the potential temperature and local wind fields.

4   Development of Transfer Functions for Temperature and Wind Characteristics

Transfer functions calculate the deviations of the micro-scale weather conditions from the regional weather conditions at certain receptor points for selected typical weather characteristics. Representative spots have been selected as receptor points to generate transfer functions generally representative for the urban environment properties. The occurrence of strong local influence from building walls and corners or special open space properties has been avoided by allocating the points in some distance to the buildings.

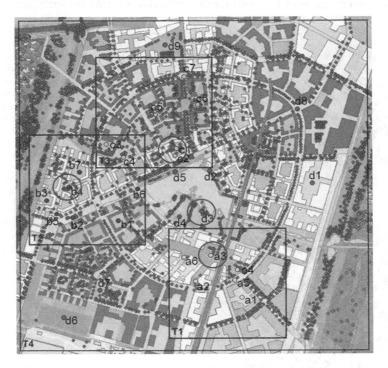

Fig. 8. Receptor points (red circles) in the selected reference areas of Aspern where transfer functions shall be applied

4.1   Functions to Transfer Regional to Local Temperature

To derive transfer functions to estimate local temperature starting from the regional climate simulations, the regional climate model results have to be compared with the diurnal temperature dynamics as conducted by the ENVI-met model.

The variation of the local temperatures during a day are expected to be rather high because of changes in radiation, shading, surface properties in terms of reflection and as well as in terms of soil humidity supporting evaporation and thus cooling.

Fig. 9 compares different temperature indicators as modelled for the 4 receptor points during a day - the mean radiant temperature shows the highest peaks (left diagram) - due to full sunlight exposure and additional exposure from reflections from the surface and the surrounding facades. The surface temperature (centre diagram) shows still a high variation, depending on the surface properties: humid open grassland provides some cooling which lowers the amplitude. Concrete or asphalt surfaces (the blue line of receptor point a3) operate more as heat storage. (Both two indicators are influenced by temporal shades which provide some cooling around 14h). The potential temperature (right diagram) excludes all effects of direct solar radiation and reflection. The amplitude seems to be too low for all receptor points.

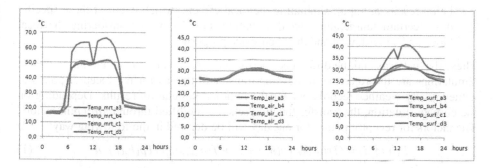

Fig. 9. Comparison of diurnal temperature dynamics (hourly data): mean radiant temperature (Temp_mrt), potential (air) temperature (Temp_air) and surface temperature (Temp_surf), for the 4 receptor points a3,b4,c1,d3 (as shown in Fig. 8)

As no actual air temperature is delivered by the model, the actual temperature (as observed by weather monitoring equipment) is estimated by taking the potential temperature and applying reverse equations to calculate the potential temperature out of relative humidity, atmospheric pressure and the gas constant.

Further the hourly temperatures of the 10 peak days of the year 2043 have to be extracted from the regional climate simulations. (Here shown for the "open space" receptor point d3 near the lake shore). Fig. 10 compares the temperature dynamics of these 10 hot days for receptor point d3.

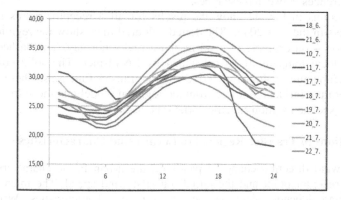

Fig. 10. Diurnal temperature-variation extracted from the regional climate simulations for peak days in June and July 2043

Finally the diurnal variation of the actual temperature at the receptor points will be compared with the day dynamics of the regional climate simulations. The basic assumptions are:

- The diurnal temperature variations of the regional climate simulations describe the daily weather around Aspern.
- The local temperature variations for the 4 receptor points in Aspern as derived by ENVI-met (with 7 m resolution) for certain days take the regional climate simulation results as input, simulating the local effects, which occur at these specific days (certain temperature, wind, radiation, cloud cover), considering the local block and street layout and the open space properties.

These day patterns and the differences between the regional climate and microclimate simulations are the reference to develop transfer functions for the receptor points to achieve daily weather records out for the regional simulation results. Depending on the climate situation, the transfer function sets are modified through different factors. The factors for receptor point i for one day will be derived in the following way:

$$F(h,tg_y,i) = (Tr(d_x,h)/Tp(h,i) + ...+ T(d_{x+1},h,r)/(Tp(h,i)\ )\ /n \qquad (1)$$

where:
$F(h,tg_y,i)$ = factor for hour h for day-type y at receptor point i
$Tr(d_x,h)$ = regional temperature for hour h at day d_x ; $x = \{a,..,n\}$,
n = number of selected days for averaging the hourly factors
$Tp(h,i)$ = receptor point temperature for hour h; at receptor point i

The local day- and hour-specific temperature at the receptor point - $Tp(dx,h,i)$ - is carried out by:

$$Tp(dx,h,i) = Tr(dx,h) * F(h,tgy,i), \qquad (2)$$

where
factor set F() is selected, depending on the day type and the initial regional temperature at the respective day. The number of alternative day types depends on the intensity of differences between these types.

The diagrams in Fig. 11 show the results for all 4 receptor points for different summer days in the year 2043. The dotted coloured lines show the regional temperature variation – on example of a warm and a really hot day. The dashed black line shows the local temperature as calculated by ENVI-met. The solid coloured lines show the temperature patterns as derived by the transfer functions. These lines reflect both temperature influences: those from the regional model and those from the microsimulation (see the location specific variations in shape!).

4.2 Functions to Transfer Regional to Local Wind Characteristics

The local wind direction change depends on the urban fabric characteristics of the respective receptor point and the initial regional wind speed. The intensity of wind speed change depends again on the urban fabric characteristics. Wind transfer-functions will be derived through comparison of the regional wind characteristics with the local ones derived by ENVI-met and extracted for the respective receptor points.

This has been carried out by simulating wind fields with predefined wind speed and wind direction taking 8 major wind direction classes. Transfer functions are estimated with the help of non-linear curve fitting models (log-, exponential-, polynomic

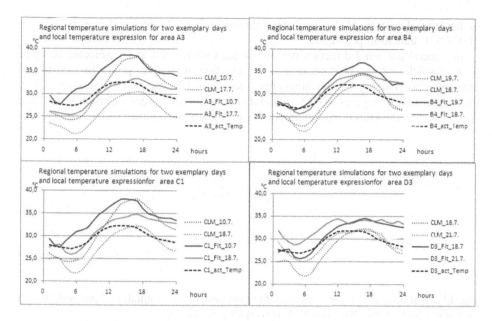

Fig. 11. Temperature-variation for two different summer peak days in June und July 2043 (for all 4 receptor points / areas)

functions) to calculate local wind-speed decline, depending on initial (regional) wind direction and regional wind-speeds, and to calculate the local wind direction deviations from the regional wind directions.

The following diagrams in Fig. 12 show the wind speed decline for one receptor point as example for two wind directions. The details are not relevant to describe the approach, but generally wind speed decline is different for different wind directions with respect to the urban fabric characteristics which serve - more or less - as barrier.

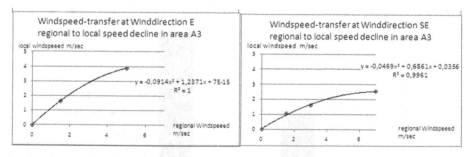

Fig. 12. Transfer-functions for local wind speed decline by initial regional wind speeds as example for two main wind directions at receptor point a3

Change of wind directions is different depending on the receptor point location (Fig. 13 presented for one point for 2 wind directions). The developed transfer functions do not deliver new local wind directions in degrees but deliver an either positive or negative deviation of the local wind direction from the regional one, to avoid < 360° / > 0° transition-problems.

In general the wind direction deviations are rather small at the selected receptor points (which was expected because of the selection of receptor points in undisturbed environment). The highest deviations reach less than 10% which is 36 degrees. Often they arc within a range of +/- 2 % which is less than 10 degrees. Certainly the local wind direction deviations tend to diminish with declining (regional) wind speed.

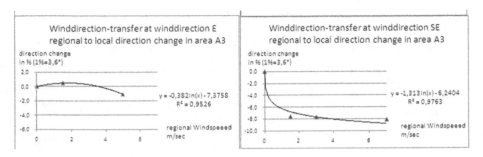

Fig. 13. Transfer-functions for local wind direction deviation by (initial) regional wind speeds as example for two main wind directions at receptor point a3

5 Conclusions

The transfer functions turned out to be applicable to generate hourly data of temperature and wind characteristics for synthetic weather records for future climate which have been applied to simulate thermal building performance and to estimate the energy demand for different settings building properties, considering different surface conditions, different open space layout and different building orientations [7]. Fig. 14 compares the energy demand for heating and cooling for a virtual test building to be erected at one of the receptor points in the Aspern area.

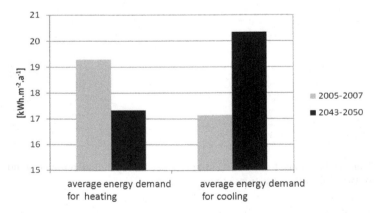

Fig. 14. Estimated changes in energy demand for heating and cooling for different climate situations for a defined building concept -an application example applying the synthetic weather records described above. (Source: Ohrehounig et al. [7])

In the future these methods will be applied to different urban fabric settings in order to explore the effects of these settings on micro-climate conditions systematically. It is finally planned to carry out a set of synthetic weather records for future climate for certain representative urban environments.

References

1. Bruse, M., Feer, H.: Simulating surface-air-plant interactions inside urban environments with a three dimensional numerical model. Env. Modelling and Software 13, 383–384 (1998)
2. City of Vienna: Aspern Airfield Masterplan (English, German), by Tovard Architects & Planners AB; Magistrat der Stadt Wien, 1082 Wien (2008)
3. Hageneder, C., Hinterkörner, P.: Aspern, Die Seestadt Wiens – nachhaltige Stadtentwicklung. In: Conference Proceedings, CORP 2010, Wien, pp. 989–994 (2010)
4. IPCC: Climate Change: The Physical Science Basis. Final Report Working Group 1, Intergovernmental Panel on Climate Change, Assessment Report 4, Geneva, Switzerland (2007)
5. Loibl, W., et al.: Reclip:century - a project conducting 21st century regional climate simulation runs focussing on the Greater Alpine Region. EGU General Assembly, Vienna 2010. Geophysical Research Abstracts 12 (2010)
6. Loibl, W., Jäger, A., Knoflacher, M., Köstl, M., Züger, J.: Urban Streetscapes responding to changing climate conditions - Effects of street layout on Thermal Exposure. In: Proceedings BAUSIM 2010, Technical University Vienna (2010)
7. Orehounig, K., Mahdavi, A., Hagen, K., Trimmel, H., Stiles, R., Knoflacher, M., Loibl, W.: Maßnahmenkatalog für Bauträgerwettbewerbe betreffend Oberflächengestaltung von Fassaden und Freiräumen. TU Wien (2011)

Using a Commercial Optimisation Tool for Fine Tuning of Parameters of an Eutrophication Model

Albrecht Gnauck[1], Bernhard Luther[1], and Wilfried Krug[2]

[1] Brandenburg University of Technology at Cottbus, Dept. of Ecosystems and Environmental Informatics, Konrad-Wachsmann-Allee 1, D-03046 Cottbus, Germany
[2] DUALIS –IT Solutions GmbH, Tiergartenstraße 32, D-01219 Dresden, Germany
{Albrecht.gnauck,luther}@tu-cottbus.de, wkrug@dualis-it.de

Abstract. Simulation models are well-known informatic tools to manage environmental knowledge. Current approaches to ecosystems modelling are theoretically based on information theory, thermodynamics, topology, or systems theory. Water quality models are used for managing eutrophication problems. In the past, the Cottbus Eutrophication Simulator (*CEUS*) has been designed on the base of *MATLAB* and *SIMULINK*, which enables an user to couple the simulator with different software tools. To quantify these relations differential equations, some site constants and model specific parameters have to be specified. The fine tuning of parameters of an ecological model can be considered from the perspective of a suitable optimization procedure. Especially the commercial optimization software *ISSOP* realised different optimization algorithms which are traced back to one standard form of discrete optimization. In the paper, results of parameter optimisation will be presented for important water quality indicators. The results of parameter fine tuning and possibilities of parameter optimisation are discussed.

Keywords: Optimisation, water quality modelling, eutrophication, parameter estimation.

1 Introduction

Modern environmental management decisions are based on mathematical models of ecosystems or ecological processes. To get suitable simulation results for management purposes the process of setting up of parameter values and initial conditions is of high importance. Management options for eutrophication control will be obtained by scenario analyses with changing parameter values [5].

The problem of parameter optimisation can be described related to a models quality and accuracy. Under the prerequisite of well-founded initial parameter settings a higher accuracy can be reached with the help of iterative optimisation. The optimisation procedures refer to goal functions including the output variables of the model. The term of parametrisation in ecological modelling denotes the determination of quantitative values of parameters. Three different approaches can be taken:

J. Hřebíček, G. Schimak, and R. Denzer (Eds.): ISESS 2011, IFIP AICT 359, pp. 618–624, 2011.

- A preliminary estimate is obtainable from laboratory and field observations of processes and effects by means of correlation analysis or by parameter estimation techniques.
- Combinations of parameters in keeping with a modelled situation may be obtained by means of estimation from parameter optimisation techniques.
- Estimates of parameter importance of a simulation model may be obtained by sensitivity analysis.

The goal of sensitivity analysis is to determine how sensitive the model is to changes of parameter values, which is the basis for model validation and parameter estimation. Investigations of parameter changes are carried out for an eutrophication model of a lowland river basin.

2 The Optimisation Tool ISSOP

Krug [3] developed a software tool *ISSOP* to support manufacturing, organisational and logistic processes. It includes an optimisation interface of *MATLAB* models. The *ISSOP* architecture of discrete optimisation methods used is shown in fig. 1.

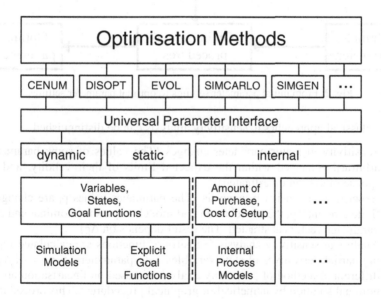

Fig. 1. The ISSOP optimisation architecture

The dialogue between external and internal models and optimisation methods is realised by a universal parameter interface. Following optimisation methods are included: CENUM – component wise enumeration, DISOPT – a quasi-gradient method, EVOL – an evolutionary optimisation strategy, SIMCARLO – optimisation by Monte Carlo method, SIMGEN – optimisation by a genetic algorithm. Other optimisation procedures can be added. Before starting an optimisation run each simulation problem is automatically transformed into the standard problem of optimisation. On the lowest level of this architecture simulation models, goal functions and internal process models are given explicitly. External static and dynamic simulation models can be implemented without any restriction. Convexity of goal functions is not necessary.

3 Parameter Optimisation and Sensitivity

The parameter sensitivity according to the output variables gives information how to select and weight the parameters and on which range and accuracy they have to be treated (fig. 2).

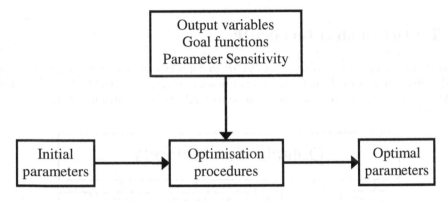

Fig. 2. From initial parameter settings to optimal parameter settings

Three classical approaches to sensitivity analysis can be distinguished:

1. Sensitivity to major parameter changes (The values of some parameters are arbitrarily changed within the expected limits of their validity, and the response of system investigated).
2. Experimental sensitivity analysis (The parameter values p_i are changed by a finite amount Δp, the model rerun and model outputs for nominal and changed parameter vectors abstracted. The result depends on Δp).
3. Analytical sensitivity analysis (Sensitivity functions are calculated representing partial derivatives of state variables u_j to parameters: $S(p_i) = \partial u_j / \partial p_i$. This differential method of sensitivity analysis is based on linearisation around the nominal solution by numerical or graphical procedures). This procedure is not covered within this paper.

Estimating sensitivity to external parameters, those connected with driving variables or site constants, a picture is getting how a given freshwater ecosystem would behave under different conditions. One particular problem is the sensitivity to sampling intervals or kinds of approximation of driving variables. For internal parameters, those characterising state variables, the goal is to determine the importance of parameters for the approximation of the model to reality. Attention has to be devoted mainly to those parameters, to which the model is most sensitive [4].

4   Results and Discussion

To investigate parameter optimisation and sensitivity a *MATLAB* based stationary 1D eutrophication model for shallow water bodies [2] was coupled with the commercial optimisation tool *ISSOP* [3].

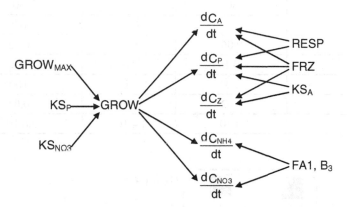

Fig. 3. Direct and indirect relations between model parameters and model variables

Concerning the eutrophication process in figure 3 an overview is presented on direct relationships of important model parameters to model variables. The parameters themselves can be assigned to essential processes in the water body and in the sediment.

The overall growth rate of phytoplankton mainly is determined by the production of algae biomass and the half saturation constants KS_P (of phosphorus) and KS_{NO3} (of nitrate). It is restricted by an upper bound $GROW_{MAX}$ for the nutrient uptake of the phytoplankton. So the constants $GROW_{MAX}$, KS_P and KS_{NO3} directly affect the phytoplankton concentration and the concentration of the nutrients nitrogen and phosphorus. The nitrogen fraction of algae biomass FA1 and the ammonification rate B_3 directly affect the nitrogen compounds ammonium and nitrate. The half saturation constant KS_A in the balance equation of zooplankton affect zooplankton and phosphorus. The filtration rate FRZ of zooplankton has a direct influence on zooplankton only, and the respiration rate RESP of phytoplankton connects phytoplankton and phosphorus.

For the eight parameters $GROW_{MAX}$, KS_P, KS_{NO3}, KS_A, FRZ, FA1, B_3 and RESP initial values (p*) are given (table 1). On the base of these values any parameter p has been varied in the interval Δp. According to these parameters a ranking of the variables x = {CHA, o-PO_4-P, NH_4-N, NO_3-N} is presented by means of a Hasse diagram [1] in fig. 4 regarding the global differences

$$\tilde{\Delta}x = \max_{p,t} |\Delta x| = \max_{p,t} |\Delta x_p(t)| = \max_{p,t} |x_p(t)-x_{p*}(t)| .$$

Table 1. Reference values and ranges of the eight parameters

Parameter p	Reference value p*	Lower bound $p_{lower} = 10\% \cdot p^*$	Upper bound $p_{upper} = 200\% \cdot p^*$
GROWMAX	5	0.5	10
KSP	30	3	60
KSNO3	0.1	0.01	0.2
KSA	0.06	0.006	0.12
FRZ	0.1	0.01	0.2
FA1	50	5	100
B3	0.02	0.002	0.04
RESP	$1.4 \cdot 10^{-5}$	$1.4 \cdot 10^{-6}$	$2.8 \cdot 10^{-5}$

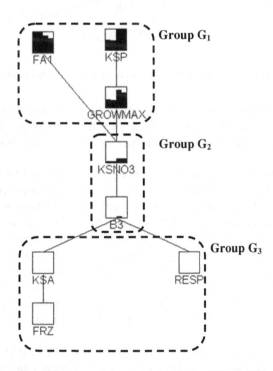

Fig. 4. Hasse diagram of the variables CHA, o-PO$_4$-P, NH$_4$-N, NO$_3$-N

It is noticeable that the four parameters GROW$_{MAX}$, FA1, KS$_P$, and KS$_{NO3}$ that directly affect the algae growth form the upper half of all rankings. The lower half is formed by the filtration rate of zooplankton, the respiration rate of phytoplankton and the parameters B$_3$ (ammonification rate) and KS$_A$ (half saturation constant in the balance equation of zooplankton). The two latter mentioned can be seen as parameters of sea-internal driving forces.

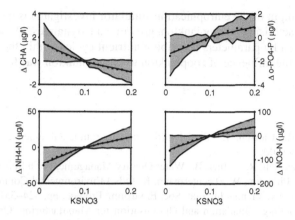

Fig. 5. Sensitivity of the variables CHA, o-PO$_4$-P, NH$_4$-N and NO$_3$-N to KS$_{NO3}$

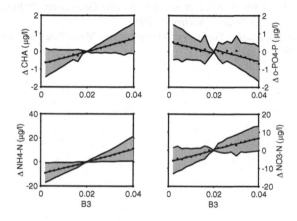

Fig. 6. Sensitivity of the variables CHA, o-PO$_4$-P, NH$_4$-N and NO$_3$-N to B$_3$

More precisely all of the four variables show a partition of the parameter set into three groups:

- Group G_1 = { GROW$_{MAX}$, FA1, KS$_P$ }   highest sensitivity
- Group G_2 = { KS$_{NO3}$, B$_3$ }   mean sensitivity
- Group G_3 = { KS$_A$, FRZ, RESP }   lowest sensitivity

Figure 5 shows the sensitivity of the variables CHA, o-PO$_4$-P, NH$_4$-N and NO$_3$-N according to parameter KS$_{NO3}$, figure 6 shows the results for parameter B$_3$.

5 Conclusions

Investigations of parameter sensitivity are essential tasks of the modelling procedure. Especially for complex systems like freshwater ecosystems these investigations are necessary to mark the parameter range of validity for environmental management decisions. The output of the eutrophication simulator investigated is most sensitive for parameters characterising phytoplankton growth and dynamics. A second level of sensitivity is given by parameters describing nutrient cycles within the water body. In opposite of that, the influence of zooplankton to phytoplankton was found very stiff.

References

1. Brüggemann, R., Carlsen, L.: Partial Order in Environmental Sciences and Chemistry. Springer, Berlin (2006)
2. Gnauck, A., Heinrich, R., Luther, B.: Water Quality Management of a Sub-Watershed of the Elbe River. In: Pillmann, W., Tochtermann, K. (eds.) Environmental Communication in the Information Society, Vienna. Internat. Soc. Environm. Protect., pp. 524–531 (2002)
3. Krug, W.: Modelling, Simulation and Optimisation for Manufacturing, Organisational and Logistical Processes. SCS Europe Publishing House, Delft (2002)
4. Luther, B., Gnauck, A.: Parameter Sensitivity of an Eutrophication Model. In: Wittman, J., Flechsig, M. (eds.) 2009: Simulation in Umwelt- und Geowissenschaften, Workshop Potsdam 2009, pp. 125–133. Shaker, Aachen (2009)
5. Straškraba, M., Gnauck, A.: Freshwater Ecosystems – Modelling and Simulation. Elsevier, Amsterdam (1985)

Downscaling of Short-Term Precipitation Time Series for Climate Change Impact Assessment

Jonas Olsson[1], Lars Gidhagen[1], and Akira Kawamura[2]

[1] Swedish Meteorological and Hydrological Institute, 601 76 Norrköping, Sweden
[2] Tokyo Metropolitan University, 1-1 Minami-Osawa, Hachioji, Tokyo 192-0397, Japan
jonas.olsson@smhi.se, lars.gidhagen@smhi.se,
akira.kawamura@tmu.ac.jp

Abstract. A future increase of short-term precipitation intensities may lead to problems in sewer systems, such as increased overflow volumes and flood risks. To quantify the consequences, downscaling of climate model precipitation is required to the scales relevant in urban hydrology. In the SUDPLAN project, a system where users may upload historical time series to be used as a basis for such downscaling is being developed. In this paper, the method (Delta Change) is outlined along with brief descriptions of the technical solution and result visualization.

Keywords: climate model, urban hydrology, SUDPLAN.

1 Introduction

Precipitation is often accumulated in time to days, months or years, but in some cases the short-term rainfall is the most interesting. With short-term we mean rainfall observed with a very short time step, e.g. 1 minute or even finer. In contrast to long-term accumulations, which represent averages over long periods, short-term precipitation thus corresponds to the instantaneous intensity (and intensity changes) that we perceive during a storm event.

Short-term precipitation is of particular interest in urban hydrology. Because of the large fraction of impervious surface in the urban environment the runoff process is very fast. Storm water moves rapidly on the surface to a sewer system inlet after which the flow is concentrated in the sewer pipe network. To simulate the flow response to an actual storm in a computer model of the urban environment, a time step of 1 min or shorter is required to capture the variability of the runoff. Thus also the input, i.e. precipitation time series, needs to have a very high time resolution. Such observations are commonly obtained using a tipping bucket gauge that registers a time stamp every time a small amount of rainfall (e.g. 0.2 mm) has accumulated. Further, urban catchments are generally very small, on the order of 1 km², so typically observations from only one gauge is used as input.

Short-term precipitation intensities are expected to increase as a function of the global warming. Both theoretical considerations [1] and climate model projections [2, 3] generally support this hypothesis. This implies an increased load on sewer systems with potential consequences in terms of increased overflow volumes and flood risks

J. Hřebíček, G. Schimak, and R. Denzer (Eds.): ISESS 2011, IFIP AICT 359, pp. 625–630, 2011.

[4]. To estimate the consequences quantitatively, sewer model simulations with precipitation input representing the future climate are required. A key problem, however, is that the spatial (and, to a lesser degree, also the temporal) resolution of Regional Climate Models (RCMs) is too coarse for directly applying the precipitation results in sewer system models. Climate model results represent a mean precipitation over an area of typically 1000-2000 km² whereas sewer models, as mentioned above, needs precipitation observed in a single location. Thus, some form of downscaling from the climate model grid scale to the local grid scale is required [3, 4].

In this paper, the method and system for short-term precipitation downscaling used within the project SUDPLAN (Sustainable Urban Development Planner for Climate Change Adaptation) is described. The downscaling is based on the Delta Change concept, i.e. a rescaling of historical observations in line with the expected future changes. The technical solution as well as result visualization is briefly described.

2 Downscaling Method: Delta Change

Precipitation time series downscaling is performed by Delta Change, which generally means that future changes of some climate variable (e.g. precipitation or temperature), as estimated from climate model data, are transferred to historical observations of the same variable [5]. In the SUDPLAN application, future changes of the frequency distribution of 30-min precipitation intensities, which is the shortest time step available in climate model data, are transferred to historical short-term rainfall observations.

After the historical time series to be rescaled has been defined, the first step in the procedure is to extract 30-min precipitation time series from climate model projections. Data from two 30-year periods are used; one reference period centered over the historical time series and one selected future period. The frequency distribution of the precipitation intensities in each period is calculated, after which the ratio of each future percentiles to the same reference percentile is calculated. This ratio is called Delta Change Factor (DCF; >1 implies increase, and vice versa).

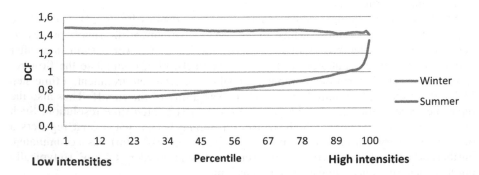

Fig. 1. Example of future changes of rainfall intensities as estimated from a Regional Climate Model. DCF=1 implies no change, DCF<1 a future decrease and DCF>1 a future increase.

Fig. 1 shows an example of DCFs and illustrates how this approach makes it possible to handle rather complicated future changes, such as increased high intensities but decreased intermediate and low intensities (summer in Fig. 1). Fig. 1 also demonstrates the need for performing the downscaling on a seasonal basis, as future changes may be radically different for different seasons. It should be mentioned that the methodology requires an assumption that DCFs estimated from data on the RCM resolutions in time and space are valid also for the higher resolutions of the historical observations.

Finally, the calculated DCFs may be transferred to the historical observations. This is achieved by firstly aggregating the observations to a 30-min time step, to correspond with the climate model output. Secondly a frequency analysis is performed to identify each 30-min value's corresponding percentile and, in turn, DCF. In the last step, the volume of each registration is rescaled in line with the DCF of the corresponding 30-min value. For further details on the approach, see [3].

3   Technical Solution

In SUDPLAN, the data flows and model executions involved in the downscaling are managed by a Scenario Management System (SMS) and a core of Common Services (CS), where the latter includes modules for downscaling of not only precipitation but also air quality and hydrology (Fig. 2). Two types of user specifications are needed to launch a model simulation. (1) CS receives from the SMS the coordinates for the station, the data from which are to be downscaled, together with some identification

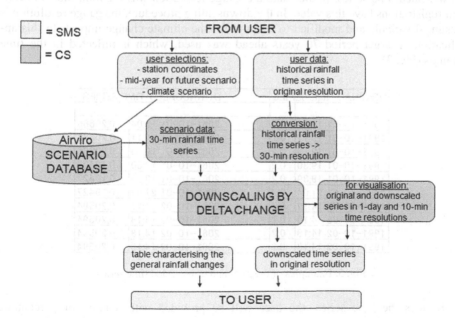

Fig. 2. Components of and data flows between Scenario Management System (SMS) and Common Services (CS) for precipitation downscaling

of the coordinate system and map projection. The user has also specified which climate scenario to use and which future 30-year time period to perform the downscaling for. (2) Short-term rainfall observations from a tipping-bucket gauge or equivalent on a specified format, time stamp (resolution: minute or higher) followed by a rainfall registration (mm).

The model execution includes the following steps. (1) Extraction of 30-min rainfall time series from the CS Scenario Database, in five RCM grid boxes surrounding the station. (2) Conversion of historical time series to 30-min time resolution, to be compatible with scenario data. (3) Downscaling by Delta Change, including (*i*) estimation of future changes from the scenario data and (*ii*) transfer of the estimated changes to the historical time series. (4) Calculation of general rainfall changes from reference period to scenario period. (5) Conversion of both historical and downscaled time series to 1-day and 10-min time resolutions, for visualization.

4 Output and Visualization

The main output is a time series which differs from the uploaded one in two ways. (1) In each time stamp, the observation year has been replaced by a future target year. (2) Each rainfall registration has been re-scaled to account for future changes in the probability distribution of short-term rainfall intensities (Fig. 3).

The automated CS downscaling function has been developed and verified using short-term rainfall data from Kalmar, Sweden, that are well known to the developer and thus optimal for this purpose. Figure 3 shows the first part of the original and downscaled time series. In this data, the gauge resolution was 0.2 mm; thus all original registrations have this value. In the downscaling procedure, the gauge resolution is assumed variable and modified to account for the climate change impact. In this application, a target period 70 years ahead was used, which is reflected in the time stamps (Fig. 3).

ORIGINAL TIME SERIES		DOWNSCALED TIME SERIES	
1991-10-01 19:04	0,2	2061-10-01 19:04	0,20666
1991-10-01 19:11	0,2	2061-10-01 19:11	0,20666
1991-10-01 19:15	0,2	2061-10-01 19:15	0,20666
1991-10-01 19:30	0,2	2061-10-01 19:30	0,19427
1991-10-01 19:39	0,2	2061-10-01 19:39	0,19427
1991-10-01 21:04	0,2	2061-10-01 21:04	0,19427
1991-10-02 14:17	0,2	2061-10-02 14:17	0,20594
1991-10-02 14:18	0,2	2061-10-02 14:18	0,20594
1991-10-02 14:18	0,2	2061-10-02 14:18	0,20594
1991-10-02 14:19	0,2	2061-10-02 14:19	0,20594

Fig. 3. Examples of original and downscaled time series

Besides the time series, the user will be provided with a table of percentage changes in different key rainfall properties (mean, maximum and frequency), separated into seasons. Further, visualization as outlined in Fig. 4 is suggested. The upper

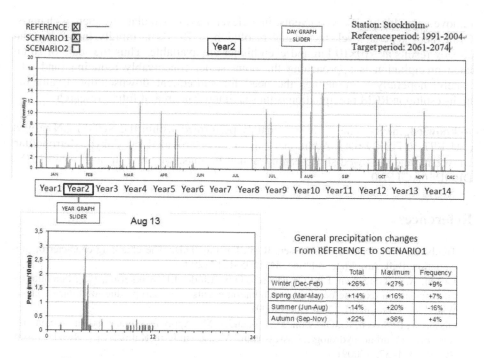

Fig. 4. Suggested approach for short-term rainfall time series visualization

graph shows daily rainfall on an annual basis, where the year can be selected using a 'year graph slider' below the graph. In the annual graph, by a 'day graph slider' a particular day can be selected and in the lower left diagram, 10-min rainfall during the selected date is shown. If both a reference and a scenario time series are selected, the lower right table shows the general rainfall changes from the reference to the scenario.

5 Concluding Remarks and Future Prospects

The precipitation time series downscaling functionality in SUDPLAN makes it possible for e.g. sanitation engineers and urban planners to obtain data for climate local change impact assessment studies. The methodology based on Delta Change (DC) a straight-forward and not without limitations. One general limitation is that the downscaled data will be strongly influenced by the properties of the historical data, with respect to e.g. variability. Another limitation is that any change in precipitation frequency is not taken into account in DC-based downscaling. Despite these limitations, in our opinion a DC-based approach is the only practicable solution in an automated system like this.

Future work will include development of the DC-approach to also be able to handle frequency changes. Preliminary analyses indicate that future precipitation frequency changes are generally caused by a change in the number of precipitation events rather than changes in event durations. Thus it may be possible to either remove or multiply observed events, in a clever way, to simulate frequency changes. On a more general level, the spatial resolution of RCMs is rapidly increasing and already results at ~10×10 km and even higher are available. Thus the scale of simulated precipitation is approaching the point scale, conceivably reducing (and ultimately, hopefully, eliminating) the need for subsequent downscaling. Evaluating high-resolution RCM precipitation is thus an important area of future research.

Acknowledgments. The study was mainly performed within the SUDPLAN project (EU FP7 ICT-2009-6.4). Additional funding was provided by Tokyo Metropolitan University and the Swedish Research Council Formas, the latter through project HYDROIMPACTS2.0.

References

1. Trenberth, K.E., Dai, A., Rasmussen, R.M., Parsons, D.B.: The changing character of precipitation. Bull. Am. Meteorol. Soc. 84, 1205–1217 (2003)
2. Larsen, A.N., Gregersen, I.B., Christensen, O.B., Linde, J.J., Mikkelsen, P.S.: Potential future increase in extreme one-hour precipitation events over Europe due to climate change. Water Sci. Technol. 60, 2205–2216 (2009)
3. Olsson, J., Berggren, K., Olofsson, M., Viklander, M.: Applying climate model precipitation scenarios for urban hydrological assessment: A case study in Kalmar City, Sweden. Atm. Res. 92, 364–375 (2009)
4. Semadeni-Davies, A., Hernebring, C., Svensson, G., Gustafsson, L.-G.: The impacts of climate change and urbanisation on drainage in Helsingborg, Sweden: Suburban stormwater. J. Hydrol. 350, 114–125 (2008)
5. Hay, L.E., Wilby, R.L., Leavesley, G.H.: A comparison of delta change and downscaled GCM scenarios for three mountainous basins in the United States. J. Am. Water Resour. Assoc. 36, 387–397 (2000)

Integrating Climate Change in the Urban Planning Process – A Case Study

Stefan Sander[1], Holger Hoppe[2], and Sascha Schlobinski[3]

[1] Stadtverwaltung Wuppertal
stefan.sander@stadt.wuppertal.de
[2] DR. PECHER AG
Holger.Hoppe@pecher.de
[3]cismet GmbH
sascha.schlobinski@cismet.de

Abstract. The ongoing European collaborative project SUDPLAN is targeted on the development of a software framework that allows the integration of climate change aspects in urban planning processes. Besides the implementation of the generic modules SUDPLAN comprises the implementation of four tangible pilot applications of the framework, one of them in the German City of Wuppertal. This "Wuppertal pilot" deals with urban storm water management and the prevention of infrastructure damages under present and future climate conditions. It can be considered as a case study for the integration of climate change in an actual, long-term urban planning process. This article describes the basic conditions of the case study and the building blocks of the intended decision support environment for urban planners, including the local models used for the simulation of storm water runoff, both in the sewers and on the surface.

Keywords: climate change downscaling, model integration, urban planning modelling experiments, SDI.

1 Introduction

The effects of climate change will expose European cities to environmental pressures ranging from heat waves to increased heavy rain falls e. g. [1]. Many processes in environmental planning are affected by these effects. This is valid particularly for the dimensioning of sewer systems and flood protection based on precipitation-runoff-models [2]. Therefore sustainable urban planning needs to take climate change into account as an integral part of the planning and decision making process [3], [4]. Obviously this requires access to global and local climate change information and the possibility to include this information in the individual workflows of local planners and decision makers.

In the present case study we focus on the use of climate change information in a real, long-term urban planning process. Due to the effects of climate change the city of **Wuppertal** (Germany) faces extremely localized runoff events from increased heavy, short-term rainfall. The potential damage of public infrastructure and of

J. Hřebíček, G. Schimak, and R. Denzer (Eds.): ISESS 2011, IFIP AICT 359, pp. 631–640, 2011.

private property is a major concern for the city managers. The needs for future investments are huge, considering that the city has to cope with runoff from many natural and canalised creeks and a sewer system of 1,500 kilometers. As in most urbanised areas, in the city of Wuppertal the dynamics of urban development have eclipsed the preservation of natural watercourse patterns. Numerous discharging streams have become part of the sewer system in the course of industrialisation. Apart from a few exceptions, a separate sewer system is used for domestic drainage in Wuppertal [5].

In a nutshell, the present case study is based upon two guiding ideas:

- The first is the development of a tool that enables the responsible planners to define and run simulations of 1D-2D sewer and surface runoff in the course of heavy storm water events and to visualise the results of these model runs.
- The second is to consider the effect of climate change on the future rainfall patterns by using downscaled rainfall data that is input to the simulations.

2   Case Study – Basic Conditions

The city of Wuppertal, a town with approximately 350,000 residents, is the biggest town in Germany that is situated in hill country (from 98 to 353 m above mean sea level). It is located in the steep, narrow, and long valley of the river Wupper. There are several creeks on both sides of this valley that open into the storm water sewage system before they finally end in the Wupper. During an extreme rainfall event that is exceeding the design storm events [6] the city's storm water sewage system might be blocked by those swollen creeks causing the precipitation to run off on the surface. The storm water runoff may thereby affect valuable public infrastructure and private property. Due to the complex geography where a heavy rainfall event might occur is completely unpredictable and therefore whether there will be flooding and where it will run off is unknown.

2.1   Objectives

Up to now the mid- and long-term planning of the storm water sewage system has been accomplished with iterative model runs of a hydrological model (for the natural creeks) and a hydrodynamical model (for the canalised creeks and sewage system). This planning process is called "Generalentwässerungsplanung" (GEP), which could be translated as 'General Drainage Strategy'. Wuppertal's main objectives are as follows:

The *first main objective is to update the existing GEP* for all areas in Wuppertal in the next several years.

The *second main objective is the modelling of surface runoff during heavy rainfall events* that should be integrated into the planning process. To achieve this objective, among others, a combined 1D-2D-hydrodynamical model has to be used to detect the critical spots (i. e. those with a high risk of flooding plus valuable and vulnerable facilities).

The *third main objective is to mitigate the risk of flooding for the detected critical spots*. The traditional strategies to achieve this are either the enlargement of the profiles of the sewage system or the construction of retention basins. Given these two options the potential needs for investments would be immense, considering that the city faces the water runoff from 350 kilometres of creeks (over 800 creek sections) and 650 kilometres of storm water sewer system. An alternative and much more cost-efficient strategy is to look for localised planning options which are likely to prevent damage. Examples of such structural measures are the alteration of street profiles by means of higher road kerbs or the installation of mobile or stationary walls.

Therefore the *fourth main objective is to find the most cost-efficient measures for flood risk mitigation for each critical spot*. These measures must reduce the probability of damage, but should still be practical to implement, especially within the increasing financial constraints of the city. See [7] and [8] for more information on Flood risk management.

The *fifth main objective is to provide the responsible planners and hydraulic modellers in Wuppertal with a tool that enables them to simulate a multitude of scenarios* with the model components for the sewer system and surface runoff, both to detect the critical spots and to simulate the effects of different structural measures at the critical spots. The tool should be able to store the parameters and results of such a model run and to visualise the results.

2.2 Requirements and Deficiencies

Climate change is expected to have an increasing impact on the frequency of heavy storm water events in Wuppertal and possibly on the maximum intensity of such events as well. This makes it necessary to include climate change effects both in the long-term planning of the storm water sewage system and in the simulations of surface runoff. In other words, the intensity and duration of a rainfall event of a given probability (e. g. one time in 30 years) is a crucial parameter in every single modelling experiment. If climate change is ignored in these simulations, the suggested structural measures would possibly not be effective in the long run.

Currently the main deficiency is the lack of any systematic knowledge about the critical spots with regard to flooding after heavy storm water events. Wuppertal intends to establish this knowledge in the forthcoming years. But there is still a deficiency in understanding the dynamic processes of floods triggered by heavy storm water events in combination with possible climate change effects. Wuppertal expects to get a deeper understanding of this by running a multitude of modelling experiments, with the model component for surface runoff, for different catchment areas and with different precipitation patterns.

2.3 Supported Tasks

The intended simulation tool will allow an analyst to predict areas of urban flooding within the City of Wuppertal for two purposes. The first is to be able to inform owners of low-lying assets about possible threats ("Flood Risk Assessment"). For example, the owners of a commercial building that contains telecommunications equipment in the cellar might be informed that (in the future) their assets might be under increasing risk of inundation and destruction. This will give them an opportunity to undertake changes to protect this equipment from such risks. The second is to consider possible alterations that might reduce the risk of damage due to flooding ("Flood Risk Mitigation"). In this case there might be infrastructure changes which could be planned to prevent damage anticipated by the first analysis. For example, kerbs might be raised, barrier walls could be erected, or storm water retention basins might be constructed. While the primary concern is in regard to flood events likely to occur within a near-term horizon (e. g. a return period of 5 to 30 years), there is also interest in the long-term ramifications of global climate change with respect to urban flooding. Both of these tasks have as their primary goal the protection of both personal and public property from damage due to urban flooding during storm events.

2.4 Targeted Users

There are two types of primary users who will make regular and direct use of the intended simulation tool: *Storm Water Managers* and *System Administrators*. Wuppertal's storm water managers are hydraulic modellers employed either by the City of Wuppertal or the Wuppertaler Stadtwerke AG, the municipal utility that runs the sewage system on behalf of the City of Wuppertal. These individuals are very comfortable with computers. As modellers they will want to interact with the hydraulic models used and they may have some familiarity with precipitation-runoff-models. However, they will likely have little to no experience with global climate models. They may or may not have sophisticated GIS experience. The System Administrators are City of Wuppertal staff members who are very comfortable with computers, computer networks, and software installation. They are sophisticated GIS users, comfortable with installing and configuring both spatial and non-spatial databases. In general they have no expert knowledge regarding climate, precipitation, or urban precipitation-runoff-models.

Secondary users of the intended simulation tool consist of those *property owners* whose assets might be endangered by flooding. Property owners in Wuppertal will be shown results by the planners and may interact with the system together to engage in "what if" scenario sessions. They may or may not have technical backgrounds.

In addition *city politicians/managers* and the *general public* will interact with the system only in the sense that they will be shown results or reports whose content was produced by the system (tertiary users).

3   The Solution

The Wuppertal case study was performed as part of the ongoing FP7 ICT project SUDPLAN [9]. SUDPLAN's two main projected software results are:

1. The SUDPLAN Scenario Management System (SMS) which is a highly interactive graphics-based decision support environment [10] that allows the end-user to access environmental information and to manage both the model runs and related information (Figure 1).
2. The Common Services that provide environmental information for European cities under present and future climate scenarios, in support to long-term urban planning.

3. Common Services deliver downscaled information on extreme rainfall events, rainfall time series, hydrology and air quality that can be used to parameterize and/or set boundary conditions for local models

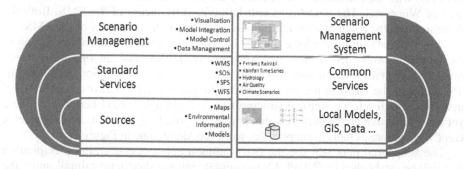

Fig. 1. SUDPLAN Architectural Layers

The access to sources of information regardless of their origin (model, data base …) is decoupled via a service layer consisting of standard compliant services, and is therefore to a large extent independent of the underlying source. This is the key to achieving a significant degree of transferability [11] of the project results to other European municipalities.

The Scenario Management System and some of the the Common Services are integral parts of the presented urban planning workbench that is called "Wuppertal pilot" in the terminology of the SUDPLAN project (cp. Figure 2).

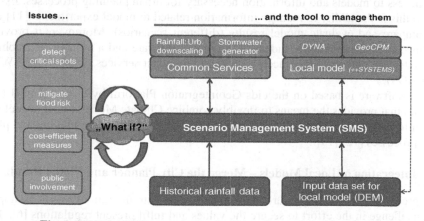

Fig. 2. SUDPLAN Wuppertal pilot for Urban Stormwater Management

To tackle the issues described in section 2.1 the Wuppertal municipality will use the Wuppertal pilot to run simulations of 1D-2D sewer and surface runoff in the course of heavy storm water events. Running such a simulation involves the execution of external local models provided by the software products *DYNA* (for sewer runoff) and *GeoCPM* (for surface runoff). Both are components for *++SYSTEMS*, a geographical information system (GIS) for the urban water management domain (cp. section 3.2). In order to keep the processing time to the order of a few hours a model run deals with the catchment area of merely an individual creek rather than the whole area of Wuppertal. The model runs will be defined by means of the SMS. Both the definition and the result of a model run will be stored in the repository of the SMS.

The input data set for the local models includes precipitation data, a description of the sewer network needed for the execution of *DYNA*, and an optimized high-resolution digital elevation model (DEM) necessary for the execution of *GeoCPM*. The setup of the DEM in the form of a triangulated irregular network with detailed modelling of all relevant vertical structures (e. g. buildings or road kerbs) is a single yet labor-intensive preparatory task that has to be carried out for each catchment area. *GeoCPM* comprises tools to support this work (cp. dotted line in Figure 2).

The Wuppertal pilot will use the two Common Services concerning precipitation that will be established in SUDPLAN to simulate intense short-term rainfall under the predicted future climatic conditions: "Urban downscaling" (already implemented) and "Stormwater generator" (under development). To use these services it is necessary to provide historical high resolution precipitation data for the area that a simulation covers. The SMS again will be used to upload these data to the Common Services, to receive the predicted precipitation data (time series or intensity-duration-frequency curves) and to insert it into the input data set for the local models.

3.1   The Urban Planning Workbench – Supporting the Planning and Decision Making Process

The urban planning workbench has the objective of supporting seamless integration of and access to models and information necessary for urban planning processes. Essential to this is the ability to manage information related to model experiments [11] and to compare and evaluate model results (different scenarios). Moreover, it provides advanced visualisation independent of the model software and a number of graphical user interface components to access standard compliant services (OGC WMS, WFS, SPS, SOS).

The software is based on the cids Geointegration Platform by cismet GmbH (cismet.de) that provides the means to flexibly combine Climate Model, Local Model and GIS information and therefore to effectively support urban decision making and planning processes [12],[13].

3.2   Integration of Local Models – Merge the City Planner and Model Results

The prediction of flooding in urban areas caused by extreme rain events is an important challenge in the effort to secure the values and fulfil present regulations [6]. Traditional 1D-hydrodynamic sewer simulation models provide the main information for robust flood protection. For further and detailed investigations the interaction between sewer and surface runoff has to be considered by using a bi-directional connected model of the sewer system and surface runoff with combined 1D-2D models. Therefore detailed information about the relevant sewer structures and the structures on the surface are needed (e. g. a classical sewer model combined with airborne laser scan

Fig. 3. SUDPLAN Scenario Management System based on the cids Geointegration Platform

data and local topographical survey). As the current calculations for the sewer system in Wuppertal are carried out with the well-established 1D(3D)-hydrodynamic model *++Systems-DYNA* by Pecher Software (Erkrath, Germany) and tandler.com (Buch am Erlbach) the combined 1D-2D calculations are carried out with the newly developed software model *DYNA-GeoCPM* by tandler.com. Figure 4 shows a visualisation of first results attained by means of a combined *DYNA-GeoCPM* model run for the test-catchment area. Further description of the approaches for modelling of urban flooding can be found in [14]. Integration into the Urban Planning Workbench is accomplished by exposing the model's functionality via a service interface with the objective of being able to obtain a high degree of modelling software independence. This will allow, for example, the use of different models in the same workbench or the replacement of modelling components, if needed, without effects on the overall workbench.

3.3   Integration of Climate Change Information in City Planning Processes

To include climate change effects in modelling experiments the software that is used for the definition of the parameters of such an experiment needs to be able to process information concerning climate change, e. g. future precipitation data.

The Wuppertal pilot will use the SUDPLAN Common Services to simulate intense short-term rainfall under the predicted future climatic conditions, as it is crucial to the modelling of surface runoff to consider the effect of climate change on future precipitation patterns. To use the urban downscaling service it is necessary to provide local historical high resolution precipitation data (cp. section 3). The required rainfall data are available for two gauging stations in the wastewater treatment plants "Buchenhofen" (keeping records since 1960) and "Schwelm" (keeping records since 1970).

Fig. 4. First results of the 1D-2D-hydrodynamic model *DYNA-GeoCPM* for the test-catchment area "Lüntenbeck" in Wuppertal [15]

The storm water generator will take the starting point and the direction of a heavy storm water event as input, along with current maximum rainfall intensity. The output of the generator will be a grid of time variation curves for precipitation, thus describing the spatiotemporal progression of a synthetic storm water event for present or future climate conditions. This service will provide an easy way to generate precipitation data for the different runs of the surface run-off model and to study the influence of the direction a storm water event is moving in.

3.4 Benefits of the Wuppertal Pilot

The main focus of the present case study lies in the establishment of an easy to use decision support environment that allows planners both in the Wuppertal municipality and in cooperating organisations to introduce climate change considerations into their everyday modelling work. Climate change is a complex matter and a municipality is not expected to have any expertise in this domain. Therefore the knowledge threshold for dealing with climate change effects has to be lowered significantly to achieve a sustainable change of the planning workflows. Introducing a tool like the SUDPLAN Wuppertal pilot seems to be a promising way to reach this goal.

The availability of the Wuppertal pilot will enhance the working environment of the planners in many different ways compared to the tools currently at hand: it will enable them to identify cost-efficient planning options for flood risk mitigation in Wuppertal by playing what-if games in a highly interactive way. Moreover, they will be able to share the results of their modelling work with city managers, politicians and the general public by means of vivid 3D/4D visualisations that go far beyond current approaches used by standard modelling software.

Other benefits follow from the generic architecture of the SUDPLAN software. This will enable the City of Wuppertal to develop applications similar to the Wuppertal pilot in a quick and cost-effective way. The SUDPLAN software will provide new generic components for Wuppertal's Spatial Data Infrastructure (SDI). These components will comprise services (e. g. access control and security) and application components (e. g. for 3D visualisation). The new components will offer further application options for Wuppertal's SDI and thus will intensify the use of the existing spatial data.

4 Summary and Future Research

The present case study illustrates the introduction of climate change considerations in a long-term urban planning process. The featured example is urban storm water management with an emphasis on the prevention of infrastructure damages. The initial point of the study is the implementation of a tool that enables the storm water managers to deal with tangible climate change predictions and to use them as input data for local models. Generic building blocks for such a software system are under development in the ongoing FP7 ICT project SUDPLAN which runs from January 2010 until December 2012. The climate change information in SUDPLAN comes from the *Common Services*, a set of standard compliant Web Services that supply environmental information under present and future climate conditions on the scale of a European city. For the case study services are used that deliver downscaled information on extreme rainfall events and rainfall time series. The second predominant SUDPLAN module is the *Scenario Management System (SMS)* that is used to communicate with the Common Services, to execute local models and to store and visualise the results of the model runs, all in a highly interactive manner. The application of these generic components for the case study – the so-called *Wuppertal pilot* – is part of SUDPLAN as well. It integrates sophisticated local models (*DYNA/GeoCPM*) that allow combined modelling of the sewer system and surface runoff for different storm water events. In order to get reliable results for the surface runoff an optimized high-resolution digital elevation model (DEM) has to be compiled for each catchment area that is subject of a model run. These are derived from high resolution airborne laser scan data that are available for the whole of Wuppertal.

For the future, the City of Wuppertal envisions a city wide standard that allows the city planners to easily combine models with the data sources necessary for their execution and to be able to create modelling chains consisting of several models linked together. This standard will define a common interface for new modelling components and thus will ensure that new models can be seamlessly integrated in the city's information infrastructure.

Acknowlegments

SUDPLAN is a Collaborative Project (contract number 247708) co-funded by the Information Society and Media DG of the European Commission within the RTD activities of the Thematic Priority Information Society Technologies.

References

1. IPCC, Fourth Assessment Report Climate Change 2007: Synthesis Report (2007), http://www.ipcc.ch/pdf/assessment-report/ar4/syr/ar4_syr.pdf (visited March 23, 2011)
2. Hoppe, H.: Impact of input data uncertainties on urban drainage models: climate change a crucial issue? In: Conference Proceedings. 11th International Conference on Urban Drainage, Edinburgh, Scotland, UK (2008)
3. Ashley, R.M., Balmforth, D.J., Saul, A.J., Blanksby, J.D.: Flooding in the future – predicting climate change, risks and responses in urban areas. Wat. Sci. Tech. 52(5), 265–273 (2005)
4. Ashley, R.M., Tait, S.J., Styan, E., Cashman, A., Luck, B., Blanksby, J., Saul, A.: L. Sandlands, Sewer system design moving into the 21st century – a UK perspective. Wat. Sci. Tech. 55(4), 273–281 (2007)
5. Hoppe, H., Messmann, S., Giga, A., Gruening, H.: A real-time control strategy for the separation of highly polluted storm water based on UV-Vis online measurements – from theory to operation. In: Proceedings of the 7th International Conference on Sustainable Techniques and Strategies in Urban Water Management, NOVATECH 2010, Lyon, France (2010)
6. DWA, STANDARD DWA - A 118E Hydraulic Dimensioning and Verification of Drainage Systems. DWA, Hennef (2006)
7. Arun, K.: Handbook of Flood Management: Flood Risk Simulation, Warning, Assessment and Mitigatio, vol. I. SBS Publisher (2009)
8. Schanze, J., Zeman, E., Marsalek, J. (eds.): Flood Risk Management: Hazards, Vulnerability and Mitigation Measures. NATO Science Series: IV: Earth and Environmental Sciences. Springer, Netherlands (2006)
9. Denzer, R.: A Decision Support System for Urban Climate Change Adaptation. In: Proceedings of the 44th Hawaii International Conference on System Sciences (HICSS-44), CDROM. IEEE Computer Society, Los Alamitos (2011)
10. Swayne, D.A., Denzer, R., Lilburn, L., Purvis, M., Quinn, N.W.T., Storey, A.: Environmental Decision Support Systems – Exactly what are they?, Environmental Software Systems. Environmental Information and Decision Support, vol. 3, pp. 257–268. Kluwer Academic Publishers, Dordrecht (2000)
11. Denzer, R.: Generic Integration of Environmental Decision Support Systems & State-of-the Art. Journal Environmental Modelling & Software, EMS (2004)
12. Denzer, R., Güttler, R., Swayne, D.A.: Integrated Spatial Decision Support, Environmental Software Systems. Environmental Information and Indicators, vol. 4, pp. 227–235 (2001)
13. Güttler, R., Denzer, R., Houy, P.: User Interfaces for Environmental Information Systems – Interactive Maps or Catalog Structures? Or Both? Journal Advances in Environmental Research 5, 345–350 (2001)
14. Obermayer, A., Guenthert, F.W., Angermair, G., Tandler, R., Braunschmidt, S., Milojevic, N.: Different approaches for modelling of sewer caused urban flooding. Wat. Sci Tech. 62(9), 2175–2182 (2010)
15. Pecher, K.H., Hoppe, H.: Future Design of Sewer Systems (Kuenftige Bemessung von Kanalisationen). Korrespondenz Abwasser Abfall 58(2), 121–127

Decision-Support System for Urban Air Pollution under Future Climate Conditions

Steen Solvang Jensen[1], Jørgen Brandt[1], Martin Hvidberg[1], Matthias Ketzel[1],
Gitte Brandt Hedegaard[1,2], and Jens Hesselbjerg Christensen[2]

[1] National Environmental Research Institute (NERI), Department of Atmospheric Environment,
Aarhus University, Denmark
`{ssj,jbr,mhv,mke,gbh}@dmu.dk`
[2] Danish Meteorological Institute (DMI), Danish Climate Centre (DKC), Denmark
`{jhc,gbh}@dmi.dk`

Abstract. Climate change is expected to influence urban living conditions and challenge the ability of cities to adapt to and mitigate climate change. Urban climates will be faced with elevated temperatures and future climate conditions are expected to cause higher ozone concentrations, increased biogenic emissions from vegetation, changes in the chemistry of the atmosphere and changes in deposition of particulate air pollution. This paper describes a conceptual outline of a decision-support system for assessment of the impacts of climate change on urban climate and air quality, and for assessment of integrated climate change and air pollution adaptation and mitigation strategies.

Keywords: Decision-support system; climate change; dynamical downscaling; urban heat island effect; urban air quality; adaptation; mitigation.

1 Introduction

Climate change is expected to increase the global temperature, raise the sea level and alter the storm activity and precipitation patterns that give rise to flooding and drought events. These parameters affect urban living conditions and challenge the ability of cities to adapt to and mitigate climate change. Under future climate conditions it is expected that we will have higher ozone concentrations, increased biogenic emissions from vegetation, changes in the chemistry of the atmosphere and changes in how particulate air pollution is washed out of the air or otherwise removed. These changes may pose health risks to the population. Urban climates will be faced with elevated temperatures due to an increased urban heat island effect. At the same time, many cities are growing with challenges in urban, traffic and energy planning in a situation where a low-carbon economy needs to be developed to reduce climate impacts. Continued reductions in air pollution and greenhouse gases are important, as they pose serious threats to both people's health and the environment.

The aim of this paper is to describe a conceptual outline of a decision-support system for assessment of the impacts of climate change on urban climate and air quality, and for assessment of integrated climate change and air pollution adaptation and mitigation strategies.

J. Hřebíček, G. Schimak, and R. Denzer (Eds.): ISESS 2011, IFIP AICT 359, pp. 641–650, 2011.
© IFIP International Federation for Information Processing 2011

2 System Description

Figure 1 shows a conceptual outline of sub-models in a decision-support system for assessment of the impacts of climate change on urban climate and air quality, and for integrated assessment of climate change and air pollution adaptation and mitigation strategies.

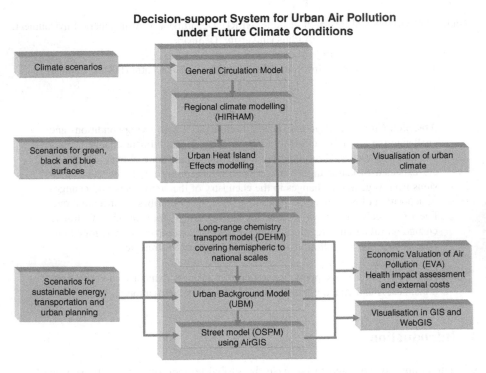

Fig. 1. Conceptual outline of sub-models in a decision-support system for assessment of the impacts of climate change on urban climate and air quality, and for integrated assessment of climate change and air pollution adaptation and mitigation strategies

Dynamic climate downscaling to regional level is based on the HIRHAM regional climate model developed at the Danish Meteorological Institute (DMI). The HIRHAM simulations can then successively be used to simulate Urban Heat island effects by setting up a very high resolution meso-scale model where urban effects are described. This model setup can predict future regional climates under different global climate scenarios, and it can be downscaled to predict future urban climates around the world. Scenarios that target the reduction of urban temperatures can be modelled through adaptation measures.

The air pollution modelling part of the system includes interlinked air quality models to model regional (Danish Eulerian hemispheric Model (DEHM)), urban background (Urban Background Model (UBM)) and street concentrations (Operational Street Pollution Model (OSPM)) developed at National Environmental Research

Institute (NERI). Regional concentrations represent conditions in rural areas outside cities and are influenced by all sources within a very large region, urban background levels represent the general pollution level in the city e.g. at roof top level in a city or in an urban park and are due to the regional concentrations including the urban increment from urban sources, and street concentrations include the urban background concentrations and the street increment due to vehicle sources in the street.

The Danish Eulerian Hemispheric Model (DEHM) provides predictions of future regional air quality based on meteorological predictions from the climate model and based on future emission scenarios to obtain certain climate conditions. This model covers the Northern hemisphere.

Urban background modelling may be based on the Urban Background Model (UBM), and modelling of street concentrations by the Operational Street Pollution Model (OSPM). Mapping of air quality at street scale for en entire city can be carried out by the AirGIS system. AirGIS is able to generate street configuration and traffic data for the OSPM model based on digital maps and databases that enables estimation of air quality levels at a large number of addresses in an automatic and effective way. The impacts to future air quality on urban and street scale can be evaluated for different emission scenarios e.g. scenarios on sustainable energy system, fuel and technology changes in road transportation, urban planning etc.

Health impact assessment and assessment of the external costs of air pollution are based on the EVA-system (Economic Valuation of Air Pollution) developed by NERI. External costs included are the costs associated to the health effects of air pollution. In a cost-benefit analyse of different policy options the EVA-system will provide the benefits (reduced costs) of reductions in emissions. The air pollution part of the EVA-system is based on the DEHM and UBM models and hence provides assessment of external costs at the regional and urban background level.

3 System Features

The decision-support system includes the following features:

(a) Climate and air pollution models that will enable simulation of changes to regional climate and air quality at different spatial scales under different future climate scenarios.

(b) Assessment of the impacts on regional as well as urban climate with focus on modelling of the urban heat island effect causing significantly warmer metropolitan areas than surrounding rural areas.

(c) Modelling and assessment of air quality; health impacts and associated external costs of air pollution as input to cost-benefit analysis of different policy options.

(d) Impact assessment of climate change adaptation measures to urban heat island effects (e.g. changes in black (asphalt, concrete etc.), green (vegatative) and blue (water) surfaces).

(e) Impact assessment of mitigation measures within urban and traffic planning and sustainable low-carbon energy utilisation as a basis for identification of optimal integrated climate change and air pollution mitigation scenarios.

(f) Visualisation of emissions, air quality and urban climate on different geographic scales using GIS. Relevant data may also be visualised using WebGIS for internet dissemination of results in a user friendly and interactive way to the general public.

4 Sub-Models

4.1 Regional Climate Modelling

Increasingly reliable regional climate change projections are now available for many regions of the world due to advances in modelling and understanding of the physical processes of the climate system. Atmosphere-Ocean General Circulation Models (AOGCMs) remain the foundation for projections while downscaling techniques now provide valuable additional detail e.g. [8] [9] [25]. GCMs cannot provide information at scales finer than their computational grid (typically of the order of 200 km) and processes at the unresolved scales are important. Providing information at finer scales can be achieved through using high resolution in dynamical models or empirical statistical downscaling. Development of downscaling methodologies remains an important focus and downscaled climate change projections tailored to specific needs are only now starting to become available [11] [15]. Here we propose to use a chain of models, where a GCM is the first link in the chain. These relatively coarse resolution simulations are then providing lateral boundary conditions for a dynamical downscaling set up with the regional climate model HIRHAM [10]. Information originating from the GCM about atmospheric temperature, moisture content, wind and surface pressure is passed to the regional model every 6 hours at the lateral boundary as is sea surface conditions (temperature and sea ice if present), except this information only is updated once per day.

The HIRHAM model has been applied in such a set-up for many regions of the world, including Europe, North America, the Arctic, Africa and East Asia e.g. [9] [26] [24]. Different resolutions have been applied including very high resolution (e.g. 5km) and experiments have been performed that spanning periods up to 150 years.

The HIRHAM simulations can then successively be used to simulate Urban Heat Island effects by setting up a very high resolution meso-scale model (~1km horizontal grid scale), where urban effects are described or parameterized.

4.2 Urban Heat Island Effect Modelling

The modified land surface in cities affects the storage and radiative and turbulent transfers of heat and its partition into sensible and latent components. The relative warmth of a city compared with surrounding rural areas, known as the urban heat island (UHI) effect, arises from these changes and may also be affected by changes in water runoff, pollution and aerosols. Urban heat island effects are often very localised and depend on local climate factors such as windiness and cloudiness (which in turn depend on season), and on proximity to the sea. From a modelling perspective, it is simple to assess the importance of an urban heat island. Experiments can be designed and performed in which different surface characteristics describing the urban area is introduced. This will allow for a detection of the localized UHI effect as well as more remote influences, which may be of some importance if the urban site is a mega-city or consists of a larger conglomerate of several major cities. An increase of surface temperatures up to 5-10°C have been reported as the effect of UHI in US [28].

Methods of monitoring and modelling UHI must involve mapping of land cover. Most methods use mapping by remote sensing of mainly two parameters that can roughly be categorized as 'black surfaces' and 'green surfaces'. Black surfaces are not all black, but characterised by having 'black body' like radiation reflection and emissivity. These are typically asphalt, concrete, and various roof materials that all are good absorbers of solar radiation and mostly with high heat capacity. Green surfaces are often reflected by a vegetation index, e.g. NDVI. This parameter describes the surface cover photosynthetic properties, and is a proxy for vegetation cooling by evapotranspiration. 'Blue surfaces' (water faces) also have UHI properties highly different from black surfaces, and should be included in any modelling if present. If available, thermal infra-red images of night time surface temperatures can contribute considerably to local understanding and will potentially increase model accuracy. All relevant parameters can be retrieved from commercially available satellite images.

Measures against increasing UHI includes mainly vegetation, and with less effect, the use of lighter-coloured materials. The use of 'green roofs' has a cooling effect and also a positive effect in case of extreme precipitation events. Trees and larger plants can also cast shadow as well as contribute with transpiration. 'Living roofs offer greater cooling per unit area than light surfaces, but less cooling per unit area than curbside planting' [27]. Optimally the combined use of vegetation and materials with favourable reflective, emissive and heat capacity properties should be considered.

4.3 Regional Air Quality Modelling

The Danish Eulerian Hemispheric Model (DEHM) is a three-dimensional, offline, large-scale, Eulerian, atmospheric transport and chemistry model developed to study long-range transport of air pollution in the Northern Hemisphere and Europe [4] [6] [7] [12] [13]. The model domain covers most of the Northern Hemisphere, discretized in a 96 × 96 horizontal grid, using a polar stereographic projection. The projection is true at 60° north, where the horizontal grid resolutions for the coarse, medium and fine grids are 150 km × 150 km, 50 km × 50 km, and 16.67 km × 16.67 km, respectively, using two-way nesting [13]. The vertical grid is defined using the σ-coordinate system, with 29 vertical layers. The model describes concentration fields of 58 chemical compounds and 9 classes of particulate matter ($PM_{2.5}$, PM_{10}, TSP, sea-salt < 2.5 µm, sea-salt > 2.5 µm, smoke, fresh black carbon, aged black carbon, organic carbon). A total of 122 chemical reactions are included. Furthermore, the model includes options for describing persistent organic pollutants and mercury.

Wet deposition, included in the loss term, is expressed as the product of scavenging coefficients and the concentration. In contrast, dry deposition is solved separately for gases and particles, and deposition rates depend on the land-cover. Emissions are based on several inventories, including EDGAR, GEIA or RCP, retrospective wildfires, ship emissions both around Denmark and globally, and emissions from the EMEP database. The model has undergone an extensive model validation where model results have been validated against measurements from the whole of Europe over a 20 year period.

To calculate the marginal difference in regional ambient concentration levels due to a specific emission source or sector, DEHM includes a 'tagging' method [5], to examine how specific emission sources influence air pollution levels, without assuming linear behaviour of atmospheric chemistry, and reducing the influence from the numerical noise. This method, used as a basis for the EVA model system (see below) is more precise than taking the difference between two concentration fields. DEHM has been used to study climate change impacts on future air pollution levels by couple the model to climate data [17] [18].

4.4 Local-Scale Air Quality Modelling

For urban areas an interlinked modelling approach is implemented that applies the modelled regional climate and air pollution as boundary conditions for local-scale modelling of urban background concentrations that again are boundary conditions for modelling of street concentrations. In this case, urban background concentrations are modelled with the Urban Background Model (UBM) and street concentrations with the Operational Street Pollution Model (OSPM).

Urban background levels are defined to represent conditions at roof top level in a city or in an urban park. Hourly urban background data are modelled with the Urban Background Model (UBM) [3], a simple area source based dispersion model. Contributions from individual gridded area sources are integrated along the wind direction path assuming linear dispersion with the distance to the receptor point. Horizontal dispersion is accounted for by averaging the calculated concentrations over a given wind direction sector that is dependent on the wind speed and centred on the hourly average wind direction. The model includes simple photochemistry to predict NO_2 formation, and requires inputs on emissions, meteorological data and regional background concentrations, as well as land-cover data to estimate surface roughness. A model region of e.g. 35 km x 50 km may be defined with a grid resolution of 1 x 1 km^2 for emission inputs for vehicle emissions that is a major source in larger urban areas. Contributions from sources other than vehicles may also be taken into account including industries, space heating, non-road etc.

Concentration levels within the street canyons are calculated with the Operational Street Pollution Model (OSPM) [2]. The calculation points are chosen so as to be representative of locations in front of the buildings at user-specified heights. The OSPM requires information about street geometry (e.g. street orientation, street width, building height in wind sectors), hourly traffic emissions, meteorological parameters and urban background concentrations. The model computes pollution levels as the sum of the direct contribution from traffic and the contribution from the wind-generated recirculation of air pollution inside the street environment. The direct contribution is described by a plume dispersion model and the recirculation contribution by a box model that takes into account the exchange with the urban background air. The influence of traffic induced turbulence is taken into account and it is especially important for low wind speeds. Traffic induced turbulence depends on vehicle density in the street, horizontal area occupied by vehicles and vehicle speed. The model also includes simple photochemistry involving NO, NO_2 and O_3 for estimation of NO_2 concentrations. The OSPM model has been successfully tested against monitor stations in Denmark, other European countries and in US and Asia [22].

The AirGIS system is a deterministic exposure model system based on the OSPM model and urban background concentrations (UBM model) together with digital maps, register data, traffic data, and Geographic Information Systems (GIS) for estimation of air pollution and human exposure in urban areas [19] [20]. One of the unique features of AirGIS is that it is able to generate street configuration and traffic data for the OSPM model based on digital maps on road links with traffic data and building footprints with building heights. This enables estimation of air quality levels at a large number of street locations in an automatic and effective way in urban areas [23].

Demonstration of linked modelling of regional, urban background and street air quality has been shown in studies for short-term forecasts [4], as well as for future air quality assessment under climate mitigation measures with focus on utilisation of hydrogen [21] and biofuels in road transportation [16].

4.5 Economic Evaluation of Air Pollution

The concept of the integrated EVA (Economic Valuation of Air pollution) model system is based on the impact pathway chain [1] [14] [5]. The site-specific emissions are causing (via atmospheric transport and chemistry) a concentration distribution, which together with detailed population data is used to estimate the population-level exposure. Using exposure-response functions for health impacts and economic valuations, the exposure is transformed into impacts on human health and related external costs.

The EVA system consists of the regional-scale air pollution model DEHM, address-level or gridded population data, exposure-response functions and economic valuations of the impacts from air pollution. The essential idea behind the EVA system is that state-of-the-art methods are used in all the individual parts of the impact-pathway chain. Other comparable systems commonly use linear source-receptor relationships, which do not accurately describe non-linear processes such as atmospheric chemistry and deposition. The EVA system has the advantage that it describes such processes using a comprehensive, state-of-the-art chemical transport model when calculating how specific changes to emissions affect air pollution levels. All scenarios are run individually and not estimated using linear extra-/interpolation from standard reductions.

The EVA-system is able to estimate the external costs of health-related air pollution based on e.g. emission reduction scenarios. In a cost-benefit analyse of different policy options the EVA-system will provide the benefits (reduced costs) of reductions in emissions.

5 Conclusion

A conceptual outline has been presented of a decision-support system for assessment of the impacts of climate change on urban climate and air quality, and for assessment of integrated climate change and air pollution adaptation and mitigation strategies. The model system includes dynamic climate downscaling to regional level under different future global climate scenarios as well as subsequent Urban Heat Island effect modelling. The air pollution modelling part of the system includes interlinked air quality models to model regional, urban background and street concentrations. The regional concentrations are based on meteorological predictions from the climate model and on associated future emission scenarios. Health impact assessment and assessment of the external costs of air pollution are also estimated and may provide input to cost-benefit analyse of different policy options.

The impacts to future air quality on urban and street scale can be evaluated for different emission scenarios e.g. scenarios on sustainable energy systems, fuel and technology changes in road transportation, urban planning etc.

References

1. Andersen, M.S., Frohn, L.M., Brandt, J., Jensen, S.S.: External effects from power production and the treatment of wind energy (and other renewables) in the Danish energy taxation system. In: Deketelaere, K., Milne, J.E., Kreiser, L.A., Ashiabor, H. (eds.) Critical Issues in Environmental Taxation: International and Comparative Perspectives, vol. IV, pp. 319–336. Oxford University Press, Oxford (2007)
2. Berkowicz, R.: OSPM – A parameterised street pollution model. Environmental Monitoring and Assessment 65(1/2), 323–331 (2000a)
3. Berkowicz, R.: A simple model for urban background pollution. Environmental Monitoring and Assessment 65(1/2), 259–267 (2000b)
4. Brandt, J., Christensen, J.H., Frohn, L.M., Palmgren, F., Berkowicz, R., Zlatev, Z.: Operational air pollution forecasts from European to local scale. Atmospheric Environment 35(sup. 1), S91–S98 (2001)
5. Brandt, J., Silver, J.D., Frohn, L.M., Christensen, J.H., Andersen, M.S., Bønløkke, J.H., Sigsgaard, T., Geels, C., Gross, A., Hansen, A.B., Hansen, K.M., Hedegaard, G.B., Kaas, E.: Assessment of Health-Cost Externalities of Air Pollution at the National Level using the EVA Model System. CEEH Scientific Report No 3, Centre for Energy, Environment and Health Report series, p. 96 (2011), http://www.ceeh.dk
6. Christensen, J.H.: The Danish Eulerian Hemispheric Model – a three-dimensional air pollution model used for the Arctic. Atmospheric Environment 31, 4169–4191 (1997)
7. Christensen, J.H., Brandt, J., Frohn, L.M., Skov, H.: Modelling of mercury in the Arctic with the Danish Eulerian Hemispheric Model. Atmospheric Chemistry and Physics 4, 2251–2257 (2004)
8. Christensen, J.H., Carter, T.R., Rummukainen, M., Amanatidis, G.: Evaluating the performance and utility of regional climate models: the PRUDENCE project. Climatic Change 81(sup. 1), 1–6 (2007), doi:10.1007/s10584-006-9211-6
9. Christensen, J.H., Christensen, O.B.: A summary of the PRUDENCE model projections of changes in European climate by the end of this century. Climatic Change 81(sup. 1), 7–30 (2007), doi:10.1007/s10584-006-9210-7
10. Christensen, O.B., Drews, M., Christensen, J.H., Dethloff, K., Ketelsen, K., Hebestadt, I., Rinke, A.: The HIRHAM Regional Climate Model. Version 5. DMI Technical Report No. 06-17. [Available from DMI, Lyngbyvej 100, Copenhagen Ø, DENMARK] (2006)
11. CORDEX, cited as 2010,
    http://copes.ipsl.jussieu.fr/RCD_CORDEX.html

12. Frohn, L.M., Christensen, J.H., Brandt, J., Hertel, O.: Development of a high resolution nested air pollution model for studying air pollution in Denmark. Physics and Chemistry of the Earth 26, 769–774 (2001)
13. Frohn, L.M., Christensen, J.H., Brandt, J.: Development of a high resolution nested air pollution model – the numerical approach. Journal of Computational Physics 179, 68–94 (2002)
14. Frohn, L.M., Andersen, M.S., Geels, C., Brandt, J., Christensen, J.H., Hansen, K.M., Nielsen, J.S., Hertel, O., Skjøth, C.A., Madsen, P.V.: EVA - An integrated model system for assessing external costs related to air pollution emissions. In: A contribution to ACCENT T&TP, Proceedings from the 2nd ACCENT Symposium, p. 10 (2007)
15. Giorgi, F., Jones, C., Asrar, G.: Addressing climate information needs at the regional level: The CORDEX framework. WMO Bulletin 58, 3 (2009)
16. Gross, A., Jensen, S.S., Brandt, J., Christensen, J.H., Ketzel, M., Frohn, L.M., Geels, C., Hansen, A.B., Hansen, K.M., Hedegaard, G.B., Silver, J.D., Skjøth, C.A.: Regional Air Quality Assessment of Biofuel Scenarios in the Road Transport Sector. In: International Conference on Energy, Environment and Health, – Optimisation of Future Energy Systems, Carlsberg Academy, Copenhagen, Denmark, May 31-June 2 (2010)
17. Hedegaard, G.B., Brandt, J., Christensen, J.H., Frohn, L.M., Geels, C., Hansen, K.M.: Impacts of climate change on air pollution levels in the Northern Hemisphere with special focus on Europe and the Arctic. Atmospheric Chemistry and Physics 8, 3337–3367 (2008)
18. Hedegaard, G.B., Gross, A., Christensen, J.H., May, W., Skov, H., Geels, C., Hansen, K.M., Brandt, J.: Modelling the Modelling the Impacts of Climate Change on Tropospheric Ozone over three Centuries. Atmospheric Chemistry and Physics Discuss 11, 6805–6843 (2011)
19. Jensen, S.S., Berkowicz, R., Hansen, H.S., Hertel, O.: A Danish decision-support GIS tool for management of urban air quality and human exposures. Transportation Research Part D: Transport and Environment 6(4), 229–241 (2001)
20. Jensen, S.S., Larson, T., Kaufman, J., Kc, D.: Modeling Traffic Air pollution in Street Canyons in New York City for Intra-urban Exposure Assessment in the US Multi-Ethnic Study of Atherosclerosis. Atmospheric Environment 43, 4544–4556 (2009), http://dx.doi.org/10.1016/j.atmosenv.2009.06.042
21. Jensen, S.S., Ketzel, M., Brandt, J., Frohn, L.M., Winther, M., Nielsen, O.-K., Jørgensen, K., Karlsson, K.: Impacts of large-scale introduction of hydrogen in the road transport sector on urban air pollution and human exposure in Copenhagen. In: International Conference on Energy, Environment and Health, – Optimisation of Future Energy Systems, Carlsberg Academy, Copenhagen, Denmark, May 31-June 2 (2010)
22. Kakosimos, K.E., Hertel, O., Ketzel, M., Berkowicz, R.: Operational Street Pollution Model (OSPM) - a review of performed validation studies, and future prospects. Environmental Chemistry 7, 485–503 (2011)
23. Ketzel, M., Berkowicz, R., Hvidberg, M., Jensen, S.S., Raaschou-Nielsen, O.: Evaluation of AirGIS - a GIS-based air pollution and human exposure modelling system. International Journal for Environment and Pollution (in press, 2011)
24. Kiilsholm, S., Christensen, J.H., Dethloff, K., Rinke, A.: Net accumulation of the Greenland Ice Sheet: Modelling Arctic regional climate change. Geoph. Re. Lett. 30 (2003), doi:10.1029/2002GL015742
25. Kjellström, E., Giorgi, F.: Introduction to special issue. Climate Research 44, 11–119 (2010)

26. Pan, Z., Christensen, J.H., Arritt, R.W., Gutowski, W.J., Takle, E.S., Otieno, F.: Evaluation of uncertainties in regional climate change simulations. J. Geophys. Res. 106, 17735–17752 (2001)
27. Rosenzweig, C., Solecki, W., Parshall, L., Gaffin, S., Lynn, B., Goldberg, R., Cox, J., Hodges, S.: Mitigating New York City's heat island with urban forestry, living roofs, and light surfaces. In: 86th American Meteorological Society Annual Meeting, Atlanta, Georgia, January 31 (2006)
28. Zhang, P., Imhoff, M.L., Wolfe, R.E., Bounoua, L.: Detecting urban heat island drivers in northeast USA cities using MODIS and Landsat products. In: AGU Fall 2010 Meeting (2010)

Towards User Requirements for an Information System of the Integrated Rhine Programme

Thomas Usländer[1], Rainer Junker[2], and Ulrike Pfarr[2]

[1] Fraunhofer IOSB, Fraunhoferstr. 1,
76131 Karlsruhe, Germany
thomas.uslaender@iosb.fraunhofer.de
[2] Regierungspräsidium Freiburg, Bissierstr. 7
79114 Freiburg im Breisgau, Germany
{rainer.junker,ulrike.pfarr}@rpf.bwl.de

Abstract. The Integrated Rhine Programme (IRP) is a strategic integrated measurement programme of the German federal state of Baden-Württemberg that aims at an improvement of flood control as well as the preservation and/or the restoration of the Upper Rhine plains. The implementation of the IRP shall be supported by an integrated and sustainable Information System for the IRP (IS-IRP) as an extension of the Environmental Information System of Baden-Württemberg. This paper describes how the analysis and design methodology SERVUS is applied to gather and document the functional and informational user requirements for the IS-IRP. SERVUS denotes a Design Methodology for Information Systems based upon Geospatial Service-oriented Architectures and the Modelling of Use Cases and Capabilities as Resources.

Keywords: Integrated Rhine Programme, Environmental Information System, IS-IRP, Requirements Analysis.

1 Introduction

The Integrated Rhine Programme (IRP) is a strategic integrated measurement programme of the German federal state of Baden-Württemberg that aims at an improvement of flood control as well as the preservation and/or the restoration of the Upper Rhine plains [1]. Over a time period of more than 30 years it proposes and implements the creation of flood retention areas at 13 sites located in the alluvial floodplains on the Baden-Württemberg side of the Rhine. Moreover, it aims at achieving the preservation and restoration of the alluvial floodplains on the Upper Rhine to the largest possible extent. The ultimate goal entails attaining the level of flood protection that existed prior to the construction of the hydroelectric plants and locks.

Each individual measure requires an intense planning period over several years and includes the involvement of all stakeholders in the respective region including the citizens. A multitude of data has to be gathered from various sensors, databases and

J. Hřebíček, G. Schimak, and R. Denzer (Eds.): ISESS 2011, IFIP AICT 359, pp. 651–656, 2011.

systems (e.g. surface and groundwater gauges, ecological data of fauna and flora, operational data of controlled weirs, input and output parameters of groundwater models, flood hazard and risk maps) such that an assessment and a justification of the measures is possible. Due to ongoing and lasting discussions with public and private stakeholders the argumentation line for a particular measure shall even stand up in courts after several years. Hence, there is a need for an integrated and sustainable Information System for the IRP (IS-IRP). It is designed as an extension and dedicated module of the encompassing Environmental Information System (EIS) of Baden-Württemberg [3]. One of the major design objectives is to avoid redundant data storage as far as possible.

In order to clearly understand the needs of the IS-IRP end-users as well as the capabilities of the existing EIS modules an intense requirements analysis phase is being carried out in 2011. Due to the multitude of involved persons and the interdisciplinary nature of this activity there is a need to follow a design methodology supported by an information management platform. For this purpose, the method SERVUS is being applied. SERVUS denotes a Design Methodology for Information Systems based upon Geospatial Service-oriented Architectures and the Modelling of Use Cases and Capabilities as Resources [2]. It is described in more detail in these proceedings [4].

This paper highlights the current status of the IRP implementation (section 2) and the approach of the requirements analysis (section 3). Furthermore, it presents a use case example (section 4) and concludes with an outlook about the consequences for the IS-IRP design from a broad architectural perspective (section 5).

2 Implementation of the Integrated Rhine Programme

By preserving the ecological goals the final objective of the IRP, once being fully implemented, is to restore protection in the Upper Rhine Valley against a 200-yearly flood event. The fulfillment of this objective requires a total retention volume of 256 Mio m^3 with a shared contribution of the adjoint regions (167,3 Mio m^3 for Baden-Württemberg, 30,3 Mio m^3 for Rhineland-Palatine and 58,4 Mio m^3 for France).

As of today, three out of 13 measures and retention areas (polders) that are foreseen in the Framework Concept for the Integrated Rhine Programme of Baden-Württemberg are operational. See their geographical locations and implementation status in figure 1. Two of them, the polder of Altenheim and the cultural weir near Kehl/Strasbourg have successfully operated for almost 20 years now. The polder of Söllingen/Greffern was brought to completion in 2005. This type of flood control operation helps retain 67 Mio m^3 of water [1]. The retention are of the Rheinschanzinsel is currently under construction. Over the next years, further flood retention areas will be built.

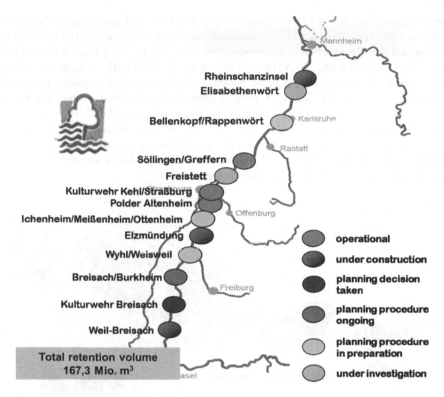

Fig. 1. Current status of measures and retention areas of the Integrated Rhine Programme

3 Approach for the Requirements Analysis

In the first half of 2011, an analysis project in order to identify, collect and assess the functional and informational requirements for an IS-IRP is being carried out. Hence, as of today, just early results can be presented. As a first step, preliminary use cases have been proposed by the IRP experts of the regional governmental agencies (Regierungspräsidien) of Freiburg/Breisgau and Karlsruhe whose task is the thematic planning and implementation of the IRP including the consensus finding with the various stakeholders. These use cases are classified into four major domains according to the major data categories that are concerned:

1. Operational data of retention area facilities (dams, weirs,…).
2. Groundwater and surface water monitoring data
3. Ecological sampling data (including soil data) and ecological assessment data
4. Groundwater modeling

After their identification these use cases are discussed and refined in workshops with the end-users and stakeholders. These workshops need to be facilitated and documented by a system analyst. As a starting point they are described in structured natural language according to a template in tabular format that just requires the name, the description, the major actors, the required information resources (input information objects) and the resulting information resources (output information objects) to be specified following the SERVUS methodology [4]. Optionally, a sequence of actions to carry out the use case may be added. It is then up to the system analyst to transform this semi-formal description into a formal representation, which, according to SERVUS, comprises a representation of the use cases and related information resources in the Uniform Modeling Language (UML). It is the advantage of this formal transition step already in an early analysis phase to detect inconsistencies and missing information as quickly as possible. The UML specification helps to (re-)discuss and check the use cases together with the thematic experts.

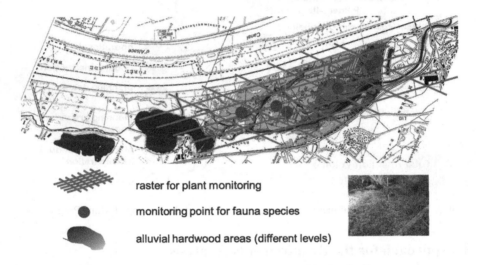

raster for plant monitoring

monitoring point for fauna species

alluvial hardwood areas (different levels)

Fig. 2. Monitoring in the Alluvial Floodplains of Breisach, Germany
[derived from a source figure of the RP Freiburg, 2011]

4   Use Case Example

As an example one use case of the ecological domain is presented in more detail. It is dedicated to fulfill statutory obligations stipulated in decisions of official planning approvals for the assessment of polder landscapes. This may be to validate that ecological floodings improve the mixture of fauna and flora species in the designated areas of the alluvial floodplains. Ecological floodings are controlled flooding events of a floodplain according to a defined procedure. Their purpose is to habituate the fauna and flora to flooding situations and, hence, to foster the formation of an alluvial forest.

Such a validation procedure requires the selection of indicator species, e.g. selected plants that characterize alluvial landscapes or epigeal fauna species such as ground beetles or snails. For these indicator species dedicated ecological monitoring programmes have to be defined. Especially, it has to be decided at which points in the alluvial floodplain the ecological observations should take place. As indicated in figure 2, a regular raster grid may be defined for plant monitoring, whereas individual points may be selected for fauna species.

The use case chosen is the performance of the monitoring programme as indicated above. The corresponding UML use case diagram is shown in figure 3. It is carried out by case officers in the IRP agency. It needs, among others, to read water gauges and further input data from groundwater information systems. It requires read and write access to nature protection data, e.g. to store the observation results of the flora and fauna monitoring as explained above. As a sub-ordinate use case the production of an ecological report is illustrated. As output information resource it produces an ecological report in pdf representation format.

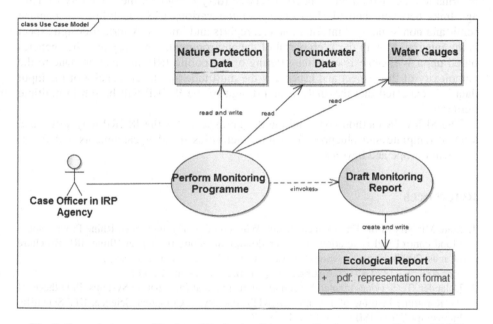

Fig. 3. Example use case "Perform Monitoring Programme" to be supported by the IS-IRP

5 Conclusion and Outlook

This paper discusses how the process of analyzing the user requirements for the Information System, that shall support the implementation of the Integrated Rhine Programme in the Upper Rhine valley of Germany, is being carried out. It is a report about the practical application of a scientifically sound analysis and design methodology. The use case analysis is currently being performed in 2011 for all of the data categories listed above. In several workshops that include representatives of all stakeholders and thematic experts use cases as well as requested information resources are being identified. The workshops and the whole use case analysis process is supported and documented by a Web-based information management system. As an early result it may be said that the rigid but flexible and end-user oriented methodology heavily facilitates the discussion and consensus finding between the thematic experts and the IT specialists. Of particular help is the immediate documentation of the use case descriptions in a Web-based content and community management system. This system is available to all project participants with dedicated read and write access rights according to their roles.

The next step will be to derive an information model for the IS-IRP and discuss the consequences and the challenges for the design of the IS-IRP system architecture in the context of the other thematic applications of the Environmental Information System of the German federal state of Baden-Württemberg [3]. Particular emphasis will be put on the question how the generic services of the EIS Baden-Württemberg may be re-used for the IS-IRP, too. Service examples to be considered are a geographical information acquisition and rendering service (disy GISterm), the capability to manage links between thematic EIS objects or the various EIS capabilities to manage semi- and non-structured information, e.g. reports and images. A further design aspect is the integration with the Web portal of the environmental ministry and the agencies based upon WebGenesis® for the offering of the public IRP information. Due to the complexity of the project and especially the multitude and heterogeneity of the input data it is expected that the analysis and design of the IS-IRP will be run in multiple iterations.

The SERVUS methodology and the design aspects for the IS-IRP may serve as a kind of template and blueprint for similar activities in other catchments and floodplains in Europe and beyond.

References

1. State Ministry of the Environment Baden-Württemberg: The Integrated Rhine Programme – Flood control and restoration of former floodplains along the Upper Rhine. IRP Brochure (August 2007), http://www.rpbwl.de/freiburg/abteilung5/ referat53.3/faltblaetter-irp/kurz-irp-engl.pdf
2. Usländer, T.: Service-oriented Design of Environmental Information Systems. PhD thesis of the Karlsruhe Institute of Technology (KIT), Faculty of Computer Science, KIT Scientific Publishing (2010) ISBN 978-3-86644-499-7, http://digbib.ubka.uni-karlsruhe.de/volltexte/1000016721
3. Keitel, A., Mayer-Föll, R., Schultze, A.: Framework Conception for the Environmental Information System of Baden-Württemberg (Germany). In: Hřebíček, J., et al. (eds.) Proceedings of Towards eEnvironment, pp. 461–468 (2009) ISBN 978-80-210-4824-9
4. Usländer, T., Batz, T.: How to Analyse User Requirements for Service-Oriented Environmental Information Systems. In: Hřebíček, J., Schimak, G., Denzer, R. (eds.) ISESS 2011. IFIP AICT, vol. 359, pp. 161–168. Springer, Heidelberg (2011)

E-HypeWeb: Service for Water and Climate Information - and Future Hydrological Collaboration across Europe?

Berit Arheimer, Patrik Wallman, Chantal Donnelly,
Karin Nyström, and Charlotta Pers

Swedish Meteorological and Hydrological Institute,
SE-601 76 Norrköping, Sweden
berit.arheimer@smhi.se

Abstract. The hydrological scientific and operational communities are faced with new challenges. There is a demand for detailed water information for large regions and new environmental issues to deal with, which request advanced technical infrastructure merged with up-dated hydrological knowledge. Traditionally, the hydrological community is disaggregated. In this paper we suggest a collaborative approach and invite both researchers and operational agencies to participate in the development of a common European core service providing free access to water information. We present the idea of starting from the new E-HYPE model and its advanced technological infrastructure and open source cod, using a bottom-up approach.

Keywords: catchment hydrology, modeling, pan-European, technical infrastructure, open source community, E-HYPE.

1 Introduction

Information about water quantity and/or quality is required by any societal sector dealing with natural resources, ecosystem services, or watercourses. Accordingly several European directives deal with water access and status, e.g. the Water Framework Directive, WFD (2000/60/EC) and the Marine Strategy Framework Directve, MSFD (2008/56/EC). Hydrological predictions by numerical models are often used to produce water information and related decision-support for societal safety or production efficiency. The predictions may be used for e.g. early warning services, hydropower regulation, infrastructure planning, agricultural practices, water allocation, shipping guidance, environmental control, or climate change adaption.

Both scientifically and operationally, the water community in Europe is diverse and disaggregated. Traditionally, hydrological model systems have often been site specific for water bodies and catchments, or small enough to be manageable by a single actor. Because of the economic interests in the water business, many commercial companies have developed their own tools for specific assessments and forecasts. Often institutes have specialized on a single model concept

J. Hřebíček, G. Schimak, and R. Denzer (Eds.): ISESS 2011, IFIP AICT 359, pp. 657–666, 2011.

for decades [1] giving answers to a few questions. SWAT [2] and HBV [3] are examples of models that are frequently used for specific catchments in Europe, and sometimes also for operational transnational use in large river basins [4]. New challenges, however, have appeared for European water authorities related to new policies for environmental control, climate change adaption and uncertainty analyses. Today's requirements on hydrological models are going in the direction of higher spatial and temporal resolution for larger regions. Developing such tools requires a lot of resources, both when it comes to technical infrastructure, computational power and hydrological knowledge.

Setting up an integrated hydrological modeling and monitoring system is maybe not only a national concern today as information is requested also for pan-European issues and cooperation would reduce costs. This has been recognized since decades among meteorologists and oceanographers, who are sharing both code development and operational systems in the international collaborations of e.g. HIRLAM/ALADIN, MACC, HIROMB, NEMO and MYOCEAN. The experiences show that it is not only beneficial for scientific and technical development, knowledge and data exchange, but it is also economically sound to share the costs of both development and maintenance of these large systems between several partners. These cooperations could serve as blue-prints for the hydrological community, when increasing ambitions to cover the whole European domain and developing a core service for hydrological information.

The most ambitious European collaboration around a common hydrological model code is probably the SHE initiative that started some decades ago, between European institutes in Denmark, UK and France [5]. For transnational analyses, some hydrological models have recently been applied for the pan-European domain, such as VIC [6], WaterGap [7,8], WASMOD [9] and LIS-FLOOD [10,11]. However, none of the mentioned initiatives combines collaborative code development and operational production in common.

In this paper we present and suggest a platform that will enable intensified collaboration among water scientists as well as operational institutes, to provide water information with high resolution for Europe. This will presumably speed up the work with European directives in the European Union, as included model components, databases, simulation platforms, and model results are suggested to be open access for all member states. Such a collaborative core service could also enable a flora of commercial decision support systems appointed to specific needs of end-users.

2   Material and Methods

2.1   The HYPE Model

The Hydrological Predictions for the Environment (HYPE) model is a dynamic, semi-distributed and process-based model based on well-known hydrological and nutrient transport concepts [12]. It can be used for both small and large scale assessments of water resources and water quality.

In the model, landscape is divided into classes according to soil type, vegetation and altitude. The soil representation is stratified and can be divided in up to three layers, each with individual characteristics and hence calculations. The model simulates water flows, transport and turnover of nitrogen, phosphorus and inert trace substances. These substances follow the same pathways as water in the model: surface runoff, macro pore flow, tile drainage and groundwater outflow from the individual soil layers. Rivers and lakes are described separately with routines for turnover of nutrients in each environment. Model coefficients are global, or related to specific characteristics of Hydrological Response Units (HRU), i.e. combinations of soil type and land-use. Internal model components are checked using corresponding observations from different sites [13]. The HYPE model code is structured so that the model can be easily applied with high spatial resolution over large model domains, which is also facilitated by linking coefficients to physical characteristics and by the multi-basin calibration procedure [14].

2.2   The European HYPE Model Set-Up (E-HYPE)

So far, the HYPE model has been set up pan-European for water, while nutrients are only modeled for the Baltic Sea basin (Balt-HYPE), se Table 1. The E-HYPE model calculates water balance, hydrological processes (snow, glaciers, soil moisture, flow paths, groundwater contribution, and lake dampening) and final routing to the surrounding sea, i.e. the Atlantic, Mediterranean, Black and Baltic Seas. The model domain covers most of the European continent, from the British Isles to the Ural Mountains, and from Norway to the Mediterranean Sea.

It serves as an operational high-resolution model and production system delivering daily data. This achievement was possible thanks to readily available regional and global databases, which are handled in a specially designed system of methods for automatic generation of model input data, WHIST [15]. The first version was uncalibrated but a second version is currently (spring 2011) being set up and calibrated against observed time-series.

2.3   HYSS

The source code of HYPE is embedded in the HYdrological Simulation System (HYSS, 2.2), which is the infrastructural part of the model source code. HYSS handles the simulation instructions, provides the hydrological model with variables containing data on the model set-up, time and current forcing data (i.e. precipitation and air temperature) and writes the result files. It also provides variables for model state, model parameters and output, which are used and set by the model. In this way, the hydrological algorithms are separated from the model infrastructure in its own module. HYSS can thus be coupled to several different hydrological modules with different model structures and process descriptions. HYSS leaves it to the hydrological process code to define parameters and output variables, and calculate state variables during a time step. Currently, HYSS only handles ASCII-files which are used both for input data and output.

Table 1. Model application set-up and input data

	Balt-HYPE	E-HYPE1.0[1]
Areal extent	1.8 million km2	9.6 million km2
Med. Sub basin area	325 km2	120 km2
No. Sub-basins	5128	57436
Topography/routing	Hydro1K [17]	Hydrosheds [16],(Hydro1K for latitude > 60°
Forcing Data	ERAMESAN 1980-2004 [18], Resolution = 11 km.	ERAMESAN 1980-2004 [18], Resolution = 11 km.
Landcover	Globcover 2000	Globcover 2000
Soil-types	ESDB [19]	ESDB [19]
Runoff data	GRDC[20], BHDC[21]	GRDC EWA[22], BHDC[21]
# calibration stations	35	Not calibrated
# validation stations	121	16 (river mouths only)

[1] Version 2.0 will cover 8.9 million km2, 36 314 sub basins and use Corine land cover [23]

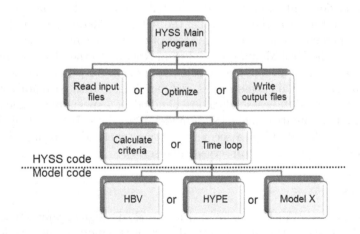

Fig. 1. Schematic picture of HYSS and its linkage to hydrological algorithms

2.4   E-HypeWeb and Balt-HypeWeb

E-HypeWeb is a publically available web service with open access where you can easily download daily and monthly simulations of discharge (m3/s) for one or several sub basins in Europe or river outlet to the sea. Data for download can be chosen by either specifying a sub basin ID or selecting areas from a map. Balt-HYPE is restricted to river outlets but also includes data of nutrient transport to the sea.

E-HypeWeb allows both zooming and panning in the maps shown in the web browser. To make the application reasonably fast the maps for different zoom levels are pre generated using cloud technology with access to several servers and parallel processing is achieved.

3   Results

The E-HYPE is a modeling tool that, on a daily timescale, and at a high spatial resolution:

- calculates water discharge *at all sub basin outlets on the European continent*
- calculates water discharge *to European Seas* (and nutrient load to the Baltic sea)
- can be used operationally to give *past* and *current* conditions and *forecast* all variables
- can be used as a tool for examining the effects of *climate change, land use change* and/or *nutrient reduction measures*, and
- uses quality-assured data and will soon be *calibrated* and *validated* against independent observations, according to sound scientific principles [24]

Pan-European analyses show that the model captures major hydrological variability for the continent 2.4. Comparisons of preliminary model results towards

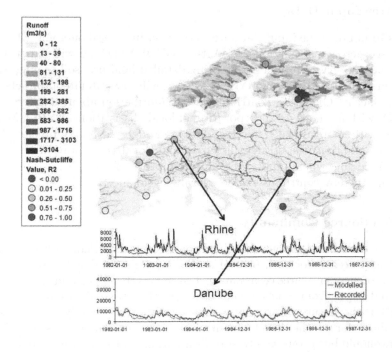

Fig. 2. First evaluation of time-series from the uncalibrated E-HYPE model vs. observations

observed values [24] also show that the model is able to reconstruct dominant features of water quality and dynamics for the continent. Although, there is a need for more detailed input data and local adjustments to achieve more useful results for water authorities on the sub basin scale.

4   Discussion and Visions for the Future

When applied for Sweden, the HYPE model (then called S-HYPE) has shown to be a very useful tool both for hydrological forecasts (for early warning services and hydropower industry) and sustainable management of water resources [25], e.g. for nutrient reductions and climate change adaptation. The process to develop a similar hydrological core service for the entire European domain with free access to water information has just started. In accordance with earlier pan-European attempts, the first E-HYPE results clearly show that quality improvements are needed before the results can be useful for local multi-purposes. The strategy for further development must include better input data, local knowledge on dominant hydrological processes, and advanced technology. For successful implementation and cost efficient development we ask for a bottom-up approach and inclusion of e-science. Some of the main building blocks in such an ambition are presented in the three steps below.

4.1   Better Input Data

Attempts to improve the input data are performed in several on-going EU FP7 projects (see acronyms that follow). Within GEOLAND2 we will experiment with new satellite-based products regarding detailed land use, soil sealing, phenology and soil moisture. In CRYOLAND we will try satellite products for snow and glaciers. GENESIS contributes with information about aquifers, and SUDPLAN with methods for incorporation of local observations. EURO4M will contribute with more detailed forcing data and high-resolution precipitation products. In addition, the strategy is to initiate local collaboration and participatory modeling where input data can be improved for a specific domain of interest, and thereby contribute to the overall development.

4.2   Open Source Community

For efficient code development and inclusion of local knowledge on dominant hydrological processes for each part of such a large model domain, we will try the concept of an open source community. The code is then open and can be seen, changed and learnt from, and all code users are then treated as co-developers. It lies within the nature of an open source project to be highly modularized, and this allows for parallel development of independent components. Users/co-developers should be encouraged to submit additions to the software, code fixes, bug reports, and documentation etc. Early versions of the software should be released as soon as possible to increase chances of finding co-developers early.

An open source community also needs a dynamic decision making structure that makes strategic decisions depending on changing user requirements and also manage/release new code versions. The open code and system related to E-HYPE could be hosted and managed at SMHI to serve the needs of local and continental issues and demands. The community should also cooperate with other national services and end-users linked to the operational production systems for full implementation.

4.3   Hydrological Laboratory and New Technologies

The proposed modeling system will also be used as a "hydrological laboratory". At present the HYSS system manage the HYPE and the HBV models, but the ambition is that more models should be plugged in relatively easily. This facilitates ensemble runs using several different models for the same domain and with the same input data. In addition, the HYPE model code is relatively easy to follow, which allows experiments with different hydrological algorithms. This would enable scientific elaboration of hydrological hypothesis and increase the knowledge base of European water systems.

New challenges in hydrological modeling include e.g. high spatial and temporal resolution, Monte Carlo simulations for uncertainty estimates, sensitivity studies, ensemble modeling, water quality estimates and climate change effects for the next coming hundreds of years. All these applications need high computational capacity. Hydrological models are traditionally run on PCs, but the new challenges thus ask for new technologies. Cloud services using several processors are already applied in the production system within SMHI hydrology to generate maps for the web products. Future modeling system may use this technology

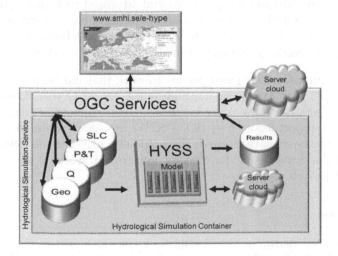

Fig. 3. Schematic picture of the future E-HypeWeb production system

also to run the hydrological models themselves 3. This will soon speed up the computational time significantly.

Moreover, new technology is currently developed for visualization of E-HYPE results in decision support systems, for data extraction and automatic model calibration to local observation. This development is done in the EU FP7 preoject SUDPLAN and will result in interactive user interfaces, including model runs and data access.

All together, the step strategy could thus lead to improved quality, credibility through transparency, collective learning and international cooperation. Each step would benefit on linkage to new e-science to be efficient. If the overall development is successful, E-HYPE has a large potential to form a hydrological core service for Europe in the next coming years. This would then combine collaborative code development and operational production in the same service.

5   Conclusions

- A pan-European model is available, providing high-resolution water information with free access through a web product http://www.smhi.se/e-hype, and water and nutrient load to the sea through
  http://www.smhi.se/balt-hype
- The first preliminary model results show that the model is able to reconstruct dominant features of water quality and dynamics for the continent. However, collaborative development is needed both for producing more useful results for water authorities on the sub basin scale, and for further operational pan-European implementation.
- A three step strategy is developed for further development and implementation using a bottom-up approach. Focus is put on better input data, local knowledge on hydrological processes and advanced technology. Much of the work will rely on EU FP7 projects, an open source community, and hopefully new e-science. The ambition is to combine both collaborative code development and operational production in this new water service.

Acknowledgments. This paper relates to work that has been partly financed by the EU FP7 projects Geoland2, Sudplan, Genesis, Cryoland and OPERR. National projects that have contributed are Hydroimpacts2.0 financed by Formas, and Ecosupport financed by BONUS. We are very grateful for the funding and the confidence we have received. We would also like to thank Peter Karlsson, SMHI, and the "water team" for efficient and fruitful work on the E-HypeWeb and Balt-HypeWeb products.

References

1. Arheimer, B., Lindström, G., Olsson, J.: A systematic review of sensistivities in the Swedish flood forecasting system. Atmospheric Research 100, 275–284 (2011)
2. Arnold, J.G., Fohrer, N.: SWAT2000: Current Capabilities and Research Opportunities in Applied Watershed Modelling. Hydrological Processes 19, 563–573 (2005)

3. Bergström, S.: Development and application of a conceptual runoff model for Scandinavian catchments. SMHI Reports RHO No. 7, Norrköping (1976)
4. Berglöv, G., German, J., Gustavsson, H., Harbman, U., Johansson, B.: Improvment HBV model Rhine in FEWS. Final report. SMHI Hydrology report No. 112, Norrköping (2009)
5. Refsgaard, J.C., Storm, B., Clausen, T.: Système Hydrologique Européen (SHE): review and perspectives after 30 years development in distributed physically-based hydrological modeling. Hydrology Research 41(5), 355–377 (2010)
6. Arnell, N.W.: A simple water balance model for the simulation of streamflow over a large geographic domain. Journal of Hydrology 217(3-4), 314–335 (1999)
7. Döll, P., Kaspar, F., Lehner, B.: A global hydrological model for deriving water availability indicators: model tuning and validation. Journal of Hydrology 270, 105–134 (2003)
8. Alcamo, J., Döll, P., Henrichs, T., Kaspar, F., Lehner, B., Rósch, T.: Development and testing of the WaterGAP 2 global model of water use and availability. Hydrological Schiences Journal 48(3), 317–338 (2003)
9. Widn-Nilsson, E., Halldin, S., Xu, C.: Global water-balance modelling with WASMOD-M: Parameter estimation and regionalization. Journal of Hydrology 340, 105–118 (2007)
10. Feyen, L., Vrugt, J.A., Nualláin, B.Ó., van der Knijff, J., De Roo, A.: Parameter optimisation and uncertainty assessment for large-scale streamflow simulating with the LISFLOOD model. Journal of Hydrology 332(1), 276–289 (2007)
11. van der Knijff, J.M., Younis, J., De Roo, A.P.J.: LISFLOOD: a GIS-based distributed model for river-basin scale water balance and flood simulation. Intrnational Journal of Geographical Information Science 24(2), 189–212 (2011)
12. Lindström, G., Pers, C., Rosberg, J., Strömqvist, J., Arheimer, B.: Development and test of the HYPE (Hydrological Predictions for the Environment) model - A water quality model for different spatial scales. Hydrology Research 41(3-4), 295–319 (2010)
13. Arheimer, B., Dahné, J., Lindström, G., Marklund, L., Strömqvist, J.: Multivariable evaluation of an integrated model system covering Sweden (S-HYPE). IAHS Publ. 345 (2011)
14. Donnelly, C., Dahné, J., Lindström, G., Rosberg, J., Strömqvist, J., Pers, C., Yang, W., Arheimer, B.: An evaluation of multi-basin hydrological modelling for predictions in ungauged basins. IAHS Publ. 333, 112–120 (2009)
15. Strömqvist, J., Dahné, J., Donnelly, C., Lindström, G., Rosberg, J., Pers, C., Yang, W., Arheimer, B.: Using recently developed global data sets for hydrological predictions. IAHS Publ. 333, 121–127 (2009)
16. Lehner, B., Verdin, K., Jarvis, A.: New global hydrography derived from spaceborne elevation data. Eos, Transactions, American Geophysical Union 89(10), 93–94 (2008)
17. Geological Survey, U.S.: Hydro1k Elevation Derivative Database, http://edc.usgs.gov/products/elevation/gtopo30/hydro/index.html
18. Jansson, A., Persson, C., Strandberg, G.: 2D meso-scale re-analysis of precipitation, temperature and wind over Europe - ERAMESAN Time period 1980-2004. SMHI Reports, Meteorology and Climatology no. 112, Norrköping (2007)
19. Joint Research Centre: Eurpoean Soils Database, http://eusoils.jrc.ec.europa.eu/ESDB_Archive/ESDB/index.htm
20. Global Runoff Data Centre: River Discharge Data. Koblenz, Federal Institute of Hydrology, BfG (2009b)

21. BALTEX Hydrological Data Centre: BALTEX Hydrological Database, http://www.smhi.se/sgn0102/bhdc
22. Global Runoff Data Centre: European Water Archive (EWA). Koblenz, Federal Institute of Hydrology (BfG)
23. European Environment Information and Observation Network: Central Data Repository (2003), http://cdr.eionet.eu.int
24. Donnelly, C., Dahné, J., Rosberg, J., Strömqvist, J., Yang, W., Arheimer, B.: High-resolutio, large-scale hydrological modelling tools for Europe. IAHS Publ. 340, 553–561 (2010)
25. Hjerdt, N., Arheimer, B., Lindström, G., Westman, Y., Falkenroth, E., Hultman, M.: Going public with advanced simulations. In: Hřebíček, J., Schimak, G., Denzer, R. (eds.) ISESS 2011. IFIP AICT, vol. 359, pp. 587–593. Springer, Heidelberg (2011)

Development of an Information Portal for the Lake Winnipeg Basin Initiative

Isaac Wong[1], William G. Booty[1], Phil Fong[1], and Sarah Hall[2]

[1] Environment Canada, 867 Lakeshore Road, Burlington, Ontario, L7R 4A6, Canada
[2] Environment Canada, 200 Blvd Sacré-Coeur, Gatineau, Quebec, K1A 0H3, Canada
{Isaac.Wong,Bill.Booty,Phil.Fong,Sarah.Hall}@ec.gc.ca

Abstract. The Lake Winnipeg Basin Initiative was created as part of Canada's Action Plan on clean water. Its focus is to deal with excessive lake inputs of nutrients from surface runoff and municipal wastewater. Understanding the dynamics of nutrient loading, the associated algal blooms and resulting changes in fish populations, beach closures, and ecosystem imbalance requires access to various sources of data, information, knowledge, expertise and tools. Such critical components are delivered through the Lake Winnipeg Basin Initiative Information Portal, which integrates multiple geospatial and non-geospatial datasets of information pertaining to the basin and serves as a data, information and modelling portal. With data coming from many disparate sources, the Canadian Geospatial Data Infrastructure standards are applied to ensure interoperability. The "Community of Models" allows the modellers to post their model and results, and also allows the portal users to comment on the results to ensure a healthy dialogue.

Keywords: Lake Winnipeg; environmental information portal; knowledge discovery; data mining; metadata.

1 Introduction

Lake Winnipeg is the sixth largest freshwater lake in Canada. For several years water quality in Lake Winnipeg has been deteriorating. Nutrient loading from agricultural run-off and municipal wastewater effluent had led to advanced eutrophication of the lake; this is the primary issue. These excessive nutrients are contributing to the growth of toxic blue-green algae which, in turn, deplete lake oxygen levels and affect the local commercial fishing industry and recreational activities. Recognizing the severity of Lake Winnipeg's environmental situation, the Canadian government decided to invest $18 million towards cleaning up the lake. Part of the funding for this Lake Winnipeg Basin Initiative (LWBI) is devoted to both monitoring and research, and is aimed at understanding and solving some of the water quality challenges facing Lake Winnipeg. Solutions will be found by identifying and assessing key water quality issues within the lake and its contributing watersheds.

To help ensure decision-makers and water managers have access to relevant scientific information and tools to guide and evaluate water management, a single window information portal to promote data sharing with key federal partners is being

J. Hřebíček, G. Schimak, and R. Denzer (Eds.): ISESS 2011, IFIP AICT 359, pp. 667–674, 2011.

developed. This portal will ensure consistent and reliable delivery of relevant information and will also facilitate data sharing among partners and contributors. In addition, the Portal also provides a mechanism to compile and review information on point and non-point sources of pollution. The result will also lead to better informed decision support and priority setting for compliance promotion and enforcement activities. Additionally, the Portal will enable the identification of gaps and priorities for further collection of information through monitoring and research. Finally, the LWBI Information Portal will serve as a hub to integrate various land and water models being used in the LWBI research and provide their results to the project partners and the public.

2   LWBI Information Portal Considerations

As stated in the introduction, the key objective of the LWBI Information Portal is information sharing and discussion among research personnel in the web environment [1]. Since the Portal must be designed to receive data from various partners whose data formats and methods of data delivery are not the same, multiple considerations must be made at the design level. Information sharing is an important component of the Portal. For proper decision-making, it is essential to have the data and information as accurate as possible. The desire of individuals, groups and organizations working within the watershed to share their information has a direct impact on the success of the Portal. The most common factors of information sharing rely on trusting relationships and good personal contacts [2]. The Portal must present solutions which encourage collaboration and data sharing with an enabling infrastructure that promotes open exchange of data, information and knowledge. This approach will provide a good comfort level to the users and will encourage multi-way partnerships.

The Portal must also be designed to handle information overload. Users will want to pinpoint the appropriate data at the temporal and spatial scale needed to answer their specific question or query. Also, there is the added pressure that users sometimes feel that ownership of their information is lost when it is shared. Users express concerns that information might be misused or misrepresented and in some cases, choose to withhold information, especially raw data, if they haven't yet completed a full interpretation of the information.

To assist decision makers and to support complex environmental issues such as Lake Winnipeg eutrophication, environmental modellers are often asked to investigate and understand the inter-relationship of the ecosystem across multi-media, such as the watershed and lake. No single model can handle such complex conditions alone and it is required to have a Community of Models framework (CoM) to provide a better understanding of the impact to Lake Winnipeg.

Since each model is operated by domain experts in their own field, it is a challenge to integrate various models from various sources and personnel. The models may have to integrate together in a certain configuration and model to model data exchange is an ongoing challenge. The CoM needs to ensure that model results are synchronized seamlessly among all models. This includes guaranteeing consistency among the variables and respective units of measure, temporal and spatial scales. It is important for the CoM that all key personnel, including modellers and data holders, "buy-in" to the approach to avoid any pitfalls and failure.

High quality data minimize errors and reduce uncertainties about the model results. In general, successful calibration and validation of the models requires large amounts of high quality data and a strong background knowledge on the data inputs.

Timeliness of the data is another issue. In many cases modellers frequently update their models with better calibration and new model results will follow. New input data may also become available occasionally. With each new update of new model results and data, it requires all stakeholders within the CoM to know and revise their own results. This trickles down within the CoM until all the results are updated.

3 LWBI Information Portal Architecture

In designing the Lake Winnipeg Basin Initiative Information Portal, significant effort has been invested in the capture and delivery of standards-based metadata, portal functionality, web personalization and a seamlessly integrated modelling framework. Fig. 1 illustrates the components of the LWBI Information Portal. It highlights the use of the CGDI (Canadian Geospatial Data Infrastructure) metadata standard concept, the rich functionality allowing users moving from one component to another while retaining personal preferences by means of web personalization, and finally, a CoM allowing modellers to share information among models.

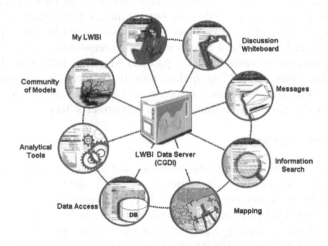

Fig. 1. The LWBI Information Portal components

3.1 Using Standards as the Backbone of the LWBI Information Portal

The Portal endorses data ownership, encourages collaboration among users and provides decision support as well as handles integrated environmental modelling. Compliance with metadata and geospatial standards is important [3]. The backbone of the Portal is based on the CGDI standards. The CGDI standardizes the way information in many of the databases is stored, accessed, and presented online. These standards are endorsed by the Government of Canada and are the same standards often applied to geospatial data infrastructures operated by other countries. Thus, the interoperability of data from standards-based Canadian and foreign sources is intact. This is an important aspect because it enables the users to understand exactly what data that they are retrieving. The Information Portal is a distributed system that attempts to leave data at source. Sharing data directly from the source, rather than adopting a data warehouse approach, ensures that users receive the most accurate and current data from a single, authoritative source. This removes problems with data duplication and redundancy. Users know that the data complies with the standards and that there will be no surprises, i.e. non-standard data delivery that often requires a huge effort to make it usable.

Depending on the nature of the dataset, there are up to two levels of metadata information. The first level is the overarching collection level metadata. At this level, information such as the description of the dataset, data owner, access privileges, bounding extents and information contacts are among the key mandatory metadata elements. The second level allows definition of station level metadata. This permits the capture of more detailed metadata information from an environmental dataset containing station information.

The LWBI Information Portal is built on the foundation of the CGDI standards. Ideally, data should be stored at source. In practice, however, this can be quite challenging because of implementation issues that may have to be addressed. There may be differences in the levels of information management and technology (IM/IT) expertise from the various partners. While some of the partners are capable of following the CGDI standards and providing data through web services such as Web Map Service and Web Feature Service, this may not be the case for others who have low IM/IT capacity. Although these partners have valuable data to share, they may be constrained by a lack of technical expertise and often require assistance in building up their capacity. In extreme cases, there are partners who are simply unwilling to invest their time and resources in building up that capacity because it is not seen as a critical component of their core business. To secure access to this critical information, the Portal must provide acceptable hosting options for partner's data.

3.2 Portal Functionality

Understanding complex environmental problems and making informed resource management decisions requires the integration of scientific data and knowledge across multiple disciplines and diverse landscapes. Ever increasing demands for timely, accurate and spatially explicit information requires that environmental modellers deploy the latest information technology. Such modern technologies provide decision support capability to the Portal and enable informed decisions surrounding point source pollution, non-point source pollution, and lake eutrophication. The Portal uses the Decision Support System (DSS) approach [4] to assist users in the various decision making processes. For example, the Portal utilizes data and models to tackle the nutrient problem in the LWBI.

There are many design issues for the LWBI Information Portal. These include the problem of information overload, the reluctance of data and information sharing, the wide spectrum of technical capacity of the partners and the consistency of heterogeneous datasets. We will describe some of the functionality currently built into the Portal which provides tools for overcoming these barriers.

3.3 Web Personalization

As more and more data is added to the Information Portal over time, a situation of information overload may result. The expanding knowledge base may lead to usability challenges, perhaps limiting users' ability to efficiently obtain the information that they need. It will be critical to ensure provision of quick access to data for these various users, in order to maintain their long-term interest in the Portal.

To improve the usability and secure user retention of the Portal, web personalization is implemented [5]. The principle components of web personalization provide an environment for categorizing and pre-processing of data and information, linking heterogeneous datasets together logically and providing services that are tailored for the web personalization.

"My LWBI" is an avenue in the Portal to allow the users to save their favourite settings. Users can save the weather information of a city within the Lake Winnipeg Basin, Know Your Watershed information, geospatial boundary of a region of interest, datasets, stations and water quality variables as a "My LWBI" project. Users can save as many projects as they want and can designate any one of their favourite projects as their default project.

The use of metadata searching tools to pinpoint appropriate data and information is an important feature of the Portal, especially when large amounts of information are involved. Since the metadata XML records are based on CGDI standards, it is possible to search information using all the elements of these metadata records. The Portal makes use of a Catalog Service for the Web to hold and query all of the metadata. Users can easily search for relevant information against these collection level metadata records.

Station level metadata of the collection dataset can subsequently be used to select water quality stations. Once the water quality stations are selected, the Portal will dynamically return the list of the available water quality variables for these stations.

The metadata approach does not stop at the collection and station levels. The Portal also provides metadata information about the water quality variables that are chosen. It is capable of identifying the number of sampling points among each station and the duration of sampling. This feature allows users to further refine their information requests. Since the Portal uses the CGDI standards, it is, by default, designed to increase interoperability. Heterogeneous datasets can be combined to provide additional information. In this manner, the Portal not only deals with information overload, but is also capable of information aggregation. User retention is the key to the success of any information portal. In order to promote regular user revisits, the LWBI Information Portal employs a number of strategies. First, the Portal offers a single window to the Lake Winnipeg Basin information. It is critical that the users understand that the Portal is providing up-to-date data and information about the basin. By combining various datasets through the CGDI standards, the Portal offers interoperability among datasets. This allows users to access and retrieve various datasets even when the data are stored at source. Secondly, the components of the Portal are tightly integrated. Users can use "My LWBI" to define the areas of interest and to select appropriate datasets and water quality stations. All of these selections are "memorized" and migrate automatically to other Portal components including analytical tools and models. Users can expect the same responses from all the components of the Portal without any surprises. Thirdly, the Portal makes use of data selection methods and provides water-related analytical tools to allow the users to understand the data better. These tools include environmental statistics, statistical graphs, tables and thematic mapping.

3.4 Knowledge Discovery Platform

Since knowledge is power, a discussion whiteboard is made available for the users to share information and local knowledge, to ask questions about specific LWBI issues and to expand networking with other like-minded users. Users can discuss specific topics regarding the LWBI. They can also upload relevant information such as spatial layers, photos and spreadsheets to share among their peers. This greatly increases the usability of the Portal since new information will be created dynamically.

The additional supporting tools include a message system allowing users to get help from the Portal system administrators, a "Who's Who" page allowing users to discover the expertise of individuals and organizations that are participating in the Portal, the "What's New" page conveying new information from the Portal administrators to the users and the "Knowledge Exchange" module which allows the users to learn from each others' experiences.

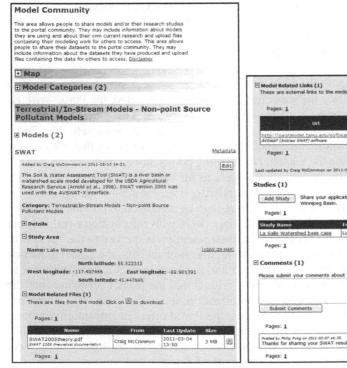
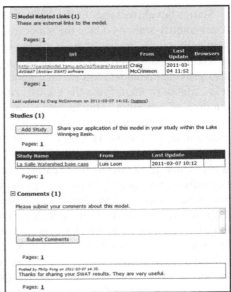

Fig. 2. Community of Models web page

3.5 Community of Models

The use of computer modelling to simulate environmental processes and the interactions between ecological and anthropogenic systems is very common. In the Lake Winnipeg Basin, there are many known models being applied to evaluate, understand and predict the environmental fate of pollutants, their impacts on human health and the environment, and the costs and benefits of alternative policies. However, it is a challenge to set up a modelling framework within the Information Portal that caters to all levels of users [6].

In some modelling, the model may be reasonably accurate to a certain spatial or temporal threshold or both, beyond which point the output becomes thoroughly undependable. These thresholds, where they may exist, tend to be poorly defined. Often, the effectiveness of the communication between the portal user and the modeller is lacking, resulting in the modeller attempting to answer the wrong question or the user asking a question in a way which makes it extremely difficult for the answer to be produced by the model. To alleviate this problem, a common modelling framework of communication for the Lake Winnipeg Basin called "Community of Models" page as shown in Fig. 2 is created. Modellers can deposit their models and model results into the portal in the way that they would like to communicate with the portal users. The assumptions, limitations, inputs and outputs of the models are described and discussed. Users can comment on the model use and directly engage with the modellers.

4 Conclusions

The LWBI Information Portal requires careful consideration to overcome information overload, user buy-in and user retention. In designing the LWBI Information Portal, we employ a number of strategies. To overcome information overload, we use web personalization so that users can customize their preferences with the "My LWBI" option. Session memory is also retained from component to component to allow for better navigation. Search of relevant information and useful environmental data analysis are also important functionalities to combat information overload.

The Information Portal is a distributed system that leaves the data at source but offers a single window access point for the users. The deployment of the CGDI metadata standard concept allows the Portal to address the issue of data interoperability. It is now possible for heterogeneous data to be aggregated. The synergy encourages more buy-in.

The whiteboard forum to exchange information, knowledge and ideas is one of the key retention strategies. It allows like-minded users to have a platform for discussion. In addition, a message system is set up to assist users with technical problems. The response time is kept to the minimum so as not to irritate users. Finally, data and information download is the main goal of the Information Portal. It allows users to search and retrieve data in a friendly data format.

The "Community of Models" framework allows the modellers to communicate their models and results with the Information Portal users. This exchange allows the knowledge about the pollutant transport, eutrophication and algae growth issues in the lake to be shared. The end result of the LWBI Information Portal is to develop wisdom among users with data mining, information sharing and modelling exchange on how to protect the basin.

Acknowledgements. We thank the Lake Winnipeg Basin Initiative Program of Environment Canada for supporting Lake Winnipeg Basin Initiative Information Portal Project, especially J. Lawrence, N. Hnatiuk, M. Conly, R.C. McCrimmon, L. Leon, S. Ross and O. Resler. Special thanks to D.C.L. Lam, R. Kent and D.A. Swayne for their invaluable input. We acknowledge contributions by our partners: Agriculture and Agri-Food Canada, Algal Taxonomy and Ecology Inc., City of Winnipeg, Ducks Unlimited Canada, Fisheries and Oceans, International Institute for Sustainable Development, Lake Winnipeg Research Consortium Inc., Manitoba Water Stewardship, Red River Basin Commission, Salki Consultants Inc., Saskatchewan Environment, University of Guelph and University of Manitoba.

References

1. Xiang, X., Madey, G., Huang, Y., Cabaniss, S.: Web Portal and Markup Languages for Collaborative Environmental Research. In: Scharl, A. (ed.) Environmental Online Communication, pp. 113–126. Springer, London (2004)
2. Forslund, J., Larsson, J.: A Portal Implementation for Information Sharing. Master Thesis in Informatics, IT University of Göteborg, Sweden (2005)
3. Kruse, F., Uhrich, S., Klenke, M., Lehmann, H., Giffei, C., Topker, S.: PortalU, a Tool to Support the Implementation of the Shared Environmental Information System (SEIS). In: Proceedings of the European conference TOWARDS eENVIRONMENT, Prague, Czech Republic, March 25-27 (2009)
4. Alter, S.L.: Decision Support Systems: Current Practice and Continuing Challenges. Addison-Wesley, Reading (1980)
5. Eirinaki, M., Vazirgiannis, M.: Web Mining for Web Personalization. ACM Transactions on Internet Technology 3(1), 1–27 (2003)
6. Gordov, E.P., Lykosov, V.N., Fazliev, A.Z.: Web Portal on Environmental Sciences "ATMOS". Adv. Geosci. 8, 33–38 (2006)

Erratum: An Environmental Decision Support System for Water Issues in the Oil Industry

Ralf Denzer[1], Fernando Torres-Bejarano[2], Thorsten Hell[3], Steven Frysinger[1,4],
Sascha Schlobinski[3], Reiner Güttler[1], and Hermilo Ramírez[2]

[1] Environmental Informatics Group (EIG), Goebenstrasse 40, 66117 Saarbrücken, Germany
[2] Mexican Petroleum Institute (IMP), Eje Central Lázaro Cárdenas
152 Mexico D.F., Mexico
[3] cismet GmbH, Altenkesseler Strasse 17, 66115 Saarbrücken
[4] James Madison University, Harrisonburg, Virginia, USA 22807
ralf.denzer@enviromatics.org

J. Hřebíček, G. Schimak, and R. Denzer (Eds.): ISESS 2011, IFIP AICT 359, pp. 208–216, 2011.
© IFIP International Federation for Information Processing 2011

DOI 10.1007/978-3-642-22285-6_73

The name of the second author is "Franklin Torres-Bejarano" and not, as stated by mistake, "Fernando Torres-Bejarano".

The original online version for this chapter can be found at
http://dx.doi.org/10.1007/978-3-642-22285-6_23

Author Index